LITERARY HISTORY
OF THE
UNITED STATES

CONTRIBUTORS

RANDOLPH G. ADAMS

CARLOS BAKER

RICHARD P. BLACKMUR

BRAND BLANSHARD

HAROLD BLODGETT

DAVID BOWERS

SCULLEY BRADLEY

HENRY SEIDEL CANBY

WILLIAM CHARVAT

GILBERT CHINARD

HENRY STEELE COMMAGER

ALEXANDER COWIE

MALCOLM COWLEY

MERLE CURTI

RALPH H. GABRIEL

MAXWELL GEISMAR

ERIC F. GOLDMAN

GORDON S. HAIGHT

HAROLD F. HARDING

ARTHUR PALMER HUDSON

EVERETT L. HUNT

THOMAS H. JOHNSON

HOWARD MUMFORD JONES

ADRIENNE KOCH

JOSEPH WOOD KRUTCH

LEWIS LEARY

HARRY T. LEVIN

TREMAINE MC DOWELL

LUTHER S. MANSFIELD

F. O. MATTHIESSEN

H. L. MENCKEN

JOHN C. MILLER

KENNETH B. MURDOCK

ALLAN NEVINS

HENRY A. POCHMANN

J. H. POWELL

CARL SANDBURG

TOWNSEND SCUDDER

ODELL SHEPARD

HENRY NASH SMITH

ROBERT E. SPILLER

WALLACE STEGNER

GEORGE R. STEWART

WALTER F. TAYLOR

HAROLD W. THOMPSON

STITH THOMPSON

WILLARD THORP

FREDERICK B. TOLLES

CARL VAN DOREN

JOHN D. WADE

DIXON WECTER

GEORGE F. WHICHER

STANLEY T. WILLIAMS

LOUIS B. WRIGHT

MORTON D. ZABEL

LITERARY HISTORY
OF THE
UNITED STATES

Editors
ROBERT E. SPILLER · WILLARD THORP
THOMAS H. JOHNSON · HENRY SEIDEL CANBY
Associates
HOWARD MUMFORD JONES · DIXON WECTER
STANLEY T. WILLIAMS

VOLUME I

1948
THE MACMILLAN COMPANY · NEW YORK

ACKNOWLEDGMENT

PERMISSION to quote copyrighted material is acknowledged to publishers and authors as follows: Albert & Charles Boni, Inc.—*Collected Works of Ambrose Bierce*, 1909–1912; Doubleday & Company, Inc.—*The Octopus*, by Frank Norris, copyright, 1901, by Doubleday & Company, Inc., and *The Responsibilities of the Novelist*, by Frank Norris, copyright, 1901, 1902, 1903, by Doubleday & Company, Inc.; Harcourt, Brace & Company, Inc.—*Collected Poems 1909–1935*, by T. S. Eliot, copyright, 1936, by Harcourt, Brace & Company, Inc.; *Essays Ancient and Modern*, by T. S. Eliot, copyright, 1936, by Harcourt, Brace & Company, Inc., *The People, Yes*, by Carl Sandburg, copyright, 1936, by Harcourt, Brace & Company, Inc., and *Criticism in America: Its Function and Status*, by Joel E. Spingarn, copyright, 1924, by Harcourt, Brace & Company, Inc.; Harper & Bros.—*Mark Twain: A Biography*, by Albert Bigelow Paine (1929), and *The Mysterious Stranger*, by Mark Twain (1916); Harper & Brothers and Edward C. Aswell as Executor—*The Web and the Rock*, by Thomas Wolfe (1937, 1938, 1939); Harvard University Press—*Literary Pioneers: Early American Explorers of European Culture*, by Orie W. Long (1935); Henry Holt & Company, Inc.—*Collected Poems of Robert Frost*, copyright, 1930, 1939, by Henry Holt & Company, Inc., copyright, 1936, by Robert Frost, and *Chicago Poems* by Carl Sandburg, copyright, 1916, by Henry Holt and Company, Inc., copyright, 1943, by Carl Sandburg; Houghton Mifflin Company—*Mont Saint Michel and Chartres*, by Henry Adams, copyright, 1905, by Henry Adams, *The Education of Henry Adams*, by Henry Adams, copyright, 1918, by the Massachusetts Historical Society, *Letters of Henry Adams*, ed. Worthington C. Ford, copyright, 1930, 1938, by Worthington C. Ford, *The Life of George Cabot Lodge*, by Henry Adams, copyright, 1911, by Houghton Mifflin Company, *Journals of Ralph Waldo Emerson*, ed. Edward W. Emerson and Waldo Emerson Forbes, *Outlines of Cosmic Philosophy*, by John Fiske, and *Some Imagist Poets*, by Amy Lowell; International Publishers, Inc.—the introduction to *Proletarian Literature in the United States*, by Joseph Freeman, 1935; Alfred A. Knopf, Inc.—*Not Under Forty*, by Willa Cather, copyright, 1936, by Willa Cather, *Imaginary Interviews*, by André Gide, 1944, and *Prejudices:*

Fourth Series, by H. L. Mencken, 1924; Little, Brown & Company—*The Complete Poems of Emily Dickinson,* ed. Martha Dickinson Bianchi and Alfred Leete Hampson, 1924, 1929, 1930, 1936, 1937; The Macmillan Company—*Collected Poems,* by Vachel Lindsay, 1925, *Collected Poems,* by Edwin Arlington Robinson, 1937, and *The Autobiography of William Allen White,* 1946; The *Nation*—"Individualism and the American Writer," by Newton Arvin, Oct. 14, 1931; *Poetry,* Chicago—the article "Private Experience and Public Philosophy," by Philip Rahv and William Phillips, *Poetry,* May, 1936; Princeton University Press—*The Poetical Works of Edward Taylor,* ed. Thomas H. Johnson, copyright, 1939, Rockland Editions, copyright, 1943, Princeton University Press; *Publishers' Weekly* and Lovat Dickson—"The American Novel in England," *Publishers' Weekly,* Oct. 29, 1938; Charles Scribner's Sons—*Gondola Days,* by F. Hopkinson Smith, 1897, and *This Was a Poet: Emily Dickinson,* by George F. Whicher, 1937; University of California Press—*Singing for Power,* by Ruth M. Underhill, copyright, 1938, by the Regents of the University of California; The Viking Press, Inc.—*A Story Teller's Story,* by Sherwood Anderson, 1924; Yale University Press—*Collected Essays,* by William Graham Sumner, 1934, *Notes While Preparing Sketch Book, etc.,* by Washington Irving, ed. Stanley T. Williams, 1927.

Also acknowledgment is made to Mrs. Millicent Todd Bingham for permission to quote brief passages from *Letters to Emily Dickinson,* ed. Mabel Loomis Todd, 1931; to John Dos Passos to quote from *The Big Money!,* copyright, 1933, 1934, 1935, 1936, by John Dos Passos; to the editors of *Fortune* magazine to quote from the article on Thoreau, in the May, 1944, issue; to the Ralph Waldo Emerson Memorial Association and the Widener Library of Harvard University for the use of manuscripts of Ralph Waldo Emerson; to the Committee on Higher Degrees in the History of American Civilization, Harvard University, to quote brief passages from the MS *Billy Budd,* by Herman Melville; to the Library of Harvard University to quote from the Howells papers, Jan. 31, 1902, and from the Ticknor Letter Books, May 10, 1851; also to the Henry E. Huntington Library and Art Gallery to quote from the letters of Harriet Beecher Stowe; to The Executive Council of the Modern Language Association of America to quote from *The English Language in America,* by George Philip Krapp, 1935; to Mrs. Dorothy Pound and Yale University Press to quote from *Make It New,* by Ezra Pound, 1935; and to G. P. Putnam's Sons for "Herman Melville: Adventurer," preprinted by them with permission of the editors in *A Man's Reach,* ed. Thomas H. Johnson, copyright, 1947, by G. P. Putnam's Sons.

PREFACE

Each generation should produce at least one literary history of the United States, for each generation must define the past in its own terms. A redefinition of our literary past was needed at the time of the First World War, when the *Cambridge History of American Literature* was produced by a group of scholars. It is now needed again; and it will be needed still again.

At mid-point, the twentieth century may properly establish its own criteria of literary judgment; indeed, the values as well as the facts of modern civilization must be examined if man is to escape self-destruction. We must know and understand better the recorders of our experience. Scholars can no longer be content to write for scholars; they must make their knowledge meaningful and applicable to humanity. As our part of that task, the editors, associates, and contributors have undertaken and completed this work.

Such a history could be the work of one or a few hands, or it could be a collaboration of many. But the United States, in its life of less than two centuries, has produced too much literature for any one man to read and digest. Its literary history can therefore be best written by a group of collaborators, whatever the risk of differences of perspective or opinion.

Those who have joined in this undertaking are historians and critics rather than specialists in a narrow sense. Their contributions are related to one another within a frame rather than separately composed essays. Each member of our company has a proportional share in the whole enterprise rather than an exclusive interest in his part of it.

The drawing of the design and the assignment of chapters took a year of conferences in which every point was discussed to a satisfactory conclusion. Seven men took part in this planning: the four editors and the three associates. Each of the additional forty-eight contributors had at hand a detailed outline of the entire work and a statement of basic principles before he agreed to write. Upon his acceptance, he was asked to meet, either individually or in group conferences, with the editors and associates and with the authors of allied chapters, and discuss the problems presented by his assignment. Three years were given to the writing; two more, to the editing and publishing. During this period each of the three editors who had undertaken major tasks of detail was granted a year of freedom from professional duties in order to give full time to the work, and in some instances contributors received grants-in-aid. All the bibliographical essays were written by one editor in close collaboration with the authors of relevant chapters.

A genuine collaboration requires some sacrifice of the individual in the interest of the group. The authorship of each chapter is given on pp. 1393–96, but the chapters are unsigned in the text. Many of them have been substantially revised in order to fit them into the larger plan, and parts of some have been lifted and incorporated elsewhere. The editors have themselves written many chapters and have supplied necessary links; but individual opinions and styles have not been altered in substance. The result is, they believe, a coherent narrative, with valuable differences on individual points. Principles of orthography in quotations have been left to the judgment of the respective contributors.

The almost ideal conditions which made this procedure possible were created by The Macmillan Company and the Rockefeller Foundation, with supplementary aid from the American Council of Learned Societies, the American Philosophical Society, and the institutions with which several of the editors were connected—Swarthmore College, Princeton University, the University of Pennsylvania, and the Lawrenceville School. The disruptions of the war and postwar eras, far from presenting handicaps, have stimulated interest by emphasizing the need for cultural redefinition.

It would be impossible to make specific acknowledgment of indebtedness to the scholars who indirectly contributed to this work. In some instances, the debt was immediate and personal, but more often it took the form of dependence upon the great body of critical, historical, and analytical studies that the past quarter of a century has produced. The mere listing of names and books here or in footnotes would be meaningless. The bibliographical essays, which attempt to be critical both in their selection and in their arrangement of entries, must serve as confession of obligation on almost every point. There would be little reason for attempting again the task which the *Cambridge History* undertook for its generation were it not for the pioneering work of such historians as F. L. Pattee, A. H. Quinn, W. B. Cairns, P. H. Boynton, and V. L. Parrington; the stimulation of scholarship by these and other such teachers as Norman Foerster, J. B. Hubbell, R. L. Rusk, and H. H. Clark; the bibliographical work of E. E. Leisy, Gregory Paine, and their associates; the invigorating perceptions of such critics as W. C. Brownell, John Macy, Stuart P. Sherman, Van Wyck Brooks, and Edmund Wilson; and the specific investigations of a host of careful scholars.

The entire text of this book was prepared specifically for it under individual contracts with contributors for their respective parts of a single overall plan.

CONTENTS

LITERARY FULFILLMENT

CRISIS

VOLUME II

EXPANSION

THE SECTIONS

THE CONTINENTAL NATION

THE UNITED STATES

A WORLD LITERATURE

TABLE OF AUTHORS

INDEX

ADDRESS TO THE READER

THE literary history of this nation be-
gan when the first settler from abroad of sensitive mind paused in his
adventure long enough to feel that he was under a different sky, breathing
new air, and that a New World was all before him with only his strength
and Providence for guides. With him began a different emphasis upon an
old theme in literature, the theme of cutting loose and faring forth, renewed
under the powerful influence of a fresh continent for civilized man. It has
provided, ever since those first days, an element in our native literature,
whose other theme has come from a nostalgia for the rich culture of Europe,
so much of which was perforce left behind.

It is not surprising that our own writers in the first three centuries of
New World history were more often purveyors of this nostalgia than recorders of the warmth of the American imagination kindling in novel scenes.
They believed that their mission was to be importers and middlemen for
America of this European culture. They encouraged nostalgia, even while
spreading civilization, and they were often insensitive to the effect upon the
imagination of the novel experiences developing upon this continent with
extraordinary rapidity and force.

Yet the literature of the new country was to be shaped more by a hope
for the future than by a clinging to the past. Observers from across the seas
have noted from the beginning the buoyancy of our writing, its richness in
spiritual conflicts, carried in such great writers as Poe and Melville, and in
such moderns as William Faulkner, Ernest Hemingway, and Thomas Wolfe,
to the bounds, and sometimes beyond the bounds, of neuroticism. They
have been impressed by the vigorous self-assertion, expressed in the lesser
men as naïve pride. The slow emergence of an articulate racial mixture—a
race of races, as Whitman called it—had deeply interested them, for this was
an experience not known in Europe since the Roman Empire; and they have
seen that the remark of Michel Guillaume Jean de Crèvecœur, one of our
most sympathetic immigrants, was true: English dogs after two or three
generations in the new land became in habits and experience American; and
so it was with men and with literature.

xiii

The first historians of American literature wrote of it as if they were describing transplanted English flowers and trees. A later school of historians discovered its democratic, psychological, and economic differentiations; but in their zeal for argument and their eagerness to establish our originality, they often left unemphasized the timeless values in our writing. The Emersons, the Mark Twains, the Whitmans emerged from the criticism of these historians with new depths of national significance; the Poes, the Hawthornes, and all writers who were primarily artists, and whose merits often did not depend upon the peculiar circumstances of American history, were less adequately estimated.

The time has now come, and the materials of research and criticism are available, to strike a balance between those who protested against European dominance and those who did not. To draw a new and truer picture of our literary tradition is the intention of the chapters that follow.

2

It is quite possible, and indeed necessary, to write of American literature in terms of its European, and especially its British, sources. That was the way in which Longfellow viewed our literature, the way in which Howells seems to have felt that it could be best understood. It was the approach of teachers, critics, and historians in general until the 1920's. From the academic point of view, American literature was simply a hoped-for extension of the great literature of the English-speaking peoples. And so it is; and such a history, as far as it goes, is entirely valid. Even the radical Walt Whitman insisted that in this new continent we should absorb, not discard, our European past. We could not discard it, if we willed to do so. The progenitors of our literature are in a European and usually in an Anglo-Saxon past. Chaucer, Shakespeare, the folk ballads, the great religious literature of the English seventeenth century, are as deep in our ancestral strain as in the genealogy of modern British writing. The English eighteenth century, English romanticism, the English novel of character, and all later and vital English literature, have a family resemblance to ours, and a family influence, with which any other source for the American imagination outside our own terrain is by comparison weak indeed. A history of American literature exclusively in terms of democracy or the frontier is no less false than a history of American writing regarded as a colonial extension. There is a blending of elements in our culture which is inevitable in a newspaper editorial or in *John Brown's Body* or the *Song of Myself*.

Obviously, our literature is a *transported* European culture, bringing with it the richness of its sources in the classical world, the Middle Ages, and the

Renaissance. Obviously, the roots of our literary culture reach down into British literature which itself has absorbed so long and so much. Yet it is equally true that our literature is a *transformed* culture. It has been written in a new continent, and under conditions definitely and impressively different in the vast majority of instances from the circumstances of Great Britain, or of Europe in general. Slowly, yet inevitably, it has found its own accent, as has American speech. But the divergence has been much greater than that between American and British habits in the use of the English language, because literature is speech made expressive of values, and from the very beginning the values, the expectations, the experience of life in America have been different, with a difference that would continue to increase were it not for the influence of America upon Europe, now making itself strongly felt.

Progress, for example, as a concept may have little general validity; but whether we call it progress, or change, or development, increasing power and vitality are extraordinarily characteristic of the American nineteenth century with which so much of this book is concerned. Never has nature been so rapidly and so extensively altered by the efforts of man in so brief a time. Never has conquest resulted in a more vigorous development of initiative, individualism, self-reliance, and demands for freedom. Never have the defeats which preceded and accompanied this conquest of nature led to more surprising frustration, decadence, sterility, and dull standardization. All this is in American literature, and the causes of both our successes and our failures are implicit, and often explicit, in our early national books. James Fenimore Cooper, for us, is more significant than Sir Walter Scott, although he only rarely equals Scott as a novelist. Melville and Whitman mean more to an American, and are more revealing for our own times, than Thackeray and Wordsworth.

The mobility of the Americans throughout their history has been another transforming factor in their life, and therefore in their literature. They moved across a continent, and continue to move, from habit as much as necessity. And although their speech is English and their political and social organization largely Anglo-Saxon they have assimilated millions whose cultural background was not English at all. Tradition in America is not the same as tradition in Europe. Our national tradition has been acquired by study and by imitation as often as by childhood inheritance of an environment. Thus the relation of what is called the American way of life—which really means the American way of thinking and feeling—to the national unity is extremely important. Our national unity does not and cannot depend upon blood or upon inherited tendencies. Thus very naturally our literature, which is a record of our experience, has been deeply, often subconsciously, aware of its responsibility in the making of a nation from a complex of peoples in voluntary union. It has been an inquiring, an exploratory, literature from the beginning—asking questions of the New World, challenging the effects of sudden release and expansion upon the spiritual nature, delighting in adventure, whether along the Indian borders or on the Mississippi or in the trek across the continent, easily elated in a Whitman, easily depressed in a Hawthorne or Poe. It has been a literature profoundly influenced by ideals and by practices developed in democratic living. It has been intensely conscious of the needs of the common man, and equally conscious of the aspirations of the individual in such a democracy as we have known here. It has been humanitarian. It has been, on the whole, an optimistic literature, made virile by criticism of the actual in comparison with the ideal.

All this has been transforming, and has given to American writing, even to American style, qualities which no Aristotelian criticism, no study of literary influences from abroad, can explain. Our contemporary literature, which from comic strip to satiric novel is really the adult education of most Americans, can be rightly understod only by readers who have followed the history of this American tradition.

3

Such readers of this book as are neither critics nor specialists in scholarship are probably more interested in the literature itself than in the vast historical changes which it reflects. Fortunately for them American literature is not merely in a state of becoming. Our national history is already long enough to have had its periods of maturing and fruition. We do not have to leave our readers confused and bored by writing in which imagination is only half formed and half worded. We are not dependent upon the topical and the timely, the imitative or the unconsciously intuitive, upon the half-gods of journalism, or the sprawlings or conventions of experimental or commercialized fiction. These are all in the background, but we have had a sufficiency of great writers representative of whatever in our history could in their time and by them be put into the forms of art. In this book the approach will be through the varied and extensive experience of a national culture on its way, but the objective of the history will be to record and explain the great men and women who have made this culture speak to the imagination. Literature as they have written it, and as the term is used in the title of this book, is any writing in which aesthetic, emotional, or intellectual values are made articulate by excellent expression. It is the record of man made enduring by the right words in the right order. It is a feeling or thought which by some inner necessity has created for itself a form. Literature can be used, and has been magnificently used by Americans, in the service of history, of science, of religion, or of political propaganda. It has no sharp boundaries, though it passes through broad margins from art into instruction or argument. The writing or speech of a culture such as ours which has been so closely bound to the needs of a rapidly growing, democratic nation, moves quickly into the utilitarian, where it informs without lifting the imagination, or records without attempting to reach the emotions. History as it is written in this book will be a history of literature within the margins of art but crossing them to follow our writers into the actualities of American life. It will be a history of the books of the great and the near-great writers in a literature which is most revealing when studied as a by-product of American experience.

Inside these margins are so many notable writers that the emphasis in the following chapters will inevitably fall upon men rather than upon movements and institutions, although these will not be neglected. There is available for discussion the enlightened common sense of Franklin, the first to make a modernizing Europe feel that there was a still more modern America. There are the astonishing intellects of a Hamilton and a Jefferson arguing great causes in documents and letters which became the political classics of their times. We have the communicable fire of Thomas Paine, the most effective propagandist of modern times before Hitler, and the antithesis of Hitler in the history of human liberty. In the youth of the nation the art of style was mastered by Irving, suave in a tumultuous commonwealth. In the same decades the equally great art of story-telling was enriched by Cooper, who added to the sagas of the world the heroic myth of Red Indian and pioneer. There is the somber beauty of Hawthorne, the moral romancer as Milton was the heroic poet of Puritanism; the fierce humor of Thoreau's individualism; the shrewd saintliness of Emerson, who spiritualized expansion; the soul-plunging adventures of Melville's imagination; the prophecy of Whitman, seeking and finding new rhythms in which to sing democracy and the future of the common man. We have had historians who were also men of letters, and statesmen like Lincoln who could say the word which makes aspiration articulate. There was Henry James, looking both ways across the sea from an Atlantis of his own creating; and Emily Dickinson who saw eternity through the windows of Amherst; and Mark Twain, tasting the bitterness of uncharted freedom while he told tall tales of an expanding America. There are the modernists of our twentieth century. Both in prose and in poetry they have pushed through the mists and illusions of romance and idealism and given us pictures of psychological oppression and moral divergence in a vast society transformed by industrialism. These and subtler strides of spiritual change have enlarged the boundaries of literary truth. The chapters that follow will be an account of such writers and their background and their associates and of a literature which must be known more fully in order to estimate their contribution to the country and to the world.

4

It may enlighten the reader of these introductory remarks to think of American literature as the record and analysis of a series of cultural waves beating in from across the Atlantic to our shores in a continuous series and changing their form and nature and sometimes their direction as they sweep over the New World.

The first waves that came with the explorers and the settlers of the seventeenth century retained their European characteristics with only slight modifications from circumstance. When the wilderness became new towns and organized communities, and immigration swelled into the floods of the eighteenth century, the waves became more numerous and more complex. For nearly two centuries they were dammed by the long walls of the Appalachians, yet their contour and content were subject to changes only less extensive than the novelties in the actual experience of millions of settlers now committed to a life in which opportunity, hardship, and danger were in equal proportions.

After the Revolutionary War and the establishing of independence, itself a modifying influence of tremendous force, the wall of the mountains was breached in a dozen places, and waves from the seaboard pool and new waves from across the sea swept into the Mississippi Valley and on toward the Western mountains and the Pacific. Here in this vast frontier the colonial culture of the East, and later the powerful literature of what was now an old New England and a mature East and South, were fertilized by pioneer experience, dynamized by the sense of a continent in unity, and transformed by the needs and new imagination of a people no longer European. Sectional literature became national literature. And while new ideas from abroad were continually absorbed, currents typically American in their influences began to roll back toward Europe and the rest of the world, a reversal that had begun with Cooper and Emerson in the early nineteenth century.

By the twentieth century and especially after the First World War, the United States was no longer a New World. Culture was now not immigrant here except on a basis of equal exchange, and the complex interactions of democracy and industrialism and the new struggle for economic democracy outweighed in importance any pressures from abroad. By the mid-century American fiction and the American drama of the screen were beginning to dominate the imagination of the masses throughout the world, although of this striking fact the American intellectual was as yet scarcely aware.

To write a simple account of these complex developments is not easy; and a chronology of writers and their books is obviously insufficient. But if a historian will view in perspective a century of this nation's history from any one place and time he will discover a logical pattern in its literary growth. He will see the raw and objective records of the explorers and settlers, usually our earliest writing, developing into documents of politics and religion. Gradually the sense of art awakes as primary needs become more certain of fulfillment; but art in this stage is either primitive or imitative. Not until the settler or his descendant is thoroughly at home in his new world can he create an art which is an organic expression of his experience. A century is not too long for the full cycle of this process, whether the place be New England, Virginia, Ohio, or California. Because this cycle unrolled in all regions, and because there was no single time schedule for the various parts of the continent, nor even a consistent tempo of westward movement, the historical account must be complex, however simple and oft repeated this formula of literary evolution.

Yet the imagination often discovers truths where complications of fact obscure it; and the imagination responds to two great movements in our literary history: the era of Emerson, Melville, and Whitman; and the age in which we are living today. The first epoch is evidently the climax of a long growth from colonial beginnings to a self-conscious and organized nation, but a nation on the brink of a destructive Civil War and a westward expansion transforming in its character. The other, the era of complete national fulfillment, shows its beginnings in the earliest hints of a country that was to be continental in scope and cosmopolitan in population, but that would not realize itself completely and make its voice heard and its power felt in the world at large until the twentieth century. These two main cycles of growth overlap and intervene, and one American author, Whitman, is clearly a pivot upon which sectional America swings into its continental phase. Yet they afford a pattern for marshaling facts and for tracing developments, and thus provide a ground plan for this book. The details will range far but find their organization in this view, which we believe to be an accurate view, of American literary history.

5

We shall tell in the following chapters the story of the importation into our New World of European ideas and shapes for the imagination. We shall show that American literature differs from all the modern literatures of Europe in that it depends both upon an imported culture and upon the circumstances of a New World radically different in human experience from the Old, and thus has a quality which will presumably be characteristic of the literature of the future in a world society more mobile and yet more integrated than our own. We shall discuss the instruments of our national culture as they existed and developed. We shall set in order the progress from colonies to republic, from republic to democracy, from East to West, from sections and regions to a national unity. We shall treat at length these regions and sections, and discuss the rise and fall of literary dominations, the schools and coteries, the prophets and mythmakers, the interactions of politics, economics, and religion with literary expression, and those strong impulses toward escape and refinement and toward revolt and the needs of the common man, so characteristic of the United States. We shall correlate American literature with the successive swings of this country, which sometimes have been toward an ideal of leadership in all human progress, and sometimes have been away from the world we have helped to make smaller by our own energy and into an isolationism where we hoped vainly to solve our own peculiar problems. And we shall pause where genius emerges; for this is a history of literature, and literature, unlike politics, can never be measured by quantity, but only by the crystallization of strong imagination in words.

THE COLONIES

--- importation and adaptation

1. THE EUROPEAN BACKGROUND

THE world in which the mainland colonies in North America were founded and out of which American letters were to grow was a world at once incredibly remote from modern man and strangely like his own. In the sixteenth century "Europe" was a tiny island in a dim, gray universe. To all intents, "Europe" was Great Britain, the Low Countries, the Iberian Peninsula, France, Italy, and "Austria," with a few adjacent territories. The Scandinavias and Germany existed, one had commercial relations with them, but they existed as remote and savage parts of the world—travelers describing German inns, for example, as if they were writing about nineteenth century Siberia. Distant in the East, "Muscovy," a part of mankind even less known to western man than is Soviet Russia, loomed darkly; southward from it, the Turks pressed into Hungary and besieged Vienna in 1529. As late as 1602 Captain John Smith's travels in Wallachia had a remote, fantastic air.

Little vessels kept to the northern half of the Mediterranean to reach the Levant, avoiding, their masters hoped, the Moslem pirates of Tripoli. Southward from the Mediterranean stretched something huge and unknown called "Africa," where dwelt the anthropophagi and men whose heads do grow beneath their shoulders. Somewhere beyond was the flashing splendor, the brilliance intermittently revealed, of "Asia," where Prester John, Cipango, Kambalu, and the Spice Islands were all jumbled together. As for the western outlook, there was for Englishmen the savage and inhospitable land of Ireland, beyond which lay the gray Atlantic main and such legendary islands as O Brasil. Past these cloudy archipelagoes—and it was difficult to distinguish actual Iceland from mythical Cibola—there was perhaps something called America. Writing *A New Interlude and a mery of the nature of the .iiij. elementes* about 1519, John Rastell said that "westwarde be founde new landes," and thought they were "muche lenger than all christendome," but Englishmen were not overly eager to find them out.

Small groups of educated men labored throughout the century to inform themselves and their countrymen more accurately about the globe. But the efforts of Thorne, Barlow, Eden, Hacket, Dee, Hakluyt, and others to

3

improve the knowledge of geography scarcely touched the general mind. We do not know the rate of illiteracy in the kingdom of Gloriana, but we know that the vast majority of Englishmen could not read. The art and mystery of chart reading was even more severely restricted by the regulations of the guilds, governmental policy, and the profit motive of merchants and mariners; in the next century, when John Donne was writing about the round earth's imagined corners and Milton could not make up his mind whether to be a Ptolemaist or a Copernican, it is probable they were picturing the general confusion of the English imagination. Most of the great library of travel literature available to middle-class readers, moreover, was not published until either very late in the sixteenth century or in the seventeeth.

In the art of landscape painting Tudor England lagged woefully behind the continent; and though New World flora and fauna began to appear on canvases painted in sixteenth century Italy or Spain, England had no comparable pictures. What was worse, the technique of landscape description in literature, by which the small reading public might have been familiarized with America was, even as late as Hakluyt's *Principal Navigations* (1598, 1600), still struggling to pass beyond the medieval stereotypes which had satisfied literary workmen from Chaucer through Spenser. The consequence was that only a few visualized America. When Jamestown was at last founded, the world was certainly wider and better known than it had been to Sebastian Cabot; but, so far as the average literate middle-class Englishman was concerned, it was a world still vague in outline, still filled with inexplicable miracles and stupefying terrors, an inhospitable world, in which only a dogged determination not to be swallowed up by Spain drove the English out of the bastions of their island fortress set in a silver sea. This determination explains why, for many decades, the West Indies seemed to Tudor statesmen far more important than the mainland. You could raid the Spanish silver fleet with vessels based on Barbados; the James River and the Charles were much too far north.

The four million Englishmen who inhabited the southern portion of Great Britain when Elizabeth came to the throne seemed to themselves to be greatly crowded together. The suppression of the monasteries, which ended the obligations of celibacy for about ninety thousand persons; the weakening of the guild system, a social pattern which had postponed marriage for apprentices; the prosperity of the towns and the contrasting poverty of the countryside—these and other causes had increased the number of inhabitants from an estimated two and one-half million in the fifteenth century to a probable four million in 1558. This increase in population had two important effects upon the image of America. The first was to increase the confidence of Englishmen in themselves, to make them feel that along with Spain,

Portugal, and France, England deserved a place in the New World sun. If the Queen was, indeed, the "Great Ladie of the greatest isle," that isle should be the center of an empire of her majesty's subjects

through the speciall assistance, and blessing of God . . . searching the most opposite corners and quarters of the world, and . . . compassing the vaste globe of the earth.

Hakluyt continued with Miltonic majesty:

For, which of the kings of this land before her Majesty, had theyr banners ever seene in the Caspian sea? which of them hath ever dealt with the Emperor of Persia, as her Majesty hath done, and obteined for her merchants large and loving privileges? who ever saw before this regiment, an English Ligier in the stately porch of the Grand Signor at Constantinople? who ever found English Consuls and Agents at Tripolis in Syria, at Aleppo, at Babylon, at Balsara, and which is more, who ever heard of Englishman at Goa before now? what English shippes did heeretofore ever anker in the mighty river of Plate? passe and repasse the . . . straigth of Magellan, range along the coast of Chili, Peru, and all the backside of Nova Hispania, further than any Christian ever passed?

These achievements were, however, principally the work of a dedicated few.

The second effect of the increase in population, together with the new economic forces at work in Europe, was to demand relief from poverty through emigration. The enclosure movement had followed upon the Wars of the Roses. When Henry VII put down livery and maintenance, he ended the necessity for great lords to maintain bands of followers through their connection with the land. And as mines in the New World poured gold and silver into Europe, coinage, agricultural prices, rents, and wages were thrown into confusion. The slow emergence of a spending economy led to the rise of a race of *novi homines* replacing the ancient nobility, whose ranks had been depleted by civil war and sectarian strife. The wool market boomed while new trade arrangements led to the growth of towns. The old common lands were obviously in better use for sheep grazing than for "strip" farming or the pasturage of occasional cows; and, moreover, sheep required fewer attendants. Said Latimer: "Where there have been many householders and inhabitants, there is now but a shepherd and a dog." The *novi homines,* wanting estates, got them by enclosure; and the villeins, no longer permitted their old pasture and farm lands, owning no acreage, unable to pay rent, and unhired as plow hands, were thrown upon the roads or crowded into the evil-smelling cities. They formed the race of sturdy beggars against whom statutes were passed, and for whom the Elizabethan poor law was written.

Some of these landless men were lured into the unprofitable enterprise of colonizing Ireland, and others were enlisted for service in the Low Countries. But in the opening years of the seventeenth century propaganda pictured a New World paradise where farms could be acquired by mere manual labor; and relieving the pressures of superfluous population became a standard theme in colonial promotion. Those who could not read listened to sermons.

Thus it was that the attractions of empire and the pressures of poverty operated to overcome the vagueness, the indifference, the parochialism, the prejudice, and the terrors of the Tudor world. Thus England eventually entered the colonial race to compete with the Latins. If the delay seems to many Americans inexplicable, we who are children of the colonial fathers must remember that we read into the records of their random enterprises a sense of importance subsequent to the event. The English did not consciously create the United States. If it is not flattering to think of Jamestown and Boston as being founded in fits of absence of mind, they were founded at least in fits of absence of plan, for the sufficient reason that neither Tudor government nor Tudor theory had any clear notion of "plantations." The astonishing thing is not that English discoveries were made at random or that colonies were nourished by neglect; the astonishing thing is that out of the social confusion of the Tudor world there emerged any colonial enterprises at all.

2

The social confusion of Tudor England was, then, great; great also was its cultural disharmony. Three opposed systems of life fought for supremacy over the Tudor mind and, in some degree, for supremacy in the New World—medievalism, the Renaissance, and the Reformation. Despite the brilliance of Spenser and Shakespeare, the massive structure of the medieval world order did not crumble at the discovery of America; on the contrary, even Marlowe's *Dr. Faustus,* with its immortal passage on the pagan Helen, contains the Seven Deadly Sins and a description of hell as vivid as that in Jonathan Edwards' famous sermon.

Tudor Englishmen in truth still looked upon the visible world as a bridge between two bottomless eternities. In relation to these the earth was but a fretful midge; but because the age of the world was less than seven thousand years the story of mankind was essentially without historic change, Troy being a town like London, and the relation of sinful poets to Christ being very like those of medieval vassals to their lord. As mankind marched across this narrow span, the chief concern of each individual was still that relation—in other words, the salvation of the soul. Catholicism may have been altered to the Church of England; Christian eschatology in the days of Ben Jonson was what it had been to St. Augustine.

History began when God, fulfilling an ancient purpose, called the visible universe into being and created Adam and Eve for his glory. These twain disobeyed him of their own free will; wherefore God placed the curse of travail and death upon their descendants from Cain and Abel to Sir Walter Raleigh, who, though he imagined he saw the grave where Laura lay, saw also heaven as a place where Christ, as an unfeed king's attorney, got his clients off. For God was not merely just, he was also kind, and offered to save some part of mankind, first through a succession of symbolic events like the preservation of Noah, and afterwards through the birth, ministry, crucifixion, and resurrection of Christ. History would come to a fitting end at the Day of Judgment, when the souls of the saved were to rejoice in the presence of God. If this be Christian orthodoxy in the modern Bible belt, we forget that it is a medieval inheritance.

Crossing the bridge of life, sinful man was surrounded by various supernatural beings of superhuman power. A great angel had instigated the original fall. This angel had evil companions, driven with him out of heaven. He was Satan or the Devil, whose chief purpose was to prevent as many human souls as possible from attaining salvation; he, with his confederates, therefore delighted to work mischief, both grotesque and terrifying. Though his power was less than God's, his followers were enabled to do magical things. These followers might be witches and wizards—human souls gone wrong; or they might be human beings who never had opportunity to go right. Such were, for example, the American Indians, whose origin could best be explained by supposing they were the offspring of Satan. Human history was (as conducted by Divine Providence) an enormous campaign between Satan and Christ; therefore colonial historians like Bradford and Winthrop anxiously examined and recorded special providences revealing the cosmic significance of striking events. Even a hard-boiled character like John Smith wrote that Lord De La Warr's coming to Virginia showed "how God inclineth all casuall events to worke the necessary helpe of his Saints."

Had the medieval world persisted unchanged in Europe, the governing concepts of a single church, a single state, and a single ordering of knowledge might have been transferred to the colonies there to shape a culture comparable to the culture of the Latin-American colonies south of the Rio Grande. In fact, nationalism, sectarianism, and the New Learning had already arisen to wreck the old unity. Yet elements descending from the medieval unity persisted, notably in New England. That human reason unaided by divine revelation could go but a partial way toward understanding the causes of things was a proposition no more unsympathetic to the New England minister than to his remote scholastic progenitor. The logic of Peter Ramus of Paris replaced Aristotelian traditionalism in the search for a lost accord; and, with the entrance into the United States of Roman Catholic education, the old scholasticism was in a sense reborn. So likewise the American colonial, though he hated the Pope, could think of the realm of the spirit as a *civitas Dei* or polity of God, as Augustine had taught, and differed chiefly from his Catholic contemporary by considering that Rome was in schism, not New England. Finally, the shadowy concept of unity in Christian society was not lost in crossing the Atlantic. All that Rome had to do was to turn Protestant.

In the feudal system man had status. Status consisted of the place he occupied in the social hierarchy, together with the rights and duties appropriate to his social function. This was his "calling." Status extended beyond military and political duties; it included the economic order, or that "practical life" which existed in order that man might fulfill his chief obligation, to glorify God and serve him. "Business" was therefore also a part of the great drama of time and eternity. Buying and selling were not something done by individuals for private personal gain, but occupations to be directed toward the great religious purpose set for mankind. This control emanated from the church, the feudal order, and various professional and occupational associations. The church, for instance, long frowned upon interest ("usury") as a violation of Christian charity, and church and state likewise denounced such forms of individual profit as "engrossing," or cornering the market. Economic life was supposed to conform to an ideal order; and since a part of this ideal was the assumption that everything had its just price or ideal value (fixed partly by custom and partly by the relation of the cost of production to the selling price) law and custom demanded and frequently secured a stabilization of price and wage. Guilds, furthermore, were organized to guard particular occupations; and as the guild (together with the town) might properly seek to fix the just price of anything, so it might also properly regulate the number of apprentices admitted to a calling. Fundamental to this system, so far as trade is concerned, was the tacit assumption that the town or community is the true economic unit. In Jamestown, in Plymouth, and in other early colonies, these assumptions had considerable vitality, and the communal idea of economic activity was for a time accepted as a matter of course.

The medieval notion of a community of goods cannot be pushed too far inasmuch as men have fallen from that state of innocence which alone would make possible a holy communism. The individual's desire for wealth is the result of man's imperfection since the Fall. But God so manages history that in commanding Adam to earn his living by the sweat of his brow and so sanctioning both private property and profit, he had still in mind his own glory. Only through property can the individual keep that status in society to which God has called him; only through the love of wealth can human industry increase the amount of private riches sufficiently to make charity possible. Only, in fact, through property can God's church be maintained from the gifts of the faithful. Communism was, indeed, the original ideal, reflected in the practice of the primitive church and in such institutions as the monastery, but over the institution of private property medieval doctors managed to throw a sacred veil; and private property thus indirectly received from the medieval world a sanction which in America it has not lost.

3

The most striking, influential, and permanent influence of medieval thought upon American development was, then, the concept that the primary values of life are theological. But the British colonies were founded after the European Renaissance and the Protestant Reformation, which obliterated some parts of the medieval inheritance, altered others, and added to that inheritance elements of their own. The gifts of the Renaissance to American development were manifold; here there is space to particularize only a few: scientific curiosity; a particular kind of individualism; and the concept of the commonwealth as an autonomous structure.

John Addington Symonds' haunting definition of the Renaissance as the rediscovery of the world and of man, despite repeated attempts to point out its inadequacy, will not down, because it contains a living truth. Doubtless Roger Bacon was not the only man of a scientific turn of mind in the Middle Ages. Doubtless if the New World had been discovered in the twelfth century, men's curiosity would have been as great as it was later, things would have had to be named, and despite metaphysical realism there would have been a pragmatic approach to problems arising from the discovery. But the New World was a Renaissance invention; and it was unnecessary to consult the schoolmen about its prodigious natural wonders. It was possible to catalogue its phenomena with a certain innocence of the eye, to describe things as they really were and not as they appeared in bestiaries—to begin, in other words, founding natural science in the United States. The reports of voyagers and settlers are strewn with specific observations, with lists of words, with careful documentation about river and cape, thunderstorm and iceberg, the increase of plants, the habits of animals, the life of Indians, manifestations of natural wealth, the operation of religion, anthropology, and much else to which we give our modern names. Medieval travelers could report, and report vividly; the Renaissance voyager was nevertheless by comparison of a more scientific habit of mind. The *Ymago Mundi* of Pierre d'Ailly, the excellent geographical compilation from the fifteenth century which fascinated the imagination of Columbus, begins by postulating nine spheres "according to the opinions of the astrologers," though Aristotle "admits of eight only." The heavens do not share in the four elements and possess none of their qualities; therefore they are neither generative nor corruptible. If we contrast this appeal to authority and dogma with Winthrop's experimental study of Atlantic weather as he went his way to Massachusetts, we see the immense distance men had come, even though Winthrop's contemporaries frequently appealed to authority and even though Pierre d'Ailly himself is capable of experimental observation.

If we turn from the thing observed to the observer, we are face to face with Renaissance man. The man of the Renaissance has been often and variously described, but always in terms of eminence, superiority, *virtù*, the conscious development of extraordinary capacities. This emphasis upon superiority and leadership is an important clue to understanding the history of the discovery and settlement of British North America, since, at least in its earlier phases, the history was to a surprising degree determined by men of *virtù*. The great names in this history—Lok, Frobisher, Gilbert, Raleigh, Drake, Smith are representative—share in greater or less degree the quality of *noblesse oblige,* even if they are of the middle class. Expeditions to the New World are, as it were, each a *posse comitatus*; one almost expects the giving out of gold rings as in *Beowulf,* so immediately does the personal capacity of the man in charge as statesman, mariner, economist, writer, and general fill the imagination. One forgets the humbler joint-stock enterprises that sent them forth. Products of a culture in which the old, rigid class structure was yearly less evident, these men, violent, capable, headstrong, command only by the sheer weight of personality; at that immense distance from England the authority of king or queen, parliament or city company, is meaningless, and they stand alone, confronting their mutinous and headstrong crews. What drove them forth? They thirsted for an immortality of fame which for them eclipsed a promised immortality of soul. The works of Captain John Smith open with complimentary verses comparing him to Moses, Caesar, Monluc, and Homer:

> Like *Caesar* now thou writ'st what thou hast done,
> These acts, this Booke will live while ther's a Sunne.

Shakespeare cannot promise more to the mysterious W. H. But these verses merely say what Hakluyt and Purchas have said, what Drayton repeated:

> Thy voyages attend
> Industrious Hakluÿt,
> Whose reading shall enflame
> Men to seek fame.

This individualism is, furthermore, a completely masculine individualism. A few like Raleigh, when in England, were aware of the softer side of Renaissance culture, wrote sonnets to their mistress's eyebrow or capered to the lascivious pleasing of a lute; but for the most part elegance and scholarship did not cross the ocean main until the second third of the seventeenth century. The explorers, the founders, were men brought up in the turbulence of Tudor England, of a Europe torn by civil strife and religious warfare. They scarcely knew the humanitarian virtues, rationalizing the slaughter of Indians or papists with the sublime indifference they brought to the slaughter of the wild Irish. Their careers were under the guardianship of Fortuna, that survivor from the Middle Ages, who, after presiding over the destinies of Wolsey, Cromwell, and Lady Jane Grey, came as it were to preside over the destinies of Edward Maria Wingfield, Captain John Smith, the "Lost Colony" at Roanoke, or any other strange bit of early American history. In such a situation the Platonic Academy, Petrarchan amorousness, or nice differences about meter or prose style were meaningless; fortitude and statesmanship, a bravura recklessness, the kind of unlicensed egoism that fascinated Marlowe and Shakespeare, were the qualities needed for success. If these men read, their libraries were those of Captain Myles Standish: Plutarch, "Bariffe's Artillery Guide and the Commentaries of Caesar," and somebody on the art of war were more to the point, not Ovid.

But the personal qualities that will lead unlettered men into the wilderness are not necessarily the same as those that will create settlements; the fishing post yields to the plantation; the marauder is replaced by the statesman; and a colony is born. The most striking fact about these colonies is that they are states in little, autonomous commonwealths, miniature nations, not those dependent invertebrate settlements which to this day helplessly dot the African coast line. An older generation of historians traced the ancestry of the Mayflower Compact to the traditional liberties of the German *Volk;* it is more historical to note that Jamestown, Plymouth, Massachusetts Bay, Providence, Hartford, each of these little settlements is conceived in the spirit of *respublica,* even when (as in the instance of Maryland) one is studying a proprietary colony. The commonwealth may be tiny, but it is a commonwealth, a single state usually with its single church, in the best manner of Renaissance theorizing. If, as Louis Le Roy wrote only thirty years before Jamestown was founded, Providence guides the transition of prosperity from state to state, the colonial founders were conscious of an historic mission; the course of empire took its way westward in men's minds long before Berkeley wrote.

These little states followed current Renaissance theory. In them as in Europe the emphasis was long upon subordination, hierarchy, and order. It was assumed as a fact in nature that there must be a ruling class, the "people" being subordinate. Government was necessarily by a minority. Citizenship was not a right but a privilege; and the dwellers in a given community did not *ipso facto* become citizens of the state. Government was something divinely sanctioned, the necessity for order arising from the spiritual corruption of mankind whether in France or in Virginia, on the coast of Maine or in Italy. The contract theory, so far as it operated, was not as with Rousseau a compact of individuals mystically conscious of their natural rights; on the contrary, "contract" was characteristically a covenant between the ruling classes and Deity, to which such minor matters as royal charters or the directives of a trading company were but codicils. We misunderstand the early years of the American colonies if we read their history through the eyes of Locke, Samuel Adams, Freeman, or Theodore Roosevelt. They grew up, not in anticipation of the Glorious Revolution, the Declaration of Independence, or the "Germanic" theory of liberty; they were creations, imperfect, tiny, obscure, but typical, of Renaissance speculation about the nature of government and the commonwealth; and the transition from these postulates to nineteenth century liberalism was as painful in the New World as it has been in the Old.

4

To remark that the Reformation was also a basic factor conditioning American cultural development is surely a work of supererogation. The rest of this history is lengthy proof of the fact that the spirit of American letters is predominantly Protestant. To the disentangling of the many threads of this Protestant influence whole subsequent chapters are given. It would be idle here to argue such vexing questions as whether Lutheranism or Calvinism was the more democratic faith; whether there was a distinctive and unique American Puritanism; or whether the protest of Protestantism and the dissidence of dissent appearing in such nineteenth century faiths as Mormonism and Christian Science are lineal descendants of the European Reformation. It is a commonplace that colonial clergymen were learned men who continued the traditions of humanism, and who sought to found Christian utopias (strictly limited to godly of the right sort) up and down the Atlantic coast. Latterly, ink has been spilled to show that Puritanism had an aesthetic, that the Pilgrims liked strong liquors and were lusty fellows. For intellectual history these questions are not so important as is the realization that in northern Europe Protestantism conquered humanism in the degree that Calvin was no Pico della Mirandola and Luther was no Erasmus. The American colonies were the children of north European Protestantism.

If humanism was the rediscovery of a literature, Protestantism was the rediscovery of a book. American colonials, even in Virginia, became the people of that book. Displacing ancient Israel as the chosen of God, the founders of American plantations regarded themselves as divinely appointed to increase the kingdom of a Protestant Christ and to further the cause revealed by Deity in the Old Testament and continued in the New World. Bibliolatry took shape as an attempt to legalize in the wilderness the Mosaic code and to learn from the cloudy pages of the prophets the American signs of the times. A kind of *sortes Biblicae* aided the magistrate; whether at Geneva or at Salem, orthodoxy became the primary test of citizenship. One has only to study, as Otto Benesch has done, the Renaissance art in northern Europe to see how profoundly Protestantism alters values; out of this alteration of values America was born. Contrast portraits by Dürer, Cranach, and Holbein with canvases by Raphael, Titian, and Tintoretto. The difference is not that the Puritan is opposed to art and the Catholic embraces it, nor that the Teutonic world distrusted paganism and the Latin culture went out to meet paganism with open arms; the difference is that in the one culture life is the education of a character, in the other it is the cultivation of a personality. The grave faces which look out at us from the pictures of the northern masters are the faces of men of affairs, men whose integrity is a credit-making virtue, who do not deny that recreation has its place in life, but to whom pleasure is never spontaneous because they have read in the Book that there is an appointed time for everything. Theirs is, in sum, a Biblical culture, not, as in the Mediterranean world, a spontaneous one.

For such men, belief is an inner experience; seeking to evaluate that experience, they are filled alternately with enthusiasm and melancholy—not the sensuous melancholy of Da Vinci's portraits, but that melancholy which transcends all wit in Dürer's most celebrated engraving. Translate this melancholia into New England theology, it becomes the inwardness, the perpetual dubiety and concern for the symbolical significance of trifles that make the diary of a man like Cotton Mather so curious and remote. A world whose deepest significance lies within is not a world of pictorial splendor, architectural magnificence, colorful theater, or sensuous verse. In America baroque architecture appears only in the Latin colonies; the spare, geometrical lines of our seventeenth century houses are boundaries about a life within, not, as in the case of Spanish-American cathedrals, a reaching outward into the air and the sky. The Spaniards and the Portuguese found theaters, give concerts, produce architects, painters, poets who really rival Camoëns; in North America there are sermons, domestic architecture, the handicraft arts, political controversy, and the most erudite colonial literature the world has ever seen. But the erudition is principally theological and looks within. Life is not an artistic affair, it is sober duty; thrift, industry, carefulness, the qualities of Poor Richard, the economic virtues do not conceal this inward-ness. The most characteristic production in stone of New England culture is the tombstone, on which the local cutter engraved an hourglass, a skeleton, or a winged head.

In sixteenth century Europe Protestantism was a fighting faith. In an either-or world there was no room for the tolerant grays of modern lati-tudinarianism; the century which saw the Massacre of St. Bartholomew was understandably suspicious of mere toleration. To modern readers the harsh, bounding line of any religious faith in the period is repellent and strange. It was, however, as necessary to be clearly and definitely an Anabaptist, a Quaker, a Lutheran, a Calvinist in that epoch as it is today to be definitely a Communist, a Fascist, or a democrat. He who was not for you was against you, and he who was against you was also against God and therefore capable of any wickedness. Elizabethan gentlemen undoubtedly treated Spanish grandees with the courtesies due to class and breeding, and there are records of the polite reception of even Jesuits in seventeenth century New England. We are, however, so bemused by the historical fame of Mrs. Hutchinson, Roger Williams, and other victims or examples of intolerance in an intolerant time that we overlook the darkest heritage of the Reformation in American history—the hatred of the Catholic faith. Not merely were Tudor voyages directed toward defeating Spain; not merely did Elizabeth encourage legends about Catholic plots against her life; but this prejudice also landed at James-town, at Plymouth, swarmed up the Shenandoah Valley, ended the well meant experiment of Baltimore in Maryland, and, save for a brief period during and after the American Revolution, still conditions the folkways of "old Americans" in dealing with their newer fellow citizens. It is also an unexpressed assumption of American literary history that Protestantism is intellectually more important than Catholicism, and that, for example, Jona-than Edwards or Emerson is of greater cultural importance than Bishop England of Charleston or Cardinal Gibbons of Baltimore. The United States derives from the Protestant Reformation a *Kulturkampf* like in kind, though not in present intensity, to that of sixteenth and seventeenth century Europe. It is one of the longest-lived and one of the most baffling inheritances to reach us from the sixteenth century world.

It has been already here remarked that the world which brought the first English colonies into being was a strongly masculine world. But among the most important legacies of the Reformation to the United States was the position of women. In the annals of Latin America women figure as poets, as religious mystics, as great ladies in colonial courts; but they figure always within the confines of customs that are both Catholic and Mediterranean. The

Protestant world being both mercantile and middle-class, women were primarily wives and daughters. In American legend Priscilla Alden is seated at her spinning wheel, and the heroic pioneer women engage in domestic economy. In a world without nunneries, without viceregal courts like those in Lima or Mexico, the Virgin was replaced by the mother; and the curious and singular purity of the history of womanhood in the United States is no less a product of the Protestant Reformation than is Woolman's *Journal* or Emerson's Divinity School Address. American culture produced no *belle dame sans merci* (until Hollywood); and it is characteristic of its mores that the first cabinet crisis of its first frontier President, Andrew Jackson, concerned a chivalric defense of Peggy Eaton. In the United States female wickedness comes from France—from, in other words, a Latin and Catholic culture. Classic American literature is without sexuality, but has domesticity; its most serious description of passion is *The Scarlet Letter,* a book taught in the public schools; and when the Protestant imagination of Longfellow finished with anthropological lore, Minnehaha was as properly a bride of Hiawatha as ever Mrs. Lapham was of Silas the paint king. Doubtless the domestic virtues are the middle-class virtues; but in the New World the middle class was originally Protestant, and when we seek the origin of their codes of conduct we are led backward to the world of the Reformation, which, in the name of domestic morality, attacked indulgences and replaced celibacy by the marriage of its prelates. From the point of view of the influence of feminine taste upon culture, the place of women in Protestant domesticity is one of the most important facts in our inheritance from sixteenth century Europe.

By the end of the seventeenth century the English mainland colonies, absorbing every other racial stock settling from Maine to Florida, were launched upon an autonomous cultural life. To the north and west the Catholic French were unabashed and defiant; from Florida and Alabama to the river Plate His Most Catholic Majesty of Spain held sway. Any map of the New World for 1700 shows only a ribbon of coast belonging to the English. If they were later to absorb most of the continent, the long delay allowed them time to adjust to new conditions, to put down roots, to adapt their heterogeneous Old World inheritance to a new environment. They developed colonial education, colonial books, colonial publishing, colonial literary art. Out of this came in time a national culture. The chronicle of this development now follows. It is the history of a complex European inheritance, by slow degrees and ceaseless experimentations becoming so unique a phenomenon that modern transatlantic observers have difficulty in recognizing its Old World roots.

2. COLONIAL LITERARY CULTURE

THE Protestant communities which sprang up in Virginia, New England, and elsewhere in America were much like country towns and villages of England. The people for the most part were hard-working, simple folk without much acquaintance with belles-lettres, and it would have been a miracle indeed if polite literature had suddenly bloomed in the American woods. The truth is that the majority of settlers had little or no literary background. They were a plain people faced with the task of subduing a wilderness.

Though some of the stricter Puritans and Quakers were actively prejudiced against many forms of imaginative literature, which they conceived to be idle and frivolous, they nevertheless placed a high value on certain forms of learning. The Puritans emphasized Biblical and theological learning; the Quakers stressed practical studies which served for the relief of man's estate. The significant fact is that colonial Americans cherished learning even when they did not share it, and in spite of great difficulties they fashioned instruments of culture which made possible a literary development in the eighteenth century.

Frontier conditions are rarely conducive to literary production, and the frontier of the seventeenth and early eighteenth centuries was particularly unfavorable. Some colonies, notably in the South, lacked the means of printing until well along in the eighteenth century. The lack of towns was also a serious deterrent in the South to the development of literary activity. Inspiration may come from vernal woods, but sustained literary production is a characteristic of urban rather than rural environment. Until the colonies along the Atlantic seaboard achieved settled towns, citizens with a modicum of leisure, and the paraphernalia of urbane life—such as schools, libraries, booksellers, lecture platforms, printing presses, and discussion clubs—literature was in abeyance.

But, from the very first, American colonists showed a deep concern lest their children grow up barbarous in the wilderness. This concern was equally great in New England and in Virginia, though the methods of meeting the danger varied with differing conditions. In New England villagers quickly set up schools for their children, and the Puritan fathers in 1636 established Harvard College to insure a learned ministry and provide a nursery of learning for their sons. In Virginia the wealthier planters hired tutors, and the less well-to-do organized plantation schools and shared the expense of a teacher; those who were able sent their sons, and sometimes their daughters, to England for more advanced education. In 1693 Virginians established the College of William and Mary from the same motives that had prompted the founders of Harvard.

By 1760 some cities, particularly Boston and Philadelphia, had excellent grammar schools, and throughout the colonies public-spirited citizens were laboring to increase educational opportunities. Stern Calvinists were convinced that education was necessary to combat the devil, and easy-going deists were equally certain that education was needed to bring about man's perfection. The doctrine of universal educational opportunity, which Thomas Jefferson was to advocate near the turn of the century, was already incipient, and movements were on foot which would transform the ideal of education into something akin to a religious fervor for Americans in the nineteenth century. Before 1760 the colonies could take pride in six colleges which freed them from dependence for higher learning upon the Old World. In addition to Harvard, and William and Mary, these institutions were Yale (1701), the College of New Jersey (1746—later Princeton), King's (1754—later Columbia), and the Charity School in Philadelphia (1740—later the Academy and College of Philadelphia, and eventually the University of Pennsylvania). Vernacular belles-lettres, it is true, had small place in formal education in this period; but classical rhetoric and the prose and poetry of Greece and Rome exerted a profound influence in the development of a literary consciousness.

2

Despite the laborious tasks faced by the earliest settlers, both North and South, they did not entirely neglect the benefits of letters. Indeed, the books which they brought with them were remarkable for their variety and significance, and the importance of little household libraries in the transmission of the literary tradition can scarcely be overemphasized. Seventeenth century inventories show a wide dispersion of books throughout the colonies. Before the end of the seventeenth century Boston had a half-dozen or more booksellers. One of the earliest of these was Hezekiah Usher, who at his death in 1676 left a comfortable fortune made in the book trade. Peddlers often carried books and pamphlets in their packs. Cotton Mather proposed to induce an itinerant hawker to "fill this Countrey with devout and useful

Books"—from Mather's own pen—but complained, years later, that peddlers were corrupting good manners by disseminating ballads and foolish poems. In the tobacco colonies, where local booksellers were virtually unknown, English factors supplied the literary needs of planters. Letters from Virginia and Maryland to merchants in London or Bristol contain frequent requests for specific books, though the planters sometimes asked their factors to send the latest things in the booksellers' stalls and left the choice of titles to the agents' discretion.

The subject matter of the books imported in the seventeenth and eighteenth centuries is indicative of the serious purpose of the colonists. In the broadest sense, their selections were utilitarian, and books designed merely for entertainment or amusement found small place in their household libraries. Picaresque narratives, jest books, ballads, and other literary frivolities were not unknown, it is true; but little money was squandered upon idle reading. This concentration upon "useful" books was as characteristic of Virginia planters as it was of New England Puritans.

Although the New England and the Southern colonists showed differences of emphasis in literary taste, they showed more striking—and perhaps more significant—similarities. The books having the widest circulation before 1760 can be broadly classified as religious and pious. Many of the same religious books were read by Calvinists in the North and Anglicans in the South. Though preachers and some laymen bought and read strictly theological works, the majority of readers preferred less controversial handbooks of piety. Books which had pleased middle-class Tudor and Stuart Englishmen remained standard reading in the colonies for generations. Lewis Bayly's *Practice of Piety* and the sermons of the Reverend William Perkins edified alike merchants and apprentices in Boston and Philadelphia and gentlemen in the region of Chesapeake Bay. Households possessing no other book might have a well thumbed copy of the King James Version of the Bible; a remarkable number had Foxe's *Acts and Monuments*. The appetite of the seventeenth and early eighteenth centuries for pious reading should not be discounted too cavalierly in appraising the cultural development of Americans. Many books of piety were written with a conscious effort at simplicity and clarity to appeal to the understanding of plain men. In such works colonial readers found not only lessons in ethics and good morality but patterns and forms of expression.

Historical works, both classical and modern, were second only to religious literature in the favor of colonial Americans. From Greek and Roman historians, they drew lessons of statecraft as well as facts about the ancient world. Tacitus was a favorite author, for example, and Thomas Jefferson, who read him in his youth, declared later in life that he was the wisest of all writers. Raleigh's *History of the World*, Bishop Gilbert Burnet's *History of the*

Reformation in England, and many another English work entertained and instructed colonial readers.

Books of conduct, instructions in domestic relations, political treatises, legal discussions and handbooks for the amateur as well as the professional lawyer, medical books, and sundry guides to farming, navigation, surveying, and other practical pursuits were among the useful books which colonists bought and treasured.

The most influential writers in the eighteenth century were probably Joseph Addison and Richard Steele. Countless Americans who bought and read the *Tatler* and the *Spectator* could not entirely escape the moral and social lessons which the authors intended. Neither could they avoid being affected by the style. Benjamin Franklin was not the only colonial writer who deliberately imitated the *Spectator* essays.

By the end of the seventeenth century, poetry and drama had come to have a larger place in colonial reading, and the appetite for belles-lettres gradually increased. A few men and women of advanced literary taste dipped into Spenser's *Faerie Queene* and Milton's *Paradise Lost*; considerably more read the poetical works of George Herbert, Francis Quarles, and Abraham Cowley. By the mid-eighteenth century, Shakespeare's plays were frequently found in gentlemen's libraries. By the same period, booksellers had discovered a considerable market for chapbooks, fiction something less than edifying, and other trifling works which serious folk still regarded as frivolous and perhaps iniquitous.

During the seventeenth century most libraries were gathered for the immediate utility to their owners; but by the end of the century book collecting in almost a professional sense had begun. Cotton Mather in Massachusetts and William Byrd in Virginia during the early years of the eighteenth century gathered substantial libraries; and at death each had nearly four thousand volumes divided among the various branches of learning. By 1751 James Logan had gathered in Philadelphia a library of approximately three thousand volumes, which he bequeathed to the city for public use. To the collecting instinct of the Reverend Thomas Prince of Boston, we are indebted for the preservation of many rare books and manuscripts of the period. Many other private libraries of substantial proportions were gathered during the colonial period and helped in the dissemination of learning. Records of book borrowing show that the influence of the private libraries extended far beyond the households of the owners.

Institutional libraries date from the founding of the first colleges. John Harvard's bequest of his books to the college at Cambridge established a library that continued to grow in importance and usefulness. By the middle of the eighteenth century Yale also had a respectable library, and the other colleges had working collections of learned books.

A systematic effort to foster piety and learning by the circulation of books was started near the end of the seventeenth century by the Reverend Thomas Bray, moving spirit in the founding of the Society for the Propagation of the Gospel in Foreign Parts. He devised a plan for sending parish libraries to the colonies for the use of the Anglican clergy and their parishioners. By his efforts it is estimated that approximately thirty-four thousand volumes reached America and were widely distributed, chiefly in regions where Anglicans were most numerous. In 1700 the provincial legislature at Charleston, South Carolina, made Dr. Bray's parochial library a public institution.

Public and semipublic libraries began to develop in the seventeenth century and by 1760 were fairly numerous. A merchant, Robert Keayne, by his will in 1653, established a public library in Boston which in some degree served the needs of the populace for several generations. In 1700 the Reverend John Sharpe, chaplain to the governor, bequeathed his books to found a public library in New York; although this benefaction was augmented somewhat, it made little impression until a group of citizens in 1754 took up a subscription, bought about seven hundred additional volumes, and rejuvenated an institution which eventually grew into the New York Society Library, a proprietary institution. Benjamin Franklin was instrumental in founding the Library Company of Philadelphia, incorporated in 1742 but actually started by subscription some time before. A few years later, in 1747, a merchant, Abraham Redwood, provided funds for the Redwood Library in Newport, Rhode Island; and a year afterward "seventeen young gentlemen" founded the Charleston Library Society in South Carolina. All of these institutions, which still exist, exerted an important influence. Benjamin Franklin, in his pride over the Philadelphia Library Company, wrote in his *Autobiography* that such libraries had made common tradesmen and farmers as intelligent as gentlemen elsewhere and had contributed to the ability of Americans to defend their privileges.

3

Before an indigenous literature could develop in the colonies, an adequate means of printing was essential. Massachusetts led all the other colonies in this endeavor with the press established at Cambridge in 1639 and operated by Stephen Day for the widow Glover. From this press came the Bay Psalm Book, the earliest laws of Massachusetts, and many religious and learned works. Day was succeeded by Samuel Green, whose descendants later carried the art of printing to several other colonies. Before the end of the century the Cambridge press had competitors in Boston, which soon became an important center for New England publishing. There James Franklin had his shop, and there his half-brother Ben learned the craft. After Boston, Philadelphia became the most important printing center, and by the middle of the eighteenth century it had equaled if not surpassed its northern rival. William Bradford, the first printer in Philadelphia, was also responsible for the establishment of a press in New York in 1693.

Printing got under way more slowly in the South, where royal governors took a sour view of printing presses and at first sought to suppress them (if Massachusetts Bay had not been virtually independent of royal interference for most of the seventeenth century, it is certain that the press there would have enjoyed much less freedom). In 1682 William Nuthead attempted to establish a press at Jamestown, Virginia; but he soon became involved with the authorities, and his efforts were suppressed by order of the governor. In 1685 he transferred his activities to the proprietary colony of Maryland. Thereafter no press was attempted in Virginia until 1730, when William Parks came over from Maryland to Williamsburg and set up a print shop. In 1731 three printers working separately tried to start presses at Charleston, South Carolina; but it remained for Lewis Timothy, a partner of Benjamin Franklin, in 1733 to become the first successful printer there.

By 1763 printing was firmly established in each of the thirteen colonies. Although censorship varied from colony to colony and from time to time, printers had achieved considerable freedom by the mid-eighteenth century, and had become potent influences in shaping public opinion. After the beginning of the eighteenth century nearly every printer aspired to be the proprietor of a newspaper, for newspaper publishing—along with the printing of official documents—was regarded as essential to a printer's prosperity.

A writer in the *Gentleman's Magazine,* in November 1796, observed that "the newspapers of Massachusetts, Connecticut, Rhode Island, Pennsylvania, and Maryland are unequaled whether considered with respect to wit and humour, entertainment or instruction." And he added that "every capital town on the [American] Continent prints a weekly paper; and several of them have one or more daily papers." The journalism that excited the admiration of this writer had not suddenly flowered after the Revolution, but had developed over a long period of years. Indeed, newspapers from the mid-eighteenth century onward provided a means of expression which had a far-reaching influence upon the literary, as well as the political, development of the country.

The first newspaper was Benjamin Harris' *Publick Occurrences,* which appeared on September 25, 1690, in Boston and expired four days later when the governor and council "disallowed" its further publication because Harris had presumed to make his venture without permission. The next endeavor of this kind was made in the same city by a cautious Scot, John Campbell, who, in 1704, founded the *News-Letter,* which lasted until the Revolution.

By 1735 Boston alone had five newspapers, and other cities of the Atlantic seaboard were not far behind. By 1750 all the colonies were well provided with newspapers, published weekly and in some cases oftener.

Many of the early papers were partly literary in content. James Franklin, for example, mingled poems and humorous pieces with the news items in the *New-England Courant*. The stated purpose of this journal was to be entertaining, amusing, and instructive. Benjamin Franklin contributed anonymously his first literary efforts to his brother's paper. Many another American achieved a brief literary life in the columns of newspapers. Among the more literary papers were the Boston *Evening-Post*, the *Virginia Gazette*, and the *South Carolina Gazette*. The last-named paper published extensive selections from contemporary English authors as well as from the pens of local writers.

Benjamin Franklin and Andrew Bradford founded rival monthly magazines in Philadelphia in 1741, but both periodicals soon collapsed for lack of support. Magazines were to be a later development in American letters. Even earlier, Samuel Keimer, a visionary printer of Philadelphia, had endeavored to give a literary quality to the weekly paper which he founded in 1728 under the title of *The Universal Instructor in all Arts and Sciences: and Pennsylvania Gazette*. Besides attempting to reprint a contemporary encyclopedia, he started the serial publication of Daniel Defoe's *Religious Courtship*. The heavy instructional and literary quality of the paper was too much for Philadelphia, and Franklin bought it for a song the year after its establishment. The new publisher made the *Pennsylvania Gazette* more lively—if less consciously "literary"—and the publication flourished.

Of several attempts to establish foreign-language newspapers during this period, only two achieved success. Christopher Sower and Heinrich Miller published German-language papers, religious in sentiment, at Germantown and Philadelphia respectively.

An event of vast import for the freedom of expression in the colonies was the fight made in 1734-1735 by John Peter Zenger, publisher of the New York *Weekly Journal*, against the persecution by the governor's party. His imprisonment and trial for libel, and his vindication by the jury, made a great stir, not only in New York but in all the colonies, and quickened men's zeal to defend the liberty of speech and press.

4

The tradition of public discussion in the colonies was a strong influence in the training of men's intellects. Long before newspapers gave an outlet for written thoughts, colonial citizens were practiced in self-expression. In the legislative assemblies, political debate was not the exclusive monopoly of the rich and well born. An occasional speech or state paper, preserved in the records of the popular assemblies, is written in vivid and sinewy prose. The town meetings of New England and the political gatherings in the Southern colonies are more famous for their effect upon the development of democratic institutions, but their influence upon literary expression should not be overlooked.

The pulpit, particularly in the seventeenth century, was a forum for learned exposition on religion, ethics, sociology, science, politics, and almost any phase of the life of man. Puritan sermons are amazing in the variety of subjects treated directly or incidentally. Here and there preachers succeeded in putting their thoughts into moving prose; and even though the literary qualities of the clergy have been exaggerated by later historians they at least furnished a pattern of logical reasoning and taught their audiences useful lessons in formal expression. The Puritan clergy of New England were far more influential than ministers elsewhere, but an occasional Anglican clergyman in the middle and Southern colonies furnished intellectual stimulation in his region.

Informal clubs and discussion groups helped to foster literary as well as scientific interest. Most famous was Franklin's Junto in Philadelphia, the later American Philosophical Society, but nearly every town of importance had some sort of discussion club by the mid-eighteenth century.

Religious opposition to theatrical performances was widespread throughout the seventeenth century. Besides a prejudice against plays on moral grounds, a lingering belief among middle-class folk that stage productions were frivolous and wasteful of precious time helped retard theatrical progress. The first professional actors to perform in the colonies presented a play in Charleston in 1703. Within a year of production in London, George Lillo's sentimental drama *George Barnwell* (1731) was published serially in the *New-England Weekly Journal,* which recommended it to readers on the ground that it tended to promote virtue and piety, though Boston censorship forbade dramatic activity in the city for many years to come. Professional companies appeared in New York after 1732, and Philadelphia and Williamsburg witnessed mid-century performances, often written or acted by college students. But on the whole the theater was late in development, and its influence was relatively unimportant in this period.

During the first century and a half of settlement and development, the colonists spent their main energies in practical and utilitarian pursuits, as would be expected in a raw and unexploited continent. Although the colonial contribution to literature was small, these busy settlers salvaged time for intellectual interests and attached great importance to schools, books, libraries, and other influences above and beyond material considerations. The foundation for a later manifestation of remarkable intellectual and literary capacity was laid in the period before 1760.

3. REPORTS AND CHRONICLES

THE earliest writing to come from the New World can be called literature only by stretching the meaning of the word. Before the English had settled their strip of coast, men of many nations had explored the continent from Newfoundland to Mexico and from the Atlantic to the Pacific. The records of their adventures, many of them crude and utilitarian, are our first literature. They are letters home, diaries written in the midst of dangerous actions, chronicles compiled while the memory of the actions was still warm. They were written in the languages of the explorers—Spanish, French, Dutch, and the Scandinavian—some were written in or translated into Latin, others English. Some were published at the time, some were excerpted for collections of voyages, some remained in manuscript for centuries. Together they form a body of documents recording one of the great adventures of man, the opening and settling of the western hemisphere. In them, American literature made a cosmopolitan beginning which was narrowed to the Anglo-Saxon cultural tradition only after two centuries. The story of these reports and chronicles is vast and complex; only its main outlines and principal documents can be noted. But unless it is told, our literature would seem more provincial in its origins than it was. The British colonial period was but an episode—a major episode to be sure—in our cultural history.

2

Suppose that one Leif Ericsson did sail west from Greenland about A.D. 1000, and suppose that ten years later one Thorfinn Karlsefne did the same thing—what reports of their adventures exist?

Three manuscripts, the *Flateyjarbók, Hauksbók,* and a document known as A[rna]–M[agnean] 557, which contains the story of Eric the Red, are in the Royal Library at Copenhagen. Written in the thirteenth or fourteenth century, these tell of events which had occurred about four hundred years earlier. They are the oldest extant writings containing traces of the reports on "Vineland"—which may have been anywhere between Labrador and Long Island. What these "sagas" have to tell did not get into print until Adam of

Bremen's "Ecclesiastical History" was published in 1595—more than a century after Christopher Columbus got his story into type. These sources have been often republished, translated and reproduced in facsimile, while critical works about them multiply, and authorities continue to agree vaguely, or disagree openly as to what they mean. It may be, indeed it has been said, that the history of America would be precisely the same if no Norseman had ever steered his Viking ship west from Greenland. As reports these manuscripts are not contemporary, and as chronicles they are not trustworthy. They are merely parts of that Scandinavian literature which has occasionally inspired American writers from Longfellow to the present.

3

Spain got a head start with respect to "voyages" to and through the "Newe Worlde." "It is therefore apparent that the heroical facts of the Spaniards of these days deserve so great praise that the author of this book (being no Spaniard) doth worthily extoll their doings." Thus Richard Eden, in his *Decades of the Newe Worlde* (1555), introduced the first collection of "voyages" to the English reading public in its own language. His magnanimity to Spain may have owed something to the fact that the English sovereign was the Catholic Mary who had temporarily forged a bond with Spain's Philip. More than sixty years had elapsed since the first printing of Columbus' own "Epistola" in 1493. Of that book, in which the discoverer published his own story, there were at least seventeen "incunabula editions"—but not one in English.

So let the literary history of the United States begin in Texas. Between 1528 and 1536, Alvar Núñez Cabeza de Vaca, Spaniard, walked across the present area of Texas, New Mexico, and Arizona and wrote a book about his wanderings. His *Relación* appeared in print in 1542, has been translated into many languages, and reprinted in every century since. Colored by the religious zeal of his time, it is not altogether the work of a mere superstitious observer though he lived in a day when impossible wonders found their way into the literature of travel. De Vaca's inaccuracies are gratifyingly few, and he provided the first report on two animals without which American literature would be the poorer: his opossum was to become a character in the writings of Joel Chandler Harris, and what would be the literature of the trans-Mississippi West without the buffalo?

The next "overland narrative" tells of Hernando de Soto, who between 1539 and 1542 marched his Spanish expedition from Florida to North Carolina, thence west to the Mississippi. There his death and dramatic burial in the Father of Waters ended his career. The chronicler of this exploit lives only as "The Gentleman of Elvas," an unknown Portuguese who accompanied De Soto and whose *Relaçam verdadeira* was published in 1557. His work was introduced to the English reading public by Richard Hakluyt (of whom, more, later) as *Virginia richly valued* (1609). Said Hakluyt, quite correctly: "This work . . . though small in show, yet great in substance, doth yeeld much light" upon the immensity of the area and resources of what was to become the United States.

In 1540 Francisco Vásquez Coronado started from Mexico into our South-west. Searching for the "seven cities of Cibola," Coronado certainly got as far north as the present state of Kansas. His chronicler was Pedro Casteñeda, who did not write the full and fascinating "Relación de la jórnada de Cibola" until twenty years after the expedition's return to Mexico. It lay in manu-script (occasionally transcribed by men who had no share in the original work) for more than three hundred and fifty years. Not until 1896 were the Spanish text and a translation into English printed for the first time. Partly because the region explored was sparsely settled (discoveries are still being made there), partly because of the ever-changing place names, and partly because the Southwest was not much exploited by European colonization at the time, the Coronado-Casteñeda story has only recently assumed its proper place in the literature of the United States. The expedition was one of the last of those swashbuckling and panoplied raids for God, glory, and gold, wherein Cortez and Pizarro succeeded in Mexico and Peru, but Coronado failed because the gold was not found. The "Conquistador" has persisted in national legend.

Less well known than Coronado is Antonio de Espejo, who roamed the Southwest in 1582 and 1583. His work produced a book in English, the author-ship of which is credited to him: *New Mexico: otherwise the voiage of Anthony of Espeio . . . translated out of the Spanish copie printed first at Madreel [Madrid], 1586, and afterward at Paris, in the same yeare* (London, 1587). The modern reader will find the elaboration in Hakluyt's *Voyages*, as these early Spanish and French editions are hard to come by and the English edition survives in a single copy in the Huntington Library; but translations and successive reprintings are some measure of the significance of a book.

4

The first Frenchman who wrote satisfactory reports on what is now the United States was Samuel de Champlain, soldier, explorer, and "Father of New France." He knew how to make bold decisions and to act with dispatch, suggesting a clearheadedness which, in turn, reveals itself in clarity of style. What he saw, he described vividly and in detail. In the 1613 edition of his

Voyages he first reports upon his mapping of New England and his celebrated "battle" with the Iroquois, which had far-reaching effects since it allied the French with the enemies of that all-powerful league. Champlain's powers of description are well illustrated by his reports on such matters as the effects of scurvy and by word pictures (often with engraved maps) such as that of Port St. Louis (Plymouth, Massachusetts). Despite the many printings of his works, it was 1922 before a complete and satisfactory edition in English began to appear; yet many a traveler has followed Champlain's routes, text in hand, and been able to check and verify the accuracy of his observations. The reader of Champlain's *Voyages* may be reminded of Caesar's "Commentaries." Both captains were dealing with a disorganized and semibarbarous foe. As Caesar played off the Gauls against one another, so Champlain allied himself with Algonquins against Iroquois. Both were able to view and to describe their enemies objectively, admiring their meritorious qualities while pointing out less desirable characteristics. Champlain's description of his attack on the Iroquois fort is a miniature of Caesar's siege of Alesia. Both writers seem fascinated by mechanical details, and enjoy describing them. At times a reader is apt to feel that Champlain had a more genuine sympathy for, and understanding of, the American Indians than Caesar ever had toward the Gauls. It is entirely possible, if anything may be inferred from such a comparison of their writings, that Champlain was more deeply and sincerely concerned with the glory of France than Caesar ever was with that of Rome. On the whole, a critic might well conclude that Champlain was the greater of the two. His report of wandering in upper New York State in 1615 appears in the 1627 edition of the *Voyages et decouvertes*. His personal explorations ended in 1616, and the final summing up of all his work appears in his longest and last book *Les Voyages de la Nouvelle France* (1632).

Promotion writing is sometimes literature. The annual reports of a commercial corporation, a government bureau, or a missionary society may be literature if they are well written, and if they are widely read throughout the years for more reasons than the original reporter anticipated. Such is that series which has come to be known as the "Jesuit Relations." They were originally prepared to tell the superiors of the Order what the Jesuit missionaries were doing in New France, to secure financial support, and to inform the pious of the great work "ad majorem Dei gloriam." The Jesuits covered the world, but the expression "Jesuit Relations" has come to designate the group of reports which came from the area of the Great Lakes in the seventeenth century, more particularly between 1632 and 1673 when they were being published by Sébastien Cramoisy in Paris. A substantial part of them recount what was going on in the areas of the present states of New York, Michigan, Illinois, Wisconsin, and Minnesota. The "Relations" tell of the folklore, the mores, the economic condition, and the daily life of an Indian people now practically vanished. They were written by men who combined the physical endurance of the athlete with the scholar's academic training, for these Jesuits had to be, and were, rigidly educated in rhetoric, the humanities, and what would today be called psychology. Although the driving force back of this writing was religious zeal, the intellectual curiosity of these missionary reporters led them to record all sorts of phenomena so that generations of readers have found the "Relations" a source of information in many fields. After enjoying a considerable and significant popularity, the "Jesuit Relations" sank into relative obscurity for two centuries, to be revived in the latter half of the nineteenth century, possibly because of their republication by the Canadian government (1858), the popularity of Francis Parkman's *The Jesuits in North America* (1867), and the publication of the series with translation into English by R. G. Thwaites in seventy-three volumes. The expression "Jesuit Relations" should not be permitted to obscure the fact that these volumes were written by individual authors, many of whom became martyrs to their faith at the hands of the Indians. Any consideration of them should record the names of Paul Le Jeune, Barthélemy Vimont, Jérôme Lalament, Paul Ragueneau, Claude Allouez, Claude Dablon, Jean de Brébeuf—and Jacques Marquette. They were trained men with a thirst for adventure, a zeal for Catholicism, and an unusual ability to express themselves.

A by-product of these writings was the "War of the Orders," the rivalry between the Jesuits and Franciscans (Recollects, in this case). The administrators, explorers, and traders of New France were inclined to favor the Franciscans because they were more tolerant than the Jesuits, particularly with respect to using brandy as legal tender to the Indians. Foremost among these Franciscans is Brother Gabriel Sagard, historian of the Hurons, whose first book appeared in 1632 with a dictionary of the Huron language. His *Histoire du Canada* (1636) sums up his previous works and first accounts for the arrival in the present area of the United States of one Etienne Brulé who probably reached Mackinac and the Sault a year before any Pilgrim got to Plymouth. Father Chrétien le Clercq's *Premier etablissement de la foy dans la Nouvelle France* (1691) is a compilation of original accounts of La Salle's voyages, especially that down the Mississippi, and particularly the writings of Father Zenobius Membré. But the most widely read of these Recollects was Father Louis Hennepin, whose *Description de la Louisiane* (1683) is a more reliable account of his work, particularly in the upper Mississippi Valley, than his subsequent *Nouveau Voyage* (1696)—story of a journey he probably never made but plagiarized from Membré's account in Le Clercq. Although Hennepin's writing is marked by the literary egotism characteristic of his day, his geographical observations and his comments on men and manners are excellent. It may be that something has been lost in the continued reliance upon the seventeenth century English translation. Does "This Calumet is the most mysterious Thing in the world among the Savages" express quite the same thought as "Il faut avouer, que le Calumet est quelque chose de fort mysterieux parmi les Sauvages du Grand Continent de l'Amerique Septentrionale"? Hennepin's books ran to thirty-five variant editions in five languages.

Among these Frenchmen was the charming Baron Louis-Armand Lahontan. While the Jesuits and Recollects were minutely describing the American Indian, Lahontan philosophized about him. The fifty-two editions of Lahontan's *Nouveaux Voyages* (1703), which appeared in five different languages, provide some quantitative measure of his work. A more subtle evaluation of his influence is suggested by a modern critic who has pointed out the significance of Lahontan's "noble savage" Adario. That imaginary Indian describes "man in a state of nature" in a manner which is a perfectly logical outcome of many descriptive writings by the Jesuits and the Recollects in the previous decades. French critics have been the first to point out that Montesquieu and Rousseau drew their inspiration from these French reporters and chroniclers of the Indian in New France, and have suggested that the French Revolution actually takes its origin in Huronia

5

In that seventeenth century when the Thirty Years' War eliminated Central Europe from the colonial game, the maritime nations played for high stakes—overseas. In America, two lost out. Both were Protestant, both apparently had the resources and energy for expansion. Both favored the region between New England and Virginia. But, while failing in North America, the Dutch succeeded in the other hemisphere, whereas the Swedes elected to attack Russia and lost out in the east as well as the west. England displaced both in the river valleys of the east coast of North America.

A Florentine, Giovanni da Verrazano, in the service of France, probably looked in at New York harbor in 1524. But from then until 1609 that water was relatively undisturbed by the white man. Emanuel van Meteren published the first account of Henry Hudson and his *Half-Moon,* which bore the flag of the Dutch West India Company. Said Meteren in 1610: "They reached 40° 45′ where they found a good entrance, between two headlands and entered on the 12th of September into as fine a river as can be found." With this, the Hudson River gets into American literature; but Meteren never came to America—he wrote that simply as a part of his story of the Netherlands. More important is the account given by Robert Juet, an English sailor on the *Half-Moon* whose story appears in 1625 in Purchas' *Pilgrimes*. Better than either is a book published in that year by Johann de Laet. He was himself a director of the West India Company, a learned business man, and an associate of the great publishing house of the Elzevirs with whom, under Abraham of that name, he published his *Nieuwe Wereldt* (1625), the first work devoted solely to these Dutch colonies of which New Amsterdam was only one.

So much for the "North," or "Hudson," River. A reporter of the "South," or "Delaware," River is David Pieterszoon de Vries whose *Korte historiael*, published in 1655, recounts his travels in the "four quarters of the globe"— which seem based on some sort of contemporary journals or notes. He went out to the previously abandoned Dutch settlement at Swanendael (near the present Lewes, Delaware), did a bit of trading, then went to the more promising settlement at New Amsterdam, where his descriptions cover the years 1633 to 1643. As a patroon he displays a natural prejudice in favor of that system and is often critical of the administration of the West India Company. His observations show him to have been a person of energy and ability, with a style that is both quaint and vivid. His book is illustrated by exceedingly well executed etchings on copper (including a portrait of the author), which like the narrative sometimes betray a naïve plagiarism.

A somewhat more reliable volume is Adriaen van der Donck's *Beschryvinge van Nieuw Nederlant* (1655). The author was a Dutch lawyer who, as a young man, was brought out to manage the finances, particularly to collect the rents, on the patroonship of the great Kiliaen van Rensselaer. He got into difficulties with that worthy because he seemed to understand the point of view of the tenants who could not always meet their obligations. This led to his preparation of the *Vertoogh van Nieu-Neder-Land* (1650), one of the first of a long line of "remonstrances" stating the grievances of the tenant farmers in the Hudson Valley, a line which did not end (if indeed it is yet ended) until the days of the Anti-Rent War in the mid-nineteenth century. Although this book was begun under the approval of Governor Petrus Stuyvesant, van der Donck quarreled with that worthy, and when writing the *Beschryvinge* was refused access to the official records. His work is less a narrative than a description—and a very satisfactory description at that.

The short-lived colony of "New Sweden" follows the usual literary pattern —some books published at the time, and at least one important report which was not fully published until two centuries afterward, yet was drawn upon by later writers. Peter Mårtensson Lindeström, engineer, visited these Swedish settlements on the Delaware, 1653–1654, then returned home and spent the last years of his life compiling his *Geographia Americae* (published 1925). The first detailed chronicle was *Kort beskrifning om provincien Nya Swerige* (1702), by Tomas Campanius Holm. This author never came to America but composed his work from the journals left by his grandfather, Pastor Campanius Holm. The latter was for six years minister to the colony and made a translation of Luther's catechism into the Lenape Indian language that was printed in 1696. Possibly the best of these Swedish chroniclers was Israel Acrelius who was pastor of the church at Christina (Wilmington, Delaware) 1749-1756. His *Beskrifning om . . . Nya Swerige* (1759) is somewhat ecclesiastical but contains a good description of the land and people. Mention should also be made of a curious series of "theses" on America published at the University of Upsala in the eighteenth century, one of which, by Tobias Erick Biörck, may be accounted the first such "dissertation" about Pennsylvania by a native Pennsylvanian (1731).

6

The literature of the British conquest of America owes an inestimable debt to Richard Hakluyt. This scholar, collector, and editor introduced the English-speaking public to the American discoveries by the Cabots, Verrazano, and Ribaut in his slender volume *Divers Voyages* in 1582. Although he has been variously called a geographer and historian, Hakluyt was, above all, a collector of narratives in the time when it was most important to rescue them. In 1589 appeared *The principal navigations, voiages, traffiques and discoveries of the English nation,* a folio volume which through subsequent editions down to 1600 trebled in size. For America the work is supremely important as gathering the then known narratives of what the explorers were finding, and making these first-hand accounts available to posterity. Stylistically the sections are uneven, varying with their authors; but the value of the source material transcends any consideration of literary quality. At his death Hakluyt had a mass of unused material. By good fortune it was bequeathed to one with similar tastes, Samuel Purchas, who carried on the work by publication of his *Hakluytus posthumus; or, Purchas his Pilgrimes* (1625). Purchas used much material that he had himself gathered as well as what Hakluyt had left him. On the whole his editorial work is far less satisfactory than Hakluyt's, but even so posterity is grateful for it.

The first English book on the first English colony in what is now the United States was *A briefe and true report of the new found land of Virginia* (1588) by Thomas Hariot, professor of mathematics at Oxford. He was especially selected by Raleigh to go with the expedition of 1585 to observe and to report. The result was a slim volume which must ever be "Number One" in the literary history of the British colonies which form the present United States. It is an excellent illustration of the fact that a clear and precise thinker can produce an accurate and readable statement. The economic resources of the North Carolina coast, the manners and customs of the Indian inhabitants, and the possibilities for colonization are succinctly set forth. The book was promptly translated into Latin, French, and German and republished. But its pre-eminence in the literature of history lies also in the fact that Raleigh, besides sending out so expert an observer, sent with him an artist, John White, who painted scores of water-color drawings of what he saw. At the same time Theodore De Bry, publisher in Frankfurt-am-Main, conceived the idea of combining the text of discoveries currently being made with illustrations in full-page engravings made from the drawings the explorers were bringing back to Europe. These De Bry produced periodically, somewhat in the manner of the modern *Illustrated London News* or *Life*. The first "part" combined the text of Hariot and the pictures of John White (1590)—and it had to be reprinted at least nineteen times before 1625. The extent to which the Hariot text was borrowed and the White and De Bry pictures were plagiarized by subsequent writers and artists for the next two hundred years is evidence of the widespread influence of the volume. No other English colony in America ever produced anything comparable to it. De Bry did the same thing with René Goulaine de Laudonnière's *L'histoire notable de la Floride* (1586), the tragic history of the Huguenot colony in Florida, conceived by Admiral Coligny, and planted by Jean Ribaut, which ended in a general massacre by the Spaniards. Laudonnière was also accompanied by an artist, Jacques Le Moyne, whose paintings got back to France and were used by De Bry to provide illustrations for his edition of *La Floride* (1592).

Here let a distinction be made between "adventurers" and "planters." The former "adventured" (invested) their money, not their lives, wives, and labor. The latter "planted" homes as well as seed in the soil. The word "plantation" did not connote a lush growth of tobacco, sugar cane, or rice, but was used to characterize so agriculturally unpromising a place as "Providence Plantation." Thus advertising literature, designed to sell an idea to an absentee "adventurer," had to precede such a book as *Advertisements for the unexperienced planters of New England, or anywhere* (London, 1631), the author of which now enters the story.

For the Old Dominion of Virginia, there is, instead of the careful Hariot, that cheerful romancer and valiant soldier, Captain John Smith. The fact that he was "Governour in Virginia" has, rightly or wrongly, overshadowed the fact that he was also "Admirall of New England," and strove for most of the last years of his life to plant a colony farther north than Chesapeake Bay. The puzzle of his writings is well illustrated by the story of Joseph Sabin's *Dictionary of Books Relating to America*. That great work began publication in 1868, and foundered in 1892 when it reached "Smith, John." "Sabin" stayed on the rocks for twenty-six years before a combination of scholars, foundations, and book collectors pulled it off and arranged the works of John Smith in order. Critics and bibliographers alike have spent three hundred years trying to ascertain exactly what John Smith did write, and did publish—and, worse than that, just what he meant. In those Jacobean days writers did not always observe the canons of scholarship current in the twentieth century. If a traveler writing of what he has seen departs from accuracy, he is apt to be checked up and contradicted by some other member of his expedition. Cortez told his own story of the conquest of Mexico and provoked his companion Bernál Díaz to correct him with yet another book. But the curious thing about John Smith is the manner in which his contemporaries ignored rather than contradicted his yarns. Consider the Pocahontas story—and one cannot well avoid it. Smith's own account in 1608 is matter-of-fact. When he retold it in 1624, the story had become gorgeously and glamorously enlarged. Perhaps the 1608 text is history and the 1624 version is literature. Mark Twain characterized this kind of wisdom after the event in a single word: "embroidery." John Smith may have had that adventure with the comely Indian girl, but he does not mention it in his first account, and his companions, Edward Wingfield, Ralph Hamor, and Christopher Newport, did not record it. Then there is the story of the first Church of England service in America. It is told by others besides Smith, but Smith alone gives us a word picture of that rude first Episcopal church, in his *Advertisements for the unexperienced planters,* published in 1631 nearly a quarter-century after the event. One will never know whether his description is correct, but no artist, sculptor, or even dioramist would dare reproduce that memorable scene without putting in the hewn-log seats and the roof of "sayle" cloth, for the existence of which John Smith is the sole authority. Three of his books are "musts": *A True relation of . . . occurrences in Virginia* (1608); *The Generall historie of Virginia* (1624); and *New Englands trials* (1620). His descriptions of what he saw, what happened to him, his narrow escapes, his bad luck, his triumphs, and his unappreciated greatness give us a picture of an egoist who must have been thoroughly delightful if not always reliable.

7

During the seventeenth century a change came over the temper of the pioneers to the New World, and with it a change in their reports and chronicles. After 1607 the attempted settlements of the Atlantic coast began to succeed. The letters and diaries of the seventeenth and eighteenth centuries are records of hardships encountered and overcome, of plans for living that finally worked. Still contemporaneous in their interest, the stories of these permanent settlements—most of them British—become a more immediate part of our literature. They constitute the first step in our cultural tradition in its specific and dominant Anglo-Saxon phase.

Although Champlain described the harbor of Plymouth, it was Captain John Smith who, in 1614, put "Plimouth" on the map in the position it still occupies. Not until six years later came that band of English Separatists who produced and provoked some notable specimens of literature of their own. The first book about the "Pilgrim" colony seems to have been compiled from memoranda sent back by William Bradford and Edward Winslow in the returning *Mayflower*. But because the volume was seen through the press by one George Morton, of the original Scrooby congregation, he was credited with the authorship of *A relation or journall of the beginning and proceedings of the English plantation settled at Plimoth in New England* (1622)—a title so long that the book was at once dubbed "Mourt's Relation." Its importance lies in the facts that, unlike Bradford's own Journal, it was written at the time the events took place, that it contains the only contemporary account of the voyage of the *Mayflower,* and that it tells of what happened in the first few months of the life of the Plymouth colony.

Far better known are two journals: that of William Bradford, perennial governor of Plymouth, and that of John Winthrop, Sr., who was similarly persistent governor of Massachusetts Bay. Both journals remained in manuscript for a long time, Bradford's until 1856 and Winthrop's until 1790. None can deny the simplicity and sincerity of Bradford's literary style, nor the fact that he reveals the Puritan at his best. Winthrop's character was slightly more complex, and he did not always display the Christian charity of his contemporary at Plymouth.

These articulate founders of New England, and others who will be mentioned below, not only were educated gentlemen, but were well educated. Within certain narrowing limits of their religious beliefs, they were able to discern and to think clearly. They were "planting" as well as "adventuring" in a new country in which they proposed to make permanent homes. It was inevitable that they should want to write about what they were doing. To select the more significant of these men and generalize about them and their writings, would betray a lack of understanding. They were individuals and individualists—that is why they came to America in the first place. They displayed in common the pietism of their sect, and they thought in terms of their own consequent concept of the Deity. But it must be remembered that if occasionally they displayed intolerance, they had been the victims of intolerance; if they seemed inhospitable to other emigrants such as Quakers and Catholics, whose views were at variance with their own, this may well have been because the Puritans felt that America was big enough for all and that the dissidents ought to go elsewhere. The heterodox should find other open spaces even if the Puritans had to whip them or imprison them to make that point clear. True, they made a fetish of hard work; but that was not only because these people had work to do in making new homes in a comparatively unfertile land with a chilly climate, it was also because they genuinely enjoyed hard work.

The language in which they expressed themselves was the language of their day, contemporaneous with the publication of the King James Version of the Bible, and all that that implies with respect to the standardization of literary expression and form. Because the King James Version is still readable, so are these Puritan books.

Although the literature of New England in this period is more fully treated in later chapters, mention should here be made of those reporters and historians whose works first chronicled the process of settlement. A thorn in the side of the serious people at Plymouth was Thomas Morton, "Gent.," who persisted in conducting a rum-and-gun-running house (even worse) at "Merrymount" between Boston and Plymouth. The Plymouth people threw him out bodily twice, whereupon he wrote *New English Canaan* (1637), which had to be printed in Amsterdam. In it he "reports" what was going on from a point of view quite different from that of the patient Governor Bradford who had to handle him. There was not likely to be any agreement with an author who always referred to Myles Standish as "Captain Shrimp."

A very different Morton was Nathaniel of that name, actually one of the original "pilgrim fathers," and a minor politician at Plymouth. He used the unpublished works of Bradford and Winslow in the preparation of his *New-England's memoriall* (1669), and reported from his own knowledge the painstaking character of the life of his region. More readable is *New Englands prospect* (1634), wherein William Wood describes the natural features of the country with an easy grace and intersperses really meritorious verse in his prose. In contrast is Edward Johnson's *History of New England* (1654), which covers the period 1628–1652, and which he wanted known by its ponderous subtitle "Wonder-working providence of Sion's saviour in New England." This is a homely record of workaday facts to which other chroniclers are apt to be superior. But to provide such facts was not Johnson's purpose in writing it. His design was to prove that the Deity in person ordained the success of the Bay Colony and that he took a personal interest in such matters as the price of cattle and the accuracy of Myles Standish's aim when shooting at an Indian. The book is revivalistic in style, and the text is garnished with original verse of questionable merit. Better balanced is John Josselyn, who hovered on the border line between herbalist and botanist, and whose *New Englands rarities discovered* (1672) was noticed by the Royal Society. This encouraged him to write *An account of two voyages to New-*

England (1674), which combines scientific lore with hints to settlers and sly digs at the Puritans.

Toward the close of the seventeenth century the colonies had become so firmly established that they had histories to be written. Among the historians whom New England produced, three—William Hubbard, Thomas Prince, and Thomas Hutchinson—wrote about their own day as well as of earlier times. Hubbard was a clergyman, and his *A Narrative of the troubles with the Indians in New England* (1677) is a graphic account of those wars which later came to be associated with the name of the Indian King Philip. Hubbard lived through those struggles, and though one feels that sometimes he agreed with General Sheridan that the only good Indian was a dead Indian he did interpret his own times. A more ambitious work was his *A general history of New-England from the discovery to MDCLXXX,* based on the previous works of Morton and Winthrop. It was not published until 1815, but the manuscript was drawn upon heavily by subsequent historians, notably Cotton Mather and Thomas Prince. Unlike Hubbard—an historian who happened to be a clergyman—Prince was a clergyman who made an historian of himself. He must have been a precocious youngster. He got into print by issuing sermons, which led to his writing an introduction to a life of Cotton Mather, thence to a deep collector's interest in Matheriana and the planning of his ambitious *A chronological history of New-England,* the first volume of which appeared in 1736. In this noteworthy work Prince seems to have outgrown his earlier subject-matter limitations and developed a style which was both lively and fairly objective. But his praiseworthy love for verifying details bogged down his history.

Thomas Hutchinson was a chronicler of a different and far broader experience than these clergymen. He was a cultivated gentleman, a merchant, a lawyer, a man of the world, and Governor of Massachusetts. The first volume of his *The History of the Colony of Massachusetts Bay* appeared in 1764, and although it is rather dull reading today, its reception encouraged him to continue work so as to bring his story down to 1750. His conservative position in the Stamp Act troubles led to disorders wherein his house was invaded by a Boston mob and his papers scattered. Rescuing them the next day from the mud (which may still be seen on the manuscripts) and undeterred by the ill manners of his fellow townsmen, he pushed his second volume to conclusion and wrote with facility and grace on happenings of which he himself had been a witness. On the losing side in the Revolution, he colored his third volume with his prejudices and displayed a failure to appreciate that his world was changing.

When the Dutch yielded New York to the British, two little books appeared which, because of their extreme rarity, are probably less known than they should be. Daniel Denton, a native Long Islander, published in 1670 *A brief description of New York: formerly called New Netherlands*. Since this is the first separate publication in English describing New York, it is note-worthy that the author insists he has "writ nothing, but what I have been an eye witness to all or the greatest part of it" and deliberately cries down the extravagant claims of both the Indians and the Dutch as to the possibilities of the real estate—yet he concludes with a not-too-subtle statement that the poor of the Old World will find haven here. In the next year appeared a tiny volume by the first American minister to have a charge in New York, Charles Wolley. His *A two years journal in New-York* (1701) is worth while if only for his anecdote on how he reconciled the pugnacious Lutheran and Calvinist ministers whom the Dutch had left behind. These two, says Wolley, "behav'd themselves one toward another so shily and uncharitably as if *Luther* and *Calvin* had bequeathed and entailed their virulent and bigotted Spirits upon them and their heirs forever."

Of the many published writings of William Penn, few deal with his great colony. His *Some account of the province of Pennsylvania* (1681) was written before he set sail—yet gives us this phrase: "Colonies are the seeds of nations." His *Frame of Government* (1682) suggests, "Any government is free to the people under it where the laws rule and the people are a party to the laws." This antedates by a century John Adams' adaptation from Jean Bodin, "to the end that it shall be a government of laws and not of men." After Penn reached Philadelphia, he reported to the "Free Society of Traders" in London, by *A letter from William Penn* (1683), a document which is largely descriptive but contains a priceless introductory paragraph in which he gently corrects the reports by his enemies in London about him, and explains that he is not dead and is not a Jesuit. Upon his return to London he published his *Further Account* (1685), wherein he sums up by saying to prospective emigrants, "Be moderate in Expectation, count on Labour before a Crop, and Cost before Gain"—than which no entrepreneur ever gave better advice.

As what Penn had to say about Pennsylvania was the least of his literary output, the investigator must turn to Thomas Budd's *Good order established in Pennsylvania & New Jersey* (1685), a delightful seventeenth century im-print wherein the author tries to summarize the entire book on the title page. Few specimens of colonial promotional literature state so succinctly that the capitalist system will do Christian work and produce 7 per cent:

Taking into consideration the distressed Condition that many Thousand Families lie under in my Native Country, by reason of the deadness of Trade, and want of work, and believing that many that have great Store of Money, that lies by them unimploy'd, would be willing and ready to assist and encourage those poor distressed People, by supplying them with Monies, in order to bring them out of Slavery and Poverty they groan under, if they might do it with safety to themselves, these Considerations put me on writing this small Treatise, wherein I hope . . . that the Rich may help relieve the Poor, and yet reap great Profit and Advantage to themselves by their so doing.

The practical tone of Budd's advice was predominant in all the reports and chronicles, as well as the other literature, of the Southern colonies discussed in the next chapter. Even indentured servants like John Hammond and George Alsop praised the pioneer life in a gay and worldly spirit reflected, in more serious vein, in the histories of Robert Beverley and William Stith. Characteristic of these writers are John Lederer and Thomas Ash.

Tourists of the future will become more and more familiar with the "skyline" drive along the Blue Ridge, Shenandoah Valley, and the Great Smokies, in the back country of Virginia and North Carolina. The earliest reporter of this country was one of whom little is known save his book, *The Discoveries of John Lederer in three several marches from Virginia to the west of Carolina* (1672). Lederer introduced the geology, botany, and native inhabitants to the English-reading world. Of German origin, he wrote in Latin, whence his book was rescued by a member of the Virginia "Council" and translated into English because the author was "a modest ingenious person, and a pretty scholar." There is reason to think that Lederer was first to climb the Appalachian Divide and look over into what was to become the Middle West.

For writing that is picturesque one turns to Thomas Ash who, as "T. A." in *Carolina* (1682), describes the synthesis of the elements of the social history of the region. Noteworthy among these are two derivatives of corn: hominy and a beverage wherein the corn is treated "by Maceration, and when duly feremented, a strong spirit like *Brandy* may be drawn off from it, by the help of an *Alembick*." Both Ash and Governor John Archdale, whose *A new description . . . of Carolina* appeared in 1707, are careful writers within the limits of the scientific knowledge of their day. Archdale betrays the fact of his previous residence in the Bible commonwealths to the north when he suggests that it "pleased Almighty God to send unusual sicknesses amongst" the Indians since, in order to make room for the white man, "there seemed a Necessity of thining the barbarous *Indian* Nations." Yet he has misgivings and comforts himself with the assurance that the English colonists "in comparison to the Spaniard, have but little *Indian* Blood to answer for."

Thus the discovery, opening, and settlement of the continent was recorded by those who took part in the adventure. There is the charm of the primitive, not only in the expression but in the format of these old books. But their principal appeal lies in the fact that they present the feelings of the man who was there at the time the event took place and not what some later interpreter, however learned, may have felt. If the "end of all scribblement is to amuse," there are those who are entertained by these efforts at expression on the part of many a stout Cortez who was not content to remain silent upon a peak in Darien.

4. WRITERS OF THE SOUTH

THE earliest literature of the permanent English settlements came from the Southern colonies and was, for the most part, descriptive and factual, concerned in some fashion with the land itself. Less introspective than the Puritans of New England, the writers of the agrarian South turned their attention to the world outside their doors. Though verse writers frequently were imitators of conventional themes in poetry, a few devoted their efforts to describing their own milieu, sometimes satirically, but with attention to external life in the colonies. Southern writers of prose and poetry rarely, if ever, wrestled with their souls in the manner of Cotton Mather; to most of them, the exposure of one's innermost thoughts and feelings would have seemed indecent. Even when, like William Byrd of Westover, they kept diaries, they were more reticent about their thoughts than about their behavior; and their meditations were more often upon politics and social relations than upon metaphysics.

To its London readers the Reverend Alexander Whitaker's *Good News from Virginia* (1613) described an earthly paradise. In Virginia men might live in ease supported by the fruitfulness of the soil and take their pleasure in sport which the Creator provided, for the woods abounded in wild turkeys, swift as greyhounds, and with pigeons, ducks, geese, partridges, and other game birds, and the rivers teemed with the finest fish: "Shads of a great bigness, and rockfish . . . trouts, bass, flounders, and other dainty fish . . . [and] multitudes of great sturgeons, whereof we catch many." The author vouches for the abundance of the fish which he himself had caught— "with mine angle." Therefore, he advises his readers, "since God hath filled the elements of earth, air and waters with his creatures, good for our food and nourishment, let not the fear of starving hereafter, or any great want, dishearten your valiant minds from coming to a place of so great plenty." If Whitaker's book stirred the hopeful imaginations of Englishmen to contemplate the virtues of the New World, that was his intention. And that, indeed, was the purpose in one way or another of much of the writing in the colonial South.

The first strictly literary work, however, was an exception to this most characteristic type of colonial writing, for it linked the New World with the great cultural past and was prophetic of that interest in the classics which the educated groups in the colonies retained and fostered for many generations. The work was Ovid's *Metamorphoses,* translated into English verse by George Sandys, son of the Archbishop of York and brother of Sir Edwin Sandys, the noble-spirited secretary of the Virginia Company of London. Sandys came to Virginia in 1621 and remained seven years, taking an active part in the colony's administration and defense.

The more cultivated members of the colonial ruling class inherited something of Sandys' zeal for the classics. This tradition, a legacy of the Renaissance more evident in the reading and in the oratory of Southerners than in their literary productions, helped to modify and transmute some of the materialism which frontier conditions induced. Generations later, colonial gentlemen read Sandys' Ovid as they read another of his works, *A Paraphrase upon the Psalms of David* (1636), and they approved of both.

The contrast between the classical interests of Sandys and the literal record of Whitaker provides a revealing introduction to the study of Southern colonial writers. The same contrast is to be found in the person of the master of Westover, William Byrd the younger, most representative Southern colonial writer. A man of means and learning, he collected perhaps the finest private library of colonial times; but his own writing is a record of his life on his plantation and on his surveying expeditions into the interior. The Southern books that have come down to us from these early days are concerned with the things of this world rather than of the next. Behind Thomas Jefferson's *Notes on Virginia* (1784) there is a tradition of scientific, descriptive, and promotional literature unequaled in the colonies to the north.

2

To defend both Virginia and Maryland from traducers, John Hammond in 1656 published in London a little tract entitled *Leah and Rachel, or, the Two Fruitful Sisters, Virginia and Maryland: Their Present Condition, Impartially Stated and Related.* Hammond had lived for nineteen years in Virginia, he tells us, and for two years in Maryland, until dissensions during the Cromwellian period forced him to flee to England. This pamphlet, written after his arrival, describes nostalgically the goodness of the land in the Chesapeake region, where men and women can live in ease and plenty. By contrast England is an abode of misery. "And therefore I cannot but admire," Hammond declares, "and indeed much pity the dull stupidity of people necessitated in England, who rather than they will remove themselves, live here a base, slavish, penurious life, . . . choosing rather than they will forsake England to stuff Newgate, Bridewell, and other jails with their car-casses, nay cleave to Tyburn itself." Like Crèvecœur more than a century later, Hammond vividly emphasizes the opportunities of the new life in America, where everything is inviting, a country "not only plentiful but pleasant and profitable, . . . pleasant in . . . the brightness of the weather, . . . pleasant in their building, . . . pleasant in observing their stocks and flocks of cattle, hogs, and poultry, grazing, whisking, and skipping in their sights, pleasant in having all things of their own, growing or breeding with-out drawing the penny to send for this and that, without which, in England, they cannot be supplied."

A few serpents had invaded that Eden, notably Maryland, and Hammond is emphatic in his distaste for troublemakers, particularly one of the leaders of a turbulent faction, Will Claiborne, "whom ye all know to be a villain." The earlier tract, *Hammond versus Heamans, or, An Answer to an Auda-cious Pamphlet, Published by an Impudent and Ridiculous Fellow Named Roger Heamans* (1655), was a vigorous but less literary diatribe against the ship captain who had espoused the cause of rebels against the government and had helped to drive Hammond himself out of Maryland.

The most vigorous and original work of the middle decades of the seven-teenth century was George Alsop's *A Character of the Province of Maryland,* printed in London in 1666. The author, who had served four years as an indentured servant in Maryland, wrote in stout defense of life in that colony, even the life of a servant, which he found far pleasanter and more promising than the drudgery and the hopeless poverty of England.

Alsop's descriptions, written in colorful and idiomatic prose, have the rhythms of the Elizabethans and their zest for the world about them. His style is not unlike that of Thomas Dekker's pamphlets. With a boisterous humor that is sometimes coarse but never dull, he tells about the country and its customs, the Susquehannock Indians, and the mutual benefits of trade between England and Maryland. At the end of the book are several letters written to friends and kinsmen about his voyage to the New World and his experiences there. Occasionally Alsop inserts a poem, displaying an ease of versifying and a quality not often encountered among early writers in the colony.

That Alsop is a man of some cultivation appears from his literary allusions. He has read the prose of Dr. John Donne, and, when ill and threatened with death, he quotes from a sermon by the learned dean and includes a philo-sophic observation: "We are only sent by God of an errand into this world, and the time that's allotted to us for to stay is only for an answer. When God, my great Master, shall in good earnest call me home, which these warnings tell me I have not long to stay, I hope then I shall be able to give him a good account of my message."

Like certain Cavalier poets, Alsop's muse requires no theme of vast importance. When someone sends him a purple cap he lets his imagination range on the possible uses of this piece of velvet headgear. Perhaps it once graced Oliver Cromwell's head, which, Alsop is pleased to note, has lately been hoisted on Westminster's roof:

> Say, didst thou cover Noll's old brazen head,
> Which on top of Westminster'[s] high lead
> Stands on a pole, erected to the sky,
> As a grand trophy to his memory?
> From his perfidious skull didst thou fall down,
> In disdain to honour such a crown
> With three-pile velvet? Tell me, hadst thou thy fall
> From the high top of that cathedral?

Elsewhere in prose and verse, he is equally disdainful of Puritans and their kind. For example, he attributes the ready market of Maryland's pork with ship captains of New England to the stiff Calvinists' need for some kind of softening, "because their bodies being fast bound up with the cords of restrigent zeal, they are fain to make use of the liniments of this non-Canaanite creature physically to loosen them."

Alsop's little book reads less like a promotional tract than most of the descriptive works written in the colonies. He gives the impression of sincerity and truth in his descriptions, as in the passage defending the system of indentured servitude. Those who cannot pay their passage to Maryland, he writes, "may for the debarment of a four years' sordid liberty go over to this province and live there plenteously well. And what's four years' servitude to advantage a man all the remainder of his days, making his predecessors happy in his sufficient abilities, which he attained to partly by the restrainment of so small a time?"

Most of the descriptive prose of the early eighteenth century was less boisterous than Alsop's. Typical of a long series of such works was *The Present State of Virginia and the College* (1727), prepared by a committee of Virginians consisting of Henry Hartwell, James Blair, and Edward Chilton, who presented their report to the Board of Trade in London on October 20, 1697. The author of the portion describing the College of William and Mary was that institution's founder, the Reverend James Blair, an irascible Scot, who as "commissary" of the Church of England was the Bishop of London's personal representative in Virginia. He labored unceasingly to make the College of William and Mary a nursery of Anglican clergymen, and he was the author of a popular series of homilies entitled *Our Savior's Divine Sermon on the Mount,* five volumes, published in London in 1722. A second edition was called for before the author died in 1743, and the work attracted so much attention that it was translated into Danish and published in Denmark in 1761.

By the end of the seventeenth century, settlers in the oldest English colony were beginning to feel a maturity not yet manifest in the newer colonies. Writers began to display an incipient nationalism, a loyalty to the new land as their native region. An anonymous Virginian published in London *An Essay upon the Government of the English Plantations on the Continent of America* (1701) and in place of his name proudly subscribed on the title page the words "By an American." Some evidence suggests that the writer was Robert Beverley, or perhaps his father-in-law, William Byrd the elder. Certainly it was some member of the Beverley-Byrd group of planters. The tract is an earnest and clearly written plea for more intelligent understanding and administration by the colonial authorities in England, and it makes one of the earliest proposals of a plan of union for the English colonies.

Robert Beverley exhibited an originality and self-conscious pride in his Virginia origins that sometimes irritated his contemporaries, especially his socially ambitious brother-in-law, William Byrd the younger, who was pleased to hang the walls of his house at Westover with portraits of English noblemen. In 1705, a London bookseller brought out *The History and Present State of Virginia . . . by a Native of the Place.* On a handsomely engraved frontispiece, Beverley acknowledged the authorship with his initials. Writing with humor, and occasionally with biting sarcasm, he did not spare the feelings of his contemporaries. He was sharply critical of various royal governors, particularly Francis Nicholson, and he ridiculed the lack of enterprise of his fellow planters who had become utterly dependent upon tobacco and the English market. He also suggested somewhat satirically that his fellow Virginians would have been better off if they had followed John Rolfe's example and had intermarried with the Indians. Although the historical narrative for the early years is largely derivative from Captain John Smith and other chroniclers, the sections dealing with the Indians and with contemporary observations are an important contribution to history.

In 1722, the year of his death, Beverley finished and published a revision of the *History* which omitted the acerbities of the earlier version. The second edition, reprinted in the nineteenth century, is less colorful but more charitable. The *History* was translated into French and had four printings on the Continent by 1718. Beverley had written his book with one eye on prospective immigrants, especially French Huguenots, and he must have been pleased at its popularity abroad. It is an early instance of how the patronizing tone of British writers on the colonies could stir the "native" pride to reply.

3

The writer from the Southern colonies best known today is William Byrd the younger, author of the *History of the Dividing Line,* and of an extensive diary lately discovered and published. The son of one of the wealthiest planters in Virginia, Byrd received an English education and while a student of law at the Middle Temple cultivated the acquaintance of literary and social lions. A familiar friend of Wycherley and Congreve, he played with the idea of being a man of letters and wrote dainty or satirical verses, some of which found their way into an English miscellany. Since scientific specu-lation at the turn of the seventeenth century was both fashionable and appeal-ing, Byrd determined to make himself a man of learning and a virtuoso in science. Flattered by an invitation to join the Royal Society, he submitted a paper describing an albino Negro and for the rest of his life prized his status as a corresponding member of the Society. Although Byrd was called back to Virginia in 1704 on the death of his father, he later spent considerable time in England as agent for the colony, and until the day of his death in 1744 he corresponded with titled and learned friends in the mother country.

His diary indicates a methodical devotion to classical learning; he is care-ful to record the daily reading of Greek, Latin, or Hebrew, interspersed with an occasional effort at literary translation. A free rendering of the tale of the Matron of Ephesus from the *Satyricon* survives. He also continued to write verses, a few of which are in existence, and he turned his hand to science and mathematics. Fancying himself something of an amateur in medicine, he dosed his household and neighbors when opportunity offered, and wrote *A Discourse Concerning the Plague with Some Preservatives Against It* (Lon-don, 1721). This forty-page pamphlet is the only complete work from Byrd's pen known to have been published in his lifetime.

Byrd's diary, kept in shorthand, probably through most of his adult life, is a significant and revealing document with occasional glints of humor. Three portions are known, two of which are now in print. The Virginia Historical Society, which owns a section covering the years 1717–1721, has declined to permit its publication. In this suppressed part Byrd describes with Pepysian frankness his amatory adventures in London, where he pursued without discrimination whores, chambermaids, and great ladies. Most of his diary, however, concerns the matter-of-fact and fairly decorous existence of a man intent upon maintaining his classical learning, managing his estates suc-cessfully, and fulfilling his responsibilities to the commonwealth.

Byrd's most important literary contribution is the *History of the Dividing Line Run in the Year 1728,* a narrative of the boundary survey between Virginia and North Carolina in which he commanded the party of Virginians. Although he was clearly ambitious to be regarded as a man of letters, he preferred to pursue his avocation in the genteel manner, without rushing precipitately into print. From a journal kept during the survey, Byrd made a draft of his well known narrative which he called *The Secret History of the Line*. This version, which contained fictitious names of the participants, the author revised, expanded, and polished; but he never brought himself to publish the finished text. Not until 1841 was any version of the narrative printed, though manuscript copies had circulated among Byrd's friends and had attracted their favorable attention, as did two shorter works, *A Journey to the Land of Eden, Anno 1733* and *A Progress to the Mines in the Year, 1732.*

These are all spirited narratives. Writing with the zest of youth and the maturity of a man of the world, Byrd conveys to the reader some of his own adventurousness and commands attention with his shrewd observation and commentary. He spices his story with humor, as in the passage describing the laziness of North Carolinians encountered in the back country:

> They make their wives rise out of their beds early in the morning, at the same time that they lie and snore, till the sun has risen one-third of his course, and dispersed all the unwholesome damps. Then, after stretching and yawning for half an hour, they light their pipes, and, under the protection of a cloud of smoke, venture out into the open air; though, if it happens to be never so little cold, they quickly return shivering into the chimney corner. When the weather is mild, they stand leaning with both their arms upon the cornfield fence, and gravely consider whether they had best go and take a small heat at the hoe: but generally find reasons to put it off till another time. Thus they loiter away their lives, like Solomon's sluggard, with their arms across, and at the winding up of the year scarcely have bread to eat. To speak the truth, it is a thorough aversion to labor that makes people file off to North Carolina, where plenty and a warm sun confirm them in their disposition to laziness for their whole lives.

4

The defense of North Carolina, its products and its native people, was undertaken by John Lawson, a Scottish adventurer who landed at Charleston in 1700 and became surveyor-general of the colony. First published in London in 1709 as *A New Voyage to Carolina,* it is generally referred to as *The History of Carolina* from the title given to the second edition of 1714. Lawson's book, a brisk and readable account from first-hand observation, achieved considerable popularity. A third English edition appeared in 1718, and it was translated into German and published in Hamburg in 1712 and

1722. Like Beverley's *History,* it served as propaganda for immigration to the Southern colonies. " 'Tis a great misfortune," Lawson observes in the preface, "that most of our travellers who go to this vast continent in America are persons of the meaner sort, and generally of a very slender education . . . uncapable of giving any reasonable account of what they met withal in these remote parts, tho' the country abounds with curiosities worthy a nice observation. In this point, I think, the French outstrip us." To correct the balance, Lawson expanded the journal of his travels; but he warns the reader that he has aimed at truth and accuracy instead of entertainment, "which is, indeed, the duty of every author and preferable to a smooth style accompanied with falsities and hyperboles."

The most readable part of his narrative is the description of the Indians and their customs, which attributes to them, particularly the women, many attractive qualities, albeit a lack of inhibitions shocking to a Puritan but not to John Lawson. Of a companion of his travels whose fair comrade of the night made off with her lover's shoes and personal possessions, Lawson remarks, "Thus early did our spark already repent his new bargain, walking barefoot in his penitentials like some poor pilgrim to Loretto."

Lawson's earthly and literary career was cut short in 1711 by these selfsame Indians. In company with the Baron de Graffenried, a Swiss promoter of colonization, he made another journey into the hinterland and was captured by the savages, who put him to death. De Graffenried escaped to tell the tale and blame Lawson's rashness for the catastrophe.

The chief literary monuments during the remainder of the colonial period were descriptive histories or narratives. The Reverend Hugh Jones, professor of mathematics at the College of William and Mary, the author of the first American grammar of the English language, published in 1724 *The Present State of Virginia,* a brief factual account, which announced on the title page that the book was designed "for the service of such as are engaged in the propagation of the gospel and advancement of learning, and for the use of all persons concerned in the Virginia trade and plantation." Jones' book is simple and clear without any effort at rhetorical adornment.

The most voluminous historical work in the Southern colonies up to its time was William Stith's *The History of the First Discovery and Settlement of Virginia: Being an Essay towards a General History of this Colony* (Williamsburg, 1747). Stith's 331 pages of small type brought the narrative of Virginia down only as far as 1624. Though his detailed account of Virginia's early history proved tedious to the busy master of Monticello, the work exemplifies a new ideal of historical investigation and a zeal for accurate research hitherto unknown in the American colonies. His preface is a readable and significant landmark in the story of American scholarship, and the main body of the text is far from deserving Jefferson's censure. Like more recent historians, Stith found much to commend in Captain John Smith's own observations, but lamented the confusion of his work and deplored the inattention to documentary evidence displayed by Smith's successors. "And I can further declare with great truth," he says, "that had anything of great consequence been done in our history, I could most willingly have saved myself the trouble of conning over our old musty records, and of studying, connecting, and reconciling the jarring and disjointed writings and relations of different men and different parties."

Stith's uncle, Sir John Randolph, had contemplated an account of the development of the government of Virginia, and had collected many records and public documents which at his death he left still unused. Furthermore, William Byrd, who had procured a manuscript copy of the records of the Virginia Company, made this document available and encouraged Stith to pursue his research. "Neither could I well excuse myself," Stith comments, "if I did not likewise acknowledge with what humanity and politeness that well-bred gentleman and scholar not only communicated those manuscripts to me, but also threw open his library (the best and most copious collection of books in our part of America) and was himself ever studious and solicitous to search out and give me whatever might be useful to my undertaking." Stith's history, which he intended to continue to a later period, was an example of the newly awakened American point of view. For example, his interpretation of King James' interference with the Virginia Company as the machinations of a hostile tyrant—a view which grew ever more congenial under the mistakes of the Georges—became the traditional explanation until our own time.

Somewhat akin to the historical and descriptive narratives was a brilliant satire and an exposé of conditions in Georgia by a group of disgruntled enemies of the founder, General James Oglethorpe. Their tract, *A True and Historical Narrative of the Colony of Georgia* (1741), was published in Charleston, South Carolina. The authors—who announced themselves on the title page as Patrick Tailfer, M.D., Hugh Anderson, M.A., David Dougles, "and others"—had taken refuge there after antagonizing Oglethorpe's agent in Georgia. Prefaced by a dedication of mock deference to Oglethorpe, the book calmly and devastatingly ridicules the vanities and weaknesses of the philanthropist. Jonathan Swift himself need not have been ashamed of the satirical skill demonstrated in the dedication. After referring to the generous governments of certain colonies and the prosperity which commerce had brought, the authors comment that "your Excellency's concern for our perpetual welfare could never permit you to propose such transitory advantages for us. . . . You have afforded us the opportunity of arriving at the integrity of the primitive times by entailing a more than primitive poverty on us. The toil that is necessary to our bare subsistence must effectually defend us from the anxieties of any further ambition. . . . The valuable virtue of humility is secured to us by your care."

Among the grudges which the authors held against Oglethorpe were his injunctions against Negro slavery and the importation of rum. Although promotional tracts had lavished hyperboles on the wholesomeness of the air and water in the colony, they thought a little rum would be a benefit to health, for "the experience of all the inhabitants of America will prove the necessity of qualifying water with some spirit." They were particularly hostile toward John Wesley, whose residence in the colony had encouraged such "attendances upon prayers, meetings, and sermons" as to "propagate a spirit of indolence and of hypocrisy amongst the most abandoned" who by a show of religion managed to live in ease from the public stores.

Although the tract is plainly partisan, its authors display an urbane cultivation, a familiarity with contemporary literature, and a detachment unusual in eighteenth century controversial writings. That its barbs went home is evident from a solemn defense made by the Reverend William Best in a sermon before the trustees for the colony of Georgia, entitled *The Merit and Reward of a Good Intention* (London, 1742)

5

The muse of poetry inspired few Southerners in the colonial period to write from their hearts about their own world. When they wrote verse, the most formalized type of composition, they became self-conscious and imitative. Rarely could they escape the diction, the manner, the style, or the themes of the reigning dictators of poetry in England. Dryden and Pope had their slavish and uninspired disciples on the banks of the James, as well as the Thames. Even incipient democracy was sung in formal measures in the Southern colonies.

The verse with which George Alsop decorated his prose account of seventeenth century Maryland demonstrates that indentured servants were often men of considerable schooling. It is possible that another indentured servant was the author of one of the noblest poems of this period. The rebellion in 1676 of Nathaniel Bacon against Sir William Berkeley, governor of Virginia, inspired both a narrative tribute and a poetic one, which are preserved in a manuscript usually called the Burwell Papers (published 1814). The unknown prose narrator, clearly no partisan of Bacon's, inserted the poem at the conclusion of a passage recounting the rebel's death. The elegy ends:

Mars and Minerva both in him concurred
For arts, for arms, whose pen and sword alike
As Cato's did, may admiration strike
Into his foes; while they confess withal
It was their guilt styl'd him a criminal.
Only this difference does from truth proceed:
They in the guilt, he in the name must bleed.
While none shall dare his obsequies to sing
In deserv'd measures until time shall bring
Truth crown'd with freedom, and from danger free
To sound his praises to posterity.
    Here let him rest; while we this truth report;
He's gone from hence unto a higher court
To plead his cause, where he by this doth know
Whether to Caesar he was friend or foe.

Such praise was certain to bring forth an answer, and another unknown
writer replied with a poem beginning:

Whether to Caesar he was friend or foe?
Pox take such ignorance, do you not know?
Can he be friend to Caesar that shall bring
The arms of Hell to fight against the King?

Thus in the midst of civil war and Indian forays, men of action could take
time to express their emotions in verse that had a depth of feeling and sometimes a grace and ease of diction. Clearly the wilderness of Virginia was far
from destitute of literary talent, though few examples have survived.

    More in the realistic tradition of Southern colonial writing is a boisterous
satire, *The Sot-Weed Factor* (London, 1708), which took for its subject of
ridicule the contemporary scene in Maryland. Unfortunately for American
literature, its author, who signed himself Ebenezer Cook, declared that he
was an Englishman.

Condemn'd by Fate to wayward curse
Of friends unkind and empty purse,

he had been obliged to make a dismal voyage to a rude and ribald land.
Twenty-one quarto pages of couplets relate the poet's unhappy adventures
in Maryland, where he tried to set up as a tobacco merchant but was roundly
cheated by the inhabitants. With his last lines he curses the country:

May wrath divine then lay those regions waste
Where no man's faithful nor a woman chaste.

Belles-lettres in Maryland and Virginia found a fresh stimulation after the arrival of William Parks, the printer, who by the spring of 1726 had established a press at Annapolis, and by 1730 had opened a printing shop in Williamsburg. Parks was more than a printer. He had literary taste and a flair for journalism. In 1736 he established the *Virginia Gazette*, which opened its columns to ambitious poets and essayists. They responded with an assortment of occasional verse and miscellaneous commentary.

The most important poetical work to issue from Parks' Annapolis press was *The Mouse-Trap, or the Battle of the Cambrians and Mice* (1728), a translation by Richard Lewis of Edward Holdsworth's Latin poem *Muscipula*, satirizing the Welsh. Lewis, who served as a schoolmaster in Annapolis, displayed a genuine talent for versification, and a learning which would have been a credit to Augustan London. His verse dedication to Governor Benedict Calvert concludes:

> Yet—hear me!—while I beg you to excuse
> This bold intrusion of an unknown muse;
> And if her faults too manifest appear
> And her rude numbers should offend your ear,
> Then, if you please with your forgiving breath,
> Which can reprieve the wretch condemn'd from death,
> To speak a pardon for her errors past,
> This first poetic crime shall prove her last.

Governor Calvert encouraged the translator by heading a list of one hundred and fifty Marylanders who subscribed for one or more copies of the book. Lewis was the author of a few later poems, but the translation was his most ambitious undertaking. His preface in prose to that work is an urbane, polished, and learned bit of literary criticism, worthy of an Elizabethan courtly scholar.

Two years after the publication of *The Mouse-Trap*, the Annapolis press issued *Sotweed Redivivus, or the Planter's Looking-Glass,* by E. C. Gent. [Ebenezer Cook?] (1730), written in obvious imitation of the earlier satire, *The Sot-Weed Factor,* which had proved popular; but the new work lacked the vigor and the robust humor of the original. The following year Parks brought out a volume bearing the hopeful title of *The Maryland Muse,* which, in addition to a versified account of Bacon's Rebellion, included a third edition of *The Sot-Weed Factor.*

Fittingly William Parks chose to publish as one of his first labors at Williamsburg, J. Markland's *Typographia, an Ode on Printing* (1730). With a panoply of classical allusion, Markland praises King George and Governor Gooch, and then pays tribute to Parks, the printer:

From whom Virginia's laws, that lay
In blotted manuscripts obscur'd,
    By vulgar eyes unread,
Which whilom scarce the light endur'd,
Begin to view again the day,
    As rising from the dead.
For this the careful artist wakes,
And o'er his countless brood he stands,
    His numerous hoards
Of speechless letters, unform'd words,
Unjointed questions, and unmeaning breaks,
Which into order rise, and form, at his command.

If Markland's ode has no great originality it at least displays able craftsmanship in a genre popular in the age of Pope.

Governor Gooch, to whom Markland dedicated his ode, was himself a
man of no mean skill in letters. To popularize a new law regulating the
inspection of tobacco, he wrote in spirited prose and had Parks publish
*A Dialogue Between Thomas Sweet-Scented, William Oronoco, Planters,
and Justice Love-Country, Who Can Speak for Himself* (1732). For lightness
of touch and humor, Gooch's piece of propaganda surpassed the usual work
of this type.

The Williamsburg press brought out in 1736 *Poems on Several Occasions,*
by "a Gentleman of Virginia." The unnamed author was William Dawson,
a graduate of Queen's College, Oxford, and professor of moral philosophy
at the College of William and Mary who later became its president. Dawson's statement in his preface that "the following pieces are the casual productions of youth" is confirmed by the quality of the poems. No verse in
the volume shows the slightest glimmer of inspiration from the New World.
Though Dawson's poems are not without skill, they can hardly be described
as contributions to American literature, for they were most certainly written
before he took up residence in Virginia.

A somewhat better claim for a small niche in the annals of American
letters can be made for James Sterling, Anglican rector of St. Paul's Parish,
in Kent County, Maryland. An Irishman who had already achieved a modest reputation in Dublin as a playwright and poet, Sterling is believed to be
the author of an anonymous poem, *An Epistle to the Hon. Arthur Dobbs,
Esq. in Europe, From a Clergyman in America* (London, 1752). This work
in sixteen hundred lines is a display of patriotic verbosity glorifying the
promoter of a voyage in search of the Northwest Passage. Other poems
attributed to Sterling appeared in the *American Magazine* between October,
1757, and October, 1758. These ranged from "A Poem, On the Invention of

Letters and the Art of Printing" to "The Royal Comet," praising the King of Prussia as the champion of Protestantism. Sterling's muse inspired him to fluency rather than depths of feeling.

6

By the mid-eighteenth century, the Southern colonies had developed a considerable literary activity, thanks largely to the establishment of local printing presses and newspapers which gave an outlet. Much of the writing was far removed from belles-lettres, but it illustrated the needs and interests of the people. The argument over inoculation for smallpox, for example, precipitated a controversy in 1739 between James Killpatrick and Dr. Thomas Dale, which Lewis Timothy chronicled in pamphlets from his press in Charleston, South Carolina. Doctors in Virginia and Maryland likewise published their observations on various diseases in books which are of considerable interest for the history of American medicine, if not for literary history. Religious disputes often resulted in the publication of controversial sermons. George Whitefield's evangelical tour of South Carolina aroused the ire of Dr. Alexander Garden, rector of St. Philip's in Charleston, and called forth an exchange of letters between the two which Peter Timothy duly published in 1740. Three years before, Lewis Timothy had advertised an edition of hymns and psalms by John Wesley, earlier by nearly a year than Wesley's first London edition. Some of the most interesting bits of writing are to be found in old private letters, which now and then exemplify literary skill. Though they usually wrote about business, an occasional letter of William Fitzhugh or Robert Carter of Corotoman in Virginia, or of Eliza Lucas Pinckney of South Carolina, reads like a little essay on some theme of intrinsic interest.

The growth of an interest in belles-lettres was diverted after the middle of the century by the gathering storm of controversy over the colonies' relation to the mother country. From 1750 onward there was an increasing flood of political writing, and by 1760 literary effort was already being translated into the kind of oratory, satirical verse, and polemics which would occupy such a large place in the intellectual activities of the Southern colonies in the Revolutionary period. For those activities, the substantial and circumstantial accounts of such men as Byrd, Beverley, and Stith provided a solid background in the realities of life in the New World.

5. WRITERS OF NEW ENGLAND

Wɪᴛʜ different motives for colonization from their Southern neighbors, the early settlers of New England wrote in order to guide in daily living, to educate and to edify, rather than merely to describe. It is extraordinary that colonists preoccupied with the great task of building a durable state in a new land found time to write so much and so well. But they did so because they were convinced that effective writing was a necessity for a healthy commonwealth. Books were useful tools for teaching. If they gave pleasure, well and good; but to write merely to please would have seemed to the northern colonists usually a dangerous waste of time. They left us no novels, no drama, and very little that can be classified as belles-lettres, not because they were aesthetically blind but because they were sure that there were better uses for their talents. Most of their work was designed to convey religious truth or to give sound instruction on immediate practical issues, political, social, or economic, because they were confident that such work was essential for the building of a vigorous and virtuous state.

If the modern reader is to appreciate colonial New England literature, he must have some familiarity with the state of mind loosely called "Puritanism." In general, the early writers of New England shared that state of mind, and although attitudes shifted quickly after 1700, many of the old ideas and the literary habits fixed by them persisted. Even the work of the few non-Puritan writers in colonial New England was affected by the prevailing intellectual tastes of the community.

The Puritan author, ever striving to make his books useful, recognized that they could be so only when they presented truth understandably and attractively. He chose his methods from those which seemed to have proved useful in practice and also to be in accord with God's laws. Art was a means, not an end; but the New Englander's realization that some degree of artistry was required if his writing was to be effective made him a careful workman and led him to develop a definite, although limited, theory of style.

The theory was shaped by his religious beliefs. He was an extreme Protestant, and saw the Reformation as a great victory of true Christianity

54

over the man-made tenets of the Church of Rome. He was sure that the universe centered not on man, but on God, and that all man's energies must be devoted to God's service. God absolutely controlled all creation. Man was his creature, inherently sinful, and could be freed from evil only by the arbitrary gift of divine grace. Neither his own deeds nor the intercession of a church could help him—although he might do something to escape the fear of damnation by proving that he could persistently do God's will. That will he could best comprehend from the Bible, the precepts of which might be supplemented, but never challenged, by a patient study of God's operations in creating and controlling the world. To claim knowledge of the divine will by direct inspiration was arrogant and "enthusiastic" heresy. God did not speak directly in man's heart, but through the Bible and through the orderly plan of the universe. Those to whom he vouchsafed his grace could and should use their reason to learn what the Bible and God's creations meant; logic, metaphysics, science—any conceptions with which the mind could deal— were serviceable only because God had benevolently granted to some of his fallen children the power to reason. The would-be righteous must hope that God's grace was in them so that their reason might bring them knowledge of his truth. In this hope they must struggle to inform themselves, with all the aids of logic and philosophy, as to God's will and the means of carrying it out on earth. Inevitably they revered scholarship: to be good in any real sense they must learn; they needed both knowledge and faith. As John Cotton, a pioneer Boston divine, put it: "Knowledge is no knowledge without zeal"—that is, without religious conviction—but "zeale is but a wilde-fire without knowledge." The classics, the heathen philosophers, the teachings of Renaissance humanism were all grist to the Puritan's mill, all helps in his effort to use his reason for the carrying out of divine law.

Such thinking, in its essentials, was common to most Protestants in the sixteenth and seventeenth centuries. The elements in it which affected literary standards are therefore reflected in the writings of Anglicans and Puritans alike, in the religious artists of the Old World as well as the New. But the latter differ markedly from the former in content and style, because Puritanism, of the variety prevalent in early New England, gave special emphasis to certain tenets of Protestantism and developed accordingly some special points of view toward literature.

Starting from the idea that the Bible is God's word, to be believed even when its validity could not be demonstrated by human processes, Puritan and Anglican agreed that reason furnished arguments for the infallibility of Holy Writ. But the Anglican tended to supplement the Bible with other authorities, holding that it stated the fundamental Christian principles but need not be looked upon as a complete guide for every detail of life. Those details were regulated by reason, by the rules of a church taught by experience, and by the judgment of devout men. The Bible was not to be taken so literally as to leave no place for men to act freely when no essential Scriptural precept forbade. But the extreme Protestant—the Puritan—was more strict. If the Bible was God's word, and God was infinite, why suppose its authority to be less than infinite? Why was not its authority complete and binding, regardless of changing human conditions and aspirations, all of which were, after all, decreed by God? The Puritan took his Bible literally as a manual of instruction for every phase of conduct. In it he thought he found precise rules for the structure and polity of the true church, and he was sure that there should be nothing in worship or church government not specifically authorized by it. Inevitably he rejected many elements of the Catholic and Anglican service and polity because he could find no warrant for them in the sacred text. Thus he seemed to conservatives to be a rebel, not because of any basic theological unorthodoxy, but because his conception of a true church was unlike that of English ecclesiastics.

The New England Puritan's difference from the Anglican or Catholic in worship and polity dictated differences in literary theory. His literal attitude toward the Bible left little excuse for any religious art not somehow justified by its text; and the ardor of his Protestantism led him to reject anything traditionally associated with the Church of Rome. Organ music, stained-glass windows, incense, rich vestments, ornate altars, religious images —these were all adjuncts to Catholic, and to some extent to Anglican, worship. Their "Papist" associations were enough to make them anathema to the Puritan. Catholics commonly held that things which appealed to the senses could be fittingly used in the service of religion. The Puritan could not agree. He distrusted sensuous appeals in worship because they usually involved objects and practices not specifically endorsed by Holy Writ, because they smacked of Rome, and because he believed that "fallen man" was likely to become the prey of his senses, subject to the tyranny of passion rather than the dictates of right reason and faith.

This meant that the Puritan writer could not use, as his Catholic and Anglican contemporaries did, a body of material and a set of devices calculated to charm sensuously and to "adorn" his work—such charming and adornment seemed to him dangerous. He wanted to reach men's reason and to convince them of truth, not to lull them to acceptance by drugging their minds with potions all too likely to stir the carnal passions so powerful in the descendants of fallen Adam. The Puritan usually rejected imagery which served merely to delight, accepting only that which seemed to him to make the truth more easily understood, and preferring that which he could find in the Bible. He would rather talk of plain glass, letting in all the light, than of stained-glass windows, which seemed to him empty adornment symbolizing man's aptness to dim the light of truth. Anything which appealed to the senses so strongly as to endanger concentration on what must be grasped by reason, was dangerous. Good writing was to teach; its method must make directly and clearly comprehensible what man most needed to know.

Naturally, early New England writers of prose concentrated on sound and logical structure, and on clarity. The logic and rhetoric of Peter Ramus, the great French anti-Aristotelian logician of the sixteenth century, were adopted by Puritan pundits partly because they seemed to offer useful rules for good expository prose. But more immediately important than such rules was the Puritan's consciousness of the nature of his audience. It comprised men who were neither trained critics nor expert writers, but were, usually, earnest Christians, eager to learn. They were humanly fallible, and if a page, however clear, seemed dull, their thoughts strayed. Therefore the Puritan preacher and writer, although he advocated the "plain style" and objected to adornment for adornment's sake, seasoned his prose with imagery and used whatever literary devices seemed to him legitimate and necessary to make his instruction palatable. Anything in words which might rouse evil passions was forbidden, but picturesque phrasing and evocative images were allowable if their associations were innocent or if they had Biblical precedent.

The last point is important. The Bible had for the Puritan supreme literary value. It was the work of an omnipotent God, who used language perfectly because all that he did was perfect. Allegory, figures of speech— even frankly sexual imagery—crop up often in Puritan writing, sometimes in ways that are startling if we forget that its authors knew that men's "affections" must be charmed if their attention was to be held, and were sure that any literary method used in the Bible had divine sanction. New England authors avoided the rapturous expression of Catholic or Anglican mystics as too sensuous and too redolent of "enthusiasm"; they closed their eyes to much in the great religious literature of seventeenth century England because they did not want to tempt their readers' passions or to cloud their understanding of the truth by too elaborate rhetoric. Moreover, symbols and images, linked with the Mass and with ritualistic forms of worship, were suspect to the Puritan, and, in general, he looked coldly upon the ingenuities of style, the extended similes, the complicated metaphors (often sensuous or even sensual in suggestion), the elaborate prose music, and the rhetorical decoration, which characterized much of the best English writing in the late Renaissance. The Puritan was thus cut off from many sources of literary effect; but mercifully the Bible gave him others. He had no qualms about using its imagery, its rhythms, and its stylistic devices for his own pious purposes.

Part of his success with his audience depended on what he learned from Biblical style; he profited also by his understanding of other means by which he could hold his audience's attention without concessions to its baser appetites. He spoke and wrote principally for fishermen, farmers, woodsmen, shopkeepers, and artisans. However little they knew about classical literature or about rhetorical niceties in English prose and verse, they knew a great deal about the sea, gardens, village life, and the concrete concerns of pioneers busily establishing prosperous colonies in a wilderness. They enjoyed seeing an author drive home his point with a simile or a metaphor that touched their familiar experience; and their experience was rich with homely material. When Thomas Shepard wrote in his *Sincere Convert* (1655 edition), "Jesus Christ is not got with a wet finger," he meant, "Salvation cannot be had by mere study of books"; but his metaphor made a commonplace statement expressive and vivid for his readers by calling up the picture of an earnest student wetting his finger whenever he had to turn a page. Such metaphors and similes abound in Puritan writing. Their purpose is obvious; their effect is to give to pages which might otherwise be abstract and dull the taste of life.

Some New England writers broke away from the usual Puritan conventions of style. They were all to some extent influenced by non-Puritan ways of writing; many of them were English university men, well trained in literary traditions; and those whose work has merit enough to deserve mention today were individuals never completely subjugated by rigid convention. But the variations from orthodox Puritan practice are usually minor, and, so far as the work of any group can be summed up in a formula, the Puritans' can be. The formula called for clarity, order, and logic as supreme stylistic virtues. It admitted some concessions to the reader's liking for sensuous appeal, but limited that appeal to what was unlikely to stimulate man's baser nature and distract his mind from truth.

2

Nathaniel Ward, who came from England and preached at Ipswich, Massachusetts, in the early days of its settlement, is a useful example both of the Puritans' literary theory and of the permissible deviations from it. His *The Simple Cobler of Aggawamm in America*, a vigorously intolerant plea for Puritan orthodoxy, which was first printed in London in 1647 and ran through four editions in a few months, is full of word coinages, jingling phrases, and other forms of verbal display, and its style is certainly far less "plain" than that prescribed by strict Puritan theory. But Ward knew

what he was doing. He defended himself against the charge of "levity" by
writing:

> To speak to light heads with heavy words, were to break their necks; to clothe
> Summer matter, with Winter Rugge, would make the Reader sweat.

In other words, he was trying to make his style fit his material—and his
audience. He virtually admits that he has now and then adorned his prose
too much:

> I honour them with my heart, that can express more than ordinary matter in
> ordinary words: it is a pleasing eloquence; [I honour] them more that study
> wisely and soberly to inhance their native language. . . . Affected termes are
> unaffecting things to solid hearers; yet I hold him prudent that . . . will help
> disedged appetites with convenient condiments.

Ward wrote to teach, and he chose what seemed to him to be an effective
method for his audience. If he offended against the strictest Puritan standard
in using too many stylistic "condiments," he observed it in his reliance on
homely imagery and in his exclusion of anything likely to stir sinful passions.

As for Cotton Mather who, in most of his work, departed from the plainest Puritan "plain style" by peppering his pages with allusions, quotations,
and pedantic playings upon words, he knew quite well that he followed a
fashion not universally approved in New England. He did so deliberately.
He had thought a little about style, knew what he wanted to accomplish, and
believed there were good ends to be served by varying from stylistic plainness. But even Mather, although he wrote his ecclesiastical history of New
England, the *Magnalia Christi Americana* (1702) in the full tide of an enthusiasm for a prose encrusted with rhetorical eccentricities and learned allusions, in many another book used a style as simple and direct as the most
conventional Puritan's. He could ape the new prose writers of the Restoration
and the early eighteenth century in England, as well as the rhetoricians of
1630 or 1640. His *Political Fables* (about 1692) are in impeccably lucid prose;
his *Christian Philosopher* (1721), an exposition of the arguments for Christianity to be found in the study of the natural world, has its flowery passages
and is loaded with quotations and allusions, but the stylistic core is simple
expository prose; his *Bonifacius* or *Essays to Do Good* (1710), beloved of
Benjamin Franklin, was aimed at plain folk and is appropriately homespun
in texture. So in all his voluminous writing—some four hundred and fifty
books and pamphlets—Mather chose the kind of prose which seemed to him
best suited to his purpose, without ever lapsing into a style so sensuously
appealing as to be dangerous for fallen man. The *Magnalia,* he hoped, might

reach the erudite abroad, and for such a book a style "richly trimmed" with learned trappings was appropriate. For less pretentious offerings he chose a simpler style, because he understood his audience and, like other good Puritans, held that his first task was to make truth intelligible to it.

The main stream of early New England literary practice is best shown in the chronicles and histories treated elsewhere in this volume, and in the sermons and other religious prose of Cotton Mather's generation and before. His own father Increase, for example, wrote numerous works chiefly striking for their typical Puritan emphasis on clarity and order; so did hosts of other New Englanders before 1700. Their zeal for ordered simplicity and their distrust of the sensuous too often makes their work seem to us cool and thin, colorless, and imaginatively tame. But with the faults went virtues—an effect of patterned dignity and, often, skillful use of homely realism.

This realism appears everywhere. Samuel Sewall, a Puritan layman, writes a paragraph about New England in *Phaenomena quaedam Apocalyptica*, a pamphlet on the Book of Revelation, and we hear of "the hectoring Words and hard Blows of the proud and boisterous Ocean," beating against Plum Island, of the salmon and sturgeon in the Merrimac, and of the "free and harmless Doves" perching in the "White Oak." And Sewall's famous diary is full of vividly realistic phrasing. How could the behavior of an angry man be more sharply pictured in a single phrase than in the diarist's account of the minister, who "with extraordinary Vehemency said, (capering with his feet)"? Even in the pages of a scholar as formidable as the Reverend John Norton, Augustine's "A good life is requisite in respect of ourselves, but a good name is requisite in respect of others" is pointed up by the observation "The gratefulness of the most excellent liquor unto the stomach depends in part upon the quality of the vessel." And elsewhere Norton remarks: "The hen, which brings not forth without uncessant sitting night and day, is an apt emblem of students." Roger Williams, although his advanced democratic ideas and his championship of complete religious toleration made him seem to many New Englanders a dangerous heretic, wrote with the authentic Puritan ring. He tells us of "the day of our last farewell, the day of the splitting of this vessel, the breaking of this bubble, the quenching of this candle." He reminds us that we are mere sojourners on earth, "strangers in an inn," "passengers in a ship," who "dream of long summer days." We "dwell in strange houses" and "lodge in strange beds," and pass like "smoke on the chimney's top" when the time comes for "the weighing of our last anchors." We are "poor grasshoppers hopping and skipping from branch to twig in this vale of tears."

The literary virtue stemming from the Puritans' insistence on order and logical structure as essential for conveying truth appears in a passage from

Samuel Willard's election sermon, *The Character of a Good Ruler* (Boston, 1694):

A People are not made for Rulers, But Rulers for a People. It is indeed an Honour which God puts upon some above others, when he takes them from among the People, and sets them up to Rule over them, but it is for the Peoples sake, and the Civil felicity of them is the next end of Civil Policy; and the happiness of Rulers is bound up with theirs in it. Nor can any wise men in authority think themselves happy in the Misery of their Subjects, to whom they either are or should be as Children are to their Fathers: We have the Benefit of Government expressed, 1. *Tim.* 2:2. *a quiet Life and a peaceable, in all Godliness and honesty,* and it lies especialy with Rulers, under God, to make a People Happy or Miserable. When men can injoy their Liberties and Rights without molestation or oppression; when they can live without fear of being born down by their more Potent Neighbours; when they are secured against Violence, and may be Righted against them that offer them any injury, without fraud; and are encouraged to serve God in their own way, with freedom, and without being imposed upon contrary to the Gospel precepts; now are they an happy People.

Or, to take a more complicated example, here is Thomas Hooker, in *The Application of Redemption* (London, 1659), expounding a point important both theologically and in its implications for literature:

It is by the Spiritual Operations and Actions of our minds that we meet with the Lord, and have a kind of intercourse with the Almighty, who is a Spirit. For al outward things are for the body, the body for the soul, the soul is nextly for God, and therefore meets as really with him in the Actions of Understanding, as the Eye meets with the Light in Seeing; which no other Creature can do, nor no action of a bodily Creature doth. Our Sences in their sinful and inordinate swervings, when they become means and in-lets of evil from their objects, they meet with the Creature firstly, and there make the jar: It's the beauty of the Object that stirs up to lust by the Eye, the daintiness of the Diet that provokes to intemperance by the tast, the harsh and unkind language that provokes to wrath and impatience by the Ear: But the Mind and Understanding toucheth the Lord directly, meets with his Rule, and with God acting in the way of his Government there, and when it goes off from the Rule as before, and attends its own vanity and folly, it justles with the Almighty, stands in open defyance and resistance against him.

In this the effect comes both from the structure and from the vigorous realism of such phrases as "there make the jar," or "justles with the Almighty." Samuel Willard's sentence, in his *Mercy Magnified* (1684),

There is a great deal goes to the eternal life of a soul, and thou hast none of it; thou wantest the love of God, which is better than life; thou wantest grace which is indeed the inward principle of life in the soul; thou wantest the promise which is the support of the soul here in this life,

hits its mark because of its balance and its flavor of simple speech. Hooker writes of "meditation," in *The Application of Redemption* (1659):

> The second End of Meditation is, *It settles it effectually upon the heart*. It's not the pashing of the water at a sudden push, but the standing and soaking to the root, that loosens the weeds and thorns, that they may be plucked up easily. It's not the laying of Oyl upon the benummed part, but the chafing of it in, that suppleth the Joynts, and easeth the pain. It is so in the soul; Application laies the Oyl of the Word that is searching and savory, Meditation chafeth it in, that it may soften and humble the hard and stony heart: Application is like the Conduit or Channel that brings the stream of the Truth upon the soul; but Meditation stops it as it were, and makes it soak into the heart, that so our corruptions may be plucked up kindly by the Roots.

The pattern is plain; its effect is enhanced because it is clothed with images thoroughly familiar to men and women who weeded gardens and treated one another's ailments.

3

Not only in his prose but in his poetry the Puritan displayed his fundamental literary creed. Early New Englanders wrote a great deal of verse, and in it, as in their prose, they chose the methods which seemed to them best adapted to their audience and most consonant with the Puritan view that all good writing must teach. Of course distrust of sensuous appeals does more injury to poetry than to prose, and the Puritan's verse suffered accordingly. Too often his poems are merely versified prose, expounding a useful lesson. Too often they are flat reiterations of pious truisms, adorned with some of the poetic artifices which the seventeenth century appreciated more than the twentieth. The devices were the more innocent ones sanctioned by the time, the ones least likely to arouse unruly and dangerous emotions; but some of them were intricate and "witty" to a degree uncommon in Puritan prose. The New England colonist gave a little more license to his verse writers than to the preacher or the writer of theological tracts, but he still kept them on a tight rein. The result is that their feeling, however genuine, too often quite fails to reach the readers of their verse.

That they wrote as much verse as they did, however, is sufficient refutation of the old heresy that Puritans were "hostile" to poetry. They were not. They found in it a way of expression necessary to them, but their theories limited their freedom in writing it. Also their utilitarian attitude toward all literature often put verse in the light of a luxury, since there was so much that needed to be said in sober prose. Most of the poetry written in New England before 1760 was never printed; most of it was circulated, if it was circulated at all, in manuscript, or committed to the pages of diaries or volumes of family memorabilia.

There were exceptions, though, and some New England verse found its way into print in the seventeenth and eighteenth centuries. The almanacs, indispensable to colonial farmers and fishermen, gave space to many stanzas, and there were even a few whole volumes of verse. Most famous of these is the "Bay Psalm Book," *The Whole Booke of Psalmes Faithfully Translated into English Metre,* printed in Cambridge, Massachusetts, in 1640, celebrated not for any poetic merit in its clumsy stanzas and tortured lines but because it was the first book issued in the English colonies in North America. Its authors, Richard Mather, John Eliot, and Thomas Welde, all devout and learned ministers and capable craftsmen in prose, knew that they were not writing poetry and said so. They wanted a literal translation of the Psalms which would fit metrically the tunes familiar to Puritan congregations. Accuracy and serviceability for worship were more important than literary excellence. The book was designed to be useful to ministers and their flocks, and was therefore a proper offering to God. If it was rough and graceless in form, it did not matter, since, as its authors wrote, "God's altar needs not our polishings."

Other New England books had more pretensions and more success as poetry. Most famous in its own day was Michael Wigglesworth's *Day of Doom* (1662), a colonial "best-seller." Its jog-trot ballad measure seems to us curiously inappropriate for an account of the Judgment Day, but it has a few flashes of sensitive poetic expression. So have some of Wigglesworth's other poetic efforts. But he was first of all a Puritan divine, and saw his main task as the teaching of sound Christianity. Therefore he chose a meter familiar to his readers, and versified standard Puritan doctrine, hoping that the rhyme and rhythm might make it more gratefully received and more easily remembered than it could be in prose. That he succeeded seems to be proved by the fact that *The Day of Doom* had at least ten editions before 1760.

Anne Bradstreet's verses were never as popular as Wigglesworth's; but they were well enough received to make possible three editions before 1760. The daughter of Thomas Dudley, steward to the Earl of Lincoln and, later, Governor of Massachusetts, she married Simon Bradstreet and came with him to Massachusetts in 1630, when she was seventeen. She had apparently read widely, and although she was a faithful Puritan wife, she could not always accept in entire docility the sterner aspects of the New England variety of

Calvinism. The last stanza of her little poem on the death of a grandchild is revealing:

> By nature Trees do rot when they are grown.
> And Plumbs and Apples throughly ripe do fall,
> And Corn and grass are in their season mown,
> And time brings down what is both strong and tall.
> But plants new set to be eradicate,
> And buds new blown, to have so short a date,
> Is by his hand alone that guides nature and fate.

The simplicity of the diction and the limited but accurate imagery carry a genuine emotional effect until, suddenly, Anne Bradstreet realizes that she is perilously close to writing rebelliously against God's decrees. She pulls herself up in the last line. It falls flat, even metrically, because it is dictated not by real feeling but by deference to orthodox doctrine. In other poems she is content simply to versify learning, sedulously imitating the pious French poet Du Bartas, whose work, in the English translation of Joshua Sylvester, she loved. Many of her pages are dull; many are merely "instructive" verse, using the devices of poetry but rarely rising above the attitudes of prose. But there are also pages in which she wrote simply and well of things close to her heart, and let her emotion, although always decorously expressed, warm her lines. Her *Contemplations,* for example, although overformal by modern standards, is a brave attempt to express poetically some sense of the physical beauty of Massachusetts; her lines in praise of Queen Elizabeth have defiant vigor and wit:

> Now say, have women worth? or have they none?
> Or had they some, but with our Queen is't gone?
> Nay Masculines, you have thus taxt us long,
> But she, though dead, will vindicate our wrong.
> Let such as say our Sex is void of Reason,
> Know tis a Slander now, but once was Treason.

Many a minor English poet of her day, more celebrated than Anne Bradstreet, wrote nothing that is better than her best, even though her best conforms to the Puritan's utilitarian view of art and to his distrust of the frankly sensuous.

A host of other New England colonial poets published only an occasional verse, or are known in print only by lines prefixed to books or collected by Cotton Mather in his *Magnalia*; but many of them left poems in manuscript. Mather says, for example, that the Reverend John Wilson, a pioneer divine in Boston, left at his death enough verse to fill a folio; but a very small book would contain all of it that was put into type for his contemporaries. He was a diligent anagrammatist, addicted to the then admired device of rearranging the letters of a man's name to make a phrase which could be used as the theme for a set of verses. Such contrivances seem to us mere ingenuity, but we should not forget that in Wilson's time anagrams were sometimes thought to have a mystic significance, and that to write verses on themes suggested by them was an intellectually reputable pursuit. Here, as in most Puritan poetry, the modern reader is handicapped by the fact that it is poetry written to meet outmoded standards. The great English poets who were publishing, and were winning applause, while the colonial New Englanders were constructing rhymes in the intervals of arduous lives in a "wilderness," adapted those standards to the uses of great poetry. The New Englander usually followed the convention expertly enough, but rarely made his finished work memorable for anything but competent craftsmanship. He was partially cut off from the tradition of great poetry by his specifically Puritan theories. He was reluctant to stir emotions too deeply, and he disliked the Anglicanism or Catholicism of many of the poets who might have taught him most. He was hampered by the lack of an artistically experienced audience, and he was too often blinded to poetic values by his intense concentration on the idea that the writer's first task was to put useful doctrine into the most immediately intelligible form. This is not to say that the Puritan was emotionally cold or poetically insensitive; there are proofs to the contrary in both Wigglesworth and Bradstreet. Nor is it to say that he could never write memorable lines; there are several in Urian Oakes' *Elegy upon the Death of the Reverend Mr. Thomas Shepard* (1677), and others in the usually awkward rhymes which Edward Johnson sprinkled through his *Wonder-Working Providence*. Any reader with a taste for good technique in expository or didactic verse will be rewarded in the pages of Benjamin Tompson or Richard Steere, who, for all their defects in imagination, were good enough workmen to give pleasure by the neatness with which they satirized New England's foibles or used the devices of Dryden and his school to make useful precepts and sound learning palatable to the colonists.

4

The greatest poet of New England before the nineteenth century was Edward Taylor, a Puritan minister of Westfield, Massachusetts, in the late seventeenth and early eighteenth centuries. His work, and his apparent attitude toward it, illustrate admirably the working of the Puritan theory of poetry, and his successes and failures are useful indices of the general poetic condition of the New England he knew. Very little of his verse was published in his day, but he left enough in manuscript to fill a large volume, with the request that it be not printed. We cannot be sure why this request was made, but Taylor probably knew that his poetry was not quite orthodox, and that it might seem to the more sober of his brethren a reflection upon his godliness or upon his understanding of man's sinful nature. His poetry is, in general, more sensuous, richer in luxurious imagery, and more daringly expressive of an essentially mystic emotion, than that of most Puritans. There are in Taylor decorated altars, jewels, spices, perfumes; there are strong echoes of such poets as John Donne and Richard Crashaw; there are whole poems which play more directly than most Puritans approved on men's love for color, gems, scents, and the delights of the flesh. Of course Taylor's poems were pious in intent; he was passionately devout—but he chose to express his pious devotion in terms which, as he may well have recognized, savored strongly of this world. He seems to have been not only more imaginatively endowed than his contemporaries, but also more defiant than they of the restrictions imposed on poets by the Puritan's fear of the passions of fallen man. For us his poetry gains by this. Where Bradstreet and Wigglesworth give hints of poetic power, Taylor gives proofs; where other Puritan poets rise only to ingenious expression or deft exposition in verse, lighted by very occasional flashes of imaginative insight, Taylor at his best writes poems so vivid in emotional evocation that they attain an artistic immortality quite independent of their doctrine.

Taylor's virtues do not stem merely from his enlargement of the limits of conventional Puritan practice; one source of strength in his work is his skill in using the kind of image most dear to Puritans—the homely image drawn from the simplest daily experience of simple folk. With this goes his adroit use of homespun diction, made more effective often by a contrast between the earthiness of a word (or a figure) and the loftiness of his theme. The soul is a "Bird of Paradise" in a "Wicker Cage," and there it "tweedles" praise to God. God "grinds, and kneads up into this Bread of Life, . . . the Purest Wheate in Heaven, his deare-dear Son." The result is "Heavens Sugar Cake." Man is to be a "Spinning Wheele" for God:

> Thy Holy Worde my Distaff make for mee.
> Make mine Affections thy Swift Flyers neate,
> And make my Soule thy holy Spoole to bee.
> My Conversation make to be thy Reele,
> And reele the yarn thereon Spun of thy Wheele.

The poem goes on to the weaving and dyeing of the cloth, until man is at last "Cloathd in Holy robes for glory."

The image is ingenious in the typical "metaphysical" mode, and is effective by virtue of its realism. No Puritan could have taken exception to it except possibly in so far as its ingenuity might seem to him to smack too much of current Anglican verse, and to be too apt to delight the reader to the point of distracting him from the truth the poem was written to express. But many Puritans might have had doubts about

> My Lovely One, I fain would love thee much,
>   But all my Love is none at all I see;
> Oh! let thy Beauty give a glorious touch
>   Upon my Heart, and melt to Love all mee.
>   Lord, melt me all up into Love for thee,
>   Whose Loveliness excells what love can bee,

or

> Shall I not smell thy sweet, oh! Sharons Rose?
>   Shall not mine Eye salute thy Beauty? Why?
> Shall thy sweet leaves their Beautious sweets upclose?
>   As halfe ashamde my sight should on them ly?

Was there not room for fear lest such lines work perilously on the carnal nature of sinful man? There might be offense, too, in

> But now my Heart is made thy Censar trim,
>   Full of thy golden Altars fire,
> To offer up Sweet Incense in
>   Unto thyself intire.

Censers, golden altars, and sweet incense had Biblical precedents, to be sure. But was not this verse too redolent of the ritualism against which the Puritans rebelled? There are other lines of the same sort in Taylor; others, too, in which love fills heaven, love runs over, blood is linked with love. The intensely emotional tone of many of Taylor's poems, and their specifically physical connotations, might well frighten critics who believed the senses could betray the reason, and had no use for the dangerous "enthusiastic" idea that man could ever achieve on earth a rapturous union with God.

Today, fortunately, no such scruples get in the way of our appreciation of Taylor's imaginative power and dramatic skill. His emotions may have been too strong for the tightest bonds of Puritan theory, but he adroitly used some Puritan literary conventions to give contrast and dramatic tension to his work. His constant use of homely and realistic diction and imagery brings ecstatic religious vision and the actualities of earth together in his verses, striking poetic sparks from the contrast. Again and again he makes articulate the drama inherent in man's quest for a beauty which is beyond earth but realizable only in images of earthly delights.

5

Taylor died in 1729. By then New England had changed greatly. The old religious fervor had abated; the concept of a universe centered in God had weakened before that of one centered on man; and more and more colonists, especially in the properous seaboard towns, were interested in trade and in aping the amenities of English society rather than in conquering new lands for Christ. They paid lip service to the old theology, and church membership was still a mark of social respectability; but the zeal for teaching and the fierce concentration on the dilemma of sinful man had lessened, and literature reflected the change. More and more the grace and urbanity of the English periodical essayists came to be admired; the robust vocabulary and rhetoric of the original colonists were toned down to the level of easy fluency; concrete realism often gave way to well turned generalizations couched in abstract terms. In verse Taylor's ardor and his love of dramatic contrast were replaced by smooth couplets and neat stanzas obviously reminiscent of Dryden, Watts, and Pope. Between 1700 and 1760 New England produced plenty of good prose and plenty of graceful verse; but much of it seems tame when compared with earlier work because the feeling behind it was less intense. "Good sense" was in vogue; "reasonableness" and "politeness" were more important than they had been to Puritan preachers and tract writers. Compare almost any line of Taylor, or almost any stanza, however clumsy, of *The Day of Doom* with this bit from a "Poetical Meditation" by Roger Wolcott of Connecticut, published in 1725:

> Vertue still makes the Vertuous to shine,
> Like those that Liv'd in the first week of time.
> Vertue hath force the vile to cleanse again,
> So being like clear shining after Rain.
> A Kind and Constant, Chearful Vertuous Life,
> Becomes each Man, and most Adorns a Wife.

True enough, any Puritan would have agreed; but few earlier Puritans would have put it so blandly, with so little sense of man's helpless vileness before God or of the miracle of God's grace vouchsafed to his elect. The change in attitude—and in style—from the earlier writers, shown in Wolcott and many eighteenth century New Englanders, illustrates some of the ways in which deism, the new rationalism, and changed English literary fashions affected the original Puritan outlook.

There were some literary gains. The newer theory flowered in Benjamin Franklin's best essays, skillfully written by a "sensible" man for "sensible" folk, with their eyes on this world more than on the next, and in the scientific and philosophical works of Jonathan Edwards. The brilliance of the prose in which the Reverend John Wise defended the original New England church polity in *The Churches Quarrel Espoused* (1710) and *Vindication of the Government of New-England Churches* (1717), shows how much he had learned from English stylists of the school of Dryden and Swift.

Furthermore the increasing secularization of society, the relaxing of the old dominant preoccupation with religion, opened the door to pleasant excursions in fields unvisited by the earlier Puritans. Mather Byles, for example, the nephew of Cotton Mather, was a minister, but achieved almost as much fame for his punning as for his preaching. He was also a rhymer, and an admirer of Pope and of the English poets of his day, and dashed off a few verses which his ancestors would have considered too trivial—or too frivolous —for a divine. The early Puritans had humor, of course—to take but two examples, Samuel Sewall in his diary and Nathaniel Ward in his *Cobler,* showed theirs; but usually the seventeenth century colonial preacher would have considered it a waste of paper and ink to display wit (in the modern sense) or humor in published writings. Nor were there, in the early days of Massachusetts, merchants like Joseph Green, ready to entertain themselves and their less pious neighbors with verses on the joys of drinking, or on the death of Mather Byles' cat, or with even more direct ridicule in rhyme of the minister of the Hollis Street Church. New England's notion of the purpose of literature changed fast after 1700. Good writing was seen no longer as simply a way of serving God by communicating divine truth as directly as possible; there was room for work designed merely to entertain. There was also an increasing interest in discussions of purely literary and stylistic matters. John Bulkeley, in 1725, wrote for Wolcott's *Poetical Meditations* a preface which is pious enough but devotes more attention than do most earlier colonial writings to purely literary values. Cotton Mather's famous essay on style, inserted in his *Manuductio ad Ministerium* (1726), a manual for theological students, takes a broader aesthetic view than the preface to the "Bay Psalm Book" or Michael Wigglesworth's unpublished "Prayse of Eloquence."

It is unlikely that more than a few pages of poetry and prose of New England before 1760 will ever achieve popular literary immortality. There are, none the less, memorable passages not only in the chronicles and histories, but in the great mass of sermons, tracts, essays, poems, and pious verse written by the colonists; and there are hundreds of other passages which lack the stamp of greatness but still have interest for, and may give excitement to, the modern reader who can read them with the understanding they deserve. That understanding involves first of all some knowledge of colonial conditions, some realization of the circumstances under which they were written and of the purpose and the audience for which they were designed. It involves, too, an appreciation of the literary conventions which were accepted by our fore-fathers and, in spite of serious limitations, had value. Order, logic, clarity, are still virtues in writing, even though the devices by which we try to achieve them are unlike the Puritans'. Homely imagery, earthy phrasing, and the use of simple and realistic figures to make abstract ideas or emotions concretely realizable are traits still characteristic of much of the best American writing. Emerson admired "language of nature." He found it in the speech of a "Vermont drover" and said that "in the 17th century, it appeared in every book." For an example he cited Thomas Shepard's "And to put finger in the eye and to renew their repentance, they think this is weakness." Obviously he was thinking of the homeliness so characteristic of Puritan prose; obviously too, much of his own best work shows the same quality. Emerson, and others, found in the Puritan's stylistic theory something adaptable to the needs of the idealist in any age. The early New Englanders' eyes were on God; but they were busy men with a wilderness to subdue and the divine will to carry out on earth.

Jonathan Edwards wrote on science and philosophy more effectively and more attractively, at least for modern readers, than most of his seventeenth century predecessors. Such men were exceptional, but they profited from some of the new methods in English prose popularized in the late seventeenth and early eighteenth centuries—methods by which many other New England writers before 1760 made their work palatable. The Puritans' literary prac-tice grew out of the search for some way to express both the spiritual emotion that controlled them and their vigorous desire to make practical use of it, and to teach others to do so, in daily life. They never succeeded, perhaps, in realizing their aim, either in literature or in life, but only those of us who are too limited in vision to see the gallantry of their quest will refuse them respect for what they did and wrote.

6. JONATHAN EDWARDS

THE East Windsor parsonage where Edwards was born October 5, 1703, was a rambling Connecticut farmhouse which easily accommodated the eleven children of Timothy and Esther (Stoddard) Edwards. In the gently sloping meadow at the rear, by a brook, the youthful Jonathan built the booth where he and his boy companions came to meditate and pray. It was in the immediate neighborhood that he observed the flying, or balloon, spiders in his twelfth or thirteenth year and reported on them in an account celebrated as the earliest natural history essay written on the subject. Timothy encouraged his only son in tasks that required painstaking accuracy, and the boy's imaginative mind responded to the discipline. The son was under the tutorship of a parent better remembered as a teacher than as a preacher, one who was especially successful in preparing students for Harvard and Yale. The power to evoke an "admirably rich and delicate description," as William James characterized *A Treatise Concerning Religious Affections* (1746), was foreshadowed in the youthful considerations of natural phenomena, of insects and rainbows, seen on a Connecticut hillside. Thus endowed, the boy entered Yale College in the autumn of 1716.

The pattern of Edwards' thinking was first displayed in the "Notes on Natural Science" and "The Mind." They were responses to courses in "natural philosophy," or physics, taken in the junior and senior years. This was the time when his conning of the new science, through the pages of Newton and Locke, bewitched him into self-discovery. The quiet young man, whose dependability won him the honor of a college butlership, as supervisor in the dining hall, was already a citizen of the realm of mind. The "Notes" pose the questions: What is reality? What are the metes of human knowledge? Wherein consists true liberty? And, most important of all, is it possible for a man to love anything better than himself?

Here Edwards first attempted to integrate the principles of morals, art, and being. The note on "Excellence" concludes:

Wherefore all Virtue, which is the Excellency of minds, is resolved into *Love to Being*; and nothing is virtuous or beautiful in Spirits, any otherwise than as it

71

is an exercise, or fruit, or manifestation of this love; and nothing is sinful or deformed in Spirits, but as it is the defect of, or contrary to, these.

However technical as doctrine, this early attempt to set down a philosophical ideal on nine sheets of foolscap is the kernel of everything that later took root. It is Edwards' first effort to harmonize emotion and reason, mercy and justice, fate and free will. To read the world in terms of love was Edwards' unique contribution to the philosophic system of Calvin.

All his study of theology, undertaken in the two graduate years after he received his bachelor's degree in 1720, was now absorbed into abstract reflections, as were the scientific speculations. The idealism of "The Mind" and of the better known "Of Being" may or may not be traceable to the English idealist George Berkeley. One thing is sure. The stretch of Edwards' mind is observable from his youth. Rumors of new and exciting speculative theories were in the air: that the world of the senses is a direct expression of divine ideas; that mind and spirit are more important than their manifestation in matter. Such perceptions he had doubtless discussed, for they are convictions toward which he was moving.

The final and certainly determining event in his student years, described so charmingly in the "Personal Narrative" written twenty years after, was his mystical conversion at seventeen: "I often used to sit & view the Moon, for a long time; and so in the Day-time, spent much time in viewing the Clouds & Sky, to behold the sweet Glory of God in these Things: in the mean Time, singing forth, with a low Voice, my Contemplations of the Creator and Redeemer." All that he witnessed as manifestations of the sensible world became shadows of divine truths. The concrete image henceforth was to be the symbolic fact. From now on, nature was an analogy, as it has been felt by mystics from the beginning of time. Among American men of letters in the next century, Bryant came to express it in his own way; and Emerson, most articulately of all.

The apprentice preaching in New York during 1723 at a newly congregated church in William Street lasted but eight months. Edwards' haste to accept an invitation by a group in Bolton, Connecticut, may imply that the world of wharves and brick houses was not congenial to the New England youth now first separated from homestead, woodland, and meadows. The "new Sense of Things" as reflected in the universe round about, which had first possessed him at college, was never to alter.

A pressing community need released him almost immediately from his Bolton commitments. In 1724 his alma mater offered him the senior tutorship at a most stormy moment in the early days of the college, a position which Edwards held for two years, acting virtually as president. Then came the call as colleague pastor to his grandfather's church at Northampton. The aged "Pope" Stoddard, who dictated church polity in a manner no Boston minister dared emulate, would shortly retire. Edwards was settled in February, 1727, and in the same year married Sarah Pierrepont of New Haven, a woman of spirit and great sensitivity. These were the years when the burdens of raising a family and the task of preparing biweekly sermons and writing an occasional book occupied him fully. Indeed, the stately Mr. Edwards, spare of limb, was becoming an author of repute, though his townsmen would recall him walking, lost in thought, across the village common or riding with loose rein through the back pastures, his coat dotted with paper slips, notes set down lest he forget the ideas which absorbed him. It was Sarah Edwards that encouraged this life of plain living and high thinking, and uncomplainingly shared with her husband the heartbreaks of the later Northampton years. She accepted as he did, without self-pity or remorse, the humble missionary station after their transfer to the small Stockbridge Indian outpost in 1751.

2

The root of the Northampton trouble which led to Edwards' dismissal in his forty-seventh year from the most influential Connecticut Valley parish can be traced to the idealism implicit in the youthful notes on "The Mind." Edwards had been embroiled in "issues" from the day he matriculated in Yale College at the age of thirteen. His forthright honesty clearly produced them, and he was now willing to court his dismissal because any earlier doubts were resolved. The good of mankind was inseparable from the manner in which that good must be obtained. The *Farewell Sermon*, preached in July, 1750, spotlights the drama of his life in mid-passage. "You need one," he concludes, remarking of a successor, "that shall stand as a champion in the cause of truth and the power of godliness." And the opinion ruefully evaluates his administrative limits, not his principles.

The willingness of Edwards to accept into church membership only those who professed "renovation of heart," a conviction of spiritual regeneration, seemed intolerable to the majority. The shadow of his grandfather Stoddard, dead these twenty years, was yet upon the community, for Stoddard had taught his congregation to believe that under special circumstances the sacred seal of the Lord's Supper might in itself be a "converting ordinance." That is to say, Edwards was at last convinced that the sacrament was for those only who felt it to be the symbol of a conversion already achieved by the participant. His tragic realization of the place of evil in the scheme of things, his conviction of the irreversible reality of human isolation, were now fully reasoned. The revolution he was effecting in an attempt to abrogate Stoddard's decision, and the issue he joined, were to be made clear in the treatises he would soon write in the frontier settlement at Stockbridge during the remaining eight years of his life. For the moment he seemed an isolated reactionary, lost to the times because he would not compromise with them. Need religion be more than regular church attendance, profession of a reasoned belief in godly living based on good breeding and humanitarian interests in the welfare of one's neighbors? Edwards thought it should be. He was ready to express himself in a series of independent metaphysical speculations which have in fact given permanent direction to spiritual culture in America.

3

Edwards did not codify his analysis until after the apparent failure of his career in 1750. Of the five works which compass his scheme, only *Religious Affections* was written before he left Northampton. The remaining four appeared very late. *A Careful and Strict Enquiry . . . of That Freedom of Will . . .* was issued in 1754; *The Great Christian Doctrine of Original Sin Defended,* in 1758, the year of his death; and the *Two Dissertations* on "The Nature of True Virtue" and "Concerning the End for Which God Created the World"—capstones of his philosophical edifice—were brought out posthumously in 1765. The orthodox theology of Calvinism, on which Edwards had been nurtured in East Windsor and at Yale College, was not a shackle limiting the range of his ingenious faculties. Taking, as he did, all human nature for his province, he absolutely required some frame of reference. Calvinism served him admirably as material for the creation of a new idealism.

In a strict sense Edwards, like Emerson, did not construct a systematic philosophy; but the pattern of his interpretation of man's struggle is laid out in the early "Notes," and the later treatises expound the doctrine. From Locke he took the concepts that knowledge must be supplanted by faith, that man's ideas are derived from sense-impressions, even though he diverged widely from Locke in his exposition of the limits and value of knowledge. To Edwards the process was intuitive: man cannot achieve moral grace by an act of will or reason, but must passively receive it through the senses. From Newton, Edwards learned to observe how immutable natural laws, working harmoniously, reflect the great Geometrician. He began by attacking the problem of man's limitation and failure. His weapon was the language of Calvinistic theology.

Calvinism was never synonymous with Puritanism. Archbishop Whitgift, who crowned James I, was a Calvinist; but not so the men he drove to seek out a new plantation in the Bay Colony. Boston and Salem were not touched by Calvinism, nor the dynasty and followers of the Mathers. Edwards, better than any other spokesman, articulated it as a working philosophy, and this Connecticut Valley phenomenon was carried by his supporters into New Jersey and Virginia. Edwards as the first American Calvinist did not emphasize, like Thomas Shepard, Thomas Hooker, and other leaders among the seventeenth century Puritans, the covenantal relation between God and man, whereby the Sovereign was as fully bound by the contract as the subject. Edwards' Calvinism made the Deity more awesome and arbitrary. It emphasized sin as a property of the species. The "immensity and spirituality of the essence of God," in the words of Calvin, were not to be apprehended by an act of reason or bound by man in too legal a contract.

At great pains Edwards reasserted the reality of evil and the assurance of salvation, not to all, but to the "elect." Those so saved, he emphasized, are the regenerate: men and women infused by some external, supernatural grace which they are powerless to win by inclination alone. The regeneration is passively received by way of a new sense. Men may not be sure of election, but they must never cease yearning, with a heart laid passively open to receive the mystical grace. To see God in a rainbow or a buttercup is a reassurance and a challenge. Both the pantheism and the mysticism of Edwards are harmonized in a Calvinistic dogma.

In common with all Puritans, Edwards made clear distinction between the two activities of God, and set them forth in the "Treatise on Grace," written during the Stockbridge years but not published until 1865. There is first God's "common grace," working through secondary causes, to be seen in his providence—his decreeing will—observable in events; and in his commanding will—the Bible. There is secondly, and most important, his "supernatural grace," his regenerative power, an emanation, a new radiation reaching directly to man, overleaping regular channels. It is the supernatural grace that is peculiar to the elect, for it is an irresistible force depending on no antecedent condition or preparation. It reaches beyond the flawless regularity, the implacable justice of cosmic laws. Such mystic union cannot be rationalized. But this "Divine and Supernatural Light, Immediately Imparted to the Soul by the Spirit of God," as Edwards called it in the title of one of his earliest published sermons in 1734, is coexistent with God's common grace. Without the lesser, the greater cannot work. Since God's decreeing will is clear to all who will read their Bible, the preacher is under obligation to advocate hell-fire and brimstone now and then, in order to remind men forcibly that "conversion" is a matter of immediate urgency. The minatory sermon, though seldom used by Edwards in fact, is especially associated with the Calvinism he expounded, and was a traditional part of the Puritan ideology. Edwards' sermon on the sovereignty of God and depravity of man, *Sinners in the Hands of an Angry God* (1741), has fascinated and horrified succeeding generations of readers as much, apparently, as it did the hearers at Enfield, Connecticut, when it was first delivered; but, removed from its contextual place in the scheme of salvation which Edwards expounded, it tends to misrepresent him as one who despised men when in fact he loved them as fellow beings sometimes forgetful of the warnings of a compassionate Father.

The position of Edwards has thus far been stated in the language peculiar to Puritan theology. When it is reassessed as a living philosophy its idiom is seen to have universal truth. Edwards was Calvinistic especially in that he asserted the persistent reality of sin. Its existence, he felt to be inevitable and inescapable. Created free, with power of choice, man has yet one compulsion laid upon him: that he shall not, as a human creature, overstep the limits which his humanity had fixed. He must not seek to be as a god. The fruit of the tree of knowledge is not his to eat. For Edwards there was a twofold significance to the story of Adam's fall, and in both instances the implication, though tragic, was spiritually invigorating. Act and consequence are inseparable. For Adam's wrong act there must be an appropriate consequence which men call justice. Yet men know that as *human* beings their blindness and ignorance are so necessary that, if justice is to be satisfied, the doctrine of God's absolute sovereignty, with respect to salvation and damnation, can admit of no doubt. "The doctrine has very often appeared exceeding pleasant, bright, and sweet," Edwards remarks in his "Personal Narrative." "Absolute sovereignty is what I love to ascribe to God."

And the second implication is profounder still. Had Adam been allowed to remain forever in Eden where the fruits hung ripe for his picking and no physical problems taxed his ingenuity, what conceivable pleasure could he or his descendants ultimately have found in such virtual condemnation to the life of Lotus-Eaters and Struldbrugs? It is at this point that the concept of Mercy or Redemption is required, for were there no mitigation of justice somewhere, man could have no purpose in living. "Use every man after his desert," said Hamlet testily to Polonius, "and who should 'scape whipping?" No theme more surely postulates the issue of Being. Milton had chosen it for his great epics because he believed it the profoundest subject in the world. And Edwards as a Calvinistic metaphysician expounded the theme with originality. His efforts to uncover the roots of religious experience were greater even than those of William James, since James did not share his conviction that the roots were discoverable. The attempt schematically begins with the "Treatise on Grace," already mentioned, and with the *Freedom of the Will*. It concludes with the essay on God's end in creating the world. The projected *History of the Work of Redemption*, a vast design which was to have epitomized his philosophy by embracing all three worlds, heaven, earth, and hell, was left unfinished.

4

In order to understand *Freedom of the Will*, it is necessary first to know the problem Edwards had to meet. The fact that the treatise is a polemic, directed at certain contemporary "heresies," is today inconsequential except in so far as Edwards hacked at them to provide a clearing on which to establish his city of God. Any child of the eighteenth century knew that the proper study of mankind is man; and Edwards began and ended with man. His probing of the psychology of desire is a courageous facing of the rigors of existence, one that avoids the cosmic optimism of thinking mere flawless regularity is enough. *Freedom of the Will* is an essay on human liberty wherein the will and the emotions are seen to be indistinguishable: "And he that has the Liberty of doing according to his will," Edwards says, "is the Agent or doer who is possessed of the will; and not the will which he is possessed of." Morality, then, is an emotional, impulsive process, not a rational one. Edwards does not deny man's freedom, but states that it is qualified by man's "previous bias and inclination"—by such antecedent complexes as inheritance and childhood conditioning. Here are established both the basis of motivation—that is, self-love—and the limits of achievement. Shades of Mandeville and Hobbes! Had Edwards been their apologist he could hardly have argued their position more cogently. The fact that Edwards had never read Hobbes, though he considered him by way of secondary sources to be a "bad man," gives added force to Edwards' philosophical integrity. "Let [Hobbes'] opinion be what it will, we need not reject all truth which is demonstrated by clear evidence, merely because it was once held by some bad man." The will, then, is passive, the creature is "possessed" by it, and the doctrine of necessity equates with Greek fate. Both transcendentalism and pragmatism have roots in a Puritan past, and this essay with its insistence on passivity is one of then

To follow the scheme of man's relation to the cosmic plan as it is seen to unfold in Edwards' analysis, one must note that he had established at this point the causal relationship of reason and emotion. A resolution of the struggle between justice and mercy must be attempted, and Edwards faced the issue in the essay on *Original Sin*. Though it was not completed until shortly before his death, it assembled material Edwards had long been pondering: What is the cause of evil? Where are its roots? The logical objection to the position Edwards assumed is that, since God is admittedly the creator of man's moral capacity, any apologist of "original sin" must find God the author of it. Edwards met the argument by contending that sin is original in the sense that it is a "property of the species," that God ordained a system which allows it, that therefore necessarily sin will come to pass. But the sin, Edwards contended, is man's act, not God's; hence the punishment is just. The system which God, the All-Good, ordained, is indeed desirable. Nothing but suffering will answer the Law. The thought is St. Paul's, and is integral with all Christian thinking. If this be tragic, it is the tragedy of an infallible nexus. Let more comfortable men stress the benevolence of Deity, Edwards insisted. Logic and the experience of mankind give no warrant for the assumption. Sin is a universal malady, common to all mankind, one which they must endure from their coming hence until their going thither. It is one illness definitely not contracted from rats, lice, and other vermin. Thus man is unique among creatures. To Edwards the story of the origin of evil, traced to our own hereditary taint, was beautiful as well as disturbing. The fact that it is disturbing should not lead us to deny its truth. Its beauty is manifest by the incentive which man is hereby given to contemplate the mystery of God's inscrutable design. Boldly to avow the reality of sin is to enhance the terror of God's sublimity and compel acknowledgment of humanity's dependence.

The essay does not make easy reading, but the conclusion justifies the labor. "It appears particularly, from what has been said," he remarks in final summary, "that all oneness, by virtue whereof *pollution* and *guilt* from *past* wickedness are derived, depends entirely on a *divine establishment. . . .* And all communications, derivations, or continuation of qualities, properties or relations, natural or moral, from what is *past,* as if the subject were *one,* depends on no other foundation." And here is the second of the elements which gave later transcendentalists a kinship with their inherited past: truth is forever and everywhere one and the same.

A Treatise Concerning Religious Affections has long been widely known as a notable discussion of the psychology of religion. It grew out of Edwards' concern for the problems of human destiny, and constitutes a minute observation of revival meetings when they were recurrent during the 1730's and 1740's. Indeed, his hospitable reception of George Whitefield, the most spectacular exhorter of the century, his endorsement of the many "awakenings," made him suspect among the more urbane ministers of the colony. Though Edwards' support made itinerant evangelism theologically acceptable for the next hundred years, the real importance of *Religious Affections* was not felt until later. Like William James, he was concerned with the psychology of religion in general, and with abnormal psychology in particular; and he analyzed the soul's experience with utmost acumen. The experience is emotional, not rational, Edwards believed; and he traced the steps and gave his witness to the workings of the Holy Spirit, reintroducing emotion as a valid shaper of the good life. He perceived the philosophic meaning which lesser exhorters overlooked: "that the essence of all true religion lies in holy love; and that in this divine affection, and an habitual disposition to it, and that light which is the foundation of it, and those things which are the fruits of it, consists the whole of religion." This was Edwards' pattern for living. What he later systematized in *Freedom of the Will*, he was accounting for in the emotions of men. The union of man and God lay through the mysteries of the heart, and Edwards' bold examination established him as a student of the psychology of mysticism. His care, here as always, is to avoid identifying mere intuition with the voice of God, or fusing God and nature into one substance of the transcendental imagination. The work in this respect is unique and remains an initial force in one cultural tradition, through Emerson to the present.

The *Nature of True Virtue* (1765), properly a sequel to *Religious Affections*, is something of an achievement, for it is mysticism shaped by dogma. It proceeds by contending that acts receive moral quality from the motives that inspire them. True virtue consists of love to Being in general and thus to God as the sum of being. Since no man, Edwards concludes, can have this love unless he is supernaturally charged by some immediately imparted agency, no man can actively work toward becoming truly virtuous. If such a doctrine seems to imply that man should be glad to be damned for the glory of God, it also presents a surpassing moral ideal. How supreme the love can be! How complete becomes the virtuous man's humility when he is able to love others rather than himself! The virtuous man is motivated by good emotions—good because of their beauty, not because of their usefulness or benefits. In the companion dissertation, *Concerning the End for Which God Created the World*, he pushes the implications to final limits. God created the world as the Supreme Artist or Genius, for the pure joy of creating. "It is certain that what God aimed at in the creation of the world, was the good that would be the consequence of the creation, in the whole continuance of the thing created, . . . aiming at an infinitely perfect union of the creature with himself . . . to satisfy his infinite grace and benevolence." God intended the emanation of his fullness, Edwards here states, since beauty, goodness, and existence are all manifestations of the same Principle. The union is one for man to establish, not by will or action, but through passive receptivity. The essay is written for those who would hear, in Milton's phrase, "the unexpressive nuptiall Song."

Edwards has been analyzing pure goodness in a manner no poet has successfully done. Milton and Goethe both succeeded in portraying evil. Edwards, believing that sin is inherent—that man, to the extent that he partakes of common humanity, is "possessed" as well by good will as by bad—is presenting the conclusion that the good man is the continent of Satan. The convincing symbol of goodness must *contain* evil—experiencing it, transmuting it, dissolving it. How could so magnificent a system, Edwards implies, be postulated without the damnation of sinner and election of saint? He has added to Calvinism the mystical and pantheistic overtones; and thus emerges a symbol of sensuous experience philosophically derived.

Each of Edwards' great treatises was written to answer the arguments of insignificant publicists. The issues concerned him, not the stature of the opponents. The recognition of the dislocation as extended to the social order, the tragic vision, though less central in Edwards' thinking than in that of novelists and poets who re-create human action, is none the less clearly present. "Dear children," he said, addressing the youth of the congregation assembled to hear him preach his Farewell Sermon, "Dear children, I leave you in an evil world, that is full of snares and temptations. God only knows what will become of you." Edwards' treatises are documents to which men may turn for enlightenment on a subject of inescapable concern to man. Most of them were composed in a frontier stockade, in a wilderness village beset by trivial bickerings, by one who, while he set spelling lessons for Indian boys, was giving shape to the American destiny.

As a writer of prose, alike in his sermons and in his treatises, Edwards was sensitive to the requirement of his aim. The dissertations hold to the integrity of the syllogistic method, the sermons avoid flights of oratorical fancy. His ear for prose cadence was developed by conscious attention, and he was expert in writing a "plain" style which, in those moments when he abandoned the syllogism to describe the memory of some boyhood experience, effectively communicates the glow of his own heart.

5

Edwards' call to the presidency of the College of New Jersey followed ten years of great productivity and increased renown. His almost immediate death in 1758 deprived the young institution of a celebrated name. "Edwards of New England," as Boswell refers to him, was better known abroad than at home, where he had never been intimate with the religious spokesmen of his time. Inevitably one contrasts him with Franklin, already something of a power, though by no means yet the world figure he was shortly to become. The two, born in the same decade, in the same province, are recognized counselors of their century. Might Edwards, who never did so, have enjoyed meeting Franklin? Neither of them, one suspects, would have understood the other. Both were speculative, ingenious, and basically concerned for the welfare of mankind. But Franklin, with a patriarchal wisdom never the birthright of Edwards, was the mediator. Taking men and things as he found them, he knew how to mold issues without sacrificing principle. Edwards was an austere logician whose compassion yearned toward mankind rather than toward men. He was a dweller in the Augustinian City of God, where the symbol suggests the meaning, where reason and emotion alike are disciplined by contemplation of the principle itself.

Edwards' mystic doctrines were variously reshaped in the nineteenth century; but the tragic intensity, the dwelling upon the reality of sin, the violent imagery, the concern with symbolism were downright shocking, as Holmes acknowledged, to the men of a later generation. To many, but not to all. One thinks first of Hawthorne who, though a skeptic, transmitted much of the essence of Edwards into fiction. Is there not the elf-child Pearl, humanized only when her mother's sin is expiated? Is there not the recriminatory violence of one Maule, and the minatory apostrophe of lonely Judge Pyncheon? And Hawthorne's friend Melville, darkly brooding of a summer's night in the Stockbridge hills, expressed similar aspects of man's incapacity, failure, and turbulent striving. Emerson dedicated Transcendentalism—which never fought Edwardean Puritanism, but absorbed it—to a new preoccupation with the old symbolism of nature. "We do not determine what we will think. We only open our senses, clear away, as we can, all obstruction from the fact, and suffer the intellect to see." Emerson too was well aware, as he speaks here in his essay on "Intellect" of the will's limitation, of the correspondence of the thing and the word, the object and the spirit. Whitman's bold language shot into fresh tangents, but he wrestled with good and evil, the flesh and the spirit, in poems such as "Chanting the Square Deific." Did the idealism within the pessimism of Henry Adams, intensely cultivating self-analysis, attempting to piece "the singulars" together into rules of art through the symbols of the Virgin and the dynamo, derive more than he would have conceded from a New England inheritance? The voice, through these many American years, is the voice of Hawthorne, and Melville, and Emerson, and Whitman, and Adams. But the hand is the hand of Jonathan Edwards.

7. WRITERS OF THE MIDDLE COLONIES

Between the Wilderness Zion of the Puritans and the plantation colonies of the South lay the provinces which for want of any common characteristics save their intermediate location have been known as the middle colonies. Yet the fact that these provinces—New York, New Jersey, Pennsylvania, and Delaware—were not dominated like New England by a single theological system or like the southern colonies by a peculiar social system, was itself a most significant common characteristic. By virtue of their linguistic and cultural variety, their relatively democratic social and political institutions, their easy tolerance, and their material prosperity, they were the typically American region.

Few areas of the earth embraced such a conglomerate population. There were Dutch patroons on the Hudson; Anglican, Jewish, Huguenot, and Dutch Calvinist merchants in New York; English Quakers and transplanted New England Puritans on Long Island and in New Jersey; English and Welsh Quaker merchants and farmers in Philadelphia and the surrounding counties; industrious German sectarians farming the fertile hinterland of Philadelphia; hardy Scots-Irish Presbyterians on the frontiers; descendants of Swedish and Finnish traders along Delaware Bay; Negro servants and slaves; Iroquois, Delaware, and Susquehanna Indians. This mixed race, restless and inquiring, was always on the move; by the middle of the eighteenth century it could no longer be contained in the region drained by the Hudson and the Delaware and had begun to spill over into the watershed of the Susquehanna, where it entered the arena of Anglo-French imperial conflict. Here were the people from whom, as Crèvecœur was to write, "that race now called Americans have arisen."

Most of the books produced in the middle colonies were concerned with the topography and history of the inner and the outer worlds; few of them were written with conscious literary intent. In the older towns, however, where economic prosperity had created a stable society, a vital literary culture was coming into being. In spite of a relatively late start among the English colonies, the region advanced rapidly towards cultural maturity, and the quarter-century preceding the Revolution witnessed in New York and Phila-

82

delphia a literary flowering which foreshadowed the intellectual leadership to be assumed by those centers in the early years of the Republic.

2

Over the greater part of the middle colonies religious freedom prevailed, resulting in a typically American babel of sects and churches. The most distinctive note was contributed by the Quakers, a religious minority whose ideas, operating as a leaven, have had an influence in American life quite out of proportion to their numbers. It was a note of persistent moral idealism, drawing its strength from a religion of pure inner experience, and manifesting itself practically in the quick response of a sensitive conscience to human suffering.

The central figure in early American Quakerism was William Penn, perhaps the greatest of colonial statesmen, who organized the colonies of New Jersey, Pennsylvania, and Delaware on the basis of religious toleration, political democracy, and pacifism. He was a prolific writer on theological, moral, and political subjects, but his chief claim to attention as a literary figure rests upon his moral and religious aphorisms, of which the most extensive collection is *Some Fruits of Solitude* (1693). A singular compound of devout Quaker and man of the world, Penn distilled into his maxims a morality which was at once intuitively religious and shrewdly utilitarian, prefiguring in its latter aspect some of the sayings of Poor Richard. In *Fruits of a Father's Love* (addressed to his children on the eve of a voyage to Pennsylvania in 1699) he described the Inner Light, the root principle of Quakerism, as

the Light of Christ in your Consciences, by which . . . you may clearly see if your Deeds, ay and your Words and Thoughts too, are wrought in God or not. . . . And as you come to obey this blessed Light in it's holy Convictions, it will lead you out of the World's dark and degenerate Ways and Works, and bring you unto Christ's Way and Life, and to be of the Number of his true self-denying Followers.

The characteristic literary expression of Quakerism was the journal or spiritual autobiography. There were in the colonies scores of obscure men and women of uncommon spiritual sensitivity who traveled in the ministry as "public Friends," and left these records behind not as monuments to their own spiritual achievements but as guidebooks to others on their inward odysseys. Concerned primarily with inner states rather than outward events, the journals followed a more or less uniform pattern, beginning with a record of divine intimations in childhood, followed by an extreme compunction over youthful frivolities, passing through the spiritual conflicts of adolescence to "convincement" of the truth of Quakerism, and conversion, in which the will was utterly surrendered to the divine leading. As if repeating one another, most of the journalists recorded the same turning-points in later life: entrance upon the vocal ministry, the adoption of "plain dress," the decision to curtail the volume of outward business, and the awakening of the social conscience.

As the structure of the Quaker journals tended towards uniformity, so did the style. Its keynote was an austere simplicity. "Ye that dwell in the Light and walk in the Light," George Fox, founder of the Society of Friends, had urged, "use plainness of speech and plain words." William Penn's advice was to the same purpose: "Affect not Words, but Matter, and chiefly to be pertinent and plain: Truest Eloquence is plainest, and brief Speaking . . . is the best." The emphasis on plainness had been part of the total Quaker revolt against the "world" of the mid-seventeenth century when English literary prose had been loaded with farfetched tropes, inkhorn terms, learned quotations, and other ostentatious rhetorical trappings. In pursuing the ideal of unadorned simplicity, the Quakers were careful to strip their writings of superfluities that served only to please the carnal mind. In their insistence upon plainness of diction, they fell in with, indeed they anticipated, the trend of English and American prose style. Failing to match in syntax the simplicity which they achieved in language, the Quakers retained in their writing an archaic structural element which was to distinguish the plain style of Woolman from that of his contemporary Franklin. Just as the "plain dress" of the eighteenth century Friend was essentially the costume of Charles II with its ornaments removed, so the basic sentence structure of the Quaker journals remained tortuous and intricate in the manner of Browne and Burton, while the diction had all the simplicity and plainness of Swift and Defoe.

The uniformity of the Quaker style blurred but could not wholly erase the individualities of its users. The robust piety of a seagoing Philadelphia Quaker was revealed in the *Journal, or Historical Account, of the Life, Travels, and Christian Experiences, of that Antient, Faithful Servant of Jesus Christ, Thomas Chalkley* (1749); for all its austerity, Chalkley's language retained a salty flavor as he related the nautical and spiritual adventures of a life spent in the triangular trade with the West Indies and England. With the *Journal of the Life, Travels, and Gospel Labours of . . . Daniel Stanton* (1772) the Quaker style showed signs of becoming stereotyped; after repeated usage expressions which had originally been vivid metaphors of spiritual experience—"to dig deep," "to outrun one's Guide," "to keep down to the root"—came to be colorless, drained of imaginative content. In the hands of the saintly John Churchman of Nottingham, Pennsylvania, on the other hand, the Quaker style could be a subtle and sensitive instrument. Thus in his journal (1779) he described the manner in which a religious "concern" to travel "in the love of the Gospel" to Europe had come to him:

One day walking alone, I felt myself so inwardly weak and feeble, that I stood still, and by the reverence that covered my mind, I knew that the hand of the Lord was on me and his presence round about, the earth was silent and all flesh brought into stillness, and light went forth with brightness, and shone on Great Britain, Ireland, and Holland, and my mind felt the gentle, yet strongly drawing cords of that love which is stronger than death, which made me say, Lord! *go before, and strengthen me, and I will follow whithersoever thou leads.*

The possessor of the sweetest spirit, the tenderest social conscience, and the purest prose style among all the eighteenth century Quakers was John Woolman, the tailor of Mount Holly, New Jersey. He was early convinced, as he wrote in his *Journal* (1774) "that true Religion consisted in an inward life, wherein the Heart doth Love and Reverence God the Creator, and learn to Exercise true Justice and Goodness, not only toward all men, but allso toward the Brute Creatures." Humanitarianism was in the air in the eighteenth century, but the source of Woolman's social concern lay deeper than the transient mood of an age. The poignant consciousness of God's infinite tenderness and love was constantly renewed in him, and these moments of mystical awareness were the wellsprings of his dedicated life, causing him eventually to realize that he was so "mixed in" with the mass of suffering humanity that henceforth he could not consider himself as a distinct and separate being. This realization impelled him, as he traveled to the southward, to labor lovingly with the planters, urging them to renounce slaveholding, which struck his sensitive spirit "as a Dark Gloominess hanging over the Land." It led him to travel unarmed on a visit to hostile Indians on the frontier that he might "feel and understand their life, and the Spirit they live in"; to sympathize with the poor brutalized sailor lads on the Atlantic crossing; and to seek the elimination of the seeds of war from society.

In *Some Considerations on the Keeping of Negroes* (1754, 1762), he spoke out clearly for racial equality, and called attention to the deleterious effects of slavery on the slave owners. His *Plea for the Poor* (published posthumously in 1793) and *Conversations on the True Harmony of Mankind* (first published in 1837) left no doubt that he was equally sensitive to other forms of social injustice, that he was conscious of the rift opening up even in the midst of provincial plenty between the wealthy merchant and the workingman. "To labour for a perfect redemption from this spirit of Oppression," he wrote, "is the Great Business of the whole family of Christ Jesus in this world."

The ideal of perfect simplicity by which his life was guided led him in his writings to strip away every superfluous word and phrase. The man who insisted upon traveling steerage to England because he "observed sundry sorts of carved work and imagery" on the outside of the more comfortable cabin, and "some superfluity of workmanship of several sorts" in the cabin itself, applied the same rigorous standards to his own prose, eliminating from it everything designed merely to please the "creaturely" mind. By banishing non-essential or merely decorative adjectives, adverbs, and modifying phrases, he laid bare the structure of the introspective process. His prose was lacking in warmth and grace and color, but it had a purity which enabled his essential meaning to emerge unclouded, uncolored, undistorted, like something seen at the bottom of a clear spring of water. Thus in spite of his indifference to art, or because of his scorn for the merely ornamental, Woolman created out of the plain style which was his inheritance a medium of expression that was a triumph of functional art. In its crystal purity it was, as William Ellery Channing was to perceive, continuous with the saintly simplicity of his life.

In the realm of purely religious writing the many sects and churches of the middle colonies produced nothing to match the distinctiveness and literary charm of the Quaker journals. But in the field of philosophical speculation, a field which was alien to the Quaker mentality, learned Anglican and Presbyterian divines exhibited notable intellectual acumen and vitality. American philosophy in general has tended to oscillate between the poles of absolute idealism and naïve realism, and it was characteristic of this region of diverse peoples and liberal intellectual climate that it should have fostered, almost simultaneously, both of these diametrically opposed systems—the one originating in Ireland and given currency here by an Anglican clergyman, the other stemming from Scotland and reformulated by a Presbyterian minister.

Samuel Johnson, a Yale graduate who took orders in the Church of England, was at one with the unphilosophical Woolman and with the young Jonathan Edwards when he wrote: "I must account it the greatest perfection and happiness of every intelligent creature to depend on a perpetual intercourse with the Deity for all his happiness and all his hopes." Reacting from the Calvinism of Yale, Johnson moved towards rationalism in religion, composing a "rhapsody" called "Raphael; or, The Genius of English America" in which he pleaded for the use of reason in the pursuit of truth. He drew back as the realization dawned that in the ordered universe of Newton and Locke there was no room for the idea of God as a sustaining presence. At this point the philosophical idealism of Bishop Berkeley came to his rescue, providing a rationale for the sense of the divine presence and a safeguard against skepticism and materialism. Johnson's *Elementa Philosophica* (1752), the first philosophical textbook written and published in America, was dedicated to the Irish bishop, whom he followed closely in insisting that spirit was the only substance, that matter existed only in the mind of the perceiver, and that nature was simply the succession of ideas that God presented to our minds. Johnson's textbook was used at King's College in New York, where he was President, and at the College of Philadelphia, where the Anglican William Smith was Provost.

Idealism enjoyed a brief vogue at the College of New Jersey; but it ended abruptly in 1768 when the Reverend John Witherspoon came from Scotland to be President, bringing with him the Scottish philosophy of common sense. As a theologian Witherspoon occupied a commanding position wherever the influence of Calvinism extended. Quite as much as Johnson he was concerned to vindicate the Christian religion from the corrosive attacks of rationalism and natural science. Dismissing idealism as "a wild and ridiculous attempt to unsettle the principles of common sense," he bluntly maintained that the existence of an object was completely independent of the mind that perceived it. Furthermore, as the external senses assure us infallibly of the existence of the material world, so through the "internal senses" we are made aware of the existence of God and the validity of Christian principles. This naïve realism was the more successful in combating the deists and materialists in that it made use of their own empirical methods. "It is safer," wrote Witherspoon, ". . . to trace facts upwards than to reason downwards." With its empirical methods and its uncritical acceptance of hard facts, the realistic philosophy which Witherspoon introduced into America found a congenial environment. Radiating from Princeton, its influence was to permeate American thought for a hundred years until it came to be regarded as "the American philosophy."

3

Although the broad region occupied by the middle colonies formed the keystone of the colonial arch, it was almost *terra incognita* to English-speaking people until the last third of the seventeenth century. The forested reaches of the Alleghenies and the Ohio River valley hardly entered the consciousness of Englishmen in the colonies or the mother country until the middle of the eighteenth century, when pioneer traders and settlers from the middle colonies came into fateful conflict there with outposts of the French empire. As each of these areas was successively opened for settlement, the colonists rushed into print with accounts of the lay of the land, its flora and fauna, its aboriginal inhabitants, and the momentous affairs being transacted there. These utilitarian reports and chronicles were in the oldest tradition of American literature; but they differed from the exuberant accounts of the Elizabethan sea dogs and traders in that they were informed with something of the scientific spirit that entered British thinking after the middle of the seventeenth century.

The earliest accounts of the region were sober, factual reports, designed to attract settlers but distinguished by accuracy in observation and moderation in language. Thus Daniel Denton in his *Brief Description of New-York* (1670) declared:

> I . . . have writ nothing, but what I have been an eye-witness to all or the greatest part of it: Neither can I safely say, was I willing to exceed, but was rather willing the place it self should exceed my Commendation.

He did not hesitate to compare the New World favorably with the Old, both in economic opportunities and in natural beauties:

> Yea, in *May* you shall see the Woods and Fields so curiously bedecke with Roses, and an innumerable multitude of delightful Flowers, not only pleasing the eye, but smell, that you may behold Nature contending with Art, and striving to equal, if not excel many Gardens in *England*.

William Penn, whose *Letter to the Free Society of Traders* (1683) was the first comprehensive report on Pennsylvania, was a Fellow of the Royal Society, and the scientific temper was apparent no less in his meticulous survey of the natural resources of his colony than in his first-hand observations on the culture of the Lenni-Lenape Indians. Fifteen years later, his account was expanded and brought up to date as *An Historical and Geographical Account . . . Of Pensilvania and of West New-Jersey* by the Welsh Quaker Gabriel Thomas, who added to Penn's sober and temperate language a certain Celtic sparkle and playfulness. With ebullient optimism he enunciated the theme of the promise of American life, setting over against the incredible bounty of nature on the shores of the Delaware a dismal picture of the laboring poor in England "half-starved, visible in their meagre looks, that are continually wandering up and down looking for Employment, without finding any, who here need not lie idle a moment." Only occasionally did Thomas' penchant for hyperbole or his enthusiasm for his new home lead him to transcend the facts, and when he did, it was in a manner that would be regarded in years to come as the typically American vein of humor:

> There are among other various sorts of Frogs [he solemnly reported], the Bull-Frog, which makes a roaring noise, hardly to be distinguished from that well known of the Beast, from whom it takes its Name.

From these early reports and chronicles stemmed two types of writing—

natural history and political history—both dominated by a utilitarian purpose and both characterized by the spirit of careful observation and accurate reporting. These books stood in contrast to much of the contemporary writing in the other provinces in that they were the work not of clergymen, but of lawyers, physicians, teachers, and merchants—men of affairs with a cosmopolitan outlook limited neither by theological dogmatism nor by parochialism and excessive provincial pride. The historians among them wrote from a broad imperial point of view, and the writers on natural history were always conscious of belonging to the international community of scientists. Both groups wrote primarily for a European rather than a colonial audience.

Lieutenant Governor Cadwallader Colden of New York was both historian and scientist. Indeed he was a typical eighteenth century *virtuoso,* equally at home in history, medicine, botany, mathematics, physics, and metaphysics; he was a correspondent of Linnæus and Gronovius in Europe and of the leading members of the Royal Society in England. His *History of the Five Indian Nations* (1727) was drawn largely from Jesuit sources, eked out by his own experiences among the Mohawks. Using these same materials a century later, Francis Parkman was to create a magnificent historical drama. Colden lacked Parkman's historical perspective, his dramatic power, and his architectonic skill in relating incidents to a single overarching theme. His narrative consisted of a succession of apparently unrelated forays, council fires, and peace treaties. The chief distinction of style was contributed by the Indians themselves, whose formal orations, faithfully reproduced, were studded with picturesque and striking metaphors. However inadequate his achievement, there was grandeur in Colden's conception, nor was he unmindful of the momentous lesson implicit in his formless narrative; his avowed purpose was to demonstrate that the Five Nations were of crucial importance to British America as a buffer against the French and a means of holding the West.

"I have sometimes thought," Colden declared, "that the Histories wrote with all the Delicacy of a fine Romance, are like *French* Dishes, more agreeable to the Pallat than the Stomach, and less wholesom than more common and courser Dyet." Thirty years later, William Smith, Jr., an able New York lawyer, found himself in agreement with this dictum, although in politics he was ranged on the opposite side from Colden. Smith's *History of the Province of New-York* (1757), written to dispel British ignorance of colonial affairs, was a full-dress chronicle of New York under British rule, with a prologue on the Dutch period and a comprehensive concluding survey of the trade, religion, and politics of the province at mid-century. The narrative was written for the most part in plain, lawyerlike English, but it was punctuated and enlivened by a series of brilliant set-pieces in the form of mordant sketches of the royal governors. Smith's design, he confessed in his preface, was "rather to inform than please":

> The ensuing Narrative . . . presents us only a regular Thread of simple Facts; and even those unembellished with Reflections, because they themselves suggest the proper Remarks, and most Readers will doubtless be best pleased with their own. . . . no Reins have been given to a wanton Imagination, for the Invention of plausible Tales, supported only by light Probabilities; but choosing rather to be honest and dull, than agreeable and false, the true Import of my Vouchers hath been strictly adhered to and regarded.

Animated thus by a scientific ideal which tempered his partisanship, Smith produced a work second among colonial histories only to Thomas Hutchinson's *History of the Colony of Massachusetts Bay.*

In Pennsylvania, historians were preoccupied with the problem of the Indian on the frontier, and scientific objectivity gave way before the emotions aroused by that ever-present reality. Another William Smith, Provost of the College of Philadelphia, enlisted his literary talents on the side of the aristocratic Proprietors, and launched two vigorous salvos of polemic history against the Quaker-dominated Assembly. In his *Brief State of the Province of Pennsylvania* (1755) and his *Brief View of the Conduct of Pennsylvania* (1756), he taxed the peace-loving Quakers with excessive republicanism and with having appropriated money for hospitals and libraries at a time when the frontiers lay open to Indian incursions. He exploited all the resources of the skilled propagandist, including cold statistics, gruesome atrocity stories, and charges that the Quaker opposition was "a factious Cabal, effectually promoting the French Interest." Charles Thomson, a teacher in the Friends school in Philadelphia, endeavored in his *Inquiry into the Causes of the Alienation of the Delaware and Shawanese Indians* (1759) to vindicate the Quaker policy of seeking the friendship and respect of the Indians. With sober and painstaking scholarship, though not without an obvious bias, he recounted the story of Indian relations in Pennsylvania, a story filled in his telling with fraud and chicanery on the part of the whites and climaxed by the infamous "Walking Purchase" of 1737 by which the Indians had been deprived of a large portion of their patrimony. More than a century of dishonor was to pass before another American, Helen Hunt Jackson, would come forward with an equally strong and well documented plea for justice towards the dispossessed red man.

Lewis Evans, Philadelphia mapmaker, was, like Colden, both historian and scientist, although something of the polemic spirit infected the historical and political portions of his *Geographical, Historical, Political, Philosophical and Mechanical Essays* (1755-1756). These essays, written in the first instance as analyses of his own pioneer map of the middle colonies and the Ohio River valley, contained some of the earliest descriptions of the American landscape west of the Alleghenies. "To look from these Hills into the lower Lands," he wrote as he stood high in the Alleghenies gazing westward, "is but, as it were, into an Ocean of Woods, swell'd and deprest here and there by little Inequalities not to be distinguished, one Part from another, any more than the Waves of the real Ocean." As Evans had hoped, his essays attracted attention in England, where no less a personage than Dr. Samuel Johnson thought them an indication that literature was gaining ground in America. The treatises, Johnson pontificated, were written "with such elegance as the subject admits, tho' not without some mixture of the American dialect, a tract of corruption to which every language widely diffused must always be exposed." No doubt the lexicographer was distressed by Americanisms like *branch, fork, creek,* and *run,* his pedantry thus blinding him to a significant manifestation of the vitality of the English language in America.

Evans' companion on his first reconnaissance of the Appalachian plateau was John Bartram, a tireless collector of botanical specimens from the American forest. Natural history in the eighteenth century was an exciting adventure of identifying and classifying thousands of newly observed forms of life, and a whole continent lay open before the sharp eyes of this simple Philadelphia Quaker turned deist who corresponded with the leading scientists of Europe. The laconic style in which Bartram set down his observations was a product of the Quaker tradition of plain speech reinforced by the spirit of scientific accuracy and objectivity. Traveling through the verdant Susquehanna valley in the summer of 1743, he allowed himself to note only that

the land hereabouts is middling white oak and huckleberry land. . . . we went up a vale of middling soil, covered with high oak Timber, nearly west to the top of the hill . . . from whence we had a fair prospect of the river Susquehanah.

Even in the midst of the gorgeous exotic scenery of Florida, the taciturn Quaker naturalist, distrustful of emotion, permitted himself only a restrained scientific curiosity. He remarked in a letter to Franklin that his journal contained only his "observations of particular soils, rivers, and natural vegetable productions," adding in a revealing comment, "But there was no artificial curiosities in those provinces as temples, theatres, piramids, palaces, bridges, catacoms, oblisks, pictures." A century hence, more sophisticated writers like Hawthorne and Henry James would be regretting the absence of these "artificial curiosities" from the American scene. And within a few years Bartram's own son was to interpret the American landscape in a manner which required no reference to a remote and storied past to establish its romantic character.

William Bartram, who spent the years between 1773 and 1778 botanizing in the Floridas, Georgia, and the Carolinas, added to his father's scientific curiosity a sensibility to form and color, a rich and varied vocabulary, and a pantheistic philosophy, all of which were to make a strong impression upon the romantic poets of England. His volume of *Travels* (1791), which has attracted attention from literary historians chiefly as a document in the history of romanticism in England, deserves attention on its own merits as an authentic literary masterpiece of early American romanticism.

The younger Bartram was a painter in water colors as well as a poet. He looked upon the strange and beautiful tropical landscape with all the freshness and acuity of vision which had distinguished the earlier observers; but he had the priceless advantage of an artist's eye and a richly varied verbal palette. His style—the most distinctive and accomplished style developed by any writer in the middle colonies—was loose in structure, fluent in movement, heavily ballasted with Latin botanical names, equally apt for detailed delineation and for rapid narrative. Whether he was describing a furious battle of alligators or the flowering shrub which he named the *Franklinia Alatamaha*, a tropical thunderstorm or that "inchanting and amazing chrystal fountain" that was to meander through the wondrous landscape of Coleridge's "Kubla Khan," William Bartram wrote with conscious artistry. The measure of his success can be judged by this description of a fish observed in Georgia:

It is as large as a man's hand, nearly oval and thin, being compressed on each side; the tail is beautifully formed; the top of the head and back, of an olive green, be-sprinkled with russet specks; the sides of a sea-green, inclining to azure, insensibly blended with the olive above, and beneath lightens to a silvery white, or pearl colour, elegantly powdered with specks of the finest green, russet and gold; the belly is of a bright scarlet red or vermilion, darting up rays or fiery streaks into the pearl on each side; the ultimate angle of the branchiostega extends backwards with a long spatula, ending with a round or oval particoloured spot, representing the eye in the long feathers of a peacock's train, verged round with a thin flame-coloured membrane, and appears like a brilliant ruby fixed on the side of the fish.

Occasionally Bartram lapsed into rhapsodic ejaculations, full of pseudo-classic epithets and periphrases, revealing that, for all his romanticism, he was not wholly emancipated from eighteenth century conventions. His attitude towards the Indian owed something to his Quaker background, but probably more to the current literary stereotype of the noble savage; nevertheless, his observations on the culture of the Creeks, Seminoles, and Cherokees were anthropologically sound. His romantic pantheism, which so attracted Wordsworth, sprang from the union of his ancestral Quakerism, with its ideas of divine immanence, and the scientific deism which he absorbed from his father; he was probably unconscious of the degree to which the two influences merged in such a passage as this: "Let us rely on providence, and by studying and contemplating the works and power of the Creator, learn wisdom and understanding in the economy of nature, and be seriously attentive to the divine monitor within." With William Bartram the middle colony tradition of scientific observation and description reached a culmination. In his *Travels* the raw materials with which his predecessors had been struggling for a century were finally given form by the shaping hand of a scientific observer who was also a sensitive artist.

Not until thirty years had passed did any other American naturalist emerge to carry to greater heights the work of the Bartrams in what was to be a great American tradition of writing about nature. Starting also from Philadelphia, John James Audubon studied and painted the birds of the neighboring areas, extending his journeys eventually from the Alleghenies to the Mississippi and from the Cumberland Gap to the Louisiana bayous. He intended that his *The Birds of America* should include every American bird known to man. The great folio of beautifully colored plates was accompanied by five volumes of text, *Ornithological Biography* (1831–1839), in which species and their habits are set against romantically described landscapes and lively narratives of Audubon's adventures on the frontier. "My work," he said, "shall be not a *beacon* but a *tremendous lighthouse!*" And so it has proved to be. The light from it has thrown into undeserved shadow the pioneering work of his quiet Quaker predecessors, the two Bartrams.

4

Self-conscious literary life in the middle colonies was associated chiefly with the colleges established in the mid-eighteenth century. In two respects educational ideals in the middle colonies differed from those which had led to the founding of the older colonial institutions: education was conceived primarily as training for civic responsibility, and the English language was given a place beside Greek and Latin as a proper subject of college study. Both William Livingston in *The Independent Reflector* (1752–1753) and William Smith in *A General Idea of the College of Mirania* (1753) echoed Archbishop Tillotson's dictum that classical or speculative learning which had no practical usefulness was "but a more specious and ingenious sort of idleness, a more pardonable and creditable kind of ignorance." Regular opportunities for practice in English rhetoric and oratory were provided in disputations and literary exercises held in the college halls. The ideal college graduate in the middle colonies was thus not primarily the polished country gentleman or the learned minister but the useful and responsible citizen, skilled in the elegant and persuasive use of his mother tongue.

William Livingston, a brilliant lawyer and leader of the liberal party in the politics of provincial New York, did much by precept and example to foster this ideal. In 1747 he published a poem entitled *Philosophic Solitude,* a faint echo of *The Choice,* an enormously popular English poem written a half-century earlier by the Reverend John Pomfret. In correct heroic couplets, with a slight Miltonic flavoring, Livingston's poem described the simple felicity of life in a rural retreat, and culminated in a mild paean to a Deity whose existence was inferred, in typical eighteenth century fashion, from the beauty and harmony of the creation. Both the mood and the measure of the poem harked back to Augustan England. It is interesting chiefly for its revelation of the influences which had formed Livingston's mind and tastes. In enumerating the authors whose works he would chose for his library, he named the writers of classical antiquity; the French authors Fénelon and Montesquieu; Milton, Dryden, Pope, and Isaac Watts among the English poets; Raleigh, Swift, and Addison among the prose writers; and Bacon, Boyle, Newton, and Locke, chief architects of the eighteenth century cosmology.

Livingston's strong sense of social responsibility led him to place his literary gifts at the service of the liberal causes to which he was committed. He was the principal author of *The Independent Reflector* (1752–1753) and *The Occasional Reverberator* (1753), two series of periodical essays in the tradition of Trenchard and Gordon's *Independent Whig.* Although he denied any literary purpose ("In subjects meerly literary," he wrote, "I shall rarely indulge myself"), he achieved genuine distinction as a writer of prose. His style was formal and balanced, barbed with satire, full of carefully contrived antitheses and climaxes, rising occasionally to a pitch of stately eloquence. For vigor and trenchancy it was unsurpassed by any other periodical writing of the day either in the colonies or in the mother country.

Livingston left no room for doubt about the cause in which his literary talents were enlisted.

'Tis the cause of truth and liberty [he wrote]; what he intends to oppose is superstition, bigotry, priestcraft, tyranny, servitude, public mismanagement, and dishonesty in office. The things he proposes to teach are the nature and excellence of our constitution, the inestimable value of liberty, the disastrous effects of bigotry, the shame and horror of bondage, the importance of religion unpolluted and unadulterate with superstitious additions and inventions of priests.

Himself a Presbyterian and the descendant of Dutch Calvinists, Livingston nevertheless deplored sectarianism, and was suspicious of any interference by the church in secular affairs. In theology he was a liberal, believing religion to be "plain and simple, and to the meanest capacity intelligible." In politics he was a Whig, bent upon vindicating the authority of the provincial Assembly against the encroachments of the royal governors.

When it became known that the proposed college in New York was to be chartered by the Crown as an Anglican institution, Livingston launched a literary campaign to have it incorporated by the Assembly and kept free from denominational control. Returning again and again to the attack in successive numbers of *The Independent Reflector,* he underlined the importance of intellectual freedom, not neglecting the opportunity for animadversions upon Harvard and Yale where the tender minds of the future ruling classes, he maintained, were filled with illiberal Puritan doctrines that were bound to filter down through the whole of society. Behind Livingston's plea for academic and religious liberty one could detect stirrings of a more far-reaching revolt against authority that was to culminate before many years in a revolution.

Livingston's liberalism and literary skill made him something of a hero to the undergraduates at the College of New Jersey who gathered in Nassau Hall every afternoon at five under President Witherspoon's direction to hear orations declaimed by their fellow students. Livingston's essays were frequently used for declamations, and one of the two undergraduate literary societies at the College was named after Livingston's pseudonym, "The American Whig." The leading figures in the American Whig Society were three young men destined soon to take prominent parts in the founding of a national literature. As undergraduates Philip Freneau, Hugh Henry Brackenridge, and James Madison expended their literary energies chiefly in directing coarse and vigorous satires against the rival Cliosophic Society.

For the Commencement of 1771 Brackenridge and Freneau composed a long poem in blank verse called *The Rising Glory of America.* Their imaginations were fired by the same imperial vision which had inspired Colden and Evans. They foresaw new towns springing up along the Ohio, and "nations" on the Mississippi, American poets arising by the Susquehanna, in the Alleghenies and the Tuscarora hills, a new civilization burgeoning on the Appalachians, in the Carolinas,

and the plains
Stretch'd out from thence far to the burning Line.

Moved to hyperbole by their regional pride, they celebrated New York as the "daughter of Commerce" hailing from afar

her num'rous ships of trade
Like shady forests rising on the waves.

And Philadelphia they hymned as

mistress of our world,
The seat of arts, of science, and of fame.

At the College of Philadelphia Provost William Smith held sway as a sort of provincial Great Cham of literature. Like Dr. Samuel Johnson, his English contemporary, he is remembered not so much for his writings as for his personality and his influence on younger writers. The little circle of poets which he gathered around him in the fifties and sixties was the first self-conscious poetic "school" in America, the first group of American writers who regarded poetry not as a handmaid to ethics and religion but as a craft to be practiced for its own sake. The *American Magazine and Monthly Chronicle* (1757–1758), which Provost Smith edited, served as a vehicle for their literary efforts, establishing itself in the brief twelve months of its existence as the most brilliant and original literary periodical in colonial America. The artistic vitality of the group was further manifested by the fact that it included the first American composer of secular music, Francis Hopkinson; the first American dramatist whose work was professionally performed, Thomas Godfrey; and the first American painter to achieve international recognition, Benjamin West.

Even before the founding of its college the Philadelphia region could boast of considerable classical learning. Between 1718 and 1730 David French, Prothonotary of the Court of Newcastle in the "Lower Counties" (Delaware), had rendered into English verse some of the frankly pagan and sensual odes of Anacreon. The Quaker James Logan, who had come to Philadelphia as William Penn's secretary and had remained to become Pennsylvania's most distinguished scholar-statesman, published a translation of the *Moral Distichs* of Dionysius Cato in 1735 and of Cicero's *De Senectute* in 1744. His publisher, Benjamin Franklin, hailed the former as "the first translation of a classic which was both made and printed in the British Colonies," and the latter as "a happy omen that Philadelphia shall become the seat of the American muses." The classics were not neglected at the College of Philadelphia; but by the fifties the tide was beginning to set in another direction.

The college poets of Philadelphia were caught in the same crosscurrents and confusions of taste that affected English verse in this transitional period between the decline of the classical ideal and the emergence of full-blown romanticism. It is instructive to compare them with their English contemporaries, Collins, Gray, and the Warton brothers. There was the same devotion to the Pindaric and Horatian ode-forms and to the youthful poetry of Milton;

the same addiction to the stock epithets and personified abstractions of the Augustans mingled with glimmerings of sentiment that forecast the Romantic mood; the same scholarly urbanity alternating with effusive sensibility. If the poetry of Philadelphia was derivative, so was the best English poetry of the day. Before condemning these provincial poets out of hand for seeking their literary inspiration abroad, one should reflect that they regarded themselves after all as English poets, that they had no indigenous poetic tradition to draw upon, that they lived and wrote in an academic atmosphere, and that, like many later American poets, they felt, or professed to feel, radically out of sympathy with the bustling mercantile society in which their lot was cast. The day of appreciative patrons is past, lamented Nathaniel Evans, young Anglican clergyman,

> And we are in a climate cast
> Where few the muse can relish;
> Where all the doctrine now that's told
> Is that a shining heap of gold
> Alone can man embellish.

The artificialities of the moribund pastoral tradition exercised a singular fascination over the Philadelphia poets. Thomas Godfrey and Francis Hopkinson were at one with Nathaniel Evans in his resolution to naturalize the eclogue in America, to

> wake the rural reed
> And sing of swains, whose snowy lambkins feed
> On Schuylkill's banks with shady walnuts crown'd.

Streams bearing the names of Schuylkill and Delaware appeared in many of their poems, but the landscape through which they flowed was always the conventional bucolic backdrop derived from Theocritus, Virgil, and Pope, further conventionalized by the persistent use of such "poetic" epithets as "spicy vales," "gay, enamell'd groves," "the finny brood," "the feather'd tribe."

No doubt Provost Smith must be held partly responsible for the vein of academic classicism in the poets of his circle, but he also encouraged them in the expression of an inchoate Romanticism. His own principal literary contribution to the *American Magazine* was a series of essays written under the pseudonym (itself a typical pre-Romantic stereotype) of "The Hermit," in which a didactic purpose was invested with an atmosphere of romantic melancholy and awe at the sublimity of nature. In praising the work of his special protégé Thomas Godfrey, the untutored son of a glazier, he employed phrases which betrayed his sympathy with the emerging Romantic conception of poetry. He wrote of the young poet's "poetic warmth," his "elevated and daring genius," and cited Godfrey's own lines as descriptive of his work:

> In beautiful disorder, yet compleat,
> The structure shines irregularly great.

Godfrey's "Night Piece" (1758), written in the stanza of Gray's "Elegy," was redolent of the atmosphere of contemporary "graveyard" poetry; and his *Court of Fancy* (1762) and "The Assembly of Birds" (1765) reflected the current revival of interest in Chaucer. Francis Hopkinson's "Description of a Church" (about 1762) was an American echo of the current English vogue of Gothicism. All three of the major poets of the group shared their generation's adulation of Milton, and paid him the homage of imitation. They were in their happiest vein when they took their inspiration from the Elizabethan and Caroline lyrists. In his lines "To Celia," Thomas Godfrey succeeded in capturing something of the gay *insouciance* of Waller and Herrick:

> When in *Celia's* heav'nly Eye
> Soft inviting Love I spy,
> 'Tho you say 'tis all a cheat,
> I must clasp the dear deceit.
>
> Why should I more knowledge gain,
> When it only gives me pain?
> If deceiv'd I'm still at rest,
> In the sweet Delusion blest.

Both Evans and Godfrey died young, and Provost Smith, suspected of Loyalist sympathies, was under a cloud in the seventies; but Francis Hopkinson was to live on into the first years of the Republic, providing a link between the literary life of the provincial metropolis and that of the political and cultural capital of the new nation. This "pretty, little, curious, ingenious" man, as John Adams described him, was the most versatile of the group: he was a musician and composer, an amateur portraitist, a poet, satirist, and writer of graceful Addisonian essays, as well as a dabbler in science, a lawyer and judge, and a member of the Continental Congress. During the Revolution he exploited the satirical vein first revealed in the pungent humor of his burlesque fragment "Dirtilla" a decade earlier. To the patriot cause he contributed a number of rollicking ballads like "The Battle of the Kegs" (1778) and a series of political allegories in verse and prose of which *A Pretty Story* (1774) and "Date Obolum Belisario" (1778) were the most effective.

Combining in his own person a gift for pure literature and a readiness to devote his talents to the public weal, Hopkinson carried into the literary life of the Republic the ideal which had flourished in the college towns of the middle colonies. In 1787 he celebrated the adoption of the Federal Constitution with a ballad called "The New Roof: A Song for Federal Mechanics," employing an elaborate metaphor which he had used earlier in prose to defend the Constitution against its traducers. In vigorous and homely images he sang:

> Come muster, my lads, your mechanical tools,
> Your saws and your axes, your hammers and rules:
> Bring your mallets and planes, your level and line,
> And plenty of pins of American pine:
> *For our roof we will raise, and our song still shall be,*
> *Our government firm, and our citizens free.*

In 1788 he dedicated to George Washington a volume of songs of which he had composed both words and music. In these stanzas, with their Shakespearean echo and their romantic imagery, the lyric note which had been intermittent with the poets of colonial Philadelphia finally reached clear and sustained expression:

> The traveller benighted and lost,
>   O'er the mountains pursues his lone way;
> The stream is all candy'd with frost
>   And the icicle hangs on the spray,
> He wanders in hope some kind shelter to find
> "Whilst thro' the sharp hawthorn keen blows the cold wind."
>
> The tempest howls dreary around
>   And rends the tall oak in its flight;
> Fast falls the cold snow to the ground
>   And dark is the gloom of the night.
> Lone wanders the trav'ler a shelter to find,
> "Whilst thro' the sharp hawthorn still blows the cold wind."
>
> No comfort the wild woods afford,
>   No shelter the trav'ler can see—
> Far off are his bed and his board
>   And his home where he wishes to be.
> His hearth's cheerful blaze still engages his mind
> "Whilst thro' the sharp hawthorn keen blows the cold wind."

Already the various race which inhabited the middle colonies was revealing through its spokesmen certain traits which were to become constants in the American character. A strain of idealism, of stubborn faith in a higher law and a deeper reality behind appearances was combined paradoxically with a shrewd realism, an insistence upon hard facts and utilitarian values. The literature that came out of the experience of these archetypal Americans, a literature which achieves first rank in the writings of Benjamin Franklin, expressed something of the freedom and newness of the American continent with a freshness of feeling tempered by the objective spirit of scientific inquiry. And around the newborn colleges of the region was springing up a promising literary life that was to reach its flowering in the early days of the young American republic.

8. BENJAMIN FRANKLIN

BENJAMIN FRANKLIN, though he was born in Boston, was little affected by its earlier, sterner traditions. His father was a tradesman who had come from England in 1683, and the son grew up in a generation to which the theocratic concepts of the founders of New England seemed remote if not preposterous. He enjoyed *The Pilgrim's Progress,* particularly because it "mixed narration and dialogue," and he read other books by Bunyan; but the inquiring boy soon tired of his father's "books of dispute about religion" and preferred Plutarch's *Lives* and Xenophon's *Memorabilia.* Neither the polemic habits which Franklin first picked up nor the Socratic method to which he turned during his juvenile disputatious period stayed with him long. Reading the orthodox arguments against the deists when he was fifteen, he was converted to a lifelong deism. Reading the arguments in favor of natural religion at nineteen, he set out to prove that whatever is is right, in a pamphlet called *A Dissertation on Liberty and Necessity, Pleasure and Pain* (1725). As he did not linger with theology, neither did he with metaphysics. He burned all but a few copies of his *Dissertation,* and would not bother to print a short treatise on prayer which he wrote at twenty-four. "The great uncertainty I found in metaphysical reasonings disgusted me, and I quitted that kind of reading and study for others more satisfactory."

Yet here and there in Franklin traces of theology, New England and older, appear. From either or both of two epitaphs printed by Cotton Mather in his *Magnalia* Franklin probably took for his own *Epitaph,* written at twenty-two, his often repeated image which compares the resurrection of a man with a new edition of a book; and he was certainly indebted to Mather's "Essays to Do Good." In Franklin's *Articles of Belief and Acts of Religion,* composed in 1728 for his own spiritual guidance, there is a strain of Puritan self-searching as well as a philosopher's code of morals. In his efforts to attain moral perfection he made laboratory notes on his daily successes and failures in a manner much like that prescribed by Loyola in his *Spiritual Exercises,* which Franklin may not have heard of. In one of his electrical papers, where he speaks of "adoring that wisdom which has made all things by weight and measure," he seems to be quoting from Augustine. Years of experience brought Franklin to the conviction that "God governs in the affairs of men." But the divine government, Franklin held, was a vast order to be studied, not a mystery to be sought in ardor and torment. However intense his youthful perturbations were, he soon mastered them and thereafter lived at reasonable peace in his spacious universe.

2

His life was one of the great lives of all time, and his writings are full of great, if fragmentary, autobiography. It is hard to distinguish between the plans Franklin made and the instincts which impelled him. In his boyhood he wanted to go to sea, disliked his father's trade of tallow chandler, and at twelve was apprenticed to his brother James, a Boston printer. While the younger brother was speedily learning the printer's trade, he was also teaching himself the writer's art. He began with broadside ballads, now lost, on contemporary incidents, then took to prose in painstaking and skillful imitation of Addison's *Spectator*. Franklin was "extremely ambitious" to excel in writing prose, which he afterwards said had been "a principal means of my advancement." His *Dogood* papers, contributed to James Franklin's *New England Courant* in 1722, were Addisonian but also Franklinian, remarkably precocious for an apprentice of sixteen. Before Benjamin Franklin had completed his apprenticeship he had outgrown his status, and he ran away from his brother-master in 1723 to Philadelphia, thereby committing an act which in a tradesman of that age was almost as culpable as desertion in a soldier.

In Philadelphia, and in London in 1724-1726, Franklin worked at his trade as a journeyman. During his voyage home, recorded in a lively *Journal* which is the earliest of his autobiographical writings, he drew up a Plan for his future conduct as if he were making a "regular plan and design" for a poem. He resolved to be frugal, industrious, and strictly truthful, and to speak ill of nobody. That he made such resolutions seems to indicate that he thought he then lacked such qualities, at least in a sufficient degree. His self-discipline had begun. This discipline, and the impassioned inner life of his next few years, did not interfere with Franklin's swift and simple success in business, but did enlarge his mind in preparation for his subsequent career on wider stages. In 1729 he acquired a newspaper, the *Pennsylvania Gazette,* and in 1733 he began to publish an almanac called *Poor Richard* which was soon famous throughout the British colonies. In 1736 he was chosen clerk of the Pennsylvania Assembly, and in 1737 appointed Postmaster of Philadelphia.

One of the least solitary of geniuses, Franklin, while striving to perfect his own character, had been no less busy in his efforts to improve the society in which he lived. The Junto, the club of young tradesmen whom he brought together in 1727, founded in 1731 the subscription library which has survived as the Library Company of Philadelphia; and in 1736 the Union Fire Company, the first in the town. From these Junto beginnings, Franklin and its members and later a widening circle of public-spirited men, particularly after he was elected to the Pennsylvania Assembly in 1751, went on to reform the city watch, encourage the paving and lighting of streets, propose the Academy which was to become the University of Pennsylvania, establish the Pennsylvania Hospital, organize the armed defense of the Quaker province, and generally to develop in Philadelphia the forms of active and enterprising life which made it long the chief city of America.

Philadelphian and Pennsylvanian, Franklin was at the same time American. His *General Magazine, and Historical Chronicle, for All the British Plantations in America* lasted for only six months in 1741; but the American Philosophical Society, which he initiated in 1743 in the hope of uniting American scientists everywhere in a common effort, is still the first of American learned societies as it was the earliest. In 1753 Franklin became the Crown's joint deputy postmaster general for North America. In 1754 his Plan of Union was adopted by the Albany Congress which had been called by the Crown in the desire to see the English colonies united against the French power in Canada. The Plan of Union having been rejected, Franklin had to go back to affairs in Pennsylvania, where he was a leader in the struggle of the people of the province against the British proprietors. That struggle was for Franklin a rehearsal of the part he was afterwards to play in the struggle of the United Colonies against the British Parliament.

In brief intervals snatched from business and politics Franklin incredibly found time to perform the experiments in electricity, mostly in the years 1747–1753, which made his the first great name in that branch of science and produced, in his successive volumes of *Experiments and Observations on Electricity* (1751–1774), the principia of electrostatics. In 1752, apparently in June, he flew his famous electrical kite; in October of that year he announced in *Poor Richard* the invention of the lightning rod. These achievements brought him the official thanks and compliments of Louis XV of France, the Copley gold medal of the Royal Society in London and election to the Society, and honorary degrees from Harvard, Yale, and William and Mary. When, in 1757, Franklin was sent to London to manage the appeal of the Pennsylvania Assembly from the proprietors to the King, he went not only as Pennsylvania's agent but also as, what David Hume called him, America's "first philosopher, and indeed the first great man of letters, for whom we are beholden to her."

For the years down to about 1757 Franklin's *Autobiography* (first published in Paris, 1791) tells the story that is known round the world. But in countless letters and other private and public papers written afterwards it is easy to find as full, if not so formal, a record of his later life. He returned to America for a short stay in 1762-1764, only to go back to England with Pennsylvania's petition to be made a royal, not a proprietary, province. He returned again in 1775-1776, to serve in the Second Continental Congress, and by it to be sent to France as commissioner—and in time minister—from the rebel colonies which had declared themselves the independent United States of America. Everywhere his renown grew, as wizard in science and wit in letters, philosopher and sage, beloved friend to men, women, and children. Yet his method in dealing with affairs remained essentially what it had been in Philadelphia. By deft and tireless persuasion he sought to draw like-minded people together to bring a just political order out of the confusions of prejudice and special interests. The English thought him too American, the Americans thought him too English. As he had risen from local to intercolonial concerns in America, so he rose in England to imperial concerns, and worked year after year for a broader conception of the British Empire. When his vision of that Empire as "the greatest political structure human wisdom ever yet erected" was ruined by the outbreak of hostilities between the parts on the two sides of the Atlantic, he turned himself with all his weight and charm to the business of uniting America and France, not only in resistance to England but also in support of the rights of man in any nation. What he did was of less importance than what he was. When at last, in 1785, he left Europe for America again, he was the most famous private citizen alive. His life had roused the universal curiosity with which his *Autobiography* was greeted the year after his death by contemporary readers, and its record has ever since been cherished in virtually every language that has a printing press. He had written his biography, so far as it went, as well as he had lived his life.

3

Not only his final *Autobiography* but also a large part of his written work had followed the steps of his life, recording it. In his youth, whether as Mrs. Silence Dogood in the *New England Courant,* or as the Busy Body in the *American Weekly Mercury,* or as Richard Saunders in *Poor Richard,* Franklin assumed a fictitious role and wrote in the first person. When in time he put off these disguises and wrote as himself, he continued to write more or less autobiographically, whether in his accounts of his scientific experiments or in his records of his diplomatic activities or in his statement of the various ideas upon which he hit in many fields of speculation. Though he wrote always with care, drafting and revising, he looked upon writing as his means, not as his end. With all his inventive gifts he invented no new forms of writing, but was satisfied with those ready at hand, and with the fresh uses he could put them to.

When late in 1732 Franklin issued his first *Poor Richard,* for the year 1733, he was simply a printer risking his money and labor on an almanac, as many other printers were then doing in America and Europe. His brother James, now removed to Newport, had an almanac called *Poor Robin.* An earlier English almanac, *Appollo Anglicanus,* had been compiled by an actual Richard Saunders. Benjamin Franklin, taking over the name of Richard Saunders for himself as compiler, and adapting the title *Poor Robin* to *Poor Richard,* fell smoothly into step with a familiar tradition. His circumstantial prophecy that a rival almanac-maker, Titan Leeds, would die on the coming October 17, merely imported to Philadelphia the hoax played by Jonathan Swift on John Partridge in London twenty-five years before. *Poor Richard's* forecasts of sunrises and sunsets, high and low tide, lunations and eclipses through the year were mathematical and naturally the same as those in any other almanac. What was new in Franklin's almanac was the humorous character of Poor Richard the philomath, and the range of laconic wisdom tucked in along the margins of the crowded pages.

Poor Richard, in his annual appearances from 1733 to 1758, did not in reality tell much about himself. He lived in the country, made some profit out of his almanac but had to share it with the printer, engaged in altercation with his wife Bridget, and was pestered by people who wanted him to tell their fortunes. Yet the brief strokes with which he was displayed, year after year, were drawn with a skill which could have made Franklin a first-rate novelist if he had cared to write novels. The earliest well-known character of fiction created by an American, Poor Richard, though only an outline, is still as amiably, eccentrically alive as ever.

The marginal Sayings of Poor Richard are some of them in character, more of them not. For they come from Franklin's, not Poor Richard's, reading and reflection during that formative quarter-century. He drew upon such identifiable sources as Rabelais, Bacon, La Rochefoucauld, Dryden, Swift, Pope, Prior, Gay, anthologies of verse, and collections of proverbs. Besides sayings in English, there are also a few in Latin, Spanish, French, German, and Welsh. Now and then Franklin set down one of his own recent moral conclusions, as in 1739: "Sin is not hurtful because it is forbidden, but it is forbidden because it is hurtful. . . . Nor is a duty beneficial because it is commanded, but it is commanded because it is beneficial." La Rochefoucauld's "Cunning and treachery are the offspring of incapacity" became, either directly or through some intermediary version, in 1751 Franklin's "Cunning proceeds from want of capacity." Franklin, returning to the matter in 1754, spoke more definitely in his own idiom: "A cunning man is overmatched by a cunning man and a half." In 1749 he formulated his thoughts about revenge with a neatness found in none of his predecessors: "Doing an injury puts you below your enemy; revenging one makes you but even with him; forgiving it sets you above him." In one of the most characteristic of all his sayings, not yet traced to any earlier source, Franklin in 1752 summed up his principle of tolerance for erring mankind: "The brave and the wise can both pity and excuse when cowards and fools show no mercy."

So many of Franklin's sources remain unidentified that it is impossible to tell with precision how much he only passed on, and how much he added to, the stream of proverbial wisdom which flows down from the past through him into the living human language. But it is easy to see that he bettered most of the sayings which he reworked, thanks to his genius for terse clarity and his delicate ear for cadence. For example, since 1572 a common English-Scottish proverb had been put by several writers into as many forms: "A gloved cat can catch no mice"; "Cuffed cat's no good mouse-hunt"; "A muffled cat was never good mouser." In 1754 Franklin gave it the form which it has since kept: "The cat in gloves catches no mice." The Scottish "Fat housekeepers make lean executors" became in Franklin, in 1733, "A fat kitchen, a lean will." A saying as old as Chaucer or Shakespeare, in one set of words or another, and printed in 1670 as "Three may keep counsel, if two be away," was pointed up by Franklin in 1735 to "Three may keep a secret if two of them are dead." As far back as Plautus it had been said that no guest is welcome longer than three days. Lyly in *Euphues* and Cervantes in *Don Quixote* had compared guests with fish as soon ill-smelling, and Herrick in his *Hesperides*. Franklin may have come upon the saying in John Ray's *English Proverbs* (1670) as "Fresh fish and new come guests, smell by they are three days old"; or in James Kelly's *Scottish Proverbs* (1721) as "Fresh fish and poor friends become soon ill sar'd"—that is, ill savored. In Franklin's handling the proverb settled in 1736 into its vernacular idiom and cadence, "Fish and visitors stink in three days," which sensitive editors print with a politer verb.

If the merely prudential maxims of Poor Richard, which are in fact fewer than the others, are better known than all the rest put together, this is partly an accident of printing. In July, 1757, when Franklin was crossing the Atlantic to London as Pennsylvania's agent, he wrote a preface, longer than usual, for the next year's almanac, which was to be the last edited by him. That preface, known as *The Way to Wealth,* has since then been reprinted more often than anything else by Franklin except his *Autobiography*; while the less specialized sayings have lain unread in the original almanacs or have had to be content with few and limited reprintings. Consequently the prudential part of Poor Richard's counsel has been mistaken for the whole of Franklin's wisdom. But it must be remembered that in *The Way to Wealth* the imaginary speaker, Father Abraham, is an old man at a country auction urging people not to pay more for things than they are worth, and quoting Poor Richard as his authority. Of course he restricts himself to the economical maxims, and has no occasion to quote Poor Richard on all the larger topics with which he had concerned himself. Franklin, for whom frugality was discipline, not nature, had insisted too much on penny-saving and so left behind him a reputation which belies his character and is contradicted by his career.

4

Though Franklin early made up his mind that any writing, in order to be good, ought to be "smooth, clear, and short," and though his own writing from first to last invariably had those merits, he experimented with more different styles than have been commonly noted. They ranged from the sly bawdry of his letter of advice to a young man on marriage (dated June 25, 1745, and called by Franklin *Old Mistresses Apologue*) through the homespun splendor of the opening paragraph of his neglected *Some Account of the Pennsylvania Hospital* (1754) to the elevated and harmonious prose of certain of his later political papers, not to mention the varied tones of sharp wit and easy candor and warm affection in his private correspondence. Slow and hesitant in speech, in English as well as in French, he was at his best only when he could write what he had to say. He is immensely quotable, yet never annoyingly sententious. His years of practice at adapting and perfecting maxims for *Poor Richard* no doubt bred in Franklin the habit of felicity, but it was his felicity, not something borrowed from other writers.

"If you would not be forgotten as soon as you are dead and rotten, either write things worth reading or do things worth the writing," Franklin said in *Poor Richard* for 1738. In his own life he aimed to do both, though his writing, as the pressure of affairs upon him increased, frequently lagged behind his living. By the end of 1741 he had invented the Franklin stove, which he described in his *Account of the New-Invented Pennsylvanian Fire-Places* (1744). This was at once a promotion pamphlet written for a Junto friend to whom Franklin had given the right to manufacture the stoves and also, in effect, the first published contribution to science by a member of the new American Philosophical Society. Franklin, secretary of the Society, found its members less active in general science than he had hoped they would be, and he himself turned aside in 1747 to the special electrical studies which brought him fame. His originality in research was equaled by the force and grace with which he reported his discoveries to the learned world and to general readers alike. It never occurred to them, or to him, that such writings did not belong to literature in the large true sense of that term.

Nor did it occur to Franklin that he was free, however well his electrical studies were under way, to confine himself to them in the midst of the public troubles which beset Pennsylvania and the rest of America. Though he retired from business in 1748, his interests expanded rather than contracted. In August, 1750, he had observed that the pigeons in a dovecot on the wall of his house increased in number as fast as he provided room for them. From this he proceeded to his germinal idea, expounded in *Observations concerning the Increase of Mankind, Peopling of Countries, etc.* (published 1755), that population depends on subsistence and will grow as long as supplies hold up. His idea developed into a confidence that the people of America must before long outnumber the people of the British Isles, and the conviction that the coming change in the balance of population must demand a new organization of the British Empire in respect to its dominions overseas. This confidence and this conviction guided Franklin in all his political and diplomatic efforts down to the American Revolution, and were implicit if not explicit in his Canada pamphlet called *The Interest of Great Britain Considered* (1760), *The Examination of Doctor Benjamin Franklin* (1766) before the House of Commons, *Causes of the American Discontents before 1768* (1768), and many of his more casual pieces. Though he had to suit himself in his particular actions to events as they came, he was remarkably consistent in his major principle.

His fundamental political consistency is sometimes lost sight of in the bewildering, if charming, variety of his scientific, moral, and humorous utterances. He did not cease to seem a wizard and a wit while he became a more and more important politician. In 1769 he brought together a "corrected, methodized, and improved" edition of his *Experiments and Observations on Electricity . . . To which are added, Letters and Papers on Philosophical Subjects*; and in 1773 he aided in the publication in French, at Paris, of a still more extensive collection of the *Œuvres de M. Franklin*. In the scientific papers there were then bound to be many "conjectures and suppositions," as Franklin had earlier insisted. "I own I have too strong a penchant to the building of hypotheses; they indulge my natural indolence." But to his readers it appeared that here was the evidence of a tireless mind inquiring with masterly ease and success into all the mysteries of nature. They could only wonder, since they could not know which of his guesses (in fact the majority of them) would be confirmed by later experiment, and which would turn out to be inadequate or erroneous

While it might seem strange that a politician was also a scientist, it seemed stranger still that he could moreover be so delightful a humorist. Humor, with a satirical intent, was one of Franklin's social and political methods. His specialty was the hoax. As early as 1730, in his fictitious account of *A Witch Trial at Mount Holly,* he ridiculed the witchcraft superstition. In *Exporting of Felons to the Colonies* (1751) he gravely proposed that as a kind of return for the felons the Americans might export rattlesnakes to Britain. In a letter *To the Editor of a Newspaper* (1765) he made fun in London of tall tales about America with his comment on the pursuit of the cod by the whales into American fresh waters: observing, with unquestionable though elusive accuracy, "that the grand leap of the whale in that chase up the Fall of Niagara is esteemed, by all who have seen it, as one of the finest spectacles in nature." In 1773 he parodied the British claim of a right to rule America in *An Edict of the King of Prussia,* wherein Prussia made what Franklin offered as a parallel claim on Britain. In 1782 he printed in Paris his *Supplement to the Boston Independent Chronicle* purporting to prove that the British commanders in America had paid regular bounties to Indians for scalps from American settlers they had killed. Readers fooled at first by such hoaxes might soon see through them, but they would also see these matters in a new perspective, and would remember Franklin's serious meaning as well as his witty expression of it.

The bagatelles with which Franklin amused himself and his circle at Passy, near Paris, while he was Commissioner or Minister to France, were merely a further, lighter application of his hoaxing method. Because Madame Brillon smilingly refused his smiling request that she be more than daughter to him, he wrote, and printed at his little private press, *The Ephemera* (1778), a fantasy on the passage of time and philosophic resignation. When Madame Helvétius declined his proposal of marriage, Franklin in *A Notre Dame d'Auteuil* (1778?) lightheartedly told her how he had slept and gone to the Elysian Fields, where he had found her former husband now married to Franklin's former wife. "Here I am; let us avenge ourselves." If gallantry was expected of a diplomat in France, Franklin could be a master in that pleasant art; just as, if he was expected to be a sage, the Solon of the New World come back to the Old with news of a Golden Age ahead, he could be sage and Solon. These were not disguises he put on, as with Poor Richard, but his own character touched up with deft dramatic art. The years had taught him how to become fully what he was.

The most substantial writings of his later years, outside his *Autobiography,* belong to the literature of diplomacy, in which no other writer has surpassed him. Even his routine dispatches, if any can be called that, were written with a statesman's grasp of the diplomatic situation, a philosopher's insight into the minds and motives of the persons involved, and a wit's happy knack at making everything alive and intelligible. About two of the most interesting chapters in his diplomatic history Franklin was too busy to write much: the passage and repeal of the Stamp Act, and the negotiation of the treaty of alliance with France. But he told as much as it was then possible for any one man to know about three other important chapters, in his *Tract relative to the Affair of Hutchinson's Letters* (1774), *An Account of Negotiations in London for effecting a Reconciliation between Great Britain and the American Colonies* (1775), and *Journal of the Negotiation for Peace with Great Britain* (1782). For the first two of these affairs Franklin remains the chief and almost the sole authority: of all of them he is the classic chronicler in whose pages the bones of those old controversies get up and walk in convincing flesh and blood.

For writing out these chapters at such length Franklin had different specific motives. His narrative of the Hutchinson affair was his vindication of his conduct though it had cost him his Crown office. His story of his negotiations with the British ministry during the winter of 1774–1775, set down on his voyage home while those events were still fresh in his memory, was his testimony that he had done everything he thought possible to avert hostilities. His detailed record of the early peace negotiations in Paris was intended not only for the Continental Congress but also for his fellow commissioners, not one of whom was in Paris when the first moves were being made. But in every case Franklin wrote autobiographically because he had already begun his *Autobiography,* and knew that these recent events must have a place in what was yet to be written.

5

He had begun the *Autobiography,* which Franklin himself never called anything but his Memoirs, at Chilbolton, the house of Bishop Jonathan Shipley near Twyford in Hampshire, in August, 1771. Shipley, pro-American among the British bishops, had a large family which was devoted, young and old, to Franklin whom they regarded as a modern Socrates. They asked him for anecdotes of his childhood, so different from theirs, in far-off Boston. They insisted, at least the older among them, that he owed it to the world to tell the story of his life. Their suggestion seems to have roused a responsive impulse in him, and the unusual expectation of "a week's uninterrupted leisure" furnished him an opportunity. In "the sweet retirement of Twyford, where my only business was a little scribbling in the garden study," as Franklin later put it, he wrote the first part of his *Autobiography* in the thirteen days of his visit, and probably less than that. Since no form of writing was so natural to him as autobiographical letters, and since he had written many of them to his son William, now royal Governor of New Jersey, the father cast his Memoirs in the form of an autobiographical letter to the son. On the first day of writing, it appears, Franklin began with a rush of family anecdotes about his ancestors, his parents, and his early childhood; then, again it appears, he resolved to write "more methodically" and drew up the Outline which thereafter he followed, not too methodically, through all four parts down to the year 1757. The first part is the happiest and sunniest of them, with its carefree recollections of one of the best known of all boyhoods.

After that August, 1771, Franklin for thirteen years found no time, or impulse, to resume his story. On his voyage home in the spring of 1775 he was expected, by his eager friends at Twyford, to do it, but he chose instead to write for his son about the past winter's unsuccessful negotiations. The outbreak of the Revolution interrupted any plans for the Memoirs that Franklin may have had. Not till 1784 did he turn back once more to his youth and go on with the narrative. He had left the manuscript of the first part in America, and could not remember exactly where it broke off. Estranged from his son, who had sided with the British government in the late conflict, Franklin would not now write as to him, and did not feel disposed to give so much space as before to "little family anecdotes of no importance to others." What he wrote in 1784 was "intended for the public" which, through certain of Franklin's close friends and advisers, was demanding that he recount the instructive adventures of his rise to world renown.

Yet even in the congenial air of triumph at Passy, after the peace, Franklin wrote only a short second installment of his Memoirs. Living so richly in the present as he did, he found it difficult to relive the remote past. For that he needed a more pressing personal vanity or literary ambition than he had. His last voyage home to America, in the summer of 1785, he spent on scientific speculations which interested him more than his own history. And at home, where there was no such leisure as he had looked forward to, he put off his Memoirs, in spite of many urgings, till August-October, 1788, when he wrote the third part. He was now too old and infirm to plan, or hope, to do much more. In November, 1789, he sent revised (and somewhat formalized) copies of Parts I-III to friends in France and England, asking their advice whether to publish the work at all. After that he wrote the few pages of the fourth part, probably in the last weeks of his life. The final lines of the manuscript are crooked, as if he were writing in bed.

Because Franklin had delayed so long, his Memoirs met with strange fortunes for so desired and desirable a book. It first appeared in 1791, in an unauthorized and unexplained French version, promptly retranslated into English by some unknown London journalist. That version was often reprinted, even after Franklin's grandson in 1818 printed an authorized version from one of Franklin's revised copies of 1789. Not till 1868 was the original manuscript discovered in France, and the *Autobiography*, including the hitherto omitted fourth part, printed as Franklin had written it.

This bungling introduction of a masterpiece did not too seriously handicap it. The meat of the matter was there in any version, as it was in time to be in any language. This was of course not the earliest of autobiographies. Augustine had told of his struggles between flesh and spirit, Benvenuto Cellini of his fiery life as artist and lover, Rousseau, very recently, of his career among raptures and neuroses. Franklin, telling his straightforward story in a language so transparent that few readers noted his amazing art, seemed to them hardly to be writing a book. This was a life. The book fixed the mode which most realistic autobiographers have since then followed. Franklin is still known to the world at large for his *Autobiography*, which is a fragment, and for *The Way to Wealth*, which is only a selection from his memorable sayings. Probably he will always be best known by these pieces of himself he left behind. Posterity can hardly be trusted to fit the whole of him together in one record if he could never do it. Nor has posterity a good excuse for asking that a man who did so much should have somehow managed to do less in order to write and publish more.

Franklin, summing up his world and at ease in it, left behind him the essence and living image of colonial America in the years when it was realizing its power and achieving its independence. The first to be called the father of his country, he came, after the rise of Washington's fame, to be thought of rather as his country's grandfather. In America, more than elsewhere, he has been popularly remembered for his grandfatherly qualities of prudence, geniality, humor. But the history of his fame has been notably marked by the rediscovery, decade after decade, of his other qualities of originality, audacity, and searching wit. One after another his prophetic forecasts have been justified by events. It increasingly appears that he conformed to the revolutionary spirit in his age, not to its complacency. Revolutionary as well as prophet, he helped shape the future. If he was full of contagious energy in the eighteenth century, so is he in the twentieth. No other early American writer is anything like so well known as he, so often reprinted, or so widely read and enjoyed. A large part of the American character lay in him as in a seed, and it has gradually unfolded by a process not unlike that of his own individual growth. Some great men cast a shadow over posterity. Franklin throws a light, which has affected American life, literature, and science ever since his own day and is still undimmed. He survives as a tremendous national symbol, and yet has never ceased to be a familiar and beloved person.

THE REPUBLIC

--- inquiry and imitation

9. REVOLUTION AND REACTION

B<small>Y</small> 1763 the British colonies on the North American continent had attained a degree of political and economic maturity which ill fitted them for the restraints and prohibitions of British colonial policy. Moreover, the conquest of French Canada by the combined forces of Great Britain and her colonies produced in America an exuberant confidence and expansionism which led Benjamin Franklin to urge the extension of the British Empire—and the liberty for which he believed it stood—around the globe. This lusty sense of power and freedom constantly overset the best-laid schemes of British imperialists who sought, after 1763, to curtail the liberties of Americans with direct taxation by the British Parliament and a stricter enforcement of the Navigation Acts. Balked in their efforts to bend the Empire to their ideals, Americans directed their new-found feeling of unity and strength into the struggle for independence from the mother country.

In order to protect their liberties from the efforts of English administrators to centralize in London power over the Empire, Americans turned—as they had repeatedly done in the past—to Locke, Harrington, and other philosophers of the natural rights school. Their first line of defense against British tyranny was natural law, upon which, they contended, the British constitution itself was based. "Who," asked John Dickinson of Pennsylvania, "are a free people? Not those over whom government is reasonably and equitably exercised but those who live under a government so constitutionally checked and controlled that proper provision is made against its being otherwise exercised." By this philosophy, King and Parliament could not do what God and Nature had clearly forbidden. Above all, they could not impose taxation without representation. God and Nature, to Americans, were Reason; and they sought to apply the cardinal principles of the Enlightenment—the faith in reason and human perfectibility—to the British Empire. Until 1776, far from seeking to destroy the Empire, they strove to ensure its prosperity and perpetuation by bringing it into harmony with the laws of nature. But what the laws of nature were, Englishmen and Americans could not agree: "Were my countrymen now in England dipped once in the River Delaware," remarked an Englishman, "I dare say, that it would make an almost miraculous change in their opinions." Americans stoutly insisted upon the privilege of interpreting natural law—which, Englishmen objected, was to submit the laws of the Empire not to God or Nature, but to a "Jury of Bostonians" with Sam Adams and James Otis as judges.

Because of its universality, natural law became a bond of union among Americans, giving New Englanders and Carolinians alike a common ground upon which to rest their case against British oppression. As a philosophy of the liberty of the individual against the state, natural law was one of the most fruitful sources of democratic ideas. Whether debated by the Rev. John Wise as determining the proper form of government for New England churches, or by Robert Beverley as determining the relationship of the Virginia planters to the mother country, the issue of natural rights *vs.* civil authority was familiar to thinking Americans at least a century before the Revolutionary War.

When applied to the problems of empire, Americans' interpretation of natural law led to decentralization and the exaltation of local liberties. Fearful of the authority of the government at Westminster, they glorified their provincial assemblies into local parliaments, bound to the mother country only through a common king. In the opinion of Englishmen, these ideas pointed not so much to liberty as to provincialism and isolationism—in short, to the break-up of the Empire. When compromise failed, Americans declared their independence—and in so doing inherited the problem which the English government had been unable to solve: how local liberty in the Empire could be reconciled with the existence of central government.

2

Conflicting ideologies gave rise to a war of words which raged for ten years before Americans and Englishmen resorted to blows to settle their differences. During the decade before Lexington, the colonists sought to persuade the British government by means of arguments, reinforced by non-importation agreements directed against British merchandise, to respect their rights. Literature became a weapon in the struggle for liberty: the art of whipping up public opinion by propaganda became the chief study of many American writers. As the conflict grew more embittered, less attention was paid to the niceties of the constitutional argument as developed by James Otis and John Dickinson: British atrocities, the wickedness of the ministry of Lord North, and the depravity of the English people increasingly became the subject matter of American pamphleteers and newspaper writers. This literary outpouring materially helped to prepare public opinion for the

Declaration of Independence and to sustain American morale during the days that tried men's souls. Edmund Burke said that Americans sniffed tyranny in every tainted breeze: it would be more exact to say that they read about it in their newspapers.

As long as the revolutionary movement remained an effort to win for Americans the rights and privileges of Englishmen within the Empire, the colonists were united and "Toryism" was relatively unimportant; but when the goal of independence and Republicanism was held up to Americans early in 1776 by Thomas Paine, it became apparent that the revolution was to be a civil war in which Americans fought Americans. A large number of colonists—perhaps one-third of the population—continued loyal to Great Britain, not merely out of love for King and Parliament and veneration for the mother country, but because they feared that a democratic upheaval would be the first result of American independence. The Declaration of Independence gave these conservatives no comfort. In pronouncing that "all men are created equal," Jefferson seemed to have opened the floodgates of revolution at home; it was now certain that the patriot leaders intended not only to sever the connection with Great Britain but to usher in a new order based upon the principle that government was created for the welfare of the common man.

Not all conservatives took the hard and thorny road that led to Toryism and exile; many threw in their lot with the patriots and, in consequence, the revolutionary party itself became a battleground between radicals and conservatives. Conflict centered on the questions of who should rule at home and how democratic the United States was to be. Some patriots resisted all reform and strove to confine the revolutionary movement within the narrow channel of resistance to Great Britain; others wished utterly to sweep away the old aristocratic order and to turn the country over to the new men— chiefly from the small-farmer class—who boldly promulgated the right of the majority to rule. But neither radicals nor conservatives won a clear-cut triumph: it was rather the moderate reformers who carried the day. Over the protests of the embattled reactionaries, the state churches were disestablished and the principle of religious freedom avowed; primogeniture and entail were swept away; slavery was abolished, usually by gradual means, in the Northern states; and the preambles of the new state constitutions proclaimed that the people were the source of all political power. Yet in most of the states "the people"—in the sense of those qualified to vote and to hold office—remained essentially the same; and the West was denied its fair share of representation lest it should seize control of the state governments from the conservative East.

These reforms were the most important achievements of the Enlightenment in the United States during the revolutionary period. The eighteenth century was the era of enlightened despots: for a brief span in European history, philosophers were kings. It was a period when ideas, long germinating in the minds of philosophers, began to bear fruit in the form of humanitarianism. Thus the United States was conceived in an age of reform—but it was reform from above, the work of paternalistic and arbitrary rulers. The American patriots of the revolutionary generation proved that republicans were not less enlightened than despots and that the people themselves could do, and do better, what kings and philosophers sought to do for them.

The changes introduced by the Revolution did not destroy aristocracy in the United States. In abolishing primogeniture and entail, Jefferson believed that he was striking a blow at the roots of aristocracy; but he soon found that he had merely lopped off one of its limbs. Privilege had yielded only a few of its outer defenses to the democrats: its citadel remained unshaken. Moreover, the Revolution spawned its own aristocracy: the *nouveaux riches* created by privateering, profiteering, and speculation, having already moved into the houses of the departed Tories, quickly adopted their manners and ideas. These beneficiaries of the Revolution became the backbone of the Federalist party and the most redoubtable enemies of the "principles of 1776."

Perhaps the greatest service rendered by the Revolution to the cause of democracy in the United States was throwing open the West to settlement. Quite rightly, many British statesmen had foreseen that, once Americans were permitted to stream unimpeded across the Alleghenies, the cause of authoritarian government would be gravely weakened. But the westward advance was too powerful to be long held in check by any governmental fiat: the Federalists sought to oppose the growth of the West and, like the British government before them, went down to defeat. The party of Jefferson, on the other hand, allied itself with the West and thereby with the future of American democracy.

If the American Revolution seemed to many democrats an "unfinished" revolution, it likewise fell short of the expectations of those who wished to establish a powerful national government. During the darkest hours of the Revolutionary War, these patriots had been sustained by the hope that the United States would emerge from the struggle a strong and united nation. But under the Articles of Confederation, the republic was weak, disunited, and seemingly drifting into anarchy. To alarmed nationalists, the United States seemed a certain victim of hostile European states; yet the mass of Americans remained unconscious of their danger, unheedful of warnings that weakness was an invitation to attack.

Instead, the American people, spurred on by a postwar depression, attempted to apply the ideals for which they had fought to conditions at home. They demanded laws for the benefit of debtors, fair representation for the West, office holding open to all, manhood suffrage, and curbs upon the power of wealth—in short, Jacksonian Democracy fifty years before Jackson became President. The small farmers gained control of many state governments and proceeded to enact legislation in their own interest; and where the conservative, privileged class refused to yield, as in Massachusetts, the people rose in armed rebellion.

These events produced a sharp reaction in favor of strong government. The people, who in 1776 had been hailed as the source of wisdom and virtue, now began to be regarded as a "great beast" which must be kept securely under leash. To reconcile order with liberty and to create a strong central government capable of resisting foreign foes and American populists alike, plans for "a more perfect union" were drawn up at the Constitutional Convention held in Philadelphia in 1787. Here was contained the answer of American statesmen to the problem that had wrecked the British Empire: how local liberty could exist alongside strong central government. It was also the answer of Americans to the age-old problem of whether man lives for the state or the state is his servant, created for his benefit. Despite the strong feeling against popular "licentiousness," the framers of the Constitution made clear that Americans were not to be mere creatures of the state but citizens endowed with inalienable rights beyond the reach of government.

3

If a nation had been created by the American Revolution and the Federal Constitution, the question remained: What kind of nation was it to be? Was the United States to become an industrialized country of cities, with an aristocracy of wealth looking to the federal government for bounties and protection, or was it to be a country of small farmers, led by an aristocracy of talents, and with the fostering of individual liberty the paramount concern of the states? Herein lies the crux of the struggle between Jefferson and Hamilton, between Republicans and Federalists—the struggle that was to preoccupy the American mind until, merging with the slavery question, it produced the elements of civil war.

The contest between Jefferson and Hamilton, involving as it did the future of American civilization, was intensified by the outbreak of the French Revolution. In the United States, discontented democrats hailed the work of French revolutionaries and began to clamor for a second American revolution, to be based upon the principles of "Liberty, Equality, and Fraternity" and directed against the home-grown brand of aristocracy and privilege. Conservatives rallied to the defense of the established order, resolved to resist any change whatever lest it prove the opening wedge for revolution.

In this struggle, Thomas Paine's *The Rights of Man* became the Bible of the radicals while conservatives found an arsenal of arguments in the counterrevolutionary writings of John Adams and Alexander Hamilton. The New England clergy—the "black regiment" of war days that had given its congregations rebellion and theology in approximately equal measure—now fulminated against the infidelity and license of the French Revolution, picturing the horrors that awaited Americans if they followed in the footsteps of the French. "Shall our Sons become the disciples of Voltaire and the dragoons of Marat," exclaimed the Reverend Timothy Dwight of Connecticut, "or our daughters the concubines of the Illuminati?" But American democrats staunchly upheld the cause of revolution both at home and in France: in their eyes, opposition to the French Revolution was "a war of Kings and Nobles against the equal Rights of Men" and the Federalists were reactionaries who sought to deny the American people the freedom that was their birthright.

4

It is significant that even before the Constitution had been adopted, an ardently nationalistic school of American writers had appeared: the so-called Hartford Wits. The idea that the United States was to be the new Athens of the arts and sciences had been frequently expressed during the Revolution: as long as they remained British colonists, it was said, Americans had reflected all the prejudices and insularity of Britons, but now, as free men, they stood prepared to embrace the world, drawing inspiration from all cultures and all men. In the eyes of some patriots the separation had come just in time: another generation of British rule, said an American, and the colonists would have "learned to eat and drink, and swear and quarrel like Englishmen." Happily, their eyes had been opened in time and they could now perceive that France, for example, was "the most enlightened nation in the world" and its people the most civilized and polite. France had polished and refined Europe: the next step was for this gifted nation to remove the last vestiges of colonialism from the United States. To Thomas Paine, the alliance of the United States with France was like a breath of fresh air stirring among the dead leaves of provincial America, promising a golden age of American literature. "We see with other eyes," Paine exclaimed; "we hear with other ears; and think with other thoughts than those we formerly used. . . . Every corner of the mind is swept of its cobwebs, poison and dust, and made fit for the reception of generous happiness."

In this frame of mind, Americans rushed into print to proclaim their declaration of intellectual independence, grimly determined to stand and die in the literary trenches rather than submit to any return to colonial bondage in things of the spirit. Inevitably, they were led to use American scenes and materials—and thus helped prepare the way for the American Renaissance of the nineteenth century. If America had not come of age in literature—and the work of these early writers is the best evidence that it had not—at least the first stirrings of a vigorous and promising adolescence were evident.

Yet polemics continued to engross the American mind: Philip Freneau, the most promising poet of his generation, spoke as Jefferson's champion against Hamilton and devoted to politics talents that belonged to literature. Party warfare tended to make the American a "newspaper reading animal," to borrow the phrase of an English traveler, and to make American writers propagandists and pamphleteers. Seemingly a grave disservice was thereby done to the cause of literature; but, by developing a great mass of readers, the newspapers made possible a wide and expanding market for books.

By 1820, the triumph of democratic ideals and the ending of the menace of foreign intervention enabled Americans to turn their attention to the business of settling and developing the continent. The purely polemical phase of American literature was passing, and writers could give literary expression to something more enduring than the political passions of the day. America, it began to be recognized, in its size, color, and diversity furnished the man of letters with a wealth of material for his pen. No longer wholly concerned with hewing out a livelihood from a forest wilderness, and now imbued with a desire to exploit the literary resources of their country, Americans were prepared for the long awaited, and long delayed, American Renaissance.

10. THE MAKING OF THE MAN OF LETTERS

Education was the first need, and the colonial schools and colleges had made a good start toward providing it. The early colleges survived the era of revolution and maintained well into the following century their modified classical curricula, their small and socially selected student bodies, and their emphasis on preparation for the law, the ministry, and public life. To the eight colonial colleges were soon added Virginia and many others. The church drew fewer of their graduates, and the law and politics more. Gradually there was less temptation to send likely youth to Oxford or Cambridge, London or Edinburgh, for the fundamentals that make a gentleman.

On the other hand, the habit of going abroad for advanced study in medicine, the fine arts, science, and still to a large extent the law became even more firmly established in the first half-century of independence, and, particularly in science, continued to our own day. The American-born president of the British Royal Academy, Benjamin West, spread his giant historical canvases on the walls of Windsor Castle and Greenwich Hospital, and trained almost all our early painters in his London studio, at least until one of them, Charles Willson Peale, broke the tradition and helped to found in 1805 the Pennsylvania Academy of the Fine Arts. Similarly our early physicians went as a matter of routine to Edinburgh and London for their training until they in turn could establish medical schools at home. And the study of language and literature took George Ticknor, Longfellow, and many another young professor to England and Germany during the years that followed. The former colonists were typically adolescent in their attitude toward their parent cultures. They cultivated the strut of independence in voice and manner while sedulously learning from and aping their elders.

On other levels of education, this attitude brought good results. The rampant nationalism of the lexicographer Noah Webster and the geographer Jedidiah Morse did much to popularize a more genuine and less traditional system of elementary and secondary schooling, combating the limitations of the colonial grammar schools, dame schools, and private tutors of the socially privileged. The district and "charity" schools which, after the Revolution, provided the democratic foundations for our modern system of public instruction, were slow of development. Although Massachusetts had had a public-school law since 1647, most of the state constitutions made no such provisions, and even the federal constitution was silent on the subject. During the eighteenth century, the training of youth was still a responsibility of the home.

Into this situation, Webster in 1783 injected his "blue backed speller," a challenge to traditionalism and complacency. On the principle that learning must be close to experience, it proclaimed an American language and set out, by properly training the youth, to make this country "as independent in *literature* as she is in *politics*—as famous for *arts* as for *arms.*" The campaign was carried forward by his own reader, grammar, and dictionary, by Morse's *The American Geography,* "calculated early to impress the minds of American youth with the idea of the superior importance of their own country," and by Jefferson's proposal of 1817 for a comprehensive plan of mass education, starting with county schools and culminating in a university in which should be taught "all the useful sciences in their highest degree."

It was a century or longer before natural democratic man took his place in the councils of the colleges. In spite of the liberal and rational views of such planners as Franklin, Jefferson, and even the American Samuel Johnson, first president of King's College (Columbia), the classical and theological ideals of the colonial period, born of sedulous loyalty to the tradition of Oxford and Cambridge, persisted through early national days. Our first literary men had a colonial training and a colonial heritage. They were the select few, presumably masters of Latin, Greek, logic, rhetoric, theology, mathematics, and perhaps science in its early form of natural philosophy. In college, "that temple of dullness, that roost of owls," as Joseph Dennie described it, discipline was strict and learning carefully divorced from life. Occasionally the more spirited students were rusticated for misbehavior as was Dennie, or dismissed outright, as was James Fenimore Cooper when, it is reported, he opened the door of a friend's room by a miniature blast of gunpowder tucked into the keyhole.

Other and better outlets for youthful spirits were the literary and debating societies, such as the Linonia and Brothers societies at Yale, the American Whig Society in which Freneau and Brackenridge were active at Princeton, and the Philomathean and Zelosophic societies at Pennsylvania. These groups were usually paired, and their rivalries provided the focus of undergraduate life. They supplemented the classroom by promoting debate on current topics in politics and literature, sometimes so successfully that the resulting pranks and brawls led to petty bloodshed. But, most significant for our purposes, their surviving libraries show a preponderance of the currently imported and popular books, which must have compensated for the narrowly academic collections built up by the administrations. It was out of them rather than the formal classroom that the modern American college grew, and it was in their meetings that the combative and creative interests of our later political and literary leaders were formed and nurtured.

2

Once out of college, the American youth found even less stimulus to a purely literary life. If he had learned to read, analyze, and declaim in the classroom, he had also learned in his societies to debate current issues and to enjoy current English and American books. His mind might be stored with Latin and Greek, theology, logic, rhetoric, and mathematics, but his veins secretly pulsed with the gentle rhythms of Addisonian prose or the emphatic couplets of Pope while his ears rang with the phrases of Patrick Henry and Samuel Adams. It was all very confusing and thwarting if one wished to write, as college graduates do. The simplest answer to the problem was to read for the law, and then to enter the political or business world, saving literature for the idle moment and watering it down to belles-lettres. There were so many immediate issues to be settled; there was so much work of the pioneering world to be done!

For one thing, there were no publishers in the modern sense, and few printers would take a chance on a book by an American when English authors could be pirated at will. Franklin had republished *Pamela* in 1744, and the example had been followed with no qualms by later printers. These printers, of whom there was a steadily increasing number in all the coastal cities, were primarily equipped to issue broadsides, currency, pamphlets, newspapers, and occasionally a magazine. Until about 1825, American authors published their own books, taking all or the greater part of the financial risks. Most of our printers had learned from the example of Hugh Gaine, of wartime notoriety, to change their opinions with the weather and to seek out such business as the market afforded. Our first publishers in anything like the modern sense—Isaiah Thomas and Mathew Carey, who had ambitions and ethics of their own and the initiative to implement them—were exceptions. Yet even these two were primarily printers, only incidentally publishers.

The reading public, which grew rapidly during this period, was also in part responsible for hampering the immediate encouragement of native work because the prestige of English authors more than satisfied the increasing demand for popular forms of literature. Colonial libraries had been composed of the works in the classics, history, philosophy, and theology which their owners had learned to value in college; and the stock-holding subscribers to the libraries of pre-Revolutionary days like the Philadelphia Library Company, the New York Society Library, and other athenaeums and library societies from Providence to Charleston, merely extended the pattern to New Orleans (1805) and to Boston (1807). Even though these societies bought generously from the lists of native printers, their subscribers demanded even more urgently the London imprint and the standard or popular work.

The craze for novel reading which hit the British public toward the close of the eighteenth century, and the subsequent popularity of the Romantic poets and the familiar essayists of the early nineteenth, soon found reflection in this country. American presses were reprinting English novels in quantity by 1790, and soon long listings of "new books (mostly travel and fiction) by the ship Electra from London," sales of private libraries, and offerings of "books, fancy articles, &c. for Christmas" were occupying almost as much space in the newspapers as were announcements of importations of gloves, cotton goods, wine, tea, salt, and soap. Cooper could not hope to find a publisher who would pay him adequately for his first success, *The Spy,* in 1821; but when it appeared, in December of that year, there were four booksellers in New York City alone ready to advertise that they had it for sale.

The novelist Charles Brockden Brown was the first American, and the only one before Cooper and Irving, to attempt the literary profession by reliance on the book market alone; and he failed. He experimented with a bookseller as well as with local printers as publishers for his American Gothic tales. The list of fiction in the circulating library of one William Caritat (1804) supplies the causes of Brown's failure with both, and the reason why he, like so many of his fellows, turned from writing to magazine editing for subsistence. Caritat, a fashionable bookseller, in that year had some two thousand French and English novels on his shelves, reprinted in this country or directly imported. A study of this list reveals why Brown was hopeful of the popular moral tale of horror as a medium for his literary ambitions; but it also explains why his inspiration dried up so suddenly in the face of foreign competition.

3

Our printers were quicker than our authors to learn how to profit by the unequal situation. By the time *Waverley* appeared in 1814, the war was on, and Scott became its principal victim. John Miller, a hack publisher of London, acted as agent for his most successful American counterpart, Mathew

Carey in Philadelphia. It was his task to see that the sheets, or even the proofs if he could get them, of any potential British success were in Carey's hands by fast packet (about thirty days) almost before the bound volumes had appeared in the London bookshops and well before any of them could be imported. Carey paid Miller, not the British author or publisher, for this service. "We have rec'd *Quentin Durward* most handsomely," he writes Miller on June 17, 1823, "and have the same completely in our own hands this time." He had won the race if he could be first to get sufficient copies to the local booksellers and into the van of the picturesque Parson Weems, peddling his wares through the countryside and fiddling his way to the hearts of his customers.

When the sheets of a new book were received, they were at once divided among three or four typesetters who worked night and day in shifts and sometimes produced a reprint in twenty-four hours. Even one or two days' priority assured financial success. It is perhaps significant that when this traffic was at its height, about 1815, popular books of American authorship were virtually nonexistent. The first group of writers had given up the struggle and were depending on a precarious magazine market to issue the literary by-products of their more substantial pursuits, while the second had not yet overcome the increasing obstacles to success. It is also significant that almost all the prominent early American printers of books—the Wileys, Appleton, the Harper brothers, and the Careys, as well as other and lesser men—were violently opposed to any form of international copyright.

The problem remained unsolved until about 1825, when Irving and Cooper discovered the cause of the difficulty. They were the first to realize that Noah Webster's patriotic zeal had overreached itself, for the Copyright Act of 1790 allowed protection only to American authors, whereas in England protection could be claimed under common law or gentlemen's agreement on the basis of prior issue and regardless of the author's nationality. For an entire literary generation this legal difference had remained unnoticed and merciless pirating gone unchecked on both sides of the water. Both British and American authors suffered; but British prestige made the lot of the American hopeless. "What publisher," wrote Cooper to Carey, "will pay a native writer for ideas that he may import for nothing?"

Great as this temporary sacrifice of native talent may have been, perhaps it was a necessary preparation for the writers who were still to come. However unethical the copyright situation, it built up and educated a reading public in a great European literary tradition, and it taught American writers that they could not compete with that tradition by imitation alone. The full force of this education would not be felt for another generation, when the spirit rather than the mere forms of older cultures had been absorbed and the values rather than the bare facts of the American experience had begun to be understood by native writers.

4

If the book market was, in this transition period, practically nonexistent for the American author, the outlets for his work provided by the magazines and the theater were little better. The four principal post-Revolutionary magazines of the eighteenth century—the *Columbian*, Carey's *American Museum*, the *Massachusetts Magazine*, and the *New-York Magazine*—all were addicted to the scissors and the paste-pot, although they occasionally published original essays, poems, and tales with scrupulous anonymity. Dennie's *Port Folio* occupied the central place among American literary magazines during the first quarter of the nineteenth century and achieved the longest run of any such journal up to that time. It offered safe harbor to John Quincy Adams and Richard Rush when their impulses turned from diplomacy to poetry and essay, and to men like Charles Brockden Brown and Dennie himself, for whom writing was an end in itself. The ambitious "Knickerbocker" authors, Irving, Paulding, and their friends, long before the *Sketch Book* days, relied on the newspaper and the pamphlet rather than on the book or the magazine for their Addisonian *Salmagundi* essays, as did Dickinson and Paine for their political tracts during the Revolution and Halleck and Drake for their verse satires, *The Croaker Papers,* in 1819. Yet even the scant market provided by the magazines and newspapers, by an ironic paradox, may have had some bearing on the cultivation of the tract, the essay, the short story, and the lyric poem by American authors at a time when novels were obviously the choice of their readers.

The theater too afforded little encouragement to native talent. Probably there was no time during colonial days when some form of play-acting had not been practiced, however primitively or secretively. The problem of what to do about it was among the first of the agenda of our forefathers. As early as 1610 it had seemed wise to Virginian authorities to forbid the immigration of actors from England because of the evils associated with them. In 1665 three young men of Virginia were charged with "acting a play of yᵉ Bare and yᵉ Cubb." New England's hostility toward the drama has been proverbial, yet in 1712 Samuel Sewall was disturbed by "a Rumor, as if some design'd to have a Play acted in the Council Chamber, next Monday." In Charleston, South Carolina, the "Court room" was used for theatrical performances (in 1735) long before a regular theater was established. In the meantime New York had probably had its first taste of professional acting about 1700 when Richard Hunter apparently was granted a license to present plays. By 1732 there was some sort of "play house" in New York. Strolling players turned up from time to time in many of the major towns and cities of the Atlantic seaboard: Boston, New York, Philadelphia, Annapolis, Williamsburg, Charleston. Sometimes a nucleus of professional actors (generally British) worked in conjunction with local amateurs. In the absence of adequate theaters, performances took place in coffeehouses, stores, or barns. Occasionally, to avoid arousing the ire of municipal authorities, a flimsy, impermanent structure was devised or adapted on the outskirts of a town.

The more consecutive history of the American theater begins about the middle of the eighteenth century. In 1749 a "Company of Comedians" presented the tragedy of *Cato* in Philadelphia. New York was accorded its first notable Shakespearean performance on March 5th of the next year when, with the permission of his Excellency the Governor of the Province, the "Comedians" presented *Richard III*—"Wrote originally by *Shakspere,* and alter'd by Colly Cibber, Esq." Another notable "first" was the presentation of *The Merchant of Venice* at Williamsburg, Virginia, on September 15, 1752, by the "American Company." This occasion was the more historic because it marked the first American production and performance of the Hallam family, among them Lewis Hallam the younger, who was to dominate "the stage of the New World" for "nearly a quarter of a century." It was this initial performance of which John Esten Cooke wrote a glamorous (and not entirely accurate) account in his *Virginia Comedians* (1854). From about this time on, the record indicates a rapid expansion of the theatrical activities, professional, amateur, and "unofficial." When authorities frowned, plays were sometimes advertised as "readings" or "lectures." Private performances, which were hard to censor or suppress, whetted the appetite of play lovers. Students at some of the colleges began to put on performances despite administrative disapproval. In a moment of irritation one former tutor of Yale College complained to the president (in 1777) that students had "left the more solid parts of learn^g & run into Plays & dramatic Exhibitions chiefly of the comic kind & turn'd College . . . into Drury Lane."

The professional theater slowly acquired confidence and prestige. The establishment of more or less permanent buildings was a material gain. The first of these, the Southwark Theater on South Street, Philadelphia, was built in 1766. A brick-and-wood structure painted "a glaring red," it lasted fifty-five years as a theater before becoming (what the opponents of playgoing did not fail to mark) a distillery. The John Street Theater (opened in 1767) in New York was of the same general type as the Southwark. In Annapolis a theater was built in 1771; and Charleston's "elegant" new theater, larger than either the Southwark or the John Street Theater, was opened on December 22, 1773.

With the erection of substantial buildings, the play business became more and more institutionalized. A common practice was to have performances on

Mondays, Wednesdays, and Fridays, with the bill changed for each night. Performances generally began at six or seven o'clock, and the standard bill included a regular play and an "afterpiece," which might be a farce or ballet or a comic opera. The "society" which attended was of course mixed, but it was by no means riffraff. In the South, ladies of the better families were often seen at public amusements, as Josiah Quincy of Boston noted to his astonishment when visiting Charleston in 1773. The frequency and virulence of tirades against the theater everywhere lessened in proportion to the increasing social distinction of its patrons. When General Washington himself attended dramatic performances—as, the records indicate, he did on scores of occasions —who should presume to say that the theater was an altogether degrading and iniquitous place? Alert managers learned to advertise the fact that he would be present, sometimes with a party including brilliantly appareled ladies. Surely on occasions such as these the theater had "arrived." But the best that can be said of it in this period is that it was not a bad imitation of the British. Where Byron and Keats failed, American poets can hardly be blamed for inadequacy. It produced a successful actor in John Howard Payne, whose fame rests equally on his playing of Young Norval in Home's *Douglas* and on the perennial "Home, Sweet Home" from his own *Clari*; but it failed to make a playwright out of himself or his friend Washington Irving, however hard they tried.

5

For self-protection as well as for sociability, these writers gathered together in mutual encouragement societies. The most famous of such groups was the "Hartford Wits," originally composed of four men of varying political views —Joel Barlow, John Trumbull, Lemuel Hopkins, and David Humphreys— but later to include Timothy Dwight, Elihu Hubbard Smith, and many others who shared with them either an enthusiastic patriotism, a religious conservatism, or a love of rhyming couplets. When Dr. Smith moved to New York City in 1793, he became the center of the Friendly Club, a group composed of William Dunlap, Charles Brockden Brown, Dr. Mitchell, and Noah Webster. The fellowship which gathered about Dennie's *Port Folio* in Philadelphia, known as the Tuesday Club, and Peter Irving's Knickerbocker group on the *Morning Chronicle* of New York, were not dining and writing clubs in as strict a sense; but they performed similar functions, as did the later Bread and Cheese Club which forgathered with Fenimore Cooper in the "Den" back of Charles Wiley's bookshop in the City Hotel, and which survives as the Century Association in its dignified home off modern Fifth Avenue.

Under such circumstances, the false literary dawn of the nineties and the "dark ages" which followed seem to lend themselves to ready explanation. Not only was the creative genius of our best minds channeled into politics and practical affairs, not only were we intellectually dependent on England long after we obtained political independence, but we had as yet inadequate means for producing a literature of our own. The struggles of Poe, Cooper, Irving, Halleck, and Bryant did not meet with even modest success until well after 1825; the first half-century of our national life was spent mainly in preparing for the writers and readers to come.

11. THE WAR OF THE PAMPHLETS

E<small>VEN</small> though excellence in the deliberately "literary" forms of literature had to wait more settled times, the Revolutionary era was ideally suited to the pamphlet. The writer of 1776 might have said of his book, as George Gascoigne said in 1576 introducing Humphrey Gilbert's *New Passage to Cataia:* "It is but a Pamphlet & no large discourse, & therefore the more to be borne withall: since the faults (if any be) shalbe the fewer, because the volume is not great."

The first three hundred years of American history coincided with the age of the pamphlet. In these centuries, pamphleteering became a distinct profession with its own techniques and forms, the pamphlet the dominant vehicle of propaganda and debate. Promotion of colonies in the sixteenth century and the rise of contending religious sects, political revolutions in the seventeenth century, the issues of imperial organization and national wars in the eighteenth century, finally the American and French revolutions at the end of the pamphlet era, were episodes perfectly suited to brief, controversial, and popular treatment.

The literary controversies of the American Revolution were conducted in little books—books inexpensive to print (though well printed), cheap to buy, easy to read, and, more significant, easy to write. About nine thousand books, newspapers, and broadsides were emitted by some two hundred American presses between 1763 and 1783; of these, perhaps two thousand were pamphlets on the political issues of the day. This is the corpus of literature of the American Revolution—a couple of thousand little books with their pretentious and formidable titles, intended for instant circulation, designed to change men's minds, addressed to urgent problems, sometimes touching the universal issues that confront men everywhere, any time, in civil society.

In a literature of such fugitive productions and such voluminous mass, individual dimensions were likely to be slight. The man and his book had to be considered in relation to a host of men and their books which, taken together, expressed the thoughts and feelings of two million Americans embroiled in a common experience of appalling magnitude. The pamphlet, even

131

a great one like Dickinson's *Farmer's Letters* or Paine's *Common Sense,* never stood alone. It took its place in the stream of action and the stream of thought. Nor did its influence end with its publication. Often an essay would have prepublication readings, as did Otis' *Rights of the British Colonies* before the Massachusetts Assembly, and Governor Stephen Hopkins' treatise on the origin and nature of law before the legislature of Rhode Island. Sometimes, too, it would have public readings after publication, around a drumhead in a militia camp or in meetings of the Sons of Liberty. Some loyalist tracts received public burnings after being heard. Frequently, a little book had appeared first in a newspaper, or was reprinted in news columns afterward. Moreover, it was the nature of the pamphlet to evoke other pamphlets— rejoinders, refutations, responses of all kinds. Samuel Seabury's five "West-chester Farmer" tracts explain and are explained by the prodigious rejoinders of young Alexander Hamilton. One little book did not make a literary figure, nor a political leader. Only when a man had written several pamphlets, and developed in them a reasoned, coherent program of thought and action, did he rise to personal eminence as a writer among writers.

Some men did just that. A few pamphleteers—Otis, Dickinson, Paine, Franklin, Jefferson, Hamilton, Seabury, Galloway—wrote so effectively and so often that for them the little book became a literary career. Each had something more than ordinary to say; each, through special insights or unusual learning, saw in discrete instances of political conflict the permeating principles of universal application that enabled Americans to feel their cause akin to the historical purpose and destiny of man.

The pamphleteers of the Revolution received their training in local political struggles in each colony before 1765. There were American political pamphleteers before there was any unifying American point of view. The Parson's Cause in Virginia had produced the early tracts of Patrick Henry; Daniel Dulany argued a taxation question in Maryland; the prolonged attempt to overthrow the Penn family's proprietorship in Pennsylvania occasioned pamphlets from the famous Franklin and from men like Joseph Galloway and John Dickinson who were not yet so famous; in Boston James Otis, Josiah Quincy, and a brace of Adamses became the leaders of a radical faction in Massachusetts politics. All these writers developed in their partisan little books the contentious tone familiar to America from the religious polemics of the Great Awakening; but the orientation of their thinking before 1765 was narrowly provincial. A sense of purpose common to all America was lacking. After 1765, however, provincial issues were swallowed up in imperial polemics. When the British government embarked on its program of reforming the Empire, American writers rose from local squabbles to general political principles. The Stamp Act and the laws of Parliament which followed not only forced the several colonies into a kind of union; they also obliged the American pamphleteers to rise above their local orientation and become philosophers. The philosophy of the pamphleteers gradually won Americans from fundamentalist attitudes of colonial political thinking to secular attitudes of revolution.

2

The literary career of James Otis comprehended the early stages of the movement (1761-1769). Massachusetts-born and Harvard-trained, Otis in 1761 was a successful lawyer in his middle thirties. His sister, Mercy Otis Warren, was a playwright, poet, and historian, whose *History of the Rise, Progress, and Termination of the American Revolution* (1805) was to stimulate the patriotism of a generation. Otis had published a textbook in Latin prosody and composed another in Greek, but his tastes were not really academic. He was by nature partisan and worldly. An eloquent courtroom speech against the new parliamentary measures made him the chief spokesman of the local radicals, and as leader of this faction he wrote the five pamphlets on which his great reputation rests. They were controversial and intemperate works, reckless and sometimes coarse, but they stated tersely and vividly (if not always logically) an American constitutional theory. The first tract, *A Vindication of the Conduct of the House of Representatives of the Province of Massachusetts Bay* (1762), written in angry tone on a trivial issue of local politics, developed the principle of representative taxation as a basic requirement of constitutionally limited government. The second, *The Rights of the British Colonies Asserted and Proved* (1764), marked Otis' transition from local to imperial issues. Written "amid the continual solicitations of a crowd of clients," after "one single Act of Parliament has set people a-thinking, in six months, more than they had done in their whole lives before," this pamphlet was a testament of fundamental political faith. Supreme power, Otis asserted, was "*originally* and *ultimately* in the people." The people delegated power to whom they pleased, but only as one man gives another a possession to hold in trust for him. Thus government was a fiduciary trust. "The *end* of government being the *good* of mankind, points out its great duties: It is above all things to provide for the security, the quiet, and happy enjoyment of life, liberty and property." The tract, conservative in spirit, was designed to justify opposition to Parliament. Otis hoped to persuade Americans "to behave like men, and use the proper legal measures to obtain redress." The next year, in an acidulous pamphlet, *Considerations on Behalf of the Colonists* (1765), he retorted to the English writer Soame Jenyns, stressing the dependence of the colonies on Britain but warning:

"Revolutions have been. They may be again." In later pamphlets the violence of his writing increased, at times approaching "a mere shriek," and the contours of his thinking failed to alter with changing issues. After 1769 he was silent, living in a disordered half-world until he was struck down by a bolt of lightning in 1783. But his work had really reached fruition, for in his virile tracts he had exhibited the literary technique of resistance, and had given, in Moses Coit Tyler's words, "a conservative and law-respecting race, a conservative and lawful pretext for resisting law, and for revolutionizing the government."

A large amount of James Otis' fame is due to the repeated encomiums heaped upon him by John Adams, from whom we have the only contemporary description of Otis' Writs of Assistance speech. Although Adams continued to praise the older man as long as he lived, he produced himself four essays on the Stamp Act more profound than anything Otis was capable of, treating the new measures as episodes in the ageless struggle in western civilization between corporate authority and individual rights. These essays, originally published in newspapers, were issued in pamphlet form as *A Dissertation on the Canon and Feudal Law* (1768)—the first of a long series of distinguished works by Adams which are more properly considered as philosophical literature than as political pamphlets. To Adams also is due much of the reputation of the Rev. Jonathan Mayhew, whom he termed a "transcendent genius." Author of a dozen significant published sermons and tracts, Mayhew represented the spirit of the Enlightenment in New England dissent, and epitomized the combination of religious leadership with political emancipation. Just before his death at the age of forty-six he published *The Snare Broken* (1766), a sermon on the repeal of the Stamp Act in which he justified civil disobedience even to the point of rebellion. The "great and primary law of nature" was self-preservation, he averred, and the measure of political action (as of spiritual truth) was now as always private rather than public judgment.

A bewildering number of little books by a host of young men had appeared before the Stamp Act controversy was over. One, by an older hand, appealed to readers in all provinces. Daniel Dulany, eminent Maryland statesman whose gracious personality and immense learning had placed him, in the Chesapeake colonies, at the very summit of the newest American profession, the bar, wrote a brilliant, persuasive tract against the power of Parliament to legislate for the colonies, *Considerations on the Propriety of imposing Taxes in the British Colonies* (1765), which went through many editions and endured as a strong influence in American constitutional thinking. "No taxation without representation" had been a slogan to Otis; to Dulany it became the foundation principle of free government.

3

The Stamp Act also marked the beginning of John Dickinson's leadership as a writer of the little book. Dickinson was thirty-three years old in 1765, a product, like Dulany and so many other leaders of the middle colonies, of the wealthy farm-proprietor group of the Chesapeake Bay region. He had prepared for three years at the Middle Temple, and had built a conspicuously prosperous business as lawyer, merchant, and landowner. Studious, frail, modest, diffident, he lived elegantly in the most polished Philadelphia society; he wrote with good humor and poised assurance. "The cause of *liberty* is a cause of too much dignity to be sullied by turbulence and tumult," he observed. "Those who engage in it should breathe a sedate yet fervent spirit, animating them to actions of prudence, justice, modesty, bravery, humanity and magnanimity." Dickinson's literary career extended over forty years and ranged over many subjects. The basic principles of his philosophy were broad enough and his mind was fluid enough to adapt to the successive crises of revolution, constitution, nationalism, and democracy. Dickinson stood between extremes. He was moderate in all things. He presented the picture of the thoughtful legislator, the adroit political manipulator, the able administrator, moving slowly but firmly toward well defined goals. His extensive learning, his ever keen sense of political conflict, his winning style as a writer, his analytical ability, and his impelling moral convictions gave his books immediate popularity and imposing stature. Tyler has called the appearance of the *Farmer's Letters* "the most brilliant event in the literary history of the Revolution."

The early pamphlets of Dickinson on Pennsylvania politics—he wrote eight in five months—not only reveal his mastery of this technique of propaganda, but also reveal how ephemeral the tract on transitory issues could be. When he turned to the greater questions of colony and empire he explored permanent values of freedom and order. His powerful state papers and pamphlets on the Stamp Act made his voice the most effective of the resistance movement, since he wrote for a broader audience than Otis had reached. Dickinson described all the various classes of colonial society and their relations with one another, analyzing the economic situation of each class, and the meaning of freedom for each. He warned that while the colonists were instinctively loyal, oppression would undermine that loyalty: "we never can be made an independent people, except it be by *Great-Britain* herself," he declared, "and the only way for her to do it, is to make us frugal, ingenious, united, and discontented."

When the Townshend Acts were passed, Dickinson wrote his *Letters from a Farmer in Pennsylvania* (1767–1768), which were published in all but four of the twenty-five American newspapers, and in eight book editions; Richard Henry Lee edited them in Williamsburg, Otis in Boston; in England Franklin wrote a preface for the first of two editions; in France also two editions were published, translated and edited by a noted liberal. Dickinson made a triumphal tour of England, was awarded an honorary degree by Princeton, was toasted in John Wilkes' prison lodgings in London; he was to be known for the rest of his life as "the Pennsylvania Farmer." He formulated the American interpretation of the British constitution in terms of the principles of liberty.

For WHO ARE FREE PEOPLE? [he asked]. Not *those,* over whom government is reasonably and equitably exercised, but *those* who live under a government so *constitutionally checked* and *controuled,* that proper provision is made against its being otherwise exercised.

He developed a theory of imperial federation in which colonies and empire were perfectly balanced. In such an empire, Americans could "support the character of *freemen* without losing that of *faithful subjects.*"

From 1774 to 1776 Dickinson led the moderate party in the Continental Congress; and he wrote many of the state papers of that body. As chief executive of two states, Delaware and Pennsylvania (1781–1785), he wrote proclamations and messages on the nature of political power, on the suppression of vice and immorality, on social inequality, and on free governments as the expression of the American spirit. He participated in the Constitutional Convention, wrote the *Letters of Fabius* (1788) urging ratification, and in 1797, when American politics turned upon the axis of the French Revolutionary Wars, produced his most reflective and most eloquent pamphlet, another series of *Letters of Fabius* (1797), in which he recommended the French cause, enjoining his countrymen:

Let us assert and maintain *our true character—sincerity* of thought, and *rectitude* of action; and convince the world, that *no man,* or *body of men,* whatever advantages may for a while be taken of our *unsuspecting confidence,* shall ever be able to draw this nation out of the direct road of an honest, candid, and generous conduct.

The length of Dickinson's career, and the distinction of his writing, made him one of the most constructive and successful pamphleteers of his generation—among them all, one of the surest of his ground. In a "chaos of politics and morals, in which strength and weakness, safety and ruin, virtue and iniquity, strangely met together, and wrought in wild conjunction," he strove for order and principle, for intellectual integrity. "I am acting a very small and a very short part in the drama of human affairs," he told his critics. "I shall little trouble myself how your applause or your censures are bestowed."

4

The year 1774 was the watershed of Revolutionary literature. The meeting of the First Congress gave continental expression to all the various bodies of opinion. Production of pamphlets increased, and the state papers of the Congress, instead of emphasizing the areas of agreement among the American writers, polarized the elements of disagreement. Three parties appeared: moderates like Dickinson, loyal extremists of the right, and the independence party of the left. The loyalists were among the ablest literary figures. They .had a worthy cause, and they were as American in their orientation as the moderates and independents, expressing—only with different emphasis—the same intellectual and emotional currents that moved in the revolutionists. There was a loyalist philosophy, akin to the fundamentalist conservative philosophy of all social crises. Jonathan Boucher, Virginia clergyman, developed in bold sermons the theme of a natural aristocracy and a divinely ordained government. Robert Proud, pedantic Latinist and schoolmaster, argued in almost medieval spirit that men were born to obey. But not all Toryism was backward-looking. By more realistic men a positive reform program was developed, which can be seen in such spirited essays as *A Friendly Address to all Reasonable Americans* (1774) by President Myles Cooper of King's College, and the five great "Westchester Farmer" pamphlets (1774–1775) of Samuel Seabury. Most original of the loyalist writers was Joseph Galloway of Pennsylvania, whose plan for union between Britain and the colonies was first presented to the Continental Congress where it was rejected, then published in various pamphlets, and after Galloway's migration to England developed through three more stages, the last appearing as late as 1788. Galloway's productivity included more than a score of the little books. His nobly conceived plan of a federal empire was one of the significant intellectual achievements of the American mind of this period.

Meanwhile, after 1774, the extremists on the left steadily gained adherents, and with the beginning of hostilities in April, 1775, independence tracts secured an ever widening audience. The war itself was the cradle of a more exuberant literature, in which the poetic careers of Philip Freneau, Francis Hopkinson, and John Trumbull were nurtured. These satirists as well as radical leaders like John and Samuel Adams continually urged independence; but at the end of 1775 America was still paralyzed by indecision. Then in January, 1776, a new little book appeared in Philadelphia, by a writer theretofore unknown, who with this work began to assume international significance as a pamphleteer of revolutions. The pamphlet was *Common Sense,* its author the one-time English artisan, Thomas Paine.

Paine belonged to no country, his doctrines to no age. Of all the writers of the American Revolution, he was the least American in background, in spirit, and in purpose. He had not participated in the fifteen years of constitutional debate that had qualified the colonial mind for contention and produced such achievements as Galloway's simple federalism and Dickinson's complex matrix of constitutional limitations, for throughout these years he had been still in England. His cause was not America; it was revolution. He differed in every essential respect from the major writers who had preceded him: his learning was slight, his personal standing inconsequential, his ability in systematic philosophy or organized presentation of argument almost nonexistent. Still, having missed the previous debates with their constitutional metaphysics, he was uninhibited by them. He felt, he sensed, he reacted. He did not complicate his emotional processes with intellectual refinements. He was the exotic radical, the revolutionary prototype. He wrote with urgency, excitement, and bold simplicity; he furnished straightforward, uncomplicated guidance for artisans, mechanics, and farmers. He carried the new philosophy to the masses of the American people, and turned the resistance movement into revolt.

Once a corset maker of Thetford in Norfolk, later a sailor, then a careless exciseman, later still a teacher, successively a tobacconist, a grocer, and once more a crown servant, Paine had lived a singularly disorganized and unfulfilled life before he came to America in 1774 at the age of thirty-seven. Possessed of a lively intellectual curiosity but lacking the capacity for sustained application, he had learned a little about a great many subjects. He became an editor in Philadelphia just as the cumulative force of the resistance movement was supplied with a national focus, the Congress, and in Pennsylvania was entering a proletarian phase. He responded both to the aspirations of the lower classes and to the humanitarian zeal of such enlightened men of position as Benjamin Franklin and Dr. Benjamin Rush, who were his patrons. His newspaper articles on abolition, women's rights, dueling, titles, and the freedom of British India constituted a significantly different preparation for writing revolutionary tracts from that furnished by local political contention and legal study to Henry, Otis, Dickinson, Dulany, and Galloway. The battle of Lexington awakened Paine to the magnitude of the Revolution in a way that constitutional arguments and congressional papers had not. Deciding that, "in a country where all men were once adventurers," his recent arrival did not preclude his uttering opinions, he set out to win America's thoughts from dependence to independence. He concluded that the issue had passed beyond the subtleties of constitutional law, had indeed become a matter to be solved "by man's instincts for truth, decency, and fairness"—that is (Dr. Rush suggested the title), by *Common Sense*.

The impact of the pamphlet was amazing. In a few months more than a hundred thousand copies were published in America and four European editions appeared. The total number eventually circulated was not much less than half a million. Every contemporary felt its effect. Washington found it "working a powerful change in the minds of many men." A South Carolinian declared it had made independents of a majority of Americans. Seldom if ever had a book enjoyed such an immediate popularity. Paine rejected all political theorizing over sovereignty and federalism; he scoffed at loyalty to George III. Instead, he presented the doctrine of separation as inevitable: a continent could not remain subject to an island. "The period of debate is closed," he wrote. "Arms, as the last resource, must decide the contest." In violent language he attacked "the royal brute of Britain" and ridiculed the institution of the crown. "Of more worth is one honest man to society, and in the sight of God, than all the crowned ruffians that ever lived." He painted the picture of three million Americans "running to their seacoast every time a ship arrives from London, to know what portion of liberty they should enjoy," and he contended that the colonies had reached a maturity that made their state of pupilage both farcical and dangerous. Finally, he challenged America to build a freer state than existed anywhere in the world:

O ye that love Mankind! . . . Every spot in the old world is overrun with oppression. Freedom hath been hunted round the globe. Asia and Africa have long expelled her. Europe regards her like a stranger; and England hath given her warning to depart. O! receive the fugitive; and prepare in time an asylum for mankind.

Paine was, like Jefferson and Rousseau, a master rhetorician. In this lay the strength of his appeal. His arguments were crudely simple, his presentation of issues blandly elementary. The canons of good taste scarcely applied to his works; he was not above referring to the stricken George III as "His Madjesty," and he approached the subtleties of politics with blundering passion. But his very simplicity and the heat of his febrile writing brought him the attention of masses of readers whom the careful, reasoned arguments of others had not touched. "The world is my country; to do good my religion," he exclaimed, and in the confident way of inspired agitators he proselyted for his faith.

That faith contained two stable and enduring elements: a belief in the ability of natural reason to govern, and a conviction that all men everywhere were united in the fellowship of freedom. Neither idea was original, nor had Paine as profound an appreciation of their meaning as had certain of his greater contemporaries. But he proved better able than anyone else to translate them into the vernacular of the common man, and his books were then and have ever since been range-lights of liberalism.

Common Sense made Paine the spokesman of the independence party. *The American Crisis* (sixteen papers he contributed at irregular intervals to the *Pennsylvania Journal* during the next seven years) made him the journalist of the Revolution itself. The first *Crisis* opened with the famous words that became a battle-cry:

> These are the times that try men's souls. The summer soldier and the sunshine patriot will, in this crisis, shrink from the service of their country; but he that stands it *now,* deserves the love and thanks of man and woman. Tyranny, like hell, is not easily conquered; yet we have this consolation with us, that the harder the conflict, the more glorious the triumph.

He attacked the complacency of those who wished for peace in their day, if it meant war for their children's generation; and he praised the sturdy resolution of the patriots who had endured the defeats of the first year of campaigning.

> I love the man that can smile in trouble, that can gather strength from distress and grow brave by reflection. It is the business of little minds to shrink; but he whose heart is firm, and whose conscience approves his conduct, will pursue his principles unto death.

Later numbers dealt with the threatening issues of the war years: financial chaos, loyalist opposition, military conspiracy, national union, a just peace, and adequate government. Busy with minor offices and with many essays besides the *Crisis,* Paine became enmeshed in the details of political life. His essential philosophy remained, but he did not again achieve the originality, the vitality, the unifying definition of the American overcause that had in *Common Sense* helped to make "thirteen clocks strike together."

But there was no confusion in his philosophy of freedom. "My own line of reasoning is to myself as straight and clear as a ray of light," he wrote; and as he watched the slow and painful victory of the American people he developed the concept of revolution as the emancipation not of Americans alone but of common men everywhere from the worship of their antique idols in their antique symbolism. Revolutionism became Paine's basic faith. It had little application in American politics after the peace, even less after the reforms in government of 1787–1789. In this country, the Revolution was over. In Europe it was just beginning, and Paine, who went abroad in 1787, was its self-appointed evangel. Like Archimedes, he felt that, "had we a place to stand upon, we might raise the world." The French Revolution gave him his platform. Ineffectual in his efforts of personal leadership, he gave all his intense convictions and restless energies to his writings. *The Rights of Man* became a textbook for world revolution, and has remained the democrat's breviary of two continents. *The Age of Reason,* confronting the connection between political and theological doctrine—always present but never before so explicit in his thought—stated the case of deism crudely but so overtly that Paine incurred the enmity of hosts of the common people who had once been his admirers and followers. *Agrarian Justice* was an examination of the problem of poverty. Could civilized man, who begat poverty, eliminate it by social action? To answer this question in the affirmative, Paine proposed a system of state taxes and pensions. He had moved from the democracy of the seventies to the nationalism of the nineties.

The French Revolution ended, as the American had; France entered a constructive, aggressive phase, to which Paine had little to contribute. He returned to a strange America in 1802, spent a few pitiful years, poor, ill, and outcast; he died in 1809. Thriving on social turmoil, he languished in times of peace; apt to stir emotions, he affronted sober judgment; yet he had wrought marvelously in the processes that undermined the ancient pieties of men; he had crystallized the conviction that reason, rather than accepted authority or revelation, is the surest guide in politics, religion, and morality; and he had added to the vocabulary of politics stirring phrases of courage, determination, and faith that have not lost their magic in the passing years. If doubt still lingers as to which nation should take Paine unto itself, there is at least no doubt that, in giving memorable expression to American life at its most decisive moment, he made his place in the formative literature of the new republic.

5

There was only one Otis, one Dickinson, one Galloway, one Paine; yet the age of the little books produced many other notable literary careers. There was, for example, gentle Anthony Benezet, whose humanitarian ministry of good works included five sensible tracts on abolitionism, the slave trade, temperance, Quaker doctrine, and the treatment of the Indians. There was the vain, half-educated mountaineer, Ethan Allen, who wrote pamphlets on the Vermont controversy, an account of his captivity during the war, and shared in a barbarous presentation of deism, *Reason the Only Oracle of Man* (1784). Most copies of this tract were accidentally destroyed by fire and some were burnt on purpose; but enough remained to cause a brief uproar among orthodox clerics, and it has unaccountably received serious attention by historians since. There was Benjamin Rush, scientist, philosopher, reformer, statesman, and educator, whose great works on chemistry, diseases, medicine, and madness do not entirely eclipse the scores of essays and tracts he wrote on social and political questions. And there were many more. But for several years after the peace (1783) fewer pamphlets emerged from the run of little books to achieve either literary distinction or a wide audience. Controversy scarcely abated, but the issues of controversy were not so often the great universal issues of political experience. Religious contention, social reform, currency problems, and economic ills were the subjects of the little books, while larger books were appealing to the dominant moods. War-nurtured nationalism was gratified by the publication of military journals and patriotic histories of the Revolution. These were noncontroversial works that were not part of the literature of propaganda and debate.

The proposal of the new Constitution in 1787, however, was the occasion for another spate of pamphlets, in volume second only to that the independence controversy had caused. The debate on ratification extended over twenty months, and produced examinations of first principles of political organization as searching and as significant as any of the revolutionary pamphlets of the previous decade. Historical traditions have conferred such an accolade upon *The Federalist* that other tracts of literary merit, particularly those opposing the Constitution, have been all but forgotten. Yet writers of ability, reputation, and learning, in little books simpler and more popular than the great classic of Madison, Hamilton, and Jay (which was "not well calculated for the common people"), laid the cases for and against the Constitution at the bar of public opinion. Elbridge Gerry's *Observations . . . By A Columbian Patriot* (1788), criticized the new plan as a scheme "of military combinations, and politicians of yesterday." In New York the partisan leader George Clinton attacked the proposed frame as tyranny and corruption, in *Letters of Cato* (1787-1788), to which Alexander Hamilton, as *Caesar,* replied. Albert Gallatin, Luther Martin, James Monroe, Patrick Henry, George Mason, and Samuel Chase were among the pamphleteers who wrote little books and newspaper essays against the Constitution; but the most effective antifederalist tract, and one of the most persuasive pamphlets of the whole period, was Richard Henry Lee's *Letters of the Federal Farmer* (1787-1788), which went through four editions in as many states in three months, and became a handbook of the opposition to the new frame of government. It evoked vigorous rejoinders, among them an elaborate refutation by Timothy Pickering. Lee's writing was spare and firm. He preserved a calm dignity. His arguments were careful and thorough. He was neither narrow nor contentious in spirit, but earnest and constructive. "We are making a constitution, it is to be hoped, for ages and millions yet unborn," he wrote, and warned that the defects in the proposed instrument would doom it to failure. Lee spoke for what he termed "the honest and substantial part of the community," as Henry and Gallatin spoke for the lower income groups. His *Letters* were a powerful influence in bringing about the first ten amendments (the Bill of Rights) which as Senator from Virginia he helped put through Congress in the following year (1789). The pamphlet also deserves notice as the principal literary achievement of this sturdy, quiet, somewhat austere character who had been throughout a long public life above the reproach either of interest or of enthusiasm. Ever since his bold oration against slavery in the House of Burgesses in 1759, Lee had been in the forefront of the resistance movement. His stately petitions and official papers had been on a plane with Dickinson's. He it was who had written and introduced the resolution of independence in 1776; he had shared in composing the North-West Ordinance, had served long in Congress as member and for a while as president. Above all the Virginia statesmen, Lee represented what the classically trained revolutionary generation meant when it spoke of Roman virtues.

On the other side of the ratification question were writers equally distinguished and apparently even more effective. Dickinson's *Letters of Fabius*, published in a Wilmington newspaper, helped to make Delaware the first state to ratify. Noah Webster, John Jay, Edmund Randolph, Alexander Hamilton, James Iredell, Hugh Henry Brackenridge, Hugh Williamson, and Tench Coxe joined the lists of the Constitution's champions, under a bewildering array of pseudonyms. James Wilson, ineradicably Scotch, inordinately learned, incurably romantic, had led the Convention through its most tortuous philosophical difficulties. To the ratification polemic he contributed a precise explanation of the principles he had concocted, *Address to a Meeting of the Citizens* (1787), pronouncing the Constitution "the best form of government which has ever been offered to the world." Trained in law by John Dickinson, associated with him in opposition to the Stamp Act and later regulations, author of the *Considerations on the Nature and Extent of the Legislative Authority of the British Parliament* (1774) and other pamphlets, Wilson had always represented the opinions of the Philadelphia mercantile and professional classes. His style was sober and heavy, his arguments sometimes turgid, but he had attained a very extensive influence. His lectures on law at the University of Pennsylvania mark the beginning of the public study of jurisprudence in America. His brilliance as a thinker and writer and his effectiveness as a statesman were alike marred by his immoderate speculations in land companies. Perhaps because his life closed amid sordid scenes, his substantial contributions to American literature and statecraft have been insufficiently valued.

6

Of all the little books of 1787-1788, none has a stronger claim upon the student of literature than *The Federalist,* written by Madison, Hamilton, and Jay. These papers formed the best exposition of the principles of the new government, and after its adoption gained the authority almost of constitutional law. They appeared first in New York newspapers, and were issued in two volumes in March–May, 1788; republished in many American cities and in two French editions during the nineties; praised by German reviewers; and reprinted on the occasion of South American and Central European revolutions in the nineteenth century. *The Federalist* occupies a unique place in American journalism, for it summarizes the most original contributions the revolutionary generation of pamphleteers made to the discussion of government. As Paine's *Common Sense* marked the height of revolutionary radicalism, so *The Federalist* signalized the success of the conservative, constructive, consolidating processes which shaped the new nation in postrevolutionary molds. The ideas of distributive powers, checked by correlative limitations upon power, the colonists had found in their political texts: Montesquieu, Harington, Sidney, and Locke. They had given their own expression to these ideas in their first pamphlets on imperial organization in the Stamp Act year. Dulany, Wilson, Dickinson, and especially Galloway had proposed a federal scheme for the empire, and Galloway had developed his proposals into a well articulated structure of administrative and legislative units. The members of the Constitutional Convention, though young men, had in one sense been truly as Gerry had charged "politicians of yesterday," for they were directed by the writings and experience of the previous two decades. *The Federalist* papers, written by a strangely assorted trio—a conservative New York lawyer, a convinced monarchist and nationalist, a pedantic constitutional theorist— were the result not so much of the discussions behind the closed doors of Independence Hall during that hot summer of 1787, as of all the American experiments, literary and actual, with federal forms since the dimly remembered days of the Confederation of New England. This book was a sort of codification of American conservative thought. It signalized as much the end of an era as the beginning of a nation.

The ratification controversy was the last great American chapter in the age of the pamphlet. The form itself did not disappear; every national election and every national issue for many years was to see a flood of the little books. But American writers were already by 1790 presenting larger and longer works to an expanding reading audience. The pamphlet, a ready instrument in conflict, was being relegated to a minor place in the currents of reconstruction and nation building. The literary career of Tench Coxe, our first original economic thinker on a national scale, bridged the two eras. Most of his score of works (1787–1820) were pamphlets, varying from thirty-eight to one hundred thirty-five pages in length; but his *View of the United States* (1795) ran to more than four hundred pages, and was popular enough to appear in three editions in one year. Coxe and his contemporaries had to be more than pamphleteers, because the processes of thought and opinion set in motion by the pamphlet literature of the Revolution had been completed. The techniques of communicating major ideas in simple words had been refined to a point where the philosopher, the political leader, the reformer had an almost instantaneous hearing in the public forum. The newspaper and the magazine at one level, the printed book at the other, took the place of the pamphlet. The age of the little book, like the American Revolution itself, had come to an end.

12. PHILOSOPHER–STATESMEN OF THE REPUBLIC

No LESS contemporaneous in its inspiration than the writing of the pamphleteers, but far more substantial and enduring, was the writing in all forms of those philosopher-statesmen who did most by thought and action to bring the First Republic into being.

The founding fathers were men of remarkably broad interests with an uncanny aptitude for political analysis and for the adaptation of theories to practice. There are some who describe this phenomenon as no more than the heritage of humanism which the American enlightenment merely reembodied. Certainly the statesmen who shaped the Republic in its first form were confronting essentially the same issues as those formulated by the Renaissance humanists: the attempt to reconcile speculative thinking on the nature of man with the immediate task of creating a new political and social order. But these modern humanists differed from More and Erasmus in being under more pressure to apply their theories to the urgent task at hand. Yet there is something breath-taking about the reembodiment of broad humanist principles in a struggling and relatively unsophisticated people, beset on every side by the problems of living. The "fathers" therefore deserve either spontaneous admiration or informed respect, whether we study their ideas and actions as we find them, or trace their intellectual heritage to another age.

Of the first statesmen of the Republic, four—Jefferson, Madison, John Adams, and Hamilton—trained their sights higher than any of the others. Addressing themselves to more than practical considerations, they seemed to be genuinely inspired by the historical uniqueness of the experience open to them, to launch a new civilization on a large scale. In final outcome, they proved equal to the challenge of planning republican government, and they could only have become so because they tried to understand not only the buried sources of power, but the moral objectives of good government. In a sense they were, as Hamilton once contemptuously declared, "speculative" thinkers and "empirics." Even Hamilton belonged to the company he criticized, for he, with the others, assessed what he already found in existence as social habit and political tradition; he built upon that which was already

146

"given," and recommended, according to his lights, the best direction of change.

Jefferson, the greatest of them all, was conspicuously devoted to the theory and practice of good government. Further, he was actively critical of his own methods of establishing political judgments, and he was intellectually prepared to examine the logical, philosophical, scientific, or sentimental elements in his views of society. He learned to style himself an "ideologist," identifying himself with his friends the French philosophers, who had founded a school of thought known as "Ideology" in the Napoleonic period. Hamilton, Madison, and Adams as well as Jefferson contributed characteristic ways of thought, individual tempers of belief which were to be important not only in the era of the Republic but for America thenceforth. The principles of the four philosopher-statesmen taken together almost define the range of our national ideology—our objectives, our character as a people, our economic and social patterns, our "Americanism."

The challenge of creating a new form of government gave rise to an atmosphere of intellectual adventure, in which the Platonic vision of the philosopher-king could for one brief period take on American reality. "Until philosophers take to government, or those who now govern become philosophers," Plato had boldly written, "so that government and philosophy unite, there will be no end to the miseries of states." In the timeless analogy of the cave in the *Republic,* the philosophers who struggle to free themselves from the chains of ignorance and superstition make their way to the light outside. They see the truth. Loving its clarity, they would bask in its light. But the thought of the chained multitude below gives them no rest, and they understand, as Platonic seekers of truth must, that they cannot fail to carry glimmerings of light to the poorer minds who inhabit the cave.

The four great philosopher-statesmen of the American "Enlightenment" conform admirably to the Platonic pattern. They grope in authentic Platonic fashion for the true principles of social order, accepting the responsibility of administering the affairs of their less farsighted fellow men; yet they reject the Platonic ideal as an explicit inspiration. They are willing to exemplify it if they must; but justify it, direct from its ancient source, never. Plato, even for Jefferson who had the most developed philosophic predilections of the group, was too full of metaphysical flights and trances to prove sympathetic to the common-sense orientation of the new nation. Yet the double drive of philosophy and leadership, thought and action, vision and its fortifying concrete detail is heeded by Jefferson, Madison, Adams, and even Hamilton. From the time of Franklin to the present this double drive, common to all humanity but intensified by life in a new continent, has dictated a double destiny for the American nation and a dualistic orientation for its literature. In the great period of American political literature, both forces were present without fatal conflict, and lend a peculiar divided charm and predictive importance to this body of writing.

2

In its literary guise, the issue faced by the philosopher-statesmen was the reconciliation of potent ideas with traditions of style formalized by eighteenth century English writers and imitated by our early writers of fiction, essay, and poetry. The methods of belles-lettres were inadequate to the urgent demand for clear and effective expression. These public-minded men wrote their state papers, their reports, their tracts, and their letters with some care for the form as well as the content, but they subordinated the formal demands of art to the immediate need for communication. John Adams, who was himself a tyro in the "literary" essay, had made it all too plain: "substance" was to take precedence over "elegance." He had written: "The simplest style, the most mathematical precision of words and ideas, is best adapted to discover truth and to convey it to others, in reasoning on this subject [politics]." That Adams himself, who once boasted that he had never had "time" to compress his written pieces nor to prune them of repetitions, did not always live up to the severe criteria of clarity and communicability he invoked, in no way affects the importance of the ideal. Amusingly enough, some of Adams' most notorious departures from this standard produced his best prose, the nervous and animated passages so eloquent with his erratic brilliance. Jefferson and Madison never quite forsook the rounded and urbane prose line which by now seems characteristic of the Virginia political dynasty with the notable exception of George Washington, who strove, not always successfully, to restrict himself to a "plain stile." Yet even the Virginians never hesitated to put communication and content above consideration of style or form. Madison, ever judicious and temperate, best conformed to the utilitarian ideal. In criticizing a political pamphlet, he commented that it would have been "much improved by softer words and harder arguments," and he found the style attractive in that it had "the artless neatness always pleasing to the purest tastes." Hamilton, in the calculated fixity of his desire to convince, to silence the opposition by a brilliant show of fire before an enemy gun could shoot, did not hesitate to employ rhetorical ornament and insistent, obvious rhythm. Although he too agreed that "our communications should be calm, reasoning, serious, showing steady resolution more than feeling, having force in the idea rather than in the expression," he often lapsed into purple passages whose melodramatic tones are as trying as they are insincere.

Throughout, the unorthodoxy of this political literature is a consequence of the fact that these statesmen were primarily devoted to the issues and principles growing out of a serious national undertaking. The motivation of interest seems to have been so compelling that communications tended to become direct colloquial exchanges, discussions of ideas, selfless presentation of the "argument" without stopping for artifice or formal discipline. For this reason it is a great pity that the most often quoted of their political "classics" have tended to come from the public documents and official papers of the nation's archives, rather than from the enormous correspondence which more truly characterizes this age of statesmen. This correspondence, in fact, should be the mainstay of our knowledge of the political thought and of the social continuum of the early Republic. In a sense, its excellence may be regarded as the nation's unearned reward for having once lived in an age with inadequate media of communication. It is hardly an exaggeration to say that there is no Jefferson, no Adams, and no Madison without the body of letters they left. To understand Hamilton and Madison, notes for their speeches in the Constitutional Convention and elsewhere must be added to the justly famous papers they separately contributed to *The Federalist* (1787–1788).

All the statesmen had been trained in Congress or had read deeply in the law. None in the country knew better than they the amount of power that could be borrowed from the logical ordering of material, the legal-rhetorical habit of defining terms. A truly impressive endurance also marks the longer writings of Jefferson and his colleagues, as they patiently investigate detailed charges and sternly cleave to the political issues under discussion. Their writing is suffused with a kind of lofty passion born of the consciousness of the cosmic importance of the "infant nation" with which they identified themselves so intimately. What a terrible disaster it would be, they seem to say, if the "ark, bearing as we have flattered ourselves the happiness of our country & the hope of the world" (Madison's phrase), should be shipwrecked! It is not surprising that an earnestness of moral tone is the keynote of this literature which in general is neither original in metaphor nor polished in style.

On occasions, the utilitarian limitations upon expression are conceived of as a moral question, intimately related to the simple and severe needs of republican society. Jefferson, gentle lover of the fine arts, was keenly aware that America differed from Europe in being not yet ready for the highest and most cultivated art-forms. His journals of travel through Italy and France conscientiously record technical improvements in agriculture and contain long passages on how to make wines and cheese. This attitude is at war, all through Jefferson's varied European sojourn, with such projects as the adaptation of Palladio's Villa Rotunda to his plan for the second Monticello and his general enthusiasm for the ancients in literary form and moral leadership, and to the highest expression of what was then "modern" music, painting, "beauty" in general. John Adams, prone to state reasons for his actions, epitomized the stage of American literary and artistic needs by declaring:

It is not indeed the fine arts which our country requires; the useful, the mechanic arts are those which we have occasion for in a young country as yet simple and not far advanced in luxury, although perhaps much too far for her age and character. . . . The science of government is my duty to study, more than all other sciences. . . . I must study politics and war, that my sons may have liberty to study mathematics and philosophy, geography, natural history and naval architecture, navigation, commerce, and agriculture, in order to give their children a right to study painting, poetry, music, architecture, statuary, tapestry, and porcelain.

Jefferson had clearly announced that in "a republic nation, whose citizens are to be led by reason and persuasion, and not by force, the art of reasoning becomes of first importance," and had recommended the speeches of Livy, Sallust, and Tacitus as "pre-eminent specimens of logic, taste and that sententious brevity which, using not a word to spare, leaves not a moment for inattention to the hearer." Amplification, he thought, was the "vice of modern oratory," and he avoided speech-making when he could. But it was Jefferson who developed that flowing and "felicitous" line for which John Adams, the Continental Congresses, and all America since came to know him—the rhythmic yet thoughtful line that moves unchecked in our most famous public *Declaration,* in our early official papers and documents, and in that remarkable corpus of Jefferson letters with which no subsequent political correspondence can compete.

Madison we have noted as the advocate of the tightened composition of logical demonstration. He felt that the "only effectual precaution against fruitless and endless discussion" was the definition of our political terms. Hamilton nursed a notorious and constitutional fear that republican government would not weather the storm; but in his *Federalist* essays, when he was promoting the cause of the new constitution, he shared the general excitement over political innovation.

The people of this country, by their conduct and example [he wrote], will decide the important question, whether societies of men are really capable or not of establishing good government from reflection and choice, or whether they are forever destined to depend for their political constitutions on accident and force.

Adams, paternal watchdog of his beloved New England, had further called attention to the specific virtues found in the self-government local to his region. These virtues he kept in mind from his early directives on government in his influential letters, "Thoughts on Government" (1776), to his last review of the revised constitution of Massachusetts, half a century later. Madison added to his theoretical contribution a practical demonstration of superior journalism in the unique service he performed by reporting the Constitutional Convention. Demonstrating selfless honesty, patience, and comprehension, he early set a high standard for American political reporting. Thus, in different ways, the statesmen of the American Republic demonstrated their sense of a supreme political mission, and it was this dominant aim of constructing a government compatible with freedom which gave unity to their writing— not in the sense of formal arrangement or style, but in the homogeneous conviction which flowed from their dedication to political ends.

The very issue of English versus American idiom adds the final touch to the thesis that there was a separate quality in American political writing as early as the formative years of the new Republic. The British critics who mocked American writing for forsaking "purity" of standard English form and style were met with singular equanimity. Jefferson, for example, whose use of the word "belittle" in *Notes on Virginia* (1784) had been the occasion for reproof by the *Edinburgh Review,* was unperturbed. Languages, he explained, had always grown by innovation. They fattened on flexible adaptation and change. Who would expect a vast new American nation, with its very different regions, to bind itself in an iron cask of ready-made English speech and prose? No, "neology" must clearly replace purism, since the price of purism was stagnation.

Had the preposterous idea of fixing the language been adopted by our Saxon ancestors, of Peirce Plowman, of Chaucer, of Spenser, the progress of ideas must have stopped with that of the language . . . what do we not owe to Shakespeare for the enrichment of the language, by his free and magical creation of words? [To be sure] uncouth words will sometimes be offered; but the public will judge them, and receive or reject, as sense or sound shall suggest.

No matter how often the debates in Congress, or the individual statesmen in writing, might call upon the eloquent models of antiquity; no matter how much the balanced sentence of the English essayists, Addison and Steele, or the English political theorists of the seventeenth and eighteenth centuries might be copied—a sense of the American scene in all its heady potentialities was so strong in the minds of these architects of the Republic that they could scarcely avoid giving direct expression to nascent American culture. In the authentic idiom of American thought and speech the statesmen of the greatest experimental democracy in history put pen to paper.

3

The ideology of American democracy began its career with a set of political principles termed "Republican." Although John Adams was quick to
warn of the shifting meanings of "Republic," the term became a fixed pole of
reference in American political theory, directly contraposing that other pole,
Monarchy, against which the Revolution had been waged. Adams himself
believed in republican doctrine and, like the other political leaders of his day,
made standard references to the ancient republics as the historical alternative
to monarchy and to feudal hierarchic society. Almost everyone in early
America agreed on the minimal connotation of the term, either explicitly or
by implication. Like late eighteenth century philosophers elsewhere, they understood that a republic was a government which derived its power from the
people "originally," referred back to the people for an ultimate court of
appeal in "crucial" questions transcending the ordinary affairs of legislation,
and exercised its granted powers through representatives chosen by a
majority of the voting citizens. In theory, at least, these voting citizens were
further supposed to represent the "will of the people"; and, while they confided specific powers to their representatives, it was understood that a republic
was essentially a government of laws rather than of men.

Were one to try to locate the maximum adherence to this republican ideal,
one could project an imaginary political line with the left terminal point
designating "maximum faith" and the right terminal point "minimum
faith." We should then have to place Jefferson at the left and Hamilton at the
right. John Adams accordingly must occupy the middle ground, to the left
of Hamilton and the right of Jefferson; but he is also to the right of Madison,
who is closer to Jefferson on most fundamental political matters—although
it is important to note that Madison is sometimes closer than either Adams or
Jefferson to Hamilton in economic questions.

Had Jefferson written no more than the initial draft of the *Declaration of
Independence* he would probably have earned his place on the radical left of
our American political line. The achievement of the *Declaration,* if it proves
nothing else, certainly establishes its author's title to the greatest pen in the
patriotic cause. Certain contemporaries, either through faulty judgment or
through jealousy of his ability to fashion a line of fundamental national
policy that could sing itself into the country's ears, challenged the author on
the score of "originality." Madison was incensed, for he knew that it was
absurd to cavil thus.

The object [he protested] was to assert not to discover truths, and to make
them the basis of the Revolutionary Act. The merit of the Draught could only

consist in a lucid communication of human Rights, a condensed enumeration of the reasons for such an exercise of them, and in a style and tone appropriate to the great occasion, and to the spirit of the American people.

But if the content of the *Declaration* alone is not enough, Jefferson is established in his preeminence on the left by his *Notes on the State of Virginia* (1784), the first American book to become an accidental "expatriate," published in England and France in pirated versions before it reached print in the country of its origin. This series of informal essays ranges far and wide over disputed questions in philosophy, science, politics, and morals, and is the natural discourse of a born humanistic rationalist. Proud of his friend's prowess as a thinker, Madison once observed that Jefferson was "greatly eminent for the comprehensiveness and fertility of his genius, for the vast extent and rich variety of his acquirements; and particularly distinguished by the philosophic impress left on every subject which he touched." And then, as if the *Notes* had come to mind, Madison hastened to add: "Nor was he less distinguished from an early and uniform devotion to the cause of liberty, and systematic preference of a form of Government squared in the strictest degree to the equal rights of man."

Although Madison had been a friend, follower, and co-worker of Jefferson's for many years when he wrote this tribute, it is notable that in all the advancing and receding waves of historical interpretation the residual significance of Jefferson's contribution to the American tradition has grown rather than diminished. Of American Presidents, this statesman of the "Enlightenment" most closely approximates the Platonic philosopher-king. No other incumbent of the Presidency, and no other of the liberal philosophic spirits of his age—many-sided men like Franklin, Benjamin Rush, and Thomas Cooper—could match Jefferson's happy union of learning, independence, and competent judgment in diverse fields such as social morality, government, education, natural science, agriculture, and the arts. What Washington began to do for the American personality by example and by the sheer weight of personal decency and leadership, Jefferson molded into an intellectualized ideal of social order. The entire development of American affairs, as the definition of our national ideology, is consequently more indebted to Jefferson than it is to any other single man.

This is not to say that Jefferson was an illustration of that cliché, the crusader of eighteenth century enlightenment who preached the gross "goodness" of man and the inevitable rational progress of society. Jefferson, who never wearied of reading history—he knew excellently the classical and the best of modern historians—had come to recognize the hazards of evil in human as in social affairs. He had so acute an awareness of the consequences of entrenching evil men in public positions that he concluded no society would be safe without an informed, alert citizenry participating actively in government. Devoted to human possibilities of growth, he outdistanced the faith of the other philosopher-statesmen—although Madison and Adams both had their areas of hope and solid, if less generous, funds of good will. Another way of viewing the difference between Jefferson and all others is to recognize his philosophy of education for what it was—a conscious "ideological" program to create right-thinking, tolerant citizens whose management of local affairs would be but a neighborly orientation for their wise judgment and activity in the affairs of the Union. It was a program fitted to practical needs and political responsibilities, and yet attuned to the highest cultivation of the arts, the sciences, and belles-lettres.

If it was Jefferson who recommended the fullest participation in political control, just as he sustained the greatest confidence in the educability of the American people, it was Hamilton who had most concern for government as a force, who saw little to worry about in its suppressive intrusions upon local or personal rights. It must be understood that the whole of the political line ranging from Jefferson to Madison to Adams and to Hamilton operated within realistic limits. Each statesman feared different contingencies, each phrased his hopes in typical or unique terms, each seized upon symbols of approbation or aversion sympathetic to his own personality and to the range of his ideational life. One might almost conclude: therefore, the republic was made possible—through the very variety and divergence of the founders' visions, ideas, and wishes.

Hamilton, for instance, saw very clearly the vast economic potentialities of America if the government would ally itself with the possessors of large fortunes and legislate in the direction of the expansion of financial and commercial activities. In the "people" Hamilton held virtually no stock. He thought they might listen to a debate and repeat with fair accuracy another man's line of argument, but were by and large susceptible to the flatteries and the manipulations of natural politicians. When left to his own selfish and irrational devices, the "great beast" might actually retard the productive energy of the nation, rather than build it up.

It was some time after Hamilton's memorable project of the *Federalist* (1787-1788)—that lucid exposition of constitutional republican government, not always consistent in its internal logic, but always impressive in its powerful defense of the need for national unity—that he began to voice his gloomiest thoughts about the survival of the republican experiment in self-government. "It is yet to be determined by experience whether it be consistent with that stability and order in government which are essential to public strength and private security and happiness," he wrote in 1792, having already tasted the strength of Jefferson's principled opposition. He seemed eager to give voice to his fear that republicanism might not "justify itself by its fruits." His progress Tory-wise, away from what he had called "the fair fabric of republicanism . . . modelled and decorated by the hand of federalism," was complete. In this shortsightedness Hamilton showed himself less of a philosopher and less of a statesman than one would desire. Were it not for the towering importance of certain of his administrative and governmental principles, his temperament and the transparency of his self-interest would hardly qualify him as a philosopher-statesman. But there is great penetration in his theory that the extension of national prerogative is indispensable for achieving internal uniformity and efficiency in a genuinely "central" government. And there is undeniable truth in his perception that this is the first essential of defense against foreign powers. Another realistic principle of capitalist development appreciated by Hamilton early in the nation's life was that it was a direct obligation of the government to foster the development of the productive resources and activities of the nation—by whatever combination of interests might prove effective. The first of these principles figures in Hamilton's masterful *First Report on the Public Credit* (1790), when he unhesitatingly decides, "If the voice of humanity pleads more loudly in favor of some [classes of creditors] than of others, the voice of policy, no less than of justice, pleads in favor of all." The second principle is the key argument of his classical treatise on protectionism, the *Report on Manufactures* (1791).

By a peculiar concentration of interest, Hamilton attained a definiteness in the body of his belief which sounds surprisingly modern in tone. Read today, his justification of strong, efficient government comes close to a native American defense of totalitarian political management. But, clever though his analysis was, it did not succeed in reconciling the two inseparable demands of prospering republicanism: national power, exercised to the full by an unimpeded, energetic central administration, and mature responsibility vested in the people of a free society.

The conservatism and legalism of John Adams and Madison explain almost as much about the success of the American Republic as they do about the absence of their names from most of the emotional appraisals of the early American tradition. Adams was a testy man, given to incalculable fits of temper that could shake his soul and harden his behavior to the utmost expression of stubbornness. Madison was naturally prudent, neither commanding in person nor captivating in his imaginative vistas. He did not permit himself the occasional exaggerations of the genius which he himself detected in Jefferson, while Adams, unlike Hamilton, kept steadily in view his high duty to guard the national interest and subordinate his own political welfare to the paramount needs of the American Republic. Adams was therefore saved from the extravagances of Hamiltonian ambition. Since the "mean," in politics, is not golden—not, at any rate, in the "memory of the race"—both Adams, the unorthodox Federalist, and Madison, the conservative Republican, paid the political price of hewing to the Aristotelian middle. Without Adams, the preservation of the dignified ideal of lawful, responsible government and a great example of Bolingbroke's ideal "Patriot King" who comes to guard like an "angel" the destiny and the long-range interests of his country might not have been realized. Without Madison, the amelioration of factional (including "class") strife would not so early have been made a governmental objective; nor would the allocation of sovereign power in the federal and in state contexts have found so subtle an expositor.

The surety of republican foundations, one might say, depended upon the Jeffersonian "left," with its key insights that the preservation of individual freedom and the moral development of cooperative society were the ultimate objectives of free society. It depended upon the Hamiltonian "right" with its knowledge that governments need effective organization and the power which comes from having the substantial productive and financial forces in the nation solidly united behind the administration. The stability of the Republic and its true course depended much upon the labors of Madison, with his realistic conviction that the main purpose of a government is the protection of the many and diverse economic interests into which every country is divided—and with his belief that this protection can be accomplished through a limited, federal republic capable of preventing the monopolistic dictation of one faction or combine over the people of the nation. The experienced conclusion of the elder Adams, that republicanism would not dispel the disparities of wealth and station and their attendant aristocracies, was a grave note of warning. When Adams added that the chief function of wise governors would be to protect the separate but "balanced" powers delegated to them, by compact with the people, and thus prevent tyranny, chaos, or the anarchy of the impassioned mob, he further safeguarded the Republic from what the ancients had been pleased to characterize as the "inevitable" degeneration of the good society.

The main task of republican government, in the long view of John Adams, appeared to be the prevention of excessive power in the hands of any one group. Believing that "vice and folly are so interwoven in all human affairs that they could not, possibly, be wholly separated from them without tearing and rending the whole system of human nature and state," Adams had to put his trust in the rare statesmanlike leaders who would possess wisdom to formulate just laws, and discipline to abide by them. Adams thought the network of checks and balances would defeat the ambitious and power-hungry few who might design to capture government for their private ends, and would insure fair representation of the interests of every region in the nation, thereby allowing the propertied and "responsible" citizens who were the mainstay of each region a voice in governmental affairs. By these devices, he thought he could make the most of fallible human nature. A republic, devoted to the interests of the people and operating through their own representatives, should be the outcome of these precautionary mechanisms. Adams accordingly thought his own republicanism as firm as that of anyone, including the leader of the Republican party, his good friend and occasional enemy, Thomas Jefferson, who, in Adams' opinion, differed from himself only in that he was for "liberty and straight hair. I thought curled hair was as republican as straight."

Madison's starting point was less psychological and more sociological. It began with the observed differences in group interests, differences which he took to calling "factions." Factions for Madison were special-interest groups arising out of the fundamental conflict present in every society between those who are rich and maintain their riches, and those who are poor and struggle to relieve their condition.

All civilized societies are divided into different interests and factions [he wrote in the crucial year 1787], as they happen to be creditors or debtors—rich or poor— husbandmen, merchants or manufacturers—members of different religious sects— followers of different political leaders—inhabitants of different districts—owners of different kinds of property, etc.

The advantage of modern republicanism over other governments Madison expected to find in its ability to impede the full force of factional combinations, preventing them from controlling the state, and from usurping the rights of one or more minorities. Madison as a Virginian feared the added danger that the majority (the North) might suppress the rights of the minority (the South), and contended in a letter to Jefferson:

Where the real power in a government lies, there is the danger of oppression. In our Governments the real power lies in the majority of the Community, and the invasion of private rights is chiefly to be apprehended, not from acts of Government contrary to the sense of its constituents, but from acts in which the Government is the mere instrument of the major number of the constituents.

Madison thus called to the attention of all men the inflexible requirement that democracies protect the civil rights of minorities from the real or reported "will" of the majority.

Madison and Adams made more of property rights than Jefferson did, but neither of them deserted the democratic theories of natural rights, popular sovereignty, limited government, antimonarchism, and antiaristocracy. Nor did the two conservatives ever approach Hamilton's justification of plutocracy. Both Adams and Madison inclined to the ideal of a republic which was economically agrarian at base, but supplemented by mercantile and manufacturing interests. Madison perhaps a little more than Adams realized the vital role of credit and of government-financed expansion of the country's natural resources and communications—the role which John Adams' son, John Quincy Adams, was to develop fully in his program of "Internal Improvement." Theoretically, therefore, it was Hamilton, of doubtful birth, who thought most exclusively of the moneyed interests of the country, partly because he saw in them the source of national strength, while Jefferson, graceful and learned "landed squire," cared most deeply about the widespread independent well-being of the "people," farmers and laborers included. Adams and Madison, aristocratic in taste in the typical styles of Massachusetts and Virginia, but far from dazzling in the family fortunes to which they were born, were actively promoting a scheme of society favorable to widespread middle-class prosperity and power.

4

The ethical theories of these men had pronounced influence upon the political and economic views they maintained. As character is the inner side of habit in the individual, so in society its outward crystallized structure is government. Save for these four philosopher-statesmen of the Republic, the American character might never have been given more than haphazard or perfunctory significance. Jefferson, Madison, and John Adams all understood the importance of character for those who would be leaders in a republic, and Hamilton sometimes did but sometimes paid only lip service to the ideal. Jefferson and Madison and Adams advocated that "the purest and noblest characters" (Madison's phrase) should serve as the people's representatives, since they alone would do so from the "proper motives." Because these men dedicated themselves to the cause of their country before they consulted their immediate personal needs, the inceptive principles of the American republic betoken seekers of truth and wisdom, and good citizens in the Roman sense, rather than mere men of office.

Jefferson, perceiving that government was necessary for the release of man's fullest potentialities, liked to speak of it as of secondary or instrumental value—a habit which was later perversely construed to mean that government was evil. The range of realistic political choice for Jefferson lay entirely between repressive government and republicanism, and he identified the essence of republicanism as "action by the citizens in person in affairs within their reach and competence, and in all others by representatives, chosen immediately, and removable by themselves." For this reason, a republic was the "only form of government that is not eternally at open or secret war with the rights of mankind." To achieve republican freedom, citizens must pay a price, the wakefulness of "eternal vigilance," and therefore a citizenry trained in the principles of government, an educated citizenry, is the indispensable support of freedom.

Thus, subtly and indirectly, a moral climate had been postulated for the America in which republicanism was to be tried. Benevolence and moral sense, self-created will rather than coercive force, are the dynamic daily agents in free society as well as the purely theoretical factors of its ethics. "Natural" moralism is opposed to the reputed "natural" rule of force, which Jefferson saw as the breeder of authoritarian society, whether of "kings, hereditary nobles, and priests" or, in the language of a later day, of leaders, demagogues, and commissars. Jefferson's agrarianism, so often made the catchword for his variety of democracy, is in reality a by-product of an almost sentimental preference for the simplicity of classical republicanism joined to the supposed purity of "primitive" Christianity. Yet when Jefferson realized that the evolution of his nation demanded the self-sufficiency and expansion of her manufacture and trade—when he perceived that free society would be jeopardized if it were unable to defend itself on the high seas—he protested that "he . . . who is now against domestic manufacture, must be for reducing us either to dependence . . . or to be clothed in skins, and to live like wild beasts in dens and caverns. I am not one of these; experience has taught me that manufactures are now as necessary to our independence as to our comfort." Despite this, Jefferson's instinctive trust reposed in the fair and free interchange of nation with nation, as in citizen with citizen—which is to say that he was a man of peace, conceiving productive society basically as a peaceful society, an earnest judgment in which he was fully joined by James Madison.

Economically and politically, to Hamilton's expert eye, the softer fringe of social morality was not a subject for enthusiasm nor even for belief. "The seeds of war are sown thickly in the human breast," Hamilton had written, and the rivalry that precipitated wars, in his view, stemmed partly from "the temper of societies," and partly from the human disposition to "prefer partial to general interest." Coming to terms with self-interested reality was accordingly Hamilton's basic preoccupation, whether that "reality" meant strong armies and navies for defense against foreign powers, or a strong system of national credit. His ultimate separation of himself from his idealistic associates, whom he termed "political empirics," finds expression in an important unfinished paper called "Defence of the Funding System" (about 1795), where he identifies the "true" politician as one who "takes human nature (and human society its aggregate) as he finds it, a compound of good and ill qualities, of good and ill tendencies, endued with powers and actuated by passions and propensities which blend enjoyment with suffering and make the causes of welfare the causes of misfortune." Afraid to warp this fundamental human complex by urging a happiness not suited to it, the true politician supposedly aims at the social measures designed to "make men happy according to their natural bent, which multiply the sources of individual enjoyment and increase national resources and strength." The great objective of the statesman should thus be to find the cement for compounding diverse elements of a state into a "rock" of national strength.

Governments would not need to be afraid to take power, Hamilton believed, could they strip themselves of false attitudes of modesty. In the logic of economic stability and national expansion, of credit and appropriations and "sound policy" versus the misguided pleadings of "common humanity," Hamilton saw an unanswerable imperative: to wit, that the "sacred" right of property must be defended by the laws and by the constitutions of the land, and that even the non-propertied groups in the community should protect property rights lest the "general principles of public order" be subverted.

John Adams, the self-styled "John Yankee" who could not bear to kowtow to "John Bull"—nor for that matter to any foreign power—seems more at home in Jefferson's and Madison's company than he is with Hamilton, the "boss" of his own party. Without Adams, the democratic precedent of the New England meeting hall, the training green, and the system of self-support for local schools, churches, and cultural institutions might have spoken only with muffled voice in the American tradition. The political "virtues" of Massachusetts even Jefferson commended, pointing to that state as the best exponent of the theme that knowledge is power. In Adams' championship of New England there is a nucleus of national pride useful and perhaps necessary to a rising nation. To this Adams personally added the dignified appeal that, however much republican government consisted of equal laws justly administered, it further required consistent benevolence and encouragement for the arts and sciences. Almost a humanist but never quite freed of a Puritan sense of guilt and sin, Adams privately reveled in the classics just as Jefferson did. The late correspondence which flourished between the two aged statesmen as they enacted the roles of sages in retirement, with great éclat, is a phenomenon of tireless learning and peppery jest, joined in a correspondence the like of which is not known in the annals of American statesmen.

5

Such were the philosopher-kings of the American Enlightenment. However often they may have erred—in description, in prognosis, in emphasis, and sometimes in behavior as statesmen—they seem to have possessed that rare wisdom about human and political affairs which never quite exhausts its power to suggest. On occasion, it restores its own original vitality and suffices to sanction an important change in national or international policy. We know that in the curious reversals of history, the truths of an age are likely to suffer sea change. As Lincoln pointed out, the maxim "All men are created equal," once thought a self-evident truth, is termed a "self-evident lie" once we have "grown fat, and lost all dread of being slaves ourselves." So it may be with the far-ranging insights and veridical principles of the philosopher-statesmen of the Republic. Since the advent of the Jacksonian age—a "calamitous" Presidency in Madison's prediction—the objectives of tempered democracy have been often ignored or ingeniously misinterpreted. As the letters and state papers of the Republican era again come under review, it is apparent that democratic ideology can still benefit by its own very articulate original. The foundation of our national literature is present here, in the practical literature of ideas, as well as in the imitative experiments of the deliberately "literary" work of the day.

13. POETS AND ESSAYISTS

THE writing of the pamphleteers and of the philosopher-statesmen thus frequently rose to the level of literature, but it did not satisfy the demand for a national expression in that first of the arts. Independence to be complete, declared the poet-politician Freneau and many another young man, must produce for America its own Miltons and Addisons and Swifts, its Popes and Goldsmiths and Wordsworths. The times that tried men's souls demanded iron purpose, tempered to the single task of creating the framework of a strong republic; but the coming of peace brought the need and the desire for fuller expression of the national "genius."

Here was a paradox: On the one hand, patriotism demanded a national literature; on the other, the urgency of events made its creation seem an idle and unworthy occupation. The difficulty, of course, lay in the sophistication of art developed by the English neo-classical writers and as yet unsuccessfully challenged by the romantics. The standards and forms for the epic, the pastoral, the novel, the essay, the comedy, the tragedy, which had evolved in the self-conscious literary atmosphere of eighteenth century London, could not easily be bent and stretched to contain the ideas and the experiences of the young republic; yet bent and stretched they must be if that republic were to have a literature of its own. Imitation of established or current literary modes contended therefore with the unruly spirit of nationalism during the first half-century of independence in an effort to create overnight an American literary tradition.

Young men all over the new nation fumbled for words to explain themselves and the busy tumult about them. None were more active than the group in Connecticut, known as the "Hartford Wits." But practical considerations often sprawled into the path of literature. John Trumbull would have liked nothing better than to be allowed to become a man of letters, an "American Swift," the sting of whose satire reminded contemporaries of their comic inadequacies. Couplets came easily to him. He liked the tone of Prior and Churchill, the quick cantankerousness of Pope. Such satirical pose allowed him to correct without seeming pontifical, to flick incisive little wounds into complacency and pretense:

> Were there no fools beneath the skies,
> What were the trick of being wise?

He could do this kind of thing rather better than he could write seriously in the mood of Milton or Gray, though the notebooks in which he experimented privately indicate that he did not easily convince himself of his own limitations. It was gratifying to be admired, as he was admired, to be compared publicly with Pope, applauded as equal to Samuel Butler and Jonathan Swift. But the young man was also a Trumbull, with reputation to maintain and his way to make in the world. Satire, even when good-naturedly modulated, hurt people, and people who were hurt turned in anger. Their humorless opposition made difficult, perhaps impossible, the road to judgeship and political renown which a sensible young man should follow.

The lesson was learned early, when Trumbull's sprightly, but corrective essays, first called "The Medler" (1769–1770) and then, less truculently, "The Correspondent" (1770–1773), led him into controversy. It was learned most pertinently when *The Progress of Dulness* (1773) landed him in the midst of distressingly public quarrels. Today the poem seems innocently amusing, well worth an evening's reading. There is good humor behind Trumbull's probings into the aspirations and hapless adventures of the dullard ministerial student Tom Brainless, of the fop Dick Hairbrain, and of the modish young belle Harriet Simper. Idiosyncrasies of manners, dress, and education, religious bigotries and reading habits are dissected with such impish skill that we chuckle as we remember similar small absurdities among our own neighbors. We recognize Tom, Dick, and Harriet as ancient literary types, long familiar in England, but livened by Trumbull's deft wit into characters whose foibles seem distinctively American. The author's contemporaries read more knowingly into the poem to discover local men or favorite local institutions impiously ridiculed, and they struck back at him viciously in print and with ominous threats of violence. He replied manfully, denying what he could of personal intention, but affirming the satirist's traditional responsibility to expose incompetence and dishonesty wherever he found them.

Such undignified public wrangling certainly could not be permitted to continue. Little was accomplished, except that a young man's career was jeopardized. Thus Trumbull learned to soften his stroke: his next, and most popular, satire, the Revolutionary *M'Fingal* (1776), was so cautious in ridicule both of Tory and of Patriot that it could be reprinted in London without apparently causing a ripple of comment. Perhaps Honorius, who ranted pompously at the town meeting with which the poem opens, was intended to represent John Adams, with whom at the time Trumbull was studying law; certainly no such satirical intention could be openly expressed. *M'Fingal* is effective burlesque of the bombastic oratory of the early Revolution; it is ironical in analysis of Tory argument, but is not pitched in a key calculated to incite vacillating men to action. Even in 1782 when Trumbull lengthened the poem, he reached his now more strongly patriotic climax only with the tar-and-feathering of Tory M'Fingal and the ignominious hoisting of his ally, the constable, to the "sublimest top" of a liberty pole. The verse is competent, objectively humorous, sometimes quotable:

> No man e'er felt the halter draw,
> With good opinion of the law.

Such moderation helps explain the enormous post-Revolutionary popularity of M'Fingal, which went through some thirty editions and was frequently quoted in political campaigns and school readers during the next half-century. Avoiding extremes, it became a well of good-tempered ridicule into which later countrymen of whatever political persuasion could dip for aptly phrased commentary on affairs of their own times. John Trumbull seems to have been little moved by the American Revolution: he viewed it dispassionately, not quite as a disinterested spectator, but as one who allowed himself neither shrill cries of triumph at patriot successes nor thunderous encouragement when victory seemed remote. M'Fingal is the least topical of Revolutionary satires, and the best worth reading. We may overlook its literary debts to Swift and Butler, accept its impertinent burlesque of Virgil and Milton, forget even the minor position to which it must be assigned in the history of the English mock-epic, and still enjoy what it has to say of our ancestors and, obliquely, of us.

Though by 1782 Trumbull had virtually abandoned literature for a more respectable career as a jurist, his influence remained pervasive among contemporaries in New England. As tutor at Yale until 1773, he had led friends and students to an examination and imitation of modern English authors—to Addison, Pope, and Milton. "I have learned more about English style from Jack Trumbull," said one of his students, "than from any other man." David Humphreys probably expressed the opinion of many of his Yale friends when he playfully blamed the "ill company" which he kept with Trumbull for having induced him to "turn scribbler." Trumbull's was a witty and intellectual leadership which appealed to young men. When he looked forward to the literary future of America in his Essay on the Uses and Advantages of the Fine Arts (1770), he struck a spark which glowed to fine imitative fire among his younger friends:

> This land her Steele and Addison shall view,
> The former glories equall'd by the new;
> Some future Shakespeare charm the rising age,
> And hold in magic charm the listening stage.

It was not for lack of trying that Trumbull's protégés failed. Literature to them was the hallmark of superiority, a method of instruction whereby men who knew the way pointed it clearly to their less fortunate fellows. Such a guide was David Humphreys, whose armload of solid volumes taught industry and patriotism and humble recognition of the wisdom of one's betters. Such, too, was Timothy Dwight, who grew to be one of America's giants, created in the image of his own honest ambition. One of Yale's great presidents, a teacher whose solidly authenticated theological doctrines spread through all the expanding young country from the close-written notebooks of his students, he became an oracle whose voice inspired no one so greatly as himself. People like his brother-in-law, William Dunlap of New York, who read William Godwin and wrote plays, found him narrow and censorious. They called him the "Protestant Pope of New England," but they squirmed under the confident vigor of his disapproval.

At nineteen Dwight conceived a poem, an epic of high moral purpose which would combine the sublimity of Milton and Fénelon with more modern notions of what a great poem should be. Its rhyme would be the heroic couplet of Pope's Homer. Its theme would be Biblical—Joshua's hard-won entry to the promised land. When fourteen years later *The Conquest of Canaan* (1785) appeared, readers had little trouble convincing themselves that patriotic analogy was intended, that Joshua was Washington, and that other American heroes strode thinly disguised through its eleven tedious books. "He who would learn," suggested William Cowper in England, "by what steps the Israelites possessed the promised land, must still seek his inspiration in the Bible." Another Englishman, Thomas Day, whose *Sandford and Merton* was a best seller on both sides of the Atlantic, defied "the most resolute reader to wade through" Dwight's poem "without yawning an hundred times." The elements so storm in sympathetic energy with the martial strivings of its heroes that Trumbull suggested it be provided with lightning rods. In it also, says the best and most sympathetic of Dwight's critics, stalwart eighteenth century Americans with Hebrew names talk like Milton's angels and fight like prehistoric Greeks.

After 1785 Timothy Dwight left literature almost as completely as did John Trumbull. His single subsequent trial at belles-lettres was a charming bucolic and didactic poem called *Greenfield Hill* (1794), which represents the landscape and the people of a small Connecticut village. The scene is perhaps less familiar to one who knows New England than to one with some acquaintance among the poets of England. Lines are so admittedly imitative of Beattie, Dyer, Gray, Goldsmith, Thomson, and Pope that any reader, if he pause at all over the poem, may simply hold in one hand a copy of, say, *The Deserted Village* and, with *Greenfield Hill* in the other, completely deflate Dwight as a creative artist. He was not essentially a creative artist:

he was a moralist, a powerful and successful teacher, a righter of great wrongs. With a practical job to do, he did it effectively by taking what he could where he could find it. Yet the America of his day, with his concurrence, accepted him as one of her principal men of letters. The fault was as much with America as with Dr. Dwight.

As a moralist, Dwight was most persuasive in his sermons, where he could undisguisedly correct to his own pattern. He is strongest in protest, as in *The Triumph of Infidelity* (1788) which attacks what Dwight interpreted as the influence of Voltaire in America. It is a bitter and a coarse poem, published anonymously and never, even in the face of public accusation, acknowledged by Dwight. As a clergyman, he was fond of talking of the "Duty of Americans," "The Genuineness and Authenticity of the New Testament," and "The Nature and Danger of Infidel Philosophy," and he simplified, explained, and defended his theology in a series of sermons delivered to many college generations at Yale. Outsiders found him an autocrat who talked so much they could get no word in themselves. He puttered every day in his garden for his health's sake, and he spent the long college holidays exploring byways of northeastern America. His wanderings are recorded—where he had been, what he had seen, what needed correction— in a journal which, published as *Travels in New-England and New-York* (1821–1822), preserves not only delightful pictures of countryside and people but also a candidly revealing self-portrait of its author.

Other men from Yale turned in other directions. Younger than Trumbull and Dwight, Joel Barlow grew in New England under the influence of both until search for livelihood took him to Europe. There, always impressionable, he found in new masters exciting new sources of enthusiasm. He was to move familiarly among the liberal political circles of Horne Tooke, William Godwin, and Joseph Priestley, to absorb the intoxicating doctrines which promised rights to all men. He would advise with Lafayette on the future of France, with William Hayley on the future of poetry, or with Mary Wollstonecraft on the future of women. Futures fascinated him, and he overflowed with optimistic good talk. His friends remembered him as "so far gone in Poetry, that there is no hope of reclaiming . . . him."

As one of the international gadflies attracted by the bright promise of the French Revolution, Barlow joined in the attack on Edmund Burke, until that stout-hearted statesman brushed him off contemptuously as "Joel the Prophet." His *The Conspiracy of Kings* (1792) unleashed a young man's best store of conventionally rhymed invective against the designs of scheming and undemocratic men. Less heatedly, his *Advice to the Privileged Orders* (1792) defended in prose the superior claim of human rights over property rights and sounded the revolutionary's traditional warning that a better day must dawn. Fox applauded the pamphlet in Commons, but the Pitt ministry ordered it burned and the author arrested. Thereafter, like his friend Paine, Barlow became a marked man, for people were attracted by his simple logic and paused to think—nothing seemed more dangerous. The French Assembly voted him an honorary Citizen of the Republic. But friends in New England were shocked: they wished there were some way to "relieve him of his enchanted castles"; Barlow's brains, they thought, needed settling. Sober Noah Webster could not understand what maggot gnawed at his old schoolmate. John Adams considered even Tom Paine "not a more worthless fellow."

Before this, as a young man at Yale, Barlow had also conceived an epic. He hurried it to completion as *The Vision of Columbus* (1787), in nine rhapsodic books which told of the past, but particularly of the future of the brave, new American world. A young man's poem, and choked with little of the pedantry of Dwight's epic, it nevertheless breaks down in spite of—or perhaps because of—its breathless verve and easy patriotism. Barlow had dashed off page after page at single sittings, and neither his imagination nor his control of verse was equal to the strain. Yet failure in poetical technique and confusion of thought never quite dull the *Vision's* assertive enthusiasm. Foreshadowings of Barlow's later and less restricted notions of human freedom are there, sufficiently submerged beneath conventionalities to allow his conservative friends to greet the poem with hosannas of loud praise. That more precise critics in England found it pretentious, as they found Dwight's epic pretentious, was unimportant; that critics in England noticed it at all was a sign of success.

Within a year after publication of the *Vision,* Barlow had left New England to become the apostate whose change of political coloration increasingly distressed old friends. He poured out his heart in long letters to his young wife, as he was to do every time they were separated during the next thirty years—in letters which Ruth Barlow faithfully preserved and which re-create today an idyl of married love which is, quite inadvertently, among the finest monuments of her husband's career. There is humor and playfulness in Joel Barlow, sincerity, and a great fund of often completely impractical idealism. Homesick for New England and corn-meal mush (though he detested the word), he composed the mock-epic *The Hasty Pudding* (1796), a completely American adaptation of an ancient gastro-literary theme, and a poem so admired by anthologists that it sometimes promises to be all that remains of Joel Barlow.

Barlow developed into one of the most cosmopolitan and useful Americans of his generation, Minister Resident to Algiers, Ambassador to France, adviser and confidential friend to Jefferson and Madison. He worked with

Fulton on the steamboat; thrilled to the promise of the age of canals. As he grew older his enthusiasms were more controlled, but he never lost them. Nor did he ever forget the epic which had not been exactly right as he first presented it. When he had mulled over it for twenty years, it was ready again, rewritten and expanded for second publication as *The Columbiad* (1807), and heralded by public fanfare such as no American book had received before. It was a beautiful volume, a credit to American printers and bookbinders, a collector's item enhanced by engravings from his friend Robert Fulton. It is better articulated than the *Vision,* more mature and more correct in versification; but *The Columbiad* is best known today as one of America's great failures, the book nobody reads, the tin-plated epic.

The tragedy of Joel Barlow is not that he is not remembered, but that he is remembered for the wrong thing. Every textbook pauses for a paragraph to review the epic failure of *The Vision of Columbus* and *The Columbiad*. Few remind us of the armor of bright prose with which this early American Lochinvar girded himself as he crusaded for doctrines which never quite spread from the new Western world. Like Timothy Dwight, Barlow was a greater man than his writings ever reveal him. Like too many others of his time he still awaits the biographer who will detail his sincere and wholehearted small contribution to the articulation of democratic thought.

These three—Trumbull, Dwight, and Barlow—are traditionally listed as outstanding among the larger group, variously called the Hartford Wits, the Yale Poets, or the Connecticut choir. There were others: Humphreys for the bulk of his earnestly patriotic verse is sometimes admitted as a fourth; Richard Alsop, Noah Webster, Lemuel Hopkins, Mason Cogswell, and Theodore Dwight, to list them in an arbitrary, rough order of excellence, were the principal remaining members—not to forget the younger Elihu Hubbard Smith, never completely of their company, who extracted from them generously when he edited our first all-American anthology in 1793. The aim of the Wits was chiefly political and remedial: in one combination or another they produced *The Anarchiad* (1786–1787), *The Echo* (1791–1805), *The Political Greenhouse* (1799), and other serviceable satires directed against the absurdity of anyone disagreeing with solid, New England views. Such barbs more often than not found tender marks and called for retaliation, until the acrimonious exchange produced some of the most readable, if not the most refined verse of those times. It was a rough-and-tumble battle of poets with shirt sleeves rolled, the effects of which lasted long enough for Fenimore Cooper half a century later to throw his weight in satire against the New Englanders, not realizing perhaps that another man of letters from the Middle States, Philip Freneau, had already done the job very well indeed.

2

"The writings of an aristocratic, speculating faction at Hartford, in favor of monarchy and titular distinctions," wrote Freneau, "are sufficient to convince any candid person that the old *insular* enemy to independence and prosperity in America has her hired emissaries at work in that part of the union." The Wits, he continued, openly profess the same principles as the "old, defunct Tories of 1775." His statement, of course, was not quite true, but the men of Connecticut had found in this hard-bitten veteran an opponent who could stand to them blow for blow. Freneau represented, as did the apostate Joel Barlow, the democratic principles of Jefferson, even of Thomas Paine. Therefore he was an enemy, subject to attack as a party tool and, in contrast to the epic poets of New England, a "mere writer for newspapers": by others far less original than he, he was ridiculed as an imitator, a plagiarist. Literature had so become the handmaiden of politics that, "amidst the mutual clamours of contending parties, not one reader in a thousand cares three cents about the literary honour of his country."

It was not, as James Madison said more pointedly, the time for poetry. Nor perhaps could it be expected to be. Men in leather aprons rose early to insure expansion of American commerce; hands toughened at the plow were raised in committee room or assembly; come-uppers were coming up, and there was no time for dallying. Literature was for ladies, for clergymen with leisure, or for young men who had not yet found more proper and productive work. But America had then among her young men one poet whose talent, caged within the utilitarian necessities of his times, was allowed frequently to beat itself to doggerel. Might-have-beens have no place in literary history, but the early promise of Philip Freneau, displayed in the Keatsian insight of "The Power of Fancy" (written in 1770) and the philosophic searching of "The House of Night" (written possibly in 1775), foretold achievement which could have placed him among our greater poets. Even thwarted, he developed the most original, though not consistently original, poetic voice of his generation. He sang of American men and American achievements, of his fine hope for America, and of the bitterness of his disappointment that she seemed so often to fail. He had none of the mellow inclusiveness of Walt Whitman, and he wrote more often in anger than in understanding, but not before Whitman was his country to produce a poet more completely or more devotedly her own.

As a young man at Princeton Freneau had also written prophetically of the future of his fair Western world. With his classmate Hugh Brackenridge he composed *A Poem on the Rising Glory of America* (1772) as a commencement piece which, like Trumbull's, looked forward to more than a march of material progress.

> I see a Homer and a Milton rise
> In all the pomp and majesty of song, . . .
> A second Pope, like that Arabian bird
> Of which no age can boast but one, may yet
> Awake the muse by Schuylkill's silent stream, . . .
> And Susquehanna's rocky stream unsung, . . .
> Shall yet remurmur to the magic sound
> Of song heroic.

This was not only a schoolboy's poem of optimistic augury. It was the personal dedication of a young poet, steeped in the lore of his calling. Freneau would be a poet, and he would sing a clear new song. Where are the glories of yesteryear? he asks in "The Pyramids of Egypt."

> —all, all are gone,
> And like the phantom snows of a May morning
> Left not a vestige to discover them!

Vast and unexplored, filled with promise such as the modern world had never known, America would be his theme, she and the opportunities she offered for fulfillment of the ideals of which great poets had always sung. An apprentice to the art of these, his masters, Freneau soon developed his own elastic lyric idiom which, avoiding much of the stereotyped pattern of his contemporaries, contained echoes of young Milton and promise of young Keats. Thus at eighteeen he invoked his muse in "The Power of Fancy":

> Wakeful, vagrant, restless things,
> Ever wandering on the wing,
> Who thy wondrous source can find,
> Fancy, regent of the mind; . . .
> Come, O come—perceiv'd by none,
> You and I will walk alone.

This was the kind of poetry for which busy America could make no room, and it was what Freneau most wanted to write. Nevertheless, when revolution broke over America, he dutifully put poetry behind him, though not without hesitation and false starts, to enlist his talent for rhyming in the shrill war of words which played accompaniment to military and political maneuverings. Mercurial, sensitive, quick to speak in anger, Freneau in his satire showed neither the moderation of John Trumbull nor the infectious good humor of Francis Hopkinson. He spat derisively at every enemy, whether among the faint-hearted in America or among the false-hearted abroad. He wrote jubilant songs on patriot victories, spurred laggard spirits when defeat seemed most certain, and denounced the "gorged monsters," "infernal miscreants," "foes to the rights of freedom and of man" who "spare no age, no sex from lust and murder." He became the authentic "Poet of the American Revolution," who wrote of what he had known at first hand as a militiaman, of what he had suffered in his poet's pride as a prisoner of war. With the memory of his experience hot within him, he wrote *The British Prison-Ship* (1781), as intensely bitter a poem as America has ever produced. He called on his countrymen to "glut revenge on this detested foe" which pants "to stain the world with gore." Banish them forever. "Defeat, destroy and sweep them from the land." Then only might America be free for, among other things, the kind of poetry which Freneau wanted most to write.

This hatred for England, bred of his war years, colored the rest of Freneau's life and his literary production. What had been America's crime, except that she had raised her arm to stay an assassin's knife? Pride, greed, lust, avarice, each cruelty which kept mankind in chains was exhibited by that same land from whose poets he had drawn his early poetic vision. As the Revolution dragged through its last weary phases, Freneau, now editor of the *Freeman's Journal* in Philadelphia, found it necessary to combat not only the foreign tyrant but new tyrannies of compromise with and imitation of England which appeared within his own country. Drawn ever deeper into petty quarrelings, he became increasingly disillusioned. How many fine sentiments were on people's lips, how few in their hearts! With what faint courage men of letters in America faced their future! He ridiculed David Humphreys who seemed sycophant in seeking literary honors, just as he later ridiculed Washington Irving for seeking reputation abroad. Would America ever be truly independent of England?

> Can we ever be thought to have learning or grace,
> Unless it be sent from that damnable place?

One of Freneau's unique characteristics was complete sincerity in meaning exactly what he said. His were no catchwords designed to rouse the rabble to defense of special privilege. He had learned to speak plainly, in simple idiom, of simple things which common men understand, about things like liberty and the right of every man to happiness. When, after ten years of patriotic satire, he retired from controversy in 1785 to become a sea captain plying between New York and Charleston, he avoided the grandiose schemes, the epic attempts which had attracted him as a collegian. He turned to simpler subjects, less traditionally poetic—to rugged, unpretentious themes like "The Virtue of Tobacco," "The Drunken Soldier," "The Pilot of Hatteras," "The Roguish Shoemaker," and, best loved of all, "The Jug of Rum." He wrote of "the red-nosed boy who deals out gin," "the quack that heals your negro's bruise," the ranting evangelist, native Americans all, "who did as they pleased and who spoke as they thought." No poem was very long, none very serious, and all were greatly popular among men who read their newspapers quickly.

Here was what America seemed to want, simple songs of American things, in stout American idiom, brightened with humor which recognizes even its own shortcomings. No moth-wing aspiration here for the sentimentalist, no learned claptrap for the intellectual. These were clearly stamped as of domestic origin, songs of and for the people. The pity is that the more finely wrought poems that Freneau produced during these busy years were unrecognized and virtually unread. In England Sir Walter Scott purloined a line from the elegiac stanzas "To the Memory of the Brave Americans" who fell at Eutaw Springs; Thomas Campbell took another from the contemplative "The Indian Burying Ground." But "The Wild Honey Suckle" (1786), which surpassed them all, was seldom reprinted during the poet's lifetime. The tone of muted wonder and the fresh clarity of diction which here consider the "frail duration" of beauty amid American swamplands place Freneau chronologically at the head of America's poets. Burnsian it is, and written in the year which greeted the Kilmarnock edition of the Scotch poet; Wordsworthian, too, and twelve years before *Lyrical Ballads*. America cannot afford to forget "The Wild Honey Suckle," for here at last were fused the two elements of native scene and native expression, and here, too, was poetry.

Moods productive of poetry were seldom allowed to Freneau again. When principles for which the American Revolution had been fought seemed threatened and democracy held in contempt among his countrymen, he emerged once more as a partisan propagandist who lashed out courageously, even boisterously, to defend rights of the common man, the poor soldier fleeced of his earnings, or the farmer crowded to poverty by greed of industrialists. Hard-headed and sharp-tongued, he became the first powerfully effective crusading newspaperman in America, and lost, as editor of the *National Gazette* (1791–1793), much of his reputation as a popular poet. Plain people still understood him as he reduced national issues to their own plain language, but men in power struck back with blows that left permanent marks. Alexander Hamilton wrote him down publicly as a liar. Washington damned him as a rascal. The Wits of New England, when they could not withstand the logic of his argument, attacked him as a poet. But he saved our Constitution, said Jefferson, when it was "galloping fast into monarchy." Few men have done more, and with less reward. When defeat of John Adams in 1800 made the place of the common man seem at length secure, Freneau retired again, to the sea, finally to a "few sandy acres" of homestead in New Jersey, to re-phrase, more quietly now, his tenacious convictions. He continued to publish volumes which sold poorly, or unnoticed verses in obscure periodicals, even after he was seventy; but America passed him by. Bryant remembered him only as "a writer of inferior verse . . . distinguished by a coarse strength of sarcasm."

Freneau's coarse strength can be better understood and better treasured today. His stubborn refusal to compromise seems even admirable, as he extended it to include "such rhyming dealers in romance" as Joel Barlow, who failed to forge their songs to the simple, democratic temper of America. As editor of the *Time-Piece, and Literary Companion* (1797-1798), Freneau had offered its columns for the display of poetical wares from his countrymen. And what had he received? Echoes of English verse, sentimental and sac-charine, as beaux and bluestockings parried traditional compliments, prettily phrased and insipid. Where was American virility, the solid, self-assertive strong phrases in which a new country should sing herself to the world? Nothing was more popular than the limpid lines with which young Joseph Brown Ladd, as "Aroeut," addressed his fair "Amanda," or which Robert Treat Paine as "Menander" exchanged in Boston with the "American Sappho," Sarah Wentworth Morton, known to each reader of sensibility as "Philenia," the "warbling eloquence" of whose harp stirred such polite, such sad and sweet response. The air was filled with melancholy strains inspired by Goethe's *The Sorrows of Young Werther,* with liquid rhapsodies distilled from Ossian, with inconsequential nonsense hung—so spoke one critic—with "garrish ornament and tinsel decoration, which are necessary to satisfy expec-tation." Against this background, Freneau's unpretentious work stands out, homespun among faded satins, durable, woven of native fiber to a pattern adapted to native requirements.

Like his verse, Freneau's prose became progressively more indigenous. During the Revolution he had been satisfied with that stock figure of the eighteenth century periodical essayist, the learned hermit who surveys the world from a quiet, woodland retreat. The voice with which "The Pilgrim" (1781-1782) pleaded for simplicity or railed against bestial servilities of Eng-lishmen was a deep-throated expression of Freneau's new-found national creed, but the words were old, and the mood and the setting. "Tomo-Cheeki, the Creek Indian in Philadelphia" (1795-1797), an unidealized American aborigine who found strange foibles among his white neighbors, represented an advance, but along trails already clearly marked by Goldsmith and Mon-tesquieu; "Hezekiah Salem" (1797), the defrocked Yankee deacon who spoke variously and sometimes amusingly in ridicule of domestic eccentricities, was more genuinely a home-grown product; but most American of all was "Robert Slender." As first presented in 1788, he was a stocking weaver who liked to record sly observations on such things as young men in love, the frustration of garret-pent poets, or the peculiarities of American businessmen; but he grew as Freneau grew until, when resurrected in 1800 to comment on the upheavals which brought Jefferson to power, he had become a native type whose literary and political descendants have been numerous among us. He was the simple country boy, who knew nothing of affairs except what he read in the newspapers. His rustic interpolations and naïve misgivings, his optimistic assurance that everything must come out right are in the best tradi- ton of American political burlesque.

Freneau's failure is most simply explained by his headstrong refusal to compromise his conception of a literature divorced completely from "that damnable place" which had threatened American liberties. He had few fol- lowers, no imitators, for he was not quite respectable. He was a radical who, even when right, went too far. He addressed the wrong people, and proper people scorned him. His strictures on the writings of contemporaries went unnoticed or were explained as grumblings of a disappointed man who prostituted his own talents to politics. His nativism thus became an under- current which was seldom to emerge during the next fifty years, and never in the pristine and unworkable state in which he conceived it. In person he was known as an opinionated gaffer, eccentric in insisting on smallclothes and cocked hat long after they were out of fashion. So also in poetry he refused the easy sentimentality which became popular in America. His stark and didactic idiom, founded on rational principles of human justice, seemed old- fashioned and harsh in the 1820's beside the smooth, more modern phrases of Fitz-Greene Halleck and Rodman Drake. His prose, for all its sturdy inde- pendence, was seasoned so strongly with reference to local events that it repelled all but the most expertly trained palates. Forgotten in his own time, too seldom remembered in ours, he left as his testimony:

> To write was my sad destiny,
> The worst of trades, we all agree.

This worst of trades attracted few experienced workmen. Almost every- thing presented as literature was apprentice work by young men who later in self-protection turned to other things. We read copybooks in which stu- dents painstakingly traced moods and themes in which other men had suc- ceeded. Scott, Byron, Moore, even Gray and the older poets were eagerly read in America: in what better manner might young men write if they too wished to be read? "Piddling poetasters," their practical countrymen called them, and this they were, swaying sensitively, as young poets must, to every breath of influence. They sang of solitude, of broken harps, and of genius—how they liked the word!—allowed to wither unrecognized. Theirs were juvenilia beside which Freneau's simplest "newspaper verse" seems extraordinarily mature.

3

Americans were proud of their newspapers. What other country on the face of the globe could boast a larger proportion of readers? This was America's literature—she had no time for more. Almost every newspaper or short-lived magazine had its poets' corner, and had also its essayists dressed in motley patched with shreds of Addison, Swift, Goldsmith, or Johnson. Noah Webster's homely "The Prompter" (1790) was popular and inspirational. Brockden Brown's "The Man at Home" (1798) contained the first draft of scene and incident later to find place in his novels. William Wirt's "Letters of the British Spy" (1803) was panoramic in literary learning. Each was corrective, some were pointedly satirical. Thomas Greene Fessenden was "Christopher Caustic"; New York had its "Tobey Tickler," Boston its "Tim Touchstone," and Philadelphia its "Tobey Scratch-'em," all lampooning with the conventionalized audacity of their English betters. Following them came the Irvings and James Kirke Paulding who in *Salmagundi* (1807–1808) simply did so much better what had often been done before.

Satire was condoned as a useful occupation, but polite literature was something quite different. William Wirt inquired of St. George Tucker whether being known as an author would harm his legal reputation and seemed not at all surprised at the older writer's answer that it very well might. At best, what sensible men liked to call "scribbling" was what they also liked to dismiss as "an avocation of idle hours," something almost surreptitious, certainly anonymous, for one dared not acknowledge many hours idle. Only a few hardy souls attempted literature as a livelihood; and they failed, like Freneau, and like Brockden Brown who capped his brilliant brief successes as a novelist with hack work little above that of an almanac maker.

Fresh from brilliant journalistic triumphs in New England, Joseph Dennie was also resolved to make writing a profession. He was equally resolved to create a standard for native literature in no degree inferior to that demanded in England. In fact, to this young Harvard man the standards were the same. His own prose rang so true that Timothy Dwight could claim him as the "Addison of the United States, the father of American belles lettres." Hawthorne recalled him as "once esteemed the finest writer in America," and Irving began his career in the contagion of Dennie's influence. It was as "Oliver Oldschool," a precise and opinionated champion of tradition, that he first edited the *Port Folio* (1801–1808) in Philadelphia, just as it was as

"The Lay Preacher" who restrained American folly that he had made his earlier reputation. Like Freneau, he was contemptuous of the sentimental and the extravagant: "a childish taste prevails and childish effusions are the vogue." Unlike Freneau, he refused even by implication to accept inferior products just because they were linsey-woolsey from homemade looms.

A critic rather than a creator, Dennie himself produced little that recommends him to our day. His essays seem prim, crotchety, sometimes sophomoric. His humor is condescending. His occasional easy familiarity is that of a well informed superior who stoops self-righteously to instruct. Above all else, however, he did love literature and had a sound, sure taste when his prejudices allowed him to exercise it. He printed long extracts from his favorite English authors. He solicited original verses from Thomas Campbell. He recognized and helped promote the early promise of Leigh Hunt. He was the first American critic to notice Wordsworth. He spent charming hours with Thomas Moore, who contributed to the *Port Folio* and remembered his visits with Dennie as among the "few agreeable moments" of his American tour. He gathered young men about him, and many a fine, literary talk they had together. "Mr. Dennie," said Moore, "has succeeded in diffusing through his cultivated little circle that love of good literature and sound politics which is so rarely characteristic of his countrymen."

Someone like Dennie was necessary to America—after him came the *North American Review* (1815) and the flowering of literary New England. He helped draw together, bind up, and package for many generations a conception of literary purpose irrevocably tied in with politics and respectability: authoritative sanction was given for lifting the literary embargo against England; standards were reimported and the level of excellence set high. He supplied an atmosphere in which Irving could grow to favor and Cooper to favor and disfavor, in which Freneau could be disregarded and Bryant hailed as a fresh, clear American voice; which made it possible for Longfellow to flourish, and necessary for Emerson to sweep aside the debris of tradition in clearing a path for Whitman.

Not everyone was convinced: "Dependence is a state of degradation, fraught with disgrace; and to be dependent on a foreign mind, for what we can ourselves produce, is to add to the crime of indolence, the weakness of stupidity." But, for all the protest of Freneau or anyone else, literary independence was as unrealized by 1820 as when Trumbull had called for it half a century before. After Campbell published *Gertrude of Wyoming* in England, Rodman Drake rephrased in the twenties the old complaint:

> No native bard the patriot harp hath ta'en,
> But left to minstrel of a foreign strand
> To sing the beauteous scenes of nature's lovliest land.

14. THE BEGINNINGS OF FICTION AND DRAMA

THE history of fiction and of the drama during this period runs parallel to that of poetry and the essay. Here too the impulse to produce an independent, indigenous literature vied with the natural tendency to carry on a distinguished European tradition.

The vogue of the novel, so pronounced in England during the latter half of the eighteenth century, was reflected in America by imported reading until about 1790. Then native authors began suddenly to write stories of their own in the three current British fashions: the sentimental (or domestic), the satirical, and the Gothic. The first to succeed was the sentimental. Its usual theme, seduction, not only permitted the discreet exploitation of thrills but lent itself to those moral lessons which made fiction acceptable. Thus William Hill Brown's *The Power of Sympathy* (1789), usually reckoned the first indubitably American novel, was designed "to represent the specious causes, and to expose the fatal consequences, of seduction . . . and to promote the economy of human life." This formal reassurance prefaces a story compounded of seduction, narrowly averted incest, abduction, rape, and suicide. The main plot tells of a young man who, upon learning that his sweetheart is really his half-sister (by a liaison), shoots himself—a copy of Goethe's *The Sorrows of Young Werther* lying on the table beside him. The secondary plot tells of an unprincipled Lothario who triumphs over the virtue of his wife's sister. The victim dies by taking poison. The diction employed by Brown is decorous to the point of obscurity, and the episodes are only obliquely described; but between the lines lie the very elements against which moralists were inveighing as likely to inflame the passions if not corrupt the heart. Still, the story was, as the title page made clear, "founded in truth." The secondary plot was so patently based on an actual case in contemporary Boston that Brown was prevailed upon to suppress his book.

Connecticut and New York soon received similar lessons—and thrills. Susanna Rowson's *Charlotte Temple* (London, 1791), one of the most popular novels ever written, relates the tragic experiences of a young English girl lured to New York on the promise of marriage, only to be abandoned there by her lover and to die in childbirth. Old-fashioned in its rhetoric, the story is nevertheless told with a sincerity and power that can be felt even today; and indeed the novel still sells. Like *The Power of Sympathy,* this narrative is based upon an actual history, that of Charlotte Stanley whose mortal remains (according to legend) lie in Trinity Churchyard under a tombstone now inscribed "Charlotte Temple." Whether as love story or as a moral emblem, *Charlotte Temple* has attracted millions of readers; it went through some 160 editions (many of them incredibly garbled) before 1860.

The Connecticut Valley also had its lurid fictional warning when Hannah Foster published *The Coquette* (1797). The novel closely followed the case of Elizabeth Whitman, daughter of a trustee of Yale College, who put her confidence unwisely in a "gentleman" speculatively identified by some as Aaron Burr and by others as Pierrepont Edwards, son of Jonathan Edwards. Her death in childbirth occurred at a tavern in Danvers, Massachusetts. In the novel the heroine (Eliza Wharton) is the victim partly of her own vanity and partly of the unscrupulousness of a glamorous military man. The narrative is quietly unfolded by means of letters, but the moral is inescapable, and Eliza's tragic end added to the mounting calendar of advice to young women.

All three of these novels are in the general stream of Richardsonian fiction in that they picture females in distress. Two of the three are told in letter form with a great deal of analysis of the "heart." All are at times heavily didactic in tone, but since the same lessons could have been conveyed by straight prose, it must be inferred that the authors preferred to be novelists rather than moralists. The quality of fiction they represent is not high. Settings are almost negligible, and dialogue sparse and generally inept. *Charlotte Temple* is the most touching as a story; *The Coquette* is the most finished as a novel; *The Power of Sympathy* is the most uncompromising as a tract.

2

The satirical novel was not so prolific as the sentimental, for its irony was disturbing to the Calvinistic mind, and its humor, often arising from sordid picaresque episodes, was objectionable. Yet the use of satire is one of the first signs of intellectual maturity, of the writer's consciousness of his art. Hugh Henry Brackenridge's *Modern Chivalry* may therefore be listed as among our more important achievements in the last decade of the eighteenth century. This massive work—as long as four or five average-length novels—was published in installments between 1792 and 1815. In outward form it is a picaresque or "rogue" novel; its intellectual core consists of a satire on bad government.

As a picaresque story *Modern Chivalry* contains many of the stock elements and devices of eighteenth century British fiction. Chief of these is the framework of roadside adventures experienced by a master and his servant— a parody, in effect, of Don Quixote and Sancho Panza. In *Modern Chivalry* the protagonist is a fifty-year-old Squire, Captain Farrago, who is described as a "peripatetic philosopher" engaged in a trip through Pennsylvania. His servant is the Irishman, Teague O'Regan, a blundering, conscienceless, irrepressible oaf who passes ingloriously from one ludicrous scrape to another, to be rescued and lectured (vainly) by his master on each occasion. Some of these scrapes are of a low order; on one occasion Teague tumbles into bed with a chambermaid, who resists his advances. When she screams for help, Teague manages, with what the author ironically calls presence of mind, to cast suspicion on a Presbyterian preacher. Urged to confess so that an innocent man should not suffer, Teague at first refuses; and he finally consents to do so only if the minister pays him "smart money": it "is a thankless thing to do these things free, you know."

But *Modern Chivalry* is no mere sequence of rogue incidents related for amusement. Teague is a walking embodiment of some of the ills of a raw republic, and his crude actions stimulate Captain Farrago's (i.e., Brackenridge's) analysis of governmental abuses. The author's basic intention was serious: he proposed to examine the state of American "democracy" as he had seen it in operation. For years a judge in Pennsylvania, he knew at first hand the rough politics of democracy; yet his point of view in *Modern Chivalry* is generally that of an objective observer.

Modern Chivalry has often been called a satire on democracy; but Brackenridge was not opposed to democratic government. Indeed he explains that to him it is "beyond all question the freest." His target in *Modern Chivalry* is not democracy itself but rather its incompetence and corruption. Teague is the fulcrum on which his satire turns. Crude and illiterate as he is, Teague is everywhere invited to assume positions for which he is totally unqualified except by a certain good-natured acquiescence. Had it not been for the interference of Captain Farrago, he would have become a preacher, a member of the Philosophical Society, and an Indian treaty maker. When on one occasion he disappears, the Captain not unnaturally fears that he will find him speaking in the Congress or lecturing at a university; but this time Teague is employed as an actor, a post for which he is as little fitted as any. Before he has finished, Brackenridge has touched satirically upon legislation, the practice of law, the ministry, higher education, the press, dueling, scientific research, political chicanery, and Jeffersonion economy. His general method is to show Teague in an incongruous situation from which he is somehow extricated by the Captain, and then to pass on to appropriate philosophical reflections regarding government and society.

But incompetence is only one of the threats to democracy; the other is corruption in high places. The untutored and arrogant masses are themselves vulnerable to exploitation from above:

The demagogue is the first great destroyer of the constitution by deceiving the people. . . . He is an aristocrat; and seeks after more power than is just. He will never rest short of despotic rule.

Thus Brackenridge thrusts at Hamiltonian politics and at the excessive power of the courts. The "rage of mere democracy" and the aristocratic urge toward domination are the Scylla and the Charybdis between which a democracy must sail. "The great moral of this book," he concludes, "is the evil of men seeking office for which they are not qualified." It was this lesson—urged when the air was full of theories of the natural rights of man—which Brackenridge tried to teach his countrymen. To him liberty is neither an abstraction nor an inalienable right; it is something sought and worked for intelligently. Because he loved democracy, he became one of its sternest critics.

Brackenridge was a deliberate craftsman with a definite theory of writing and a calculating eye on his public. He set a high value upon clarity, and he quoted with approval Swift's injunction concerning style—proper words in proper places. Embellishment for its own sake he frowned upon, and he believed that the proof of good writing is "that when you read the composition, you think of nothing but the sense." Yet he enriched his own page with many an allusion to the Greek and Roman classics, which more than any modern models (excepting *Don Quixote*) influenced his writing.

At the same time he thought of himself as an American writer. Occasionally oppressed by his lonely existence in a western wilderness, he "sighed for the garrets of London," but he was in general reconciled to his environment, and he never became (like his contemporary Joseph Dennie) an outright Anglophile. Although he seldom referred specifically to American writers, he once asserted that English is better written in America than in England, and his own prose could stand comparison with most of the best that eighteenth century England produced. He said that he intended *Modern Chivalry* for "Tom, Dick and Harry in the woods"; but its quality was such as to appeal primarily to the intelligentsia. His was one of the ripest minds of the era. While the lady novelists were dispensing simple, serious lessons in morality for young folk, Brackenridge was teaching his fellow men how to be good citizens. His was the harder task. To it he brought not only the wisdom of observation but also his wide reading from Plato to Swift.

3

Charles Brockden Brown, exemplar of the American "Gothic," was the first of our writers to make a profession of literature and the first to approach the stature of a major novelist; few have failed of "greatness" by so narrow a margin. Powers, Brown indubitably possessed; his failure lay in his inability to focus and sustain them. His work drew praise from a wide diversity of other writers as well as from critics domestic and foreign. Shelley was fascinated by him; in the opinion of one of his biographers, "nothing so blended itself with the structure of his interior mind as the creations of Brown." Keats found *Wieland* "a very powerful book." Applause came from many other foreign writers, including Thomas Hood, Godwin, and Hazlitt. In America his gifts were recognized by Poe, Cooper, Neal, Dana, Hawthorne, and others. The scene depicting the maniacal frenzy of Wieland deeply impressed Whittier, who wrote: "In the entire range of English literature there is no more thrilling passage. . . . The masters of the old Greek tragedy have scarcely exceeded the sublime horror of this scene from the American novelist."

The common factor in most of the tributes to Brown is their recognition of his originality: there was no writer quite like him even among the contemporary pre-Romantics to whom he was in some ways akin. The nature of Brown's power eludes exact definition, but its property is to compel the reader's attention irresistibly not only to the exciting narrative but also to the gravity of whatever philosophical or moral problem is implicit in it—whether it be religious obsession (as in *Wieland*), criminology (as in *Edgar Huntly*), philosophic anarchism (as in *Ormond*), humanitarian reform (as in *Arthur Mervyn*), or marriage (as in *Clara Howard* and *Jane Talbot*). His fiction was outwardly sensational, yet no device for heightening the reader's interest in tense action—and Brown commanded Gothic devices—completely effaces the reader's awareness of his high seriousness as a student of mankind.

Brown took himself seriously too. He was a writer of great ambition—perhaps too much so for the good of his health. During his bookish boyhood and effervescent youth he conceived (partly under the stimulus of Elihu H. Smith and William Dunlap) the most grandiose schemes. He would write a trilogy of epics. He would analyze the basic causes of man's misery and propose remedies. He would serve the cause of perfectibility. He would classify all knowledge. He would found important magazines—on a scale suggested by the prospectus of one of them: "to extract the quintessence of European wisdom; to review and estimate the labours of all writers, domestic and foreign." He was in fact attracted by so many ideas that his work suffered from the dispersion of his energies. The air was full of liberal theories which he brought to his desk for eager observation. He was excited by ideas which he could not finally or fully endorse, yet he acquired the reputation of a radical, for in his fiction he discussed the most "advanced" theories: freer divorce laws, political rights for women, deistic religion, a more humane treatment of criminals, amelioration of the lot of the peasant class. Many of these ideas he probably first encountered in Godwin's *Political Justice* (1793), but even less than Godwin could he implement radical thought. He was less interested in machinery than in motives. He never devised a coherent program of reform because he lacked the final qualification of the true crusader, a dynamic urge to act. He remained a liberal Utopian dreamer, resting his hopes for mankind somewhat vaguely in the rule of reason, the rejection of the incubus of Calvinism, and an appeal to benevolence in the human spirit.

In *Wieland* (1798), his best novel, Brown seems to have used for his plot an actual case of murder committed under the influence of hallucination in Tomhannock some years before; but the tone, coloring, and motivation are his own. The action is laid in the environs of Philadelphia, where Theodore Wieland has lived in pastoral tranquillity with his wife and sister until events begin to play havoc with his delicately poised mental health. He becomes the victim of a religious melancholia and hears a mysterious "voice." Actually this voice is at first the voice of a wandering, experimental ventriloquist, Carwin, who uses his special powers some eight times altogether in situations ranging from the trivial to the tragic. Finally Wieland, far gone in a religious psychosis (for which Carwin's experiments are only partially responsible), hears a heavenly "voice" (not Carwin's this time) which commands him to slay his wife and children. This he does. He is prevented from extending his dubious benevolence to his sister Clara only by the intervention of Carwin, who calls upon him to "hold!" This command brings him back to reality; but his realization of his deed converts him into a "monument of woe," to be delivered from ineffable remorse only by death.

The story, despite serious structural defects, is intrinsically as well as historically important. On the derivative level, it is obviously Richardsonian in its presentation of a persecuted heroine (Clara) carrying on in the face of incredible difficulties. Gothic terrors beset her, for she lives in seclusion in a house architecturally ideal for nocturnal terrors. Yet these horrors take on a degree of reality because of the seriousness with which Brown treated—apparently for the first time in American fiction—a case of dementia. In addition there is a Faustian motif: the ventriloquist's chief trait is his appetite for knowledge, and he pleads that his "only crime" is "curiosity." His dismay in contemplating the tragedy that he in part induced may have given Mary

Shelley the idea for her Frankenstein. Says Carwin: "Had I not rashly set in motion a machine, over whose progress I had no controul, and which experience had shewn me was infinite in power?" *Wieland* derives its strength not merely from the exploitation of sensation, but from the blending of the Gothic method with philosophical, psychological, and moral implications to create a powerful, even if unbalanced, book.

Like his own Carwin, Brown had a vast curiosity. In *Ormond* (1799), as chaotic a book as he ever wrote, he presented a glamorous, superman-like villain with a high intelligence and a low opinion of bourgeois conceptions of good and evil. His principles he has absorbed in part through contact with the secret society of the Illuminati on the Continent. He scoffs at the conventions of marriage, religion, and private property. His conduct is commensurably extravagant and violent. Yet opposite this almost caricatured villain Brown placed Constantia Dudley, who seemed to Shelley "a perfect combination of the purely ideal and possibly real." In *Arthur Mervyn* (1799–1800) there is a serious study (with emphasis on civic responsibility) of the problem of yellow fever, which Brown had observed in epidemic proportions in Philadelphia. In *Edgar Huntly* (1799) he provided his country with its first detective novel. The story has thrilling moments, but its action is finally bungled. At the same time it reflects Brown's interest in the Godwinian theme of morbid curiosity and its relationship to crime. Its "cave scene" may have inspired Edgar Poe as a source for "The Pit and the Pendulum," and Cooper, who at first scoffed at *Edgar Huntly,* later imitated its author.

Clara Howard (1801), Brown's next novel, is relatively free from the violence of the preceding stories, being mainly a love story told with emphasis upon an ethical dilemma. *Jane Talbot* (1801) treats of the problem of a sensitive young lady who makes a loveless marriage although she has met her real affinity before the wedding. The problem is handled with a finesse that surprisingly adumbrates certain stories of Henry James. The relative quietness of these last two novels reflects Brown's awareness of the relationship between a writer and his public. He was a conscious craftsman. His first three novels had made him a reputation, but they had not sold well. In April, 1800, he wrote, "Book-making . . . is the dullest of all trades." When his brother suggested that perhaps the public would find more interest in novels less devoted to "the prodigious or the singular," he gloomily agreed, and he promised less extravagance and more emphasis on "daily incidents" of the sort that the public presumably cared for. Yet he never succeeded in becoming a popular writer, and indeed produced no novels after 1804.

A late eighteenth century novelist, Brown was inevitably influenced by foreign models, for American models were almost nonexistent. Yet he was keenly aware of his position as an American writer. Even as the author of Gothic fiction, he bravely attempted to use native materials. He prided himself on the fact that in *Edgar Huntly* he had opened new sluices of power:

Puerile superstition and exploded manners, Gothic castles and chimeras, are the materials usually employed for this end. The incidents of Indian hostility, and the perils of the Western wilderness, are far more suitable; and for a native of America to overlook these would admit of no apology. These, therefore, are, in part, the ingredients of this tale, and these he has been ambitious of depicting in vivid and faithful colours.

Europe's example was to him by no means an unmixed blessing, for, he said in *Clara Howard,* "Our books are almost wholly the productions of Europe, and the prejudices which infect us are derived chiefly from this source." A substratum of American democratic thinking underlay his romantic theorizing and his moral speculation.

Without being overtly doctrinaire, Brown was unquestionably a moralist in his fiction: idea and scene coalesced to form art. His most sensational narrative episodes were the artistic counterparts of his philosophic probings into the causes of man's unrest. Even those of his characters who (like the protagonist in *Ormond*) were antisocial in act and creed revealed the basic problems of humanity. Final remedies Brown did not in most cases propose: he was not a "didactic" writer. He merely described the human tragedy with a skill great enough to enable him to produce many memorable scenes of high seriousness and compelling interest. Constantly interrupted by illness and the exigencies of business, he wrote rapidly during the time available to him, and he revised little. He rose brilliantly to heights of eloquence and as suddenly bogged down in bombast, bathos, or incoherence. Had he been able to sustain his flights, he might have been a great tragic novelist.

4

In this period the novel could experiment, with relatively few restrictions, but the drama suffered under enough handicaps and discouragements to founder any ordinary enterprise. Legal statute, clerical frowns, the exigencies of war, yellow fever, the copyright bogy—these and other factors operated to prevent the conception and hinder the growth of the American theater.

Moralists might indict the theater as the "House of the Devill," and lawmakers might legislate against it as contrary to the public good; but no amount of opposition could effectively stamp out a form of entertainment based on the virtually instinctive will to "make-believe." Not that the opposition ever capitulated completely or permanently—it was renewed, for example, during the Revolutionary War—but its severity was relaxed from time to time. At the end of the eighteenth century the American theater was pretty well established, but original American drama was far from arrival. Repertories were mainly foreign; it would have been folly to expect a native drama to compete with royalty-free plays such as *Richard III* or Dryden's *Amphitryon* or Farquhar's *Beaux' Stratagem*.

In the beginning, however, there was no thought of an American drama. To be sure, many Americans experimented with the dramatic form; but they had little hope of seeing their plays professionally produced. Out of some forty plays written prior to 1787 fewer than a half-dozen were even intended for production on the regular stage, although many of them were presented by amateurs. The first complete and unquestionably American play to be performed publicly and professionally was presented in 1767. Gradually more American writers entered the field, and between 1790 and 1820 the variety and vigor of native production was so great that our failure to bring forth a single great dramatist or a single great play is the more remarkable.

The first American play of record acted on the American stage was Thomas Godfrey's *The Prince of Parthia,* written before 1763, published in 1765, and produced at the "New Theater," Philadelphia, April 24, 1767. That the play was a tragedy was perhaps consonant with the prevailing sobriety of our national thinking at the time. That it was Elizabethan in pattern and Oriental in subject matter is not to be wondered at. The population of this country at the time was in effect that of Englishmen transplanted, but scarcely rooted, in a new land. Given the circumstances, it was natural for a playwright to utilize the tested and the universal rather than the new and the local. *The Prince of Parthia* is a reasonably good play. It tells of dark passions and violent action in the ancient and remote kingdom of Parthia. Epic enterprise and fierce personal tensions combine in melodrama sincerely conceived. Brother fights brother; father and son compete for the favors of the same woman; wife instigates the murder of husband—these are some of its bloody data. At the end the heroine, falsely told that her lover is dead, takes poison; it remains for the hero to dispatch himself on his sword. Plot elements and language from Shakespeare, and Beaumont and Fletcher, obviously inspired but did not completely dominate Godfrey's work. In *The Prince of Parthia,* tradition was put to good use by the first native American dramatist.

There was a good deal of interest in the drama during the Revolutionary War. The British, who were active in promoting it, converted Faneuil Hall for a time into a theater. Some plays were written, and a few of them remain as interesting mixtures of colonial art and politics. Tory views were sometimes dramatized, as in the anonymous farce *The Battle of Brooklyn* (1776 *)

* Except as noted, dates of plays are those of first production.

which lampoons General Washington and his officers. Notable among patriotic plays were Mrs. Mercy Warren's *The Adulateur* (published 1773), a satire on Governor Thomas Hutchinson, and *The Group* (about 1773), which bitterly satirized those persons who acquiesced in the abrogation of the Massachusetts charter. It is possible that Mrs. Warren also wrote *The Blockheads,* a coarse satirical answer to Burgoyne's satirical farce, *The Blockade,* which had been played in Boston in 1776–1777. These plays by Mrs. Warren and others are not of sufficiently high quality to command enduring interest, but they are reminders of the fact that the Revolutionary War was one of the factors responsible for the awakening of interest in the drama.

5

By the time Royall Tyler wrote *The Contrast,* the nation had emerged as an independent political unit; but its social pattern was still equivocal. *The Contrast,* the first American comedy to be presented in America, was performed at the John Street Theater in New York on April 16, 1787. It was and is an excellent acting-play. Its universally interesting theme of urban sophistication vs. rural naïveté had a peculiarly appropriate application in post-Revolutionary America, when the British, having lost political control, were still able to patronize us culturally.

The central situation in *The Contrast* shows an English cad maneuvering for the hand of a pure American girl while at the same time he is making dishonorable overtures to another intended as a "companion" to his wife. Of course he loses out ignominiously. The characterization of the "fashionable" elements in the dramatis personae is done with the authentic tone of a writer who knew his Sheridan—for *The Contrast* has much in common with *The School for Scandal*—but the prologue sounded a national note that was well sustained:

> Why should our thoughts to distant countries roam
> When each refinement may be found at home?

Patriotism was further emphasized when "Yankee Doodle" was sung during the performance. Beyond this, the action was made interesting to Americans by local references and the celebration of the American character. Colonel Manly's success in breaking up a sinister stratagem (and in his suit of the young lady he has saved from a Chesterfieldian fop) constitutes an endorsement of the American way of life in 1787. Our own social institutions must set the standards of individual behavior.

The success of *The Contrast* on the stage was probably due also to the adroitness with which Tyler manages his dialogue and to the introduction, for the first time on the American stage, of a fine example of Yankee rustic, Jonathan, whose combination of sturdy, though not inflexible, New England morality and childlike innocence makes for rollicking comedy, especially in the scene in which he unwittingly attends a theater and tries to carry out the foreign servant's instructions as to how to succeed in an amour. The play scene is almost worthy of Fielding, whose Partridge is a literary cousin of Jonathan. Jonathan's attempted amour ends in a rebuff which helps to clarify his thinking: "If this is the way with your city ladies, give me the twenty acres of rock, the Bible, the cow, and Tabitha, and a little peaceable bundling."

The Contrast was a lusty embodiment of American ideals in a play which, without pointedly ignoring English tradition, made its own way. Subscribers to its publication included, among other eminent people, George Washington and General Humphreys. Tyler also wrote other dramatic pieces, including a musical farce (a popular type at the time), but his fame as a dramatist remains vested in *The Contrast.*

The mixture of opportunity and handicap that confronted early American dramatists is further illustrated by the production of James Nelson Barker, who experimented with masque, domestic comedy, topical (political) drama, romantic comedy, and historical play. His *Tears and Smiles* (acted 1807), a sentimental comedy, reopens a vein which Tyler had mined profitably in *The Contrast,* with the foreign menace to our native institutions—this time French instead of British. Barker had "never even seen a Yankee," but at the request of the actor Jefferson he supplied Nathan Yank. The play was a moderate success. His next play, *The Embargo* (acted 1808), illustrates a current trend toward realistic political discussion. Its text has been lost, but when it was produced at "Old Drury" (the Chestnut Street Theater) in Philadelphia, a riot was instigated by those of the merchant class who objected to Barker's pro-administration bias. The drama was evidently becoming a social force to be reckoned with.

Barker's *The Indian Princess* (1808), the first "Indian play" written by an American and produced on the stage, told of the adventures of John Smith and Pocahontas, with perhaps less emphasis upon the dangers threatening Smith than upon the romantic love between Rolfe and the Princess, as well as among the lesser personnel. Realism was here no major aim of Barker. The outcome of events is happy: a conspiracy to kill the white men is quashed, and there comes (as Lord Delawar puts it) a "pairing time among the turtles." John Smith survives to envisage a time when "arts, and industry and elegance shall reign" in "this fine portion of the globe." Called a "melodrame" (a sign of increasing French influence on our theaters), *The Indian*

Princess is a light, actable play, with music and a masque added in deference to popular taste.

Superstition (acted 1824), Barker's most ambitious work, is a carefully wrought drama based on an aspect of the Regicide Judges' story, a very creditable early treatment of a theme later used by Cooper, Hawthorne, Paulding, Longfellow, and others. It is a sober and serious study of a solemn chapter in American history. If it fails to be really memorable, the reason is that Barker's derivative language was not quite equal to sustaining the mood in which the play was pitched.

Barker led an extremely active public life, and his plays form only one expression of his constant concern for the public good. He was no blind believer in an untutored democracy. He realized, as his use of the witchcraft theme in *Superstition* showed, the havoc that might be wrought by an "unthinking crowd." Yet he was basically American and republican. He was furthermore a proponent of an American theater even though he seems to have connived at manager William Wood's ruse of passing off one of his plays (*Marmion,* acted 1812) as by a British dramatist. Without being fanatically nationalistic, he staunchly did his part in building a native tradition in the drama. Compared with Tyler, he seems more earnest but less of an artist. Compared with Dunlap, he seems less significant by reason of the latter's more voluminous production and more intense devotion to the cause of the drama.

6

One of the most influential names in the earlier cultural history of America is that of William Dunlap. He fell short of genius in any single category, but he achieved distinction in several. Playwright, theatrical manager, painter, historian of the drama and of the arts of design, novelist, biographer, diarist, periodical writer, entrepreneur, he escaped the obscure fate of many men who have exhibited so much versatility. Called the Vasari of America for his services to painting, he might also be called the father of the American drama and theater. His devoted service to the drama was motivated by his conviction, "The rise, progress, and cultivation of the drama mark the progress of refinement and the state of manners at any given time and in any country." All the arts were having their troubles in America at the time of Dunlap's ascendancy, roughly from 1790 to 1820. When a man like John Adams could say, "I would not give sixpence for a picture of Raphael or a statue of Phidias," there was obviously much missionary work to be done. Dunlap objected to the practice of singling out the drama for attack. He believed that "the fine arts [are] all connected, and must stand or fall together . . . if the drama is injurious to a state, so are literature and the arts." As manager, designer, producer, and writer of plays, he exerted an influence which helped to elevate and stabilize the theater in a chaotic period. If as a writer he lacked imaginative powers of the first order, he was extremely useful to the young nation at a time when it greatly needed standards of taste and technique.

The plays Dunlap presented were both a reflection and a cause of conditions in the theater. As producer he responded to public demand; if he frequently presented Shakespeare, he also presented many of the mediocre plays of Kotzebue, that darling of the Continent as well as of the American theater about 1800–1805. But even in his partial concessions to public demand, he knew good taste and good technique even though he did not always exercise them. He himself wrote and adapted some sixty plays. If one failed to succeed, he could be ready with a new one in ten days to two weeks. He had the advantage of his own versatility; he could keep control of most of the production factors himself. First and last he experimented with many varieties of drama: comedy, farce, melodrama, tragedy, heroic plays, romantic drama, opera, domestic drama, and patriotic "spectacles" lying between drama and pageant. The scenes of his plays include America, England, Germany, France, Russia, Italy, and South America.

His first play, *The Father, or American Shandyism* (acted 1789), was a creditable but not really distinguished work written under the influence of *The Contrast*. Dunlap himself thought that the best of his plays was *The Italian Father* (acted 1799), for which he used as a model Dekker's *The Honest Whore*. Considered critical opinion now points to *André* (1798) as probably his best. It is a tragedy based on the last days of the British officer. Dramatic tension is established by a young American's attempt to save André out of gratitude for the latter's generous behavior to him. But General Washington, to whom young Bland applies, denies the appeal on the ground of patriotism. Complications arise when the British threaten to execute Bland's father (their prisoner) if André is hanged. Since the outcome of the action was known to the audience in advance, the success of the play depended on the power of Dunlap (and the actors) to invest the drama with high seriousness of mood and resourcefulness in episode. High seriousness the play does attain, but the action tends to crumble away into a diversity of separate scenes which, despite unity of time, fail to cohere. The blank verse in which the play is written is mobile and not without apt echoes of Elizabethan dramatists. The public did not greatly favor the play in its original form; but Dunlap thriftily revamped it and presented it as a patriotic spectacle with music. In this form, known as *The Glory of Columbia,* it was a commercial success. But as a dramatist Dunlap exhibited more craftsmanship than high art. To him the text, in any case, was only one of the elements upon which the prosperity of the theater depended.

All the factors of production and management interested Dunlap. He frequently inveighed against the star system, for he sensed the danger that playwrights would be guided by the whims of the star instead of the principles of sound, balanced drama. He studied the physical conditions of the theater as well as the use of appropriate sets and properties. He observed that an overlarge theater could affect a play adversely, for besides making it impossible for actors' facial expressions to be seen, it "requires an exertion of the actor's voice which destroys its melody, and renders variety of intonation impossible." He was extremely meticulous in working out details of staging, especially for Shakespeare. He once searched "several books" in order to find out what were the right banners to use for "the Britons under Cymbeline." His intelligent interest in the merging of the theater arts was exemplified when during a production of *Hamlet* he painted an interpretation of the play scene. Harassed by practical production problems and beset by the temptation to pander to the masses, Dunlap never really relinquished his high ideals.

As a producer-playwright Dunlap was not unduly concerned to stress American themes. Indeed he even queried "how far we ought to wish for a national drama, distinct from that of our English forefathers." He thought that the process of Americanization should be gradual rather than hasty and arbitrary, but in one sense he did wish the drama to be "national": he believed that most of the ills of the theater—which he attributed to the "necessities and cupidity of managers"—could be removed by a system of government patronage, citing in support of his view the experiences of Germany and France. Time and again in his *History of the American Theatre*, he reverts to this possibility of saving the drama. Perhaps such a system would have made his own career more tolerable, for he was in constant difficulties and went into bankruptcy at one time.

In his later years Dunlap had very little active connection with the theater, returning to painting and to miscellaneous writing for his somewhat precarious livelihood. In 1832 he produced his *History of the American Theatre*, a work which, despite evidences of hasty composition, remains a monument to a man who did more than any other one person in his time to promote the welfare of the American theater and drama.

7

During this period the novel fared better than the drama: Brackenridge's *Modern Chivalry* and Brown's *Wieland* probably reached a higher level of achievement than any of the plays that appeared. Yet for a long period the harvest is singularly meager in both forms. The familiar explanations of this condition are the lack of affinity between Puritanism and art, and the overinfluence of Europe. Probably the latter factor was the more deleterious. Puritanism was a direct deterrent, but it waned to a point at which it should have ceased to hamper a real artist. The influence of Europe, particularly England, was more subtle and pervasive, taking various forms. England provided us with a language and a tradition. With a ready-made literature at hand, was it not natural for us to defer our efforts? Long after we had won our political independence we remained, as Barker said, "mental colonists." A kind of provincial snobbery prevented many Americans from seeing such merit as there was in national productions. Certain critics, as he noted in the preface to his *Tears and Smiles,* had coined the opprobrious term "Columbianism" to apply to "every delineation of . . . American manners, customs, opinion, characters, or scenery. . . . They can never pardon the endeavor to depict our national peculiarities, and yet they will listen with avidity to Yorkshire rusticity, or Newmarket slang." Such an attitude was fostered by the British who, having lost the war, continued to belittle our cultural progress.

There were notable exceptions: John Howard Payne, for example, had a considerable success as an actor at Drury Lane, and his tragedy *Brutus* ran fifty nights in one season. Yet he was later to be the victim of "much prejudice" and "persecution" because of his American principles. During the first two decades of the nineteenth century an inglorious literary warfare was carried on between England and America. It was Irving's purpose in "English Writers on America" to allay this ill-feeling. He reminded England that it was beneath her dignity to attack us; and he bade Americans think indulgently of England as a "perpetual volume of reference." Yet perhaps it was unwise to seek to end this literary war by appeasing both sides. Perhaps it was necessary that we should fight for our literary independence too.

15. THE AMERICAN DREAM

W_HILE the citizens of the United States were thus struggling to create a literature fitting to the assumed grandeur of the national destiny, the idea of America was becoming itself a part of the cultural tradition of Europe. As a state of mind and a dream, America had existed long before its discovery. Ever since the early days of Western civilization, peoples had dreamed of a lost Paradise, of a Golden Age characterized by abundance, absence of war, and absence of toil. With the first accounts of the New World, it was felt that these dreams and yearnings had become a fact, a geographical reality fraught with unlimited possibilities. The first navigators had landed, not on the rocky coast of the northern part of America, but in islands swept by balmy breezes, inhabited by natives of peaceful dispositions, living without toil or industry on the natural productions of a generous soil. Their nakedness, their disconcerting absence of shame, their simplicity seemed to indicate that in some incomprehensible way they had not been as much tainted by original sin as had the peoples of Europe.

From the very beginning travelers' relations provided an inexhaustible store of material and arguments in the great debate, opened since the early days of the Renaissance, between the enemies and the defenders of the European form of life. Critics of a society which was becoming every day more closely knit, more sophisticated and artificial, never tired of comparing the simple, virtuous, and "natural" life of the Indians with the complicated, restless, and greedy existence of civilized men. Undoubtedly Shakespeare had these people in mind, when he made the honest old Counsellor Gonzalo, in *The Tempest,* draw a picture of the ideal commonwealth he would establish in an island if he were "king on't":

> All things in common nature should produce
> Without sweat or endeavour: treason, felony,
> Sword, pike, knife, gun, or need of any engine,
> Would I not have; but nature should bring forth,
> Of its own kind, all foison, all abundance,
> To feed my innocent people.

This is the "soft primitivism" also found in the French poet Ronsard or in the story of *El Villano del Danubio* retold by the sixteenth century Spanish writer Antonio de Guevara or even later in Cervantes' description of the Island of Barataria under the rule of good Sancho. To a philosopher like Locke it offered a true image of a condition which had existed before personal property and compacts had laid the foundation of human society such as we know it, for then "all the world was America." But though neither Locke, nor Vico, nor Montesquieu intended to use their praise of the savages as an argument destructive of our form of society, such was clearly the purpose of the Frenchman Lahontan, in his *Dialogues between an American savage and the author* (1703), and to a lesser extent of Jean-Jacques Rousseau. Whether they intended it or not, these advocates of a more or less complete return to nature were the forerunners of some of our modern anarchists and communistic utopians.

Admirers of a harder form of primitivism also found abundant material in the travelers in the northern parts of America, particularly in the Jesuits' relations. The good Fathers were steeped in the classical tradition, and they were delighted to find in the Indians replicas of Greek and Roman exemplars of stoic and republican virtues. On the other hand, it is no less certain that Hobbes derived from travelers' accounts his unsympathetic reconstruction of the natural state of mankind. But such pessimistic views were exceptional; what prevailed was the picture of a boundless and generous land, preserved from the evils of our modern society, and it is significant that Thomas More in 1516 set a precedent followed by countless imitators in locating his ideal state of Utopia in the newly discovered world.

This dream of an Earthly Paradise was, of course, a mirage—but it was more; it was a revolutionary force, let loose in the Western world, because it proved that the whole of mankind had not been irremediably condemned by some inherent vice to toil, suffering, oppression, war, famine, and misery. Man's faulty organization of society and not man's nature was responsible for his unhappiness. America as an idea was already at work pointing the way in the never-ending and hitherto chimerical quest of happiness.

If it had not been confusedly felt that the New World held out a hope to the whole of mankind, the indignation against the atrocities committed by its European conquerors might have been less vehement. The first eloquent outburst of indignation came from a Spanish missionary, the famous Las Casas, as early as 1552. His *Brief Relation* was translated into English in 1556 and into French in 1579, and in the Latin original was circulated throughout Europe. It marked the beginning of a long protestation in the name of humanity against the use of unjustified violence and the enslavement of innocent peoples. It was the proclamation of the rights of the so-called inferior peoples, echoed again and again during the eighteenth century. From the very excesses of the conquerors rose a new conception of the right of conquest and the right of colonization.

2

The implication was clear: what our civilization had failed to accomplish would perhaps find its fulfillment in the newly discovered lands. This "infant world, still quite naked and at the breast" suddenly presented to a senescent world another chance, perhaps the last one, to build anew the city of man.

By the middle of the eighteenth century, despite the vogue of the primitivistic dream in literature, this view had become singularly definite. The American Indians occupied a larger place than ever on the stage, in poetry, and in works of fiction, and more than ever their simple and natural virtues were opposed to the corruption of civilized men. It was only too plain that any reform in Europe would entail an enormous effort, and that new structures could not be erected without destroying the buildings still sheltering a discontented society; but in America persecuted peoples could find not only a refuge but an opportunity to lay the foundations of a better society. This dream was not limited to the British colonies, for the French had attempted in Brazil and in Florida about the middle of the sixteenth century to establish such settlements. Whether the Jesuits had succeeded or not in doing it in Paraguay was a moot question among the philosophers. At any rate, it was known that the French Huguenots, after the Revocation of the Edict of Nantes, had found a refuge in New England, on the banks of the Hudson where the Palatines had joined them, in Pennsylvania, and in the Carolinas. New England as well as Virginia had been the subject of a considerable body of "promotion literature," intended to counteract the recital of the trials and sufferings of the first colonists.

Among the British colonies, Pennsylvania occupied a privileged rank. Even the wildest dreamers among the philosophers never entertained seriously any scheme which would bring man back to a stark state of nature. The real problem was to find a form of society which would enable man to preserve his native qualities while enjoying all the benefits resulting from his association with his fellow beings; and such was the formula proposed at the end of the century by Godwin in his famous *Enquiry concerning Political Justice*. But long before Godwin the French *philosophes* thought they had discovered such an ideal commonwealth in the "republic" of Pennsylvania. To a large extent, the propaganda carried on in Europe by William Penn, in order to attract desirable immigrants, was responsible for that impression.

Pamphlets and leaflets containing enthusiastic descriptions of the advantages offered to the colonists were printed in English, Dutch, German, and French and distributed among the would-be immigrants. The Quakers, themselves a persecuted people, had substituted purchase from the Indians for conquest by force; they were true republicans using the equalitarian "thee" and recognizing no man as their master; they were philosophers who had abolished all the artificial trappings of religion, and who worshiped God in their hearts. The noble Quakers inherited all the virtues of the noble Indians, and Voltaire could declare, in his *Lettres anglaises* (1734), that Penn had brought to this earth the Golden Age, hitherto believed an invention of poets but now existing in Pennsylvania. Thus was developed through the eighteenth century a semiphilosophical and semisentimental body of literature dealing with the good Quakers and culminating in the *Histoire philosophique des deux Indes* of Abbé Raynal, in which the author contrasted the humane and philosophical development of the republic of Pennsylvania with the atrocities committed by the Spanish, the Portuguese, and all the European nations in the course of their colonial conquests.

Even admitting that the British colonists had not succeeded in establishing everywhere the city of the philosophers, the fact remained that liberty in America was much more the result of conditions inherent to the soil than the product of reasoned efforts. Such was the conclusion reached in 1774 by the editor of the *Gazette de France,* the official journal of the Court:

Those of our navigators who have studied this half of the Northern American Continent, maintain that an inborn love of liberty inherent to the soil, the sky, forests, and lakes prevents this still young country from resembling the other parts of the Universe. They are convinced that any European transported under this climate will be affected by this particular condition.

Whether through some providential design or, as Montesquieu and his disciples would have said, because of the "nature of things," the stage was already set for an unprecedented political experiment. During the earlier part of the eighteenth century, Voltaire and Montesquieu had represented England as the classic land of liberty. But Montesquieu himself had admitted that he had described not England as he had seen it, but England as it might be if the principles of the British constitution were integrally applied. American liberty, however, did not rest upon ancestral institutions and traditions; it was a new revelation, and as such it was described by Thomas Pownall, a former colonial governor and a friend of Benjamin Franklin, in his *Memorial addressed to the Sovereigns of America* (1783). It was a

New System of Things and Men, which treats all as they actually are, esteeming nothing the true End and perfect Good of Policy, but that Effect which produces, as equality of Rights, so equal Liberty, universal Peace, and unobstructed inter-communication of happiness in Human Society. . . . This is a Principle in act and deed, and not a mere speculative theorem.

This was the burden also of Crèvecœur's *Letters of an American Farmer* (first printed in English, then in French, and broadly circulated between 1780 and 1790), and of Thomas Paine, who came to Philadelphia to tell its citizens in January, 1776, that theirs was much more than a quarrel with the King of England:

The cause of America is, in a great measure, the cause of all mankind. Many circumstances have and will arise which are not local but universal, and through which the principles of all lovers of mankind are affected, and in the event of which their affections are interested.

To the enemies as well as to the friends of the Anglo-Americans, it appeared from the very beginning that from the Revolution would come answers to the problems affecting the future development of Western civiliza-tion. It was generally conceded by clear-sighted observers, even in England, that the revolt could not be crushed once for all by force. Sooner or later, the colonists would win their independence. Furthermore it would be utterly impossible to limit the conflagration, which would spread from the British colonies to the other colonies of the new world and to all European colonies, all over the globe. This meant the disappearance, or a deep transformation, of economic factors on which rested the economic structure of Europe. It meant the end of monopolies, of exploitation of colonies for the sole benefit of the metropolis; it meant also that the trade of all nations might enter hitherto restricted areas. It meant eventually the freedom of the seas and consequently the complete reorganization of international life.

This was clearly perceived in England and explains the exclamation of Horace Walpole upon hearing the "black news" of Saratoga: "Nothing will be left of England but the vestige of her grandeur." In France it was hardly less keenly felt by Turgot, Vergennes, and even such a liberal as Abbé Raynal, who dreaded the consequences which would follow the collapse of the colonial system.

Even more important and fundamental was the answer given to the social and political problem which had become acute during the eighteenth cen-tury and was simply the problem of government. Very different were the forms of government adopted by the former colonies; but all rested on the doctrine of popular sovereignty proclaimed in the Declaration of Independence and developed in the declarations prefixed to most of the state constitutions. The theory was not new, but the undertaking was unprecedented. It was an attempt to form a society in which essential natural rights would be preserved, and government from above be reduced to a minimum. Such a form of government was not to be granted by sage legislators more or less divinely inspired or by an impersonal state substituted for the monarch; it was to be determined by the decisions of the citizens, whose collective body constituted "the people." It cannot be said that all the implications of the initial expression of the Constitution, "We the people," were at first fully understood even by the philosophers. The Italian-born citizen of Virginia, Mazzei, had to explain to the French in 1788 that "the people" was not the rabble, but was constituted of all the inhabitants of the land. Mirabeau fought in vain to make the deputies in the National Assembly meet and proclaim the Declaration of the Rights of Man in the name of "the people." The old prejudices prevailed in 1789: the Deputies preferred "Nation" to "People" and the "French people" was recognized only in the preamble to the Constitution of 1793. Joel Barlow, friend and disciple of Jefferson, had to remind the French in particular and the Europeans in general in his *Vision of Columbus,* published in Paris in 1793, that the people was this

fraternal family divine
Whom mutual wants and mutual aids combine.

Condorcet himself, who, because of his efforts in favor of the rebels, had been made a "citizen of New Haven" with several members of the philosophical group gathering around Madame d'Houdetot, was puzzled to know how the will of the people could be ascertained and wrote to his colleagues of the American Philosophical Society of Philadelphia to inquire what mathematical computations would enable the Americans to have a true representation of the people. Despite these reservations, the magic words uttered in Philadelphia echoed, to quote Condorcet again, "from the Guadalquivir to the banks of the Neva." Enthusiasts like Lafayette hailed the beginning of "the American era," and Dr. Richard Price, Benjamin Franklin's old friend, could declare in 1785:

Perhaps I do not go too far, when I say that, next to the introduction of Christianity among mankind, the American Revolution may prove the most important step in the progressive course of human improvement.

Even before the final success of the Revolution, its first repercussions were felt in Europe. Nowhere were they more direct and more instantaneous than in Ireland, where ever since 1763 the progress of independence had been anxiously followed. "Look to America," cried Grattan two months after Yorktown, and already, on June 14, 1782, Henry Flood had proclaimed in the Irish House of Commons:

A voice from America shouted to Liberty, the echo of it caught your people as it passed along the Atlantic, and they renewed the voice till it reverberated here.

This fervor reached its maximum in France. It has often and justly been pointed out that the French Revolution was in fact the daughter of the American Revolution. The French Declaration of the Rights of Man follows very closely the Virginia "Bill of Rights" of 1776. The American precedent was quoted in the National Assembly and in the different assemblies which vainly tried to establish a permanent regime during the ensuing years. If later Fench historians have attempted to trace the main principles of the Declaration of Independence to Montesquieu and Rousseau, it does not seem that such indebtedness ever occurred to the French contemporaries of Jefferson. Yet, as Chamfort, the French moralist, pointed out, Louis XVI had acknowledged the legitimacy of popular government and signed his abdication when, in February, 1778, he signed a treaty of alliance with the young United States. Almost a hundred years later, Lamartine, at the end of his career, was no less justified in declaring with poetical emphasis:

One would need the discernment of God himself to distinguish America from France after their respective causes had been fused together during and after the American Revolutionary war.

3

The fight for independence had been won and a stable government established through the countless efforts of obscure American citizens, but popular imagination is fond of heroes who seem to embody all the characteristics of a people and an epoch. From the Revolution emerged two towering figures, living symbols of the country they had created: George Washington and Benjamin Franklin.

The Virginia gentleman called by Byron, after the first abdication of Napoleon,

the first—the last—the best—
The Cincinnatus of the West,

enjoyed from the early days of the American Revolution an extraordinary popularity. He was celebrated in epic poems; he appeared as the main character in patriotic dramas; no novel dealing with the Revolution was complete without some episode in which he appeared as a stern, sad, reserved, dignified figure, a great man without personal ambition, entirely devoted to his country, at all times conscious of the tremendous responsibility he was bearing on his mighty shoulders.

To him young Alfieri, in Italy, dedicated one of his odes on America in December, 1781, and seven years later he repeated his tribute "Al chiarissimo e libero uomo il Generale Washington," in the dedication of his tragedy *Brutus*. In a gesture of defiance to the Tories, young Coleridge drank Washington's health in a public inn in 1792. The French volunteers who joined the Americans unanimously acknowledged in him a military genius of the first order. Frederick II was anxious to obtain information on his tactics. Berthier, who later was to become Napoleon's chief of staff, made it a point to visit all the places where the American general had fought, and drew elaborate maps of his battles. In him they saw an organizer who had revolutionized modern warfare by leading to victory against professional soldiers an army of volunteers without any military training, poorly armed, without uniforms, "without shoes and without bread." His fame grew immensely in later years when the French, during their Revolution, had to resort to the levy in mass in order to defend their frontiers, and when Kosciuszko who had served under him attempted to repeat the tactics of his old chief during the insurrection of Poland. When the news of Washington's death reached France, young Bonaparte, then First Consul and still a republican hero, ordered a week of mourning for all the French Army and had his eulogy delivered in the "Temple of Mars" before the veterans of the campaigns of Italy and Egypt.

The foreign officers who served under Washington, the foreign visitors who saw him at Mount Vernon, when under his vine and fig tree he was living as a private citizen, readily acknowledged in him a sterling character, an impressive dignity, and a sort of melancholy most striking in a man who had had such a glorious career and had lived to enjoy the completion of his task. The only discordant notes to be heard in this unanimous praise are found in the correspondence of some French and British ministers during the troubled years between 1793 and 1797.

Of his achievements as a statesman, of the part he played in the making of the Constitution, little was known and little was said. Outside America, the names of his victories were soon forgotten, with the exception of Yorktown. His military glory was eclipsed by the fact that, once the victory was won, he had disbanded his army and resigned his commission to the hands of Congress. As the years passed, the comparison with Napoleon became unavoidable and almost obsessing, and Washington stood more and more as the prototype of the republican hero.

For obvious reasons, the tributes paid to Washington were more frequent and more persistent in France than in any other country; but they were not limited to France. The Italian Carlo Botta, writing in 1809 a *History of the War of Independence of the United States of America,* concluded his account with Washington's resignation as commander-in-chief, a significant and bold allusion to the very different course followed by Bonaparte. According to his memorialist, Napoleon himself sighed at St. Helena, "They wanted me to be another Washington" and attempted to explain that conditions in Europe did not permit him to keep his republican faith. In his "Ode to Napoleon Bonaparte" as well as in the "Age of Bronze," Byron gave Washington as a "watchword" to would-be dictators. Traveling in South America in 1817, H. M. Brackenridge found everywhere translations of Washington's Farewell Address, and at the same time the political magazine published by Chateaubriand deplored that everywhere on the Boulevard were seen portraits of Washington and Bolívar as a sort of tacit protest against the Bourbon restoration. No more eloquent tribute has ever been paid to the republican leader than the pages in which the author of *Atala,* recalling the short visit he had paid to the President of the United States in 1792, contrasted Washington and Napoleon, the man who had built a country and the conqueror who had left only ruins behind him.

The Washington hero-myth persisted throughout the nineteenth century and into the twentieth. Less eloquent than the praise of Chateaubriand, but no less striking, is the chapter at the close of *The Virginians* (1857–1859), in which Thackeray pictures Washington taking leave of his army at Whitehall Ferry, on the Hudson. More qualified and typical of many English appreciations was the estimate of Matthew Arnold, who spoke of Washington as if he had been an Englishman accidentally living in America, and maintained that Americans should think of him as a good model of the English country squire. In France admiration for Washington remained throughout the century a form of opposition to dictatorship and arbitrary power, as may be seen in the lectures delivered at the Collège de France during the Second Empire by Edouard de Laboulaye. Washington appeared again to proclaim "Liberty to the World" in *Le Nouveau Monde,* a play written by Villiers de l'Isle-Adam to commemorate the centennial of the Declaration of Independence. Again, in 1882, when France was obsessed by the fear of a dictator, Joseph Fabre in his book *Washington, libérateur de l'Amérique,* hailed the soldier-citizen. More recently, when many French liberals were seriously alarmed at the progress of totalitarian ideology and the growing popularity of Mussolini and Hitler, Louis Ferrier produced a play on Washington, to revive the old patriotic faith and, in the name of the great American, to preach the republican gospel.

Of an entirely different order has been the fame of Benjamin Franklin in Europe. His mission to France (1776–1784) marked the apogee of his European popularity, but he would not have taken Paris by storm if his reputation had not already been firmly established. His experiments in electricity were known in England through his friend Collinson as early as 1749; the French physicist Dalibard made them available to the French in 1752; and translations into German and Italian soon followed. European scientists saw in him a skillful observer and experimenter, but popular imagination magnified the American "doctor" into a modern Prometheus, a man able to control and play with a force of nature which had filled with awe countless generations.

During his lifetime, Franklin's fame extended throughout Europe even to Austria, the Scandinavian countries, and Russia. He corresponded with the most famous philosophers and scientists of his age, received from them and from monarchs the most flattering messages. He felt as much at home in Paris, although his knowledge of French was far from perfect, as in Philadelphia. After the partial publication of his *Autobiography,* printed in French and in Paris during the Revolution, he appeared as the most striking illustration of the unlimited possibilities residing in the "people," a living demonstration of the fact that in a republican society, where class distinctions do not prevent recognition of talent and genius, a poor boy may seize opportunities and rise to positions reserved to privileged classes in the Old World. No wonder the German historian Georg Forster in his *Reise um die Welt* (1784) saw in Franklin a prophet chosen to inaugurate the Golden Age of humanity, and Chamfort in his *Tableaux de la Révolution Française* (1793) hailed him as the herald of the new era of the common man. Thirty years later, the "child of poverty" who was to become a great South American leader, Domingo Faustino Sarmiento, treasured equally the only two books he had in his possession, the Bible and Franklin's *Autobiography*. As late as 1845, the French historian Mignet included a life of Franklin in a collection issued under the auspices of the *Académie des Sciences Morales et Politiques*. It was reprinted again in 1865 under the same auspices

as a biography which makes live again a good man, a master of wisdom adapted to every age, every condition, every society, and one of the founders of that American liberty which is not the privilege of a race, or of a given form of government, but pure and simple Liberty.

Franklin had not kept to himself the secret of his extraordinary success in life. Eighteenth century philosophers had vainly attempted to establish a practical code of morality which would not rest on a religious foundation and would be acceptable and accessible to the common man. In Franklin they found no metaphysical speculations, but sound and homely precepts of conduct. "The Science of Good Man Richard," the title generally given to the translations of *The Way to Wealth,* provided a sort of civic catechism soon incorporated in elementary textbooks and still to be found in fragmentary form in many of the readers used by children in the public schools of France and Italy. There is no young European who in his school days has not become familiar with the story of the whistle and anecdotes from the *Autobiography.*

Franklin also contributed another important element to the composite picture of America as it appears to European eyes. He stood, even more than Fulton, as the embodiment of the spirit, bold in its aims and yet practical, which characterizes American science; and the great English physicist Humphry Davy praised his work as justifying not only pure scientific research, but the application of science to the service of man. Franklin was the first to give the impression that through science America could achieve the impossible. Thus was established a popular tradition which was reinforced through the pseudoscientific tales of Poe and carried out in the novels of Jules Verne, in which Americans conquer the interstellar spaces and travel to the moon. Later the tradition, already well established, received a new confirmation in the inventions of Edison, "the wizard of Menlo Park," celebrated by Villiers de l'Isle-Adam, in his *L'Ève Future* (1886) not only as the man who had invented the phonograph but as a sorcerer who through mechanical devices had succeeded in creating an automaton endowed with all the manifestations of a living organism, including feeling and thought.

4

General as this admiration for America was in the days of the Revolution and later, it was accompanied in many quarters by reservations and misgivings. By comparison with the discoverers whose imaginations were haunted by visions of a recovered Earthly Paradise, many eighteenth and early nineteenth century travelers seem particularly unimaginative and "unromantic." To them, as well as to most of the settlers, nature was essentially an obstacle to colonization: it had to be tamed and subdued in order to make room for civilization and provide a living to man. As late as 1770, Oliver Goldsmith in his *Deserted Village* represented Georgia as a "dreary scene":

> Those matted woods, where birds forget to sing,
> But silent bats in drowsy clusters cling; . . .
> Where crouching tigers wait their hapless prey,
> And savage men more murderous still than they.

Occasionally happier notes occur in the accounts of foreign travelers who were sincerely interested in nature, and particularly in botany, like the Swede Peter Kalm, or in glowing descriptions of the Ohio published in Paris shortly before the Revolution and intended to attract French immigrants; but with the exception of Chastellux, who was a philosopher and a poet, the officers who accompanied Rochambeau failed to be impressed by the American scene, and Lafayette was completely blind to the beauties of nature.

British travelers generally deplored a country defaced by unsightly settle-ments and by forest fires leaving behind them bleached skeletons of trees and horrible stumps. They compared the scarred spaces surrounding the farms, the dreary and unhealthy swamps, and the eroded hills, with the well kept and humanized European countryside. Very few of them showed any real appreciation of American scenery; Isaac Weld was one of the first foreigners to perceive the beauty of autumn foliage, of the majestic landscape of the Hudson between New York and Albany, and of Niagara Falls. Here and there scattered notations could be collected. John Davis, in his *Travels in the United States* (1803), was probably the first European to celebrate the mock-ingbird. A disciple of Rousseau, he should take first rank among the romantic observers of America.

Frequent as the unfavorable comments of disgruntled travelers may have been, their effects were largely canceled by the works of two writers, the American botanist William Bartram and the French prose-poet Chateau-briand. Bartram's *Travels* was widely reprinted in Europe and was used as a source by Coleridge in "Kubla Khan" and "The Ancient Mariner," by Wordsworth in "Ruth," by Southey in "Madoc," by Thomas Campbell in "Gertrude of Wyoming" (County in Pennsylvania), by Mrs. Hemans, by Shelley, and even by Tennyson in *In Memoriam*.

Bartram's influence was multiplied in a measure difficult to ascertain because he was the chief source of the descriptions inserted by Chateaubriand in *Atala* and *Les Natchez* (1802 and 1826). In many respects, the famous prose-poem of Chateaubriand may be considered not as a revelation of an unknown world, but as a final and perfect expression of the various sorts of exoticism which had flourished during the previous three centuries. Atala and her simple lover are no longer children of nature; they are torn between the traditions, customs, and prejudices of their tribe and a new and higher code of ethics. Unable to solve the conflict, they can only suffer and die; Chateaubriand's poem sounds the funeral dirge of a disappearing race.

A generation later, the novels of Fenimore Cooper were to revive Euro-pean interest in the Indians and to start a very different tradition. Whatever may have been the intentions of the author of the Leatherstocking tales, the

French public saw in them primarily exciting adventures, with Indians lurking behind the trees, tracking their enemies with uncanny skill, scalping and slaying the white settlers. Balzac, who was a fervent admirer of Cooper, drew abundantly from him to portray not only the half-savage peasants ambushing the Republican soldiers in *Les Chouans,* but also both the criminals and the detectives constantly at war in the jungle of the Paris underworld. Thus gradually through a long series of popular novels and particularly through the many stories of Gustave Aimard, the noble savages of the early discoverers and philosophers underwent a curious evolution to become finally the *apaches,* or gangsters, of the French capital.

At the beginning of the nineteenth century, the success of Chateaubriand's *Atala* could be attributed to the magnificent descriptions of the "scènes de la nature": the Falls of Niagara, the Mississippi, the virgin forest, and the tropical swamps which serve as a frame for the melancholy love story of Chactas and the half-breed Atala. Whether or not his descriptions were embellished and magnified by his poetical imagination matters little here. They were accepted as authentic, for the author had dreamed of the American solitude, he had heard the voice of the desert, he had seen or imagined, with the assistance of Bartram, the swarming life of the swamps, the majestic cedars and the towering magnolias (*grandiflora*). He had done what many of his less gifted successors had confessed themselves unable to do, from Thomas Moore who was content to observe that the sight of the Niagara was "sad as well as elevating," to Frances Wright, who admitted that the Falls "acknowledge at once their power and immensity, and your own insignificance and imbecility." Neither the much more precise descriptions of Volney, in his *Tableau du Climat et du Sol des Etats-Unis* (1803) nor the scientific and minute accuracy of the great British geologist Charles Lyell could modify the deep and lasting impression made by Chateaubriand's little book, translated at once into all the languages of Europe and accepted as a model of description even by several South American writers. This extraordinary popularity was strengthened by Longfellow's *Evangeline* which helped further to arouse, in European travelers, exaggerated anticipations followed by an almost general disappointment when they were confronted by the actual countryside of the Eastern United States.

More serious than this concern for the contemplation of nature was the effort of European observers to find out whether natural conditions in the United States would permit and favor the development of a great civilization. During the last half of the eighteenth century, the French naturalist Buffon and the Berlin academician Cornelius de Pauw answered negatively. Judging from the accounts of travelers, they found the climate enervating, and nature itself so weak that the natives were unable to do any sustained work. Only unfavorable natural conditions could explain the fact that the New World, despite its reported fertility, had never developed a population comparable in density to the populations of Europe or Asia. The creoles (whites born in the colonies), as well as the domestic animals they had brought with them, showed signs of physical degeneration, and the wild species were decidedly smaller than the corresponding animals in the Old World. This was more than an academic question, and its political implications grew apparent as the British colonies progressed towards independence and finally formed a new nation. What faith and what hopes could be placed in the mission assigned by European liberals to the United States if this "young" people was condemned by the laws of nature ever to remain small and comparatively weak? Many of the French officers who had suffered from the extreme cold of a Rhode Island winter before being exposed to the semitropical temperature of the Virginia seashore had come to the conclusion that America was unfit for human beings. La Rochefoucauld-Liancourt and Volney, who spent several summers in Philadelphia, between 1794 and 1799, could but agree with them and insist upon the unhealthy features of the climate and the frequent epidemics.

These were some of the notions that Franklin and later Jefferson attempted to refute; but they did not succeed in convincing their opponents. The controversy found a last echo in Schopenhauer. Facts, however, spoke louder than theories: it was soon discovered that, despite certain unfavorable circumstances which could not be denied, the population of the United States increased at a regular rate independently of immigration, thus justifying the optimistic calculations of Franklin. Malthus provided an explanation: in the rapid development of the new nation he saw a confirmation of his theory that population invariably increases with the increase in the means of subsistence. The native population had remained practically stationary because of the Indians' lack of industry. It had increased as new territories were opened to cultivation and, because new land was practically limitless, it would continue to grow with the progress of agriculture.

Doubts nevertheless persisted concerning the quality of the civilization which the Anglo-Americans, as they were still called, would succeed in establishing. The first reports were far from favorable. French refugees remembering the exquisite life of the Old Regime, supercilious Britishers still considering America as a wayward child, criticized sharply or with indulgent scorn the uncouth manners of the people. In New York, Philadelphia, and Boston they missed the literary and artistic coteries, the salons, the concerts, the frivolous and yet intense intellectual life of the great capitals. Some, like the poet Thomas Moore, were so deeply disappointed as to doubt the soundness of the liberal creed in which they had placed their hope. Even the best intentioned among them fell into the common mistake of judging American society by European standards, and were disillusioned by this unexpected contact with a harsh reality. Once again was confirmed the curious separation between America as a geographical, political, and social entity, and America as a state of mind. Never perhaps had it been more strikingly expressed than in the words of Goethe in *Wilhelm Meister,* when one of the characters declares after a disappointing experience in America:

I shall return, and in my house, on my land among my home people, I shall repeat: Here and nowhere else is America. *Hier oder nirgends ist Ameriқa.*

But as Europe grew constantly weaker, torn by continuous wars and domestic strife, while the strength of the United States increased rapidly, the optimistic predictions concerning the future development of the United States made on the eve of the French Revolution seemed amply justified. Already in 1795, during the third year of the French Republic, Pictet of Geneva, summing up the observations of European travelers and the data found in Jedidiah Morse's geography, thought he was justified in examining "the causes of the greatness of America." His was not a great book; but it contained a summation of all the material available at the time, and his conclusion contrasted the country whose inhabitants had been wise enough "to submit themselves to a strong government in order to preserve their liberty," with a Europe apparently doomed "to oscillate between the cheerless tranquillity of despotism and the stormy fury of anarchy." At the same time (1793-1799), impelled by the same considerations, Christoph Daniel Ebeling published in Hamburg an enormous compilation on the United States which was to serve as the main source-book of information for several generations of German scholars.

Even more emphatic were the views presented by the Reverend John Bristed after the fall of Napoleon, the Peace of Ghent, and the reorganization of Europe. In the world of 1818, this British clergyman who had spent many years in America could see only two countries susceptible of growth: the giant Russia and the giant United States. He was too much attached to the European tradition to admire without restrictions the American ways of life; but he had to admit that the sun of Europe was setting, that none of the old nations could compete with a country capable of supporting ultimately a population of five hundred millions through its agriculture, commerce, industry, steam navigation, and mechanical inventions. It was not that the soil was extraordinarily fertile—America was "neither the Garden of Eden, nor the Valley of Tophet"—but a practically unlimited extent of territory which could be reclaimed through the tremendous energy and industry of the inhabitants offered possibilities undreamed of by the crowded populations of Europe.

Very similar was the conclusion reluctantly reached by Abbé de Pradt, the former chaplain of Napoleon, in his study *Des Colonies et de la Révolution actuelle de l'Amérique* (Paris, 1817). The contagion predicted by Jefferson and dreaded by Turgot and Vergennes had reached South America. The Spanish and Portuguese colonies, following the example of the United States, were shaking off the yoke of Europe. Thirty years after the conclusion of the Treaty of Versailles, the revolutionary influence of the United States extended over the whole New World. Considering "What is the future of the United States?" De Pradt answered that according to Franklin's calculations, which so far had proved to be correct, the United States would support 138,400,000 inhabitants by 1919. Nothing comparable had ever happened in ancient or modern times. The American flag was already everywhere, and everywhere the very existence of the United States placed monarchies in jeopardy. Going even further than Bristed, De Pradt concluded:

No human power can now stop the march of a nation destined to exert its influence all over the world and perhaps to dominate it.

In fact, it was not an influence, it was an "invasion."

Less emphatically, but no less positively, ten years later, Barbé-Marbois reiterated the warning. In the eyes of the old diplomat who had served Louis XVI and known Washington; who, acting for the First Consul, had "sold" Louisiana to the United States and remained in the diplomatic service under Louis XVIII,

the United States, even without participating actively in the affairs of Europe, will exert through their example, an influence to be reckoned with by the imperial and royal cabinets of Europe. The Prince, whether he be called a king, magistrate, or people will no longer be able to rule without paying due regard to the political liberties of the citizens.

This extraordinary prediction was intended as a lesson to the future ruler of France, since it was dedicated by the old Royalist to the heir apparent of the French throne, "Monseigneur le Dauphin."

Once again Europe was discovering America. All the predictions and misgivings of Montesquieu and his disciples had proved to be false. It was no longer possible to maintain that a republican system of government was inherently weak and that it could survive only in a small territory. Not only was America a powerful country which had recently repelled aggression, but it was the only country that had been able to establish "a stable government, standing without props, while most governments in Europe maintained a precarious existence through measures of expediency."

5

Far more extensive and pervasive than the influence exerted in Europe by the American Revolution proper, and consequently not so easily traced, was a new force, symbolized in the magic word "America" and felt throughout the Old and the New World. This new force was Democracy. All the subterranean activities which neither Napoleon nor the Holy Alliance had been able to suppress completely had slowly prepared the violent explosion which shook all the nations of Europe in 1830. To determine the part played by the American example in the elaboration of the ideas and the fostering of the movements which came to fruition at that time, would require detailed studies which are not yet available. It would be particularly desirable to ascertain the influence of Jefferson, exerted directly and personally through his extraordinarily large correspondence with the lovers of liberty in Europe.

The author of the Declaration of Independence never enjoyed during his stay in Europe the extraordinary popularity carefully exploited by Franklin in the interest of his country. The *Notes on the State of Virginia* (1784), printed in Paris and in London, were not widely circulated, and Jefferson's other writings very seldom appeared in the public papers. But to the *philosophes* he was known as the man who had drafted the "Bill for establishing Religious Freedom," who had proposed a comprehensive plan of public education. By the members of the Committee on the Constitution of the National Assembly he was eagerly sought as a wise counselor. By the Physiocrats he was highly esteemed as a practical philosopher and farmer, interested in developing the agricultural resources of his country. He became later the man who had befriended Volney, Priestley, Thomas Cooper, and Thomas Paine, and was represented as the champion of the oppressed and the protector of political refugees fleeing their country to escape prison, persecution, or worse. As long as he stayed in office he was compelled to observe great prudence in the communications he addressed to his European friends. After his retirement he spoke more openly. He did not conceal the fact that he hated Bonaparte, the man whose ambition had changed Europe into a charnel house. He applauded the first efforts of the South Americans to achieve their liberty and the attempt of the Cortes to establish a more liberal regime in Spain. He advised the Greek Coray, the Portuguese Correa, the Pole Kosciusko, the Spaniard De Onis, and encouraged even more strongly his French friends, Lafayette, Du Pont de Nemours, and Destutt de

Tracy. He corresponded with British liberals like Major Cartwright, and with philosophers like Dugald Stewart, and political and human geographers like Alexander and Wilhelm von Humboldt. He was fully aware that his letters circulated secretly among his friends, but he showed a genuine iritation when his confidence was betrayed and they were printed, on several occasions, in the public papers. He was in fact, and perhaps unknowingly, the leader of a secret resistance movement in Europe during the Empire and the Bourbon Restoration.

The few and still superficial investigations of Jefferson's influence hitherto undertaken are singularly revealing. It seems that at the origin of the Italian *Risorgimento* is to be found a combination of eighteenth century philosophy and French revolutionary theories, with Jeffersonian Americanism acting as a sort of catalytic agent. It may be shown that under the combined influence of Jefferson's theories of government and Destutt de Tracy's *Commentary and Review of Montesquieu's Spirit of Laws,* the Russian "Decembrist" Pestel wrote his book on *Russian Justice* (1825), which led to the promulgation of the first Rumanian code of laws, worked out in collaboration with the representatives of the Rumanian people in 1832. In France again, Auguste Comte acknowledged his debt to the man who had attempted to found the science and practice of government irrespective of theological and metaphysical assumptions. A selection of Jefferson's letters and speeches published in Paris in 1832 led to a long discussion of his political philosophy in Armand Carrel's *National.* The great French critic Sainte-Beuve advised the young French generation to take as a leader and master the man who had proved that one of the first functions of government was to respect the rights of the "individual." No less emphatic and enthusiastic was the *Edinburgh Review,* in October, 1837, proclaiming Jefferson "the recognized leader of the party which had effected the first, possibly the most remarkable of those revolutions, and the one that has had the greatest influence upon the fortunes of mankind." Two years earlier, Richard Cobden had already declared that the time had come to draw lessons from the American example, in words calling for a complete reorganization of the social structure:

We fervently believe that our only chance of national prosperity lies in the timely remodelling of our system so as to put it as nearly as possible upon an equality with the improved management of the Americans.

Shortly before the Revolution of 1830, the French "doctrinaire," Royer Collard, had declared, "La démocratie coule à pleins bords," and indeed Democracy seemed to be on the point of overflowing its banks and of sweeping through Europe like an irresistible flood. But "Democracy" was now a battle cry rather than a definite program, as "Liberty" had been some fifty years earlier. Even its most enthusiastic apostles had no experience with the working of a democratic system of government. At a time when a complete transformation of the European system was impending, the Americans were the only people who had somehow managed to control and to direct through well laid-out channels this apparently unmanageable force. The United States stood no longer as engaged in an unprecedented and venturesome experiment: the experiment had been conducted in a gigantic laboratory, and it was an undeniable success.

6

Such were some of the thoughts which filled and haunted the mind of the young French magistrate who, in the spring of 1831, crossed the ocean with the official mission of studying the penal system of the United States. Born of a noble family, Alexis de Tocqueville was the grandson on his mother's side of M. de Malesherbes, the fearless lawyer who had presented the defense of Louis XVI before the Convention. Recently appointed to a modest position in the judiciary, he seemed little prepared by his education and family tradition to become, if not an apostle, at least a theorist and an exponent of democracy. He did not venture on his expedition without misgivings and hesitations. He was, as he has told us himself, "under the impression of an almost religious awe" caused by the sight of that irresistible revolution, marching for so many centuries through countless obstacles and now advancing in the midst of the ruins it had accumulated. To determine whether this "phenomenon almost fatal or providential" could in some degree be limited; to discover through what means democracy could be dedicated to the great task of enabling people to govern themselves; to find out some of the reasons which had made it possible for America to avoid the pitfalls into which the French people had fallen—these were the momentous problems that this young man, twenty-seven years of age, had undertaken to solve.

This utilitarian preoccupation, this eagerness to serve his country and the cause of civilization, have secured for Tocqueville a unique place among the critics and historians of America. He had no desire to prove or disprove any theory or system. He had no preconceived idea or prejudice, but as a judge he had been trained to look for the evidence and the facts of a case. His training largely accounts for both the judicial quality and the shortcomings of *Democracy in America* (1835).

That he was an alert and keen observer, susceptible of spontaneous reactions, is amply proved by his recently published journals. He traveled extensively in the United States, interviewed many statesmen and scholars, slept in the huts of the pioneers, and even visited some Indian tribes. But he strove to rise above contingencies; he looked for what is permanent and durable under the changing surface of changing phenomena. To use again Montesquieu's phrase, he was more interested in the "nature of things" than in things themselves. He used observation to establish principles from which, through an extensive deductive process, he could derive logical consequences and ultimately lessons in the art of self-government for the use of his fellow countrymen.

The consequence and perhaps the weakness of this method is that *Democracy in America* does not present a vivid and complete picture of American life, but rather a sort of diagram of what American life might become if the principles which directed its development continued to apply. A not inconsiderable number of Tocqueville's predictions have proved to be false, but for three-quarters of a century his book was accepted as fundamental and authoritative in America as well as abroad, and even today it can be read and studied with profit.

Tocqueville concluded that the pillars on which the structure of American civilization rested were separation of church and state, and an almost excessive decentralization. Obviously, in emphasizing these features of American life, the author had always present in his mind reverse conditions and tendencies in his own country. His conclusion was that the American experiment could not be repeated in Europe, and least of all in France, without a deep moral transformation. His picture of American democracy was presented as an object lesson and not as a pattern to be exactly reproduced.

Two problems, however, were common to Europe and America. The first was how to preserve the liberty of the individual against all tyranny, whether it be the tyranny of the state or the tyranny of the majority. The second problem, no less pressing, was raised by the irresistible leveling and lowering tendencies of modern peoples. As the old aristocracies were doomed and had amply demonstrated their political incapacities, as an aristocracy of riches would entail no lesser evils than those of the old system, as on the other hand, the common people were incapable of solving directly the problems of modern life, the main question was

for the partisans of democracy to find means of getting the people to choose the men capable of governing and to give them in addition enough power to direct the latter in matters as a whole, but not in the details of their work nor the means of execution.

And in discussing, in a letter to John Stuart Mill, the first part of his work, Tocqueville concluded: "That is the problem. I am fully convinced that upon its solution depends the fate of the modern nations."

One of the unavoidable consequences of this unavoidable leveling was the disappearance of many of the features of the old civilization which were dearest to Tocqueville and most of his French contemporaries. Among them was, first of all, the gradual pauperization of intellectual and artistic life, which can thrive only where a distinct and semipermanent aristocracy is maintained. In common with almost all of the travelers and observers of American life, Tocqueville not only refused to recognize that America had made any distinctive contribution to arts and letters, but asserted that conditions in America were so adverse to the development of the arts that an acceptable mediocrity was the most that could be expected. It was an old quarrel and an old contention against which Franklin and Jefferson had protested in the eighteenth century, and which had aroused the ire of the American public on several occasions during the first third of the nineteenth century. In vain David Warden, for a long time Consul General in Paris, and later Eugène A. Vail in his book, *De la Littérature et des Hommes de Lettres des Etats-Unis d'Amérique* (Paris, 1841), had attempted to counteract the supercilious criticism of American literature published in the *Edinburgh Review,* the *Quarterly Review,* or the *Revue des Deux Mondes.* At most it was granted that in some "minor" fields like history, oratory, perhaps natural history with Bartram, Audubon, and Agassiz, American authors had attained some distinction. But even if Irving, Cooper, and later Longfellow were names ranking high in literature, their indebtedness, real or assumed, to the literatures of the old world was such that they could hardly be regarded as the leaders of a truly original and American school.

Such was the price that America had already paid, thought Tocqueville, and that sooner or later Europe would have to pay; such as it was, it was not too high. With all its imperfections and deficiencies America remained to him and to his many followers the only place on earth where a new science, the science of government, could develop with a minimum of interference from internal troubles and foreign wars. Europe had already lost its leadership. In the world of 1830, there remained only two great powers with undeveloped and practically unlimited resources, America and Russia—one representing, despite many deficiencies, an ideal of liberty and a promise to respect the rights of the individual, the other centering all the authority of society in a single arm:

The principal instrument of the former is freedom; of the latter servitude. Their starting point is different and their courses are not the same; yet each of them seems marked by the will of Heaven to sway the destinies of half the globe.

Tocqueville had made his choice early and never departed from it. Only six

years before his death in 1859, when the Union was on the eve of being torn
by a civil war, he reiterated his faith in the mission of America:

I earnestly hope that the great experiment in self government which is carried
out in America will not fail. If it did, it would be the end of political liberty in
our world.

The lasting influence of Tocqueville's book can hardly be overestimated.
It was translated into Danish, English, German, Hungarian, Russian, Serbian,
Spanish, and Swedish and went through many editions in France, England,
and America. There is little doubt that John Stuart Mill, who reviewed the
first part of *Democracy in America* a few months after its publication, would
never have written his great book *On Liberty* (1859), and would not have
insisted as he did on "individuality" and the dangers of government interference, if he had not had always present in his mind the picture of democracy
presented by Tocqueville. This impact was felt in many different quarters.
Tocqueville strengthened the faith of the European liberals by insisting upon
the checks to which popular government should be submitted, while
Proudhon in France, Max Weber in Germany, and more recently Harold
Laski in England saw in him a prophet, proclaiming the doom of the
bourgeoisie and the necessity for drawing leaders from the mass of the people.
In some respects, and particularly as an analyst of the American form of
government, he was not only complemented but superseded by Lord Bryce.
But the influence of Bryce's *American Commonwealth* (1888) was far more
limited both in time and in space, while for many generations *Democracy in
America* has remained, if not the bible, at least the handbook of liberals in
most countries of the world.

One of the most obvious shortcomings of Tocqueville was his failure to
give sufficient consideration to the new economic forces and to the industrial
revolution then taking place before his eyes. To a large extent his work was
supplemented by two of his fellow countrymen, Michel Chevalier and Guillaume Tell Poussin. Both of them were civil engineers, and both of them
foretold the gigantic industrial power of the United States. Michel Chevalier's
Lettres sur l'Amérique du Nord (1836) was somewhat overshadowed by the
success of Tocqueville's book. In common with many of his contemporaries,
he entertained a gloomy view of the future of Europe. As did so many of
them, he accepted the historical theory of the westward march of civilization
and of the decline of old societies. He was too patriotic a Frenchman to admit
that Europe was irremediably doomed, but he admitted that preponderant
influence in world affairs would soon pass to the young peoples of Asia,
among which he included Russia, and to the young peoples of America. His
only hope was that ultimately the East and the West, the civilizations of

Europe and those of the young nations of Eastern Europe and Asia, would meet on the American continent not in a death struggle, but "to join hands and mix together, and this will be the greatest fact in the history of mankind."

His contemporary, Guillaume Tell Poussin, whose ambition was to write "a complement to Tocqueville's great book," emphasized, even more than Chevalier had done, the extraordinary development of applied science in America. In the railroads and steam navigation he foresaw the end of economic isolationism and a sort of industrial democratization of the world originating in the United States. In a book significantly entitled *De la Puissance Américaine* (1845), he foretold the triumph of world democracy, following great struggles in which America would be called upon to participate. Her strength and power, which could no longer be questioned, were consequently a matter of international importance. Nor was this view limited to the French. In the Introduction to his *Philosophy of History,* Hegel, some twenty years earlier, had admitted that

America is therefore the land of the future, where, in the ages that lie befcre us, the burden of the old world's history shall reveal itself . . . perhaps in a contest between North and South America. It is the land of desire for all those who are weary of the historical lumber-room of Europe. Napoleon is reported to have said: "Cette vieille Europe m'ennuie." It is for America to abandon the ground on which hitherto the History of the World has unfolded itself.

It remained for a disciple of German thought, Edgar Quinet, in an article published in 1831 in the *Revue des Deux Mondes,* to trace the decay and death of the religions of the Old World accompanying the decline of Old-World civilizations and to predict:

A new idea of God will surge from the lakes of Florida and the peaks of the Andes: in America will begin a new religious era and will be born a new idea of God.

To a certain extent, but with an interesting modification, this was also the view expressed by the Prussian historian Friedrich von Raumer, in 1845 (*America and the American People*). In the prodigious growth of the United States he saw an almost divinely inspired achievement of "the Germanic stock marching irresistibly forward." Having little faith in the future development of Asia and Africa, unable to distinguish any indication of a rejuvenation of a sickly Europe, he concluded:

If we were forced to despair of the future progress of the Germanic race in America, whither could we turn our eyes for deliverance, except to a new and direct creation from the hand of the Almighty.

7

Such were some of the dreams to which America was giving rise. As much as during the eighteenth century, it was, in the early years of the nineteenth, still a Utopian land, or rather a land where Utopias became realities. It was the land where Lezay-Marnesia had hoped to establish a refuge for the French aristocrats and where a few years later Coleridge had planned to establish his Pantisocracy. It was the land where Robert Owen after his unsuccessful experiment in England came to build his New Harmony and where the German Rapp established his communistic village of Economy, sixteen miles from Pittsburgh. The Napoleonic exiles, after Waterloo, had come as "soldier farmers" with General Bertrand to plant "the vine and the olive" in the wilds of Texas and Alabama. It was known that, while the theories of Fourier could not be put to the test of experience in Europe, a group of New England writers managed to conduct a famous if inconclusive experiment at Brook Farm. America was the only country on earth where the French socialist Cabet could attempt to organize colonies of Icarians, because nowhere else could small groups, advocates of a new order, establish and govern themselves locally and practically without any interference from a central government. It was the land where Priestley and Thomas Cooper from England, Comte de Noailles, Talleyrand, and Volney in the troubled last decade of the eighteenth century, General Bertrand, Jérome Bonaparte, and Achille Murat after the fall of Napoleon, had found an asylum. It was the land where the Germans, the Irish, and the French after 1848 were again to come as refugees to seek a liberty which they despaired of establishing in their own countries. It was also a land of hope in another respect. It was an irrefutable demonstration that the representatives from all the nations of the world, thinkers, reformers, and generous poets who had been called to attend an International Peace Conference under the presidency of Victor Hugo, in 1848, were not wild dreamers. The United States of America was a "commonwealth of nations." It had proved the truth of one of Hegel's chief axioms, that Unity dominates the diversity of elements. As long as the United States stood, there was hope that ultimately the peoples of the Old World could be redeemed from themselves. The American dream had become part of the cultural tradition of Europe.

THE DEMOCRACY

. . . the meaning of independence

16. THE GREAT EXPERIMENT

During the years from the nonpartisan reelection of James Monroe in 1820 to the Compromise of 1850, the United States lived very much to itself. Contacts with Europe were slighter than at any time before or since. Transportation by steamship was initiated in the thirties, but it was irregular and unreliable. Communication by cable had not yet been attempted. Consular and diplomatic exchanges were few. As compared with the rate of increase from births, the increase in population from immigration reached the lowest point since 1607. For three decades, Washington and New York and even Boston moved westward across the globe—farther from Europe, nearer the Rocky Mountains.

In the period of the Revolution, American liberals had put into execution European ideas; during the early years of the Republic, conservatives had been equally willing to accept foreign thought. Now, in partial isolation, a new generation adjusted Old World concepts to their own activities and began to create indigenous symbols to represent their own experiences. Out of this ferment there emerged a way of life dominated by the two forces of self-trust and expansion. Each advanced the other, yet at the same time each contravened the other: the thrust of expansion drove individuals and the states farther apart while the pull of self-trust held them together in one nation. More often expressed in action than in words, this diversity within unity found fragmentary utterance in the speeches of Clay, Webster, and Calhoun, and in the social criticism of Bryant of the New York *Evening Post* and of Cooper. In these crosscurrents of opinion, the generation of Lincoln and Emerson came to maturity.

Self-trust, when exercised by a people, is nationalism—in this instance, the brash yet healthy assurance of a youthful country secure in its achievements and its potentialities. Born in the political and philosophical debates of eighteenth century Europe, the doctrine had first taken on a negative form in America, that of hostility to England. Later it had become a self-conscious demand for native arts, native customs, and even a native language—to be created *de novo*. Now, as the frontier moved toward the Pacific, geography gave nationalism a new context. Not only was the United States the first nation founded on the novel principle that the boundaries of a nationality should coincide with those of a sovereign state, but it was also the earliest example of a nationality taking root in the rich soil of an unexploited continent. It is true that the enthusiasm of Americans for national symbols and holidays, for native scenery and customs, and for their own past often paralleled similar enthusiasms in Europe. But the impact of a new world, with its tremendous resources and its ever-present frontier, gave to nationalism in the United States a fresh and gusty incisiveness which sometimes angered and always amazed foreign observers.

This nationalism of the thirties and forties was often provincial, and it was often noisy—never in American history were patriots more vocal. It was at the same time realistic. Statesmen in Washington, as they watched the continental European powers withdraw from the Americas, discovered that the United States could rely on the Atlantic Ocean and on the self-interest of Britain as guarantors of American independence. In 1823 President Monroe was shrewdly capitalizing on the geographical self-sufficiency of the United States and on the foreign policy of Britain when he announced that the young republic had become the protector of a hemisphere: "The American continents . . . are henceforth not to be considered as subjects for future colonization by any European powers," and any attempt of a foreign power to control any independent state in the American hemisphere will be viewed as "the manifestation of an unfriendly disposition toward the United States." It should be remembered that the President and his advisers, Jefferson, Madison, and J. Q. Adams, did not commit the United States to this bold policy until they were assured of the support of Britain. Self-confidence for Americans in that day was confidence not only in themselves but in the only foreign power which maintained a navy capable of striking across the Atlantic.

Meanwhile the American people were congratulating themselves on the success of their experiment in republicanism. The division of opinion in the later eighteenth century between monarchists and republicans now disappeared, and monarchy became a symbol of all that Americans hated. Their republic, on the other hand, was neither the mirage nor the chaos that European reactionaries had anticipated; it was a practical, going concern. Out of the older concepts of natural law and natural rights, American liberals developed the new doctrine of popular sovereignty. Then they defended the republic as the only form of government consistent with that doctrine. (Popular sovereignty was not at that time generally associated with "democracy" because the latter term was not yet in general use.) Americans, as might be expected, were confirmed in their faith by the emergence of each of the French republics, by the founding of the South American republics, by the turmoil in Europe in 1830–1831, and particularly by the revolutions of 1848–1849. Whenever a foreign political experiment collapsed, Americans congratulated themselves again on the happy state of their own nation.

A steadily increasing respect for and reliance on the idea of the Union, one and indivisible, further strengthened egocentric Americanism. Jackson made his position dramatically clear at the Jefferson Day dinner of 1830, when he repudiated a series of toasts from the nullifiers by proposing: "Our federal Union: it must and shall be preserved." Likewise unequivocal was his reaction when in 1832 South Carolina declared that the federal tariff was null and void, and that the state would leave the Union if it were coerced. Jackson issued a proclamation in which he denied that the Union is a league of independent states and insisted that it is sovereign and perpetual. He let it be known also that he would use troops to enforce national laws. Respect for the Federal Constitution continued to grow until that instrument and the doctrine of the Union became, in the minds of nationalists, the two great bulwarks of the Republic.   ,

A people as successful as the Americans considered themselves to be, and as religious as a majority of them were, inevitably credited their triumphs to God as well as to themselves. Reinterpreted in terms of the nineteenth century, the Puritan thesis that God's hand had been evident in every incident in the colonization of New England became the cult of manifest destiny. The United States had been set apart by divine Providence or by fate as the scene of a great, and perhaps a final, experiment in free government. The success of this experiment now made it evident that Americans were indeed a chosen nation. As such, they were destined to bring self-determination and republicanism to Texas, to California, and perhaps even to Canada and Cuba. They were chosen, likewise, to exemplify the ideal state for the imitation of rebels against monarchy in Europe. The honest concern of the American people for the welfare of all mankind gave a certain dignity to this theory of manifest destiny and a comfortable feeling of self-righteousness to its exponents.

The pervasive self-trust of these decades was announced, both by single citizens and by the nation, in a variety of terms. On the frontier, Davy Crockett shouted: "I kin lick my weight in wildcats!" In the White House, the President announced the nation's coming of age in state papers. In office and countinghouse, men said: Much as we owe to Europe, that continent is merely the exhausted past from which our fathers escaped; we find it expedient and profitable to be Americans. Among the older men of letters, Irving and Cooper groped for security, now abroad and now at home; but the young men put their trust in themselves and their new world. Emerson, speaking in 1837 for his egocentric contemporaries both in the United States and in Europe, declared: "If the single man will plant himself indomitably on his instincts, and there abide, the huge world will come round to him." And speaking for all high-minded nationalists of his century, he announced: "Our day of dependence, our long apprenticeship to the learning of other lands, draws to a close. The millions that around us are rushing into life, cannot always be fed on the sere remains of foreign harvests. Events, actions arise, that must be sung, that will sing themselves."

2

The spirit of expansion, at once result and cause of self-trust, wrote its own history across the map of the United States. In the years from the Revolution to 1820, the area of the Union had doubled. From 1820 to 1850, the westward migration pushed on into Texas, into Oregon, and to the Golden Gate; the territory of the United States increased by half; and the Americans were masters of three million square miles of land—an empire thirty times the area of the British Isles. The people themselves at the same time were growing with a swiftness unparalleled in history. During the two centuries from 1650 to 1850, their rate of increase per decade maintained an average of 35 per cent—that is to say, the number of inhabitants doubled every twenty-five years. Thus the population rose from nine million in 1820 to twenty-three million in 1850, when it was all but equal to that of the British Isles. American brag may have offended foreign ears, but it was often confirmed by history.

Under the thrust of expansion, no new cleavages appeared among the American people, but old frictions were intensified. Sectionalism, for example, in the 1780's had delayed the Federal Constitution and during the War of 1812 had provoked New Englanders to threaten secession. By 1840 not only the East but the South and the West were actively promoting their own interests. In New England sectionalists campaigned for protective tariffs, a centralized monetary system, and a strong federal government. In the South Hayne and Calhoun defended free trade, easy money, and states' rights. In the West, where self-interest coincided now with the interests of the South and now with those of the East, local patriots stood for easy money, a strong federal government committed to internal improvements, and free land. No one section commanded enough votes to win a national election. The South and the West in alliance were rarely able to control national affairs; only a coalition which included the East could dominate the nation. When the three sections came to a realization of these facts and of the futility of any attempt by a single state to exercise its rights through nullification, the only question which remained was this: Have the territory and wealth of the United States become so great that one of its sections is prepared to withdraw from the Union and form a new nation?

Certain of these sectional differences reappeared in the pattern of the agrarian-industrial conflict of the period. The nation was still predominantly rural, for only 7 per cent of the population in 1820 lived in towns of more than twenty-five hundred, and in 1850, only 15 per cent. The value of farm property was moved upward, exceeding three billion dollars in 1850, but the rate of increase was soon to fall off. In 1820 manufacturing ranked third as a source of national income, surpassed by shipping as well as agriculture. But the value of industrial property was doubling every ten years; the annual value of manufactures rose to over a billion dollars in 1850; and American industry was well launched on its spectacular career. Humanitarians and the early spokesmen of labor were already attacking Eastern industrialism as undemocratic. Southern planters feared its power and damned it as a peculiarly unenlightened variety of slavery. Western farmers in general agreed that industrialism was dangerous, but they were too busy with their own affairs to make an active assault on the factory. Apologists for capital remained on the defensive, content to emphasize the democratic nature of an industrial order which offers every man an equal opportunity to earn a living, to invest his savings, and to climb to the top of the ladder. The factory itself was glorified by capitalists as a Utopia where young men and women from the back country took on urban culture—an interpretation endorsed by Davy Crockett after a glimpse of the mills at Lowell, Massachusetts, and by the mill girls themselves in their literary organ, the *Lowell Offering*. But the American people as a whole remained agrarian-minded.

Deepest and widest of the cleavages in the era was that between aristocracy and democracy. In the South, where the past retained its greatest influence, Jefferson's theory of a natural aristocracy flourished but the democratic elements in his thinking were neglected. In their place, Calhoun proposed a "democracy" modeled after the society of pre-Christian Greece, in which a large population of slaves supported a small population of enlightened freemen. Moneyed aristocrats in the East (especially in Cooper's New York) adhered to the stake-in-society theory, arguing that men should participate in government to the same extent that they own property. Less materialistic patricians continued to put their trust in family; others, in the learned professions; and still others (as the Brahmins of Boston), in both. The stronghold of democracy was the new West and its new states. Here backwoodsmen and farmers kept alive the radicalism of the left-wing Jeffersonians and of Shays' Rebellion, until in 1828 their man Jackson went to the White House.

A prelude to this defeat of the patricians was the gradual extension of suffrage: by 1828 only Virginia and Rhode Island retained property qualifications on the ballot. This expanded electorate, free but of course not unanimously democratic, chose as President a frontiersman skilled in swapping horses and land, in wrestling and dueling, in killing Indians and British—the first man to reach the highest elective office in the nation without benefit of family or learning or wealth. This event threw many of the well bred into a frenzy: the young gentlemen of Harvard College burnt Andrew Jackson in effigy, and their elders fulminated against this "millennium of minnows" and the enthronement of "King Mob" in the White House.

To Jackson and his followers, the one institution which most clearly symbolized wealth, privilege, and aristocracy was the National Bank. He did not rest until it was destroyed. He also gave his support to such equalitarian practices as frequent elections, the increase of elective offices, and rotation in office, on the ground that "the duties of all public officers are, or at least admit of being made, so plain and simple that men of intelligence may readily qualify themselves for their performance." Then followed the demand of party members that the rewards of office should also rotate, and the spoils system was established. But the theory of Jacksonianism remained noble, for it proposed to achieve equality not by leveling but by raising. Andrew Johnson, the Tennessee tailor who became President at Lincoln's death, could declare in 1865:

Man can be elevated; man can become more and more endowed with divinity; and as he does he becomes more God-like in his character and capable of governing himself. Let us go on elevating our people, perfecting our institutions, until democracy shall reach such a point of perfection that we can acclaim with truth that the voice of the people is the voice of God.

3

In religion, the result of self-trust was diffusion in the form of voluntarism, secularization, and sectarianism. The process of separation of church and state, which had been initiated in the eighteenth century, came to its conclusion in 1833 when Massachusetts broke all official ties between government and religion. Legal regulation of religious practices, especially Sabbath observance, declined. Church membership and church support were now a matter of choice, and the success or failure of all religious activity became the responsibility of individual sects and their individual members. At the same time authoritarianism was weakened. In the Congregational and the Baptist churches, every man had a right to speak and hold office; in the Episcopal and the Methodist churches, secular authority increased; and among the Disciples of Christ, unpaid lay preachers filled the pulpit on Sunday and earned their own living during the week. As the nation expanded, minority groups among the Baptists, the Methodists, and the Presbyterians split off from the mother churches, to create new schisms. Even more symptomatic were the "come-outers" who devised their own religions, some as early as the eighteenth century: the Shakers, the Harmonites, William Miller and his Millerites (who announced that the world would end in 1843), the Fox sisters and the spiritualists, John Humphrey Noyes and his Oneida Community, Joseph Smith and his Mormons, and many more. During these lively years, creeds multiplied as rapidly as the swiftly multiplying population.

The success with which minorities shaped new religions to fit their own needs is illustrated by the history of transcendentalism. Its exponents were a small group of New England intellectuals who, after rejecting both rationalism and Calvinism, built their own faith around the divinity of man. Their nucleus was the informal Transcendental Club, their organ was the *Dial,* and their most influential spokesmen were William Ellery Channing and Ralph Waldo Emerson. Channing announced the fundamental principles of Transcendentalism: God is all-loving and all-pervading, the presence of this God in all men makes them divine, and the true worship of God is good will to all men. Emerson pointed up its individualistic tendencies by stressing intuition, Platonic idealism, and self-reliance.

The fashion in which less intellectual Americans cultivated their own variety of emotionalism in religion is evident in the history of the revival on the Western frontier. In the equalitarianism of the camp meeting, every man had as much right as his neighbor to renounce his sins, square his accounts with God, and choose a new way of life—all on his own volition. The Congregational church offered equality in church government, but its college-trained and college-founding ministers offered little excitement at the mourners' bench. More successful was the Baptist faith, especially among Negroes and pioneers who derived particular satisfaction from the rite of immersion. Most popular of all was Methodism, which prospered mightily in the West under the apostolic Francis Asbury and the rough and ready Peter Cartwright. A few nights of the singing and shouting, the holy laughter, holy jerks, and holy rolling of a revival gave emotion-cramped pioneers new faith in their country and their sect.

Humanitarianism in its broadest aspects may have helped to unify American society, but in the daily living of individuals it provoked dissent and acrimony. The theory and the practice of doing good, which had received their impetus in eighteenth century sensibility, were now sustained by American democracy and by nineteenth century pietism. The theory, as interpreted by the prophet Emerson, was all-inclusive: Let us not capitulate to the lie of one idea or of one reform; let us destroy, not one prison, but all prisons. Men who attempted to put this doctrine into practice—Lyman Beecher, William Ellery Channing, Theodore Parker—were hailed as universal reformers. But even those expansive souls could not cure literally all the ills of mankind; they could only give their support to certain favored causes and withhold it from the rest. And the leadership which translates good intentions into good deeds came in most instances from zealots devoted to a few related reforms or a single issue.

An instance was the temperance movement, which by 1825 enlisted more than a million Americans in a crusade directed not toward temperance but toward total abstinence. Those friends of all good causes, Beecher, Channing, and Parker, blessed the movement and made converts in the upper reaches of the electorate—important people but a minority on election day. Such universal reformers as the Sweet Singer of Hartford (Lydia Huntley Sigourney) and the staff of *Godey's Lady's Book* converted wives and mothers—but they cast no ballots. It remained for the men with one idea to bring in the votes: Timothy Shay Arthur, author of *Ten Nights in a Barroom, The Sons of Temperance Offering,* and a flood of tracts; the Washington Temperance Society, a group of reformed alcoholics; and the famous evangelist John B. Gough. These enthusiasts aroused the masses, and they in turn enacted prohibition legislation in thirteen states during the fifties.

In similar fashion, other crusades were led by men who concentrated their powers. Horace Mann and Henry Barnard were aware of more than one contemporary problem, but they specialized in educational reform. Emma Willard and Mary Lyon taught "females." Thomas H. Gallaudet, Samuel Gridley Howe, and Dorothea Dix befriended the deaf, the blind, and the insane. Lesser contemporaries, whose names are no longer familiar, organized municipal leagues, societies for prison reform, and similar agencies for amelioration. Unhappily, most idealists who were sufficiently tough-fibered to fight for a minority were too individualistic to get on with their fellows. Many a builder of the New Jerusalem erected with his right hand his own little structure of perfection, and tore down with his left hand what his neighbor had shaped.

While humanitarian movements clashed and rose or fell, one question grew more insistent: What shall be the final attitude of the United States toward slavery? As the years passed, the answer of the abolitionists gained in volume and insistence, until theirs was the loudest voice in the land. When the advocates of temperance bid for support in competition with the aroused antislavery men, the latter won and the temperance movement declined. When the campaign for women's rights ran afoul of abolition, only William Lloyd Garrison's radical minority accepted women as equals, and feminism receded into the background. The peace movement, pioneered by William Ladd and Elihu Burritt, flourished for more than a quarter-century; then it met slavery head-on, and even Theodore Parker finally admitted of war: "I hate it, I deplore it, but yet see its necessity. All the great charters of humanity have been *writ in blood,* and must continue to be for some centuries." The pressure of events thus made it evident that slavery was the one issue which could not be evaded.

4

Only a nation endowed with perfect wisdom could have effected a final reconciliation between the self-trust and the expansion of these years. Actually, the American people achieved a partial reconciliation in their thinking and a series of compromises in their public affairs. In their thinking, they brought together the familiar doctrines of the rights of man and his perfectibility, the expanding idea of democracy, and the new doctrine of progress. Out of these concepts, came their faith that by perfecting the individual they might eventually build the perfect state. Thus they reconciled the one and the many.

In the realm of public affairs, the period began and ended in compromise. The National Republican Party collapsed in the early thirties with the defeat of Clay. The Whig Party then emerged, an ill assorted band of former National Republicans, worshipers of Clay and Calhoun, nullifiers, and Antimasons, whose only common denominator was hatred of Jackson, living or dead. Jackson's party was itself in disagreement, West vs. South, over a variety of issues, particularly slavery. Men's minds were whirling with the claims of nationalism and sectionalism, industrialism and natural rights, slavery and the will of God, equality and a stake in society, revivalism, public improvements, the emancipation of women, manifest destiny, progress.

Of the three compromises which emerged from these conflicts, two involved the problem of slavery, and all three the problem of sectionalism. The first was the Missouri Compromise of 1820, whereby the South gained Missouri as a slave state and the East gained Maine as a free state, and slavery was prohibited "forever" in the greater part of the Louisiana Territory. The second was the Compromise of 1833, whereby Southern sectionalism was placated by a gradual reduction in the tariff and Unionists were appeased by the enactment of Jackson's Force Bill. The final and unavailing Compromise was that of 1850. The weary Clay, whose nationalism was ever stronger than his pronounced sectionalism, now urged the Whigs to make large concessions to Calhoun and the South in order to save the Union. The aged Webster, at last convinced that the preservation of the Union was more important than the liberalism of New England, supported Clay. By the legislation which they sponsored, the slave trade but not slavery was abolished in the District of Columbia, the reclaiming of runaway slaves was made easier, and the Missouri Compromise was repealed by the stipulation that new territories should come into the Union either slave or free, as their citizens might determine.

Compromise could go no further; civil war was inevitable.

17. ART IN THE MARKET PLACE

THE era for the making of the new literature had arrived by 1820, but no one knew the rules or had the blueprints. The air was alive with energy and experiment. Writers were relying more upon journalism and the lecture and less upon the law, politics, and the church for their support. At the same time, American culture began to develop stronger regional characteristics and to strengthen such cultural centers as New Orleans, Charleston, Richmond, Baltimore, Cincinnati, Louisville, Philadelphia, Albany, New York, Concord, and Boston. But as the business of publishing and distributing books and magazines became better organized, these widespread centers looked more and more to New York for the stimulus of literary association and for the market place of literary wares.

The spirit of self-trust and expansion in this period found one form of expression in a zeal over all of America for the country to distinguish itself in the arts, to compel the critics as well as the common readers of England to think highly of the American book. That zeal was doubly felt in the South which, after about 1830, was concerned to justify itself sectionally against the North as well as nationally against Europe. The West as it expanded felt the same double defense to be necessary. Nationalism and sectionalism can hardly be distinguished; both stimulated the demand for "mental independence," both deferred to the critics of the older cultural center. The result was a ferment of literary activity.

2

New theories of education based on the concept of the natural man had already begun to develop a new generation of readers. The textbook reforms of Noah Webster and Jedidiah Morse were carried forward by the matter-of-fact "Peter Parley" (Samuel G. Goodrich) who insisted that cows give milk as well as jump over the moon, and that the first ideas of children "are simple and single, and formed images of things palatable to the senses." Starting with pictures and common experience, he took his imaginary charges over the

228

globe, at the same time covertly attempting "to spiritualize the mind, and lift it above sensible ideas." He wrote or edited in the next twenty years 170 volumes and sold seven million copies. Emerson's philosopher-friend Bronson Alcott followed the same route from sense to spirit for the thirty children in his "Temple School" in Boston a few years later, although his climb from the sensory experience to the "spiritual" was aided by a school-room with "paintings, busts, books and not inelegant furniture," which provided "a prop round which tendrils may fasten"; while the Thoreau brothers accepted the conditioning provided by nature for their Academy and took their charges for long walks in the woods and fields of placid Concord.

The theories of Pestalozzi and of Jefferson, thus curiously mixed with sentimental idealism, were to require another century before John Dewey could urge their acceptance in a purer form, but meanwhile primary education developed rapidly. In 1827, when Peter Parley began to write, there were two "infant schools" and fifty-six primary departments in New York City, while a Massachusetts law in the same year required a high school in every town of five hundred families or more. But progress was slow, especially in the South, and it was not until 1850 that a campaign of propaganda and legislative reform, led by Horace Mann, succeeded in establishing, in principle at least, in every Northern state the provision of a common-school education for all children at public expense. "I have faith," wrote Mann, "in the im-provability of the race—in their accelerating improvability."

This faith in improvability led to the founding of some five hundred universities and colleges before the close of the century. There were two theories of state direction of higher education: that of New York which followed the French plan of administrative centralization of control over a distributed group of institutions, and the German plan of gathering the various schools of learning into one place and establishing a sprawling mammoth. The latter prevailed in most instances, and the states of the West and South almost without exception created universities within a few years of their admission to the Union. Even cities like Charleston and Louisville had by 1837 set up universities or colleges of their own on this pattern. At the same time, the various religious sects followed the advancing waves of migration and established small denominational colleges by twos and threes in each new state. The pattern of higher education for affairs as well as for ideas, which had been laid by Jefferson in the early years of national life, guided this entire period of expansion and became set as the distinctive form of organization for democratic institutions. Its chief characteristics were elas-ticity and a blind faith in "Veritas" and "Lux."

The colonial colleges adopted this pattern by a slow breakdown of the classical curriculum and of the close-knit control by the faculty over the students. George Ticknor, appointed the first teacher of modern foreign languages at Harvard in 1815, is spokesman and symbol for the changes which were national. Before taking up his duties, he spent several years of study at Göttingen—an example followed by Edward Everett, George Bancroft, and ultimately a hundred other young American admirers of the German awakening, including Longfellow and Lowell. Supplementing his studies by wide travel in England and on the Continent, he returned with books and ideas enough to overturn the settled ways of the provincial college. Long a friend of Jefferson, he admired the unrestricted freedom for intellectual exploration which the latter had made the guiding principle of the University of Virginia. Ticknor published a pamphlet in 1825 urging the adoption at Harvard of the departmentalized elective system, with a wide variety of offerings, the system finally achieved by Charles W. Eliot who became president of Harvard in 1869.

The education of women was a natural by-product of this tendency. Women were not full citizens under our original Constitution, but a few of them like Lucretia Mott, Margaret Fuller, and Elizabeth Peabody began agitation in the forties which ultimately brought them most of their "rights." In 1821 Emma Willard had established at Troy, New York, a "Female Seminary" which provided not only religious and moral, but literary, domestic, and what was called "ornamental" instruction for girls. Although the force behind this movement was moral zeal, its social implications were not long in making themselves felt. Other seminaries followed, but years passed before the education of women reached the college level on a par with that of men.

This widespread intellectual hunger produced the Lyceum and other systems of popular lectures. The surviving Lowell Institute of Boston, one of the earliest and most influential of these organizations, has been providing free public lectures in all branches of human knowledge for more than a century. The Peabody Institute of Baltimore and the later Cooper Union of New York were and are similar bodies. Supplementing the wider Lyceum movement, these local agencies soon offered a career to traveling lay preachers like Emerson, and a modestly remunerative side line for newspaper editors like Horace Greeley, as well as innumerable writers including Simms and Thoreau, Dickens, Thackeray, and later Matthew Arnold. Even museums like the Smithsonian Institution at Washington used the lecture as well as the display of their treasures as means "for the increase and diffusion of knowledge among men," and exponents of pseudosciences like mesmerism and phrenology or of causes like abolition and temperance gained an audience by combining entertainment with knowledge.

The rage of Boston has turned from parties to lectures [wrote W. W. Story in 1840]. What with Waldo Emerson and Useful Knowledge, and Lowell Institute and Grammar and Temperance, the whole world is squeezed through the pipe of science. All go to be filled, as the students of old went with their bowls for milk.

This movement owes much to Josiah Holbrook of Derby, Connecticut, peripatetic lecturer on geology and mineralogy. In 1826 the *Journal of Education* carried an outline of his plan for a national adult system of popular education. Every town was to have its own lyceum, with a library, a collection of minerals or other specimens of natural history, courses of lectures given by members, and groups for the study of science, history, and art. County lyceums were to be formed by delegates from the town societies, and in turn state lyceums and finally a national or even a world lyceum. Holbrook gave his life to the development of this vast corner in the adult education market and might have succeeded but for the rivalry of American copies of the Mechanics' Institutes of England and other local movements originating in trade and guild schools, local academies and colleges, women's clubs, and extensions of the great universities. Nevertheless, Holbrook's crusade created a hundred branches of the American Lyceum in two years and spread to nearly every state in the Union. By 1834, when the movement was at the crest, there were some three thousand local lyceums in the nation. The American Lyceum, a national federation of local units, had been organized in New York City three years earlier and held annual meetings until 1839. It influenced popular education from the common school to the college, and no one can tell how close was the connection between its popularization of knowledge and the explosive anarchy within every type of formal educational institution during this period. Whether cause or result of the forces of uncontrollable freedom in our early educational history, it did more to shape American literary history than any other agency. Not only in the East but throughout the North and West, it created a vast army of readers, listeners, and students and developed the new literary form of the popular lecture, although in the South the tradition that gentlemen could give themselves most fruitfully to politics delayed the democratization of literature.

3

New York City became in these years, by sheer mercantile superiority, the literary capital of the nation, making virtual provinces of the South, the West, and even New England. But in Boston and its environs there were literary stirrings which depended on other than mercantile factors. From the glitter of lower Broadway to the calm of Concord or Cambridge is a journey longer in mood than in miles. To discover the significance of the cultural renaissance which flowered in these New England villages in the forties and fifties, one must turn backward or forward a few pages in this book and forget the descriptions of bustling and mercantile New York. Boston, with its *North American Review* and its Harvard College, had succeeded more than any other American city in keeping aloof from the market place even though the materialism of its State Street was shocking to some. Prosperity did not avoid it in blessing the commerce of all American seaboard towns from Charleston north, but Bostonian pride succeeded in using material gains to foster rather than to overwhelm the things of mind and the spirit. The mystery of this contrast can probably never be completely resolved; with the same instruments of culture at its hands, Boston developed great orators, great teachers, great writers; and Concord, some twenty miles to the west, was her conservatory for the cultivation of her finer fruits.

Two closely related institutions, the Town Meeting and the Congregational Church served, as they had since the founding of New England, to maintain the distinct character of the region. The Congregational and Unitarian ministers, although few of them retained either the theological rigor of early Puritan days or the fiery enthusiasms of the Great Awakening, still exerted great influence. Aside from their spiritual and religious functions, they were New England's chief representatives of the intellectual life. They almost alone had leisure for study, for thought, and for thought's full expression. They were, in fact, "delegated minds" in a sense more exact than that in which Emerson could use the term in speaking of his ideal American scholar, and indeed he might never have used that term if he had not been familiar from childhood with the duties and prerogatives of the New England clergy.

In trying to estimate the probable influence of these clergymen we should have in mind not only men of exceptional ability, powerful preachers such as Joseph Stevens Buckminster, intrepid leaders such as William Ellery Channing, or scholars and thinkers like Frederick Henry Hedge, but also the far more numerous run-of-the-mill ministers who spoke from country pulpits week after week in tones none the less authoritative because they had little to say. Fair examples of this ordinary preaching are to be found in the sermons of Ezra Ripley still preserved by the hundreds in Concord's Old Manse, some of which were heard by Ripley's young kinsman, Ralph Waldo Emerson, when he was making up his mind to leave the ministry. The Reverend Mr. Ripley was undoubtedly a stout laborer in the vineyard of the Lord, but it must be said that the sermons he preached for nearly sixty years in Concord can have done very little to advance the culture of that town or, one may add, the Christianity. His sermons were empty and dull, laboriously conventional and elaborately superficial. While struggling to read them one is often reminded that their author was, as he said, a "natural Unitarian," so that he never had the intellectual discipline of thinking down into the "cast-iron logic of despair" called Calvinism nor yet that of thinking his way out of it. Compared with the rock-ribbed sermons of the great Puritan past written by men such as Thomas Hooker, Thomas Shepard, and the Mathers, these of his are woefully deficient in "fundamental brain-work." Indeed, they all but justify one of the severest remarks ever made by Emerson about any human being: "This afternoon the foolishest preaching—which bayed at the moon. Go hush, old man, whom years have taught no truth."

With such leadership the New England culture that began to be aware of itself in the third and fourth decades of the nineteenth century was inevitably conservative, moralistic, and tinged with an unimpassioned piety. Often erudite but seldom creative, it was largely a matter of reading and bookish talk, doing little to lessen that unwholesome predominance of literature and oratory over the other arts which had characterized New England from the start. And even with regard to literature a culture thus dominated was somewhat timorous and spinsterish—inclined to doubt, for example, whether Goethe could be really a great poet in view of what was known or surmised about his illicit amours. Worst of all, this culture was not an indigenous growth but a plant imported from foreign lands to take its chance among the native flora.

The prevailing mood of New England was as conservative as that of her clergy. In her detestation of Jefferson's Embargo and her lack of enthusiasm for the War of 1812 she revealed, at least among her more prosperous classes and in the vicinity of Boston, an Anglophile tendency. Members of the Federalist Party, retaining power in Massachusetts long after the party elsewhere had died out, exerted an influence out of proportion to their numbers. At the Hartford Convention in 1815 they expressed their belief that New England might at need become independent. Longfellow's father attended that convention as a delegate, and it seems likely that the fathers of Lowell and Holmes would willingly have done so.

The chief intellectual center of the region, from which most of the Congregational clergy were sent forth, was, and from the start had been, Harvard College, an institution almost two centuries old when Holmes graduated there in 1829. With fewer than two hundred undergraduates, a faculty of some fifteen permanent members, and a library of less than forty thousand volumes, Harvard did not make an extensive educational offering. The curriculum, rigidly prescribed, laid primary stress upon Latin, Greek, and mathematics, although increasing attention was given to the modern languages and science was recognized in a few lectures and "demonstrations." Courses in English composition were conducted, with signal success, by Professor Edward Tyrrel Channing, who in his many years of teaching read and castigated the "themes" of Emerson, Holmes, Lowell, Dana, Motley, Thoreau, Sumner, Parkman, and Edward Everett Hale. Compulsory chapel exercises were held twice a day.

The college was not remarkably stimulating to lads of fine intelligence, and the ordinary undergraduate probably gained less information there than is commonly acquired in a good high school of the twentieth century. On the other hand there was at Harvard a serious concern for things of the mind to which even a dullard could scarcely fail to respond. In a time and place almost exclusively concerned with crude "practical facts" it managed to inculcate an interest in abstract ideas and in knowledge for its own sake. It had a character, an idiosyncrasy of its own, which it stamped upon all its sons indelibly. There was a hint of ancient Rome and Athens in this Harvard character, and through the barnlike classrooms and dormitories there blew as it were the bracing air of Plutarch's "Parallel Lives." Most of all to its credit, the place was hospitable to odd and unclassified individuals who did their own thinking and boldly spoke it out. In training most of the New England clergy Harvard had done her share, producing a conventional and conservative culture; but now she was slowly making ready for a different kind of leadership.

4

The pulpit and the lyceum did not supersede other and more traditional agencies for the making of the literary man. The increase in population, the spread of literacy, the improvement in means of communication, the growing sophistication of both urban and rural society, and the technical advances in printing and book production conspired to build up a substantial reading public. George P. Putnam of New York, the first of the great publishers in the modern sense, estimated that in 1845 the combined college libraries in the country contained 600,000 volumes and public collections almost 900,000. "Besides these," he added, "there is scarcely a town of any importance in the Union, but has some sort of a public library, reading-room, lyceum, or athenaeum."

The effects of inventions on the spreading of the printed word soon became apparent. The old methods of hand-set type, handmade paper, and the screw-pressure press had already been superseded by the principles of levers and cylinders when in 1825 the Napier steam-driven press made its appearance. The production of 2,000 copies an hour of the New York *Daily Advertiser* seemed a miracle until in 1847 the Hoe rotary press stepped production up to 20,000. Type casting and hand setting continued, however, for editions of most books, which in 1832 averaged 1,000 copies. Stereotyping of plates was known in this country as early as 1813, but was applied mainly to Bibles and textbooks until about 1830 when the Harpers adopted it as a regular practice for their "omnibus editions" of English reprints and Carey began to use it for Cooper's novels. Paper- and ink-making processes, machine type casting, and new methods of binding and embossing kept pace with these other improvements, and the process of steel engraving in the forties started F. O. C. Darley and others on careers of book illustration which would have been altogether impractical with the less durable wood block, the copper plate, and the lithograph.

Important by-products of these improvements were the appearance of the annual or gift book and of the giant anthology or cyclopedia of literature, scenery, or other matter suitable to fine printing, binding, and illustration. Goodrich attributed the sudden vogue of such annuals as *The Token, Friendship's Offering,* and *The Atlantic Souvenir* to the invention of steel engraving. "Under such seductive titles," he wrote, "they became the messenger of love, tokens of friendship, signs and symbols of affection, and luxury and refinement; and thus they stole alike into the palace and the cottage, the library, the parlor, and the boudoir." Similarly, R. W. Griswold raised the literary anthology to new levels of luxury if not of discrimination with *The Poets and Poetry of America* (1842) and his subsequent collections of prose and of the work of "female poets." And the Duyckincks produced their ten-pound, two-volume *Cyclopaedia of American Literature* in 1855.

Mechanical improvements in book making led in two quite contrary directions. They made it possible to produce far more elaborate books at no increase in cost, to illustrate them more copiously, and to bind them more sumptuously; but competition was so acute that mechanical improvements could not be generally applied until the middle of the century, when the Townsend *Cooper* and the Putnam *Irving* appeared, dignified gentlemanly rows of stocky volumes, with clear type on heavy paper, steel-engraved illustrations, and embossed ornaments on substantial cloth covers. Such books could look down on the humble, paper-bound parts of the 1819–1820 *Sketch Book* as a well disciplined, modern regiment might view ragged mountain guerrillas.

On the other hand, competition called for a continuously increasing quantity of production and lowering of costs. This tendency reached its climax in the late thirties and the forties, when Cooper's novels began appearing in paper wrappers at twenty-five cents instead of a dollar a volume; when mammoth newspapers, four feet long and eleven columns wide, began to print the complete novels of Dickens, G. P. R. James, or Lytton in "extras" of• some seventy closely printed pages at ten cents a copy; and when the editor of the New York *Tribune,* the first great penny newspaper, could write:

What is to prevent a daily newspaper from being made the greatest organ of social life? Books have had their day—the theatres have had their day—the temple of religion has had its day.

The effect of the situation on the book market is stated by Goodrich. According to his estimates the gross amount of trade in books in the United States in 1820 was $2,500,000, of which one million was in books of kinds other than educational, classical, theological, legal, and medical. By 1850 the total had mounted to $12,500,000, or an increase of 500 per cent, of which $4,400,000 was in the miscellaneous category. And, with the general lowering of cost and quality the actual number of titles issued may have shown as much as four times this increase. At the same time Goodrich estimates the ratio of books of American authorship to those of British at 30 to 70 per cent in 1820 and at 70 to 30 per cent in 1850. Throughout the period, the Southern market remained a major outlet for Northern booksellers, and the markets of the Ohio River valley grew in importance.

"American authors," writes Putnam, "are not always deprived of just remuneration for their writings." In this respect, progress was fairly rapid, and, in the period of inflation prior to the panic of 1857, royalties were as high as they are today. But the struggle of Poe to earn a livelihood by his writing is reflected in the experiences of many others in the earlier group. Cooper offered Carey the rights to an edition of his *Notions of the Americans* in 1828 for $1,500 and usually got $2,000 for an American edition of his novels. But even with his reputation made Poe could get no return for his *Tales* in 1839 and only eight cents a copy for the small 1845 edition. Emerson followed the common practice of paying for the manufacturing of his books and let booksellers handle them on commission. It was apparently Putnam who developed the royalty method of payment, offering 10 per cent to American and even to exploited British authors in 1845-1846. The shock was almost too much for them. Carlyle, with characteristic pomp, exclaims, "Such conduct was that of men of honour." The usual method of distribution was a barter system among publishers, which, without national advertising, tended to restrict sales and so cut the return from royalties, however high their rate might be.

Book publishing was financially unrewarding unless the British market was played as well as the American and the absence of an international copyright law or protocol was thus circumvented. Cooper and Irving together found at least a temporary solution to this problem. Irving's *Sketch Book*

(1819–1820) marks the real beginning of American literature in more ways than one, in that it was the first book by an American to bring its author financial returns on both sides of the Atlantic. The formula which he stumbled upon by his presence in London and his urgent financial need was learned by Cooper when he visited England in 1827, and it became an important means of support for most of our mid-nineteenth century writers. It was, briefly, the trick of residence or of prior publication in England.

The reason for this curious situation was that the American copyright law allowed protection for their work only to *American* authors, whereas the English law based its protection on priority of publication or on residence without regard to the nationality of the author. British publishers were often willing to pay an American author cash in advance for first publication rights, whereas citizenship made prior publication unnecessary for protection at home. Thus the American author could sell his manuscript to an English publisher, have advance sheets, or pages, shipped by fast packet to America, and, by timing the issuance of the books in the two countries with an interval of a few days or weeks, outwit the pirates and obtain double returns. An English author, on the other hand, because of his foreign citizenship, could not obtain protection in the United States and was free spoil for the American publisher until, toward the middle of the century, a sense of fairness on all sides tended to equalize the situation.

The fight for international copyright stretched on for a century with both British and American laws frequently altering but never correcting the situation. For a long time authors fought almost alone, but they were slowly joined by the publishers under the leadership of Putnam. The paper and other collateral industries seem to have furnished the bitter-enders, aided and abetted by the reading public which unthinkingly wished its books to be many and cheap. The passage in 1891 of an American law providing for international copyright brought to an end a century of controversy.

Meanwhile, the magazines managed to pay sufficiently to keep both major and minor authors in pocket money by offering modest fees for original work and by allowing advances to authors in need. The vogue of the short story, the familiar essay, and the lyric poem in America may be attributed to this cause. The *North American Review* marched sedately through the period, publishing mainly critical articles; but there were many other magazines of more popular and literary caste. Among the earlier ones were the *Casket* (1826–1840) of Philadelphia, the *New England Magazine* (1831–1835), and the *Southern Review* of Charleston (1828–1832). Later the field was taken over by the *Knickerbocker* (1833–1865), the *United States Magazine and Democratic Review* (1837–1859), the *Southern Literary Messenger* of Richmond (1834–1864), and *Graham's* (1840–1858) of Philadelphia, the last two of which Poe edited for short periods. Margaret Fuller and Emerson published the distinctive organ of the transcendentalists, the *Dial,* in Concord from 1840 to 1844 while *Harper's* started publication in 1850 and the *Atlantic* in 1857. *Godey's Lady's Book* set the pace for women's magazines in 1830 with its colored fashion plates and its sentimental fiction and poetry, and continued its prosperous career almost to the end of the century; while Willis' *New York Mirror* (1823–1857) exploited the possibilities of the weekly, and for many years was supreme in that field.

Graham's, for its period, seems to have created almost a monopoly, and entered into contracts with authors for regular and exclusive rights to contributions. Its circulation in 1843 was over 100,000 copies, and Hawthorne was content with the arrangement "on account of the safety of your Magazine in a financial point of view." Its editor, R. W. Griswold, offered Mrs. Frances S. Osgood $25 each for stories and $10 for poems in that year, and about the same time Park Benjamin wrote Graham: "Would you like to have an occasional poem from Professor Longfellow? I think I could get him to write for you at $20. He asks $25." Still some minor authors wrote for love and there is no record of their offers having been rejected, but a professional attitude was becoming more common. A contemporary guess set N. P. Willis' annual earnings in four magazines at $1,200 to $1,600 a year, and Paulding contracted to write a five-page article for every issue of *Graham's* at $10 per page. "My terms," wrote H. W. Herbert, "are necessarily in these hard times cash on delivery." Even as late as 1851, the dramatist George Henry Boker could write to a friend, "Alas! Dick, is it not sad that an American author cannot live by magazine writing?"

Writing for the stage was an even less secure profession. Prior to the passage of the Copyright Act of 1856, which gave the playwright, "along with the sole right to print and publish the said composition, the sole right to act, perform, or represent the same," the only hope for protection was to keep a play out of print. Early managers and actors like Dunlap, Hackett, and Wallack sometimes rewarded their authors with a benefit "third night," but the return in any case was insufficient to encourage native talent, especially as most acting companies came direct from London with their casts and their repertories complete. Gradually American actors and managers took over, and the tendency of companies to travel less and to become identified with specific theaters encouraged local talent without providing any regular returns. Forrest's system in the forties of offering cash prizes for new plays did much to dignify the position of the playwright, but it reacted unfavorably as it meant the outright sale of the manuscript. The story of Boker's *Francesca da Rimini* is now classic: the best play by an American in the nineteenth century, it was withdrawn in 1855 after a few performances and had to wait twenty-seven years before it was revived by Barrett, when its author was too old to be stimulated to new effort by its popularity. Boker seems to have earned no more than $1,500 in all for five plays produced between 1849 and 1856. Robert Montgomery Bird, after selling several plays to Forrest for $1,000 each, turned from drama to the writing of fiction.

There were a few efforts to better the position of the writer. In 1836 a joint stock company of lawyers and literary men, called the Stationers' Company of Boston, was organized to promote the publication of more serious work. It issued Prescott's *Ferdinand and Isabella* and Hawthorne's *Twice Told Tales,* but it was not financially successful. Yet recognition was coming to authors by 1855, the year of the Duyckincks' *Cyclopaedia.* On September 27, there was held in the Crystal Palace, "the Complimentary Fruit Festival of the New York Publishers' Association to Authors and Booksellers." It "was one of the most gratifying and suggestive occasions I ever witnessed," wrote a visitor from Boston, and Everett, Sumner, Bryant, and Beecher were present to raise their voices in praise, while James T. Fields read a poem.

A word should be added for the publisher-bookseller, for he often encouraged an author when other agencies failed. Putnam did much to promote the sale of American books in his London shop, and Hawthorne wrote to his friend Fields in 1862, "My literary success, whatever it has been or may be, is the result of my connection with you." It was Fields who had suggested in 1849 that he rewrite *The Scarlet Letter* as a novel, with the result that it had three times the circulation of the book of Tales from which it was taken. The Old Corner Bookstore in Boston was Hawthorne's favorite haunt even though he sat apart from the distinguished group of men and women who made of the shop a literary club in the days of Emerson, Holmes, Harriet Beecher Stowe, and Lucy Larcom. Cooper and Irving formed similar groups in the shops of New York and Philadelphia, and by 1856 William Gilmore Simms had gathered such a group in Russell's bookshop in Charleston.

More even than Fields and other publishers, the two anthologist-editors, Rufus W. Griswold and Evert A. Duyckinck, shaped the course of literary history in the forties and fifties. Their choices became the choices of the ever widening reading public, and authors were quick to court their favor and enjoy their friendship. Griswold, whom Lowell accused of plucking alive and feeding on his literary flock, became Poe's successor as editor of *Graham's Magazine* in 1842, and later his literary executor, and with his many anthologies developed into a kind of "chief herdsman" of the "Parnassian fold" of younger writers including Thomas Buchanan Read, George Henry Boker, Bayard Taylor, and Richard Henry Stoddard. *The Poets and Poetry of America* (1842) and the companion volume of *The Prose Writers of America* (1847), together with a half-dozen other anthologies and introductions to editions of the poetry of Scott, Milton, Praed, Béranger, Bryant, Hemans, Campbell, and others, made him a sort of court of appeal in matters of taste; but he abused the authority this gave him in his treatment of Poe's life and reputation, and otherwise exercised it with breadth rather than discrimination.

Duyckinck was a man of sounder scholarship, finer taste, and broader human sympathies. Unlike his rival, who fought with Poe, he encouraged Melville when the author of *Typee* was beginning his career and most needed the kind of aid that an editor could give. A graduate of Columbia College in 1835, Duyckinck spent more than a year (1838–1839) in Europe in the expectation of a professorship of literature; when the appointment failed to materialize, he became a sort of *ex officio* professor to countless literary men, many of whom gathered weekly for far-ranging conversations over Roman punch and cigars in the basement of his New York residence. Bryant, Irving, Lowell, Simms, Taylor, and Hawthorne were his close friends. They and many others borrowed books from his well chosen library of some eighteen thousand volumes. As editor, after 1845, of Wiley & Putnam's Library of Choice Reading and Library of American Books, he was a major influence in introducing European classics to American readers and in helping American authors to find an audience. Hawthorne advised him to publish Emerson's poems because he thought Emerson's reputation still "provincial, and almost local, partly owing to the New England system of publication." Simms sought him out on a visit to the North and became one of the distinguished group of contributors to the *Literary World*—as brilliant a literary journal, under Duyckinck's editorship, as this country has known.

The *Cyclopaedia of American Literature* (1855) immediately became and still is a standard reference work. Written and edited with the aid of his brother George, it reflects his comprehensive reading, his widespread acquaintance with living authors, his extensive research in both books and manuscripts, and his indefatigable correspondence in search of facts, as well as his taste and his critical judgment. Here and in his critical articles he declared the superficiality of the popular N. P. Willis and of much of the poetry of even Longfellow and Lowell. Although out of sympathy with the principles of transcendentalism, he never doubted Emerson's greatness and was disappointed in not obtaining some of his work for New York publication; and he unqualifiedly proclaimed Hawthorne and Melville the literary titans of his day. Like most New Yorkers, Duyckinck felt ill at ease in Boston; but his friends included writers from all sections, and his home—like his native city—was a national meeting ground.

Thus mercantile giants like John Jacob Astor and Stephen Girard were not alone in learning before the middle of the century the art of focusing the diverse material of a democratic laissez-faire economy upon their own fame and profit. James Gordon Bennett, Horace Greeley, and William Cullen Bryant became powerful as editors by so marshaling these forces; George Palmer Putnam, E. A. Duyckinck, and James T. Fields did the same for book making; Willis, Graham, and Lewis Gaylord Clark, for the magazine; Edwin Forrest and William Niblo, for the theater; and finally Cooper, Irving, Emerson, Kennedy and many lesser men, for literature. Cooper, Irving, and Willis, by playing their cards with cunning and care, made possible the career of the professional man of letters in America; Emerson did the same for the popular lecturer, as Edward Everett stamped out the pattern for the occasional orator by making of his art a career. By mid-century the American literary man had come into his own.

The increasing millions of new readers created by education and migration could thus be supplied with literary fare only because there was corresponding progress in importing, producing, and circulating the printed word. At first glance one wonders, not why there was suddenly a new generation of native authors, but why this group was relatively small and why it struggled with financial obstacles almost as great as those of an earlier day. The answer to these questions is clear. In a competitive mercantile economy, the writer is in the position of the farmer, a producer of raw materials without protective tariff. Power and profit pass him by unless he too can find ways to play the game. "Democratic literature," wrote De Tocqueville in 1835, "is always infested with a tribe of writers who look upon letters as a mere trade"; Dickens spoke of the "present abject [moral] state" of the American newspaper press; and the elder Longfellow wrote sorrowfully to his son in college, "There is not wealth and munificence enough in this country to afford sufficient encouragement and patronage to merely literary men." Wealth was growing, but for many years it was to be widely distributed and was to fall for the most part into the hands of the literary manufacturer and middleman rather than into those of the author.

18. WASHINGTON IRVING

THUS America was ready for a man of letters: the lights were on; the audience assembled. The mediums for the new culture were exciting. In all those interests of man which we call cultural there was a stir, the unmistakable promise of a future. A few of our writers, a Hawthorne or an Emily Dickinson, were to live "beyond time," that is, not without aloofness to the dust and heat of their own eras. This man of letters, however, for whom the theater, the magazine, the novel, the more civilized society, and the new nationalism called so imperiously, was not to be, like Edwards or Emerson, timeless, but temporal, an inevitable creation and adroit user of those cultural mechanisms and moods; it could not, in this adolescence of our intellectual life, be otherwise. Without a skillful manipulation of these instruments of culture, success in writing was impossible; and without measurable public renown of some kind, any author might hope in vain for readers.

Naturally some of our first men of letters were men of affairs who discovered in themselves surprising talents with the pen. Before he published *The Sketch Book,* at the age of thirty-six, Washington Irving had been a lawyer, a businessman, and a soldier; in his contemporaries' eyes the crown of his career was not this famous volume, but his appointment as minister to Spain. Although at heart a dreamer and a deliberate artist, he was fascinated by these new playthings of culture, and became an urbane participant in the clubs, coteries, and literary and theatrical circles which formed a graceful backdrop to his own preeminence. In spite of his long residence abroad, his links with the "Knickerbocker Group" were real. No writer gauged better than he the demands of contemporary readers, at home and abroad; his essay of manners was not unaware of that of Joseph Dennie in Philadelphia, of Miss Mitford in England, and of Fernán Caballero in Spain. His creative life prospered not in the study, but in the drawing room, the theater, or John Murray's publishing house.

Washington Irving was our first classic. Even in his own time his sketches found their way into the schools and into the libraries beside the English masters; and he early demonstrated his mastery of the form and temper of

242

the nineteenth century essay. Byron, Coleridge, and Scott were among his admirers; he stands on the shelves with Addison, Goldsmith, and Lamb. Yet, contrary to the myth, he never imitated these essayists, nor even Scott; his own style is authentic, born of a temperament, taste, and subtlety of mind which were peculiarly his own. Hawthorne, who worshiped him, and whose writing resembled his in its singular unity of tone, felt, as did all his peers (save the bristling Cooper), the union in him of a sensitive personality and the power to express this completely. His good sense and amiability undoubtedly enhanced his prestige, as Cooper's truculence diminished his; if Irving is now unread, this may be partly the reason. Yet his place, apart from his literary pioneering and his personal charm, is secure.

For Irving is classic not only as a stylist but as a poetic interpreter of legend—local, European, and universal. The monument at the entrance of "Sunnyside" commemorates his triple achievement, in the three figures of Diedrich Knickerbocker, King Boabdil of Granada, and Rip Van Winkle. If we dismiss the romantic story of his life, that of the son of middle-class Scottish parents rising to eminence as a famous American, or if we set aside his brilliant workmanship in prose, there still remains his extraordinary intuition concerning America's heritage of world legend, his fulfillment of his early determination to enrich his country with the "colour of romance and tradition." The tendrils of Irving's finest stories lie deep in human memories and feeling. Rip Van Winkle's return is a symbol of his concept of mutation, an all-pervasive theme in his writings:

With what singular unanimity [says Thoreau] the furthest sundered nations and generations consent to give completeness and roundness to an ancient fable.

2

In retrospect, Washington Irving's golden career as a man of letters seems the result of a happy convergence of circumstances: the rapidly growing social and literary life of Manhattan; European fashions of writing; his own alert, plastic mind. Spanning the period between the Revolution and the Civil War (1783–1859), he read successively, as they came from the press, the writings of Burns, Campbell, Byron, Scott, and later, with some misgivings, those strange new books of Emerson, Poe, and Hawthorne! The early nineteenth century romantics, particularly Scott, oriented his taste, as the clubs, periodicals, and theaters of the gay, civilized little city directed his talents toward satire, the essay, the drama, and the short story.

Indulged by parents and innumerable friends as the youngest and most gifted child of a large family, he let himself drift in the pleasant currents of parties, gossip, and tea-table authorship. By his twenty-sixth year he had already composed light verse; a life of Thomas Campbell; essays and biographies for the *Analectic Magazine,* of which he was for a brief period the editor; a dim little volume of dramatic criticism (*The Letters of Jonathan Oldstyle, Gent.,* 1802); a symposium of satiric pieces, in collaboration with his brother William Irving and James K. Paulding (*Salmagundi,* 1807); and that energetic burlesque, *Diedrich Knickerbocker's A History of New York* (1809). This was our first remarkable piece of comic literature. Old New York shook with a roar of laughter.

In these years Irving knew the blessing of a light heart which defied his strain of latent melancholy. Of medium height, with chestnut hair, blue eyes, and a peculiarly pleasant, husky voice, he was friendliness itself; never as a person does he seem more winning than in these casual years when he squired the damsels of New York and Philadelphia, journeyed on a holiday trip to the Canadian frontier, played with the study of law in Judge Hoffman's office, or frolicked with *Salmagundi.* He "makes his travels go far," said his friend Henry Brevoort, alluding to a two years' grand tour of Europe bestowed upon Irving in 1804 by his fond brothers. He had returned still less in love with the family hardware business or with the bar; instead he was enamored of his little vellum notebooks, reminiscent of his wandering and germinal of many a later essay and story. Thus he had become almost the habitual dilettante when in 1809 the remarkable satire by "Diedrich Knickerbocker" (one of Irving's many *noms de plume*) revealed to discerning eyes, among them Scott's, his exceptional powers as a satirist. Yet in this very year occurred the great sorrow of his life, the tragic death of his fiancée, Matilda Hoffman; a period of doubt and uneasiness ensued, accentuated by the uncertainties of his future. During the War of 1812 he served as a staff colonel, and in 1815 he again sailed for Europe: he did not know that he was to remain abroad for seventeen years, or that he would return as "Geoffrey Crayon," the famous author of *The Sketch Book* (1819-1820).

After *Bracebridge Hall* (1822) and *Tales of a Traveller* (1824), and a winter in Dresden, he collaborated unsuccessfully in play writing in Paris with John Howard Payne. In 1826 he was on his way to Madrid to translate, at the request of A. H. Everett, Navarrete's history of Columbus. The following three years, mellowing his natural vein of romance, saw him a scholar in the ancient libraries of Madrid (where Longfellow called on him), a dweller with Andalusian peasants in the courts of the Alhambra, and a friend of the German antiquarian Böhl von Faber, and of his daughter Fernán Caballero, the Spanish novelist of manners. Such a life, seminomadic, was entirely congenial. Nevertheless, in 1829, bowing to his brothers' wishes, he accepted the post of Secretary of the American Legation in London. Three years later he returned to his own commonplace country, but not before he had published or prepared for the press four works memorializing his experience in the Spain of a century ago (*The Life and Voyages of Columbus*, 1828; *The Conquest of Granada*, 1829; *The Companions of Columbus*, 1831; *The Alhambra*, 1832).

For Irving this break with European life and thought was momentous. Though only fifty and at the height of his powers, he returned to an America appreciative of his fame but suspicious of his extended exile abroad and of his truancy to European themes. He now permitted a belated Americanization of all his interests. After a pilgrimage to the wild Southwest, he celebrated the wonders of the Osage frontier and other Western explorations in three elegant volumes for the parlor tables of his countrymen (*A Tour on the Prairies*, 1835; *Astoria*, 1836; *The Adventures of Captain Bonneville*, 1837). He was now the friend of Astor and, some said, his factotum; he dabbled in the stock market; and he was discussed for political posts. Most dismaying, he ceased, so far as we can tell, to read or to write for his craft, and on one occasion he admitted to John Pendleton Kennedy that, like most of his contemporaries, he regarded the creation of literature as merely a gentleman's avocation.

Living on at "Sunnyside," except during the years when he was the popular Minister at the court of Isabella II (1842–1846), he became an arbiter of our letters, a benevolent despot of our writers, a symbol of our thin literary culture. Uncomprehending, he beheld the rise of the great New Englanders and uttered pontifical platitudes on Poe's tales and *The Scarlet Letter*. He himself could only rifle again his old notebooks to produce biographies of Goldsmith, Mahomet, and Washington. His work was long since done; the age in which men read eagerly of the romantic wanderer in Europe already belonged to the past. Yet in the pathos of his decline we must not forget the adoration of Poe and Hawthorne; through Washington Irving, writing as an art had been born in America.

3

On all the historic events occurring within his long life of more than three-quarters of a century Irving sets down in letter or essay shrewd comment; but in his pages we look in vain for sustained wisdom concerning the movements of thought behind such events, for penetration of the intellectual life of his epoch. He wrote graphically of many famous episodes, of Waterloo or of the War with Mexico; but of Anglo-French relations or of American imperialism he has nothing to say worth hearing. He lived in England during the ferment culminating in the Reform Bill; but he merely laments the passing of the stagecoach and the yule-log Christmas. From the unrest in England and the democratic upsurge in America he acquired only a sentimental Toryism. On the meaning of democracy, of sectionalism, of the frontier he offers only pretty paragraphs communicating his personal distaste. He was simply a lover of old ways, of the romantic past.

Likewise, on more spiritual problems Irving was properly silent. His personal religious history includes his childhood with Deacon Irving, a Scotch Covenanter, his rapid progress toward skepticism and indifference, and finally, in the later years at Tarrytown, his identification with the Episcopal Church; the story reflects his natural remoteness from religious introspection. On the turmoil of Unitarianism, transcendentalism, evangelicalism, he let fall no word; he merely found New Englanders uncongenial, and popular religions vulgar. His notions on current trends of thoughts had their origin not in an analytical mind such as Melville's, nor even in a passionate partisanship such as Cooper's, but in an indolent temperament and an incurably conservative taste.

Irving's first books, *The Letters of Jonathan Oldstyle, Gent.* and *Salmagundi,* are distinguished by little save high spirits. Yet the other "youthful folly," as Irving ruefully called it, *A History of New York,* is still breathing. Prolix, repetitious, and, in consequence, mercilessly revised by Irving for later editions, it boils over with his boisterous ridicule of Swedes and Yankees, Dutch ponderosities, the pedantry of histories, and Jeffersonian democracy. It is written with gusto, on one occasion breaking into blank verse, and with such an avalanche of satiric allusion, from Cervantes and Rabelais to Walter Scott, that the latter's sides ached, so he wrote Irving, from laughing at its fantasy. In particular, the Dutch personalities of Wouter Van Twiller, William Kieft (a cartoon of Jefferson), and Peter Stuyvesant have crept into tradition, painting, and into the imaginations of subsequent generations of readers. The tough old mock epic may live; it proclaimed not only the breadth of Irving's self-cultivation, but also the vigor of mind that underlay his apparent languor.

Even as Irving corrected the proof sheets of his comic history, lovely Matilda Hoffman lay dying. The decade beginning with the publication of Diedrich Knickerbocker's learned indiscretion and ending with the appearance of *The Sketch Book* changed Irving from a callow youngster to a man; he was still amiable, still shrewd, but he was now meditative, a participant in human suffering. "I know," he wrote, "what it is to be sick and lonely in a strange land." As a refuge he turned again to writing. From boyhood he had faithfully kept journals and notebooks, and now, after his arrival in Europe in 1815, he continued to set down the titles of books, quotations, anecdotes, travel incidents, and his moods of depression; in the blurred pencil lines we may read of his unhappiness in the Liverpool office, of his study of German, of his ecstatic hours with Walter Scott: "Ah," he exclaims, "I knew happiness then!" On March 3, 1819, he forwarded to New York the first number of *The Sketch Book*.

"Crayon is very good," remarked Byron. Some even believed that he was Walter Scott. To us halfway through the twentieth century, all the virtues of *The Sketch Book* seem pallid; we can endure but not applaud the unevenness of the thirty-two pieces, the sickly pathos of such an essay as "The Pride of the Village," the naïve records of Irving's travel in England, the appropriation of the familiar legends. This last weakness in particular has attained an unpleasant emphasis in the scholars' discovery that even "Rip Van Winkle" is dependent on a literal translation from a tale in Otmar's *Volkssagen,* and that "The Legend of Sleepy Hollow" has origins in Bürger's *Der wilde Jäger* and one of the Rübezahl tales. Superficially at least, *The Sketch Book* appears to be dated, embalmed beyond all hope of a resurrection.

Yet beneath Irving's insipidities burned one strong response to life, his sadness or romantic melancholy in the presence of the law of change. The underlying idea in all Irving's best essays is that of flux. The old, forgotten books in "The Mutability of Literature"; the silence of the Boar's Head Tavern, once alive with the mirth of Falstaff; the tombs of Queen Elizabeth and Queen Mary; the grave of Shakespeare; the aged Rip Van Winkle— all declare the terrible brevity of life, the transiency of Man. Wistfully, recalling the tragic alterations in his own life, Irving dwells repeatedly in his public and private writing on "the dilapidations of time":

How [he lamented in a notebook] the truth presses home upon us as we advance in life that everything around us is transient and uncertain. . . . We feel it withering at our hearts . . . in the funeral of our friends and written on the wrecks of our hopes & affections—when I look back for a few short years, what changes of all kind have taken place, what wrecks of time and fortune are strewn around me.

Perhaps the gossamer loveliness of these sketches suffers under precise interpretations. Their symbolism is probably unconscious, involuntary; the essays' indefinitiveness of emotion may be felt as we read, but not explained. In "Rip Van Winkle" this connotative meaning is the secret of its hold upon our imaginations; in it are all the implications of the grim but romantic theme of *tempus edax rerum*. In retrospect or in prospect, Rip's free youth, prolonged sleep, fanciful dreams, and disillusioning return are all ours. The fragile piece deserves study for its debt to German literature, to American legend, to Thomas the Rhymer, to Walter Scott, and to Irving's own boyhood; for its arresting adaptation in the theater, in song, or in Spanish or

Russian translation, for its revelation of a great stylist. But its soul lies in the symbolic distillation of a universal mood. All of Irving's literary manipulation of his reading, his wandering life, and his melancholy were concentrated in a passion which made him compose the tale during a single night, pouring into it all that he had ever felt concerning man's ceaseless enemy, "time": the German romance of Otmar, stories heard from the lips of Dutch friends, memories of the shadowy Catskills and of the blue Hudson. However outworn, by familiarity, jest, and parody, "Rip Van Winkle" still belongs to the indestructible literature of all peoples.

The depths of Irving's melancholy were not meant for repetition. As the climax of ten years of uncertainty and bereavement, his sadness had nearly spent itself in "Westminster Abbey" and "Rip Van Winkle." In a sense he had spoken; never again was he to recapture the spiritual tension of these essays, even in the moonlight scenes in "St. Mark's Eve," in *Bracebridge Hall,* or in the reveries of *The Alhambra.* A professional writer, bent on consolidating his reputation, he was now destined to do *The Sketch Book* over and over again, for the most part on its lower levels. After a season as "the most fashionable fellow in London," with Gifford, Rogers, Moore, and Scott as his friends and Byron and Coleridge as his admirers, he became the author of the fifty-one miscellaneous tales and sketches known as *Bracebridge Hall* (1822). "The fault of [this] book," said Maria Edgeworth justly, "is that the workmanship surpasses the work. There is too much care and cost bestowed on petty objects."

4

Meanwhile Irving was exploring the vein which was to link his books with the more macabre studies by Poe and Hawthorne. Long before 1817, when he sat in Scott's library and watched the novelist take down from his shelves his copies of Fouqué, Grimm, Bürger, Tieck, and Hoffman, he had shared the popular passion for what Scott called "the supernatural in fictitious composition." His approach to the tale of horror, despite his laborious study of the German masters, was characteristically light; he was fond of pointing his eerie stories with a question or a whimsical smile. Was the specter bridegroom an actual being? Was not the rumble of the Catskill bowlers a thunderstorm? After all, the head on Brom Bones' saddle was a pumpkin! He understood the practical value of success in this lucrative field, but his interest in the supernatural had causes deeper than those of expediency. Late in life he declared that the essential stuff of his life had been reverie. Dreams he could express in his versions of German romantic tales; these stories of the supernatural fed his restless, playful imagination, and in addition, as in "The Spectre Bridegroom," offered provocative problems for his craftsmanship. It is not surprising to hear of him during the winter following *Bracebridge Hall* writing, so rumor had it, a "German novel."

If so, this novel was never finished, and only one of the four sections of *Tales of a Traveller* (1824) showed directly the harvest of Irving's prolonged curiosity concerning the supernatural, from his youthful days in New York through this unlucky winter in Dresden. Beginning in an intensive study of German language and folklore, this had been expended in Saxon balls, skating parties, boar hunts, and an unhappy love affair with the English girl, Emily Foster. Tenacity of purpose was not the dominant trait in Irving's nature. So the ghost stories and the robber tales, at best marionettes, were supplemented with three other sections, one on Italy (rehabilitated from the notebooks of 1805), "Buckthorne," a shallow, semiautobiographical novelette under the influence of Goethe's *Wilhelm Meister,* and flaccid tales of cabbage-growing Dutchmen and of Captain Kidd. Gothic novelists, German romancers, Italian robber stories, legends of old New York—*Tales of a Traveller* is an empty cave of echoes.

The ensuing Spanish episode was to be far more felicitous than the German. In the Madrid libraries and in the matchless collection of the bibliographer, Obadiah Rich, he lingered long, indulging his love of old books and manuscripts. His original plan of translating Navarrete's history proved difficult; finally he abandoned the translation in favor of his own free dream of the great navigator. *The Life and Voyages of Christopher Columbus* (1828), in its eighteen books and one hundred and twenty-three chapters, is a strange compilation of theatrical personages (Columbus is a "man of sensibility"), pageantry, Gothic thunderstorms, treacherous Spaniards, noble savages, mermaids, seas of milk, and careful documentation. Its tantalizing hesitation between history and romance evidently created in Irving—a natural *colorista* in his treatment of Spanish material—an indecisiveness which reached a culmination in the next year in *The Conquest of Granada,* a book which no critic has ever been able to classify. It translates the chronicles but poetizes episode and character. Professedly the work of an old monk Fray Antonio Agapida, it craved respect as history. Yet the two long volumes are really romances, beautiful in their tone and even in their monotonous, flowing style. That such things never happened, we may be sure. Yet few admirers of Irving would cancel, as part of his total achievement, the lofty, melancholy personages of Columbus and the fair-haired "El Chico," Boabdil, the last Moorish king of Granada.

In *The Alhambra,* Irving's "Spanish Sketch Book" as Prescott christened it, the frail Boabdil reappears, the legendary king living happily in the palace or pausing sadly at *El Suspiro del Moro* for his final glance backward at his "city of delights," *bellissima Granada*. In its pages Irving was more at ease; he was not a scholar nor even a historian, despite his myriad footnotes; he was an antiquarian romantic. Released from a pattern of writing which had never won his complete devotion, he was again the easy student of folk-lore, through the black-letter books he had studied for his histories, through his friendship with Fernán Caballero, and through his intimacy with Anda-lusian peasants in the palace, Dolores and Mateo Ximénez. So he described in the leisurely fashion of *The Sketch Book* the Court of the Lions and the gallery of Lindaraxa; so he revived the ancient myths of mysterious caverns, buried gold, clashing scimitars, and phantom Moors. History, legend, and the ways of Granada blend in a reverie like those inspired by the dim, blue Catskills. Instead of homespun Dutchmen, paynim cavaliers; instead of the pumpkin, the pomegranate. In the book is the gorgeous tapestry of the Moorish past; such stories as "The Legend of the Arabian Astrologer" in Irving's most civilized manner perpetuate the enduring fascination of opu-lent, barbaric Spain.

If Irving was, as Robert Southey declared, no man to write of the wars of Granada, it is equally true that his books on the Western frontier, which after his return to America in 1832 he published as a capitulation to popular demand, show the same incapacity to set down facts unadorned by sentiment. H. L. Ellsworth's literal record of adventures in the Oklahoma country, on this same journey, reveals by contrast Irving's prettifying of buffalo, wild horses, and the customs of the Osage Indians. *A Tour on the Prairie* (1835) is a drawing-room version of, to do Irving justice, a rough experience, in which he forded streams on horseback and dined uncomplainingly on skunk. Yet in the waving trees of the forest he saw the Gothic arches of the Europe for which he was still homesick; and as he rode with Ellsworth through the blackjack, he reminisced on his creation of *The Sketch Book*. The glimmering lights of the campers, the picturesque dress of the ranger, the bee hunt, the hostile Indians, the undulating reaches of prairie and forest, he refined into a Europeanized idealization of the wilderness.

Sensing the gentle wave of excitement roused by *A Tour on the Prairie* in readers who had never seen a bison or an Indian, he sat in John Jacob Astor's library, and from the diaries of trappers, authentic writing of the frontier, he spun out in *Astoria* an agreeable epic of the overland journey to the Pacific outpost and the voyage around the Horn of the *Tonquin*. In both *Astoria* and the *Adventures of Captain Bonneville, U.S.A.*, also under the patronage of Astor, he relied upon just the right composite of general reading and citation from original sources, upon velvety narrative, upon that "singular sweetness of composition" which had captivated even the hard-bitten Francis Jeffrey. These frontier narratives were not really history, though scholars quoted from them; nor were they humbug, for compared with the actual events they depicted no dream world; they merely reflected the born romancer exploiting materials which belonged to the historian.

However popular, the Western narratives proclaimed one fact: the famous Washington Irving had written himself out. Surrendering in 1839 to Prescott the great theme of the Spanish conquest of Mexico, he attempted little more until, in 1848, he revised his collected works. He now, as he said, read little, and during the four years in Spain as Minister he did not even keep a note-book. He still loved everything Spanish, even the odor of the kitchens, but his beautiful letters to his nieces concerning the court of Isabella II and Espartero remain the sole record in these years of a talent that had gone to seed. Instead of legend, his thoughts were of politics, gossip, and his return to dear Sunnyside and his nieces. Reestablished there, in the last decade of his life, he wearily replundered the old notebooks until Longfellow, who owed so much to the inspiration of *The Sketch Book,* protested at this deterioration. These articles for the *Knickerbocker,* the miscellanies, such as *Wolfert's Roost,* or the third-rate biographies of Goldsmith and of Mahomet hardly bear analysis; little remained but the worn-out themes and the perfunctory grace of the master's style. Of his decline he was conscious, and just before his death he spurred himself to one last effort; but the five huge volumes of his *Life of Washington* mirror in his tired prose merely a stolid marble bust of the founder of the Republic.

5

More and more in retrospect, Irving emerges as both the beneficiary and the victim of the adolescent American culture of the first three decades of the nineteenth century. In this period he formed standards of literary taste from which, for good and ill, he never afterward deviated. To the pre-Victorian drama (he boasted he had seen every actor of his time), to the periodicals, to contemporary idols (not Addison and Steele, but Byron, Moore, Campbell, and Scott), to literary clubs, to growing libraries and still unexhausted private collections of manuscripts, and to lax copyright laws he was heavily in debt. Although he was occasionally capable, as in the libraries of Spain, of almost monastic devotion to learning, yet constructive thought, such as that of the Concord group, was alien to him. His satire, his short stories, his personal essays, were the easy products of his travel, his life in society, his endless casual jottings in his notebooks. Tirelessly he collected these literary *morceaux;* skillfully he amplified them into story or essay; and tactfully he introduced them into the most apropriate cultural medium—the periodical, the annual, or the timely book. He was a superlative literary adventurer.

This is the first, most obvious Irving, the caterer to public taste, hardly more than the hack writer hand in glove with such eminent publishers or editors as John Murray or Lewis Gaylord Clark; this is the Irving cannily alert to fluctuations in literary fashions and sales. Yet from such habits of mind, evident to readers of his self-revealing correspondence with Murray concerning the *Columbus,* developed a second Irving, the man of affairs, the successful American, the substantial citizen of New York (mentioned as candidate for the mayoralty), the grandee of Sunnyside, the Minister to Spain. From the days of Aaron Burr, Irving had hated the sweaty nightcaps of the mob; his Tory soul shrank before Jacksonian democracy. Yet if not openly on the political stage he remained in the wings of this theater. The same disarming tact, the same shrewdness, the same comprehension of public opinion so influential in his literary career, did not harm him in this related role of the observer of American life. These two careers were intimately joined. The America of the forties loved to canonize its literary men, such as a Bryant or an Irving—and so destroy them as poets or essayists. Literary fame might mean public eminence and, turn about, public distinction might enhance literary reputation.

Yet still another Irving—there were really three—commanded the homage of younger American writers who resisted more effectually than he the corrupting influences in our callow culture. If Hawthorne and Poe beheld in their inspirer a journeyman or political meddler, they never said so; in Irving's *Sketch Book* and even in his trifles they perceived the penetrating observer, and his aspirations and his craftsmanship as an artist. This Irving they revered. This Irving wrote tolerable verse and sketched so well that for days in Rome Washington Allston pleaded with him to turn painter. This Irving's notebooks blossomed with delicate sketches; his writing was deeply in debt to this related art; the pictorial quality of his prose is evident both in its metaphors of the brush and in its transference into the drawings of Leslie, Darley, and others, and into the weird beauty of John Quidor's paintings, from "Rip Van Winkle" to "Wolfert's Roost." For this nobler Irving, no self-imposed discipline for the sake of the image or sentence was, as the notebooks prove, too arduous. Ceaselessly he rewrote; indefatigably he revised; his was, in his best moments, the happy, blessed labor of the true artist.

19. JAMES FENIMORE COOPER

Meanwhile, James Fenimore Cooper, a tyro in the more subtle aims of the novel, assumed in the history of our literature an almost giant stature. More casual than Irving toward literary craftsmanship, he triumphed by his interpretation of romantic and realistic life on the frontiers of the forest and the sea, of the development of democracy, and of the meaning of America. A man of action whose career as a novelist was superficially an accident, in him genius was "mainly an affair of energy." In preface, pamphlet, history, and novel he poured out his convictions concerning his era, employing to the full, like Irving, all (except the theater) of the new instruments of culture. Cooper's was not properly a "literary" spirit; he was Agamemnon at a desk (and in the fray, too). Yet his genius left some thirty novels, several volumes of enduring social criticism, and two or three immortal characters. The resiliency of his masculine mind defied in his time devastating attacks from his critics; and his vitality is still contagious. As we read, we breathe the air of ocean and primeval lake; we hear the crack of Leatherstocking's rifle. Not only is Cooper an indispensable critic of growing, bumbling democracy, but a golden story-teller, the creator of our own Arabian Nights of the frontier.

Born in Burlington, New Jersey, on September 15, 1789, of English, Swedish, and Quaker antecedents, he enjoyed a vigorous youth in his father's village, Cooperstown, New York, not far from the edge of the eighteenth century frontier. Here he learned, from the example of Judge Cooper, to restore the traditional right of property to the Revolutionary prerogatives: life, liberty, and the pursuit of happiness. After two years at Yale College, from which he was dismissed for some obscure disciplinary reason, after serving as a midshipman in the United States Navy, after his marriage in 1811 into the family of the aristocratic Westchester De Lanceys, he began, virtually on a wager, his career of the man of action turned fiction writer. His rise to fame seems incredible. Within four years he had written four novels that placed his name second in popularity at home and abroad to that of the author of *Waverley*.

After these preliminaries, after his first fame in literary New York, after the incomparable *Last of the Mohicans,* we may follow him for seven years through England, France, Switzerland, and Italy. His was now a triple role: the cultivated American, with his family, in quest of the traditional experiences of European life; the distinguished author consorting in London and Paris with other notables; and the aroused critic of political and social institutions abroad and, indirectly, at home. Hazlitt saw him "strutting" down the streets of Paris; he was, in contrast to Irving whom he already despised, an unabashed observer in this older civilization.

Before Cooper returned to America in 1833, he had found time, besides aiding Lafayette in the French budget controversy and composing his invaluable commentaries on Europe and a defense of America against the attacks of foreign critics, to publish seven novels, of which three concerned the past of Europe, two the life of the sea, and two that of the frontier. Human energy could hardly do more. When Cooper, refusing an invitation to a dinner of welcome by his countrymen, set foot again on American soil, he was alive with a critical spirit which was to mold his career in America until his death in 1851. His was to be a boundless and often misdirected fervor. For eighteen years he instructed his unwilling countrymen through preface, novel, and libel suit; he lived his full life as country squire and critic of democracy; and he gave to the world his flow of novels. At virtually the height of his powers he died, his personal unpopularity obscuring his brilliance as a romancer of wilderness and sea.

2

An orderly and chronological or a sharp and topical classification of Cooper's writings is almost impossible. He had begun, after his unsuccessful novel *Precaution* (1820), modeled upon Jane Austen or Mrs. Opie, with three types of American subject (the Revolution, the frontier, and the sea); these themes he was to discuss throughout his life. Almost simultaneously he had begun in *Notions of the Americans* (1828) that downright defense of American life which was to animate *A Letter to His Countrymen* (1834) and his many prefaces and articles. In particular, his first frontier novel, *The Pioneers* (1823), explored the subject in which his genius was to find its noblest expression; it began the Leatherstocking series. The five novels in this series were composed over a period of eighteen years, and their chronology, in reference to the prolonged life story of Leatherstocking, is at variance with the order of composition and publication. At the same time the Revolution, the frontier, and the sea crossed and recrossed one another in these and other tales; and through them all crackled the fire of Cooper's criticism of America.

One fact is clear, a by-product of the truism that Cooper's writings are a

paradise for the intellectual historian: he cared little for literature as literature. For him, writing was primarily an implement for his convictions about
America. Some of his ideas, such as those concerning the Navy or the antirent
laws, are as obsolete as those in Melville's *White Jacket or Mardi*; but others
anticipate the persistent problems of democracy which now meet our troubled
eyes in the newspapers. We should be aware of those which recur: his belief
in the moral quality of liberty; his nationalism; his conviction that an aristocracy of worth was not inconsistent with the democratic ideal; his notion
that native human character received its most valid self-expression in America; and his concept of the relation of all these ideas to the natural world of
forest and sea. With infinite variation in detail these great themes reappear
in all his books.

Thus in Cooper's writings we may see America in the early stages of
introspection and self-evaluation, America trying to explain its origins and
growth and to prefigure its far-off future, and America struggling for a
commensurate cultural independence. In his novels and tracts may be found
the optimism and fatalism of the frontier, the growth of class-consciousness,
the beginnings of imperialism, the stubborn resistance of property-ownership,
and a hundred other battles of a century ago. The desire to record these drove
Cooper to his pen instead of to the forum; through writing he hoped to
resolve these elements into some kind of unity. Having become an author, he
was subject to literary influences, but his fundamental conception of writing
is suggested in his statement in 1837:

It is high time not only for the respectability but for the safety of the American
people, that they should promulgate a set of principles that are more in harmony
with their facts.

Nevertheless he can never be dismissed as a social novelist. Despite his
"literary offences," as Mark Twain called them, he stands with Dumas and
Scott as one of the great romancers of all time. Thackeray, for example, paid
tribute to his heroes:

Leatherstocking, Uncas, Hardheart, Tom Coffin, are quite the equals of Scott's
men; perhaps Leatherstocking is better than anyone in "Scott's lot." *La Longue
Carabine* is one of the great prizemen of fiction. He ranks with our Uncle Toby,
Sir Roger de Coverley, Falstaff—heroic figures, all—American or British, and the
artist has deserved well of his country who devised them.

Here is a puzzle: the contrast between these "great prizemen" and
Cooper's own disregard of his famous novels, at which he was accustomed
to laugh as "light literature." His attitude toward such fiction was, of course,

typical of an era which considered writing a medium for saying what had to be said; even Irving came to believe that he must not take belles-lettres too seriously. Most of our early nineteenth century men of letters disdained, at least outwardly, the aims of the "artist."

Yet Thackeray uses this very word, and not too hastily or too flexibly. If we turn to Cooper's letters or his prefaces we shall find only simple literary principles, such as a story-teller's right to take a poetical view of his subject, or the novelist's definitions of types. Such do not seem, in the deepest sense, to be the reflections of an artist. Yet their simplicity is misleading. The fact is that Cooper cherished unconsciously an allegiance to the traditions of English fiction, precisely as he felt a deep but unanalytical devotion, especially in later life, to one of the traditional churches. We should reconsider his associations with writing not immediately concerned with "American opinions" or "American things."

Such a reexamination discovers in his reading the positive, somewhat naïve tastes which adorned his living. Certain economists and geologists he studied meticulously; he did first-hand historical research for both his fiction and his nonfiction; and he was steeped in Shakespeare. Yet deep literary intimacy, comparable to Hawthorne's understanding of Milton, is absent. His critical opinions were violent, impressionistic; throughout his letters we encounter few penetrative judgments on books, and though there is real dependence on the substance of literature, extremely few allusions occur, except for the poetic captions of his chapters. In his youth he read the lucid poetry of the eighteenth century (Pope, Gray, and Thomson); and he afterward shifted to such popular narrators in verse as Byron, Scott, and Longfellow. We do not need his sarcasms to learn what he thought of the more introspective nineteenth century poets. Shakespeare he held dear, but the writing of other Elizabethans had for him little meaning. Verse of intellectual weight bored him; he was fond of saying that Shakespeare should have written *Paradise Lost*!

Whenever the broader philosophic thought of Shakespeare or Scott touched his own simple code of living, he approved; but he was evidently less moved by such wisdom than by the power of the well told story. Here was a gift which, though he never says so precisely, must have stirred him deeply, like the bold art of historical or biographical narration. Such vital creation was worth a man's attention. Let us not be deceived by the petulance uttered not long before he composed *Precaution*: "much as I dislike writing in general." In the prefaces he sets down theories on the technique of narration. In such matters he was interested.

Thus by reading and by temperament Cooper acquired a devotion to a leading art form of the nineteenth century; namely, narrative. No definition

of his work is just without recognition of this interest, however incomplete
he was in the exposition of his theories. Perhaps this representation of action
was an escape; certainly his study of it as an art form was amateurish; but
his intuitional grasp of its methods was impressive. His love of books centered in the depiction of moving events and large natural emotion. His
writing, says his daughter Susan,

was simply the outpouring of his own nature, the expression of his own inmost
train of thought, the current of real feeling in his own breast.

Had not his early experiments in verse revealed his incapacity for rhyme,
he might well have attempted narratives like Byron's, for poetic feeling, as
Balzac pointed out, was a strong element in his mental constitution. Since
he loved narrative, he drew his literary life from the English novel. He
swallowed it whole, with all its vices, devoting himself to its main purposes
of eventful record and broad characterization.

For like reasons he admired the basic characteristics of the English novel
form: realistic action, unrefined psychology or character, luxurious description, comfortable denouements, and the use of all these elements for the
communication of social ideas. This last function of the English novel, which
enjoyed such vogue in the first decades of the century, he emphasized, often
to the detriment of his literary reputation. His great original contribution
was the theme of the frontier, but this he adapted to the standard concepts
of the novel form, concerning which he harbored no misgivings. Rebellion
and criticism he reserved for the affairs of his country. In the movements
which prophesied the break-up of the novel form or in those which strove
for an American literary independence he showed no interest whatever:

It is quite obvious [he remarked] that, so far as tastes and forms alone are
concerned, the literature of England and that of America must be fashioned after
the same models. . . . The only peculiarity that can, or ought to be expected in
their [the Americans'] literature is that which is connected with the promulgation
of their distinctive political opinions.

Accepting, with a surprising docility, a form later used by Hawthorne
and Melville, Cooper made the most of its time-honored conventions. With a
heavy, humorless style, often drawn into a terrible prolixity, he repeated in
novel after novel all the threadbare formulas. He exploited heroic action in
battle or single combat; he described secret escape and breathless pursuit;
he played with disguises and rejoiced in true love rewarded. So objective
was he, so fixed in purpose, so lacking in self-criticism, that he never foresaw
how absurd his subservience might appear to later writers, so ridiculous,

indeed, that he became a target for satire not to the intellectuals of New England but to other frontier writers such as Mark Twain and Bret Harte. He romanticized famous personages such as Washington or John Paul Jones, and for characters he often created bright-uniformed officers and high-bred maidens, strange blends of musical comedy and convent. In contrast to the natural conversation of his best characters, he frequently penned a dia-logue so artificial that we read it with suppressed laughter; such diction represents not life but only the false taste of the novel readers of his gen-eration. Everything suggests his obtuseness to what was happening in the craftsmanship of the novel.

3

Cooper's literary career, beginning with *Precaution* in 1820 and ending in 1850 with *The Ways of the Hour,* covers a period of thirty years during which he issued more than fifty books and pamphlets, exclusive of his articles and communications in periodicals. The main line of his development is difficult to trace; and in it Cooper himself had no interest. He obeyed merely his changing impulses to write on European subjects, on the bad manners of the Americans, on the United States Navy, or on frontier themes to which, had he been more sensitive to the true meaning of his genius, he would per-haps have wholly consecrated his unique powers. For convenience we may let chronology furnish us with an artificial division into three periods. The first includes Cooper's venture into fiction in his thirty-first year, his sudden triumph in his historical novel of the Revolution. *The Spy,* his comparative failure with a similar subject in *Lionel Lincoln,* and his success in special historical material of two distinct kinds—the sea and the frontier.

The second period, which includes the journey to Europe (1826-1833), beginning with *The Prairie* in 1827 and ending, according to our arbitrary division, with *The Deerslayer* (1841), consummates the novelist's richest, most varied performance. From his thirty-fourth to his fiftieth year he bestowed upon his puzzled countrymen his travel sketches, his social criticism, his satirical and allegorical novels, his romances of Europe, additional sea tales, and the three supplementary volumes of the Leatherstocking series. In the third period, which equates the last decade of his life, he played, with strength but with less inspiration, on the now familiar themes. Surveyed in this broad fashion, the three periods tell a fascinating story of his alternate blindness and vision in the creation of fiction.

Cooper's uncritical dependence upon the traditions of the English novel is evident not merely in his first novel, *Precaution* (1820), but in his second, *The Spy* (1821), in which the conventional patterns of mysterious disguise, the near-supernatural, sensibility, realistic comedy, and the mercurial rise and fall of human fortunes in chase or battle create all the surface faults and virtues of this version of a Revolutionary legend. The differences between *The Spy* and its feeble predecessor are real enough, but less so than some critics lacking the courage to finish *Precaution* have admitted. In both novels is the same Cooper, trying an increasingly deft hand at the tricks of story-telling. What delight must have filled his energetic mind as he found in the tale of "neutral ground" opportunities to use the devices culled from his wholesome but unprofessional habits of reading! Halfway through the composition of *The Spy* he must have known himself for a master of his new trade; likewise he must have realized that he had stumbled on themes suited to his unique powers.

One of these themes, invisible in *Precaution,* we may call, for want of a better name, patriotism. Often clumsily handled in *The Spy*, as in his anxious justice to the loyalists as opposed to the predatory skinners, or in his too composed, too benevolent "Mr. Harper"—George Washington transformed into a kind of fairy-godmother—this is basically a profound, almost religious emotion concerning the destiny of America. This feeling he was to express in many different ways, from the petulance of *Home as Found* to the sublimity of certain scenes in *The Prairie*. The feeling seems at best a tenuous, inconclusive weapon for a novelist, but it served Cooper well; indeed, it sheds today a glory on his writings. His meaning is inadequately conveyed in the starched words of Washington, as, at the end of *The Spy*, this Olympian figure attempts vainly to reward Harvey Birch for his unrecognized loyalty:

> That Providence destines this country to some great and glorious fate I must believe, while I witness the patriotism that pervades the bosoms of her lowest citizens.

We smile and rephrase the sentiment for ourselves; yet there remains the sincerity of Cooper's emotion. Consistently throughout his life it led him to expound and defend a Platonic theory of democratic society which, he felt, Europe needed and America did not appreciate.

Less nebulous, but equally suggestive of directions in Cooper's development, is his mastery in *The Spy* of native background; his powers of observation were remarkable. Intimate friends stressed this gift, now suddenly so apparent in these splendid scenes of the river country in autumn. Whenever Cooper's eyes fell on forest or stream he saw much; such details of nature he recombined endlessly for the settings of his novels. Thus the picturesque haunts of Harvey Birch on hillside or in mountain cavern are almost as fascinating as the spy himself.

In this portrait of the peddler-patriot we apprehend another talent of Cooper's, dim in *Precaution* and, like his intuitional sense of America, only intermittently revealed in, for example, Magua, Chingachgook, Leatherstock-ing—or now, in Harvey Birch. This talent is his capacity for creating truly original and *natural* character. So beset is Harvey by lay figures, such as the bewildered Mr. Wharton or the "lovely maniac" Sarah, that we are likely to lose sight of the unique qualities in the spy himself. This special insight of Cooper's is evident in Harvey, rather than in the tedious Smollettesque echo Dr. Sitgreaves, or even in the robust Betty Flannagan, who excited the admira-tion of Maria Edgeworth. In fact, Harvey Birch is not imitative at all, except in his incidental resemblance to the Yankee peddler type. Daringly conceived, inviting the contempt of his readers by his avarice, timidity, and meanness, he wins them in the end by the selflessness with which he faces his leader and his God. On this legend of the mysterious patriot who served Washington directly as a spy Cooper first employed that understanding which found fulfillment later in another conception, that of Leatherstocking. Thus he early revealed his comprehension of such natural men; Harvey Birch transcends the conventional formulas which control the hundreds of manikins in his novels.

It is characteristic of Cooper's experimental temper in this early period and also of his restless energy that, instead of following this successful historical novel of the Revolution with others like it, he essays in *The Pioneers* (1823) a fresh approach to American subjects. Conscious perhaps of his newly dis-covered skill in narrative, he now tells a negligent tale of Oliver Edwards and Elizabeth Temple, and of their union after the heroine is rescued from a forest fire by her lover who is finally revealed as the grandson of old Major Effingham. Jejune devices reappear, but Cooper's interest now centers on a reproduction of the frontier settlement in Otsego County, so dear to him in his youth. In an illuminating preface, written seventeen years after the first publication of *The Pioneers,* he reveals a conflict in his mind, still unresolved prior to the Leatherstocking tales. On the one hand, he is attracted by the imaginative creation of character, as in a Harvey Birch, and, on the other, by a literal accuracy tempting him in this novel to set down a true record of the life and environment of Judge Marmaduke Temple:

This rigid adherence to truth [he admits], an indispensable requisite in history and travels, destroys the charm of fiction; for all that it is necessary to be conveyed to the mind by the latter had better be done by the delineation of principles, and of characters in their classes, than by a too fastidious attention to originals.

Such in 1823 was Cooper's uncertainty; from it resulted a compromise between a dependable record of his own father's life-history on the New York frontier, and a romance destined to be third in fictional chronology in the series of five great novels dedicated to the life of the forest. Yet he had hit it at last. He had implemented his patriotism, his descriptive power, and his exploration of human character (apart from his innumerable conventional figures); he had begun his long task of memorializing the American frontier experience. Dreamlike indeed, even with their basis of fact, were the clearings of the Otsego settlement, and heroic was the gaunt, angular Leatherstocking in his middle age. Yet these were living places and persons; at least their prototypes had lived in the past. Cooper hoped, as he said later, to show them without "too fastidious attention to originals" and "by the delineation of principles," that is, by the full sweep of his imagination. If he could do this, he would re-create one of the poetic yet essentially true experiences of developing America. He was adjusting his realism and romance in the treatment of native themes. He now trod the actual frontier and there brought to life one authentic inhabitant, a human being susceptible of continuous growth in his imaginative re-creation of the wilderness.

During this same year he had written and published *The Pilot,* a further capitalization of his own experiences. It is easy to attribute the novels of this period to minor incidents: *Precaution* to his annoyance at a weak English novel; *The Spy* to a tale told him by the brother of Mr. Jay; or *The Pilot* to a dinner party at which was discussed the nautical inadequacy of Scott's *The Pirate.* The causes lay deeper. His first novel of the sea was a consequence of his intense interest in the two frontiers; the sea and the wilderness, the water and the forest, were always intimately associated in his mind—witness, in particular, the aqueous quality of *The Pathfinder.*

In *The Pilot* (1823) we may disregard the complicated plot: the love affairs of the lieutenants Barnstable and Griffith with Cecilia Howard and Katherine Plowden, the nieces of the loyalist Colonel Howard; the schemes and ghastly death of the villainous Christopher Dillon; the usual soufflé of escapes, rescues, and pursuits. With variations, such are always staples in Cooper's novels. Beneath the veneer rests the solid oak of *The Pilot*: the passage of the straits by the schooner in the storm; the battle between the frigate and the British man-of-war; and the accurate transcripts of life on the ocean during the Revolution. Cooper's novels of the sea have more authenticity than those of the frontier; he never knew well an Indian warrior. His two years in the Navy, apart from his reading in the sea tales of Smollett and Marryat, enabled him to write with precision of sheet, jib, and compass. The sailors' dread of the land, their love of the open water, their management of schooner and frigate make *The Pilot* an event in the history of the novel of the sea.

Cooper's growth toward the mastery of his "art" is evident not only in this wider frontier of the Atlantic, but in two characters. The pilot himself, a favorite of our school days, is the second in Cooper's gallery of fictionized historic figures. This misty representation of John Paul Jones reminds us of the earlier portrait of George Washington; Cooper never learned that dimness of outline and an aura of mystery did not in themselves create a heroic character. In this man without a country he attempts a tragic hero; instead he achieves a Byronic ghost, a man with secret sorrows, darkened brow, mysterious devotions, and almost comic mannerisms. From our first sight of him in his "calmness bordering on the supernatural" until he waves adieu wearing "a smile of bitter resignation" he is as vague as his platitudes on liberty, of which Cooper evidently hoped to persuade us he was the ardent defender.

Long Tom Coffin is otherwise. He is as real as the *Ariel* itself, whose first timbers he saw laid and whose death he shared. Tom's every salty word, every vigorous action with cannon or harpoon, every simple feeling, reveal these perceptions demonstrated by his creator in Harvey Birch and Leatherstocking; himself a sailor and a man, Cooper could delineate a man of the sea. We welcome Long Tom's entrances as we dread uneasily those of the Gothic pilot, and his death (surely a mistake if we consider the possibilities for him in later sea novels of Cooper's) is closer to our human sympathies than that of Captain Ahab, in Melville's greater novel. Brief as is Long Tom's literary life, he ranks with Leatherstocking.

Presumably we must attribute the unevenness of Cooper's novels to the sluggishness of his self-critical faculty. Such disparities are almost ludicrous in the last two novels published before his journey abroad, that is, the final two in the first period of his writing and the fifth and sixth in his swiftly moving career as a novelist. Few if any novels in his later work, and relatively few from the pens of other writers, have equaled in pompous dullness *Lionel Lincoln* (1824–1825), a well informed but preposterous melodrama told against an oddly contrasting background of Boston on the eve of the Revolution. No character in the novel makes common sense—neither the priggish hero, nor the mysterious father, nor "Ralph," nor the hideous, unconvincing Mrs. Lechmere. *Lionel Lincoln* is a harlequinade of absurd scenes unredeemed save by the two or three battle pieces. Momentarily Cooper throws over us his old spell as the embattled farmers drive the redcoats down the Lexington road or as they release their sheet of fire from the crest of Bunker Hill. Yet such flickers of life are hardly to be mentioned except as hints of the unfaltering genius of the sixth volume, the second in order of publication of the Leatherstocking series, *The Last of the Mohicans* (1826). Here at last was mastery; more profound studies of his great frontiersmen were to come, but never was Cooper, now thirty-five years old, to attain such unerring control over the only technique of art which really interested him; never was he to tell another story with more triumphant suspense.

For many—and this represents one real level in the book—*The Last of the Mohicans* is a breathless, unrelenting chase, unbroken save when Alice and Cora are captured by Magua, and Leatherstocking, Uncas, and Duncan Hayward, thus far the pursued, become the pursuers. Who does not, like Mark Twain, discern extravagances in the plot? Yet the pauses between the climactic rifle shots of "La Longue Carabine" are so brief; the moments of security, so insecure; the very rustle of the leaves in the red man's forest, so ominous that the reader has no peace—nor desires it. This acceleration of event is a convincing indication of the novelist's development: gone is the jerky Cooper, backing and filling between tense incident and dreary moralizing. In this novel too there is time for frontier wisdom, but from the bitter struggle of Hayward and the Indian on the rock until the deaths of Uncas and Magua, action is all!

To this unflagging suspense *The Last of the Mohicans* probably owes its universal fame and its innumerable translations into foreign languages. The student of Cooper will also observe his skill in showing the civilization of the white man through the eyes of the Indians and through the mind of the partly Indianized Leatherstocking. In *The Pioneers* we have glimpses of the wilderness; in *The Last of the Mohicans* we live there. In this novel Cooper is less interested in the trapper than in the Indian, and the latter he counterpoises not so much against his enemies, the whites, as against other types of his own race. The noble young brave Uncas, his father, the honorable chieftain Chingachgook, the treacherous Magua, the venerable patriarch Tamenund—all such commemorate Cooper's first sustained exploration of the Indian's soul. In no other of his novels do we live so intimately with the folk ways of the red man and appreciate so sharply the inevitable conflict of those ways with encroaching civilization.

Aside from their value as studies of the Indian character, in whose depiction Cooper has been so maligned and eulogized, Uncas and Magua epitomize fairly the virtues and vices which Cooper thought worthy of portrayal in human nature: in the former, loyalty, unselfish love, and kindness; in the latter, treachery, hatred, and cruelty; in both, bravery, endurance, and intelligence. Cooper had never seen such Indians, but he had known, with modifications, such men. Intensifying and magnifying these human traits, he placed them in their frontier setting; authentic, Uncas and Magua retain permanent places in the history of fiction. As for Leatherstocking, he has grown younger since his somewhat grumpy role in *The Pioneers*. Wise, counselor of the forest, chivalrous protector of women, ruthless enemy, provocative if by no means succinct philosopher, he has now reached full stature, although he is to be younger and more adventurous fifteen years later in *The Deerslayer*.

4

The appearance in the next two years in our second period of two strongly contrasted novels of respectively the sea and the prairie (on which Cooper never laid eyes) is an illustration of the vigor of his imagination. The *Red Rover* (1828) offers a magnificent drama of sailing ships in combat on the vast ocean; *The Prairie* (1827), though not deficient in incident, breathes upon us the peace of Nature and of Leatherstocking's old age and death. The story of the seaman in the Royal Navy who killed an officer and became the notorious pirate, but who loved America, flags and ends in the usual revelations of mistaken identities; the antics of Fid and Scipio Africanus cannot excuse its conventional episodes. Only the storm—perhaps the most titanic in all Cooper's writings—survives, the storm in which the *Royal Caroline* is beaten to a naked hulk.

More slow-moving than *The Last of the Mohicans, The Prairie* tells an adventurous tale in which a kidnaping, a buffalo stampede, and a prairie fire cannot divert our interest from Cooper's powerful conception of the immigrant family of Ishmael and Esther Bush and their sons. These squatters, the villainous Sioux, Mahtoree, or the benevolent Pawnee, Hard-Heart, are subordinate to the noble delineation of Leatherstocking, which, Cooper honestly believed, was to be the last glimpse of his frontier hero. This book, he wrote—not divining the future—

closes the career of Leatherstocking. Pressed upon by time, he has ceased to be the hunter and the warrior, and has become a trapper of the great West. The sound of the axe has driven him from his beloved forests to seek a refuge . . . on the denuded plains that stretch to the Rocky Mountains.

Enfeebled in arm but not in mind, Natty is still the "philosopher of the wilderness"; he dies as he has lived, serenely, calling out to his Maker, "Here." Although in this period Cooper published ten more novels, all save the two which recalled Natty from his grave on the prairie (*The Pathfinder,* 1840; *The Deerslayer,* 1841) were marred by that pedestrianism which was so characteristic of him when absorbed by some general aspect of tradition or afflicted by his heavy enthusiasm for reforming his countrymen. Thus *The Wept of Wish-ton-Wish* (1829), clumsily aiming to "perpetuate the recollection of some of the practices and events peculiar to the early days of our history," is a melodrama of King Philip's War enacted against a superficial background of Puritan Connecticut; Cooper alluded to these New Englanders' "very quaint and peculiar dogmas." He was more at home but not more convincing in *The Water-Witch* (1830), set in New York in the same century; instead of the assault on the blockhouse of the previous novel, he offered the pursuit of the pirate, "The Skimmer of the Seas." This book he wrote in Italy, while, with his fatal fertility, he was already at work on a series of three novels with European themes. This trilogy (*The Bravo, The Heidenmauer, The Headsman*) attempted to meet Scott on his own ground, by portraying European society as it would appear to an enlightened American, liberalized by his intimacy with democracy.

Some savage attacks from American newspapers on *The Bravo* crystallized his latent intention: in 1834, he published his vituperative *A Letter to His Countrymen,* in which he assailed these criticisms and prematurely announced his retirement as a novelist. He now embarked upon that fierce warfare of preface, satire, and libel suit which makes the reappearance of Leatherstocking nearly a miracle. His anger found expression in an experiment in allegory, *The Monikins* (1835), and in two complementary novels *Homeward Bound* and *Home as Found* (1838). These latter are ambitious efforts to portray contemporary American manners; the first, spiced with the usual chase and battles, shows a group of cultivated Americans returning to their country in company with less estimable members of society; the second examines American social life in town and country. Cooper's success is debatable; the elegant Effingham brothers, who represent his conceptions of the American gentleman, are as unnatural as his caricatures of our clodhoppers, Mr. Steadfast Dodge and Aristabulus Bragg. Through such charcoal sketches Cooper solidified the growing enmity of his countrymen, earned the nickname of Effingham, became involved in the famous "Effingham" libel suits, and seemed to justify his irritable decision (to which he did not adhere) that he would write no more fiction. Yet in *Homeward Bound* and *Home as Found* he bequeathed to historians sovereign documents of the social issues of the day.

About the year 1840 he had reached the peak of his activity, not only in his quarrels with his countrymen, but in his power over the written word. Since his return to America he had published, besides the works already described, four volumes on his life in Europe, his political primer for his countrymen *The American Democrat* (1838), various reviews, the pioneer history of the American Navy (1839), a masterpiece of tediousness (*Mercedes of Castile*) in the form of a novel on Columbus; and in a demonstration of the fertility of his genius, he completed the Leatherstocking series with *The Pathfinder* (1840) and *The Deerslayer* (1841). These two novels were the immortal answer, had his angry contemporaries only realized it, to all denunciations of Cooper as a man and writer. Once again he moved freely amid forest and lake; forgotten were the self-conscious allusions to his own experiences (as in *Home as Found*), and even the moralizing, which he could never entirely abandon, took on dignity from Leatherstocking's life in the wilderness. Again, all is action; and once more we share his beautiful insight into simple, strong characters, so amazing after the grotesque portraits of the Effinghams.

The Pathfinder is absorbing for its union of the two themes most natural to Cooper in fiction—adventure in the forest and adventure on the water; and in this novel the water is an inland lake, enriching the beautiful panorama of the Ontario frontier. Moreover, he obtains a secondary contrast in Cap, the salt-water sailor, watching with reluctant admiration the exploits of young Jasper Western, the fresh-water pilot of the *Scud*. No other frontier novel of Cooper's attains the variety of episode of *The Pathfinder*; even the standard blockhouse scene is pleasantly off-pattern through the character of the Indian woman, Dew-of-June; and there are no mistaken identities! Only the suspicion concerning Jasper, with his final vindication, reminds us of Cooper's stock artifices. The great central character of the series is in his prime now, like his creator; and the woods are his sanctuary as well as his battleground. Cooper wishes us to feel the deepening influence of the frontier upon this natural man, this true democrat living simply with other men. Possibly some of Cooper's own Quaker heritage enters into the scout's relations with God and Man. Leatherstocking is capable of grief in the loss of Mabel Dunham. Yet Cooper's blessing lies on the idyllic happiness of Mabel and Jasper; united at last, the lovers bid the scout farewell:

A tread whose vigour no sorrow could enfeeble soon bore him out of view, and he was lost in the depths of the forest.

Thus at this apex of Cooper's intellectual and emotional powers, sustained in *The Deerslayer,* we may observe not only his control over his material—stock characters are few in this final novel of the series—but also his deeper intuitions concerning the moral nature of the scout. In renouncing Mabel Dunham (in *The Pathfinder*), he dedicates his life to the meditative moods of the forest, and because of his conviction, already latent in *The Deerslayer,* the love of Judith Hutter finds him unresponsive. Younger now, if we follow the chronology of Leatherstocking's spiritual development, the affair prepares us for his unwillingness to wed Mabel. In his increasing imaginative grasp on the character, Cooper emphasizes Deerslayer's essential loneliness and his kinship with the forces of nature. Thus he now depicts him in its early years, the brother-in-arms of Chingachgook, taking human life for the first time and acting with youthful energy and intensity. We thrill at the fight for Tom Hutter's "castle" or mourn for the death of Hetty or shudder as Deerslayer awaits the torture; but in this culminating novel we perceive, in particular, Cooper's preoccupation with the spiritual meanings of his immortal character.

5

In *The Deerslayer* Cooper had, unaware of the precise nature of his post-humous fame, made his ultimate bid for immortality through enduring works of fiction. Nevertheless, in the dozen or so novels which were to follow, in our third period, from *The Two Admirals,* in April, 1842, until *The Ways of the Hour,* published in 1850, a year before his death, he retained his zest for narrative. Moreover, in the trilogy of antirent novels, the Littlepage Manu-scripts, he reached the zenith of another talent; he became the acute social observer. Thus there occurred no real decline of his innate force as a writer, but only, according to the laws of advancing years, a hardening of prejudices, a narrowing of opinions, and insulation from the new generation in the America he loved so dearly. It is pointless to enumerate the topics which clogged more and more his narratives and aroused his didacticism as his social vision was dissipated into concern for particular and sometimes petty causes: revelation and reason in *Wing and Wing*; Dutch and English land grants in *Wyandotté, Afloat and Ashore,* and *Miles Wallingford*; Christian conversion in *The Oak Openings*; or trinitarianism, against the odd Arctic backgrounds in *The Sea Lions*. Religion, as he himself drew more closely to its supports, and social injustice, as he realized its persistence, were now perpetually the subjects of his lectures to his readers, but his other obsessions were infinite: the Yankees, English pronunciation, or the Bay of Naples. Yet if to these crotchets we oppose a patience unknown to their possessor we may, in such a novel of adventure as *Jack Tier* (1848), learn much concerning Cooper's mind. In *The Two Admirals* (1842) the maneuverings, not this time of single ships, as in *The Pilot* and *The Rover,* but of fleets, make engaging episodes; and, despite the theology and the ever present villainous Yankee Ithuel Bolt, Cooper's complacence about *Wing and Wing,* which appeared only a few months later, is pardonable. Against a blue and gold Mediterranean back-ground, this tale of a privateer and an English frigate is enthralling—more so, indeed, than the standard blockhouse siege in *Wyandotté.* In contrast to Hawthorne, who distilled his study of Puritanism into delicately balanced interrogations, Cooper's exposition of the ideology he detested is opinionated and superficial, though hardly more so than his favorable delineation, in the same novel, of Anglicanism.

It is on his mature mastery of an impartial approach to social history in the guise of fiction that the distinction of his next two novels rests. Published within a year, told in the first person as the recollections of their hero, and relating a continuous story, *Afloat and Ashore* and *Miles Wallingford* are really one novel. The first part is in Cooper's best narrative manner, the action on the sea equaling in suspense that of *The Pilot* or *The Red Rover,* and throughout both parts we take pleasure in Cooper's own autobiography (for the lovely Lucy is assuredly Susan De Lancey, and Miles is Fenimore Cooper). Yet apart from an undeniable subacidity of manner, the two novels are remarkable for their temperate portrayal of eighteenth century life in orchards, meadows, fields, river valleys, and substantial buildings of such American farms as Clawbonny. Here is a serene picture of this solid, almost idyllic America then hardly known at all to European critics of our civilization. Here, as in *Satanstoe* and *The Chainbearer,* is the novel of manners, the fictional re-creation of the best in American society, which Cooper had always hoped to accomplish, blended imperfectly with the romance of action which he did with such natural ease.

This panorama of American life is integrated with the succeeding trilogy, *Satanstoe* (1845), *The Chainbearer* (1845), and *The Redskins* (1846). In the antirentism controversy, now a forgotten issue, Cooper saw the crisis of American idealism, and characteristically aligned himself on the side of the landlords and the rights of property. His now nostalgic patriotism had finally turned him against the equalitarian society of Andrew Jackson's America. Again, in the first of the three novels, and to a lesser degree in the second, he tells a good story, though this virtue is stifled in the preachy *Redskins.* In any case the sequential elements of the three books, as he says in a Preface, depend upon his study of "principles." The romance of Cornelius Littlepage and Anneke Mordaunt, with the usual reticulations of plot and with a black-hearted pedagogue from Danbury, Connecticut, ranks high among Cooper's plots. At the same time the social novelist diverts us from the action to the scenes themselves, to the patroons and the English in the eighteenth century, or to colonial New York, with its "Pinkster" or Dutch Festival. Such interests dominate the trilogy, even in the symbolic character of Thousandacres, the New England squatter, and in the long debates concerning the ethics of this upstart and that of the heroic figures admired by Cooper. The tone of the first two books is judicial; only in *The Redskins* does the controversy dissolve in Cooper's incoherent rage at the impending defeat of what he held so dear.

With the beguiling confession of the Littlepage Manuscripts, really Cooper's own memories related in his late fifties, and with these adventures of the trilogy, it may be said that Cooper's career as writer of the creative imagination began its decline. His five remaining novels show little weariness; they include lightning flashes of his art, as in the careful symbolism of *The Crater* (1848) or the battle between the sloop-of-war and the brig in *Jack Tier* (1848). Yet toward the close of his life his disgust with the stupidities of civilization narrowed his literary horizon; his general underlying thesis concerning the blindness of mankind to his ideal of controlled liberty was not enough. Into *The Crater,* for example, our first important Utopian allegory, he poured his dismay about humanity's need for authority; into *The Oak Openings,* his fears concerning its insensibility to conversion; into *The Sea Lions,* his ideas on the Trinity; into *The Ways of the Hour,* his hatred of trial by jury; and into all that he wrote, the thousand little familiar petulances which we still associate with Cooper's temperament. Though he fled to the mysterious island in *The Crater* or to antarctic realms in *The Sea Lions,* yet he was still harassed and stung by these gnats of the mind. It is a strange, and in retrospect, almost a comic spectacle. His powers had not failed; the old narrative skill and the social idealism were still strong, but they were cluttered by the foibles of the society in which he lived so critically.

After all, as we look back on Cooper's career, we may well be lost in wonder at the magic which this American civilization, with all its follies and grandeurs, held for him, at once its enemy and its lover. He criticized it, satirized it, and abused it, but he never ceased to find it fascinating; for him its interest long outlived his intermittent experimentation with literary craftsmanship. All his writing after *The Deerslayer* indicates that he cared less and less for form and method and more and more for what he could say through the novel as a medium. To only one phase of art he remained loyal, to the talent which he could not have abandoned had he wished, the art of telling a story; this art he never quite fused with his devoted but often misguided patriotism. Thus, estimating Cooper, we should note again that in his writing America was first indeed and the novel for its own sake a bad second. Therefore in scope and in passion, it is barely possible that Cooper the social critic will outlive Cooper the novelist of the many novels, but never Cooper the romancer, Cooper the teller of the Leatherstocking tales. Yet even those tales could never have been so passionate, so profoundly and originally American, had he not probed relentlessly beneath the surface of facts to the principles of American society and of human conduct.

20. DIVERSITY AND INNOVATION IN THE MIDDLE STATES

Between the extremes of New England on the one hand and the South on the other, New York and Pennsylvania, as the leaders of the group of middle Atlantic states, were distinguished at this time by their "middleness," as Henry Adams put it—their practical and sagacious aptitudes for compromise and the blending of interests. Uniting now with New England, now with Virginia and her Southern neighbors, serving as a balance wheel, they provided the force that in politics made a nation and in intellectual and artistic activities was ultimately to fuse divergent elements into a national culture.

Cooper and Irving were, of course, the major literary figures, with Bryant joining them in 1825 after a New England youth, and Poe later, after struggling to make his career in Richmond. It is perhaps significant that these four writers, thus drawn to a center, became recognized, when they spoke for the region, as the first literary spokesmen for the whole Republic, both at home and abroad. A region that boasted the political and commercial capitals of the nation would have little incentive to develop a strong regional characteristic in its culture. Only in its minor writers, like Paulding, Willis, Barker, Halleck, or Bird, does the too insistent influence of a Dutch, a Quaker, or a patrician British ancestry, a naïve coffeehouse or greenroom sophistication, a patriotic fervor, act as a restraint on creative power. This was the hub of the national literary life—and a wheel is small but solid at the hub.

These minor writers created in the metropolitan centers of Philadelphia and New York—and to a lesser extent in the smaller cities of Albany, Baltimore, and Washington—something of the spirit of a provincial eighteenth century London. These were the men and women who gathered in salons and clubs for literary conversation; who supplied the magazines and the stage with acceptable offerings, patriotic in accent but usually British in form and tone. They were the logical inheritors of the earlier group (Freneau, Brown, Dennie, Hopkinson, Brackenridge, Tyler), but more numerous and more successful. Many of them managed, where the earlier group had failed, to make a substantial living by their pens. Poe caught their dominant characteristic when he called them the "Literati"; N. P. Willis, their tone when he titled his essays *Pencillings by the Way*. There was scarcely an accepted literary form that escaped them, but they naturally ran to the short story, the essay, and the lyric poem because there was a market for such writings in the new magazines, or to the social comedy or the melodrama because there was a call for such plays in the new theaters.

2

James Kirke Paulding, throughout his life identified with New York State, was perhaps the most typical writer of his time and place—of the diversity and innovation so characteristic of the writings of these middle states. In his voluminous writings over several decades, he showed affinities with more literary movements and styles, even with more individual authors, than any other figure of the early nineteenth century. His virtues and his faults were those of a new nation just coming to self-awareness. He was a Cooper without Cooper's gusto, an Irving who stayed at home. His versatility, his impetuous enthusiasm for a wide variety of subject matter, his willingness to experiment with poetic epic, short story, novel, drama, literary criticism, humorous sketch, moral and social and political criticism of a Swiftian stamp—all these phases of his ever alert inclusiveness perhaps explain better than any lack of talent or perspicacity his failure to achieve the stature of a truly great writer. He was "middleness" personified, and "innovation" was his greatest virtue; he was as well a devout though sometimes noisy champion of democracy, but realistic, with his feet on the ground, and without metaphysical subtlety.

Except for minor contributions to Peter Irving's *Morning Chronicle* as early as 1802, Paulding's literary career properly began in 1807, with the publication of the first series of periodical essays entitled *Salmagundi; or the Whim-Whams and Opinions of Launcelot Langstaff, Esq., and Others,* jointly produced with William and Washington Irving, who had been his friends and literary cronies since his arrival in New York City from his native Dutchess County some ten years before. Though the collaboration of Irving and Paulding was so close as to make individual assignment problematical, Paulding is generally given credit for having first sketched the characters of the Cockloft family, modeling one of them on his own uncle. The second series of *Salmagundi,* issued in 1819, was entirely Paulding's work.

The Diverting History of John Bull and Brother Jonathan (1812), published as by one Hector Bull-us, set the tone and indeed to a large degree the pattern for a series of nationalistic political satires. This work, originally in sixteen chapters but later more than doubled in length, looked backward to Francis Hopkinson's *A Pretty Story* (1774) and forward to some of the later sections of Melville's *Mardi* (1849) in its intention and method. Bullock

Island, representing England, and the thirteen farms of Jonathan, representing the United States, are the chief locales of action, though activities are reported from the Manor of Frogmore of Lewis Baboon (Louis XVI) and Beau Napperty (Napoleon), "called Beau because he was no beau at all." The theme of the British traveler in America, which reappeared in Paulding's *John Bull in America; or the New Munchausen* (1825), is embodied here in Corporal Smellfungus. The sequel of this early work, though its inferior, *The History of Uncle Sam and His Boys* (1835), pictured Jonathan as now become Uncle Sam, with twenty-four sons (states), mostly large, though a few, "shrunk in the boiling," were "rather conceited and jealous, as most little people." Paulding's two plays—*The Bucktails; or Americans in England* (written about 1815) and *The Lion of the West* (which won a prize in 1830)—reflect this tendency of nationalistic caricature, though the major figures deserve more serious consideration as realistic character portrayals.

For most of Paulding's later serious work—whether epic poetry or fiction or drama—the keynote was sounded and the intention stated in his article on "National Literature," in the final issue of the second series of *Salmagundi*, August 19, 1820. Here, in discussing "rational fiction," Paulding attacked "servile imitation," "the ascendancy of foreign taste and opinions," "the aid of superstition, the agency of ghosts, fairies, goblins, and all . . . antiquated machinery," and advocated dependence on nature and "real life" where "events, however extraordinary, can always be traced to motives, actions, and passions, arising out of circumstances no way unnatural, and partaking of no impossible or supernatural agency." Though Paulding sometimes used foreign settings for his tales—rarely with much success—and occasionally introduced supernatural elements, for the most part he lived up to his creed. Some aspects of American life he saw through rose-colored glasses; he shared with his contemporaries an ill founded hope that pioneering and frontier life would develop only "doric simplicity" and strength of character, rarely noting that it might also develop crudity and cupidity.

Paulding's epic poem of some sixteen hundred lines, *The Backwoodsman* (1818), is less romantic than Crèvecœur's account of Andrew the Hebridean and foreshadows some of the ideas expressed in Frederick Jackson Turner's famous essay on the frontier three quarters of a century later. The story of Basil's westward trek from the banks of the Hudson to "the poor man's long-sought, new-found promis'd land" in the Ohio River valley, Paulding told "with homebred feeling, and with homebred fire," though the fire of the ruthlessly mechanical eighteenth century heroic couplets has dimmed. Indicating the success of Basil's Western career by sending him to Congress as reward is a fault more national than personal—merely another evidence of the common American belief that virtue and industry inevitably bring material reward. The descriptions of natural scenery, the pictures of the Moravians in Pennsylvania, the interspersed accounts of the Wyoming Massacre and of various historical figures—Arnold, André, Greene, Marion, Franklin, Washington—as well as the central narrative, make the poem intrinsically American.

The tales or short stories and the novels are Paulding's most important work. His leisurely manner of writing, his inclination to introduce personal comment and opinion, and his variety of interests are best adapted to happy expression in prose fiction. Assuredly the Dutch stories are the best—and Sybrandt Westbrook of *The Dutchman's Fireside* (1831) is probably his most successful full-length characterization—but settings and characters other than Dutch are also effectively handled. Woodsmen and frontiersmen, whether Sir William Johnson in *The Dutchman's Fireside* or Ambrose Bushfield in *Westward Ho!* (1832), are drawn with veracity and compulsion. Paulding's first novel, *Koningsmarke* (1823), introduced the Long Finne as a character against a background of the Swedish colonies in Delaware; his fifth and last novel, *The Puritan and His Daughter* (1849), shifted from Cromwellian England to New England, portraying Puritanism in its two main environments. *The Old Continental, or the Price of Liberty* (1846) used the background of New York during the Revolution to tell a story of the vicissitudes of Whigs in a Tory community—a theme echoed in the account of the origin of the ancestral curse that haunted the melancholy Dudley Rainsford in *Westward Ho!*

In his zealous and often self-conscious efforts to build an indigenous literary tradition, Paulding took himself and his work seriously, emphasizing throughout accuracy and morality. As he took pains to point out, he frequently used original sources, such as Mrs. Grant's *Memoirs of an American Lady* (1808) for *The Dutchman's Fireside* and Timothy Flint's *Recollections of the Last Ten Years* (1826) for *Westward Ho!* He no doubt fully agreed with the publisher's (Harper's) preface to *The Dutchman's Fireside* setting forth the moral duty of the novelist to supply to his reader

without the bitterness and danger of experience, that knowledge of his fellow-creatures which but for such aid could, in the majority of cases, be only acquired at a period of life when it would be too late to turn it to account.

By characterization, depiction of the mores of other times, dialogue, and direct auctorial comment, he inculcated the values of "doric simplicity" (a frequent phrase in *The Dutchman's Fireside*), rationality, common sense, and tolerance—the latter notably in his attack on the sadistic dogmatism of the itinerant preacher in *Westward Ho!* Sometimes he used broad satirical portraiture suggestive of Sheridan or Royall Tyler to reduce the qualities he abhorred to the absurd. The Obsoletes in *The Bucktails* are caricatures of this type, as also the suitors of Catalina Vancour in *The Dutchman's Fireside*: Barry Gillfillan, a "combustible gentleman," with "the truly Irish propensity for falling in love extempore," and Sir Thicknesse Throgmorton, the impecunious peer of "dignified stupidity." Less frequently, and most often less successfully, he embodied the admired virtues in a model character, like Sir William Johnson, also of *The Dutchman's Fireside,* or Virginia Dangerfield or Father Jacques, of *Westward Ho!*

In characterization and in handling of plot, Paulding was occasionally the equal of Simms and Cooper. Resemblances between *The Dutchman's Fireside* and Cooper's *Satanstoe* (1845), both dealing with the region near Albany during the French and Indian War, have often been pointed out. *Satanstoe* is a more compact and unified story, but Corny Littlepage's rescue of Anneke from the ice break in the Hudson was no more vividly described than Sybrandt Westbrook's saving Catalina Vancour when a violent storm flooded the island where the young people were picnicking. Cooper's hero had much in common with Paulding's: both represented the ideal fusion of Dutch and English blood; both saved the heroine's life on more than one occasion when she was threatened by a natural calamity or by Indians; both found their chief rivals in Britishers visiting the colonies. But Paulding's Sybrandt was less idealized, more bashful and lacking in assurance, less suave (indeed, even awkward), more credible thus in confronting the situations the plot involved him in, and withal more human and appealing. The author's understanding of his psychology was on occasion profound, particularly in the relations of Sybrandt and Sir William Johnson. Catalina, also, was in her womanly spirit and perversity more credible than Anneke. Paulding did not, however, produce any character so vividly compelling as Cooper's Guert Ten Eyck.

Though more fluently written, *Westward Ho!* which was published only a year later is less realistic, even less honest. Paulding did not know or understand the Virginia plantation owner type, which Colonel Cuthbert Dangerfield of Powhatan represented, as he knew and understood the New York Dutch. He was also less familiar with the topography and mores of Kentucky in the days when it deserved the name "dark and bloody ground." In his fascination for the psychological quirks of Dudley Rainsford, whose perverted guilt-consciousness is a major determinant of the plot, Paulding was on the track of profoundly dramatic material, but he was beyond his depth—unwilling to treat his character according to the superficial romanticism of Poe's practice and unable in realistic terms to understand and describe the aberrations of Rainsford's diseased mind. Thus he fell short of Charles Brockden Brown in picturing a situation reminiscent of *Wieland* (1798), when Rainsford feels religious compulsion to make a blood sacrifice of his fiancée, Virginia Dangerfield, though in a detailed transcription of the hell-fire sermon which immediately provokes the delusion, Paulding prepared the way for intense tragedy. In the character of Ambrose Bushfield he was more on his own ground. The burly and uncouth woodsman who is Colonel Dangerfield's executive officer in the conduct of the expedition down the Ohio to Kentucky and in the building of a new community is an inveterate Indian-hater, made so by the Indian massacre of all of his family in which he miraculously escaped. "Transcendent" is his favorite adjective, and he invariably desires to make the object of his wrath "smell brimstone through a nail hole." Woodsman's rodomontade—suggestive of the speeches of Nimrod Wildfire in *The Lion of the West,* which Paulding got ready for the stage about the same time—comes frequently from Bushfield's lips. Despite his eccentricities of dress, speech, and action, Bushfield is a well rounded, credible character exemplifying Crèvecœur's theories of the effects of life on the cutting edge of the frontier.

Of the Dutch short stories, "Cobus Yerks" and "Claas Schlaschenschlinger" —both included in *The Book of St. Nicholas* (1836)—are typical. The first, in mood and material suggestive of Irving's "Legend of Sleepy Hollow" though the situation described more nearly resembles that in Burns' "Tam O'Shanter," is the account of Cobus' return one night from a tavern presided over by a "bitter root of a woman." He is chased by a black dog turned "devil," and learns the fallacy of "the doctrine that spirit and courage, that is to say whiskey and valour were synonymous." In "Claas Schlaschenschlinger," the two main events are supernatural interventions by St. Nicholas; but the details of the plot and the characterizations are realistic. The psychological stories are best represented by "The Dumb Girl" and "The Ghost," though both might also be classified as stories of character or of plot. In the first, Phoebe Angevine, the title character, living a frustrated existence with her mother and idiot brother, Ellee, is attracted by the stranger, Walter Avery, allows herself to be seduced, and is deserted. Though some critics have made extravagant comparisons with Hawthorne and *The Scarlet Letter,* Paulding's tale lacks the fullness and depth to give conviction to the handicapped heroine's psychology or reality to the pathos of the story. "The Ghost," first published in both *The Atlantic Souvenir* and the New York *Mirror* in 1829, is the story of one William Morgan, who perversely delights in playing ghost, thereby occasioning trouble for others as well as himself. Paulding's characterization of Morgan and of Tom Brown—the chief victim of Morgan's pranks—and his handling of suspense and narrative are effective, direct, and convincing.

Restless like the young nation itself, Paulding was busy with political office as well as with writing—too busy ever to criticize and revise, too eager to be doing other things that also needed to be done ever to do anything quite to the best of his abilities. But he frequently did first what other writers—New Yorkers, or New Englanders, or Southerners, or Westerners—were later to do better and more memorably. Poe's comment, "Paulding owes *all* of his reputation as a novelist, to his early occupation of the field," is unjust. In his range of interest and materials, in his capacity for "innovation," in the breadth of his view of the resources out of which America could build her own literature, and in his formulation and practice of a literary creed, Paulding represents the catholicity and inclusiveness, the fusion of divergent strains, for which the whole body of literature produced in the middle states from 1810 to 1860 is most distinguished, and by which it is best characterized.

3

Closely allied with Paulding in the novel—and like him showing common traits with Cooper and Simms—was the Philadelphia physician Robert Montgomery Bird. After two novels with a Mexican background, *Calavar; or The Knight of Conquest* (1834) and *The Infidel; or The Fall of Mexico* (1835), as well as the earlier plays for Edwin Forrest which also used foreign settings, Bird turned to native material. *The Hawks of Hawk-Hollow* (1835), which Poe condemned as too much like Walter Scott, is the story of a Tory family in Pennsylvania in the year after Yorktown. *Sheppard Lee* (1836), to cite Poe's complimentary term, is a *jeu d'esprit* about a New Jersey farmer whose passage through numerous incarnations affords Bird opportunity to comment satirically on contemporary conditions ranging from fashionable life to plantation slavery. His most popular and best novel is *Nick of the Woods* (1837), the story of Nathan Slaughter, an uncompromising Indian-hater, like Paulding's Timothy Weasel and Ambrose Bushfield in many respects but a better realized character than either—or, for that matter, than any character Paulding or Simms or Cooper ever drew. Nathan the Quaker is called "Bloody Nathan" in derision for his refusal to join his fellow Kentuckians of 1782 to fight the Indians. In spite of his miraculous exploits and his weird dependence on his little dog Peter, who smells Indians and other danger afar off, he is a credible human being, the victim at times of a powerful monomania, but a consistent personality, whose actions and speech and personal appearance all fit into place. *Nick of the Woods* is a good novel, as good as any produced in America in the 1830's, with narrative directness and a skillfully handled complex plot. Bird's conception of the Indian is based on the belief that "in his natural barbaric state, he is a barbarian." Not believing the myth of the noble savage, as he affirmed in the preface to the 1853 revision of this novel, he "drew his Indian portraits with Indian ink."

Like *The Old Continental* by Paulding and *The Hawks of Hawk-Hollow* by Bird, *Greyslaer* (1840) by Charles Fenno Hoffman, a novel of the Mohawk valley during the Revolution, presented the favorite theme of the conflict between Whigs and Tories. This novel, which Hoffman based at least in a general way on the well known murder of Sharp, the Solicitor General of Kentucky, by Beauchamp, changing the locale and many other details, seemed to Poe less effective than Simms' treatment of the same event in *Beauchampe* (1842); and he thought both novels less impressive than the real events. Hoffman's talent lay chiefly in journalism. Thus one may understand the purposes and methods of the greater Fenimore Cooper by seeing his work as a part of a national movement in the novel.

4

In poetry, the field where Paulding was least successful, Fitz-Greene Halleck takes first place after Bryant. Poe in his *Literati* sketch so rated him a hundred years ago, with Nathaniel Parker Willis third. Griswold would perhaps have saved the third place for Charles Fenno Hoffman, best known for the martial lyric "Monterey" and occasional poetry like "The Mint Julep"; but Poe's ranking seems sounder. After Freneau's death in 1832, the middle states had no important poet until Whitman's emergence in 1855, except as New York could claim Bryant.

In 1819, the *Croaker* pieces, a series of humorous and satirical odes published pseudonymously in the New York *Evening Post,* launched Halleck and his friend Joseph Rodman Drake in popular poetry. Beside this joint production, Drake's fame must rest on "The Culprit Fay" (1819), a conscious attempt to utilize American scenery for poetic purposes, which though not altogether successful, hardly deserved Poe's label of "puerile abortion." The younger poet's death the following year occasioned the lines of Halleck "On the Death of Joseph Rodman Drake" (1820), by which Drake is now chiefly remembered.

Steeped in Thomas Campbell, Samuel Rogers, Byron, and Walter Scott, Halleck often seemed more a part of English literary romanticism than a native American product. True, the materials of *The Croaker* and of his own long poem "Fanny" (1821), also in the vein of social satire, were local. "The Field of Grounded Arms" (1831), about the Battle of Saratoga, "Red Jacket" (1828), eulogizing the Indian chief of the Tuscaroras, and "Wyoming" (1827), all used American settings, characters, or events, but are not distinctively American. Halleck's interest in the banks of the Susquehanna was derived from an appreciation of Thomas Campbell's *Gertrude of Wyoming* (1809); the eulogy of the Indian chief afforded opportunity to lament the good old days; the vanquished at Saratoga appealed more romantically to him than did the victors, because they represented an older tradition. His poem "Young America" (1865) was about a fourteen-year-old boy, but it was a "bonny" boy who dreamed of Titania and Diana—American, if at all, only in his desire

> to settle down in life
> By wooing—winning—wedding A RICH WIFE.

The unfinished "Connecticut," despite such intrusions as "the San Marino of the West," "delicate Ariels," and "the Rhine song," was in thought and feeling, as well as in material, the most native of Halleck's poems. Though identified in both business and literary career with New York, Halleck retained a nostalgic loyalty to his native state:

> Hers are not Tempe's nor Arcadia's spring,
>   Nor the long summer of Cathayan vales,
> The vines, the flowers, the air, the skies, that fling
>   Such wild enchantment o'er Boccaccio's tales
> Of Florence and the Arno; yet the wing
>   Of life's best angel, Health, is on her gales
> Through sun and snow; and in the autumn time
> Earth has no purer and no lovelier clime.

His love for "Greece, the brave heart's Holy Land," could make a hero of the title figure of the justly celebrated "Marco Bozzaris" (1823); a "wild rose of Alloway" could inspire a masterful appreciation in "Burns" (1827) of the poet and the Scotland that gave him birth; a visit to the "home of the Percy's high-born race" could produce his masterpiece, "Alnwick Castle" (1822)—and these three poems were their author's selection as his best work—but it commonly took the far away in time and place to evoke the poetic muse in Halleck. Employed most of his life by John Jacob Astor, he found ample occasion to lament, as he did in "Alnwick Castle," that

> The power that bore my spirit up
> Above this bank-note world—is gone;
>   .   .   .   .
> These are not the romantic times
> So beautiful in Spenser's rhymes,
>   So dazzling to the dreaming boy:
> Ours are the days of fact, not fable,
> Of knights, but not of the Round Table.

Out of a "bank-note world" and "days of fact" Halleck was unable to make poetry. Though he lived past Emerson's pronouncement in "The Poet" (1844) and into the days of Whitman's fulfillment, his outlook and habits were fixed in an earlier period, and he could not agree with Emerson that

banks and tariffs, the newspaper and the caucus, methodism and unitarianism, are flat and dull to dull people, but rest on the same foundations of wonder as the town of Troy, and the temple of Delphos, and are as swiftly passing away.

In Nathaniel Parker Willis, Poe's choice for the third most significant poet of the New York group of this period, there was generally the same failure to treat American materials with seriousness and poetic depth. Perhaps poetry is, by its nature, the last form of literature to become thoroughly indigenous; but one is tempted to agree with Lowell that

> For some one to be slightly shallow 's a duty,
> And Willis's shallowness makes half his beauty.

Willis was polished, urbane, sophisticated, but never—in poetry, plays, or prose—profound or great: a talented, versatile, and prolific writer.

As a poet, Willis seems today inferior to Bryant or even to Halleck. In bulk his poems on scriptural subjects loomed large; but a comparison of his "Absalom" with a masterpiece like Browning's "Saul" establishes the justice of Poe's verdict that though "quite 'correct,' as the French have it," they were "in general tame, or indebted for what force they possess to the Scriptural passages of which they are merely paraphrastic." In his poem "Parrhasius," the story of the Athenian painter who subjected his aged Olynthian captive to extreme torture that he might better from this living model paint the agony of Prometheus, the dramatic values somehow fall flat, and Willis shows himself unequal to the tragic theme. Of the serious poems, the "Dedication Hymn" (1829), sung at the consecration of the Hanover Street church in Boston, is simple and direct and owes its force to these qualities. "Unseen Spirits" (1843), Poe's choice as Willis' best poem, showed clearly that Willis' talent lay, not in picturing profound passion or tragedy, but in wistful sentiment. The contrast between the beauty who married for wealth and the woman who loved without marriage vows is effectively pointed by the final well known lines:

> But the sin forgiven by Christ in heaven
> By man is cursed alway.

"To M——, from Abroad" (1834) and "Birthday Verses," written to his mother, are charming examples of sentimental poetry, better suited to Willis' abilities, and, with his religious lyrics, account for much of his contemporary fame.

The bulk of Willis' prose writing was in a dozen volumes of letters of travel and personal reminiscence, beginning with *Pencillings by the Way* (1835) and extending to *The Convalescent* (1859), mainly collections of letters written for the New York *Mirror* and other periodicals of which Willis was at one time or another an editor. The earlier letters recorded excitement about Lady Blessington and her circle and the conventional tourist haunts and shrines of the Old World, but from *A l'Abri; or The Tent Pitched* (1839) onward, Willis' country estates, Glenmary and Idlewild, and his ramblings in the areas near by formed an important part of his subject matter. As he once said of an exploratory walk to the Chemung River, so it might be said of many a poem or letter or essay he wrote: "It was done *à l'improviste,* as most pleasant things are." For most of the results, in collected form, Lowell's opinion of the best known title still holds:

> Few volumes I know to read under a tree,
> More truly delightful than his A l'Abri.

At his best, Willis was, like many earlier pilgrims to the English literary scene, "a casual writer for dreamy readers." One is inclined to smile now at his more serious ideas, such as his pronouncement in 1839:

In literature we are no longer a nation. The triumph of Atlantic steam navigation has driven the smaller drop into the larger, and London has become the centre. Farewell nationality! The English language now marks the limits of a new literary empire, and America is a suburb.

Willis' short stories often showed the "casual" quality of his other prose and the sentiment of his best verse. Most of them deal in a moral tone with highly artificial situations and characters. Only in "The Lunatic's Skate" from "Scenes of Fear" (1834) did he show real depth of feeling and sense of character. Though the story elicited from Willis' biographer, Henry A. Beers, a comparison with Poe, the treatment of the material here was more realistic than Poe would have given, and without stagy romanticism or generalized sentiment. Willis' approach to the psychotic skater was more like Paulding's in Dudley Rainsford of *Westward Ho!* though the story of Larry Wynn is more concise, better written.

Late in life, in *Paul Fane* (1857), Willis attempted a psychological novel about a young American artist who determined, after being shunned by a cold English girl, to make the noble and high-born women of England accept him on a basis of equality by whatever methods were available. Though several women fell in love with him, he spurned them. Since Willis proved unable here to sustain the keenness of insight of "The Lunatic's Skate," the novel failed to come off.

5

In keeping with the diversity and innovation of the middle states literature of this period, four writers well known for fiction or poetry were also leading playwrights: Paulding, Bird, Willis, and Mathews. The two main themes of the native drama produced in New York and Philadelphia during these years were the glorification of American nationality or distinctiveness, and a romantic escape into the far away or the long ago. The most successful plays often combined these two motifs, though the best of them, Mrs. Anna Cora Mowatt's *Fashion* (1845), was frankly an American comedy of manners much influenced by Sheridan, in which Adam Trueman was something of a cross between the Yankee type inaugurated by Jonathan in Royall Tyler's *The Contrast* (1787) and the serious-minded patriot represented by Colonel Manly in the same play. Mrs. Mowatt's villain, Count Jolimaitre, was also a variation on Tyler's Dimple, though more ingenious and more dramatically effective. There was considerable penetration in Poe's assessment in the *Broadway Journal,* March 29, 1845, that "*Fashion* is theatrical, but not dramatic," and in his elucidation, perhaps too tartly expressed:

The drama has not declined as many suppose: it has only been left out of sight by everything else. We must discard all models. . . . compared with the generality of modern dramas, it is a good play—compared with most American dramas, it is a *very* good one—estimated by the natural principles of dramatic art, it is altogether unworthy of notice.

Notable among the plays with a foreign setting were N. P. Willis' *Bianca Visconti; or the Heart Overtasked* (1837 *), whose action took place in fourteenth century Milan, and his *Tortesa the Usurer* (1839), dealing with medieval Florence; Robert Montgomery Bird's *The Gladiator* (1831), a story of Rome in 73 B.C., and his *Broker of Bogota* (1834), which used a setting of the South American city in the early Spanish colonial days; and *Charles the Second; or The Merry Monarch* (1824), written by John Howard Payne with assistance from Washington Irving.

Plays on native themes which used material from the past included James Nelson Barker's *Superstition* (1824) and Cornelius Mathews' *Witchcraft* (1846), both set in late seventeenth century New England; a host of plays about Indians, by George Washington Parke Custis and John Augustus

* The dates of plays cited here are of production.

Stone; Mathews' *Jacob Leisler, or New York in 1690* (1848) and Elizabeth Oakes Smith's *Old New York, or Democracy in 1689* (1853), both of which made use of the same incident in the early history of Manhattan.

In *The Lion of the West* (1831), introducing a character suggestive of Davy Crockett, Paulding presented a salient aspect of contemporary American life not touched on in a play like Mrs. Mowatt's *Fashion*. Earlier, in *The Bucktails; or Americans in England* (not published until 1847), he had made an important contribution toward defining the American character by showing his countrymen against a European background. *The Bucktails* was a comedy of manners, often exaggerated into farce, designed to dispel the myth that all Americans were Wildfires or Crocketts. Among the few notable plays using contemporary American materials was Cornelius Mathews' *The Politicians* (1840).

Of the plays here named, only Payne's *Charles the Second* was without relevance to characteristic American themes and interests. It was an adaptation of a French play by Alexandre Duval and was originally produced on the London stage during Payne's long residence abroad (1813–1832), but was free enough of its original to be considered as part of American literature. Willis' *Tortesa, the Usurer* had a tenuous connection with the American theme of the rise of the underdog, in the success of the poor painter Angelo in winning not only the noble and beautiful Isabella de Falcone in marriage but also, through the sudden and largely inexplicable generosity of Tortesa, a sizable fortune along with her. But Willis' interest was less in American ideology than in the age-old theme of the triumph of true love over seemingly insurmountable obstacles, and more especially in effective theater.

In *Bianca Visconti,* the central character was Francesco Sforza, at the time of the action in high-pitched rebellion against the Italian dukes who were using him to fight their wars against each other while he himself was personally despised and trifled with. Sforza attracted Willis in part at least because of the dramatist's concern for democracy and the dignity of all men. Willis' interest in this character was similar to Bird's interest in Spartacus and his revolt against brutal Roman tyranny over conquered peoples, though Bird approached the subject of *The Gladiator* differently. Stone's sympathetic portrayal of the title character in *Metamora* (1829) was in the same vein, though here the dramatic impact was sharper since the oppressors of the chief of the Wampanoags, son of Massasoit, were the New England colonists of the seventeenth century, the ancestors of the audience now applauding the Indian's struggle for freedom. Jacob Leisler, in the plays by Cornelius Mathews and Elizabeth Oakes Smith, was another hero in revolt—the champion of an abortive democracy in New York of 1689–1690. The same theme appeared in Bird's *The Broker of Bogota* in the struggle of the bourgeois Baptista Febro to get his rights against people of noble birth.

It becomes apparent then that, like the essay and fiction and poetry of the day, the American drama prior to Boker's notable *Francesca da Rimini* (1855) reflects not a matured but an adolescent indigenous culture. The leading writers of the middle states between 1820 and 1850 were realistic at their best rather than merely picturesque, tolerant of variation and originality within the boundaries of intelligibility, well informed about European literary traditions and current vogues though disinclined to be swept away by passing fads, lacking in intellectual unity but thriving on diversity and innovation, catholic in interests though caring "but little for the metaphysical subtleties of Massachusetts and Virginia." In the middle of the road in opinions and tastes, the literature of this section during the decades preceding the Civil War became the unifying core of an American national culture.

21. IN NEW ENGLAND

DURING the years when Bryant, Irving, and Cooper were the major figures in American letters and the Concord-Cambridge galaxy were still schoolboys, authorship in New England was by no means confined to eastern Massachusetts. The editors of the *North American Review* and their chief contributors, it is true, were Boston men; but in that day the poets of Connecticut outranked the Bostonians and the most popular novelists lived in the Green Mountains, the Berkshires, and Maine. Thus literature in New England was shaped by the life not of any single community but of the entire region—the half cultivated, half primitive homeland of William Ellery Channing and Richard Henry Dana, Sr., of Daniel Pierce Thompson and William Cullen Bryant.

The literary tradition of Boston and its back country was overwhelmingly English, for New England at the opening of the century was closer in spirit as well as in fact to the British Isles than any other section of the United States. This is to say that the heritage of Pope was still strong, and that American romanticism was chiefly imitative. Where the great romantics in England wrote on English and Continental themes, early romantics in America copied, not American life, but English copies of English life. This literary colonialism focused the attention of New Englanders on decorum and sensibility, on the legends and history of Europe, on Old World religious and political concepts, and on both the substance and the style of the eighteenth century novelists and of the nineteenth century romantic poets. Thus the lesser New England authors were moved hither and yon by the backwash of classicism, the main current of derivative romanticism, and the ever increasing pull of indigenous American romanticism. In the poetry of William Cullen Bryant, New England found its authentic voice, not because Bryant was a rebel against the past and Europe, but because he absorbed tradition and made it his own. Other writers of his day were less successful either because they rebelled more violently or because they were swept too easily with the currents of foreign influence.

284

2

Boston, according to James Fenimore Cooper, was populated by hardened provincials, incapable of speaking either the English language or a kind word for the rest of the United States. Although the members of the *North American* group were friends—professional men in Boston and faculty men in Cambridge—with the same cultural heritage, they never actually reached the agreement concerning the national scene which Cooper attributed to them.

Provincial devotion to New England was exemplified by the first editor of the *Review,* William Tudor, who traveled in Europe and South America but wrote only one significant book: *Letters on the Eastern States* (1820). Despite his promise that the *North American* would "avoid the narrow prejudice of locality," he gave so much attention to his college, his city, and his New England that readers in other sections dubbed his periodical, the *North Unamerican.* A sane nationalism animated Tudor's friend Jared Sparks, who during his two terms as editor of the *Review* was concerned with everything American—not only North but South. As professor at Harvard, he outlined an ambitious program in the history of the United States. As author, he wrote biographies of John Ledyard, Gouverneur Morris, and Benjamin Franklin as well as many of the briefer sketches in his *Library of American Biography* (first series, 1834–1838). Even though twentieth century historians find his work inaccurate, they still honor Sparks as the man who won recognition for American history in American colleges. But it was Europe that filled the mind of Edward Everett during his years as editor, and came near to filling the pages of the *Review.* The first American to receive the Ph.D. degree from the University of Göttingen, he and his fellow student in Germany, George Ticknor, were busily reshaping Harvard College along German lines. The facile Everett later turned to American affairs and defended nationalism in his oration at Gettysburg; but in his *North American* days he was an apostle of that inverted provincialism which flourishes among the colonially minded.

Even ardent nationalists uncritically continued to evaluate their own literature in European terms; to them, a native author was successful if he could do what a foreigner did. But in 1830 one of the most distinguished of this Boston group proffered a formula for creating a genuinely American literature. William Ellery Channing brought to the criticism of belles-lettres in the United States a sound knowledge of European authors and a fine capacity for generalization. In his "Remarks on National Literature" in the *Christian Examiner* (1830), he reached these conclusions: First, we have not yet produced an American literature because, even while we protest against "dependence on European manufactures," we continue to import the "fabrics of the intellect." Secondly, the American faith in "the essential equality of all human beings" is highly favorable to creative activity. Finally, when this new world begets "great minds" and breeds "a nobler race of men," we shall then write books of the first magnitude. At the time, Bryant was moving toward the same position in his reviews of American authors, but not until Emerson delivered his Phi Beta Kappa oration in 1837 was cultural nationalism defended more cogently.

Morality bulked almost as large as public affairs, and was indeed a public issue, in the writings of the *North American* authors. Channing, for example, declared in his "Remarks" that the only force which can elevate American literature to its full potentialities is "the religious principle." Fortunately for America, his faith was a particularly enlightened variety of the Boston religion. Combining whatever was congenial to his mind in the beliefs of Separatists and Deists, Rousseau, the French Revolutionists, Godwin, and Wollstonecraft, he devised his own brand of Unitarianism. He announced, in his ordination sermon for Jared Sparks and in other addresses, that God is infinite (too great to die on a gallows) and God is love (too beneficent to predestine men to eternal flames). Man like God is good—and divine. The natural relationship between such a man and such a God can only be good; to worship God, therefore, is to live the good life. As God recognizes the inalienable rights of man's personality, "the only God . . . is the God whose image dwells in our own souls." Thus Channing laid the moral foundation for an egocentric yet devoutly religious romanticism which, in so far as it was truly self-reliant, was truly American.

Such a man as Channing found it easy to love that "outer garment of God," the physical universe. The Atlantic Ocean, the White Mountains, the forests of New England he knew and cherished, both for themselves and for their Creator. In reading these physical transcripts of deity, he was aided by Schelling and Coleridge, and by his favorite among living poets, Wordsworth. When he visited Wordsworth, the two men exchanged ideas while riding in a farmer's cart on the road from Dove Cottage to Grasmere. "We talked so eagerly," said Channing, "as often to interrupt one another, and I descended into Grasmere near sunset, with the placid lake before me, and Wordsworth talking and reciting poetry with a poet's spirit by my side."

Boston's most severe critic of outmoded classicism and its most extravagant champion of romanticism in the English manner was Richard Henry Dana, Sr. Sensitive and high-tempered, distrustful of his contemporaries and himself, he was lonely in New England. As a contributor to the *North American,* he insisted that Pope could not write poetry but that the poets of the Lake School were masters. Thereupon he was violently attacked by the reactionary majority among the Boston literati and warmly defended by his friend Bryant; he failed of election to the editorship of the *Review*; and thereafter he refused to contribute to its pages. Eager for public recognition, he was hard hit by the cool reception of his essays and tales in *The Idle Man* (published in parts during 1821–1822), of his long poem, *The Buccaneer* (1827), and of his collected *Poems and Prose Writings* (1833, 1850). In middle life, he withdrew from the world which would not recognize his genius.

Dana's heart was not in this present "age of improvement" but in that golden day when, he fancied, "all was rustic and unforced" and "the relentless curiosity of modern times had not . . . soiled and torn asunder the flower." Past-minded in politics, he remained a Federalist long after the party had disappeared, and he even argued the superiority of monarchial to republican government. He was likewise an ardent Trinitarian and, during the twenties, an outspoken foe of the heterodoxy of Channing and Bryant. In his poetry and prose, as might be anticipated, he followed many masters: in *The Buccaneer,* eighteenth century sentimentalists, Coleridge, Wordsworth, and Byron; in his tales, especially "Paul Felton," the same Englishmen and Charles Brockden Brown. Dana expressed much sympathy for Brown's "loneliness of situation," his isolation as a man of sensibility in a mechanical age, and his ultimate success in escaping from "free thought" and becoming "a true believer." Didactic as Dana was at times, his extreme romanticism entitles him to a reprieve from Poe's sentence to death by hanging for all the *North American* men. The fact remains, however, that Dana was throughout his life an ardent exponent of the inverted provincialism which colored Edward Everett's earlier years. Except for Channing, this Boston group did little to break away from England or her literature and to discover the roots of American life.

3

Connecticut, according to Washington Irving, was populated by onion eaters, hog stealers, bundlers, improvers, and slab-sided schoolmasters. Such witticisms are an index not only to the complacency of New York, but to the dilemma of genteel men of letters in Connecticut during the early century. Cut off by distance from the intellectual stimulus of Boston, and by choice from the earthy stimulus of life among hog stealers and onion eaters, they too turned directly to Europe for precedents, as had the earlier Hartford wits. Thus it happened that the most enthusiastic medievalist of the period and the most complete romantic solitary were products of Yale—and the most shameless sentimentalist was a Hartford woman. The poets were no longer stirred by the old themes of religion and politics; the graces and amenities of life took their place.

The medievalist was James Abraham Hillhouse. In "A Discourse . . . on

Some of the Considerations Which Should Influence an Epic or a Tragic Writer in the Choice of an Era," he rejected the "heathen" world of the ancients for the glorious Christian era of chivalry ("Its spirit was pitched to enthusiasm, imagination was the ruling power, and the whole tenor of its actions was extraordinary"). America, he added, is an admirable residence, but it has no past and the American writer of tragedy or epic must therefore rely on our "indefeasible . . . portion in the fame of Arthur and Alfred." These principles he put into practice in three blank-verse dramas: *Percy's Masque* (1819), based on Thomas Percy's original ballad, "The Hermit of Warkworth"; *Hadad* (1825), a melodrama of the days when there was "intercourse between mankind, and good and evil beings from the Spiritual World"; and *Demetria* (1839), a "horrid" tragedy of Italian cavaliers and ladies. Always self-consistent, Hillhouse introduced nothing of the epic or the tragic into his American poem, *Sachem's Wood* (1836), but pictured his home in New Haven solely in terms of the sentimental and the comic.

The romantic solitary was James Gates Percival. Elegant steel engravings of distinguished authors, hanging on the parlor walls of America, honored him through the twenties as the nation's chief poet, and many reviewers gave him the same rank; but the public left him to starve. He met nothing except disappointment as a tutor, a lecturer on anatomy and later on botany, a physician, an editor, a surgeon in the Army, a professor of chemistry at West Point, a lexicographer, and the author of four volumes of poetry—all within the span of twelve years. Wounded, and too timid to mix with the herd, he next voluntarily secluded himself for a decade in three unswept rooms in the state hospital at New Haven. He spent his last years on the frontier in Wisconsin, where he died in solitude.

The world of poetry into which Percival escaped from New Haven was compounded of his own undisciplined emotions and his emulation of the English romantics. When a young maniac in "The Suicide" shouts, "Give me the knife, the dagger, or the ball," he echoes his creator Percival, who in youth attempted to destroy himself in a variety of ways; but the same maniac echoes Byron when he cries, "O, hell to me is nothing,—nothing's hell." When Percival generalizes windily in "Prometheus," he follows Shelley; but his condemnation of Prometheus for sacrilegiously rending "the veil Religion hung around us" voices his own pietism. Although the mountains which rise on many of his pages are dim copies of Wordsworth's first-hand observations, it should be added that Percival could write delightfully of the American scene when, on rare occasions, the charms of Seneca Lake or a landscape in New England caught his eye.

Percival's chief weakness was loquacity, but of it he made romantic virtue. "The highest interest of a poet," he declared, is "to write only, when he feels inspired, when his subject has gained full possession of him. . . . Then . . . his language will flow abroad without effort." It is too evident that his long poems and his flood of lyrics—there are more than four hundred of them—did indeed flow abroad, with all the ease of divine madness and little of the anguished effort which Bryant, for example, was putting into his best lines. Thus Percival, instead of expending his slender talent with caution and discretion, scattered it with a prodigal hand.

Sentimentalism came to a dead end in the verses of Lydia Huntley Sigourney. She offered the public neither the violence nor the abstractions which alarmed them in Percival; instead, she gave them literalness and propriety, convention and elegance. As her reward, she was editing an annual, contributing to a half-dozen more, and selling her work to a score of magazines while Percival was hiding himself in a hospital. She knew something of the humanitarian movements of the day, but all that she did for Negroes, Indians, the poor, and the insane was to embalm them in the amber of her tears. Until Longfellow came into his own in the fifties, the most widely read American poet (she published sixty-seven volumes) was "The Sweet Singer of Hartford."

4

Even the ruggedness of the hinterland could not wean New England writers from conventional European modes. The simple realities of contemporary life in Vermont, in the Berkshires, and in Maine helped bring national and international recognition to three novelists; but the hand of the past lay so heavily on all three that they capitulated to traditional melodrama or to traditional propriety and rejected, in varying degree, the region which made them famous. They too failed to achieve the nationality or the universality of an indigenous art.

Least original of the three and least appreciative of his resources was Daniel Pierce Thompson. In a day when native novels were few, *The Green Mountain Boys* (1839) was famous as a classic of Vermont life. But its author, a rural lawyer with no literary standards and no literary conscience, was less concerned with recording New England character than with imitating the blood-pudding school of romancers. Actually, the book is not a document in social history but a violent yarn of a villain who slinks, muttering, down the valleys and a hero who strides up the mountains with the heroine held high in one arm and her Indian maidservant in the other. *Locke Amsden* (1847), frequently praised for its account of education in early Vermont, is likewise so filled with clichés and stereotypes that it has little meaning as a record of local manners.

Catharine Maria Sedgwick, like Maria Edgeworth to whom she dedicated her first book, was at first keenly interested in the manners of her own region; and in her early novels she described those manners with naïve and convincing honesty. When she recorded the meanness of Yankee rustics and defended the Friends' religion in *A New-England Tale* (1822), her brother reported, "The orthodox do all they can to put it down, . . . and New Englanders feel miffed." Thin-skinned New Englanders were miffed again by the pungent, self-willed spinster, Miss Debbie, in *Redwood* (1824); Shakers protested that the novel treated them with "irreverence and derision"; the austere Dana in Boston charged Miss Sedgwick with lack of good taste; but her friend Bryant praised *Redwood* "as a conclusive argument, that the writers of works of fiction, of which the scene is laid in familiar and domestic life, have a rich and varied field before them in the United States." Thereafter she grew more interested in the chitchat of her ladies and gentlemen than in the homely ways of Berkshire countryfolk—she was now a distinguished authoress who wintered in New York and only summered in the Berkshires. She was also so infected by the vogue of historical romance that she deserted contemporary American life for seventeenth century Massachusetts (*Hope Leslie*, 1827) and Revolutionary New York (*The Linwoods*, 1835). Thus propriety and a new fashion in novels smothered Miss Sedgwick's innate realism and made her at last an apostate to her region and a purveyor of sentimental romance to genteel females.

The most colorful and original of the trio was John Neal of Portland, Maine, a Quaker and a tempestuous individualist, a shrewd down-Easter and a citizen of the world, and withal a strident prophet of Americanism in literature. With no education beyond elementary school, he went into trade with John Pierpont in Boston and was left penniless when their branch in Baltimore failed. For a few years he studied law, wrote for the Baltimore newspapers and the *Portico,* and dashed off one novel after another—now in six or seven weeks and again in twenty-seven days: *Logan* (1822), *Errata* (1823), *Seventy-six* (1823), and *Randolph* (1823). In his first novel, *Keep Cool* (1817), he attacked dueling; he enlivened *Randolph* by biting comments on American authors and public men, among them William Pinkney. Pinkney's son challenged Neal, who refused to fight. From 1824 to 1827 Neal lived in England, where he was the first American to write regularly for the great reviews. To *Blackwood's* he contributed a series of essays on American authors—sharply critical but no more severe than his comments written in the United States for *Randolph*. Eyed with suspicion in Portland after his return to America, Neal let it be known that he was a trained boxer and fencer (he had now been read out of meeting by the Friends for knocking a man down), founded the *Yankee,* a literary journal, and in due course was accepted as a leading citizen. In the thirties Neal was one of the first to praise Poe; in the sixties he wrote dime novels for Beadle.

The young law student who turned off a novel with one hand and a review with the other had no time to search for original characters or themes. He snatched high-minded villains from Godwin and low-minded heroes from Byron, then sent them roaring and murdering through the hackneyed routines of cheap melodrama: Logan, who sheds tears and blood with equal ease; and Harold, "whose very breath is poison." The public which supped deep and often on these horrors is well represented by an Englishwoman who, according to Neal, read his novels until "the high seasoning and wild flavor of these fierce and extravagant stories had rendered all other literary aliment unpalatable," and she "died with 'Seventy-Six' in her hand."

Unlike Miss Sedgwick wintering in New York, John Neal living in London developed new respect for our native character and speech. When he took stock of American books, he concluded: "Our best writers are English writers, not American writers. . . . Not so much as one true Yankee is to be found in any one of our native books: hardly so much as one true Yankee phrase." Adapting to his own ends the romantic doctrine of uniqueness, he declared: "It would not do for me to imitate anybody. Nor would it do for my country. Who would care for the *American* Addison where he could have the English?" Neal therefore proposed to abandon *"classical* English" ("It is no natural language—it never was") for common American speech, and to plow deep into American soil. American authors, he believed, would find "abundant and hidden sources of fertility in their own beautiful brave earth, waiting only to be broken up."

Although it remained for later generations to put these precepts into full execution, Neal at least attempted to observe them in his later novels. In the early chapters of *Brother Jonathan* (1825), he reported Yankee manners and diction with extraordinary fidelity, then relapsed into melodrama. In *Rachel Dyer* (1828) he dealt honestly with the witchcraft delusion and two of the unfortunate women sentenced to death by Judge Hathorne, then wandered off into polemics. In the opening pages of *The Down-Easters* (1833) he etched a striking series of Yankee portraits, then degenerated into bombast. Neal's most significant account of the resources of our "beautiful brave earth" is his lively autobiography, *Wandering Recollections of a Somewhat Busy Life* (1869)—his most distinctly American and, as a result, his most memorable book. Here was a romantic individualist who under more favorable circumstances might have exemplified Emerson's theory that any American who writes with full self-trust becomes a true voice of America. In him, as in Paulding and Cooper, belligerence served where art was inadequate to break the ties with the past and with Europe.

5

The interest in reform which had led Mrs. Sigourney into excessive sentimentalism was more vigorously pursued by another group of New England
writers. During the two decades which followed 1820, they fought what
Emerson described as "a war between intellect and affection." The war
was won by affection, as exemplified by humanitarians who believed that
"the nation existed for the individual, for the guardianship and education of
every man." When a call went out in 1840 for a Convention of Friends of
Universal Reform, all manner of men and women presented themselves at
the Chardon Street Chapel in Boston. With as much approval as amusement,
Emerson catalogued them as "madmen, madwomen, men with beards,
Dunkers, Muggletonians, Come-outers, Groaners, Agrarians, Seventh-Day
Baptists, Quakers, Abolitionists, Calvinists, Unitarians, and Philosophers."
Among the members of the older generation who contributed to this reorientation of the New England mind were Channing, John Pierpont, and
Lydia Maria Child. As reform was their ultimate concern, their lives speak
more loudly than their books. And their books, lacking in literary distinction
as they are, speak more loudly of America than do the more polished writings
of their bookish contemporaries.

After Channing had analyzed the relationships between the members of
the Trinity and between God and man, he turned to those between men and
men. Translating into contemporary terms his "high estimate of human
nature," his "reverence . . . for human rights," and his faith in "the essential
equality of men," he warned his wealthy parishioners in Boston that "justice
is a greater good than property, not greater in degree, but in kind." He told
Southerners that a man cannot be held as property, because he is both a
rational and a moral being—but he told Abolitionists that they were too
violent. He attacked intemperance as "the *voluntary extinction of reason*"—
but he rebuked temperance agitators for their irrational attempts at coercion.
He lectured against war as incompatible with a proper recognition of "the
worth of a human being" and helped organize the Massachusetts Peace Society. He declared that "it is a greater work to educate a child, in the true and
larger sense of the word, than to rule a state" and gave his support to Horace
Mann. He rejected Franklin's dictum that a man should improve himself
to increase his earning power, and urged self-improvement as a means of
self-perfection. And the perfection of society through the perfecting of each
citizen was, of course, Channing's goal.

John Pierpont brought to the role of universal reformer less elevation but
no less devotion than Channing. He sold dry goods and went bankrupt with
his partner John Neal, wrote his widely popular *Airs of Palestine* (1816),

and pawned the family silver to pay the printer; studied divinity and was ordained as a Unitarian clergyman. American-minded, he wrote "Warren's Address to His Soldiers at Bunker's Hill" for generations of schoolboys to recite and edited *The American First-Class Book* (1823) and *The National Reader* (1827). A friend of universal reform, he opposed war, slavery, imprisonment for debt, and intemperance. When his church in Boston leased its cellar to a rum merchant as a warehouse, after a "Seven Years' War" against the enemy, he resigned in protest and was fully vindicated by an ecclesiastical council. Pierpont lived on to serve briefly as chaplain in the Civil War and to see the Negro emancipated, but not to write a line of truly memorable prose or verse.

From patriotic romances of New England to tracts in defense of humanity was an easy transition for Lydia Maria Francis Child. Encouraged by her brother, a Unitarian clergyman, the youthful Miss Francis published two novels: *Hobomok* (1824), a story of a noble red man, spawned by eighteenth century sentimentalism, and *The Rebels; or, Boston Before the Revolution* (1825), another misalliance of propriety and melodrama. "My natural inclinations," Mrs. Child confessed, "drew me much more strongly toward literature and the arts than toward reform"; but in 1833 she dedicated herself once for all to humanitarianism with *An Appeal in Favor of That Class of Americans Called Africans,* which was the most widely read of her books. It won considerable and important support for abolition, but it also killed her journal, the *Juvenile Miscellany,* reduced the sale of her novels, and deprived her of membership in the Boston Athenaeum. Mrs. Child, with occasional assistance from her husband, edited the *National Anti-Slavery Standard* from 1841 to 1849, and in 1843–1845 she sharply condemned the current scale of income and wages in the United States (*Letters from New York*). As Lowell remarked in doggerel,

> Yes, a great heart is hers, one that dares to go in
> To the prison, the slave-hut, the alleys of sin,
> And to bring into each, or to find there, some line
> Of the never completely out-trampled divine.

But there was doubtful honor and no money for her in social reform and quiet realism; until *Uncle Tom's Cabin* established a precedent, it was more profitable for the authors of New England to romanticize an unreal past than to explore the actualities of a controversial present.

The absorption of humanitarian reform into a larger view of man and society—so vital an element in the work of Emerson, Thoreau, Melville, and Whitman—was at least hinted by Richard Henry Dana, Jr. With the publication of *Two Years Before the Mast* (1840), a new generation took its place in New England letters. Dana paused midway in his college career to strengthen his eyes by a two years' ocean voyage on the brig "Pilgrim," then graduated from Harvard and became a lawyer. Out of his voyage to California came a narrative of the sea as sober and honest as his father's *Buccaneer* was extravagant. To readers of the forties who still doubted, in spite of Cooper's success with such romances, that it was possible to fill a volume with life on the sea, the book was a revelation. To a generation of patriotic Americans who found high satisfaction in the achievements of Yankee captains and Yankee crews sailing the seven seas, this account of the daily duties and the daily boredom of seamen was exciting. To humanitarians of the Chardon Street persuasion, Dana's account of flogging and other severities on shipboard was a sound indictment of the petty tyrants of the American merchant marine. And to sea-smitten boys, the book was and is a classic. For readers who know *Typee* and *Moby Dick, Two Years Before the Mast* is most significant as a specimen of the kind of raw material out of which Herman Melville created his great romances of the sea. As for Dana the lawyer, he lived quietly on in Massachusetts, where he befriended sailors (his manual, *The Seamen's Friend,* became their bible), longed for more years before the mast, and was sensibly content with a vacation in the West Indies (*To Cuba and Back,* 1859). Once a month he dined at the Parker House in Boston with Holmes, Lowell, and the other immortals of the Saturday Club.

6

It remained for the quiet poetry of William Cullen Bryant to express the unity of past and present, of America and Europe, which underlay the work of these seemingly diverse writers. On November 3, 1794, he was born into the primitive society of Cummington in Hampshire County, Massachusetts— the home of Ebenezer Snell and his daughter Sarah Bryant. Grandfather Snell was a figure from the past: a Federalist in politics and an extreme Calvinist in religion. Sharp-tongued and austere, he meted out harsh justice as squire in the town of Cummington, deacon in the Congregational Church, and head of the house of Snell and Bryant. To him, the chief temporal duties of man were thrift and industry. His grandson, he taught to plant potatoes and hoe corn. In raking hay, he put the boy in front of him; if Cullen did not make enough speed, his grandfather's rake dropped on his heels.

William Cullen Bryant was born also into the Massachusetts of his father Peter Bryant, M.D., who wrote verse in the manner of Pope but bought for his library (one of the best in Hampshire County) the poems of the late eighteenth century romantics. An able physician and an active public servant, he journeyed often to Boston as a member of the state medical society and of the state legislature. His friends in Boston and his own reading early converted him to Unitarianism. Kindly and democratic during his life, Peter Bryant at his death was mourned throughout western Massachusetts as "the beloved physician."

From the conflicting worlds of Peter Bryant and the Snells, Cullen early escaped into his own New England. To Sarah Snell, the physical world was wind and rain to be noted in her diary; to Dr. Bryant it was an herb garden for his medicines. But their son was from his earliest years "a delighted observer of external nature—the splendors of a winter daybreak over the wild wastes of snow seen from our windows, the glories of the autumnal woods, the gloomy approaches of the thunderstorm, . . . the return of spring, with its flowers, and the first snowfall of winter." Near his doorstep he found yellow violets and fringed gentians, growing beside a rivulet and in a wood. To the eastward, he roamed down the hill-meadows to the noisy Westfield River. To the west, his eyes followed the dim ranges of the Berkshires. And when he walked with nature, he declared:

> I was with one
> With whom I early grew familiar, one
> Who never had a frown for me, whose voice
> Never rebuked me for the hours I stole
> From cares I loved not.

Out of the Federalism of both Squire Snell and Dr. Bryant came Cullen Bryant's first notable publication, *The Embargo, or Sketches of the Times; a Satire,* printed in Boston in 1808 as the work of an anonymous "Youth of Thirteen." The boy's earliest lines had been pious jingles written with the approval of the Snells and sometimes rewarded by a coin from Ebenezer. Lampoons on his schoolmates followed. Then, encouraged by his father, he aimed his shafts at that "imbecile slave," the President of the United States. His angry couplets repeated current libels on Jefferson, among them the accusation that he was intimate with a Negress on his plantation, and demanded his resignation. In Boston the *Monthly Anthology,* organ of William Tudor, George Ticknor, and William Ellery Channing, and predecessor of the *North American Review,* found in *The Embargo* "no small amount of fire and some excellent lines." Such a satire by a boy of thirteen would have been in 1758 an auspicious beginning for a literary career; but in 1808 it was a piece of belated classicism to be outgrown.

Out of the religious liberalism of Peter Bryant and out of Cullen's exploration of his own New England came "Thanatopsis"—the bridge over which the youthful poet moved from Pope toward Wordsworth. The autumn of 1811 found Cullen in a somber mood. He and his father had hoped that he might attend Harvard College, where Peter Bryant had once expected to study medicine and where Sparks and Everett were now undergraduates. The Snells, however, favored the orthodoxy and the economy of Williams College, where he entered as a sophomore—only to leave before the year was out, exasperated by the intellectual poverty of Williamstown. Then he thought to transfer to Yale, where Percival was a student; but Yankee thrift again defeated him, and he attended college no more. Thrice disappointed, Cullen now rambled over the "lone and still and unfrequented" Hampshire hills, meditating sadly on life and, more particularly, on death. Sixteen years earlier, he had been born across the road from a burying ground. He had been frail, and the neighbors predicted that he would not live. As he grew older, his grandfather's prayers of death and his mother's biblical tales of death made the grave a terrible and an imminent reality. As he walked, Cullen asked himself, How shall I face death? The answer was "Thanatopsis."

Back of "Thanatopsis" lay not only long years of fear but long hours of reading among the poets in Peter Bryant's library: Robert Blair, Beilby Porteus, Henry Kirke White, Erasmus Darwin, Southey, Cowper, Milton. Back of "Thanatopsis" lay also Volney's *Ruins* and Dr. Bryant's Unitarian journals from Boston, and Cullen's knowledge that his father testified to his Unitarian belief by refusing to stand when the Trinitarian doxology was sung in the Cummington church. Behind the poem lay also the boy's exploration of nature. In the second edition of *The Embargo* (1809) he had published three crude pastorals in which he attempted, without success, to express his incipient romanticism in the diction of Pope. Now as he wandered "in the gloom of the thickets" and "the twilight of mountain groves," among the "deep-cloven falls" and beside "the rush of the pebble-paved river," he found, without benefit of Wordsworth whom he had not yet read, a vocabulary fit to voice his conception of the physical world.

Ignoring Christ and Calvin, conversion and immortality, Cullen stoically announced in "Thanatopsis" (in early texts of the poem, his own "better genius" speaks, not nature) that every man shall go to the grave serene in his own particular faith—and what that faith is, the poet does not particularize. Here he broke with the more rigorous aspects of the religion of the Snells, accepted the deistic elements in Peter Bryant's religion, and turned in death, as he had already turned in life, from mankind to nature. As this was no poem for the eye of Ebenezer Snell, Cullen hid it away for a time, meticulously revising its lines as his father had taught him.

The economic pressure which had kept him from Yale now sent him over the hill to Worthington to study law. Here he was concerned with people; he lounged in grogshops and danced in taverns; he read Byron and rhymed Byronically of maidens and love. But whenever he returned to the homestead nature spoke to him again, and he lived in his private world of stream and forest. What he heard he set down in "The Yellow Violet" and "Inscription for the Entrance to a Wood." Already professing to be weary of men, he concluded that nature is "the abode of gladness" where the birds "sing and sport in wantonness of spirit" and the wind

> That stirs the stream in play, shall come to thee,
> Like one that loves thee nor will let thee pass
> Ungreeted, and shall give its light embrace.

At Worthington Bryant read Wordsworth's poems and drew from them new symbols to express his conception of the universe; but the romanticism which was emerging in his poetry was neither English nor American; it was both.

7

At the age of twenty-one, Bryant left Cummington to make his own way in the world. During the decade which followed, his ideas, his emotions, and his poetry took on the conformations which were to mark them until his death at eighty-five. First, he came to terms with God and religion. Late one afternoon in December, 1815, he set out from the homestead to open a law office in the crossroads hamlet of Plainfield, to which he resigned himself when it became evident that there was no money in the family purse to send him to Boston. As he walked down into the gathering shadows, uncertainty crowded upon him. Very much alone, he remembered his father's God, to whom he had of late given little thought. Then his eye was caught by a waterfowl sharply outlined against the evening sky—nature's confirmation of the existence of omnipotent Goodness. Deeply moved, Bryant put himself into the keeping of nature's Deity:

> He who, from zone to zone,
> Guides through the boundless sky thy certain flight,
> In the long way that I must tread alone,
> Will lead my steps aright.

Thereafter he was a religious liberal, associating himself particularly with the Unitarians, who to the mind of the Snells and most New Englanders, were a Christless lot.

"Thanatopsis" was given to the public by the *North American Review* after Bryant had left Plainfield, not for Boston, but for Great Barrington among the Berkshires. The town had been settled by the Dutch and was now in closer contact with Albany and New York than with eastern Massachusetts; but the influence of Boston still followed Bryant. On a visit to Cummington, he left the manuscript of "Thanatopsis" on his father's desk, and the latter took it to Dana and Channing. Both were profoundly moved by the poem—the Anglophile Dana so deeply that he protested to one of his editorial colleagues: "Ah, you have been imposed upon. No one on this side of the Atlantic is capable of writing such verses!" When the *North American* printed "Thanatopsis" anonymously in 1817, it attracted no particular attention, and the world was not aware that an obscure lawyer in the Berkshires had published what was then the finest of American lyrics.

Bryant's first critical pronouncements on poetry were in close accord with his own practices. In an essay on versification, commenced when he was writing the early drafts of "Thanatopsis," he revealed that his preciosity in poetry was no accident; at sixteen, he had already concluded that the use of trisyllabic feet in iambic verse "is agreeable to that kind of measure, as well as to the habits of our language." Reviewing Solyman Brown's *An Essay on American Poetry* in 1818, he condemned the American Augustans for their "balanced and wearisome regularity." And in his own poetry he had long since freed himself from the chains of Pope and was now exploring, with true romantic delight, the varied resources of meter. No American during the twenties matched Bryant in the diversity and the refinement of his measures.

The problem of nationalism in literature also occupied Bryant's mind. He pointed out in the *North American* that contumely abroad and complacency at home were equally unjustified. So, likewise, was American subservience to foreign opinion: "We do not praise a thing," he protested, "until we see the seal of transatlantic approbation upon it." He admitted that an American author "must produce some more satisfactory evidence of his claim to celebrity than an extract from the parish register," but he insisted, despite British and American pronouncements to the contrary, that the United States was "a rich and varied field" for literature, and that authors who dealt honestly with the American landscape and the diversities of American character would deserve well of their countrymen. He was soon able to point to the novel *Redwood*, by his friend Catharine Sedgwick, as an example of honest nationalism.

An opportunity to review the history of the human race and at the same time to make a name for himself in Boston came to Bryant in 1821, when the editors of the *North American* secured for their contributor an invitation to deliver the Phi Beta Kappa poem at Harvard. For that occasion, Bryant wrote "The Ages"—a pedestrian defense of the doctrine of human perfectibility. In heavy Spenserians, he traced the progress of mankind from the early days of barbarism, through the glory of Greece and the darkness of the Middle Ages, on into modern times, and at last to America, where man shall come to ultimate fulfillment:

> Here the free spirit of mankind, at length,
> Throws its last fetters off; and who shall place
> A limit to the giant's unchained strength,
> Or curb the swiftness of his forward race?

Nothing in this familiar interpretation of history impressed the Harvard faculty, nothing in Bryant's quiet delivery caught the fancy of the public, and no one offered him a good berth in Boston. But he met Dana, and with Dana he formed the longest and closest friendship of his life. And he found a publisher for his *Poems* (1821), which included among its eight items "Thanatopsis," "The Yellow Violet," "Inscription for the Entrance to a Wood," "To a Waterfowl," and "Green River." The volume sold slowly; no important journal in New England praised it except the *North American*; and its most enthusiastic reviewer was a New Yorker, Gulian Verplanck. Although Bryant was in reality the foremost American poet of the day, he was still an unknown.

In Great Barrington, Bryant was moving toward the same stability in his affections and in his politics that he had already attained in religion. During his days as a student of law, his fancy and his pen had often toyed with love. Now he gave his heart to a young woman reared beside his Green River; in Frances Fairchild's honor he produced, after agonies of revision, the graceful lyric, "Oh Fairest of the Rural Maids"; and the two were happily married. As for his political beliefs, Bryant had been from boyhood an advocate of human liberty and of republicanism. Now he spoke out for the emancipation of Greeks, Waldenses, and Spaniards in Europe and of Negroes in the United States. He was converted to free trade by his reading in the English economists Adam Smith, Ricardo, and Thornton, to whom he was introduced by the Sedgwick brothers of Stockbridge and New York. Thus, when the Federalist Party disappeared and no antislavery party offered itself to the electorate, he was prepared to turn from the conservative majority in New England to the Democrats and free trade. Thereafter he remained a political liberal, in one party or another, until old age overtook him.

A systematic testing of his capacity for writing poetry followed in 1824-1825. From Boston came an invitation to contribute to each issue of a new semimonthly magazine, the *United-States Literary Gazette*. In response, he wrote more poetry than during any comparable period in his life. As the Berkshires and he were now intimate friends, his favored theme was nature:

"A Winter Piece," "The West Wind," "A Walk at Sunset," "March," "Summer Wind," "After a Tempest," "Autumn Woods," "November," "To a Cloud, "A Forest Hymn," and others. Bryant's regular appearance twice monthly in a new literary journal had its effect: his poems were reprinted, critics commented on them both here and in England, and his reputation grew. But in Massachusetts comment was often unfavorable, for Bryant was an America scion of the Lake School of poets and the Lakers were still anathema to most Bostonians.

At the age of thirty, Bryant left New England. Respected in Great Barrington but not universally liked, he himself was sharply annoyed by the factiousness of village life. "It cost me," he complained, "more pains and perplexity than it was worth to live on friendly terms with my neighbors." In this unwelcome atmosphere, he was

> forced to drudge for the dregs of men,
> And scrawl strange words with a barbarous pen,
> And mingle among the jostling crowd,
> Where the sons of strife [are] subtle and loud.

Practicing only in the civil courts and occupied chiefly with trivial suits for the collection of debts, he never earned more than five hundred dollars for a year's toil for the dregs of men, while the *Literary Gazette* paid him two hundred dollars a year for a hundred lines of poetry per month. In financial matters, Bryant possessed too much practicality to starve in a garret for the sake of the muse. But a salary of a thousand dollars as joint editor of the *New-York Review and Atheneum Magazine* was a conclusive argument for abandoning both the law and Massachusetts. In 1825 he became a "literary adventurer" in New York.

8

The adventurer soon found security as editor and part-owner of the *Evening Post*. There Bryant for a half-century shaped American public opinion, took on prestige and patriarchal dignity, and eventually became one of the first citizens of New York. Yet the characteristics of the New York editor all had their origins in the character of the Massachusetts lawyer. Thriftily he invested his earnings, not from profitless poetry but from his newspaper, in real estate; then the growth of New York made him a wealthy man. Once a caustic young satirist and later a hot-tempered lawyer, he horsewhipped Editor Stone of the *Commercial Advertiser* and refused, under any and all circumstances, to speak to Editor Weed of the *World*. Then he learned to curb his wrath—but even in his last years dull flames occasionally smoldered under his heavy brows. The man who had fled from men to the fastnesses of the Berkshires was in New York as shy as "a sensitive young girl"; his polished contemporary from Boston, Edward Everett, found him as nearly helpless in polite society as any famous man he had ever met. To cover all this, Bryant developed a highly formal manner ("One would as soon think of taking a liberty with the Pope as with BRYANT," said John Bigelow) and cultivated an austere silence ("Not a soul can get a word out of him without cart and horses to fetch it," complained Bret Harte). Uncritical observers soon mistook this mask for the man, and in the forties young Lowell was so far misled by externalities as to write:

> There is Bryant, as quiet, as cool, and as dignified
> As a smooth, silent iceberg, that never is ignified.

But in Bryant's last years his emotions did indeed atrophy under this rigid self-discipline, until the man whom Harte met in the seventies was truly a cold and silent iceberg.

Bryant of the *Post* was a hard-working and capable editor, but brilliance was not to be expected from a quiet country lawyer turned city journalist. When the *Post* finally became a money-maker, its prosperity came not from any superlative ability of Bryant as a newsman but from increased public endorsement of the two beliefs which he had brought with him from Massachusetts: faith in liberty and faith in democracy. In New York he was an early and often a lonely advocate of abolition, free speech, and the rights of labor. In 1836 he defended a group of tailors who formed a union and were thereupon fined for conspiracy in restraint of trade. "If this is not SLAVERY," he thundered in the *Post*, "we have forgotten its definition." When a mob murdered Lovejoy in 1837, Bryant wrote a noble plea for freedom of speech: "The right to discuss freely and openly, by speech, by the pen, by the press, all political questions and to examine and animadvert upon all political institutions, is a right so clear and certain, so interwoven with our other liberties, so necessary, in fact, to their existence, that without it we shall fall at once into despotism or anarchy." He made the *Post* an organ of the Free Soilers, of the Barnburners, and, after the Kansas-Nebraska Bill was enacted in 1854, of that radical new party, the black Republicans. He damned the Fugitive Slave Law as "the most ruffianly act ever authorized by a deliberative assembly," glorified John Brown as "one of the martyrs and heroes" of human liberty, and sponsored Abraham Lincoln on his first appearance in New York. When further compromise with the South became impossible, Bryant repudiated his youthful belief in the right to secession and became a hot advocate of relentless war upon the rebels.

Too level-headed to become a universal reformer, Bryant gave the support of the *Post* only to those movements which seemed to him both sane and urgent. In municipal affairs, for example, he campaigned with varying degrees of success for a central park, improved police and fire protection, and against corrupt politics. In international affairs, he continued to back free trade, and he became an advocate of free cultural, as well as economic, exchange between the old world and the United States. Moral considerations were never forgotten in his editorials. Although his conception of democracy is more reminiscent of Peter Bryant than of the Snells, he attributed his adherence to "the great rule of right without much regard for persons" to the influence of his mother, whose conduct taught him "never to countenance a wrong because others did." Thus when Editor Bryant pilloried such national figures as Harrison, Clay, and that "sordid apostate" Webster, he was dealing with wrongdoers just as Sarah Bryant and her female colleagues had dealt with a notorious wife-beater of Cummington when, one election day, they rode him out of town on a rail. Industry, good sense, moral purpose, honesty, courage—these made Bryant one of the great figures in American journalism.

During his early years in New York, Bryant turned his hand to prose tales on romantic themes which he had earlier treated in verse: Indians and pioneers in the manner of Cooper ("The Indian Spring," "The Cascade of Melsingah," "The Skeleton's Cave," "The Marriage Blunder"), fantasy and legend in the manner of Irving ("A Border Tradition," "A Pennsylvania Legend," "Reminiscences of New York," "The Legend of the Devil's Pulpit"), and the literature and customs of Spain ("Recollections of the South of Spain," "Early Spanish Poetry," "Phanette des Gantelmes"). From his travels in the prairie states (where his mother and brothers found a new frontier) and in Europe and the Near East, he brought back solid cargoes of fact: *Letters of a Traveller* (1850), *Letters of a Traveller, Second Series* (1859), and *Letters from the East* (1869). When his contemporaries among the romantics died, he reviewed their careers: Thomas Cole, Cooper, Irving, Gulian Verplanck. But Bryant's prose, whether fantasy or funeral oration, was heavy, and in his later years he wisely employed verse as a vehicle for his excursions into fairyland: "Castles in the Air," "The Little People of the Snow," "Cloudland," "Stella."

9

Bryant was also a pioneer in American literary criticism; his was our earliest systematic study of the nature of poetry. From "Lectures on Poetry" (delivered in 1825; published 1884) to "Poets and Poetry of the English Language" (introduction to *A Library of Poetry and Song,* 1871), he consistently defined poetry in the same familiar terms: morality, imagination, originality, emotion, simplicity. Thoroughly committed, like the entire *North American* group in Massachusetts, to a moralism at which New Yorkers were beginning to smile, Bryant never doubted that the poet should teach "direct lessons of wisdom." At the same time, he believed that poetry, as a suggestive rather than a mimetic art, addresses itself to the imagination of the reader. Then the reader, in turn, contributes to the poetic experience by sending his own imagination along "the path which the poet only points out." Admitting that every artist takes up his art where his predecessors have left it, Bryant insisted that the poet, if he is to "deserve the praise of originality and genius," must go on to discover "new modes of sublimity, of beauty, and of human emotion." And emotion, Bryant declared, is "the great spring of poetry." From this principle, it follows that "poetry which does not find the way to the heart is scarcely deserving of the name." And again: "The most beautiful poetry is that which takes the strongest hold on the feelings." Finally, he was an advocate of clearness and simplicity, particularly as they are exemplified in the "luminous style" which is "one of the most important requisites for a great poet." As for the origins of these views, young Cullen Bryant met them in his father's library in Cummington, stated explicitly or through implication by certain of the eighteenth century rhetoricians and critics who precipitated the romantic revolution in Great Britain.

General recognition of Bryant the poet came belatedly, on the heels of recognition of Bryant the editor. In 1837, Poe wrote: "Mr. Bryant's poetical reputation, both at home and abroad, is greater, we presume, than that of any other American. British critics have frequently awarded him high praise; and here, the public press have been unanimous in approbation." These superlatives were not entirely justified, for American critics were by no means unanimous in recognizing Bryant as the chief American poet. An English edition of his poems, sponsored by Washington Irving in 1832, was well received, and in the United States he reached the apex of his reputation in the thirties—only to be overshadowed at once by the next generation of romantic poets, Poe, Longfellow, Whittier, and Lowell. It is a further irony of literary history that during the years of his greatest fame, he wrote only a handful of significant poems ("To the Fringed Gentian," "Song of Marion's Men," "The Prairies") and during the four decades which followed, hardly more ("Oh Mother of a Mighty Race," "Robert of Lincoln," "The Planting of the Apple-Tree," "The Death of Lincoln"). Although he was at times too hard pressed by editorial duties to compose poetry, he had at other times considerable leisure. His scanty output is therefore to be explained on the ground that he possessed only a modest vein of genius, which he early discovered and soon explored to its full extent. From the first, he was obliged to mine that vein with the utmost industry—revising, discarding, reworking, and revising yet again. To his credit, these revisions were almost invariably fortunate. Likewise to his high credit is the fact that, despite these limitations, he earned for himself a secure place among the American poets.

Even though Bryant's early readers found his poems complex and difficult, he is in the present century read, as he would prefer to be, as a poet of simplicity. His ideas are few and familiar. God he interpreted as truth and love, justice and liberty. Man is, in terms of the immediate, a creature of "sorrows, crimes, and cares"; in terms of the ultimate, man is moving steadily toward that great day when "love and peace shall make their paradise" on earth. Nature is a serene temple for worship and a reservoir of health and joy to which Bryant continually invited his reader to escape, from

> all that pained thee in the haunts of men,
> And made thee loathe thy life.

Bryant's emotions seem to readers of the present day to be equally limited: reverence for God, wrath for all despoilers of humanity, pity for their vicitims, love for wife and child (who, to Bryant's mind, never despoil), devotion to native land (which rarely despoils), and affection for the physical world (to whose despoilings Bryant closed his eyes). But his most successful transcriptions of these ideas and these emotions are marked now by a quiet charm and again by a dignity unsurpassed, of their kind, in American poetry.

Bryant would wish to be, and should be, read also as a poet of America. His nationalism was more consistent than that of Catharine Sedgwick or John Neal and more solidly grounded than that of any contemporary New Englander except Channing. His affection for the American landscape exceeded Irving's and equaled Cooper's. As a New Yorker, he capitulated to the beauty of Long Island and the Hudson. He and Thomas Cole, the romantic painter of magnificence and grandeur, were particularly charmed by the Catskills; they are, very appropriately, the only human figures in Asher Brown Durand's painting of a Catskill landscape ("Kindred Spirits"). But Bryant, like his friends among the Hudson River School of painters, was more successful in introducing American materials into his work than in creating an American manner. Unlike Whitman in the next generation of romanticists, he was prepared neither to announce nor to put into practice the brave dictum, "The expression of the American poet is to be transcendent and new." Closely related as the substance of many of Bryant's poems is to the life of America and especially of New England, his voice was to the end the voice of an Anglo-American.

Bryant should be read, finally, as a poet of the eternal procession of mankind. He followed the march of men and of time in the ancient classics, which in boyhood he translated for pleasure and in old age, for consolation (*The Iliad of Homer,* 1870; *The Odyssey of Homer,* 1871–1872). In the Bible and in science, he traced "the great Movement of the Universe." In Massachusetts and in New York, he mourned as his family and his friends joined

> The innumerable caravan, which moves
> To that mysterious realm, where each shall take
> His chamber in the silent halls of death.

Then he drew on the events of history to trace the great procession in "The Ages" and "The Past." In terms of the physical world, he charted the progression of the universe in "The Planting of the Apple-Tree," "The Song of the Sower," and employing an even more figurative idiom, in his many poems of the winds. Drawing on his own memories, he retold the story in "A Lifetime" and "The Flood of Years." Here, with fourscore years behind him, the poet asked for the last time the question which he had first posed at sixteen: How shall a man approach the grave? And the aged Bryant replied: Go serenely, with an unfaltering trust in "the never-ending Flood of Years," a trust in that "eternal Change" which unites all men, all times, and all events in "everlasting Concord."

22. IN THE SOUTH

By 1826, when Cooper, Irving, and Bryant were making for themselves the first great names in American literature, Poe was an unknown student at the newly established University of Virginia, and the most notable author in the South was George Tucker, the Charlottesville Professor of Moral Philosophy and Political Economy. Tucker was born in 1775 in Bermuda. He came to Virginia as a youth to study law at William and Mary College under his cousin St. George Tucker, himself a native Bermudan, a famous lawyer, and an occasional author.

George Tucker's career may be taken to reflect the state of literary culture in Maryland, Virginia, and the Carolinas during the 1820's. A man of inquiring mind and conservative temper, he was led by his legal training into a serious study of the agrarian economy upon which the political philosophy of the South was deeply based, and to the publication, while a member of the National Congress, of *Essays on Subjects of Taste, Morals, and National Policy* (1822). But when he turned to the writing of literature as such, he looked for models to the London of the past century rather than to the contemporary New York of Irving and Cooper or the New England of Bryant. As a lawyer in Richmond, he is reported to have put an end to card playing among refined people by a poetical satire, and his novel, *The Valley of the Shenandoah* (1824) combines his memories of Richardson's *Clarissa* with observations of sparsely settled Virginia. After his fanciful, pseudoscientific *Voyage to the Moon* (1827), his writings both in Charlottesville and in Philadelphia, where he resided after 1845, a vigorous and productive figure, were for the most part historical and sociological.

Even more than Tucker, William Wirt, though long inactive in literature, was generally held during the late twenties to be the most important author in the South for his popular *Letters of the British Spy* (1803) and other Addisonian essays on Southern manners. A Marylander born in 1772, Wirt had married into a prominent Virginia family and moved to Richmond to practice law, where he gained repute as one of the leading orators of his day. There he wrote a life of Patrick Henry, and prosecuted the extremely sensational trial of Aaron Burr. In 1817 he became Attorney General of the

United States. From that date, through the year of his declining to become first president of the University of Virginia, till his death in 1834, he resided in Baltimore nearly all of the time that he was not in Washington. Wirt's tastes were aristocratic and conservative; in the manner of the day, he divided his energies sharply between the light satiric essay and the serious efforts of the court of law and the world of affairs.

There was surely little love lost between Wirt and his older, mercurial Baltimore fellow citizen, William Pinkney, a perennial diplomat, often esteemed the greatest lawyer in America; and of Pinkney's son, Edward Coote Pinkney, even more mercurial than Pinkney the elder, the always temperate Wirt must have entertained a poor opinion indeed. This poet was born in 1802 in England, when his father was there on a diplomatic mission, and he spent more than half of his twenty-six years either with his father abroad or in the United States Navy, which he joined at thirteen and, proud and quarreling, abandoned at twenty-two. In 1823 he published *A Serenade Written by a Gentleman of Baltimore* ("Look out upon the stars, my love") reminiscent of the Elizabethan lyrics, and *Rodolph: A Fragment*; and in 1825 he published a slight volume, *Poems,* containing "A Health":

> I fill this cup to one made up of loveliness alone,
> A woman of her gentler sex the seeming paragon.

All of this time, especially after his marriage in 1824, he was desperate for money, but his poetry, echoing Byron in morals as well as in melody, was too unconventional for sedate people, and did not help him with his law practice. What it did help him with was an appointment to the unsalaried Professorship of Rhetoric and Belles-Lettres in the University of Maryland, and later, the editorship of a political paper, which he held for a few months before his death. For its fiery spirit and its flowing rhythm, Pinkney's poetry, though scant in volume, has come to be recognized as the purest product of the romantic and conservative Old South of the twenties.

The friendship that Wirt enjoyed with another young man in Baltimore must have delighted him as much as the Pinkney phenomenon dismayed him. John Pendleton Kennedy, the patron of Poe and the Maecenas of Southern letters for fifty years, was the son of an immigrant father and a mother from the distinguished Pendleton family in Virginia. In his youth he was probably more at home on the Shenandoah Valley plantations of his mother's relatives than in his native town, where he attended school and college.

Of bookish disposition, Kennedy contributed to the newspapers at an early age, and, as an advancing young lawyer, helped publish at irregular intervals an anonymous little magazine. Though this magazine was some-what impish, it was trenchant enough to win the mild, solicited applause of Edward Everett at Harvard. In 1820 Kennedy was in the Maryland legis-lature, and early in 1822 Wirt proposed him, without his complete assent, for a diplomatic post in South America. In his mid-thirties, about the time when in Baltimore Poe at twenty-one was living in poverty and Pinkney at twenty-six was dying in poverty, Kennedy inherited a considerable sum of money and married the daughter of a prosperous and literary-minded Balti-more manufacturer. From that time, he devoted himself less and less to the law and more and more to writing, politics, and public affairs.

Kennedy's presence made Baltimore a literary center to be rivaled only by Charleston, which was in the meantime becoming notable in letters mainly through the unimportant writings of a society-wit who had come from Massachusetts and of a transcendental painter who was bound for Massachu-setts. In the late 1820's, however, a vigorous and thoroughly native group asserted themselves and William Gilmore Simms, then a slightly schooled young man of twenty, but soon to become the most prolific and popular of Southern authors, published two volumes of poetry. And two prominent fellow citizens of his, plantation men both of them—the aging banker and botanist Stephen Elliott, and the maturing lawyer and traveled scholar Hugh Swinton Legaré—inaugurated the *Southern Review* in 1828. This recondite publication was an adaptation to the Old South of the great quar-terlies then current in Britain. But its collapse after four years suggests that the editors' calculation of the degree of adaptation needed was something less than adequate.

Always a little ponderous, inflexibly honest, Legaré was a phenomenon of industry and learning in his own subject, the law, and in most phases of European history. He was too earnest and fastidious to be interested in anything but the most classic classics, and he had little respect for American literature; that is, for American creative literature. His own essays, whether published in the *Southern Review* or in the *New-York Review*, testify fully that he was ready to tolerate critical literature that was American in authorship if not in subject. The brevity of his service in Congress indicates how gravely his opposition to Calhoun injured him as a politician at home, and his appointment as Attorney General of the United States in 1841 and Acting Secretary of State in 1843 indicates how little that opposition injured him elsewhere. His death in 1843 at the home of his long-time intimate friend George Ticknor in Boston was celebrated in a memorable poem by his kinsman, James Mathewes Legaré; and in 1846 his sister edited two volumes of his writings in Charleston.

As the national Congress, a sort of haven for Southern authors, had received Legaré and George Tucker, it received in 1818—and intermittently until 1835—Richard Henry Wilde of Georgia. Wilde was born in Ireland in 1789 but grew up in Augusta. He was a lawyer at nineteen, and the author by 1815 of a long poem dealing with the Indian wars in Florida and containing the lyric "My Life is Like the Summer Rose." This widely popular, lugubrious, Byronic plaint was the center for a long time of a storm of charges and countercharges as to its originality. A Greek translation of it, passed off as a newly discovered fragment of the verse of Alcaeus, and an outright claim to its authorship by an Irish impostor kept confused an issue that was cleared up in 1871 to its true author's complete credit.

In 1834 Wilde bestirred himself valiantly in Augusta in connection with the inauguration of the Richmond magazine, the *Southern Literary Messenger,* writing articles for it and procuring a hundred subscribers. But he was disillusioned with democracy; he could find no political party that did not "require of its followers what no honest man should and no gentleman would do." In 1835 he quit America for Italy. There for five years he occupied himself with a study of Renaissance Italian literature; and in 1842 he published a book on Tasso. The severe contemporary judgments passed on his "shirking abandonment" of America for Europe—"delight to the senses, but mildew to the heart"—and his own freely expressed poor opinion of the literary potentialities of America did not cool the adulatory nature of his welcome when he returned home. He had already to some degree refuted and, it was hoped, might further refute the charge that the artistic life in America was sterile, and somebody proposed that the people of Georgia should set up a monument to him. The proposal was not carried out, and Wilde left Augusta for New Orleans, a change which he came to think a further step into the cultural badlands. Before his death from yellow fever in 1847, he taught and practiced law, contributed to Southern magazines, and made occasional trips to New York where at times he encountered his friend Simms of Charleston.

2

In 1832 Kennedy in Baltimore published as by one Mark Littleton *Swallow Barn*—not a novel, he explained, but "a series of sketches linked together"; and Southern literature to some extent broke its tie with the classical and chivalric traditions of the Old World to recognize its kinship with the young writers to the North. Whatever its species, *Swallow Barn* is highly suggestive of Irving in style and spirit. It deals with Virginia plantation life in the first quarter of the nineteenth century. The really Great Days of Virginia, Kennedy thought, had already vanished; but he presented the remains of greatness there in such a fashion as to suggest that the time and place were inexhaustibly romantic. Kennedy's scenes and characters are uniformly "aristocratic," so that the credit as an early realist goes to Augustus Baldwin Longstreet for his humorous and earthy *Georgia Scenes,* published three years later. Yet it is important to remember that the way of life which is pictured in *Swallow Barn* is more simple and casual than that represented by the alabaster columns, with human and other appurtenances, which later novelists reared in battalions all over Virginia.

Swallow Barn was well received throughout the country, and its author was recognized as the literary heir of the aging Wirt, to whom the book was dedicated in time for him to know of the compliment before his death in 1834. In 1833 Kennedy was one of a committee of three who awarded to Edgar Allan Poe, then almost wholly unknown, a prize in a literary competition for his short story "MS Found in a Bottle." Poe's talents and his poverty and general emotional wretchedness stirred Kennedy deeply, and it was through him that Poe in 1835 obtained the position with the year-old *Southern Literary Messenger* in Richmond that in a sense "made" both magazine and editor. During the rest of Poe's life Kennedy entertained the most cordial feeling for him. He helped him at times with money and oftener with what Poe indeed more truly needed but was reluctant to accept, counsel that was wise and kindly and as understanding as a man like Kennedy could devise for a man like Poe.

Two years after the appearance of *Swallow Barn,* a physician, William Alexander Caruthers of Savannah, who was almost surely a follower of the *Messenger,* published his novel *The Kentuckian in New York.* His birth in Virginia in 1800 and his schooling at the college in Lexington, if no more, made him refer to himself always as a "Virginian"; but he was also a self-conscious protagonist of the "West," of which Georgia was in his mind a part. He said that he could see Savannah in his time outstripping New York and Philadelphia, and the United States by 1870 a nation of 168,000,000 people—all of whom, he hoped, would eschew both rum and Romanism.

The Kentuckian in New York is made up of letters between two young South Carolinians and a Kentuckian, who are visiting New York, and a young Virginian who is visiting in South Carolina. The final effect is that of a voluble, high-spirited travel book, with long but interesting digressions devoted now to the tender passion, now to historical, economic, or philosophic commentary. In spite of the author's belief that there was a Northern conspiracy against Southern writers, the main thesis of his book is that if Northerners and Southerners could be brought to know one another they would inevitably love one another.

Caruthers was an affable, too credulous, but earnest and candid patriot. He deprecated the big-plantation system in the South and city "mobocracies" in the North, and he wished for the entire country, apparently with hope of realizing the wish, an economy based predominantly on small farms operated by their white owners.

In an epilogue to his first novel, he declared that he had created his talkative, Jackson-worshiping Kentuckian primarily as a humorous entice- ment for readers, and that his true interest lay in a historical romance that he would publish soon. This book, *The Cavaliers of Virginia* (1834–1835), though it deals with Bacon's Rebellion in a way deeply sympathetic with Bacon, is high-flown in its style, and generally saturated with the theory that Virginians are a race considerably apart—and apart wholly in the direc- tion of excellence. His last novel, *The Knights of the Horse-shoe* (1845), maintains the same theory in its treatment of the Old Dominion under Governor Spotswood, who led the first expedition into the Shenandoah Valley and the Appalachians.

An actual and not a merely philosophic intersectionalist was William Gilmore Simms of Carolina. Born in Charleston in 1806, he began to pub- lish very early; but when his first widely read work, the novel entitled *Guy Rivers,* appeared in 1834 he had been living in New England and New York off and on for a year or so.

Simms' mother died when he was an infant, and his father soon after- ward migrated to Mississippi, leaving the boy to be brought up by his im- poverished maternal grandmother. She gave her charge a casual schooling, put him to work in a drugstore, fed his mind with her memories of the Revolution, and attempted vainly to curtail his vast reading. The visit East in 1816 of Simms' father, by then a bona-fide frontiersman and an Andrew Jackson veteran, doubtless added its weight to the boy's discontent with life as a druggist. By 1824, when he readied himself to visit his father in Mis- sissippi, he was a neophyte lawyer engaged to be married. He remained in the West for several months, observing much that he never forgot; but, for all of his father's appeals to him never to return East, he was again in Charleston by 1825.

In that year he published a dirge in heroic couplets to celebrate the death of a local Revolutionary patriot; and in 1827 he published a volume of poems largely patterned on Byron. During 1828, while Legaré and Elliott edited the august *Southern Review,* Simms edited his ephemeral magazine, the *Tablet.* That failing, he transferred his energies to a newspaper called the *City Gazette,* which he edited with such vigorous anti-Calhoun ardor that the Calhoun victory in the next elections went very hard with him. For other reasons, too, the last of the 1820's and the first of the 1830's in Charleston were a momentous time in his life. He continued to publish poetry, one generally neglected offering after another, and he suffered the deaths of his wife, his father, and the grandmother who had reared him.

Bereaved and frustrated, politically rebuffed like Legaré, he left Charleston for the North, doubtless in a mood similar to that in which Legaré about the same time undertook a diplomatic post in Belgium. In New England and in New York City, he formed warm and lasting friendships with a number of people, the most notable of whom was William Cullen Bryant; and there he published his first prose tale, *Martin Faber* (1833), and his most important poem, *Atalantis* (1832), written in Massachusetts but having to do with the love affairs of a somewhat southerly sea nymph.

With *Guy Rivers* (1834), an action tale of gold-mining then being carried on in the wilds of North Georgia, Simms achieved his first success in romantic fiction on a native theme. After it was published he returned to South Carolina; but for the remainder of his life he made regular, frequent, and extended visits to New York. In 1835, he published *The Partisan,* a novel of the Revolution, and *The Yemassee*—always the most popular of his works—an exciting South Carolina "Border Romance" which provided, next to Cooper's more idealized portraits, the most influential fictional study of the Indian.

Simms exploited various aspects of Southern life in his many novels. *Guy Rivers* was the first of a series dealing with the Southwestern border, which he had learned about chiefly from his father; and *The Partisan* was the first of a similar series dealing with the Revolutionary War, which he had learned about chiefly from his grandmother. *Pelayo, a Story of the Goth* (1838) and its sequel, *Count Julian* (1845), both unsuccessful romances, were his response to the feeling current about him that America was in the end not a fit setting for noble literature. The story "The Loves of the Driver"— it was a Negro driver—and the two novels *Beauchampe* (1842) and *Charlemont* (1856), both turning on the same notorious Kentucky murder that Poe and Chivers set into drama, were considered offensively direct about matters best approached circuitously. But in Simms' case so very much was always happening that few could hold against him for long his occasional brief sallies, in writing, across the frontiers of what was esteemed to be propriety.

After his second marriage in 1836, Simms shifted fairly promptly and very thoroughly his political outlook to accord with that of his wife's estimable planter-father—just as in Baltimore Kennedy shifted his outlook to accord with that of his wife's estimable manufacturer-father. Both men have been blamed as craven for these sins. Both have been defended, on good grounds, for having shifted, not because of personal venality, but because the little worlds about them changed.

At length a great planter, resident at his wife's plantation, Woodlands, Simms was the head of a vast household—he became the father of fifteen children—and a host whose guest list grew always more and more voluminous. Like many other Southerners, everywhere and unremittingly harried on the score of slavery, he now found it increasingly easy to take fully to heart the ingenuous doctrine, fascinating at a moment when everything Greek was fashionable, that the South was a "*Greek* Democracy"—with a few Christian modifications. In such a society, it was maintained, any freeman might with virtue aspire to any height, and no Negro slave might so aspire, ever; but every slave could expect always, as many a "wage slave" in Boston could not expect, all of the basic necessities of existence plus a recognition of his humanity, of his brotherhood in God.

This theoretical recognition of every freeman's unlimited right to any development he can legitimately achieve is always precarious and all too likely at any moment to flicker out. For a number of reasons, it managed in the Old South to maintain itself somewhat more generally than it did in many other places. One of these reasons was the continuing existence of frontier influences. Another, apparently, was the existence of the slaves, a submerged class that could always be made to absorb readily any anti-equalitarian impulses that might assert themselves.

Simms became one of the most powerful exegetes of the Greek Democracy point of view, and it is safe to believe that as the South's position became the more dangerous and his own fame the more impressive, the one-time drug clerk was more acceptable to his fellows. There is a story of a British grandee visiting Charleston who replied to his host's question as to what he would most like to see, that he would like to see some of the great men of the place— for example, Simms. When the host indicated that at home Simms' greatness was not generally accepted, the grandee is said to have inquired who, if not Simms, was a great man in Charleston. All this may have happened; but it is probable that the phenomenal man was extolled at home quite generously, that even the more discriminating talk about him as a writer turned not so much on the carelessness of his style as on his torrential gusto and energy, on his kinship to Cooper (whom he excelled in characterization) in his treatment of the Indian, on his kinship to Scott in his heroics, on his kinship even to Shakespeare in his epic portrayal of an American Falstaff, the Revolutionary soldier Lieutenant Porgy.

The same year, 1835, that saw the publication of Simms' *The Yemassee* and *The Partisan* saw Poe become editor of the *Southern Literary Messenger,* and Wilde exile himself in Italy. In this year, also, were published Longstreet's

Georgia Scenes and a second book by Kennedy. Kennedy's novel, *Horse Shoe Robinson,* a story of the western Carolinas during 1780, was a deliberate effort to contribute to the Grand American Legend by way of romantic fiction. The central character, a veteran of the Revolution, made a living as a blacksmith; but his main business was apparently the unconscious fulfillment of the dream of the "natural man." The story was that of a man whom Kennedy had met on a trip to Georgia in 1819, and who survived long enough to vouch for most of the narrative as Kennedy set it down. Not so vigorous as Simms' stories of the Revolution in the South, the book is more seemly and precise. It was widely read and highly regarded, and in spite of its author's conviction that really important people do not care for literature, it furthered his name and fame to very practical effect throughout the seaboard states.

Kennedy celebrated the year 1838 by being elected to Congress and by publishing *Rob of the Bowl,* a loosely organized, romantic novel of Catholic and Protestant feuding in Maryland in 1661. During the forties and the early fifties politics and public affairs largely engrossed him. He published *Quodlibet,* a sharp and still very readable satire on Jacksonian Democracy, and, nearly ten years later, a biography of William Wirt. By then, he had almost come to feel that really important people care even less for politics than for literature. Accordingly, though he was flattered to serve as Secretary of the Navy, 1852–1853, and to meet and to charm the great Thackeray when he visited here, he felt that all of this was decidedly not enough.

Simms till he was a mature man, and Caruthers and Kennedy for most of their lives, were little touched with suspicion of the North. But in Williamsburg, Nathaniel Beverley Tucker, son of George Tucker, looked out when he was fifty upon a world that seemed to him heavy with malign conspiracy. Always at heart a Virginian, in spite of his residence in Missouri from 1815 to 1833, he returned home at about the time of the death of his cherished half-brother, John Randolph, to teach law at William and Mary College.

He had believed since 1820 that the South would at last resort to secession. In 1836, when his friend Thomas Dew, an irreconcilable like himself, became president of the college, he published a novel, *The Partisan Leader,* which embodied his hope for a free South unexploited by Northern tariffs. Dated twenty years after its real time of publication, the book describes a War of Southern Secession successfully concluded around 1850. The author's style was patterned upon that of Sir Walter Scott, and his conjectures as to military science were notably bad; but as a prophet within a large framework he was tragically accurate. His novel *Gertrude* appeared serially in the *Southern Literary Messenger* (1844–1845), and another, *George Balcombe* (1836), based on his memories of Missouri, stirred Poe to write, "There have been few books of its peculiar kind . . . much its superior."

3

Poe was in the North during most of the late thirties and the forties, but he was none the less a dominant figure in the Southern literature of those years. Feeling himself still a Southerner, he established relations with most of the people then writing below the Potomac. Kennedy, Tucker, Simms, Chivers, and many others were beholden to him for favorable judgments.

Because he too was a poet, the work of Thomas Holley Chivers is most closely linked to that of Poe. The son of a wealthy Georgia planter, divorced before he was twenty, Chivers was by profession a doctor of medicine. He was also a mystic poet, familiar with innumerable angels. Like Poe, he was much in the North in the late thirties, and he married a Massachusetts girl. In 1837 he published his volume of poems, *Nacoochee,* with a long preface defining Poetry as "that crystal river of the soul which . . . empties into the sea of God." Two years later he wrote his second dramatic version of the sensational Kentucky murder of 1825 used by Poe in his drama *Politian* and by Simms in two novels.

The association between Chivers and Poe began in 1840 by correspondence, and included a controversy over a pronouncement in which among other things Poe said that Chivers was "at the same time one of the best and one of the worst poets in America." The object of this verdict protested that such talk seemed likely to confirm an already widespread rumor of his insanity.

In 1842 his oldest daughter died and he memorialized this and other recent sorrows in a group of poems that both in theme and in technique were a just reflection of his own basic taste, and that were a fairly just reflection, at least, of the basic taste of Poe. These plaints were published in 1845 in *The Lost Pleiad and Other Poems.* In the same year Poe and Chivers met in New York. They were for a while intimate friends, Poe testifying to his adulation of Chivers, and leaving the avenues completely open for Chivers to advance him money. All this while Chivers, for his part, offered Poe much counsel and recurrent but vain invitations to come to Georgia as a kind of lifetime house-guest.

After Poe's death, Chivers in 1850 published his *Eonchs of Ruby* containing the much debated "Isadore," probably written in 1841, but reminiscent (or anticipatory) of "The Raven":

> While the world lay round me sleeping,
>   I, alone, for Isadore
> Patient Vigils lonely keeping—
> Some one said to me while weeping,
>   "Why this grief forever more?"
> And I answered, "I am weeping
>   For my blessed Isadore!"

The general charge, made immediately to the effect that the volume was wickedly plagiarized from the dead Poe, was met by Chivers with the charge that it was the dead Poe who had wickedly plagiarized from him. This dispute, now nearly a hundred years old, continues active among the critics. In 1853 Chivers published three volumes of verse, one of them, *Virginalia, or Songs of my Summer Nights,* carrying his metrical effects, his refrains, his suiting of sound to sense, to a point that Poe would surely have marveled over. Of far less worth than that of Poe, or even of Pinkney, Chivers' verse carries forward the interest in rhythm as such which seems to have been a dominant characteristic of Southern poetry.

Another whom Poe befriended was Philip Pendleton Cooke, author of some poetry in the *Knickerbocker Magazine* and a series of articles on early English poetry in the *Southern Literary Messenger.* His lyric "Florence Vane" —"you who were beautiful are now dead"—which appeared in *Burton's Gentlemen's Magazine* in Philadelphia in 1840 while Poe was editor, made him famous everywhere. His many prose romances were perhaps chiefly effective in establishing a domestic atmosphere in fiction that encouraged his younger brother to become a writer. John Esten Cooke was already at eighteen an inveterate writer of poetry and prose for the magazines; and at twenty-four (1854), he published two books, the first of the thirty-one volumes he achieved before his death in 1886. The most notable of all his writings are the two romances *The Virginia Comedians* (1854), dealing with Williamsburg in 1765, and *Surry of Eagle's Nest* (1866), dealing with the just concluded war.

The Southern world of the Cooke brothers was so very full of a number of enthralling things, including weather and natural prospects and field sports, that both of them always found it hard to remain for long indoors, inactive and contemplative. Yet the elder of the two loved the "fever fits" of composition, the music "coming from God knows where," the excitement of the "rapid writer," and "the gallant dash" to "round off the stanza." He affected narrative verse because that was best for reading aloud to his hunt-companions after dinner.

One of those companions actually said to him, after the success of "Florence Vane": "I wouldn't waste time on a damned thing like poetry; you might make yourself, with all your sense and judgment, a useful man in settling neighborhood disputes and difficulties." Yet Cooke continued to live in both worlds, and he was as fond of his hunting friends as he was proud of the encouragement Poe gave him. They were to him "good, kindly men, rare table companions . . . great in field sports . . . rather deficient in letters than mind . . . people whom he loved and was beloved by."

Not all of the writers whom Poe esteemed necessarily esteemed one another. Simms, for example, was too robust to care for Chivers. He thought that Chivers imitated Poe too closely, and told him so; and he admonished him, for good measure, to "be manly, direct, simple, natural." Chivers denied that he imitated Poe, and in general proclaimed himself the only American writer who had freed himself of transatlantic influences and who was absolute in his originality. This originality he said Poe himself admitted; and it is sure that Chivers, for all of Simms' condemnation, must be included among the American writers who have been influential abroad.

During the forties Poe sounded Simms' praise on every possible occasion, and in truth Simms' energy, however that alone may have impressed Poe, was enough to make him notable. In addition to his constant trips between Woodlands and Charleston and between Charleston and New York, in addition to his constant flow of novels, poems, dramas, articles, lectures, and histories, he edited the apocryphal plays of Shakespeare and wrote biographies of Francis Marion, Captain John Smith, the Chevalier Bayard, and General Nathanael Greene.

He edited during 1845 the *Southern and Western Monthly Magazine and Review*—a title that is itself indicative of his conception of himself as a kind of political strategist for the South. In that magazine he published much written by himself and much written by his other self, "Adrian Beaufain," and, when he could extract it, material by other Southern writers, one of whom lived as far inland as Arkansas.

In 1849 he took over the editorship of the *Southern Quarterly Review,* which he carried on manfully for little besides love and affection till 1856. One of the chief fruits of this work was increased association with John Reuben Thompson, the poet and editor (1847-1860) of the *Southern Literary Messenger,* which in 1845 had absorbed Simms' *Southern and Western Monthly Magazine and Review*. Thompson was a friend and memorialist of Edgar Poe, but that was less interesting to Simms than what seemed to him Thompson's bounden duty to be more aggressively Southern. Another fruit of this work with the *Southern Review* was the association it furthered between Simms and the venerable Beverley Tucker, who in turn was much interested in what he thought was Simms' bounden duty to be more aggressively Southern. Simms did his best to comply. He exulted over Tucker's never fulfilled plan to write a biography of his kinsman John Randolph, and published Tucker's scathing review of the accomplished biography by H. A. Garland. And at Tucker's death in 1851 he fruitlessly planned himself to write a biography of Tucker. But by that time the old Southern chivalric ideals were being swept aside by the impending crisis in contemporary affairs.

4

The younger group of Southern writers which made its appearance on the eve of the Civil War was torn between the old traditions and the urgent ironies of the present. Only the youngest of them, Sidney Lanier, born in 1842, survived into the period of reconstruction; but even his latest work echoes in some respects the Elizabethan and Byronic modes of his predecessors. To those who could not forecast the future, the year 1856 in Charleston seemed to hold the promise of cultural maturity. In that year there came together a sort of informal club made up of gentlemen who were somewhat formal, highly esteeming one another—highly, in fact, estimable. Most of the members, already prominent in the professions or in business, were concerned with scholarship and literature chiefly as admirers and patrons. Simms, the Nestor of the group, was primarily a writer, as were three other members, Henry Timrod, Paul Hamilton Hayne, and Basil Gildersleeve, the oldest of them only twenty-seven.

In 1857 these men inaugurated a publication which continued for three years, *Russell's Magazine*. Aside from the contributions of Simms, Timrod, and Hayne, possibly the most notable articles that this journal carried were those on political affairs written by William John Grayson. This Charleston lawyer and planter, a one-time Congressman, was turning seventy as the magazine took form. He had published in 1854 a poem in heroic couplets, *The Hireling and the Slave,* to show that the wage slavery of the North was worse than the chattel slavery of the South, and to suggest that at last the slaves would be returned to Africa.

The most enduring of prewar Southern poets, with the exception of Poe, were Henry Timrod and Paul Hamilton Hayne. Timrod was the grandson of a German immigrant and the son of a bookseller who was himself a poet. He grew up in Charleston in hard circumstances, attended briefly the college which was to become the University of Georgia, and later supported himself as a tutor. To the more notable Southern journals he contributed verses that were reminiscent of Wordsworth and Tennyson; and in *Russell's Magazine* he published some critical articles on poetry which maintained, peace to the ghost of Poe, that poems do not have to be "short" and that poetry must be powerful and true as well as beautiful. A number of his nature poems were brought together in a volume published in Boston in 1860, but he did not achieve his full stature until he was stirred by the issues of the war.

Hayne, a year Timrod's junior, was endowed more generously than his friend with apparently everything except genius in poetry. His verse even more than Timrod's was influenced by their great English contemporaries and immediate predecessors. His connection with *Russell's* was not his only experience in editing a magazine; and he published poems in the *Southern Literary Messenger* and in three independent volumes in Boston (1855, 1857, 1860).

When civil war imminently menaced the continent, there were left alive only a few notable Southern writers who had been active in the thirties. Outside the Charleston group, George Tucker was filling out his fifteen years of residence in Philadelphia, fated to die in 1861; and Kennedy and Longstreet, though they would live till 1870, were old men long since absorbed in practical affairs.

During the War, Timrod and Hayne proved incapable of extended service in the Army, and both of them poured all of their fervid spirits into martial and patriotic verse for the Confederacy. Timrod was ever exhilarated and dejected in turn: up because of his marriage in 1864, down because his verse was not, after all, published in England as he had expected it to be; up because of his appointment as newspaper editor in Columbia, down, down, utterly crumpling at last, in 1867, before the actuality of the South's defeat and of his own wretched poverty and illness. Some of his verse was noble in performance as well as in aspiration, and if Hayne's verse was always great in aspiration chiefly, his personal character was by any gauge exalted. In his memoir accompanying the *Collected Poems of Henry Timrod* (1873), this very earnest, very ambitious, indefatigable craftsman and experimenter judges and without ado declares his friend superior to himself as an artist. Certainly the militant spirit of the Confederacy is nowhere more vitally memorialized than in the ringing lines of Timrod's "Carolina":

> The despot treads thy sacred sands,
> Thy pines give shelter to his bands,
> Thy sons stand by with idle hands,
>   Carolina! . . .
>
> Thy ancient fame is growing dim,
> A spot is on thy garment's rim;
> Give to the winds thy battle hymn,
>   Carolina!

Hayne with Simms' help befriended Timrod to the limit of their very limited powers during 1866–1867. Immediately after the war, Simms had resumed his relationships in the North, and through him there were efforts on the part of some people there to be of practical help to Timrod and Hayne also. Timrod could not meet a prospective benefactor because he could not command the expenses of a trip to New York.

Hayne owned a small tract of land in the pine woods on the Georgia side of the Savannah River, and it was there, with his mother and wife and young son, that he retreated at the war's end. He swore a vow to make a living as a poet and as a poet alone, in Georgia, in the last third of the nineteenth century, and the audacity of that oath, even if he had not fulfilled it, would have made him remarkable. Timrod visited him twice shortly before his death. Simms also visited him, and when Simms died in the summer of 1870 Hayne could not, he said, accept the news; he had somehow come to fancy that Simms would live forever.

Notwithstanding Simms' regular visits to New York, and for all of Hayne's associations there after the war, both men in the last years of the sixties doubtless thought themselves unreservedly inimical to the late enemy. They must have sorely blamed Kennedy, in Baltimore, for the part he had played in the great conflict.

Over many years Kennedy had drifted into a position that made his anti-Southernism mandatory, and his *Letters of Mr. Paul Ambrose on the Great Rebellion in the United States* gave only added evidence of what was already understood. While south of the Line people cringed in poverty, Kennedy walked proudly in Maryland. He supervised the munificent Peabody Fund for the benefit of Baltimore. Or he made extended journeys to Europe. Or, agreeing perhaps with his friend and biographer Tuckerman that the war had happily ended an eagerness for mere wealth in America, he meditated on the blessings of a stable aristocracy of intellect and taste. Or, a master grievance to the South, he made a progress through that land, reporting—the same Kennedy who lately with his guest Irving had scoffed at tales of cruelty to slaves—the most wanton and direful abuses against the new freedmen.

Yet, loyal as Simms and Hayne were to their defeated Confederacy, there is something ominous from the standpoint of the Old South in the fact that both men seriously entertained the idea of moving North. A number of their peers made that move to good account for themselves. John Reuben Thompson of the Richmond *Messenger,* for instance, became literary editor of the New York *Evening Post.* It is even more ominous that before the War was twenty-five years gone, countless other Southern paladins were looking back upon the conflict more through Kennedy's eyes than through Simms'. The new upsurge of nationalism following the war with Spain carried this process further. By 1909 an influential Tennessee educator could admit that the literature of the Old South was as poor as one might care to call it. And, most ironically, a lady who was a high official in a great Confederate patriotic society could find it in her heart to apologize for Thomas Jefferson's preferring the open country of Virginia to the sidewalks of Paris.

As time ran on, notable people in the South as well as in the country at large were the agents of this reconciliation; in fact, it sometimes seemed that eminence away from home was the first condition of local eminence. But a number of brave and strong and large-dimensioned men lived on, proclaiming the old shibboleths faithfully, to go down at last quaintly regarded as doctrinaire persons by even their closest and most kindly neighbors.

23. EDGAR ALLAN POE

Concerning none of the major American authors of the nineteenth century has there been anything like the critical disagreement that still surrounds the name of Edgar Allan Poe. Even his central position in Southern literature has been disputed because of his later importance to the literary and cultural development of the middle states. Nearly a hundred years after his death the lines are still as sharply joined as when Tennyson thought him the most original American genius and Emerson pronounced him "the jingle man." He has always been a great poet in France, but to Henry James an enthusiasm for Poe was "the mark of a decidedly primitive stage of reflection." In our own day Yeats has found him "always and for all lands a great lyric poet," and Valéry has believed that Poe made an unrivaled contribution to literary method, in prose no less than in verse. But no major American poet has yet affirmed his living value in such high terms, and many have echoed the charges of Emerson and James.

The controversy even about the facts of Poe's life has been almost as violent ever since Baudelaire visualized him as the young aristocrat, "le Byron égaré dans un mauvais monde," while the Reverend Rufus Griswold pointed to his career as a satanic example and warning. A succession of scholars has at last corrected Griswold's falsifications. These began with the venomous memoir which he produced at Poe's death, where he went to the length of incorporating a passage in which Bulwer had described his morbidly egotistic villain in *The Caxtons,* and which Griswold allowed to appear to be his own characterization of Poe. As literary executor Griswold was soon to go much further by forging passages in Poe's letters to him in order to show the poet in the most unfavorable light. But the corrected version is hardly less far from Griswold's monster who exhibited "scarcely any virtue in either his life or his writings" than from the romantic legend that Baudelaire conceived, and many details of which Poe himself had done his best to foster.

The psychological insecurity that was deep in Poe's nature becomes pathetically apparent through these fabrications. Toward the end of his forty-year life he wanted to appear younger than he was, and used to give his date of birth as two or four years after that winter of 1809 when, as the son of traveling actors, he had first opened his eyes in Boston, the city of "the Frog-pondians" upon whose pretensions to dominance over American literature he was to pour out so much scorn. In his desire to give himself roots in Southern stability, he liked to state that his Baltimore grandfather Poe had been a general. He did not dwell on the fact that David Poe had started life as an Irish immigrant wheelwright, and that the title of general had been largely complimentary, the result of his having helped, as a dry-goods merchant, to supply the Revolutionary army. Poe naturally did not mention that his chief inheritance from his father may have been his high-strung liability to dipsomania, nor that when his frail and talented English mother died in poverty in Richmond when Edgar was two, his father had already permanently disappeared. Poe's description of John Allan, the tobacco exporter who then took him into his family without formally adopting him, made it sound as though Allan's connections were more with the plantation gentry and less with the merchant class than they actually were.

The poet also liked to remember from his youth the years between six and eleven that he had spent with the Allans in England, and how after his return to Richmond, while preparing for college, he had, though slight in frame, been notable as a boxer, and had swum half a dozen miles in the James—as though already to challenge the comparison with Byron. His later account of his career at Jefferson's newly founded university assumed that he had passed three years there, and had graduated with high honors. In point of fact, although he had shown marked distinction in Latin and French, the two fields which he was pursuing, he had been withdrawn by Allan at the end of a year because of gambling debts. These, Poe insisted, he had contracted simply because his foster father had not allowed him enough money to live on. Even before this the tension between the two had become so acute that, whether justly or not, Allan could say, "The boy possesses not a spark of affection for us, not a particle of gratitude for all my care." In his dealings with his foster father, Poe was to show himself at his most unstable, alternately arrogant and self-pitying, like a sick boy. But after his return from Charlottesville he determined on a break, and at eighteen he ran away from what he could hardly call home, to make his own way in the world.

This was the period which he later tried to conceal most thoroughly beneath the bright colors of legend. He spoke of having set off to join the Greeks in their struggle for liberty, but of having gotten instead into difficulties, somewhat unaccountably, at St. Petersburg. Actually he had gone no farther than Boston, where he managed to publish his first small volume of poems, and, having no means of subsisting, he had soon enlisted in the Army. He always played down his two years as a soldier—though he had risen to be a sergeant major—in order to play up his brief experience as a West Point cadet. He gained appointment there at the time when he had become temporarily reconciled with Allan through his grief over his foster mother's death. But when Allan married again Poe set out to get himself expelled, since he finally realized that he could not hope to be Allan's heir, and concluded that the Army was no career for a poor man.

If Poe had been the young aristocrat he liked to fancy himself, this expulsion would have been the last dramatic step of reckless youth. Even though disinherited he would doubtless have found some support among his wealthy connections. He had stressed to Allan his talent and his ambition. He could envisage himself as a heroic conqueror: "Richmond and the United States were too narrow a sphere and the world shall be my theater." But in cold truth he was to be faced, from the age of twenty-two, with a life of struggle and incessant poverty, for which his overwrought nervous system was desperately ill equipped.

2

His early poetry still accorded with the legend of how a young romantic poet should behave. The title piece of *Tamerlane and Other Poems* (1827), which recited the folly of risking love for ambition, was not much more than an echo of Byron's narratives. Poe was soon to speak of himself as "irrecoverably a poet," but few even of the ten short lyrics that made up the rest of this small book show any special promise. Yet his later accents can be overheard here and there, in the fervor with which he says, "Oh! that my young life were a lasting dream!" or in the characteristic image with which he ends his account of "the happiest day, the happiest hour." For even on that hour's fluttering wing there falls a "dark alloy."

His second venture, *Al Aaraaf, Tamerlane, and Minor Poems* (1829), was published in Baltimore during the interval between his release from the Army and his appointment to West Point. He had turned hopefully to Allan to underwrite the small cost of printing, but to this letter Allan had replied, "strongly censuring his conduct and refusing any aid." Poe had tried to assure him that he had "long given up Byron as a model"; but, if so, he had merely substituted the Moore of *Lalla Rookh*. Poe's narrative takes its name from the Mohammedan realm intermediate between heaven and hell, and its somewhat more than four hundred lines constitute the longest poem he ever attempted. It is also the vaguest of his many celebrations of unearthly beauty; and since a poet's theory of poetry inevitably relates to his own practice, it is not surprising that Poe should later declare that no such thing as a long poem can exist. Among the half-dozen new lyrics here, two begin to show his mature quality: "To Science," which dwells, like Keats' "Lamia," upon its withering limitations; and "Romance," which Poe himself thought "the best thing" in the volume. Here he first enunciated how his heart would feel it a crime to give itself up to the delights of music "unless it trembled with the strings."

The *Poems* of 1831, dedicated "to the U.S. Corps of Cadets" just after his dismissal from their midst, marks a great advance. He has revised much of his earlier work, as he will continue to do meticulously throughout his life, usually to its distinct improvement. But the impulse through which he has now found his own lasting direction can be discerned in the preface, his first piece of criticism. He may seem to dismiss Wordsworth far too airily, but his mind has become saturated with Coleridge. He is drawn more to *Biographia Literaria* than to *Aids to Reflection,* upon which the transcendentalists were later to build so much. In fact, Poe is later to state, after he has declared war on New England, that Coleridge has "aided Reflection to much better purpose in his 'Genevieve.' " Yet it is a remarkable tribute to Coleridge's seminal vitality that such different writers as Emerson and Poe were alike indebted to the same rich source for the immediate stimulus to their theories of language and expression. Without Coleridge the romantic movement in America would not have had the shape by which we know it.

The extent of Poe's debt may be judged by the definition of poetry with which he ends his preface. When he says, "A poem, in my opinion, is opposed to a work of science by having, for its *immediate* object, pleasure, not truth," he is giving what is to remain his opinion, but he is also following Coleridge, almost word for word. As Poe completes his brief definition, he stresses "music" and "indefiniteness," hints for both of which he has also found in the *Biographia,* though he makes them even more essential to the poetic effect than Coleridge did.

Poe completed only six new poems for this collection, but four of them are among his best known. "To Helen," he said later, was his commemoration of his first love, for Mrs. Stanard, who had died when he was fifteen. It has become probably his chief anthology piece, though its classical references are of a sort that made Baudelaire call it a pastiche. "Irene," which Poe was subsequently to name "The Sleeper," and was to regard for "the higher qualities of poetry" as "better than 'The Raven,' " is most akin to the incantation of "Christabel," in its irregular tetrameter as well as in its vision by liquescent moonlight of a strange lady from afar. "The City in the Sea" takes the stock romantic theme of the city of the dead, exploited by Byron in "Darkness," and transforms it, by means of Poe's unique command over the details of horror, into a realm where we can actually feel how Death "looks gigantically down," with an intensity unlike anything in Byron. "Israfel," the disjointed stanzas which have become the symbol for Poe's career, tells how he gained this intensity—through suffering.

With this book Poe came of age as a poet; but he was not to publish another volume of poetry for fourteen years. His work had attracted little critical attention, and he had to live. The next few years in his annals are still very obscure, though he seems to have spent them mostly in Baltimore, with his aunt Mrs. Clemm. He wrote to Allan, in the fall of 1831, in an agony of fear that he was going to be imprisoned for debt; and his final letter to his former protector, in the spring of 1833, cries out that he is "absolutely perishing for want of aid." But Allan had made up his mind that Poe's was a "debased nature," and remained unreconciled to him at the time of his own death the following year. Meanwhile Poe, determining to live by his pen against whatever odds, had turned from poetry to fiction.

3

He competed for a prize offered by the Philadelphia *Saturday Courier,* which awarded the hundred dollars to Delia Bacon for her tale "Love's Martyr" but, during the course of 1832, printed five of Poe's stories. The first of these, "Metzengerstein," already shows what was to be a characteristic feature of his fiction: it not only tells a story, but also develops an idea. Poe began here with the doctrine of the transmigration of the soul, and worked it out through a plot wherein a young baron is destroyed by a horse in which his dead enemy's unrelenting soul has become incarnated. Poe himself pointed to its source when he reprinted it with the subtitle: "A Tale in Imitation of the German." The other four are "grotesques," the intended and contemporary tone of which is not so easy to catch. They are "The Duc de l'Omelette" and "Bon-Bon," two ludicrous bargains with the Devil; "A Tale of Jerusalem," in which the offering to the scandalized Pharisees turns out to be a pig; and "Loss of Breath," wherein, applying that phrase literally, Poe demonstrates the series of disasters, culminating in premature burial, that befall the unfortunate Mr. Lacko'breath. Poe took his own humor seriously, which is a dangerous sign, and it seems never to have kindled much enjoyment in others. Putting it against its immediate background, we can see that he was dealing in some of the familiar devices of American humor: the wild exaggerations and violent destructiveness of the tall tale, the literal play on words pushed to the verge of idiocy, the gravely sustained frozen-faced manner. But Poe's handling of these devices was singularly without the saving warmth of mirth.

He had a very clear notion, however, of what he was about. He was not writing straight humor but various species of burlesque, as we can tell by glancing at his outlined scheme for *The Tales of the Folio Club,* into which he intended to fit all his early pieces. The names of some of the members of that club, who were supposed to recite the tales, may convey the tone, since they are such worthies as Mr. Blackwood Blackwood, Mr. Horrible Dictu, "who had graduated at Göttingen," and Mr. Solomon Seadrift, "who had every appearance of a fish." Furthermore, Poe was outspoken as to some of his targets. He was to give "Loss of Breath" the subtitle, "A Tale neither in nor out of 'Blackwood,' " and to say that he had been satirizing the "extravancies" of that magazine's bloodcurdling fiction. He described several of his stories as being "half banter, half satire," and in "Lionizing," a slightly later piece, he seems at once to have been quizzing the vogue for lions like N. P. Willis, and to have been burlesquing Bulwer's "Too Beautiful for Anything." When Thomas White, proprietor of the *Southern Literary Messenger,* wrote him in 1835, objecting to his taste in "Berenice"—the story in which Poe extended his horrible details to the length of making his obsessed hero rob a corpse of her teeth—Poe replied with an explicit account of the aims of his early fiction.

He agreed that his subject had been "far too horrible," but stated that the question of bad taste was "little to the purpose," since "to be appreciated you must be *read.*" He had followed current English writing very closely, and knew what had made a sensation were such productions as "MS Found in a Madhouse," "The Man in the Bell," and *Confessions of an Opium-Eater.* He had formulated the nature of such successful work:

> You ask me in what does this nature consist? In the ludicrous heightened into the grotesque: the fearful coloured into the horrible: the witty exaggerated into the burlesque: the singular wrought out into the strange and mystical.

If four of Poe's first five stories had exploited the brittle possibilities of the first or third of these alternatives, the story with which he won, in the following year, the fifty dollars offered by the *Baltimore Saturday Visiter* was a very different departure. Poe may possibly have thought of having "MS Found in a Bottle" recited by Mr. Solomon Seadrift, but here his imagination had been caught, as he dealt with both the fearful and the strange. The opening sentences struck his peculiar note: "Of my country and my family I have little to say. Ill usage and length of years have driven me from the one, and estranged me from the other." From start to finish he sustained "the presentiment of evil," the terror and wonder mounting to "a feeling for which I have no name," as his narrator's helpless craft rushed to destruction "down the unfathomable ocean."

Poe referred in 1835 to the existence by then of sixteen *Tales of the Folio*

Club, which he hoped, unavailingly, to publish as a book. He prided himself on their variety, and among the other new types that he had struck off were "Morella," his first treatment of the death and terrifying rebirth of a beloved woman; and "The Unparalleled Adventures of Hanns Pfaal," the earliest of his hoaxes, in which he sought to give the most ingenious verisimilitude to a balloon flight to the moon. An instance of how he could now take the Byronic hero and make him his own is "The Assignation." The scene opens at the Bridge of Sighs, but the slender hero, with his "singular, wild, full, liquid eyes" and his "forehead of unusual breadth" beneath lustrous black hair, is an idealized self-portrait. This is the earliest story into the texture of which Poe wove one of his lyrics, the haunting melody of "To One in Paradise." In his death speech the hero declares that "like these arabesque censers, my spirit is writhing in fire," and so introduces the term that Poe was to balance against the grotesque, as his imagination balanced his fancy.

4

Through John Pendleton Kennedy, who had been one of the judges of his prize-winning story, Poe formed a connection with the *Southern Literary Messenger,* and late in 1835 he went to Richmond to become White's editor. A letter from there to Mrs. Clemm is swept by the gusts of uncontrol to which he was to be increasingly subject. He has heard that his aunt and her daughter Virginia are deserting him, and he cries out that he will live no longer. This recently recovered letter also gives evidence that he did not marry his cousin as a matter of convenience, since it is filled with passionate messages for her. Mrs. Clemm soon came and set up their little home in Richmond, and Poe and Virginia were married the following spring. He was twenty-seven, and she was not quite fourteen.

Another phase of his legend, begotten by those who disapproved of his habits, was that Poe was one of the discoverers of Bohemia. Nothing could be further from the truth. He did not drink convivially to shock the bourgeoisie, but because he could not help it. His insecurity became ingrained. As he was to say a decade later, "the irregularities so profoundly lamented were the *effect* of a terrible evil rather than its cause." Although later Bohemians have liked to believe that Poe worked best under the release of alcohol, there is no evidence to support them. The cycle of his life from now on consisted of periods of intense industry broken off by neurotic melancholia, which sought its anodyne in drink.

His more than a year with the *Messenger* sets the pattern. He wrote its reviews, an immense number, on the average nine or ten a month and generally of essay length. He also did all the editorial drudgery, for a total pay of about eight hundred dollars a year. His work was of such caliber that it first brought both the *Messenger* and Poe to wide attention. Despite the persistent notion that he lived "out of space, out of time," his reputation in his own day, until he produced "The Raven," was almost entirely as a magazine critic. He dealt with science no less than with romance, with books on navigation and classical history and phrenology as well as with all the current literature. He won his spurs by the thoroughness with which he could excoriate the pretentiously second-rate, and he became known primarily for "cutting and slashing," in the tradition of the British quarterlies. Yet, as he pointed out in summing up his first year's work, his laudatory reviews had greatly predominated; and if we look through them now we are more likely to think that when he went astray it was through overpraise of some lady poet like Mrs. Hemans or through such a remark as "Woman is the only proper Scheherezade for the fairy tales of love." And when we find him saying, "There *may* be men now living who possess the power of Bulwer," the thought occurs that the dark clothes which became habitual with Poe may have taken their model from Bulwer's dandy-hero Pelham.

But, whatever his vagaries in taste, Poe brought to his reviews a probing intelligence such as no other American critic had shown. He made a unique stress upon "design" and "keeping," "upon a strict subordination of the parts to the whole." He was concerned from the start with a term he found in Schlegel, "the unity or totality of interest." He noted Coleridge's exceptional appreciation of "the value of *words*," and was soon making a rigorously detailed analysis of the defects in Simms' diction. The point of view from which he undertook to criticize is outlined at the opening of the most ambitious of these early reviews, the long essay in which he demonstrated, again under the aegis of his chief master, that Drake and Halleck were not poets of imagination, but merely of fancy. What most disturbed Poe in the American literary scene was the replacement of our earlier subservience to British standards by a form of provincialism that he deemed even worse, by the blatant determination to like "a stupid book the better, because, sure enough, its stupidity is American." In opposition to both extremes, Poe was to take his stand on the proposition that "the world at large" is "the only proper stage" for both writer and reader.

To be sure, he sometimes betrayed a provincialism of his own. He was so eager to prove himself a Virginian that he followed Allan's tradition, which was that of Marshall and not that of Jefferson. Poe went so far as to deplore the French Revolution, to defend slavery as "the basis of all our institutions," and to assume the scorn held by the propertied class for the democratic "mob." But, whatever his prejudices, he often showed the resilient critic's capacity to appreciate a talent far different from his own, as when he greeted with enthu-

siasm the frontier humor of *Georgia Scenes*. Most importantly, he demonstrated from the outset his devotion to the first principles of art. As he was to
declare in his *Marginalia*: "It is the business of the critic so to soar that he
shall *see the sun*."

Through his work for the *Messenger* he had learned what he could do
with a magazine. But he had had several bouts with drink, the slightest
amount of which could destroy his nervous control. Although he declared, "I
have fought the enemy manfully," both White and himself grew dissatisfied
with their relationship, and early in 1837 Poe decided to try to make his way
in the North, and left for New York.

His duties as editor had yielded him no time for new creative work, and
his *Tales of the Folio Club* had been rejected by Harper's as being "too
learned and mystical." Another objection of the publisher's, that there would
be no vogue for a collection of short tales, may have caused him now to undertake *The Narrative of Arthur Gordon Pym* (1838), whose seventy-five thousand words constitute the longest piece of work that he produced. His account
of the disasters that overwhelmed a Nantucket vessel which had started out
for the South Seas reveals his sustained fascination with the imaginary voyage,
and his ability to conjure up the kind of realistic details in which as a boy
he had rejoiced in *Robinson Crusoe*. On one level these adventures of young
Arthur and his friend Augustus, who survive mutiny and delirium and the
sight of sea gulls gorging themselves on human flesh, are merely the last
word in adolescent fantasy. But the imaginative effect of the compulsive
horror of whiteness, as the voyagers are driven at the close farther and farther
into the uncharted Antarctic, relates back to Coleridge's albatross and forward
to Melville's "whiteness of the whale," and is on a level kindred with both.

Pym met with no particular success, and Poe seems not to have been able
to find a foothold in New York, for a few months later he moved his family
to Philadelphia. He turned again to short stories, and within the next year he
produced three of his most original: "Ligeia," "The Fall of the House of
Usher," and "William Wilson." An interesting feature of the rhythm of his
production is that he was writing at the same time such pieces as his burlesque
of "How to Write a Blackwood Article"; "The Devil in the Belfry," for which
he took a hint from Irving's old Dutch material for a farce about the clock
that struck thirteen in the borough of Vondervotteimittiss; and "The Man
That Was Used Up," another drearily literal working out of a play on words.
Poe perceived that his stories fell into two main groups when he gave his first
collection of them in 1840 the title, *Tales of the Grotesque and Arabesque*. He
managed to place this collection of twenty-five pieces, all that he had written
up to then, with a Philadelphia printing-house, but only on the basis that it
was to take all profits. The title may have been suggested by Scott's famous

essay, "On the Supernatural in Fictitious Composition," but Scott had used both "arabesque" and "grotesque" interchangeably to suggest the bizarre quality of Hoffmann's imagination. In Poe's collection his "grotesques" slightly outnumbered his "arabesques," though it is the latter that are still read.

Concerning these latter, Poe raised the crucial issue in his brief preface when he maintained that their "terror is not of Germany, but of the soul." Upon the reader's felt acceptance or rejection of the truth of that statement seems to depend whether he regards Poe's work as mainly a meretricious fabrication or as a compellingly imaginative creation. Even Poe's most hostile critics have generally made an exception for some of these tales. "William Wilson," with its uncannily thorough handling of double identity, forms a sustained allegory of a man's murder of his own conscience, even if for the use of allegory Poe ordinarily had not one good word to say. "Usher" is generally rated as Poe's best, though he preferred "Ligeia." The two together present the contours of his peculiar world. Roderick Usher is the distillation of Poe's isolated, dreamy, and introspective heroes. Absorbed in occult learning, he is consumed with nameless fears, which he articulates through his poem, "The Haunted Palace," a hidden allegory on his dreaded loss of reason. The heroine matched to such a hero is Usher's sister Madeline, whose delicate beauty is heightened by disease. Or, in her fullest development, she is Ligeia, whose dangerous erudition is a match for that of the husband with whom she inhabits a remote and decaying castle. Through her Poe expressed his acceptance of Bacon's doctrine, "There is no excellent beauty that hath not some strangeness in the proportion." Through her likewise comes his most intense expression of the wild desire "for life—*but* for life," as by her naked strength of will she rises after death in brief resurrection to seize upon the body of her hated rival.

Poe said that this story had been suggested by a dream, and those who believe that he was a drug addict point to the hero's confession of being caught in the trammels of opium. But on this question, unlike that of Poe's drinking, there is no sure external evidence. It would certainly have been possible for him to imagine these sensations, as he imagined those of catalepsy or premature burial, without being subject to either. And it is interesting that, like most of its first readers, he took the *Confessions of an Opium-Eater* to be fiction. The important issue about a story like "Ligeia" is whether Poe's fantasies were merely abnormal, or whether, as Paul Elmer More believed, they had authentic roots in the same "haunted mind" that troubled Hawthorne, in the strained preoccupation with evil that had formed an inextricable strand in American experience from our Puritan beginnings.

Poe's *Tales* were favorably reviewed, but fewer than seven hundred and fifty copies were sold within three years. He had to undertake a great deal of miscellaneous hackwork for *Burton's Gentleman's Magazine* and other Philadelphia periodicals, but during the next half-decade, especially in 1841 and 1842, he displayed an access of energy in several directions. By 1845 he had more than doubled the number of his stories, and had added distinct new types. The most popular of these was the "tale of ratiocination," as inaugurated by "The Murders in the Rue Morgue." Poe, who was presently to make quite a stir as a solver of cryptograms, showed a lively enjoyment of analysis, and created in his detective Dupin a very different hero from Roderick Usher. In describing Dupin's extraordinary grip over the mind's processes of association, Poe again applied Coleridge to uses now entirely his own. For Dupin's "rich ideality" was a startling combination, both "resolvent" and "creative"; he held that "the ingenious are always fanciful, and the *truly* imaginative never otherwise than analytic." Poe had been a good student of mathematics at West Point, and in his further incarnations of Dupin, in "The Mystery of Marie Roget" and "The Purloined Letter," he attributed his hero's powers of reasoning and his ability to apprehend general truths to the fact that he was both mathematician *and* poet.

Another development of the tale of ratiocination, and Poe's most popular story in his own day, was "The Gold Bug" which, in contrast to the ten dollars he could usually expect for a story, won in 1843 the hundred-dollar prize offered by the Philadelphia *Dollar Newspaper*. "The Gold Bug" combined the fascination of cryptography with that of buried treasure. Its fresh description of Sullivan's Island near Charleston is a reminiscence of the days when Poe was stationed there in the Army, and in dealing with Captain Kidd he made use for once of an American legend.

Quite a different kind of development is apparent in such pieces as "The Philosophy of Furniture" and "The Landscape Garden," wherein he worked out his theories of taste and design. In considering the ideal interior he insisted that "an aristocracy of dollars" was far inferior to "an aristocracy of blood," that taste was ordinarily corrupted by wealth. He maintained that "keeping" was as important in a room as in any other work of art, and presented in detail such a room, the character of which was determined by a profusion of crimson and gold, wrought into "arabesque devices" in the pattern both of the wallpaper and of the carpet. Poe's longing for luxury and magnificence was in part that of a man who had been starved of them. Letting his fondness for the bizarre run riot in "The Masque of the Red Death," he devised those seven rooms of different colors, the last of which, with its tapestries of black velvet and its scarlet window panes, was a masterpiece of ballet décor for the dance of death. Taking hold of the contemporary interest in landscape gardening, he also designed his fabulous domain of Arnheim, an artificial paradise of fantastic vegetation, crowned by a mansion of "semi-Gothic, semi-Saracenic architecture." Such scenes vibrated for Baudelaire "d'un frisson surnaturel et galvanique."

Still another departure is found in his dialogues after death, such as "The Colloquy of Monos and Una," in which he first made open his scorn of the utilitarians and his rejection of the doctrine of progress, and ridiculed, "among other odd ideas," that of "universal equality." Here also he began the speculations, which were to culminate in *Eureka,* on identity after death, and conceived of a state in which the senses blended into one another and all man's perceptions became "purely sensual."

In "The Black Cat" and "The Imp of the Perverse" he enunciated the belief that sadistic cruelty "is one of the primitive impulses of the human heart," that we respond to the promptings of the perverse "for the reason that we should *not.*" In these stories, as in "The Pit and the Pendulum" and "The Case of M. Valdemar," he developed to the full his ability to convey hallucinated horror by making it immediately physical, as when rats crawl across the lips of the imprisoned man. In such stories he showed too what a thin line may separate a "grotesque" from an "arabesque." When the material treated in the two is the same, the difference depends solely on the shift in tone, whereby the ludicrous "Angel of the Odd" may become the deadly serious "Imp of the Perverse."

It is interesting also that after 1840 the proportion of "grotesques" declined to hardly one in four. He seems to have come to perceive more clearly the limitations of the genre. He stated that harmony predominates in the workings of the imagination, whereas novelty predominates in those of the fancy, novelty that may quickly turn from beauty to deformity and thus pass over into the realm of humor. In analyzing Thomas Hood's grim "struggles at mirth" he gave an unconscious definition of his own: "the result of vivid Fancy impelled by Hypochondriasis." The best of his later "grotesques" have a concrete object for satire, just as the plausibility of his balloon flight across the Atlantic hoaxed New York for a day. In "The Business Man" the quality of his mockery is obvious, but in "Diddling Considered as One of the Exact Sciences" his satire of knaves and fools has a sustained bitterness kindred to Melville's in *The Confidence-Man.* Yet to the last year of his life Poe would still be capable of the wasted ingenuity of "X-ing a Paragrab."

Another sphere of his energy during his Philadelphia years was an ambitious plan for a magazine of his own. He was among the first to discern the tendency of the age toward "the curt, the condensed, the pointed, the readily diffused," away from "the detailed, the voluminous, the inaccessible." Against those who deplored this trend as a sign of American superficiality, Poe urged that men might not think "more profoundly" than they had thought half a century ago, but that they must think "with more rapidity," since they had so many more facts at their disposal. For this reason they needed "to put the greatest amount of thought in the smallest compass": "Hence the journalism of the age." Poe often thought of himself as "essentially a Magazinist," and planned to make his journal an organ of "an absolutely independent criticism."

The money that he hoped to raise by subscription was not forthcoming, and during 1841–1842 he took the job of editor for *Graham's Magazine*. Here he reached his peak as a critic. He opened the volume for 1842 with an exordium on the proper method of reviewing. He repeated his attack on all forms of narrow nationalism, and stated that he would "limit literary criticism to comment upon art." With "the opinions" in a book, "considered otherwise than in their relation to the work itself, the critic has really nothing to do." He followed up this statement of principles with a series of masterly essays. He was the first to mark so clearly the inescapable limitations of the "pioneers," the generation of Bryant, Irving, and Cooper. He helped to establish the reputations of his own generation, while continuing to expose the mediocrity of most of our best sellers. In his resolvent analysis of the plot of *Barnaby Rudge,* in which he unraveled the mystery before the last installments had been printed, he also pointed out the common error of trying to separate practice "from the theory which includes it." "If the practice fail," Poe contended, as no one else in American criticism had done, "it is because the theory is imperfect." In his most balanced treatment of Longfellow, he objected to the "too obtrusive nature" of his didacticism, and went on to develop his own theory of poetry as the product of "supernal" longing, as "the rhythmical creation of beauty." In recognizing Hawthorne as one of our "few men of indisputable genius," he formulated his famous conception of the short story, which must be designed for "a single effect," and every word of which must be made to count.

Poe's imperfections as a critic have often been dwelt upon. Just as he was overimpressed by such pseudo sciences as phrenology and mesmerism, his tastes in literature were oppressively contemporary. When he had protested against being withdrawn from the University of Virginia, he had told Allan how far he still was from "a liberal education"; and gaps in his understanding of the past remained very apparent. Unfortunately he acted as he always did when he felt insecure. He made pretensions to erudition that he did not possess, and backed them up with quotations borrowed from some such source as D'Israeli's *Curiosities of Literature.* His critical temper was often unsteady. He was capable, as in his dealings with Lowell, of withdrawing his praise when Lowell ventured a few strictures upon his work. He exaggerated the conspiracy of New England to venerate only its own, he was

vicious in his attack upon poor Ellery Channing, and his obsession with Longfellow's alleged plagiarism grew into a mania. Yet he also fought steadily to
improve the conditions of American authorship, and his own near-starvation
had taught him "the irreparable ill" that the absence of a copyright law
wrought upon our native culture, even upon our writers' bare survival. His
originality as a critic resulted from his refusal to rest upon any authority,
from the way he considered *de novo* the capabilities of whatever art he examined. His greatest contribution was that he always insisted upon "the application of a rigorous *method* in all forms of thought."

5

After the plans for his magazine had failed for a second time in 1842, Poe
underwent a period of hopeless depression. In that winter Virginia, who had
now matured into womanhood—a fact usually overlooked by those who speak
invariably of his "child-wife"—had ruptured a blood vessel while singing, and
her condition from then on was always precarious in the extreme. Looking
back to this period, Poe said that the continual uncertainty, her partial
recovery followed by relapse, made the recurrence of his desperate anxiety
more than his nerves could stand. "I became insane," he said, "with long
intervals of horrible sanity." He also added that his enemies attributed the
insanity to his drinking, "rather than the drink to the insanity." His relations
with the proprietors of the magazines, with Burton and Graham, followed a
variant of the pattern of those with the *Messenger*. During his editorship, the
circulation of *Graham's* rose fabulously, from fifty-five hundred to forty thousand; but that brought no rise in Poe's fortunes. By 1844 he had become
thoroughly dissatisfied with any further prospects in Philadelphia, and moved
to New York, wandering, as Baudelaire conceived it, once again restlessly in
the American desert. Poe himself had now come to believe that in America,
"more than in any other region upon the face of the globe, to be poor is to be
despised." But his New York years did not alleviate his condition. He became
even less prosperous than he had been.

That remained true even after "The Raven" made an instant stir upon its
appearance in the New York *Evening Mirror*. He wrote to a friend that for
popularity his "bird" had beaten his "bug" "all hollow," and yet, "I am as
poor now as ever I was in my life." It may be impossible any more for an
adult American to have a fresh reaction to "The Raven," since it has become
such a classic of declamation and its once original tones have been drowned
out by parodies. Its repetitions and refrain, the impulse for which Poe may
have received from Chivers, and which were so startling upon their first hearing, have long become so expected as to allow Aldous Huxley to take it for

one of the showpieces of "vulgarity in literature." The suspicion of its being fabricated was given some color by Poe himself, who proceeded, in "The Philosophy of Composition," to deliver a cool account of every step in the process of designing the poem to "suit at once the popular and the critical taste." Poe spoke of this essay as being his "best specimen of analysis," but many readers have been bothered by its mechanical exactitude. Baudelaire, who delighted in Poe even as a *farceur,* detected a deliberate undertone of impertinence, whereby Poe wanted to scandalize again those who talked only of inspiration and refused to admit the necessary dependence of genius upon talent. It is possible that Poe wrote with his tongue in his cheek, since he had a fondness for what he called "funny criticism": but he also believed that an artist should possess the fullest consciousness of all the stages of composition, since "to originate, is carefully, patiently, and understandingly to combine."

As a result of his new fame Poe was able to issue, in the summer of 1845, a selection of a dozen of his tales, with a royalty of eight cents a copy on a small edition, and then a collection of his poetry for a flat payment of seventy-five dollars. This was the first time his earlier poems had any considerable audience. Griswold's widely circulated anthology, *The Poets and Poetry of America,* had included in 1842 three pieces by Poe, "The Coliseum," "The Haunted Palace," and "The Sleeper," as against seventeen poems by Lydia Sigourney and forty-five by Charles Fenno Hoffman. Poe dedicated his book to "the noblest of her sex," Miss Elizabeth Barrett Barrett, whose line, "With a murmurous stir uncertain, in the air the purple curtain," he had most certainly echoed. He said in the preface that there was "nothing in this volume of much value to the public, or very creditable to myself"; and, indeed, he had succeeded in composing scarcely ten new lyrics since 1831, the best of which, with the exception of "Dream-Land," had been incorporated into his tales. The only large addition lay in the scenes from his unfinished tragedy *Politian,* which dated from 1835 and were flatly undramatic. Yet the depth of Poe's concern over this book was apparent not only in the care with which he had revised many of his poems, but particularly when he said: "Events not to be controlled have prevented me from making, at any time, any serious effort in what, under happier circumstances, would have been the field of my choice. With me poetry has not been a purpose, but a passion." The reviews were prevailingly unsympathetic.

He was trying again to establish his magazine, and contrived for a few months to get control of the *Broadway Journal*; but the project blew up for want of funds, and because of his instability. From now on his ambition for a magazine seems to have become more overmastering as it grew less and less likely of realization; and he spoke of it in 1846 as "the one great purpose of my literary life." But in this year he had instead to undertake for *Godey's* his hack-work series dealing with thirty-eight of "the Literati of New York City." The announcement of this series fluttered the dovecotes because of Poe's reputation as "the tomahawk man," but the essays, as Poe himself knew, turned out to be hardly more than "critical gossip" of a prevailingly flattering kind.

Virginia was finally dying from tuberculosis, and sometimes there was not even enough money for a fire in their cottage at Fordham. After her death, in the winter of 1847, Poe went rapidly to pieces. One medical diagnosis at this time was that he had a "lesion on one side of the brain." He could not endure his loneliness, and threw himself into one emotional affair after another. He often behaved as though he hardly knew what he was doing, since at the very time he was trying to marry Mrs. Helen Whitman, he was torn also by his longing for the companionship of his "Annie," the wife of Charles Richmond. The only escape seemed to be suicide, and he swallowed an ounce of laudanum; but this acted as a violent emetic.

The Griswold legend was that Poe had now become diabolically possessed, and that he walked the streets with his lips moving "in the indistinct curses" of one who felt himself "already damned." Poe himself spoke of his "terrible agony." But the remarkable thing about these last years is the amount and variety of work he still managed to accomplish. Even in the midst of Virginia's final crisis, he had rallied himself and had written to Willis: "The truth is, I have a great deal to do; and I have made up my mind not to die till it is done."

Eureka was the fulfillment of prolonged meditation. In "Mesmeric Revelation" (1844) he had used the device of a trance to purvey his own doctrine of immortality, and had argued that matter is indivisible, that God "is but the perfection of matter." *Eureka*, upon which he was working through 1847, was advanced as "an Essay on the Material and Spiritual Universe." But he also called it "a Prose Poem." He was completely in earnest about the importance of his ideas, but he emphasized the beauty in their truth, and addressed himself "to the dreamers and those who put faith in dreams as in the only realities." He dedicated his book to Alexander von Humboldt, and showed himself well read in that naturalist's *Cosmos*, as well as in the nebular hypothesis of Laplace. Despite his rejection of progress, Poe shared with Emerson the contemporary concern with speculative science. He was finally giving, in *Eureka*, a full-length example of what he meant in saying that "the *highest* order of the imaginative intellect is always preeminently mathematical." Some critics have made much of the point that Poe's theories about the attraction and repulsion of atoms, and about "the stage of progressive collapse" of the universe, seem to anticipate twentieth century science. But at best these are lucky guesses of a mind untrained in physics and astronomy, and it would seem wiser to follow the course Poe urged in the last sentence of his preface: "It is as a Poem only that I wish this work to be judged after I am dead."

He started out by rejecting, in an oddly facetious passage, both deductive and inductive methods as too confined, and affirmed that for creative discovery "only Intuition can aid us." Poe's reliance upon the imagination as the discerner of truth, as the supreme faculty that brings man's soul to "a glimpse of things supernal and eternal," indicates again, despite his professed rejection of "immateriality," a belief curiously akin to Emerson's—as they both had adapted it from Coleridge. Poe once commented upon his tales of ratiocination that "people think them more ingenious than they are—on account of their method and *air* of method." The "air of method" is astonishingly sustained throughout *Eureka*, so that, whatever its originality or substance, it is a masterpiece of finesse, of intelligible and lucid exposition. At one climax, after expressing his awed admiration for the structure of the universe, he showed what kind of metaphor came most naturally to him when he added: "The plots of God are perfect. The Universe is a plot of God."

Poe ends on the note that was to become so prevalent in nineteenth century individualism, that he cannot believe "that anything exists greater than his own soul," that if God is to become "all in all," each man must recognize his own existence "as that of Jehovah." After such colossal egotism it is not surprising that Poe put an immense significance upon *Eureka,* and liked to talk of the metaphysical revolution that it would inaugurate. He had reached the stage where he was living a double identity, though not that of his William Wilson. It was as though the tortured and plunging chaos of his love letters were compensated by the way he proved that he could still conduct his intellectual processes with balance and decorum.

6

In his final years he also produced his *Marginalia,* that magnificently fertile series of suggestions on literary method. Here he condensed his leading principles of art. He gave recurrent attention to the similarities between music and mathematics, and found the basis of rhyme in our "appreciation of equality." He made his most original exploration of the unconscious by examining the images that well up at "the point of blending between wakefulness and sleep." These hypnagogic images are what surrealism has seized upon as its peculiar province; but Poe balanced his interest in them with a proposition that separated him also from most of the romantics of his day. He affirmed, "Man's chief idiosyncrasy being reason, it follows that his savage condition— his condition of action *without* reason—is his *un*natural state."

In "The Poetic Principle," which he delivered as a lecture during 1848-1849, he made a survey of contemporary poets and brought to its final stage his theory of "pure poetry," which we have already seen in formation. He betrayed again the limitations of his taste in speaking of Tennyson as "the noblest poet that ever lived," not on the grounds of depth or of intensity, but because he "is, at all times, the most ethereal—in other words, the most elevating and the most pure. No poet is so little of the earth, earthy." After such a passage one understands better why Poe thought the best conceivable subject for a poem was the death of a beautiful woman, and why both his poetry and his stories are so lacking in sensual body.

Other weaknesses in Poe's theory are manifest. The lyric, not the epic nor the dramatic poem, becomes the only norm. His occupation solely with supernal beauty risks turning even the lyric into a sustained tone, and nothing else. Atmosphere becomes not merely the envelope, but the content. The chief deficiency is owing to Poe's brittle terminology—in such contrast to Coleridge's resilience—which leads him into making mechanical and far too exclusive separations between the spheres of beauty and truth. He was so determined to root out "the didactic heresy" that he barred truth from poetry, and confined it to science and prose. In "The Philosophy of Composition" he had at least granted truth a subsidiary role in the total effect of poetic beauty, and in *Eureka* he had operated from a much broader basis and had held that "symmetry and consistency are convertible terms:—thus Poetry and Truth are one." But whatever its limitations and lapses, Poe's theory held firmly to his central conception about art, that it was not a spontaneous overflow of genius, but a designed effect. This separated it from all romantic theories of expression, and made it, in turn, the catalytic agent that quickened the French reaction from romantic disorder back to classic control of their forms.

Poe's production in fiction amounts to about seventy stories, only seven or eight of which were written after 1845. "The Cask of Amontillado" (1846) is one of the most compact illustrations of his belief that plot is not a "simple *complexity*," but "that in which no part can be displaced without ruin to the whole." "Hop-Frog" is one of the last of his "grotesques," the savage energy of which transforms it. Its story is that of a deformed dwarf who as court jester has been made drunk against his will and has watched a brutal injury to his girl. In the account of his revenge, by burning the king and his councilors to death, Poe's imagination became luridly destructive, as though in savage response to his own frustrations. In the winter of 1849 he devised the last of his hoaxes, "Von Kempelen and His Discovery," which purported to be a scientific description of how lead might be turned into gold. Poe's aim was to act as a sudden even if "temporary check to the gold-fever" of that year.

His growing bitterness to his times poured itself out most fully in "Mellonta Tauta," which looked back on that world from the vantage point of a thousand years. It defined a New York church as "a kind of pagoda" for the worship of the idols, Wealth and Fashion; but it reserved its harshest scorn for the notion that "the ancient Amriccans governed themselves." Poe traced their absurd course to its "abrupt issue" when "a fellow by the name of Mob took everything into his own hands and set up a despotism." In the latest installments of *Marginalia* he continued his attack on the pressures against the solitary thinker. He denounced "the modern reformist Philosophy which annihilates the individual by way of aiding the mass." He was still a Southerner looking at New England when he said:

The fact is, that in efforts to soar above our nature, we invariably fall below it. Your reformist demigods are merely devils turned inside out.

After "The Raven" Poe composed about a dozen poems to bring the total number to scarcely fifty. "The Bells" is a case of onomatopoeia pushed to a point where it would hardly be possible or desirable to go again. "Ulalume," appearing in the year after the death of his wife, voices a strange collision of passions, and Poe is reported to have said that its ending "was scarcely clear to himself." This poem presents all the paradoxes that have so divided Poe's critics. It uses again the hypnotic repetitions that he inaugurated with "The Raven," and subordinates meaning to music. Mallarmé deemed it "perhaps the most original and the most strangely suggestive of all Poe's poems," but Huxley thinks that its "walloping" dactyls are "all too musical." Furthermore, those whose musical tastes are severer than Poe's declare that, despite his challenging analogies between music and mathematics, he showed little technical knowledge of the subject, since he so readily confused the musical with the vaguely indefinite. Again he professed to be a craftsman devoted to perfection, and was capable of rhyming "vista" with "sister." He was a super-rational analyst, the meaning of whose poems often eludes any analysis. The limitations of his terminology are apparent once more, for he declared that "a passionate poem is a contradiction in terms." He tried rigidly to restrict "passion" to "sexual desire" in contrast to "ideal love"; but those who respond to "Ulalume" are stirred by a deeply compulsive passion.

In "Eldorado" Poe voiced the pursuit of the ideal which should supplant "the gold-fever," and in revising now one of his earliest lyrics he added the lines,

All that we see or seem
Is but a dream within a dream.

But his latest poetry was by no means all escape. He became more directly personal in his sonnet for Mrs. Clemm, whom he called his "mother," in token of his dependence upon her after Virginia's death. His stanzas "For Annie" were torn out of his knowledge of tragedy. "Annabel Lee" raises the same issue that he raised in the preface to his *Tales*. For some readers it evokes merely an imitation Gothic "kingdom by the sea." But Poe knew that his longing for remote beauty could not be divorced from mortal sadness. His prevailing theme was ruin, and the intensity of his imagination could transform even the thinnest trappings of romance into the moving climax:

> And so, all the night-tide, I lie down by the side
> Of my darling, my darling, my life and my bride,
> In her sepulchre there by the sea—
> In her tomb by the side of the sea.

This poem did not appear until just after Poe's death. He had gone back to Richmond in the summer of 1849, still in the hope of founding his magazine, and turning away again from a harsh North to a South that was actually even more indifferent to his ambitions. He spoke for the first time of "an attack of *mania a potu*." But he found some happiness, and after a swift courtship became engaged to his boyhood sweetheart, Elmira Royster, now a widow. At the end of September he started North to attend to some literary hack work and to see Mrs. Clemm. Nothing is really known about what happened during the next week until he was picked up unconscious near a polling booth in Baltimore. When he regained consciousness, he passed into a violent delirium, and kept crying out for "Reynolds"—the man whose concern with the importance of exploring the South Seas had stimulated the composition of *Pym*. Perhaps Poe's fevered mind had returned to such details as he had conjured up in "MS Found in a Bottle," the first instance when he projected his inner world through the horror of his sensation that he was "hurrying onwards to some exciting knowledge—some never-to-be-imparted secret, whose attainment is destruction." He died of acute congestion of the brain, and was buried near his grandfather in the Presbyterian cemetery. He had recently written in *Marginalia*: "There are moments when, even to the sober eye of Reason, the world of our sad humanity must assume the aspect of Hell." He was one whom "unmerciful disaster" had "followed fast and followed faster" to the end.

7

Poe's final value may hardly be judged apart from the many traditions to which his work gave rise. French Symbolism, with its desire to attain the suggestiveness of music, began at the moment when Baudelaire recognized in Poe's logical formulas for a poem his own half-developed thoughts, "combined to perfection." But Baudelaire was indebted to Poe for more than form. He took the title for his intimate journal from a phrase in *Marginalia,* "my heart laid bare," and attributed to Poe's reaffirmation of evil the recovery of human dignity from the shallowness of the optimistic reformers. Another note in *Marginalia,* "The orange ray of the spectrum and the buzz of the gnat . . . affect me with nearly similar sensations," led to Baudelaire's epoch-making sonnet, "Correspondances," and in turn to Rimbaud's further development of this same doctrine of the interpenetration of the senses. Rimbaud's masterpiece, "Le Bateau ivre," also confirmed the degree to which Poe's image of man's destiny as a frail boat out of control on the flowing waters of life was to become a major symbol for the age. Meanwhile, Gautier and the Parnassian group had found in "The Philosophy of Composition" their conception that the form creates the idea. The relevance of all these complex developments to American poetry lies in the profound attraction that T. S. Eliot and Wallace Stevens were to discover in symbolism, and thence to bring Poe back to American art by way of France.

Poe's introspective heroes begat a long line of descendants. As Edmund Wilson demonstrated so brilliantly, the remote castle that Villiers de L'Isle-Adam's Axel inhabits was inherited from Roderick Usher; and when Huysmans voiced through his Des Esseintes the doctrines of decadence, almost every artificial detail of his shut-in paradise was borrowed from Poe's interiors, as was the disordered preoccupation with what Usher himself had called "a morbid acuteness of the senses." The furthest possible withdrawal of the hero from the responsibilities of a hostile world might seem to be that in Proust, and although nationalists in criticism now view with alarm any effect in America of such European influences, the feeling that the artist is at war with a business civilization was as much Hart Crane's as it was Poe's.

This may still seem to leave Poe remote from the main currents of American thought. And although Hawthorne admired the originality of his tales, and Lowell had been quick to recognize his double gift for imagination and analysis, the first generation of realists passed Poe by. Both Howells and Twain found his method as "mechanical" as Henry James did; and for the belated dedication of his tomb in 1875, Mallarmé wrote his great sonnet, but Whitman alone among important American writers attended—and Whitman judged Poe to belong finally "among the electric lights of imaginative literature, brilliant and dazzling, but with no heat." Yet his ultimate effect upon our most popular literature was enormous. As much as anyone ever invents a genre, Poe invented the detective story. He also inaugurated the vogue for the pseudoscientific romance and for that of adolescent adventure.

Jules Verne, Stevenson, and Conan Doyle are equally in his debt. "The Gold Bug," "The Pit and the Pendulum," and "The Murders in the Rue Morgue" have now been read by millions oblivious of their author's aesthetic theories.

The notion has sometimes been advanced that the materialism of so many of Poe's interests, his fondness for inventions and hoaxes, and his special flair for journalism made him more "representative" than Emerson or Whitman of ordinary Americans. His more serious importance was noted by the Goncourt brothers, who declared in their journal for 1856 that here was "the literature of the twentieth century," an analytic literature that would be more given to what passes in the brain than in the heart. That distinction may be as brittle as some of Poe's own, but the intense investigation of the roots of Gothic horror in morbid states of mind has been part of American fiction from Brockden Brown and Poe through Ambrose Bierce and William Faulkner.

Poe wrote at a time when America was producing more real and alleged transcendental geniuses than maturely wrought poems or stories. In opposition to the romantic stress on the expression of personality, he insisted on the importance, not of the artist, but of the created work of art. He stands as one of the very few great innovators in American literature. Like Henry James and T. S. Eliot, he took his place, almost from the start, in international culture as an original creative force in contrast to the more superficial international vogue of Cooper and Irving.

LITERARY FULFILLMENT

24. DEMOCRATIC VISTAS

I~N~ quality of style, and particularly in depth of philosophic insight, American literature has not yet surpassed the collective achievement of Emerson, Thoreau, Hawthorne, Melville, and Whitman. Having freed itself in these writers from its earlier tendencies either blindly to imitate or blindly to reject European models, American literature here for the first time sloughed off provincialism, and, by being itself—by saying only what it wanted to say and as it wanted to say it—attained, paradoxically, the rank and quality of world literature, a literature authentic not only in America but everywhere the English tongue is understood.

The release was both material and social. There was, to begin with, the increasing social fluidity of the mid-nineteenth century in the East, with its accompanying sense of unlimited cultural possibilities. While the West was expanding and experimenting, those parts of the country which had by now been settled for more than two hundred years began to lose their sharp social and regional contrasts and to settle into a cultural homogeneity more like that of the older civilizations of Europe, though built firmly on a democratic base.

The social stratification of the seaboard colonies, with their mercantile and landed aristocracies, their small farmers, their squatters, and their slaves, had begun to disintegrate during the Revolution, but was not yet reshaped into the industrial class structure of the future. Regionally, colonial distinctions had also broken down with the mounting pressure of populations to the eastward—from Europe to the Atlantic seaboard and from the seaboard to the frontier. The slow process of eroding these regional differences, so important in colonial assemblies, had already achieved, by the intermingling of ideas and of local customs, the national feeling which was to culminate later in a simpler, more inclusive, division of the country into the North, the South, and the West.

Moreover, this flux of institutions and people was marked not by a sense of loss or confusion but by a sense of potentiality and expectancy. The era of good feeling following the War of 1812—a war which at first seemed lost but was miraculously retrieved—had affected all levels of the national life and, blinding men to the risk of the American experiment, revealed only its adventure. And this spirit of self-confidence had been fed by other fires: by the material promise of timber, land, and waterway, convertible at a touch into ready wealth; and by the technological promise—already apparent—of American mechanical and social invention.

Yet neither the general confidence nor the manifold promises of the period can alone explain the peak reached by American literature at this time. For this we must turn to a third and more decisive factor: the reorientation of literature under the influence of New England transcendentalism. For, by reawakening—even among its critics—an interest in the great problems of human nature and destiny, transcendentalism conferred upon American literature a perspective far wider and deeper than that proposed by its own formulated doctrines, the perspective of humanity itself. This perspective it is which gives common purpose and meaning to the otherwise divergent achievements of Emerson, Thoreau, Hawthorne, Melville, and Whitman, and accounts in great part for their manifest superiority to precedessors like Irving and Bryant whose interests were less profound and more superficially literary.

2

Transcendentalism emerged as a full-fledged movement of New England thought between 1815 and 1836. The first date marks the maturing of the liberalizing ministry of William Ellery Channing; the second, the publication of Emerson's *Nature,* the original—and probably the best—systematic expression of the transcendentalist philosophy. Thereafter the movement continued to expand, first as a revolt against the sterile Unitarian orthodoxy, then as a protest against the continuing cultural dependence of America on Europe, and finally as a profound exploration of the spiritual foundations and moral implications of the new democracy. From the beginning it attracted eccentrics no less than men of genius, and after the Civil War it gave way to weaker forms of idealism. But at its zenith in the writings of Emerson, Thoreau, and Alcott—and by its challenge to fresh speculation in Hawthorne, Melville, and Whitman—its vitalizing effect upon American art and literature and, indeed, upon the development of American democracy as a whole, remains unrivaled.

The source of this vitality lies in the intellectual background of transcendentalism: in its appropriation of certain insights of Puritan, Quaker, and other colonial theologies as they had been refracted through the secular and equalitarian ideology of the Revolution; and in its reexpression of these insights in the vocabulary of contemporary European philosophy. For in spite of its oft proclaimed rejection of authority and its frankly nationalistic bias transcendentalism was rooted both in the American past and in the Europe of that day.

To Puritanism in the broadest sense, for example, it owed among other things its pervasive moralism. Like all those early pioneers who sought freedom of conscience in a new land, the transcendentalists were ever disposed to interpret life ethically, to subordinate the aesthetic, intellectual, and even political and economic aspects of human nature to man's significance as a moral agent. Once again, after two centuries and more, this conception was used as a means of dignifying all phases of human activity, even the most humble. Thus, just as the Mathers, Edwards, Penn, Woolman, and even Franklin had alike maintained that each man is "called" to perform as faithfully as he can the duties of his particular station in life, so Emerson argued that every act of the individual springs from his inner nature as a unique embodiment of humanity, and hence no occupation is inherently ignoble.

A similar affinity may be discovered between transcendental "intuition" and the doctrine of the "inner light." For each of these theories interpreted material nature mystically as a "veil" or symbol of the divine; and each maintained that every individual can penetrate the veil to discover divine truth for himself without the aid of traditional authority or even of logic.

But none of these doctrines had been transmitted in its original form. The Puritan orthodoxy of New England had from the earliest times been subject to the filtering process of dissent, and had finally succumbed as a rigid and dominant system to the less precise and more rationalized theology of the Unitarians. The tendencies thus manifest on the level of religious thinking were even stronger on that of secular radicalism during the Revolutionary epoch. The worldliness and "common sense" of a Franklin or a Jefferson had apparently made a clean break with earlier orthodoxies while retaining their zeal for moral enlightenment; and the same tendency had but recently moved even further from theological sanction in the equalitarian theory of Jacksonian democracy. These latter-day and transplanted expressions of the Reformation and the Enlightenment, which had coalesced in the preachings of William Ellery Channing and other predecessors of the transcendental movement in New England, had in some instances added to, but in all instances had transformed, the orthodox teachings of the early religious and secular leaders.

This is illustrated in the new meanings given to the old doctrine of the sovereignty of ethics. For one thing, the equalitarian implications of the doctrine were secularized and broadened to a degree hitherto unknown in this country. Whereas in the orthodox Puritan interpretation the doctrine of the equality of man with man was largely theoretical—being restricted to a mere hypothetical equality before God and the law—and, even in the political philosophy of the Revolution, had accepted social stratification, Jacksonian individualism demanded that it be applied as a practical principle of social reform calling for local autonomy, free public education, and universal suffrage on a scale undreamed of even by Jefferson. Coincidentally, the scope of the principle had been broadened. In place of the old invidious distinction between the elect and the damned which had suggested that only a chosen few were to be admitted to spiritual equality, the Unitarian and Universalist emphasis on the brotherhood of man proclaimed the perfectibility of all.

Still more subtly, this leveling process reoriented the very concept of ethics itself. For although it was still insisted that moral obligation is transcendent in origin—is determined by more than personal whim or habit—that obligation could no longer be construed in abstract universal terms or continue to be rooted in the will of an arbitrary God. Under the influence of Unitarianism, Deity was reduced to a kind of immanent principle implicit in man everywhere, and man himself thereby was made the true source of the moral law. Also, instead of continuing to conceive moral obligation legalistically—as a kind of ritualistic observance of a general code—it was now argued that no single code fits all situations adequately and that each individual must be left perfectly free to judge for himself what his actual duty on any given occasion is. Thus theology made its final effort to provide religious sanction for equalitarian tendencies inherent in the republic from the start.

Equally radical was the transformation of the doctrine of the inner light brought about by the acknowledgment of the autonomous power of secular reason, in part aided by the accelerating conquests of natural science. For this acknowledgment—validated anew by the role of reason in formulating the principles of the Revolution, and manifested concretely both in the rationalism of Unitarian theology and in the pragmatism of frontier thought—had undermined belief in the inner light at two points.

In the first place, it challenged the theoretical competence of the inner light. Although often authoritarian in spirit itself, the new emphasis on reason was wholly antiauthoritarian in implication. Holding with Locke that all knowledge is perceptual in origin, it demanded that every truth be held subject to the test of experiment and observation. And this was a test which, with its implicit mysticism, the doctrine of the inner light as the word of God could not hope to sustain.

In the second place, the new emphasis on reason challenged the doctrine of the inner light on the score of its immediate utility. For while the older doctrine could promise only the quietistic value of bringing man face to face with God, the reason, practically applied, promised a control of nature itself and thereby the immediate satisfaction of human needs.

Yet neither the period generally, nor Unitarianism and democracy in particular, was so pragmatically inclined as to deny the possibility of religious insight entirely. The hold of the Christian tradition upon belief and imagination was still too strong. Nevertheless, certain changes in the conception of the inner light were effected. One of these was to restrict the scope of the inner light to the moral and speculative sphere and to concede to observation priority in the understanding of nature. Another and more important change was the transformation of the inner light into a wholly natural organ. Instead of being dependent, as in the early orthodoxies, upon divine Grace—upon a kind of flooding of the mind by light from without—the power of the inner light was now grounded in the nature of the mind itself, becoming merely one mental faculty among others and subject, therefore, to the same degree of individual control. It was converted, in other words, from a "revelation," an act and agency of God, into an "intuition," an act and agency of man.

It is doubtful whether these transformations of the Puritan ethic and theory of knowledge ever could have become more than vague intellectual tendencies of the time or could have achieved the degree of articulate formulation they subsequently did without the stimulus of contemporary European philosophy. There had emerged in Germany an intellectually sophisticated movement elaborately embodied in the systems of Fichte, Schelling, Schleiermacher, and Hegel, and—at a further remove—in the thought of Coleridge, Carlyle, and Victor Cousin. This movement, idealistic in nature, had its specialized formulas and idioms, its accepted premises and methods. In literature it took the form of romanticism.

It was also a movement whose influence began to be felt in New England about 1820. New England interest in German thought generally goes back much further: to William Bentley who acted as cultural ambassador between the merchants of Hamburg and of Salem in the late years of the eighteenth and the early years of the nineteenth century; and, beyond Bentley, to the correspondence of Cotton Mather with the Pietistic theologians of Halle. The interest was not widespread until after the War of 1812, when it became intellectually fashionable for younger New England to make the grand tour or to enroll in German universities, and when particular notice began to be taken of German philosophy as reflected in the writings of its English and French disciples. Later, many of the transcendentalists were to make some pretense of studying German philosophy directly; but their initial—and probably most enduring—impression of the movement was derived from such secondary sources as Marsh's edition (1829) of Coleridge's *Aids to Reflection*, Linberg's translation (1832) of Cousin's *Introduction to the History of Philosophy*, and Carlyle's *Sartor Resartus* (1836).

What was important in this influence was the fact that it made available to the New England writers and through them to American writers generally an elaborate symbolic construction capable not only of expressing the general metaphysical hesitancy of the period—its inability either to retreat into frank supernaturalism or to advance to a bold materialism—but also of providing principles and distinctions whereby this midway position could be explored and defended.

Thus, the doctrine of human individuality as both self-transcending and self-asserting—as both acknowledging its oneness with and obligation to something higher than itself, and yet ever cherishing its uniqueness and independence as a distinct being—and the further conception that individual happiness depends upon the successful synthesis of these twin tendencies, provided an almost perfect theoretical framework for a new effort to discover supernatural sanction for the swift-moving and constantly changing panorama of American life.

Similarly, the distinction found in Coleridge and Emerson alike, between the reason and the understanding—which, by a curious distortion of terminology, identified the reason with intuition and imagination, and the understanding with logic and induction—could express and justify the transcendentalist's desire to retain both the mysticism of the past and the empiricism of the present, and to assign each a sphere in experience proper to its character.

Finally, the idealistic view of the universe as an embodiment of a single, cosmic psyche, now manifesting itself as man, now as nature, and achieving through the interaction of the two in history its own secret intent, permitted the self-asserting impulse of the individual—his determination to be himself at all costs—to be explained as the consciousness of his identity with the world-psyche, while his self-transcending or outgoing impulses could be attributed to the consciousness of his own finitude, to the fact of his awareness that he is only one fragmentary expression of the world-psyche among others. The theory could also account for and validate the distinction between the intuitive and the inductive, interpreting the first of these faculties as the necessary condition for conscious union with the world-psyche, and the second as the necessary condition for survival as a separate expression of that psyche.

The initial function of this movement was thus to act as a kind of model and repository of ideas from which American, and in particular New England, writers could borrow in their self-imposed task of creating a new metaphysic for democracy out of the theological and intellectual materials of the American past. Without slavishly imitating this model, but still inspired by it in various degrees, Emerson, Thoreau, Whitman, and even, by contraries, Hawthorne and Melville were able to achieve a curious blending of the alien and the native, a blending in which specific traditional conceptions were adjusted to specific American use. This fusion is apparent, for example, in Emerson's appeal to the Over-Soul as a sanction for Yankee self-reliance, in Thoreau's discovery that Walden recapitulated the universe in small, and— by its very failure—in Melville's ambiguities. It is also apparent in Whitman's *Democratic Vistas,* which preached a new brotherhood of man in terms of the mystic unity of creation, "the divine central idea of All."

But European idealism was to act as more than a mere model for New England transcendentalism. For, working in and through transcendentalism —and reinforced a little later by the influx of roughly similar teachings from the Orient—its influence leavened American literature as a whole, including even the writings of men like Hawthorne and Melville who were actively opposed to transcendentalism proper. The general leavening consisted not so much in the transmission and implanting of specific borrowings—although this also occurred—as it did in the setting of problems and perspectives like the nature of the universe, the origin of evil, and the meaning of experience, which were destined to give American literature a universal import and eventually swing it into the orbit of world literature.

3

At first sight, Emerson, Thoreau, Hawthorne, Melville, and Whitman seem to differ from one another more than they agree. For one thing, they are divergent in temperament. Thoreau, Whitman, and—above all—Emerson are prevailingly optimistic. Hawthorne, on the other hand, is at least fatalistic in point of view; while Melville seems to have run the entire emotional gamut from optimism through pessimism to final resignation. Again, all of them differ widely in their choice of subject matter and literary form. Primarily novelists, Hawthorne and Melville are concerned with the psychological and allegorical analysis of certain types of human personality and moral situations; primarily poets and essayists, Emerson, Thoreau, and Whitman focus, each in his own way, upon the underlying relation of man to nature.

Most widely of all, they differ in their interest and capacity for sustained philosophical thought. None of them could be described as interested in philosophical theory for its own sake—not even Emerson, who is less intolerant of abstract reasoning than the rest. But even within these limits their divergency is still great. For although we can find at least traces of a comprehensive philosophical system in Emerson, the traces become progressively more rudimentary in Thoreau, Melville, and Whitman, until at last in Hawthorne they almost disappear.

Yet this incommensurability is not absolute. Common to them, as to all great writers, is a profound sense of the human predicament, of the questions that beset man as man, and of the relation of these problems to man's defects and potentialities. Their common concern surmounts all differences, as may be seen in Emerson's and Hawthorne's treatment of the problem of evil. When Emerson proclaims the non-existence of evil in an ultimate form and Hawthorne rejects this conception as tragically blind, neither writer is proceeding on the assumption that the problem of evil itself is unreal or trivial. For Hawthorne, as we know, it is the most pressing of all problems, while for Emerson—as the haunting overtones of "Experience" intimate—it is a problem which can be optimistically resolved only after the most desperate of inward struggles and only after attaining a serenity almost stripped of emotion. In other words, the difference between the two lies not in their conception of the importance of the problem but only in their conception of its proper solution.

Common also to all these writers is the framework of ideas within which they seek to understand the problem of man. Even when it provides quite divergent solutions the framework or perspective is in all instances radically humanistic.

Its basic premise is that man is the spiritual center of the universe and that in man alone can we find the clue to nature, history, and ultimately the cosmos itself. Without denying outright the existence either of God or of brute matter, it nevertheless rejects them as exclusive principles of interpretation and prefers to explain man and his world so far as possible in terms of man himself. This is expressed most clearly in the transcendentalist principle that the structure of the universe literally duplicates the structure of the individual self, and that all knowledge therefore begins with self-knowledge. But it is no less evident in the moral earnestness of Hawthorne and Melville, which leads them to dwell ceaselessly upon the allegory of the human soul and to personalize impersonal nature itself as an allegory of human experience. It is because of this, for example, that few incidents in their plots ever turn out to be wholly fortuitous or to be without symbolic significance for the characters involved in them.

This common perspective is also, in all cases, radically universalized. Its emphasis is almost never upon man as particular—as European, say, or as American—but almost always upon man as universal, upon man as freed from the accidents of time and space as well as from those of birth and talent and reduced to his common humanity. It is apparent not only in Emerson and Thoreau but also in Hawthorne, Melville, and Whitman; none of them even in the most concrete and practical moments can ever quite forget that the drama of man is clothed with the aspect of eternity. Thus, for Emerson, the "American Scholar" turns out to be simply "Man Thinking"; while, for Whitman, the song of himself merges imperceptibly into a song of all the "children of Adam," where "every atom belonging to me as good belongs to you." Thus also, in spite of a frequently high degree of individualization, the characters and situations of Hawthorne and Melville are fundamentally impersonal, emerging at their best as a fusion of particular and type but at their worst as types only.

This turning away from the current scientific view of the world and regression under the impetus of European idealism to the Neo-Platonic conception of nature as a living mystery full of signs and portents, revives a conception with which some of the five were already familiar from their reading in the literature of the seventeenth century and of religious mysticism. At the same time, a principle of correspondence is evolved which promises the reconciliation rather than the rejection of science.

Nor can we overestimate the practical importance of this conception from either the literary or the social point of view. In terms of literature, for instance, its construing of nature as inherently symbolic invests the natural faculty of imagination with a new prestige, dissolving the older literary emphasis upon wit, sentiment, and rationality, and preparing the way for the symbolist literature to come. Even more far-reaching are the social implications of the conception. For by postulating, as it does, an identity between the categories of impersonal nature and the categories of human psychology— and thereby also the unity of creation—the conception provides a metaphysical basis for the belief in democratic equality to which the social philosophy of Emerson, Thoreau, and Whitman can and does appeal.

The second assumption common to all five writers is the belief that individual virtue and happiness depend upon self-realization, and that self-realization, in turn, depends upon the harmonious reconciliation of two universal psychological tendencies: first, the expansive or self-transcending impulse of the self, its desire to embrace the whole world in the experience of a single moment and to know and become one with that world; and second, the contracting or self-asserting impulse of the individual, his desire to withdraw, to remain unique and separate, and to be responsible only to himself.

The current theory of self as expounded by Coleridge and other Europeans was adaptable here, and its importance was more than theoretical because it stated in universal terms the central goal and problem of democracy itself. On the one hand, democracy as a moral and political doctrine implied an ethic of extreme individualism, one which preserved to the individual a maximum degree of freedom and self-expression. On the other hand, the democratic self was divided. There was, first, the conflict between its traditional sense of duty to God and its new-found sense of duty to man. There was, second, the conflict between the duty to self as implied by the concept of liberty and the duty to society as implied by the other two concepts of the revolutionary triad, equality and fraternity. Hence, a doctrine which recognizes the divisions in the self and insists that their reconciliation is necessary for true self-realization defines not only the democratic ethic in general but also the specific hope of democracy that the self can be realized without sacrificing any side of its nature, altruistic as well as egoistic.

There can be no doubt that all five of the writers define the ethical ideal in these terms, although, characteristically, they disagree both on *how* the ideal is to be actualized and on the degree to which it is actualizable. Thus Emerson, Thoreau, and Whitman, who accept its actualization as a real possibility because they have assumed to begin with that the self and the cosmos express one and the same spiritual force, disagree on what specific course of action will convert their inner harmony into an outward fact. For while Emerson and Thoreau believed the harmony can be fully realized by the simple, though paradoxical, expedient of forgetting the world and being true only to oneself, Whitman seems to hold that there is needed an unlimited love of creation as such, a love that will include the self and the world as one.

In contrast to these three stand Hawthorne and Melville, who doubt whether a genuine harmony between the individual and his cosmos is possible at all. For although both assume that the destiny of man is ever to seek such a harmony, they are also deeply convinced that the self and the cosmos are victim to tragic flaws which prevent their ever realizing it. Hawthorne discovers the flaws both in the spiritual pride and spiritual weakness of the individual and in the intractability of his social environment. And Melville identifies them with a defect in the universe at large, symbolized in the inscrutability of the white whale.

But both writers hold that the flaws, in all cases, effectively block a final rapport between the individual and the world. For although the conflict between these two protagonists is sometimes susceptible of an emotional resolution—either by a daemonic assertion of the will, as in Captain Ahab, or by the will's abnegation, as in Hester Prynne and Billy Budd—the resolution is only partial since it is at the cost of eliminating either the world or the self from final moral consideration. In other words, where Emerson, Thoreau, and Whitman discover in the romantic theory of self-realization grounds for ultimate hope, Hawthorne and Melville draw from it only tragic irresolution.

The third assumption common to the five writers is that intuition and imagination offer a surer road to truth than abstract logic or scientific method. It is a corollary to their belief that nature is organic, and corresponds to the technical distinction between the reason as intuition and the understanding as logical analysis. In the specific form of this distinction, the assumption appears frequently in Emerson. But as a general principle underlying both theory and practice it is present in all.

It is illustrated by their emphasis upon introspection—their belief that the clue to outer nature is always to be found in the inner world of individual psychology—and by their constant interpretation of experience as in essence symbolic. For both these stresses presume an organic relationship between the self and the cosmos of which only intuition and imagination can properly take account.

Finally, in terms of the third assumption, all five writers were able to deduce a consequence of immense practical importance not only for their own work but for the subsequent course of American literature as a whole. Not only could the belief in the primacy of imagination be used to justify their own tendency toward the concrete, the metaphorical, and the didactic; it also had the wider implication of attaching greater significance to the craft of literature generally. Once the faculty of imagination is placed on a par with the faculty of reason, the writer as the primary exponent of the imagination acquires an importance in society at least equal to that of the scientist, the philosopher, and the theologian. All equally can then claim to be engaged in the same pursuit: the search for truth.

It is undoubtedly their faith in the imagination and in themselves as practitioners of imagination that enabled Emerson, Thoreau, Hawthorne, Melville, and Whitman to achieve supreme confidence in their own moral and metaphysical insights. It is this also that led them to conceive of the writer as a seer, and thus to exemplify in their attitude toward literature the emphasis upon its responsibility to life which is characteristic of our own day.

4

The close affinity between the idealism of contemporary European philosophy and the romanticism of Emerson, Thoreau, Melville, Hawthorne, and Whitman must not be pressed to the point of identity or to the exclusion of other influences. The sharing between European and American thinkers of common concepts and a common idiom for their expression is merely one more evidence that the young nation was beginning to lose its provincialism and to take its place in the main flow of Western culture. American philosophical thinking had remained true to its own origins, which were of course European in the first instance, through the periods of settlement, early development, and now a first maturity. Once more it could look to Europe for a confirmation by parallel of its own conclusions.

There were, however, significant differences as well as similarities. Where the Europeans of the eighteenth and nineteenth centuries were predominantly intellectual and aesthetic in their interests, the Americans were predominantly moral; and where the Europeans often tended to underscore the role of hierarchy and institutional stability in human affairs, the Americans stressed the ideas of equality and freedom from state interference.

Nor was European philosophy the only such force to act as a catalyst on the nineteenth century American mind. Its importance was taken for granted even though it was not fully understood by the earlier critics of New England transcendentalism. Recently there has been a tendency to underestimate it in favor of the obvious influences of Neo-Platonic and Oriental kinds of idealism in giving new forms and a new vocabulary to American thinkers. Historians have demonstrated the catalytic effect of Plato and Plotinus on Emerson and of the Bhagavad-Gita and other Oriental tales and poems on Emerson and Thoreau. But more often than not such influences out of the past were shared by American writers with their European contemporaries, and the precise channels or directions of their flow can be distinguished only with the greatest difficulty. The minds of Emerson, Whitman, and Melville were characteristically American in their willingness to appropriate usable ideas wherever they might be found, without too much concern for logical consistency, and it is safer to assume that these men obtained many of their principal assumptions—or at least the language in which such ideas found expression—through their alert interest in the dominant intellectual movements of the time rather than from any single source in the past.

Whatever the sources or channels of their common feeling, the fact remains that there existed between these five Americans and their European contemporaries a community of interest based upon the use of a common philosophical idiom and upon the discovery, as a result of the common vocabulary, of a common set of problems approached in a common spirit. This community helps explain the promptness with which Emerson, Thoreau, and others of the group were "discovered" and acclaimed abroad. It also helps explain the almost proprietary sense these writers themselves had in European literary and philosophical movements.

Of even greater moment was the fact that contact with European philosophy and literature established a spiritual continuity not only with their contemporaries but with the great literary and philosophical traditions of the past. For in rediscovering such fundamental conceptions of Western culture as the correspondence between man and nature and the doctrine of the poet as seer, these writers acquired something more than a set of inert principles. Rather, by means of these ideas—by accident of the fact that the ideas had been perennial to Western thought—they acquired that spirit of universality which has characterized Western literature at its greatest moments, even making it capable of absorbing the best of the Orient. Thus the preoccupation with local customs, local legends, and local scenes characteristic of the earlier writers in the seaboard states, and again of those of the frontier, was generalized, at least for a moment of literary fulfillment, into a profound concern with human nature, while democracy itself instead of continuing to be construed as a mere experiment in government was now subjected to a more thorough examination of its fundamental moral and metaphysical meanings.

In other words, European philosophical theory, acting as a primary catalyst for forces already deeply indigenous to the American mind, had effected and accelerated a reorientation of literature which was tantamount to raising it to a new plane. Having revealed the American character and experience as identical in form and substance with the character and experience of man everywhere, it had created the conditions whereby American literature without ceasing to be national could become a part of world literature. And it is one measure of the genius of Emerson, Thoreau, Hawthorne, Melville, and Whitman that they were able to transmute this possibility into an opportunity.

25. RALPH WALDO EMERSON

F~ROM~ these currents of thought and feeling Emerson emerged as the delegated intellect—his own "Man Thinking." "There are periods fruitful of great men," he wrote, "others barren . . . periods when the heat is latent,—others when it is given out." A half-century had passed since the United States had been baptized in political independence; the time had now come for confirmation in freedom of the soul. Ralph Waldo Emerson, of Concord, Massachusetts, declared the ceremony performed and became spokesman for his time and country.

His preeminence has caused our literary historians some embarrassment. America was ready for a Shakespeare, a Dante, or a Dostoevski to give literary voice to her achieved majority. She was given an apologist—an Aristotle, a Paul, a Bacon. In the wise and temperate Emerson, the heat became radiant light. It was he who brought into its first sharp focus the full meaning of two centuries of life on the Atlantic seaboard of this continent; of the economic and spiritual revolutions which had unsettled the Old World and settled the New; of the experiment in democracy which was to make a Holy Commonwealth into a world power.

He did this in two ways: by carrying to its ultimate statement the individual's revolt from authority, which marked the transition from the medieval world to the modern; and by formulating the dichotomy between the vision of a Jonathan Edwards and the common sense of a Benjamin Franklin, a conflict and a balance which has always provided the creative tension in American life. But he translated these discoveries neither into formal philosophy nor into fully formed art. His logic and his metaphysics remained without system; his art, like that of all great American romantics, retained its organic freedom.

As Emerson had no Boswell, he must speak for himself, and he spent his life in doing so. Upon an audience he played with the sure hands of a master organist; but the oft shuffled manuscripts in his study were cold. "We do not go to hear what Emerson says," wrote Lowell, "so much as to hear Emerson." A tall blond figure in black, he leaned forward across the reading desk in shy

358

Yankee awkwardness and searched the hearts of his hearers with sincere blue eyes and controlled voice.

"Where do we find ourselves?" he asks in his essay on "Experience," and he gives his answer: "On its own level, or in view of nature, temperament is final." The inner wholeness of the man is his true self; his life "is a train of moods like a string of beads"; temperament, the iron wire on which the beads are strung. Striving to give expression only and always to this central self, Emerson has left a handful of essays and poems which are to many an essential part of their religious literature; but the man himself evades discovery. "So much of our time is preparation," he explains, "so much is routine, and so much retrospect, that the pith of each man's genius contracts itself to a very few hours."

Preparation—routine—retrospect; these are the entries on the calendar, the frame of life for a reticent New England man who is Emerson the seer. He devoted thirty-three years to what he thought of later as "preparation" before he published his first book in 1836; some two decades provided the "very few hours" when his genius was at high pitch and all of his great work was produced from the essential stability and calm of "routine"; and finally there were almost thirty years of "retrospect" before his death in 1882. The central twenty years have left us our impression of a man who always stood firm on moral ground and admonished his fellows to turn their eyes from evil, to have faith in themselves and in one another, and to seek God through Nature. But the Emersonian confidence and calm were not achieved, nor were they maintained, without struggle, doubt, and self-examination.

2

The chronicle of Emerson's preparation may be reconstructed from letters and journals; it would have been alien to his temperament to leave an autobiography of the soul such as *Sartor Resartus, Dichtung und Wahrheit,* or the *Confessions* of Rousseau. But the romantic pattern of introspection, doubt, and psychological crisis found in a Carlyle or a Goethe was his as well, marked by the familiar circumstances of poverty, loneliness, illness, idealized love, and the discovery of death.

Poverty was the lot of his youth. The second of four boys, he was only eight years old when his father died in 1811 and the congregation of the "Old Brick" Church in Boston granted the "pious and amiable" widow home and subsistence for a few years, while the boys shared one winter overcoat and the housework, studied their grammar, and ended the "toils of the day," as Ralph reports to his Aunt Mary, with their private devotions.

During Ralph's school and college days this diminutive aunt, appearing suddenly out of her private wandering for visits at the Emerson home or writing admonitory letters to her adopted spiritual orphans, became the substitute for both father and conscience. Her life, writes her nephew, "marked the precise time when the power of the old creed yielded to the influence of modern science and humanity." The zeal and consecration of Puritan ancestors was mingled in the latter-day sibyl with shrewd common sense and an insatiable intellectual curiosity. Mary Moody Emerson lived this life in preparation for the next, but she lived it with gusto. The correspondence between her and her nephew charts his course as his mind and spirit grew. There is solemn thought and wiry humor in the letters of both, even though the boy's sophistication is sophomoric, that of the little old lady crisp and intricate. For Aunt Mary was both mystic and critic, Calvinist and skeptic; Ralph could laugh at her because he profoundly respected her. To her he took both his doubts and his discoveries. She sharpened his wit and deepened his perceptions. Here is at least one source for that mixture of insight and common sense which characterized his thought, that aphoristic directness which sharpened his style.

During these early years, Emerson learned the habit of introspection. His intimate experience with people seems hardly to have extended beyond the family. "The friends that occupy my thoughts," he wrote at Harvard, "are not men, but certain phantoms clothed in the form and face and apparel of men by whom they were suggested and to whom they bear a resemblance." But his intimacy with his brothers, William, Edward, and Charles, was close. The journals which he, and apparently Charles as well, kept from an early age have not all survived, for the first is now dated 1819 from Harvard; but even in these we can see the somewhat affected litterateur gradually recede and the true man emerge. By 1824, the journals have ceased to be a "motley diary" and have become a "soliloquy," a "savings bank" where he can deposit his earnings. Here is the workshop, with saw, hammer, and plane, where the raw lumber of thought, reading, and experience is stored and worked. There is a vast difference between the early and late volumes. The first four or five constitute a moving autobiography of the spirit, but the others may be read in almost any order and are most enjoyable when dipped into. Between 1820 and 1836, when his inner life was growing steadily, the record of his progress has dramatic conflict and movement. Thereafter the journals gradually become to the reader what they were to him, a mine to be worked rather than a journey to be taken.

To poverty and introspection was added a struggle with sickness and adversity sufficient to supply a romantic hero with all the sorrows he might need. For the shadow of the white plague lay across the Emerson household, and Ralph barely escaped its doom. It carried off his two younger brothers, the one more eager and self-consuming, the other less robust than he; and, if we accept his own theory, he avoided certain death when a depression and cough racked his chest only because of a "sluggish" passivity of temperament which allowed him to give in to the malady and take the rest and care which brought his recovery. But Edward's sudden mental breakdown in 1828 followed Ralph's trip to Florida in search of health by only a year, and the frailty of Charles, "the friend and companion of many years . . . whose conversation . . . has been my daily bread," kept the minds of both in secret morbid contemplation to be confessed only to private notes. "I read with some surprise the pages of his journal," wrote the elder brother after the death of Charles in 1836. "They show a nocturnal side which his diurnal aspects never suggested,—they are melancholy, penitential, self-accusing; I read them with no pleasure: they are the creepings of an eclipsing temperament over his abiding light of character."

It would be a mistake to overemphasize the similar traits in Ralph's character, but the tone of penitential self-accusation is strong throughout the college and following years, driving him in upon himself when external adversity made the way dark. Like Charles too, but again not to the same degree, this mood cultivated an insistently skeptical habit of mind which fought throughout these years a losing but bitter battle with the native optimism of his character and resulted in a strengthening of his affirmation.

Love likewise came to him in somber garb. Within parentheses he confided in 1827, "I am a bachelor and to the best of my belief have never been in love"; but the next year when he took Edward to Concord, New Hampshire, to hasten his recovery, he confessed to William: "The presumptuous man was overthrown by the eye and ear, and surrendered at discretion. He is now as happy as it is safe in life to be. She is seventeen years old, and very beautiful, by universal consent." Ellen Tucker's illness—the same as his own though more acute—had made her already an invalid and emphasized the ethereal qualities that so appealed to suppressed but dreaming youth. Delicate, deeply religious, and altogether devoted, she awoke his protective manhood, spurred ambition, inspired poetic tribute. The marriage lasted a little over a year, and her death left a "miserable apathy" rather than the morbid depression of adolescent sorrow. As pastor of the Second Church of Boston, he had meanwhile become a man. Yet Ellen remained the one great romance of his life, a dream of purity the easier to maintain because illness had protected it from the rigors of living.

Eager for experience and thwarted by his shyness, Emerson sought in books the reality he craved. His tastes were formed in early childhood. Aunt Mary had seen to it that the fatherless boys should grow up in the family tradition of religious zeal and the love of letters. She herself read beyond orthodox theology, and she encouraged her nephews to follow her devious course. Through her, Ralph discovered Milton and Bacon, Shakespeare and Burke, who were to remain through life close friends on his expanding shelves.

As he grew older and moved away from her influence, the eclectic quality of his reading increased. For the formal Harvard curriculum he had little use, and he was content to remain in the middle of his class rather than seek academic distinction. A good sermon from W. E. Channing, or an oration from Everett or Webster gave him more pleasure than the rhetorical instruction of Edward Channing or the cold rationalism of Locke. The influence of the Scottish rationalist Dugald Stewart can be traced in his later writing; but, at the time, the *Elements of the Philosophy of the Human Mind* seemed all cottages and shops after entering the gate of splendor and promise. Doubt knocked at his door in the form of Pyrrhonism, the current undergraduate fashion. Slowly, as he took over his own education, he added Plato (in the translation of Thomas Taylor), Montaigne, Newton, Swedenborg, and Plutarch (both the *Lives* and the *Morals*), to his list of imperatives. More commonly he turned to histories, anthologies, and translations as short cuts to usable ideas: Gérando, Schlegel, Staël, Cousin, Hammer's translations of Persian poetry into German, and Taylor's translations of the Neo-Platonists. Newton's *Principia* and Lyell's *Geology* opened his mind to both the old and the new science. He could read both French and German slowly, but he would "as soon think of foregoing the railroad and the telegraph" as of avoiding translations when they could save time.

In all of this reading two trends are clearly marked. He hoped to learn from the skeptics, the rationalists, and the scientists a common-sense basis for moral truth; and he hoped to meet in the mystics and romantics a validation immediate, instinctive, and final. The one brought him closer to experience, the other to God. He was feeding his moral imagination rather than disciplining his mind. The two-pronged nature of his quest was a reflection of his two-sided temperament and led to a suspended dualism, the necessary creative tension for literary expression. Always Emerson strove to make one of two; but in his own early thinking he did not clearly distinguish between the logical and the intuitive roads to truth. This distinction he owed largely to Coleridge, but it was not to become clear to him until his spirit had been melted and reforged.

The romantic crisis in his life came with his retirement from the ministry in 1832. The independence of spirit to which he had responded in the books he had read was now focused on an issue which had its roots in his own temperament, his traditions, his times. "Whoso would be a man," he wrote later, "must be a non-conformist. . . . Nothing is at last sacred but the integrity of your own mind." The choice lay before him, raw and urgent. He must renounce his own world in order to find himself.

The earnest young clergyman had chosen his profession deliberately. In one of the most remarkable passages of self-examination in all literature, he stated his prospects to his journal on April 18, 1824:

I am beginning my professional studies. In a month I shall be legally a man. And I deliberately dedicate my time, my talents, and my hopes to the Church. Man is an animal that looks before and after . . . and this page must be witness to the latest year of my life whether I have good grounds to warrant my determination.

In the following inventory a strong imagination is balanced against a proportionally weak reasoning faculty, but theology requires, in its highest form, the moral imagination rather than the "reasoning machine" of a Locke, Clarke, or Hume. Lack of self-confidence in society is a serious handicap in the ministry and entirely precludes the law; he finds in himself no taste for medicine; but "in Divinity I hope to thrive." An inherited "love for the strains of eloquence" makes "entire successs" in public preaching a reasonable expectation, even though relative failure in the functions of private influence may dull the triumph. As a teacher—he had assisted in the girls' school which his brother conducted—he had experienced little satisfaction. But his trust is that, by discipline of his weaknesses, his profession may be the "regeneration of mind, manners, inward and outward estate."

Three points emerge from this inventory, which are central to an understanding of the later Emerson: his faith in the moral imagination rather than the intellect, his lack of self-confidence, and his choice of eloquence as his natural medium of expression. At this time, he seems to have had none of the doubts about his ability to conform to the requirements of an organized church that later were to invalidate his choice.

His rebellion, when it finally came, was twofold: against the last vestiges of ecclesiastical authority over the spiritual life of the individual, and against the eighteenth century rationalism which had killed spirituality, he thought, when it denied revelation. The first pointed to a final schism in which each man becomes his own church; the second sought to provide the rules for a new and personal orthodoxy. In the end, self-reliance was sanctioned by submission to the "Beautiful Necessity." As, long before, Jonathan Edwards had paradoxically sought to bring the straying Arminians back to orthodoxy by a personal appeal to the heart as well as to logic, so Emerson attacked the intellectual liberals of his day.

For the faith of the fathers had by the early 1800's once again cooled in the growing Unitarianism of William Emerson and William Ellery Channing of Boston. The new sect had not yet declared itself, but a small company of New England clergymen, liberal in their theology, were "discarding Calvinism by silently ignoring it" and appealing to the intellect, to sentiment, and to literary taste rather than to dogma or revelation. The next step toward heterodoxy, which Emerson heard preached in the "sublime sermons" of Channing, was the doctrine of truth discoverable by the mind rather than the heart. But the spirit of Calvin stirred once more when the boy wrote to his aunt and mentor, "It would assuredly make us feel safer to have our victorious answer set down in impregnable propositions." A new orthodoxy was implied by direct appeal to the God within. His own version of the new revelation was framed in *Nature,* and elaborated in his lectures and poems. It was an indigenous growth in nineteenth century soil, but the seed was found on a high shelf of the family cupboard.

The inner drama of this struggle is written between the lines of more than 160 sermons preached between 1826 and 1832, a selection of which has been published as *Young Emerson Speaks.* In these sermons, we find most of his later and characteristic doctrines expressed in a voice straining for conviction and leaning upon logic and authority where uncertainties still cling. In his first sermon, "Pray Without Ceasing" (1826), man is declared "the architect of his own fortunes"; conscience, the predecessor of the "moral sentiment" of the later essays, is "God's vicegerent"; "the preexistent harmony between thought and things" anticipates the later convictions of correspondence between moral and natural law; and nature "helps the purposes of man."

These central ideas together with others equally characteristic are developed more fully in the sermons which follow, while other ideas, expressed perhaps with less confidence, were later modified or rejected. The painful effort to account for "Miracles" (1831) as a special "means by which God can make a communication to men" was scratched out and rewritten only to have its main argument denied in the confident "Divinity School Address" of seven years later. His wife's death made faith in personal immortality an urgently needed "Consolation for the Mourner" (1831), a doctrine which his later pantheism modified to the point of rejection. And his effort to find his vocation within the frame of the Church made him not only acknowledge the importance of the public functions of prayer and preaching, but the validity of the formal sacraments of marriage, baptism, and the Lord's Supper.

The young preacher struggled with these doubts and contradictions as long as he could; but he sensed his main difficulty from the start. With conformity in spite of conscience, he was determined to have nothing to do. In his first personal talk to his congregation he announced that he would not "be so much afraid of innovation as to scruple about introducing new forms of address, new modes of illustration, and varied allusions from the pulpit." The desire of his hearers for sanctity in style and solemnity in illustration would not deter him from the study of secular as well as scriptural wisdom and its use in his ministry. His revolt from formal sacraments might then have been predicted. Not the administering of the Lord's Supper alone, but the whole structure of formal worship was challenged.

It is perhaps ironic that the man who was to free Unitarianism from the last vestiges of dogma and from reliance upon the authority of logical argument should himself have contrasted so sharply in his discourse with the eloquence of his predecessors, W. E. Channing and Henry Ware. These sermons are cold, and the earlier of them follow careful outlines. They remain on the level of the mind and contain no evangelical buoyancy. Gradually, as personal conviction grew, a new form and a new style asserted themselves. As his personal and theological difficulties became more pressing, his heart seemed to awaken. The need for self-justification in the lonely path which was inevitably opening before him brought an emotional power to his discourse which no evangelical technique could supply. His farewell sermon on the Lord's Supper (1832) was his last effort to rest a case upon the principles of logical analysis. His real farewell came a month later in his final sermon to his congregation on "The Genuine Man," who "parts with his individuality, leaves all thought of private stake, personal feeling, and in compensation he has in some sort the strength of the whole. . . . His heart beats pulse for pulse with the heart of the Universe." With this new strength, a new eloquence was born. Hereafter Emerson would start on the plane of the commonplace and raise his hearers with himself to that of the ideal. In "The Miracle of Our Being" (1834) the form of all his later work is declared. From "the fitness of man to the earth" this sermon rises by swift ascent to "an infinite and perfect life." The seeker has become the leader and guide, with conviction in his message and confidence in his medium.

Many volumes have been written to prove that Emerson's final position was based on Neo-Platonism, German idealism, or Oriental mysticism; but a study of these sermons and of his early reading indicates that he never departed from his loyalty to the faith of his fathers, the Christian tradition as developed by Christ, Paul, Thomas Aquinas, and Calvin. Essentially romantic by disposition, he took his place with the rebels and seekers and, like Coleridge and Goethe, sought both confirmation and refreshment from all ages and quarters.

It was this growing romanticism which made the bondage of formal religion insufferable. For his final searching of the soul, he retired to Ethan Crawford's in the New Hampshire mountains, where "life is reconsidered."

There the hours passed on, bearing him to the crisis of his fate. "How hard to command the soul, or to solicit the soul." Struggling with "indignation at this windmill," recognizing that "without accommodation society is impractical," he confronted at last his inevitable choice of path: "I cannot go habitually to an institution which they esteem holiest with indifference and dislike." The issue was not one of doctrine or of form; it was a private matter of his conscience. He would not abolish the institution of the Lord's Supper if it had meaning for others; but he could no longer administer it. When he returned to Boston and once more faced his congregation, he had left all conformity behind, for he had at last grappled with himself and conquered. Fears of his own inadequacy could not block his path, for personal success no longer mattered. The self-reliance which he had preached to others was now to be his.

3

This, as Carlyle was writing at the time, is the "Everlasting Yea," the crisis and resolution of romantic doubts. But before full achievement, it must be preceded by a "Center of Indifference." Divorce from circumstance must be complete, that the inner man may expand to full self-recognition.

The way was not clearly charted when he was on the brig *Jasper* bound for Malta in January, 1833. In spite of his lifelong aversion to travel as a means of escape or refreshment, he spent most of that year in Europe. At thirty, his life lay behind him, apparently a succession of failures with no positive accomplishment to show for his efforts and a state of health and mind which promised little for the future. His mood sank to self-disgust and despair: "What under the sun canst thou do, pale face? . . . I did not put me here; yet God forbid I should therefore decline the responsibility into which I am born." With himself he was relentless: "It is doubtless a vice to turn one's eyes inward too much, but I am my own comedy and tragedy." When he warned later that the traveler "carries ruins to ruins," he was doubtless thinking of his own experience; and on his return, he sighed, "I am very glad my travelling is done. A man not old feels himself too old to be a vagabond."

Such moods were occasional only. He gave various reasons for the trip, among them illness and the desire to see great men: "to learn what man can,—what is the uttermost that social man has done." But his obvious purpose was to be alone, to confront himself, and if possible to find a new vocation unfettered by the formalities and expectations of others or by his own shortcomings. "I am thankful that I am an American as I am thankful that I am a man." His quest ended with a pledge, "if health and opportunity be granted me, to demonstrate that all necessary truth is its own evidence; that no doctrine of God need appeal to a book; that Christianity is wrongly received by all such as take it as a system of doctrines,—its stress being upon moral truth; it is a rule of life, not a rule of faith."

But his discoveries were not all moral or religious. Much to his own surprise, he was startled and ensnared by Old World culture. His senses and emotions were stirred by the incense and the music of St. Peter's, by the calm beauty of Raphael's Transfiguration, by the Sistine frescoes and the Moses of Michelangelo. He warmed to the monuments of Catholicism, but found no charm in Geneva, the home of his inherited faith, other than the surrounding mountains. In Paris, he was astounded by the collection of birds, beasts, and other specimens in the Jardin des Plantes. "I am moved by strange sympathies; I say continually 'I will be a naturalist.'" His confessed lack of human sympathy and ease of approach to strangers was belied by his friendliness with fellow Americans, the sculptor Greenough, the traveler Dewey, and innumerable others whom he joined for part of his way. But with Landor at Fiesole, Coleridge at Highgate, and Wordsworth at Rydal, his hope to discover greatness in the great was disappointed. Carlyle alone fulfilled his expectations. Emerson had come upon "the latest and strongest contributor to the critical journals" in 1827–1829 when Carlyle's articles in the *Edinburgh Review, Fraser's,* and *Blackwood's* were scorching their pages. He sought him out in his lonely farm at Craigenputtock, listened to his wry and revealing comments on the ingenuity of a pig and the immortality of the soul, and entered into a correspondence which continued through life and ultimately filled two volumes. These two met and talked through the night because they were exploring the same caverns, not because they had come out into the same sunlight. When it appeared finally that Carlyle preferred to remain a struggler in the darkness, the sympathy waned, and Emerson emerged alone into the affirmation of his middle years.

That affirmation was most intense during the ten years between his return and the *Essays, Second Series* in 1844. In that short time he delivered from carefully prepared manuscripts over seventy-five lectures, most of them in series of ten or twelve at the Masonic Temple in Boston; a dozen occasional addresses, and many sermons. His letters to Carlyle whom he met only at wide intervals of years, to Sterling whom he never saw, and to nearer friends like Margaret Fuller, Caroline Sturgis, Samuel Gray Ward, and Henry Thoreau, were platonic essays in friendship. The pages of his journal were filled regularly and fully, and poems were wrought with care at frequent intervals. Yet only *Nature* and the *Essays* from this mountain of manuscripts were prepared for the press at the time. This was to be his capital upon which he could draw with interest for the rest of his life. A few poems and essays found print in the *Dial,* the *Western Messenger,* the *Massachusetts Quarterly,* and later the *Atlantic,* and there only to help his friends and the cause of enlightenment which they shared with him, not because he wished to publish. He had found his new profession. His was to be the living message, the spoken voice. The town hall was his new church, the Society for the Diffusion of Useful Knowledge his sect.

With this rededication he discovered a new way of life. Within three years after his return from Europe all his major decisions had been made, his life put in order. In the winter of 1833-1834 he began his lectures; that summer he made Concord his home; the next year he married Lydia Jackson of Plymouth, bought the Old Coolidge house on the Cambridge Turnpike—regrettably in a meadow rather than on a hill—and delivered to his townsfolk an "Historical Discourse" on the occasion of their second centennial. In 1836 he published *Nature* and his son Waldo was born. He had home, wife, family, career, friends, and associates. "The lonely wayfaring man," as Carlyle was later to call him, was once more a citizen of this world.

But the spirit of revolt did not die in him so abruptly as these facts might suggest. He had dispersed the morbid clouds of introspection and uncertainty. He had chosen his point of issue with his age. He knew what he must accept as well as what he must reject. He was ready to speak and to act. There are two phases of romanticism, that of doubt and seeking, that of revolt in equilibrium. Emerson had reached the second phase by 1834, and his productive tension showed no sign of breaking for at least ten years.

The immediate release of that tension was *Nature*; the key to its understanding is what he called "the First Philosophy." "I endeavor to announce the laws of the First Philosophy," he wrote in June, 1835. "It is the mark of these that their enunciation awakens the feeling of the moral sublime, and great men are they who believe in them. Every one of these propositions resembles a great circle in astronomy. No matter in what direction it be drawn, it contains the whole sphere. So each of these seems to imply all truth."

The source of this cornerstone of his reconstructed philosophy may have been, as he himself implied in *English Traits,* his discovery that "Bacon, capable of ideas, yet devoted to ends, required in his map of the mind, first of all, universality, or *prima philosophia.*" But it is likely that his inheritance of Christian mysticism then drew him to sympathy with the Quakers, the Swedenborgians, and the Methodists, tempered and extended by his early absorption of Neo-Platonism and Oriental insight.

In announcing these laws, Emerson, who rejected all established doctrine, formulated a new doctrine composed of assumptions which experience had taught him were vital. With logic he could have nothing to do, declaring that "a foolish consistency is the hobgoblin of little minds." As has been pointed out, his propositions constituted for him, as it were, the persons in a drama of the mind, not the steps in an argument or system; they have also been likened to equations. They are based on the definitions of a few key words used by Cousin, Coleridge, Sampson Reed the Swedenborgian, and Thomas Taylor the Neo-Platonist, which these writers derived in turn from German metaphysics, Scottish rationalism, and the literature of romanticism in general. The similarity of Emerson's thought to that of Kant, Hegel, Schleiermacher, and Schelling is deceptive; such influences usually came to him at one or more removes. His attitude toward his assumptions had the quality if not the rigidity of the dogmatism he had rejected. He had discovered a way of setting down his victorious answers in impregnable propositions, in laws which describe relationships rather than essences. They are the stuff of ethics and faith rather than of metaphysics, theology, or logic.

Nature (1836) is the gospel of the new faith rather than, like Thoreau's *Walden*, a record of an experience of earth. Lifted by the excitement of recognition to the plane of prose-poetry, it is nevertheless a concise statement of the "First Philosophy." The primary assumption of this essay is that man, whether regarded individually or generically, is the starting point of all philosophic speculation. His functions, his relations, and his destiny are its only concerns. The self-reliance which results from this assumption is essential to vital experience. Whatever truth lies beyond or outside man can be reached only through him and by him.

Emerson opens his essay with the current distinction between the Me and the Not Me, the Soul and Nature, thereby establishing the first of his provisional dualities. The Me is consciousness, or that part of man which partakes of divinity, the Not Me is the objective of consciousness, that with which the Me is in relation. But Nature, or the Not Me, also partakes of divinity in that "outward circumstance is a dream and a shade"; its reality lies in its being "a projection of God in the unconscious." A second duality is thus established between Nature and God; and a third, between God and Man. Here is a triangle of relationships, the value of which lies not in the absolute identity of Man, God, or Nature, but in the common relationship between any two of the factors. Man may learn to worship God through the contemplation of Nature. The stars, the flowers, the animals, the mountains reflect the wisdom of his best hour, first as that which is outside of his consciousness, then as that which shares with his consciousness a "vision of original and eternal beauty," an awareness of a divine principle.

The ability to view experience in this twofold manner is the essential quality of the First Philosophy. Emerson's position, in so far as it approaches the statement of final verities, is monistic; his method invariably dualistic. He declares in the opening paragraphs of his essay that he will use the word "Nature" in two senses: the common sense in which it refers to essences unchanged by man, and the ideal sense in which it is the phenomenal expression of the soul. The possible ambiguity "is not material; no confusion of thought will occur." It is necessary to set up a provisional dualism in order to explore the ultimate unity. This method, established in the opening paragraphs of his first published book, is implicit or stated again in every word that Emerson ever wrote. As he is wholly concerned with the process of thinking rather than with the objects of thought, his position is often declared to be dualistic; it is so only in its method, but its method is very nearly all there is to it.

From Sampson Reed, and later from Swedenborg himself, Emerson borrowed the doctrine of correspondence between the natural and moral laws to validate this primary assumption. "The spiritual part of man is as really a substance as the material; and is as capable of acting upon spirit, as matter is upon matter." In each sphere there is a law the study of which may be reduced to a science; but the law in the one sphere exactly corresponds at every point with that in the other. Thus natural and moral laws are distinguishable from each other but are actually correspondent at every point. "Matter," concludes Emerson, "is a phenomenon, not a substance." "There is a law for man and a [parallel] law for things." This assumption that the one law may be treated in practice as two allowed him complete and open-minded acceptance of the progress of physical science without fear that its findings would invalidate religion. With one stroke he swept away the major controversy of the age by linking it to the persistent Christian synthesis of faith and works.

Emerson came to describe the faculty whereby man might explore the realm of the spirit as "the moral sentiment," and most of his value judgments on men and experience depend ultimately upon the presence or absence of this faculty. It is the capacity of human nature to discover the moral law by means of intuition. In *Nature* and his early essays he more commonly calls it the "Reason" as distinguished from the "Understanding," another instance of his habit of dividing in order to conquer—this time probably borrowing from Coleridge, who had stated in his *Aids to Reflection*: "Reason is the Power of Universal and necessary Convictions, the Source and Substance of Truths above Sense, and having their evidence in themselves. . . . The Judgments of the Understanding are binding only in relation to the objects of our Senses, which we *reflect* under the forms of the Understanding." "Heaven," echoes Emerson from the *Aids to Reflection,* "is the name we give to the True State, the world of Reason, not of the Understanding; of the

Real, not the Apparent." He uses these two terms specifically in this sense throughout his writing as he similarly makes distinctions on two planes between Imagination and Fancy, Talent and Genius, in common with English romantic philosophers. He thus again clearly distinguishes between the lower and the higher faculties of the mind: Understanding, Fancy, and Talent are means of dealing with immediate experience, but each has a nobler counterpart in Reason, Imagination, and Genius by which man may climb from the plane of the natural to that of moral law.

From these two assumptions, the centrality of man in his own universe of experience and the exact correspondence between the planes of material and spiritual law, Emerson developed the other principles which constituted his working philosophy. From them he derived his law of compensation or balance of conflicting forces in experience, his theory of good and evil, and his beliefs in the inevitable vocation of each man, in the idea of progress, in unimpassioned love among men, and in the Over-Soul. From the same source he developed his characteristic method for lecture and essay, starting in most cases on the level of common or material experience and rising to that of spiritual realization. From them too he derived his theory of art and poetry as an intricate system of symbols or "language" expressing through human agency an organic moral harmony.

Here was a new covenant of the spirit, built upon the foundation of Puritanism, tested by the rigors of American experience, and shaped by the architecture of romantic theory and the democratic ideal. All materials available were carefully studied and built into the structure if they could prove of use; from the past, the wisdom of Plato and his followers, the inductive method of Bacon and Montaigne, and the mysticism of Oriental religion and poetry; from the future, the naturalism of science and the rampant materialism of a growing industrial nation. The result was a tentative organization of opposing forces into a dynamic harmony rather than a static unity, a philosophy of growth and change rather than one of certainty and system. In a single essay Emerson made himself the apologist of a people because he had discovered a formula in which temperamental contradictions were reconciled if not logically resolved. The theological mystic Jonathan Edwards could speak through him across the centuries to the political idealist Woodrow Wilson; Benjamin Franklin could send through him to William James the message that pragmatism was merely "a new name for some old ways of thinking"; and the American habit of testing truth simultaneously by intuition and by action could seem to be merely a rounding out of experience, not a division of personality.

Even though *Nature* was Emerson's first formulation of his position, it was only a beginning. In spite of its organization into topics proceeding on an ascending scale from Commodity through Beauty, Language, and Discipline, to Idealism and Spirit, it asks rather than answers questions, it is a cry of astonishment at the possibilities of life rather than a record of achievement. There was much work to be done, and its author immediately set about the doing.

When Emerson stood before the Phi Beta Kappa Society at Harvard on August 31, 1837, to define the American Scholar, he was delivering an annual address on the conventional topic. Men far more prominent than he had spoken on the same subject from the same platform many times before. Current journals had for a quarter of a century been sprinkled with pleas for a national literature. There was nothing in the announced subject, the mood of the audience, or the appearance of the speaker to suggest an unusual occasion. Yet when the address was concluded Lowell declared it "an event without any former parallel in our literary annals," and Holmes pronounced it "our Intellectual Declaration of Independence." His hearers realized, as we today cannot, the depth and force of his revolt against his times.

In a series of occasional addresses between 1837 and 1844 he announced to his old associates—writers, scholars, clergymen, and men of thought in general—the revolution that had taken place in his conception of his own function and of theirs. The occasions were seized as offered, the Commencement of his old divinity school, convocations of the Dartmouth and Waterville college literary societies, meetings of library associations, or merely sponsored evening lectures at a public hall. In all of these he is eager, excited, defiant, but firm, clear, and relentless. He knew that he was issuing a challenge: "Amidst a planet peopled with conservatives, one Reformer may yet be born."

He anticipated, especially from the clergy, the violence of the inevitable response. He was speaking with deliberate intention to shock, but in carefully considered language. Each of his thrusts was strong and sure, aimed at the heart. To the scholar he said: "Translate, collate, distil all the systems, it steads you nothing; for truth will not be compelled in any mechanical manner." And again, "Man Thinking must not be subdued by his instruments. Books are for the scholar's idle times. When he can read God directly, the hour is too precious to be wasted in other men's transcripts of their readings." To the writer: "All literature is yet to be written. Poetry has scarce chanted its first song." To the student of divinity: "All men go in flocks to this saint or that poet, avoiding the God who seeth in secret. . . . Let me admonish you, first of all to go alone; to refuse the good models, even those which are sacred in the imagination of men, and dare to love God without mediator or veil," even Christ himself. And in discussing "The Times": "Our forefathers walked in the world and went to their graves tormented with the fear of Sin and the terror of the Day of Judgment. These terrors have lost their force, and our torment is Unbelief, the Uncertainty as to what we ought to do; the distrust of the value of what we do, and the distrust that the Necessity (which we all at last believe in) is fair and beneficent." The intention of all these overstatements was the same. They were designed to shock complacency into recognition that each dawn opens a new day. They did not deny the past; tradition must serve the present as one kind of experience rather than as authority. Emerson was challenging his audiences; not announcing measured and final truth.

For the present and the future he had high hope, granted that self-reliance could be restored and assured. "I speak of the politics, education, business, and religion around us without ceremony or false deference." The new literature must be neither Classic nor Romantic: "I embrace the common, I explore and sit at the feet of the familiar, the low. Give me insight into to-day, and you may have the antique and future worlds." This, he announced, is a Reflective or Philosophic age; its concern is with itself. He did not shrink from the abounding energy and the inexhaustible resources of his time and place. "Railroad iron is a magician's rod, in its power to evoke the sleeping energies of land and water." "It seems so easy for America to inspire and express the most expansive and humane spirit; new-born, free, healthful, strong, the land of the laborer, of the democrat, of the philanthropist, of the believer, of the saint, she should speak for the human race."

Emerson was not blind to the dangers in all this rampant energy. He accepted an economy of abundance based, like that of Adam Smith, on a moral law which allows self-interest full play. He believed in a natural aristocracy, in property, in immigration, in trade, and competitive industry. A laissez-faire Yankee materialist on the level of the senses, he relied on the moral sentiment to transcend and resolve all conflicts. "The materialist takes his departure from the external world, . . . the idealist . . . from his consciousness." The transcendentalist accepts both views; because his dualism is a provisional state only, he can "take his departure" from the level of the senses in full confidence that, at the same time, he is also operating from the level of the spirit. "He believes in miracle, in the perpetual openness of the human mind to new influx of light and power; he believes in inspiration, and in ecstasy."

Ecstasy is not always apparent in Emerson's own life during these ten years, nor in the many lectures which he delivered. A substantial number of them still exist, however, in manuscript, and most of them are listed or abstracted in the appendix to J. E. Cabot's *Memoir*. Their uniform emphasis upon the moral law is evident from the titles of the series: "Biography," "English Literature," "The Philosophy of History," "Human Culture," "Human Life," the "Present Age," "The Times," "New England." With the journals, these lectures bear the relationship to the *Essays* that an artist's sketch does to his finished painting. They were written out with care, but their style has the rhythm of speech, the loose phrase, the colloquial and often humorous turn.

The energy and eagerness, the security and peace which Emerson conveyed to his audiences had roots at home. His marriage and family life were steady, rich, and rewarding. Lidian, as he asked permission to call her because the *n* smoothed transition to the new name, had the qualities of a Madonna rather than of a St. Cecilia. In 1836, Waldo was born,

> Boy who made dear his father's home,
> In whose deep eyes
> Men read the welfare of the times to come—

bringing completion during his five years of life and a sorrow when he died more calm than at the deaths of Ellen Tucker and Charles. Emerson gave to his two daughters the names Edith and Ellen; to his second son, Edward. "In the dwelling-house," wrote the father, "must the true character and hope of the time be consulted," for there a man may "stand on his feet."

The town of Concord was a larger home and the circle of friends that gathered in the Emerson drawing room was but an extended family. Near-by towns had succumbed to industry, but the Musketaquid was still navigable only to canoes, and:

> Bulkeley, Hunt, Willard, Hosmer, Meriam, Flint,
> Possessed the land which rendered to their toil
> Hay, corn, roots, hemp, flax, apples, wool and wood.

The Thoreaus, Hoars, and Ripleys were native citizens, but Alcott, Ellery Channing, and Hawthorne were later comers; Margaret Fuller, Elizabeth Peabody, the mystic Jones Very, and many others of the transcendental set were never more than visitors. The Social Circle which met frequently at the Emerson home on Tuesday evenings consisted of "twenty-five of our citizens: doctor, lawyer, farmer, trader, miller, mechanic; solidest men, who yield the solidest gossip."

A very different group had formed the habit of gathering at one another's houses for an afternoon of serious conversation, whether in Boston or Concord, and so the "Transcendental Club" came into being without deliberate intention or constitution. It was, as one facetious member remarked, "like going to heaven in a swing," and Emerson himself at times mocked their earnest aspirations. "Perhaps they only agreed in having fallen upon Coleridge and Wordsworth and Goethe, then on Carlyle, with pleasure and sympathy. Otherwise, their education and reading were not marked, but had the American superficialness, and their studies were solitary," like his own. Bronson Alcott, the Orphic philosopher, existed in an ethereal sphere which he shared with Plato; Thoreau came fresh from the woods and fields; Emerson from his study; Parker, "our Savonarola," and Brownson from their churches, the one a Unitarian, the other inclining toward Rome. Margaret Fuller and occasionally Hawthorne's sister-in-law Elizabeth Peabody shot bolts of aggressive femininity into the company with their radical notion that women are people, seeking friendship on a plane transcending sex.

One such friendship, violent on Margaret's part, acquiescent but at times disturbing on Emerson's, produced "the modest quarterly journal called *The Dial*," organ of the movement for four years. George Ripley, inspired by Owen and Fourier, attempted the most famous of all communistic experiments at Brook Farm, even though the stars of the movement took only a casual part, preferring to shine each in his own sphere. A third practical—if we may stretch the word—result was the Concord School of Philosophy, founded in 1879 by Alcott in his own back yard, a highly successful pioneer of the American summer session. For at least a quarter of a century, the idyllic town was the intellectual seed pod of the nation.

In so stimulating an atmosphere, largely of his own making, Emerson expanded and matured, producing the *Essays, First and Second Series* in 1841 and 1844. These in a very real sense were new works, dependent no more on the lectures he had delivered than on the pages of the *Journals,* for he drew from both sources, running a pencil line across the chosen passage, lifting it from the page, and remolding it to its new purpose. Lectures in form and spirit still, they are written for a larger audience than any that ever could be assembled in one place. Though they retain their quality of voice, they are not meant to be spoken. In every line and every paragraph they bear the evidence of loving workmanship.

The new form which Emerson developed is neither wholly essay nor wholly lecture. Its unit is the carefully wrought sentence, "pure, genuine Saxon"; as Carlyle immediately recognized, "strong and simple; of a clearness, of a beauty." Each contains in crystalline suspension the whole meaning of the essay, of the book, an art learned perhaps in part from the gnomic sentence of Bacon or the *pensées* of Pascal, as simple and direct as the familiar style of Montaigne. "Nature will not have us fret and fume." "All things are double, one against another." "Life only avails, not the having lived." Sometimes they are but a single image: "Life is a train of moods like a string of beads, and as we pass through them they prove to be many-colored lenses which paint the world their own hue, and each shows only what lies in its focus." Longer sentences are broken and rugged, retaining their staccato quality: "The death of a dear friend, wife, brother, lover, which seems nothing but privation, somewhat later assumes the aspect of a guide or genius; for it commonly operates revolutions in our way of life, terminates an epoch of infancy or of youth which was waiting to be closed, breaks up a wonted occupation, or a household, or style of living, and allows the formation of new ones more friendly to the growth of character."

Carlyle sought coherence in the paragraph and found rather "a beautiful square *bag of duck-shot* held together by canvas." Even less closely are the paragraphs knit to their foregoers and followers, the essays to one another to make a book. But it would be a mistake to conclude that form is lacking. Each paragraph, each essay, has the structure of the circle containing smaller circles within it and itself contained in larger circles. "The eye is the first circle," wrote Emerson in the shortest of his essays; "the horizon which it forms is the second; and throughout nature this primary figure is repeated without end." His method is organic, a reflection of the structure of the universe as he sees it.

But if the movement of logical sequence is lacking, that of direct communication to faculties beyond the reason is not. The units of his style are built upon one another into a rising structure of thought and feeling. Always there is the sense of a man speaking to his audience, catching their attention, focusing it on a central meaning, expanding it to furthest limits of experience, raising it to highest levels of recognition, bringing it back to the center. Each essay opens with a challenge, either by quiet reference to ordinary experience or by sudden shock of overstatement. With text thus supplied, homiletic rather than logical principles elaborate, illustrate, and slowly unfold the theme as writer and reader are borne onward together. In most of the essays, there is a sense of rising intensity in both meaning and form, which suggests Emerson's own images of the spiral, the ladder, the swift flight upward. The conclusion brings a quiet sense of completion, of exhausted possibilities, of whole vision which has the dramatic finality of the curtain of a play.

A similar sense of structure is not discernible in the arrangement of the essays in the two companion volumes, although the first series has more coherence than the second. The wholeness of Emerson's thought is such that, touched at any point, it immediately embraces experience. The differences between the essays lie in their varying points of emphasis; each includes all. Their unity lies in the "First Philosophy" expressed, not in its expression.

The points of departure are roughly of three kinds: description of the universe and its laws (Self-Reliance, Compensation, Spiritual Laws, the Over-Soul, Circles, Experience, Nature, and Nominalist and Realist); analysis of the moral faculties in human relationships in general (Love, Friendship,

Prudence, Heroism, Character, and Manners); and studies of more nearly particular problems of experience (History, Art, The Poet, Politics, and New England Reformers). But even such broad categories soon break down as the elaboration of the primary point of any one essay includes those of all others.

The resulting unity of approach to living is the key to Emerson's hold on his own and later generations. Henry Adams called it "naïf," and others have put it away with childish things. His disregard rather than denial of evil, his lack of logical system, his staccato crispness of style, his didacticism, his appearance of being above torment and suffering, have provided blockages for many. But his morning quality of recognition and confidence, his power of distilling essences that all know to be true, his gift of innumerable texts for the problems of living and thinking, his accurate reflection of the American mind and heart in its moments of aspiration, have made these essays a book in our modern bible. "It is not yet art," wrote the sophisticated Comtesse d'Agoult when she discovered them for her people, but "the mingling heretofore unknown, of the protestant spirit of individualism, or self-reliance, with the pantheistic spirit which inspires this book, the combination and harmonizing of these two antagonisms in a superior intellect forms, incontestably, a new element from whence may be born an original art." For a moment the tensions and contradictions of American experience were held in vital suspension and, in Emerson, found their first clear and authoritative voice.

4

The "new art" of Emerson is contained in five volumes—all, except some of the poems, written within the decade 1844–1854, none published immediately. They are *Poems* (1847), *Representative Men* (1850), *English Traits* (1856), *The Conduct of Life* (1860), and *May-Day* (1867). That in this period he passed from a state of romantic tension to one of "classic" or organic restraint more suitable to the New England disposition is attested by his own statement in a lecture on "Art and Criticism" delivered in 1859:

"The art of writing is the highest of those permitted to man as drawing directly from the Soul, and the means or material it uses are also of the Soul. . . . Classic art is the art of necessity; organic; modern or romantic bears the stamp of caprice or chance." Even though he retained the doctrinal foundations of his thought in historical romanticism, Emerson developed his arts of poem and lecture-essay in this, his own, definition of the classic, by admitting the need for moral restraint in art.

His poetry was written in his own study, the product of walks in the Concord fields or to his "garden," the wood lot on Walden Pond which he allowed Thoreau to use for his cabin. The prose was a reworking of lectures delivered in England (1847–1848) and in the "West" from Pittsburgh to Cincinnati, to St. Louis and Chicago (1850–1853). During these years he was away almost as much as he was at home, and Lidian made out as best she could, caring for the children and the big white house, aided by the townsfolk and by Henry Thoreau, the master's delegate in residence to tend the fires and the garden.

Had he never written a word of prose, Emerson's achievement as an experimental and epigrammatic poet would give him a primary place in our literature. In his youth he was the admitted poet of the family, but even he refrained from taking his nonsense and imitative verses too seriously. When the time came to woo Lydia Jackson, not only to himself but to Concord, he had attained to better perspective. "I am a born poet," he wrote, "of a low class without doubt yet a poet . . . in the sense of a perceiver and dear lover of the harmonies that are in the soul and in matter, and specially of the correspondence between these and those"; but he was "uncertain always whether I have one true spark of that fire which burns in verse."

A born poet he most assuredly was, in theory as well as fact. Before the publication of his *Poems* in 1847, the United States had had but one true student and experimenter in the art, Edgar Allan Poe. Bryant, Halleck, and Freneau either had shown no deep interest in the theory and technique of poetry or had conformed to the romantic modes of Wordsworth and Byron, and to the traditions of the English lyric. The early verse of Whittier, Simms, Longfellow, Lowell, and Holmes had accepted similar models without fresh exploration of anything but the American scene. Poe alone had sought to rediscover the nature and function of poetry in itself. Emerson's originality is as profound as that of Poe, and the theories of the two supplement each other. Poe sought an aesthetic base for the art; Emerson, a moral. Poe explored mainly the possibilities of rhythm; Emerson, of symbol. Together they directed the course of American poetry since their time by turning from borrowed conventions and by seeking once more the springs of poetry. Walt Whitman and Emily Dickinson were further to exploit these breaks with the past; others would follow.

Part of Emerson's sense of inadequacy was caused by his high ideals for the poet. He is the seer, but he is more. He is also "the sayer, the namer, and represents beauty. He is sovereign and stands on the center. . . . He is a beholder of ideas and an utterer of the necessary and causal." His office is that "of announcement and affirming." He does not make his poem, "for poetry was all written before time was. . . . The men of more delicate ear write down these cadences." By characteristic overstatement, Emerson would thus make the role of the poet seem almost passive. He is an Aeolian harp that "trembles to the cosmic breath" (a favorite image). But he is also Merlin, the traditional bard, the wise man, the magician, whose "blows are strokes of fate." In the distribution of functions among men, he is the man speaking, the scholar who has an assigned course of action—to express the message he receives. By this test Plato at times seems almost to qualify as poet, and Sir Thomas Browne, Zoroaster, Michelangelo, and the authors of the Vedas, the Eddas, the Koran. George Herbert stands the test and Milton, next to Shakespeare the prince of poets because his genius is "to ascend by the aids of his learning and his religion—by an equal perception, that is, of the past and the future—to a higher insight and more lively delineation of the heroic life of man." And the Persian Saadi becomes for Emerson the prototype of the poet because

> He felt the flame, the fanning wings,
> Nor offered words till they were things.

Herein lies the insight which caused his spontaneous acceptance of *Leaves of Grass* in 1855. Whitman's words were things.

If the recording of celestial music had been to Emerson the only function of the poet, his verse might have been more melodic than it is. Rather in his prose, especially when it was prepared to be spoken, he came closest to achieving rhythmic freedom, as did Melville, whose philosopher in *Mardi* chants only when he is seized with the frenzy of prophetic vision. Before it was pruned and sharpened by gnomic insight, Emerson's style might flow with the current of his eloquence and climb by the measured but open periods of the Song of Solomon, the Sermon on the Mount, or Whitman's sweeping rhythms. In an unpublished passage from the introductory lecture to the early course on "Human Culture," he used the techniques which Whitman was later to exploit. Freed from the paragraph of prose as well as the meter of verse, his periodic lines are held to a frame by parallel phrasing, assonance, alliteration, and return:

> The philosopher laments the inaction of the higher faculties.
> He laments to see men poor who are able to labor.
> He laments to see men blind to a beauty that is beaming on every side of them.
> He laments to see men offending against laws and paying the penalty, and calling it a visitation of Providence. . . .
> He laments the foreign holdings of every man, his dependence for his faith, for his political and religious estimates and opinions, on other men, and on former times.
> And from all these oppressions is a wise Culture to redeem the Soul.

But Emerson asked more than this of the poet. The active function of poetry, as he saw it, was to make manifest and specific the correspondence between the real and the ideal, a task which rhythm alone could not accomplish. From the English metaphysical poets in prose and verse, Herbert, Donne, Milton, Browne, he learned the connotative value of the individual word, the possibilities for luster and surprise in the image. He turned to them rather than to the contemporary romantics who had acquiesced too easily in a passive pantheism. Milton and Herbert rather than Wordsworth and Coleridge felt God intensely and struggled to restore him to this world. These elder poets had striven, as did Emerson, to reconcile an intense religious faith with an equally intense challenge of science, and his method was theirs. In this, he stood alone in his times among British and American poets, for not even Matthew Arnold appreciated the full worth of the symbol, however much he struggled with the "two worlds" between which he stood. The mystic and the scientist must become one, and the symbol is the only means for the accomplishment of the union. This Emerson fully appreciated, and it is his gift to modern poetry. From Bacon he took the Aristotelian view that "poetry, not finding the actual world exactly conformed to its idea of good and fair, seeks to accommodate the show of things to the desires of the mind, and to create an ideal world better than the world of experience." To this he added the Swedenborgian view that nature must serve man for symbols, that by seeing through the phenomenon to the essence, the poet might transform the evidence of his senses to a higher use and reestablish the correspondence between the natural and the moral laws. "The act of imagination is ever attended by pure delight. It infuses a certain volatility and intoxication into all Nature." The poet is "an exact reporter of the essential law," but he is active rather than passive because he restores the harmonies of the Over-Soul through the counterpoint of experience; he supplies from his intuition the true, rather than the apparent, natural image. "The mind, penetrated with its sentiment or its thought, projects it outward on whatever it beholds." The result is a beauty not of the senses but of the moral sentiment.

The critic should not be misled by Emerson's frequent references to poetry as music, for his own verse rarely sings. "That which others hear," he confessed, "I see." Even in his poem on "Music," the images are almost all visual, and "Merlin's Song" is "of keenest eye" before it is of "truest tongue." His dissonant rhymes and limping rhythms are parts of a deliberate effort to achieve freedom of movement, and they receive at least some authority from their models. Butler used "slanted" or imperfect rhymes, Milton incomplete lines, and Shakespeare, in his later plays, a roving accent. Emerson asked for all these freedoms together. He made excessive use of rhyme, because to him it was the favorite instrument of rhythm in Nature (although again his examples are visual: reflections in a pond or the repeating forms of shadows). He also adopted the eight-syllable line because he was convinced by the theory of O. W. Holmes that periodicity in poetry is determined by human respiration. He never broke loose in his poetry as did Whitman, into the more natural freedom of colloquial speech. But within his limits, all of which he believed are imposed by Nature rather than tradition, he trusted the song as he heard it, even though his hearing was not always true. His rhymes are often little more than assonances; his meter, counted syllables that sometimes miss the count, letting the accent fall where it may.

With the visual image, Emerson's muse can safely be trusted. In his "Mottoes"—verses distilled to provide texts for his essays—he committed Wordsworth's fault of trying to deal too directly with thought. But where the image is given full play, as in "The Sphinx" (his own favorite), "Days" (perhaps his most successful), "Hamatreya" (his most direct), "Uriel," "Brahma," "The Snow-Storm" and the first part of "Merlin," it achieves an intricate pattern of conceit worthy of Herbert or Donne, but fresh from his own experience. Here the poet exerted his full prerogatives with volatile nature, using the evidences of the pines, the sea, the stars to its own purposes and revealing the correspondence of the law of things to the law of God. In other poems like "Woodnotes," "Threnody," and his odes, he achieves sureness and freedom in some passages, but falls into rhymed prose in others; and sometimes, as in "The Rhodora," the message is too explicit, the effect didactic.

At his best, Emerson's keen sensitivity to the larger aspects of nature, his mastery and daring with the visual image, his deep appreciation of the connotative value of single words (a gift not shared even by Poe and not approached by any other contemporary except Emily Dickinson who followed his course in both theory and technique), place him among the most original and provocative if not the most even poets in the language. Add to these qualities the intrinsic value of what he has to say, and his poetry becomes one of the treasures of our literature, greater in some respects than his essays because, when he allows himself full scope, he speaks from and for himself a universal language, without reference to a particular audience even by inference. His art is organic in that it reproduces the organism of moral law as reflected in nature; it is classic, as he would have it, only when his daring experiments achieve unity and, as in "Days," his intricate and climbing images merge into a single symbol of revelation.

The same quality is achieved in the prose of his maturity, *Representative Men, English Traits,* and *The Conduct of Life*. Derived from specific lecture courses, each has a distinguishable central theme upon which the parts play variations: the uses of great men; the values in modern civilization; the principles of individual action. The wise Emerson now speaks in his own church, of his own people, and to his own people. He is on sure ground, no longer defiant; the fight has been won, and he knows that he is heard.

His themes are not new. Back in 1835, in his first lecture series, he had spoken on "Biography" and examined the tests of a great man: Has he an aim to which he gives his whole soul? Is it broad and unselfish? Is it based solidly on fact? Does it set in motion the minds of others? Has it divine sanction? Two of these lectures, "Michael Angelo" and "Milton," were published in the *North American Review* and have come down to us virtually intact. The other three, "Luther," "George Fox," and "Burke," together with the introductory lecture, are unpublished or absorbed into other writing. The design for the series was his own, perhaps suggested in part by Plutarch's *Lives,* where a man's actions and distinctions are judged for their moral values; strengthened by Carlyle's *Heroes and Hero Worship,* which he welcomed in 1841—"a good book, and goes to make men brave and happy," because, from these cases, it describes and evaluates a whole system of conduct. But Carlyle's confusion of worldly with moral power was beginning to show through his transcendental intensity. On this point Emerson was clear. He did not test men for their control of others. "He is great who is what he is from nature, and who never reminds us of others." "Men are also representative; first, of things, and secondly of ideas." In contrast to Carlyle's, his criteria were the measures of democracy: self-reliance, the moral sentiment, experience, intuition.

For *Representative Men,* Emerson chose his cases carefully, each to represent a way of thinking and acting: Plato, the philosopher; Swedenborg, the mystic; Montaigne, the skeptic; Shakespeare, the poet; Napoleon, the man of the world; Goethe, the writer. All of these ways he had to some degree tried. They were tests for himself and for his hearers rather than essays in criticism. He was asking: By what measures may a man judge his own ambition? He was answering: By these I have judged my own. Only as they guide you and me in our private and single lives by their examples are great men of use.

The first four, "Plato," "Swedenborg," "Montaigne," and "Shakespeare," were written from the heart. These men had given Emerson personal aid as he emerged from the doubts and uncertainties of youth into the calm confidence of his later years. Each he had finally found lacking, incomplete for his purposes, because there is no such thing as a wholly great man. No man but one has succeeded in resolving the dualities of the law of things into the unity of the moral law, has finally identified faith and works. And Emerson did not choose to write directly of Christ, who had succeeded in fact; or of himself, who had striven in theory. But the book begins and ends, by implication, with these two. For Napoleon and Goethe he has less perfect sympathies. They were added to complete the list, for he must include at least one man who did not write, and one whose greatness depended almost wholly on the fact that he did. Carlyle had used Napoleon as the symbol of worldly power, the hero in action; Emerson through him analyzed the values in "experience" and, by revealing the dangers inherent in democracy, made one of his finest statements of the democratic faith.

In each lecture the same series of questions is asked: What is this man? What did he make of his life, and why? Are his values sound? The final test in each case is the moral sentiment, the ability to rise from the many to the one. Unlike essays on more abstract topics, these do not themselves rise except in the questions asked. Each finally records a partial failure which brings the special case back to the central thesis. Except that the weaker essays are at the end, the book thus achieves a greater unity than did the earlier *Essays*; but the individual judgment is warped to the pattern. For true perspective on the misleading final paragraphs on Shakespeare, for example, one must turn to the fragmentary tercentenary address of 1864, where, without reservation, Emerson declares that he is "the one resource of our life on which no gloom gathers . . . the most robust and potent thinker that ever was." In *Representative Men,* Shakespeare serves as a means for discussion of values beyond his own; in the later address he is confronted for himself. There is no confusion of moral with aesthetic values as some critics have affirmed.

This lecture series was delivered in Boston in 1845–1846, but it served Emerson as the chief item of his repertory while in England. On his return he prepared no single series on his impressions, but many of his lectures between 1849 and 1856 drew upon this experience to illuminate his social views. *English Traits,* in the latter year, was a book freshly written, but it drew ideas and paragraphs from both journals and lectures. At the same time he was offering his series on the "Conduct of Life" particularly to audiences in the West, the first draft of the book on the same subject.

Emerson did not enjoy himself on these travels, but they were enriching experiences both to him and his audiences. He was now carrying wisdom to wisdom, not "ruins to ruins." He was known for what he was and what he would say. In England he was guest of honor at the Grand Soirée of the Manchester Athenaeum, where he addressed several thousand people, among them such notables as Cobden, Bright, Cruikshank, and Blackwood. A few years later he faced in Cincinnati a "vast assembly, which sat for two mortal hours . . . lecture hungry," in anticipation. He met the great now on their own level: among them Dickens, Tennyson, and Carlyle again. He heard Chopin play: "Could the denying heaven have also given me ears for the occasion!" Between lectures, he traveled in the new steam trains or in ruder conveyances, was entertained in unfamiliar homes, or sat in lonely hotel rooms. He found Paris "a place of the largest liberty that I suppose in the civilized world," and "the great sweeps of the Mississippi . . . the loneliest river." In Europe, he studied people and society; in the West, he bought maps and learned geography. The demand for him was so great that he was forced to write new lectures on the road. Seldom were his audiences large— nor was he uniformly successful with them—but there were many, sometimes two within twenty-four hours, and the returns from any one were small. In one course in Chicago the "gate" for Bayard Taylor was $252; for Emerson only $37—an extreme instance. In spite of the industry and enthusiasm of Alexander Ireland who made the arrangements, the English trip apparently did not cover expenses; the American did somewhat better. But the real and enduring profit of these journeys lay in his two ripest and roundest books, *English Traits* and *The Conduct of Life*. If he had written nothing else, by these two he would deserve to be called our most representative man.

His report on British civilization was, like all the work of this later period, the fruit of years of study and speculation. For one of his early lecture series, he had chosen the topic "English Literature" and in preparation had read Warton's *History of English Poetry*. The English classics had always been favorites, but his first visit to England was a disappointment. Only when he returned in 1847 did the past become a living part of the present and the meaning of the British character become clear. "England is the best of actual nations," he wrote, "London is the epitome of our times." *English Traits* was the first record of an American's return to "Our Old Home" to achieve critical detachment without loss of sympathy; but it was also an analysis and judgment of the civilization of which America was as much a part as England. This book takes its place of fulfillment in our travel literature with ease and grace; but it marks in Emerson's own work the turn from a personal to a social perspective. In studying the English, he was concerned for the first time with the problem of man functioning en masse.

Set in the frame of his own journey, it opens with accounts of his first visit and of his voyage, and concludes with his trip to Stonehenge, his personal reception, and his speech at Manchester. The intervening chapters constitute an analysis of contemporary British civilization against a background of history. "If there be one test of national genius universally accepted," he writes, "it is success; and if there be one successful country in the universe for the last millennium, that country is England." His curiosity is piqued, and he seeks the answer in geography, ethnology, moral philosophy, economics, politics, education, religion, and literature. He finds it in a never-failing "reserve of power in the English temperament," a Saxon inheritance strong enough to absorb and use other racial strains, to profit by a favorable location, to rise above mistakes without denying them, and to exploit material resources without losing moral integrity. The mother of human liberty, England in her age is perennially young "with strength still equal to the time." She may pay absolute homage to material wealth, she may retain and develop her aristocracy, she may have her established church and her revered universities, she may cling to her traditions and rituals without great harm because she can laugh at her own mistakes and forever hold on to her "original predilection for private independence." As long as she can produce both steam engines and poets, she is sound and safe in spite of her faults.

Like Cooper and many another American traveler, Emerson returned to his own country with renewed respect for her potentialities, but sharp criticism of her crudities. The glamorous faith of his Boston lecture on "The Young American" (1844) was dulled by a keener critical sense when he began working on *The Conduct of Life* soon after his return. Not, like *English Traits,* an overt analysis of a specific civilization, this book was nevertheless his counsel to his own people in contrast to his earlier advices to men in general. He felt himself swept into the current of analysis of "the times." "By an odd coincidence," he began, "four or five noted men were each reading a discourse to the citizens of Boston or New York, on the Spirit of the Times," during the same winter. Carlyle had published *Past and Present* in 1843, and reform was in the air. "To me, however," he warned, "the question of the times resolved itself into a practical question of the conduct of life." The conflicts in prevailing ideas could only be resolved by reference to larger contexts than those of the here and now. Once more he must write a summary statement of the First Philosophy, but this time its generalizations were to be tempered by experience with the actual forces at work in contemporary society, the conduct of men at court and in the wilderness.

Now for the first time he planted his feet solidly on the ground and looked critically about him. His new task was to evaluate civilization in his day with the tools and criteria he had spent a lifetime in perfecting. No part of his earlier position, as defined in *Nature,* was denied, but no longer did he confuse what he saw of men and things with the perfection of which he believed life to be capable. The critical realism of this third period followed the balanced tensions of his earlier work with a more sharply defined duality of view: keener observation of the world as it is, on the one hand; firmer convictions of the unity of the ultimate moral principle, on the other. His conclusions and inconsistencies are now intellectual more than emotional. His equations have almost the certainty of the formula; his art is firm rather than fluid. To those who enjoy his work for its romantic fervor, this is a loss; to those who look for restraint and form, there is positive gain in firmness of texture.

The Conduct of Life marks the culmination of Emerson's work. He has become social critic as well as moral philosopher. He is willing to explore the pragmatic as well as the ideal test of conduct, and to evaluate men as well as man. Inconsistencies between the material and the ideal are the more glaring, and the ascent from the one plane to the other can no longer be made with the careless abandon of *Nature* and the *Essays*; but made it must be. A wiser and firmer spirit wrote these chapters on "Fate," "Power," "Worship," and "Beauty," because temptation, conflict, and suffering are recognized. The old optimism is not dimmed—we must still build our altars to the "Beautiful Unity" and the "Beautiful Necessity"; but the difficulties of the way are sympathetically explored before they are waved aside. "The young mortal enters the hall of the firmament. . . . On the instant, and incessantly, fall snow-storms of illusions. . . . And when, by and by, for an instant, the air clears and the cloud lifts a little, there are the gods still sitting around him on their thrones,—they alone with him alone."

5

The clouds of the Civil War were already gathering when the lectures on the conduct of life were being written; the War broke in the year the book appeared. It marked a fourth and last phase in Emerson's development, a time for retrospection. His literary powers had reached their meridian; during the last thirty years of his life, they were slowly undermined by the distractions of the times, which led him into reluctant participation in public and national affairs, and later by increasing demands and weakening powers, which made for less care in composition.

Never up to the moment of his death in 1882 did he equal the achievement of *The Conduct of Life.* He gathered together one more collection of his essays, *Society and Solitude* (1870), but a second, *Letters and Social Aims* (1875), was too much for him after the shock of the burning of his home in 1872. His friend James Elliot Cabot took over the task and completed it under Emerson's wandering supervision. Cabot culled two more volumes from the stock pile of shuffled manuscripts, and Edward Emerson a third after their author's death. In bulk, these five volumes represent almost half of his published prose; but at best they are fragmentary, however studded they may be with brilliant passages.

Part of the difficulty lies in a new habit of workmanship rather than in declining power. In his early years, Emerson borrowed freely from his own previous writing; but he always copied and revised the borrowed passage, leaving the original manuscript intact. Later, when the demands upon him grew too heavy for this practice, he took to lifting pages bodily, with the result that few of his later manuscripts were whole when the editors set to work on them. No canon of his work during these years can therefore be established, except as Cabot has done it in the listing by title of his lecture series. The lectures themselves as he delivered them are lost. The one collection that he himself prepared, *Society and Solitude,* is on a more familiar level than are his earlier essays, but it has much of the old charm and eloquence. Emerson had settled, after the war, more contentedly into the enjoyment of domestic life, farming, books, clubs, art, and old age, and he gathered together what he had said on these topics, as early as 1841, as late as 1862, to make a single book. "The central wisdom, which was old in infancy, is young in fourscore years, and, dropping off obstructions, leaves in happy subjects the mind purified and wise." This is what his mind would be; and this is what it had become.

In 1870, his lifelong wish to develop "a new method in metaphysics, proceeding by observation of the mental facts, without attempting an analysis and coordination of them" seemed gratified by an invitation to deliver a course of sixteen lectures to the students in philosophy at Harvard. But his mind was too tired to undertake so great a work as the reformulation of his theory of the law for man and the law for things, and he drew upon old lecture courses for most of his material.

His *novum organum* remained unwritten at his death. The fragments of the course which survive were published under the title he had chosen for the whole, *The Natural History of the Intellect.* In them he attempts once more to harmonize the powers and laws of thought, instinct, inspiration, and memory with the findings of natural science. The ideas are not new, but the tone is cold and clear like the atmosphere of a late autumn afternoon. Three years before, he had written:

> As the bird trims her to the gale,
> I trim myself to the storm of time,
> I man the rudder, reef the sail,
> Obey the voice at eve obeyed at prime.

The distinction in experience between the moral and natural laws, and their ideal identity, remained the primary message of that voice. It had been a long struggle from youthful doubt to wise serenity, but faith in the "each and all" had not wavered. He had defined and revealed the eternal human verities in the conflicting demands of the new man in the new world.

26. HENRY DAVID THOREAU

W HEN in 1872 the town of Concord was
dedicating its fine new library building, Ralph Waldo Emerson was the
natural choice for speaker. A river of thought, he said, is always flowing from
the invisible world into the minds of men. And he named over Concord's
makers of books. "Henry Thoreau we all remember as a man of genius, and
of marked character, known to our farmers as the most skilful of surveyors,
and indeed better acquainted with their forests and meadows and trees than
themselves, but more widely known as the writer of some of the best books
which have been written in this country, and which, I am persuaded, have
not yet gathered half their fame."

Thoreau had then been dead ten years. While he lived, only a meager
miscellany of his poems, essays, and reviews had appeared in newspapers and
magazines; only two books had been printed, *A Week on the Concord and
Merrimack Rivers* (1849), and *Walden* (1854).

Given this history of publication, and considering the peculiar man himself, there was bound to be a confusion of appraising voices—a babble taking
years to blend into anything which approximates a chorus. To William Ellery
Channing, Thoreau's companion on many walks, he was the poet-naturalist.
Amos Bronson Alcott believed him the finest possible example of the native
New Englander—a rugged, independent, inventive Yankee to show Europe
with pride. To the village selectmen, at the time of John Brown's trial, he was
a meddlesome troublemaker. Nor, though they employed him as the town's
surveyor, could they quite forgive him for once accidentally setting their wood
lots afire, on the day of Town Meeting, of all things, when he should have
been mindful of his civic obligations. In South Africa, Mahatma Gandhi, editing *Indian Opinion,* found in Thoreau's "Civil Disobedience" the way to
resist tyrannical government. Though leaning heavily on Thoreau in his own
life and writing, Robert Louis Stevenson labeled him a skulker, dodging the
responsibilities of living. A twentieth century critic, remarking on Thoreau's
immensely busy practical and creative life, characterized him as "one of the
masters of English prose, purer, stronger, racier, closer to a genuine life
rhythm, than any one of his contemporaries, in England or America." John

Burroughs, after scolding Thoreau for scientific errors, concluded that he was, first and last, a moral force speaking as a literary naturalist. George Eliot, in the *Westminster Review,* called *Walden* "a bit of pure American life (not the 'go a-head' species, but its opposite pole), animated by that energetic, yet calm spirit of innovation, that practical as well as theoretical independence of formulae, which is peculiar to some of the finer American minds." James Russell Lowell pronounced him an imitator of Emerson, an unpleasant egotist, and a failure. And Emerson himself spoke of him as *the* man of Concord.

Many of these opinions appear to be based on Thoreau himself as much as on his writings. That is readily explained, for he lived what he wrote. When his subject was nature, his intensest effort was to transfer directly to the page what each of his senses and his mind and spirit told him. When he wrote on controversial questions, he knew his thoughts were true since he had lived them—however difficult, inconsistent, or absurd they might seem to others. The electric impulses, the vital blood of his brain and body, gave life to the spirit and matter of his books. Probably more than with any other American, his acts, opinions, and literary work are one. Any attempt at comprehension, including why he wrote as well as what, begins and ends with the man himself.

2

When Emerson, still a comparative newcomer there, hailed young Henry Thoreau as *the* man of Concord, he had not long known him—though he was acquainted with his mother, for Mrs. John Thoreau, like many gentlewomen of modest means, took in boarders, among them Mrs. Lucy Brown, Emerson's wife's sister. Concord thought of John Thoreau as one of its less successful mercantile citizens. Even after the repeal of Jefferson's disastrous embargo and the close of the War of 1812, the number of merchant-bankrupts was far from small. John had failed in his storekeeping at Concord, where, on July 12, 1817, his son Henry was born. He had tried his hand in Boston and elsewhere. When Henry was five, the family had moved back to Concord, and was doing reasonably well in the manufacture of pencils. There were four children: Helen, the eldest, John, Jr., two years ahead of Henry, Henry himself, and Sophia.

Henry soon showed a bent for studies, and, with Concord township for his background, developed a liking for the country as did most New England boys who could shoulder a fowling piece, though he never became a hunter, preferring to tramp or fish. An affectionate, close-knit family, the Thoreaus pinched to send both boys to Concord Academy, not satisfied with the standards of the town school; then chose Henry as their candidate for college.

When Thoreau was at Harvard he never bothered to stand higher than the middle of his class, though his fellows soon came to think of him as a scholar. He spent many hours in the alcove of the library where Chalmers' *English Poets* were shelved—twenty-one packed volumes in which he continued his reading already begun at Concord. It was not in his nature to follow the narrow highway of the college curriculum. He preferred to cut across lots. The careful reading of books became the basis of his education.

Though content with average work in most of his courses, he was good enough in his second year to be assigned a role in Greek dialogue. Shortly after this, in the long winter vacation, he taught a term of school at Canton, Massachusetts, living with the Unitarian minister there, brilliant, erratic Orestes Brownson, who interested him in the German language and some of its literature, and perhaps in his own radical notions.

By the time Henry was a senior, he had jotted down in copy books many passages and verses from his reading—not with any definite intention, but because he wished to keep them. These were sentences the sight and sound of which he liked; these were ideas about which he wished to think.

The copy books, too, served in the composition of classroom exercises for Edward Channing, Boylston Professor of Rhetoric and Oratory. It was Channing's aim to teach his students how to express their ideas logically and in order, in a natural, lucid style. Thoreau's mind was intuitive, not logical, and there was sure to be trouble. Not that he disliked doing essays—he loved to write—nor objected to Channing's methods of teaching. Far from it—he averred this was his one beneficial orthodox experience at Harvard. But harm came with the good. Essay topics encouraged by Channing were of a sort bound to produce didactic, prosy exposition, a type of writing alien to Thoreau's better genius, yet lingering in his poorer passages.

In his extracurricular reading he had discovered certain modern British authors: Coleridge, guide to German transcendentalism; Wordsworth, whose thoughts in poems like the "Intimations" ode flowed sympathetically into the stream of Thoreau's thinking; and Carlyle. He found Carlyle highly provocative. This was the richest prose style he had met. Here also was an antidote to Professor Channing's emphasis on logical didacticism. Here was a gospel of individualism for the encouragement of young men. Thoreau enjoyed Carlyle's vigorous humor, his rank exaggeration, his readiness to burst through conventional barriers. But the Carlylese which Emerson found infecting most of the Scotsman's young American readers also took its toll of Thoreau's early prose. Before reaching maturity, he had to get rid of it.

His interest in the Elizabethans and in British authors of the seventeenth century deepened as his knowledge increased. Prose writers like Sir Thomas Browne and metaphysical poets like Donne, Vaughan, Crashaw, and Herbert became his favorites. Their eccentricity caught his fancy. But what kept his attention was the way they strove to picture with all their senses what they felt and did. The lines he liked best to repeat were these from Elizabethan Samuel Daniel:

> Unless above himself he can
> Erect himself, how poor a thing is man.

His explorations in the Harvard library also led him to old travel books like Josselyn's *New-Englands Rarities Discovered*. Aside from his interest in the subject, he valued the strong, straightforward, practical language of these cultivated men of action.

With some additions, these tastes were to remain Thoreau's favorites, and his absorption made him one of the most deeply educated of American authors. In his maturity he would tolerate no master; but books form one solid part of the foundation beneath him. The greatest impact came from his native village when, in the fall of 1836, Emerson's *Nature* was published. Our age in America, wrote Emerson, suffers from retrospection. "The foregoing generations beheld God and nature face to face; we, through their eyes. Why should not we also enjoy an original relation to the universe? Why should not we have a poetry and philosophy of insight and not of tradition?" Here was a precept to win the most from existence. Books themselves must change to drops of water in this stream of living. Nothing must impede its flow. Thus advised, Thoreau could enter into the American Renaissance directly.

On August 16, 1837, as one of the better scholars, Thoreau took an active part at Commencement, picking the negative side in a debate on the merits of the Commercial Spirit. Man's absorption by that spirit, he declared, made him turn his eyes from the world's beauty and from life's best purposes.

3

College over, he was going home. Full of joy at the thought, he was convinced he had been born in the most estimable place in the world, and in the very nick of time. "If I forget thee, O Concord, let my right hand forget her cunning," he boyishly affirmed in his class book. "To whatever quarter of the world I may wander, I shall deem it good fortune that I hail from Concord North Bridge."

To live fully, vitally, was his intent, to keep himself always at the top of his condition. But given the workaday world, how best bring this about? He was making himself useful to his family in the house and garden—no son in the village was handier—and helping his father in the pencil shop. The family meant him to be a scholar, and did not question his use of his time. He paid for his keep, like the other boarders. He continued his walks and his reading. Presently he took on the Grammar School, having taught before. But the committee's interference when he would not flog—though the discipline he kept was good—caused him to resign within a fortnight. Perhaps he would try for another school in Maine, in the South or West. Still casting about while his Harvard classmates settled down to business or the professions, he was restless, a little ill at ease, and with his back up.

Meanwhile, Emerson invited his friendship.

In his thirty-fourth year, and at the top of his intellectual powers, Emerson was delighted with this youthful scholar, deeply read in those authors whom he also found stimulating. Moreover Henry was able to read in many languages—Greek, Latin, and French with ease, Italian, Spanish, and German with more effort. He had a curiosity about the structure of language, was acquainted with Anglo-Saxon, and relished Chaucer. Though Emerson of course recognized the kinship between Thoreau's thinking and his own, he saw and hailed at once this erect, independent mind, bent on testing the truth and worth of everything it met with.

At Cambridge that August, before the Phi Beta Kappa Society, Emerson had delivered "The American Scholar." Was not this young friend the Free American he had imagined—versed in great books, responsive to nature, fit for doing as well as thinking? The better Emerson got to know him, the more he valued this firmly built man, his hands strong and useful with tools, his brain meshed beautifully with his capacity for action.

The world Thoreau entered when Emerson opened the doors of his house could be matched in few other times or places—an extraordinary intellectual universe within which Emerson and the group around him moved familiarly and with command. Easily and soon, admitted as an equal, Henry, the youngest, became a member of the circle. Sometimes, especially when the inevitable cranks were present, he rudely turned on his heel and walked out. Yet citizenship in this Athenian society was of greatest value in his development, strengthening the growth of his faith in intuitive thinking.

This group set up one target for his shafts. Farmer-friends in the village—simple, shrewd, elemental, earthy Yankee philosophers—furnished another.

"Do you keep a journal?" Emerson asked him. No, not regularly. So he began. "What are you doing now?" Emerson also inquired. Even at this experimental stage, Henry could probably never have brought himself to go permanently to Maine or the West, but he did give one more test to teaching. His brother John and he took over the old Academy and kept it for three years, incidentally using part of the summer vacation for an excursion on the Concord and Merrimack rivers. But when John's health failed Henry decided against continuing alone. The toll exacted on his freedom was out of proportion to the income. He needed more winter, as well as summer, for observation and study. Nor would he go on teaching just for a livelihood, since in his honesty he admitted that his primary objective in doing so was not the good of his fellow man.

He liked home, but a boarding house can be noisy and distracting. Sensing Thoreau's need, Emerson saw a way to gratify needs of his own. He still greatly missed his dead brother Charles, who had lived with him, and he longed for another such companion. In a letter to Carlyle, he was soon able to report: "One reader and friend of yours dwells now in my house, and, as I hope, for a twelvemonth to come,—Henry Thoreau,—a poet whom you may one day be proud of." He was finding Henry as full of buds of promise as a young apple tree. He had already presented him as a writer, having persuaded Margaret Fuller, the *Dial*'s editor, to print Thoreau's poem, "Sympathy," in the first issue along with an essay on the Roman satirical poet Flaccus. It was for introducing young men like Henry that Emerson chiefly valued the *Dial*— not to multiply writing in the old tradition, but to report life, newness, and the dreams of youth.

A young poet had one duty—to be a poet—and Emerson never doubted Thoreau's obligation. Thus encouraged and given an outlet, Henry was soon in a mid-sea of verses. But the question of how to live while writing still needed resolving, though Emerson's household arrangement gave a temporary answer. Emerson's business of lecturing seemed a possible solution, till Henry tried it. In his first year out of college he had spoken gratis before Concord's Lyceum, his subject, significantly, "Society." But offers had not poured in to speak for money. Like all Emerson's young men, Thoreau lectured with Emersonian intonations—but not with Emerson's skill nor his rich, compelling voice; and what he said was muffled to the neck in Harvard rhetoric.

A Carlylean doctrine Thoreau heartily approved of was the insistence that each man search for that one work which fits him best, then enter wholeheartedly into it. "I must confess," he wrote, "I have felt mean enough when asked how I was to act on society, what errand I had to mankind. Undoubtedly I did not feel mean without a reason, and yet my loitering is not without defense. I would fain communicate the wealth of my life to men, would really give them what is most precious in my gift. I would secrete pearls with the shellfish and lay up honey with the bees for them. I will sift the sunbeams for the public good."

Thoreau's concentration first on poetry is not surprising, since the *Dial* carried on its pages some of Emerson's best: "The Problem," "Woodnotes," "The Snow-Storm," "The Sphinx." And much of his early prose caught Emerson's manner, but little more. Margaret Fuller rejected his essay, "The

Service," for though she found it rich in thoughts, they were so out of any natural order, so choked with mystical symbolism, as to make painful reading. When Emerson took over the editorship, his protégé had better luck. "Our tough Yankee must have his tough verse," wrote Emerson to Miss Fuller when Thoreau refused to make a suggested change. He had his criticism, too, for Henry's prose. Emerson had sent "A Winter Walk" to the printer with some misgivings, he confessed, notwithstanding its fine sketches of the pickerel fisher and woodchopper. The trouble, he repeated, was Henry's *mannerism,* as if one could get the trick of rhetoric through shock; to call a cold place sultry, for example; a solitude, public; a wilderness, domestic. But Henry, developing his own style, was learning what to do. In its amended form, "A Winter Walk" is characteristic. More and more his manner sprang from and suggested the solid matter on which he based what he wrote; yet, when he wished, he could take flight thence into the realms of his imagination and thinking.

Emerson wrote to his brother William, at Staten Island, about his new housemate, praising his scholarship and poetry, his partnership in the garden and in walking. This firmly built, light-complexioned, healthy-skinned boy, his gray-blue eyes strong and serious, seemed indefatigable when bent on any labor. With Emerson's support, he had served as curator of the Concord Lyceum and, though the town meeting proved niggardly in its grant of money, had assembled as interesting a slate of speakers as the people had thus far listened to. While Emerson was away, he edited the *Dial.* Full of inventiveness and strong common sense, this young man, thought Emerson, could give judicious advice in the gravest affairs; would prove competent as leader of any Pacific exploration.

In the woods, Thoreau's spirits were most elastic and buoyant. He was developing, Emerson noticed, a passion for observation. He was furthering an intense conviction that the keys to life's secrets could be found in Concord's fields. Yet none perceived better than Henry that it is not the fact that imports, but what lies behind it. For Thoreau, every least thing, like the greatest, lay in glory, a symbol of the order and beauty of the whole.

At Emerson's or the Harvard library Thoreau was rereading the English poets. He was studying Audubon, whom he had chanced on, with delight. While a Harvard undergraduate, he had found, in Chalmers' collection, Sir William Jones' "Essay on the Poetry of the Eastern Nations," with some examples in translation. Emerson, deeply interested in the sacred books of the East—the Laws of Menu, for example, setting forth the religious ethics of the Hindus—was drawing the attention of his friends to them. Thoreau soon knew them well. But it was probably not until he left Emerson's, by 1844, that he got acquainted with the Bhagavad-Gita, which Emerson was then enthusiastically recommending. It came to be Thoreau's greatest find, as important to him as Emerson's *Nature*. What attracted Emerson was its mystical speculation. The possibility, through asceticism, of uniting contemplation and action became for Thoreau a further guide toward fulfillment.

These explorations in Hindu philosophy naturally drew closer the bond between Thoreau and Emerson. A more immediate and poignant sharing came through the sudden presence of death. In the first winter at Emerson's, Henry's brother John, whom he loved with silent intensity, unexpectedly and horribly succumbed to lockjaw. Two weeks later, Emerson's first-born son, Waldo, died. These losses make their mark in the writings of both.

Emerson had very early recognized Henry's affection for children—how heartily, like a child himself, he threw himself into their play. This affinity was like a confession that Henry was not so independent of human sympathy as he pretended. Emerson knew better than to take too seriously his friend's militant nature, though Thoreau could be prickly as a hedgehog and touchy as a snapping turtle. It seemed as if Henry's first instinct on hearing a proposition was to controvert it—a habit somewhat chilling to the social affections. But, valuing Henry for his integrity and peculiar worth, Emerson never really lost patience. Indeed, wishing Thoreau's light to become a beacon, he cast about for means to let it shine more widely than was possible in the *Dial*.

With papers like Horace Greeley's *Tribune*, New York was the nation's journalistic center. No writer of poetry, few of prose, Emerson was painfully aware, could make enough to live on in America. Still, with a letter introducing him to Greeley, Henry in New York might profit more than was possible in the village. The city might further his growth. Emerson had not seen what Henry had written in his journal: "I think I could write a poem to be called 'Concord.' For argument I should have the River, the Woods, the Ponds, the Hills, the Fields, the Swamps and Meadows, the Streets and Buildings, and the Villagers. Then Morning, Noon, and Evening, Spring, Summer, Autumn, and Winter, Night, Indian Summer, and the Mountains in the Horizon."

Sent ostensibly as tutor to William Emerson's son, Thoreau set out to explore and perhaps conquer New York. Nathaniel Hawthorne, who liked him, had also tactfully given him a lift, introducing him to John Louis O'Sullivan, editor of New York's *Democratic Review*. Horace Greeley took to young Thoreau, and began quietly to look after his literary welfare. This relationship he continued through Henry's life. For O'Sullivan's journal, Thoreau wrote an unimportant essay, "The Landlord," and a significant review of an extraordinary book by a German immigrant in Pennsylvania named Etzler who foresaw a technological age which would give man an opportunity, with a minimum of labor, to make a paradise of earth. Like a good Yankee interested in mechanical devices, Thoreau read Etzler with an open mind; but he quarreled outright with the prophet's materialistic aim. This "paradise (to be) regained" would be mechanistic and nothing else— offering an easy, hedonistic life through super-gadgetry. There was a speedier way, wrote the critic, to diversify the land, drain the marshes, secure a pleasant environment. That way must rely on the power and rectitude of the best human behavior. In his own attitude, this faith never lost its dominance over Thoreau.

New York had opened few doors, and Henry was homesick. "Am I not made of Concord dust?" he wrote to Lydian Emerson. "I carry Concord ground in my boots and in my hat." By November, 1843, he had brought it home.

4

Twenty-six years of age, Thoreau found himself again at a crossroads. Soon after leaving college, he had written: "The world is a fit theatre today in which any part may be acted. There is this moment proposed to me every kind of life that men lead anywhere, or that imagination can paint." South African planter, Greenland whaler, soldier in Florida, navigator of any sea. Now, in the summer that followed his New York venture, this proposal was repeated, literally. His friend Isaac Hecker, another explorer in living, suggested that the pair, taking nothing with them, work their passage across the Atlantic, and so through England, France, Germany, and Italy.

Henry, having weighed it, turned the proposition down. "The fact is," he replied, "I cannot so decidedly postpone exploring the *Farthest Indies,* which are to be reached, you know, by other routes and other methods of travel." Instead he would go to Walden Pond. In the metaphorical, imaginative, vigorous prose he could now command, he made a final comment on the offer. "I have been surprised when one has with confidence proposed to me, a grown man, to embark in some enterprise of his, as if I had absolutely nothing to do, my life having been a complete failure hitherto. What a doubtful compliment this to pay me! As if he had met me half-way across the ocean beating up against the wind, but bound nowhere, and proposed to me to go along with him! If I did, what do you think the underwriters would say? No, no! I am not without employment at this stage of the voyage. To tell the truth, I saw an advertisement for able-bodied seamen, when I was a boy, sauntering in my native port, and as soon as I came of age I embarked."

Emerson offered him his wood lot and field at the pond. There he would be secure of his leisure for work and study.

"I went to the woods," Thoreau later reported, "because I wished to live deliberately, to front only the essential facts of life, and see if I could not learn what it had to teach." The suspicions forming in his college days had become convictions. The mass of men led lives of quiet desperation, complaining of the hardness of their lot or of the times, when they might improve them. With man's industry and invention, when these expressed the man himself, uninfluenced by greed, Thoreau had no quarrel. It was man's exploitation of sovereign man which he deplored; man's self-delusion as to life's objectives. Everywhere, in shops and offices and fields, men appeared to be doing penance in a thousand remarkable ways. Henry was well aware that his own father, bred to the mercantile system, had worked hard only to suffer repeated failure, like so many merchants of his times. Or if they made money, they used it to ignoble ends. In his review of Etzler's book, Thoreau had pointed out that its chief fault, like that of the age itself, lay in taking for granted the idea that gross comfort is the greatest good—not the free, serene, unhampered growth of the individual. It would continue to be his purpose to dwell with a minimum of hindrance as near as possible to the channels in which his life flowed; to be in as perfect correspondence with his natural environment as possible, so as to be at home with nature. Thus he could sample and report on life with all his senses.

Not that he wanted others to follow his pattern; nor did those need advice who were already well employed. This was his present, personal answer to the problem of how to create, be happy, yet not lack food or shelter.

In the summer of 1845, in his twenty-eighth year, significantly on Independence Day, he started living at the cabin. From its door he could see the sun rise, watch the moon shine over Walden. On quiet evenings, alone in his boat under the stars, he could play his flute. He could search devotedly for images and phrases to describe the songs of birds. A master of reading, he could read more deeply.

He amused himself by keeping a record of his frugal housekeeping. He cultivated his philosophy and a patch of beans. He continued to study his world's fellow inhabitants: the otters, the foxes; Therien, French Canadian woodchopper, a primitive, Homeric man; the Irish, who, throughout sixteen hours of the day, for a pittance of sixty cents, were toiling, about one hundred rods south of his cabin, on the new railroad to Fitchburg. He often passed along the cut where they lived in stylike shanties, their bodies permanently contracted by the long habit of shrinking from cold and misery—the development of all their limbs and faculties checked. In one's prospect of society, it was certainly fair to consider that class by whose labor the distinguishing achievement of the century was being built. The sight of this slavery and exploitation outraged him, though his indignation was matched by his disgust at the human stupidity that let itself be thus imposed on. He was fascinated and repelled by the fact that, save for its wastefulness and squalor, this Irish shanty life perversely resembled the efficient simplification he was after. He turned with relief to thought of the primitive Indians, whose way of existence represented a healthier adjustment. Yet the endurance of these Irish won his admiration—especially the cheerful courage of the children, facing this new America as the earlier pioneers had faced it.

Frequently—almost daily—Thoreau visited the town, using the railroad tracks as the shortest way. The men on the freight trains waved as to an old acquaintance. And Henry liked to watch the laden cars pass, through storm and snow, a symbol of man's enterprise and adventurous spirit. In town, he called at the new house his father and he had built. He came drawn by a wish to see his family and by a typically Yankee taste for apple pies, much to his mother's pleasure, who baked them with a flavoring of herbs that was her special secret.

On request, he lectured, without pay, to the Lyceum—his subjects, the trip on the rivers, or his life in the woods. Almost daily he wrote in his journal—on his discoveries, on books, on his adventures with people, on life and its purpose. Detached somewhat from the village, he could study it the better. Though so intense an individualist himself, Thoreau favored the ideal of communal living as in keeping with the spirit of America. But this limping actuality, he condemned. Why should a village stop short at a pedagogue, a parson, a sexton, a parish library, and three selectmen, because our pilgrim forefathers got through a cold winter once on a bleak rock with these? "It is time that villages were universities, and their elder inhabitants the fellows of universities, with leisure—if they are, indeed, so well off—to pursue liberal studies the rest of their lives." Let us have noble villages of men, Thoreau pleaded. "If it is necessary, omit one bridge over the river, go round a little there, and throw one arch at least over the darker gulf of ignorance which surrounds us."

In addition to his far travels in Concord, he made two excursions: one to Maine, the other a venture into the realms of State, which ended in prison. The trip to Maine, where he climbed Katahdin, was the first of three to the north woods. He greatly enjoyed brief excursions from Concord—to Cape Cod; to Fire Island; to Canada; to see Walt Whitman in Brooklyn. On each, he kept careful records, storing up materials for future books. The trip to prison in 1846 followed the road of immediate circumstance. Negro slavery outraged Thoreau's every principle. His friends deplored it too, but most did little about it. Not so he and his family. They sheltered runaways at home, and at Walden he had already harbored one fugitive on the way to Canada. As he watched the conduct of the nation, it seemed to him that daily the slave power became more arrogant and grasping. The North, still greedy, though glutted by profits spun from cotton grown by the black man, became daily more pusillanimous and appeasing. His quarrel, he saw, was not with far-off foes but with those hundred thousand merchants and farmers, near home, who though declaring themselves opposed had their hands in their pockets, doing nothing. For himself, he was more than ever conscious of his obligation to act at any time as he thought was right. Here was a moment when truth and the Constitution were in conflict. When war broke out with Mexico during Thoreau's second summer at Walden, he saw it as an iniquitous plot by the slavery interests to control more votes through the acquisition of Texas. If government acted without principle, he must refuse it his allegiance. So he would not pay his tax.

His friend Sam Staples, the constable, did not wish to lock him up. "I'll pay your tax, Henry, if you're hard up." But Henry explained his one-man revolution. That night, much to Thoreau's disgust, someone short-circuited his protest by paying. Nothing could be done about it, so he returned to the pond. But his night in jail had developed further his ideas on the relation of the individual to the State.

At Walden he was completing, from his journals and lectures on the subject, the physical and spiritual history of the excursion on the rivers which he had taken with his brother John. He finished an essay on Carlyle and saw it printed in *Graham's Magazine*. He entertained visitors. On Sundays, some-times half a dozen railroad construction engineers—healthy, sturdy workers in clean, white shirts—would drop in for a neighborly talk.

Sometimes the hut and little hillock above the cove was lively with chil-dren—little Hosmers, little Alcott girls, who drifted out as naturally as a breeze from the village. Ellery Channing also frequently called. Henry was as close to his aim, thought Channing, as the bark of a tree. Emerson came, and Alcott. He had never known a man, thought Alcott, so thoroughly of the country. He seemed one with things, of Nature's essence and core, knit of strong timbers, most like a wood and its inhabitants. One evening, Henry read him some passages from the rivers manuscript. Fragrant with the life of New England woods and streams, Alcott found it, purely American. It could have been written nowhere else in the world, yet it profited by its author's wide knowledge of other men's books. It should become popular, Alcott decided, "winning at once the reader's fancy and his heart, inspir-ing a natural piety for nature and natural things, as surprising as it is refreshing."

Most works of major importance have been gestated with the aid of more than average love, sorrow, hate, or other emotion—experienced singly or in combination. Because to more than a usual degree what Thoreau wrote came out of how he lived, it was bound to be so with the *Week*; would be so with

Walden—though their backgrounds demanded and received a serenity of spirit which testifies to the power of creative sublimation.

Outwardly Henry's trip with his brother seems as tranquil as the riverways it followed in 1839. Inwardly there was emotion which, in recollection, was to lend beauty and strength to the writing. Henry could not jot down a single word about the excursion without the recollection that John, a year later, was dead. And thought of that loss, in itself still an anguish, was made even more poignant by the curious fact that when the brothers set out on the river, each was in love with the same girl, though probably neither ever really discussed with the other this disturbing complexity.

The girl was Ellen Sewall, daughter of a prominent, conservative New England family. She had come briefly to Concord on a visit. It is clear that she liked both boys, with whom she walked or went boating. John was the first to propose, but was rejected—Ellen probably not certain of her feelings and mindful of family misgivings. Henry, thus given his chance, at last tested his fortunes. "There is no remedy for love but to love more," he wrote in his journal, but so great was his regard for the emotion, and on so high a plane, that he expected the sensitive though altogether normal Ellen to recognize his love without his telling her. "Love is the profoundest of secrets. Divulged, even to the beloved, it is no longer Love." But the realistic acuteness of his feeling forced him at last below his transcendental level—what had begun so idyllically had become confused, painful, and needed resolving. So he proposed by letter, with little expectation, apparently, that she would take him. There is testimony in support of the notion that Ellen found it difficult to turn Henry down. And thus the affair ended. Then his brother died. At Walden, some four years later, Thoreau as he wrote lived over his feelings.

Had Ellen accepted him, it might have proved very embarrassing. Marriage, he must have seen, would have demanded compromise with his ideas, and compromise had no place in Henry's make-up. But Ellen Sewall had played her unconscious part in shaping the writer and thinker. Immediate result of this love affair was his charming poem, "To the Maiden in the East." Deferred result was his philosophy of love and friendship. After the *Week* was finished, he added to it an essay—one of the fine things in it—setting forth his idealized, spiritual conception of the affinity of friend with friend and the high, impossible requirements of love.

On September 6, 1847, after two years, two months, and two days at the pond, Thoreau left it. His friend Emerson was going abroad to lecture, and wished Henry to look after the household. That was one reason, but of course there were others, though Henry himself was not sure he could name them. He was fond of Lydian Emerson, whom he called a "mother-sister."

With Ellen Sewall, she was a factor in shaping his transcendental, Platonic philosophy of friendship. He had other lives to live; there was more day to dawn.

At the pond, he had indeed traveled far, through time and geography. With Captain John Smith, William Bradford, Josselyn, and other chroniclers, he had visited a wilder, fresher America and talked with Concord's first settlers. He had conversed with the priests of Brahma and Vishnu and Indra in temples on the sacred banks of the Ganges. He had lived closer than ever to nature. He had added to his oneness and integrity of spirit. Practically, without that stay by the cove, there would have been no *Walden,* and very possibly no *Week.* Had Thoreau lived as other men expected him to, he would not have been Thoreau, and the world would have lacked his books.

Because his mind and his journals were full of it, he wrote out and delivered a lecture, "Civil Disobedience," first given under the title of "Resistance to Civil Government," protesting against the cowardice of people who would not deny their government when it sinned against justice and eternal law. Conscience, even of the minority, must decide what is right or wrong.

5

Having finished revising the *Week,* Thoreau was seeking a publisher. Forgetful that originality has a dubious commercial value, his friends, sure that the book would find a ready market, could not understand the delay. On his travels in Britain, Emerson was full of praise for author and manuscript. "Pastoral as Isaak Walton, spicy as flagroot, broad and deep as Menu." Yet all this enthusiasm persuaded no publisher to bring the book out at his own risk.

Thoreau had waited long enough. By concentrating on the manufacture of pencils, he could meet the expense. Early in the summer of 1849, one thousand copies of the *Week* were printed. But the so-called publisher, being promised his money, made little effort to carry the book to the reader. Few critical journals noticed its existence. Only two reviews of any importance appeared. Horace Greeley carried a notice in the *Tribune*; in the *Massachusetts Quarterly Review,* James Russell Lowell, well on the way toward fame as a critic, gave the book a well meant, patronizing boost. He had obviously read with pleasure the account of the actual excursion, though he complained he had thought himself bid to a river party, and not to be preached at. Nevertheless he conceded that the writer was both a wise man and a poet.

It was not the first time Lowell had referred to Thoreau. In the witty *Fable for Critics,* he had dressed up the discovery that first had struck him when, a bored, sophisticated Harvard senior rusticated at Concord, he noticed that Thoreau seemed to be picking up the windfalls in Emerson's orchard. There had been justification for the suspicion then. Full of admiration for Emerson's *Nature,* which was contributing life and strength to his creed, recognizing his kinship with Emerson, appreciating his friendship, Thoreau, like many able young men still groping their way, quite unconsciously and naturally followed Emerson's light. But in maturity Thoreau was nobody's man but his own. Emerson himself was always surprised and hurt when anyone failed to perceive this.

The *Tribune* review, by George Ripley, might have given the *Week* a further boost, for the critic had written with that objective. But as a former Unitarian minister, though a liberal, Ripley was offended by what he called Thoreau's adherence to the "dubious and dangerous school" of the transcendentalists, and his "misplaced Pantheistic attack on the Christian Faith." In the nineteenth century, such a charge was sure to warn many away. It is hardly surprising that Thoreau's first book fell stillborn from the press. Of the thousand copies printed, most were presently returned to the author as unsalable. Close to one hundred he gave away.

At Emerson's suggestion, one copy had gone to a young Englishman to whom he had spoken of Thoreau's uncompromising life—James Anthony Froude, Fellow of Exeter College, Oxford, earnest, hard-pressed author of the reviled *Nemesis of Faith,* that "wild protest against all authority, Divine and human." "When I think of what you are—of what you have done as well as what you have written," wrote Froude, "I have the right to tell you that there is no man living upon this earth at present whose friendship or whose notice I value more than yours." Obviously not just for a book about a short excursion; from Thoreau, Froude drew strength to stand by his guns.

A Week on the Concord and Merrimack Rivers has for its architectural framework a scheme of seven chapters, one for each day. Though the trip lasted considerably longer, Thoreau's artistic judgment caused him to condense the itinerary. Nor did it suit the author's purpose to admit only observations made on the actual journey. He dipped into the journals both before and after, and drew on his work in the *Dial.* Most of his comments on the Hindu scriptures had entered his thinking later—in Emerson's library and at Walden. The book's numerous digressions—like the essay on friendship—are inserted with an unequal skill, so that Lowell's complaint that collisions with them were like bumping into snags on the river can be justified. Yet, as Lowell admitted, one would hate to miss many. With an exuberance not sufficiently controlled, Thoreau poured into his account the stream of his reading—more than three hundred references and quotations—nearly swamping his little boat. There is no denying that the *Week* is bookish, for Thoreau had not solved the problem of the artistic use of his reading, a charge that cannot be leveled at *Walden*. Yet even in the *Week*, what Thoreau read and the journey he is describing blend with the river's flow. A first venture, in which the author goes beyond basic purposes and patterns, the book inevitably displays a certain lack of know-how. It is easy to contend that the *Week*, hung together on the simplest of schemes, loses through its discursiveness any claim to artistic unity. Yet with equal validity, it can be argued that the leisurely and discursive current suggests the very spirit of Concord River, which for Thoreau and Emerson alike served as a symbol of the invisible stream that bears life on. Day slips into dreamy August day from morning to sunset, as many of the topics give the illusion of fitting the varied scene. The ending brings definite terminus. September sharpness has driven off summer's drowse, and tonight there may be frost.

The manuscript of *Walden*, Thoreau's maturest record of his life and thinking, was ready for printing as the first book appeared; but, chilled by the reception of the *Week*, no publisher would now touch it. Henry had to wait. Yet the mental and emotional incentives that created *Walden* were the guarantors of its ultimate success. Henry's devoted love of life at the pond and in Concord township, his intense religious feeling for nature (on the alert for the God behind it), his protest at the waste of life through misdirection by the code of the mercantile system, his feeling for his friends, his interest in men—all this and more enter into *Walden*. "We cannot write well or truly but what we write with gusto," he noted. "The body, the senses, must conspire with the mind." Thoreau considered no pains wasted to achieve excellence, nor resented the labor which writing cost him. His journals were the broad fields where he seeded his books, which grew to maturity at last after infinite cultivation. In composing, he profited by what he had learned of conciseness from the Greeks; but he used also his knowledge that the raciest, shrewdest, most compressed, typically American language was that spoken by farmer-friends like George Minott and Edmund Hosmer.

Thoreau's intuitional process of thinking led to the minting of individual sentences. But these often came to him in a form not yet finished for printing, nor yet perfect for apprehension, and he would copy them over and over, shaping them, thrusting them this way and that, gathering them together, finally fitting them into his plan and texture. Before *Walden* was ready for the press, he had scribbled quantities of work sheets. Several times he laboriously recopied most of the sections of the first draft.

Through the five years that *Walden*, like a chrysalis, lay dormant, Thoreau hovered over it, alert for a fault in even the most insignificant word. Meanwhile, he continued making pencils to pay for the *Week*, and, for what little extra money he needed, he practiced surveying because he enjoyed it, rather than dipping indiscriminately into his miscellany of manual skills—gardening, masonry, house painting, laying walls, carpentry. Even though Apollo was serving King Admetus, his tasks now took him into the groves and fields he loved. Daily he pursued his fluvial and terrestrial explorations.

Though nature was still religion to him, something of a change had taken place. Harvard's famous scientist, Louis Agassiz, author of the "Essay on Classification," had become his friend. Agassiz imparted to Thoreau his own absolute passion for minutely detailed description—which came naturally enough to Henry. But this approach, typical of nineteenth century science, brought no philosophy to release its practitioners from an ever-increasing rubble of facts. With Gray's *Manual of Botany* in his pocket, Henry sometimes lost sight of the God in the wood. In the early days of their friendship, Emerson had warned his friend never to find that mysterious night warbler which had always eluded his vigilance. Thoreau never made that mistake. But he now had less time for the quest, loading himself instead with a mass of detail—on depths of snow, on tree rings, and grasses, and lichens—facts he did not know quite what to do with.

Thoreau was seeing less of Emerson now than in the early days of their friendship. Forgetting Henry's manuscript of *Walden,* the gathering treasures of his journals, Emerson kept on hoping that his friend would complete the equation set forth in "The American Scholar": would prove himself the man of major action. Full of this wish, Emerson for the time being lost sight of the fact that Thoreau was making of himself a consummate artist, the native American master of expression Emerson was hoping would soon appear. Henry's prayer, in his poem of that title, that he might greatly disappoint his friends, seemed all too literally realized at that moment when Emerson confided to his journals: "Thoreau wants a little ambition in his mixture. Fault of this, instead of being the head of American engineers, he is captain of a huckleberry party."

Fortunately nature remained the common ground on which he and Emerson could meet. Like so many highly intellectual men, Emerson, though drawing inspiration from the woods, was awkward in them. When Henry took him for a walk, or boating, it was the rarest of privileges. There was not a fox or a crow or a partridge in Concord, Emerson believed, who knew the ground better than Henry. So Emerson followed as best he could his friend's striding figure, Thoreau clad in efficient homespun to brave the shrub-oak thickets: in his coat pocket, made big enough for the purpose, his notebook and pencil: under his arm, an old music book to press plants in. For birds, a spyglass; for flowers, a pocket microscope; for utility, a jackknife and twine. One must submit abjectly to such a guide, for the reward would be great.

Early in August, 1854, *Walden: or, Life in the Woods,* at last was published. A packed book, beautifully and economically written; among many things the autobiography of a mind and body in cooperation enjoying fullness of living. The structure of the whole is based on the framework of the author's life at the pond; its sense of time established by the passage of the seasons, through summer, autumn, and winter to triumphant spring—the year itself a symbol of man's lifetime. As in the *Week*, and with like purpose, Thoreau did not stick to the chronology of his stay, but considerably shortened it. Its many topics and reflections, arranged with a skillful eye on contrast or agreement, are joined with neatly managed links and transitions.

The worthy burghers of the village, oblivious to much else, fixed on Thoreau's economy and marveled that one could live so cheaply. They suspected the author's honesty, and looked for signs of cheating, recalling Mrs. Thoreau's delicious pies. This literal approach has spread far beyond the bounds of the village. Many readers, attracted by its easy concreteness, take too seriously Thoreau's account of his housekeeping, as though it represented the author's whole purpose, instead of being a diverting aside, a means to an end. In sly amusement, to catch literal minds, he attached sundry fractions to his figures, down to three-fourths of a cent, and succeeded all too well, sidetracking readers from greater matters. Channing, Emerson, Alcott, and other friends, knew better what to look for. Emerson must have loved the flashes of mystic writing, the beauty and truth of his friend's descriptions. "The little pond," he wrote, "sinks in these very days as tremulous at its human fame." Alcott, of course, fastened on Henry's social theories, and his account of the day he ran amuck against the State. "This man is the independent of independents—is, indeed, the sole signer of the Declaration, and a Revolution in himself—a more than '76—having got beyond the signing to the doing it out fully." And a boy wrote from Harvard College: "We who at Cambridge look towards Concord as a sort of Mecca for our pilgrimages, are glad to see that your last book finds such favor with the public."

Hesitant favor, however, with reviews still few and far between. Thoreau must wait for his fame. Ninety years after *Walden* was published, this appraisal could be written: "We read *Walden* as notes toward a philosophy of human happiness, with digressions into the movement of ponds, the flight of hawks, the patterns of snow, and the habits of owls. But it is most triumphant in the superb grace with which it joins the life of man to the life of nature. Its woodland jottings fold into its condemnation of greed and insincerity like the pauses of a prayer."

6

Shortly before *Walden* was published, government again ran amuck against Henry Thoreau. In 1850, the Fugitive Slave Law had been passed, turning Thoreau into a criminal, along with other like-minded New Englanders, since like them, he refused to comply with its prohibition against aiding black men. In 1854, the *Walden* year, public opinion in town meeting was strong enough to call for a discussion of the slave power. But when Henry showed up to speak on the duty of Massachusetts, he found the meeting concerned only with what was happening in distant Nebraska. On Independence Day, however, at Framingham—succinctly, jarringly, with the fearlessness habitual to him when roused by a moral concern—he gave the speech, declared out of order at Concord, attacking the complacency and complicity of Massachusetts. Only conscience and principle concerned him—to the disgust and despair of the practical-minded.

Three years later, when John Brown visited Concord, Thoreau met a man ready to act his belief. When Brown was condemned to hang for the raid at Harpers Ferry, Thoreau at once dared to defend him. The local Abolitionist Committee, the committee of the newly born Republican Party, his closest friends even, sent word it was premature. "I did not send to you for advice, but to announce that I am to speak"—and he did so, first at Concord, then at Boston. Because of this initial push, Henry Thoreau must be acknowledged one of the movers when Massachusetts finally shifted to an antislavery stand.

While this question was fevering his mind, it was hard for Thoreau to recall that wood ducks still dived in the Assabet. It was an actual effort to remember he had other lives to live, with further essays and possibly books to be written. In these final years, another barrier was his sense of obligation to his family. When his father died, Henry took over John Thoreau's business, shifted from the manufacture of pencils to the more profitable grinding of graphite. Yet the occasional essays continued: "Ktaadn," an account of his first trip to Maine, printed in the *Union Magazine*; in *Putnam's,* a description of his visits to Cape Cod. And, at James Russell Lowell's request, he was preparing for the new *Atlantic* the story of his second Maine-woods journey, "Chesuncook." It was to appear, during 1858, in the June, July, and August issues.

When Thoreau opened the July number, he was amazed to discover that Lowell had cut out from a passage describing a pine tree one sentence: "It is as immortal as I am, and perchance will go to as high a heaven, there to tower above me still." Thoreau had met with editorial tampering before, but not of this particular sort. Lowell had struck into Thoreau's very spirit. Hawthorne once jokingly remarked that Henry prided himself on coming nearer the heart of a pine tree than any other human being. But it is only needful to recall his love of the Hindu Scriptures to realize this was not just a matter for jesting. "I do not ask anybody to adopt my opinions," wrote Thoreau, "but I do expect that when they ask for them to print, they will print them, or obtain my consent to their alteration, or omission." This deletion seemed to imply that he could be hired to suppress his ideas. "I am not writing to be associated in any way, unnecessarily, with parties who will confess themselves so bigoted and timid as this implies." Was this the avowed policy of the *Atlantic*? The Editor never replied.

During Lowell's tenure, Thoreau sent no further essays. But when James T. Fields took over, and asked for more, he sent them—"Walking," "Autumnal Tints," and "Wild Apples." But Thoreau, correcting the proof of the first one, was a very sick man, destined never to see it in final print. Consumption, the scourge of his family, had at last struck him down—its attack postponed perhaps by his outdoor life, then aided by a heedless exposure; perhaps also by the unhealthy, dust-filled atmosphere of the graphite shop.

He had just returned from a trip to Minnesota made in quest of health and because the West always attracted him. By winter's end, he lay dying. Even in this final confinement, the outdoorsman remained serene. He was drawing up a list of what he had written. He was setting his journals in order. He was enjoying his friends. The porcupine quills that had guarded his independence were no longer needed. Beneath was his essential kindliness. Perhaps his one sorrow was the civil strife that was bleeding his country; while it lasted, he said, he could never get well.

He had grown to be admired and revered by many of his townsmen who had at first known him only as an oddity. Sam Staples remarked he had never seen a man dying in so much pleasure and peace. His neighbor, Reverend Grindall Reynolds, found him working over a manuscript. Thoreau looked up cheerfully, and whispered, for his voice was nearly gone, "You know it's respectable to leave an estate to one's friends."

"Henry, have you made your peace with God?" asked his pious Aunt Maria. "Why, Aunt, I didn't know we had ever quarreled!" On May 6, 1862, at nine A.M.—Henry always liked best the morning—he died in the forty-fourth year, ninth month, and twenty-fourth day of his living.

Soon after, Emerson wrote a brief biography of him—one of the finest things of its sort in the language. As for Alcott, he could hardly bring himself to realize that this oldest inhabitant of the planet had not chosen to stay and see it dismissed into Chaos—had instead slipped so quietly away from the spaces and times he had adorned with the truth of his genius. Eagerly Alcott had awaited one final work, a sort of all-inclusive "Atlas of Concord." But, had time and strength been granted, the book which Thoreau might more probably have written would have had the American Indian for its subject. In the year of his death his mind had been full of this topic. George William Curtis had seen him for the last time in the autumn of his final illness. "His conversation fell upon the Indians of this country, of our obligations to them, and our ingratitude. It was by far the best talk about Indians I have ever heard or read; and somewhere among his papers, it is to be hoped, some monument of his knowledge of them and regard for them survives." It does— but in amorphous form.

7

After Thoreau's death, further books, compiled from his periodical writings and from his journal, were brought out by his friends. The first of these was *Excursions,* in 1863, made up of such pieces as Henry's sister Sophia could readily collect. The volume included "Walking"—perhaps the finest brief statement of what he lived for—from the *Atlantic,* and the much earlier "Natural History of Massachusetts" and "A Winter Walk" from the *Dial.* In it also, among other things, appeared "The Succession of Forest Trees," a final lecture given before the Middlesex Agricultural Society. Here Thoreau set forth the results of his investigation into silviculture. Though written in his own fashion, it prompted the chairman for the day, George Boutwell, Governor of Massachusetts, to congratulate the audience on having heard an address so plain and practical.

In 1864 *The Maine Woods* appeared, bringing together Thoreau's accounts of his three expeditions into New England's northland. Not really a book, nor in the form in which Thoreau might finally have cast his material; yet here at its finest is Thoreau's zest for outdoor adventure and delight in it—save for hunting, which, as a sport, he regarded as a degradation to the human spirit. Here is his admiration for men of the wilderness like Joe Polis, the Indian guide; for Uncle George McCauslin and Tom Fowler, rivermen and pioneers, as native to the Penobscot as a brace of salmon. Because of its objectives, the book is not discursive like the *Week.* While less provocative or inspiring, it contains fewer pitfalls for the uninitiated. Henry wished it to be of help to campers. *The Maine Woods* makes excellent reading for men of action and for boys getting their earliest taste of Thoreau.

Cape Cod (1865) brought together what he had written on this subject. Unlike *The Maine Woods,* this book, departing from literal fact, has an architectural plan; but, like his travel literature in general, it is a reporter's record rather than an artist's finished product. The *Week,* thanks to the time granted at Walden, is the only one of Thoreau's excursions which escapes the limits of observant narrative. For his rudimentary scheme, Thoreau has used the record of his first trip to Cape Cod as his outline, working it into his later ventures. More than anything else he wrote, *Cape Cod* explores people along with the land and ocean. There is a warmth, a humor, a sympathetic understanding which keeps it a favorite with many readers.

Letters to Various Persons, collected and edited by Emerson, was also issued in 1865.

Thoreau, who had published only two books during his lifetime, was becoming an established author, with a lengthening list of works on each successive title page. Yet, before the next appeared, a check occurred in the march toward fame foreseen by Emerson and Alcott. In 1865, James Russell Lowell said his final say about Thoreau and the transcendental group with which he linked him. As Lowell ranked high, what he wrote carried weight. His *obiter dicta,* covering eleven pages in the influential *North American Review,* bear only minor resemblance to the opinions advanced, sixteen years earlier, in his review of the *Week.* Praise of Thoreau's artistry remains; little else. Lowell is perhaps the most intelligent commentator who chose to take very seriously Thoreau's "experiment" at Walden, looking eagerly for cheating and failure. He found Thoreau "a man with so high a conceit of himself that he accepted without questioning, and insisted on our accepting, his defects and weaknesses of character as virtues and powers peculiar to himself." Here, be it said, the critic exercises the age-old privilege of unfamiliarity with what his victim had actually written. Thoreau was indolent, continues Lowell, and excused his laziness by holding the normal activities of man unworthy. But then, Lowell had never tried to match strides with Thoreau in the woods, had never carried his surveyor's chain for him nor perambulated the bounds of Concord, had never laid walls, nor ground graphite, had not written *Walden* or the *Week,* nor seen the accumulated journals. Thoreau's solitary life, Lowell contended—having never joined the groups that gathered even at the Walden hut—cut him off so completely from men as to disqualify him as an observer of them. Thoreau, said Lowell, attacked success—as Lowell understood that word—because he lacked the qualities to achieve it. Selfish, and doing no man any good—the critic added—Thoreau lived for himself alone. But Lowell could not know about the day when a skinflint farmer claimed the prize which an Irish laborer in his employ had won, in the spading match, and Henry made up a purse to right this injustice, and burned the Yankee's ears with his blistering comments. How could Lowell know what strength Thoreau had lent to fighters in the battle, from James Anthony Froude in England to the Harvard undergraduates who acknowledged themselves heartened by what he wrote?

Alcott, who liked Lowell, was grieved by this review. Lowell, he felt, should never have written it—Thoreau and his class were so wide of his range and perception. "There is truth at the root of his estimates, and just enough to give credibility to them; but Henry's merits will survive all disparaging criticism, and justify his life and writings to unprejudiced minds." Yet, as Alcott foresaw, Lowell's strictures cannot be so readily dismissed.

There is a legitimacy about them. Thoreau stamped on the corns of worthy, public-spirited, philanthropic, hard-working, respectable men—men highly successful by average standards. He still does so. Lowell has become the spokesman for such as these. To realists, Thoreau's position will never make sense. He had a quixotic disregard for facts as they are in aiming for the right as it should be. "Either this man is joking or he's too impossible for words," scribbles one twentieth century student on the margins of a college library's copy of "Civil Disobedience." "But you don't grasp what he's driving at!!" scrawls another. Both protest and answer deserve to be weighed.

Thoreau's work kept coming out. In 1866, *A Yankee in Canada*—three chapters of observations first printed in *Putnam's*; the rest of the volume a catchall for such social and political essays as "Civil Disobedience," "Slavery in Massachusetts," and "A Plea for Captain John Brown." In it also is "Life Without Principle," given as a lecture in 1854. Only life lived *with* principle and purpose, Thoreau insisted, was worth living. Next, the manuscript journals: *Early Spring in Massachusetts* (1881), *Summer* (1884), *Winter* (1888), and *Autumn* (1892)—each book made up of appropriate selections from Thoreau's comments on nature, irrespective of the year in which written. Six years after the turn of the century, appeared a collected edition which included the journals in their chronological sequence. The first, ten-volume edition of the *Works* alone had preceded this issue by fifteen years. And in 1895, about half his verses were published under the title of *Poems of Nature*. A collection of "every available piece" of his verse appeared in 1943.

Both in composition and in reception, Thoreau's poetry has had a checkered career. Because of its unevenness, because his friends, when their first enthusiasm faded, persuaded him that prose was his higher medium, his verse had been relegated to a place of little importance. But the second quarter of the twentieth century has witnessed a revival. Thoreau's poetry, say its recent advocates, belongs not with the past but with the present—has no kinship, in its conscious and militant heterodoxy, with standard patterns such as Whittier, Longfellow, Bryant, and Lowell established. "Thoreau, like Emily Dickinson, . . . anticipates the bold symbolism, airy impressionism, stringent realism, and restless inconsistencies of twentieth-century poetry." Like these scholar poets, he too was searching for suggestions from all schools and times which he approved of—among them the classics, Chaucer's age, Ben Jonson's, and that of the seventeenth century metaphysicals, right down to Emerson's terse and gnomic didacticism. From the Greeks, of course, comes the sense of form so strikingly in evidence in "Smoke," perhaps his finest poem. Yet he loved to experiment with meters, searching for those most fitted to his moods.

When Emerson remarked that Thoreau's biography was in his verses, he meant, of course, his inner history. Thoreau's abrupt, rugged, image-crowded verse sprang from his effort to express the truth of a moment. Certainly, in the brief period during which he wrote it, Thoreau was deeply in earnest over his poetry. It is valid to argue that much of it is better than his own day supposed; that had not Emerson's advice turned him from it, Thoreau's poetry might have attained further importance. As it is, many readers will probably prefer to agree with Emerson's dictum: "The gold does not yet flow pure, but is drossy and crude. The thyme and marjoram are not yet made into honey."

With most of his work published, Thoreau's stature kept increasing through the years. His fame has grown like that heap of stones which marks where his cabin stood—a cairn begun from a single pebble picked up by Alcott at the margin of the pond, then added to by countless pilgrims from many lands. By dedicating his genius with such entire love—as Emerson put it—to the fields and hills and waters of his native town, Thoreau has proved them universal. Gone full-circle at the farthest Ganges, his Yankee words, blending even with the East, helped set up passive resistance. Translated into many tongues, his speech has reached many people. Scandinavians and Germans can read *Walden*; Czechoslovakians, Hollanders, Frenchmen, Russians, and Japanese. In England, toward the turn of the century, British liberals were carrying *Walden* in their pockets, as a spiritual sword and buckler against materialism and imperialistic sway. Indeed Thoreau must be held partly responsible for the revolt, as much social as political, of the British Labor Party. Under the title of *Life and Friendship,* pertinent selections from his writings were printed in London, to form a lay bible for its members—a pulp-paper edition cheap enough to put no great strain on the purses of such young pioneers as George Bernard Shaw, Beatrice and Sidney Webb, Edward Carpenter, and Ramsay MacDonald. Other Englishmen, of a somewhat different stamp, also discovered *Walden*. "The one golden book in any century of best books," wrote W. H. Hudson.

In Russia, during the Tsarist days, young revolutionaries found in Thoreau strength for endurance. And, in Europe and America, Thoreau speaks to a twentieth century sure to be known as the age of critical battle between the State and man's private integrity. He remains a David armed and ready to fight for himself and all men whenever government threatens to become a tyrant Goliath. Men often read meanings into classic writings which the authors could not possibly have intended—one explanation why, in a changing world, such books last. Thoreau himself countenances the practice when he advocates "sentences which suggest as many things and are as durable as a Roman aqueduct." So there is justification for reading into his attack on mercantilism, and into his one-man revolution against his government, a plea for the reappraisal of life's values in the modern industrial state, and a ringing challenge to totalitarianism. How the integrity of the individual is to be preserved within the structure of our nationalistic, intermeshed, highly mechanized, contradictory world is the twentieth century's problem, not Henry Thoreau's. But he will always speak to those who passionately love the elusive ideal of liberty; will remain "one of the prophets of that struggle for moral independence that is the deepest and most permanent of American conflicts."

To those thinkers who insist on the worth of the common man, Thoreau has become something of a hero. "When, in some obscure country town," he wrote, "the farmers come together to a special town meeting, to express their opinion on some subject which is vexing the land, that, I think, is the true Congress, and the most respectable one that is ever assembled in the United States."

8

How Thoreau lived and what he lived for is indeed the gist of all his writing—all the more reason for the reader to turn to the books themselves. Thoreau's style at its best is vigorous, terse, pungent; often epigrammatic, often racy and even colloquial, yet at the fit moment capable of a soaring beauty. Lover of spicy mountain blueberries, he had the knack of conveying that flavor to his prose. Sometimes his forcefulness betrayed him into outrageous paradox and overstatement, but he learned control of this quality as he grew older, till it became one source of his excellence. He had a remarkable gift for metaphor, and aimed, through pictures, to suggest thinking. He liked to deal in quaint, arresting comparisons, as when he spoke of a dog with a noseful of porcupine quills as the Arnold Winkelried of its race. He loved Indian names, and liked to work them, when he could, into his classic prose with a startling yet symphonious effect, like wildflowers decorating an urn in a Greek temple. In plebeian passages he was not above puns, rhymes within sentences, and other lighthearted tricks, and he was fond of alliteration, which he used for its music with a subtle skill. He spoke of the whitethroat's whistle as a wiry sound. Such was the wealth of his truth, declared Emerson, that it was not worth his while to use words in vain.

Much that Thoreau wrote found its first expression in casual speech. Leaning against a fence and discoursing of the shortness of time since the supposed creation, he remarked to a friend, "Why, sixty old women like Nabby Kettle"—an ancient crone in the village—"taking hold of hands, would span the whole of it." This he repeated later in the *Week*, adding, "a respectable tea-party merely—whose gossip would be Universal History." Sentences like these in his journals, pieced together and filled out with descriptive and discursive matter, he gathered for his lectures. These frequently became essays, and then books. Like Emerson he was an intuitive thinker, and his best statements are in the sentences his craftsmanship built to hold them. Yet it does not do to underestimate his power with longer passages. In his best paragraphs, it would seem as if he had taken the hermit thrush as his model. Their intricate phrasings and rhythms flow with the pure and spiritual beauty of its song, and with its perfect unity.

Though Thoreau did not read fiction, because he disliked it, the portraits of people scattered through his work are as three-dimensional as reality itself. To see them one need but read what he has to say of Therien, the woodchopper, of one-eyed Goodwin shooting muskrats from his flat-bottomed skiff, of Hugh Quoil, soldier of Wellington, drinking himself to death, an outcast in Concord. When he wished to, he could tell a story straight, with an arrowy directness, giving immediacy through the present tense—taking the reader with him.

Thoreau's stature as a critic of literature has steadily grown. "As good as anything ever written upon the subject," G. W. Curtis called the chapter on reading in *Walden*. "Books must be read as deliberately and reservedly as they were written," wrote Thoreau, and this attitude became habitual practice. Some of his enthusiasms suffer through his love of paradox, but the initiated can make their own adjustments. Characteristically, he is reported to have carried Whitman's *Leaves of Grass* around Concord "like a red flag," finding it "very brave and American"; and though he made the deductions he deemed necessary, he was, with Emerson, among the first to appreciate the genius of the new poet. Could he have arranged them, his comments on poetry would have made a significant essay. His critical articles are informative, analytical, and provocative. His essay on Carlyle is a clear-headed appraisal; what he says is still good after a hundred years. Furthermore, it contains some of the most perspicacious remarks on style to be found in American writing. His more occasional comments on books and reading are scattered like seasoning throughout his works.

As his life story reveals, Thoreau's absorption in nature began gradually, through a period of imperfect knowledge, till, at Concord, it developed into a religion, with the visible world as a symbol of the invisible. The force of this attitude, so fundamental to his thinking and feeling, never really weakened till toward the end, under the guidance of such classificationists as Agassiz and Gray—and here is a typically Thoreauvian inconsistency—he was led into the dry deserts of nineteenth century science. These deserts were probably never really dull to him, but they were wide enough to prevent his reaching that fruitful region in which scientists, seeking more significant answers than facts, at last allow the validity of intuition.

Yet the latter period of his observing is far from wasted. Particularly in one department of geographic exploration, Thoreau is a discoverer rather than just a pioneer. His detailed study of the behavior of natural bodies of water was a first move toward a region of scientific investigation which has not yet reached its full development. Very indirectly, the inhabitants of the Mississippi watershed owe a debt to Thoreau.

The purpose of the first editor of Thoreau's journals helped fix more firmly the American belief that his major contribution was as a naturalist. It has taken fifty years or so to modify that notion. Strictly regarded, Thoreau remains the expert amateur of nature. John Burroughs described him as so much more than a naturalist merely that he is to be thought of as a naturalist only in the largest sense. He had the philosopher's perception of identity, declared Emerson; "he referred every minute fact to cosmical laws." Sometimes, in a blinding flash or quiet revelation, his approach to comprehension fashioned mystical passages like that, in "Chesuncook," on the pine tree.

"I heartily accept the motto, 'That government is best which governs least,'" Thoreau wrote in "Civil Disobedience." Like many Americans, he noticed government mainly in times of crisis, and, like his fellow Americans, he blamed it for its iniquities. But those who hold that his political doctrine is mere anarchy do not analyze his import. His attacks on government are Thoreau keeping himself and mankind at the topmost bent, refusing compromise for expediency, demanding and expecting the noblest and best. "Seen from a lower point of view, the Constitution, with all its faults, is very good; the law and the courts are very respectable; even this State and this American government are, in many respects, very admirable, and rare things, to be thankful for, such as a great many have described them; but seen from a point of view a little higher, they are what I have described them; seen from a higher still, and the highest, who shall say what they are, or that they are worth looking at or thinking of at all?" Though he will remain the representative American in his insistence on the individual's right to self-determination, he never denied the value of enlightened communal action. He never gave up hope. The muck of man's imperfect institutions, his wars and outrages against himself, Thoreau compared to the mud at the bottom of Concord River; the water-lily became his symbol for man's emergence.

His quixotic protest against flogging, which terminated his two weeks' tenure as grammar-school instructor, has become unnecessarily famous. Much more significant is his statement that an experiment performed before the eyes of students, and with their active participation, is worth weeks of conventional teaching. As conducted by the Thoreau brothers, Concord Academy employed pioneering methods which the passage of a century has made common. Finally, he believed there should be no such thing as graduation, and held it a fault that in his day there was no adequate system for adult education.

Thoreau was among the first in America to recognize the rightness and validity of functional architecture, and, in *The Maine Woods,* he praised, as the most honest dwelling, the lumberman's log cabin. But he also foresaw the evil results that must inevitably follow what the lumberjack was hired to do. Written in a day when there still seemed no end to America's resources, this becomes a significant statement: "We shall be reduced to gnaw the very crust of the earth for nutriment." It would be worth while, he thought, in each village to appoint a committee to see that the beauty of the town receive no detriment. Highways must not be left narrow. "The road should be of ample width and adorned with trees expressly for the use of the traveller. There should be broad recesses in it, especially at springs and watering-places, where he can turn out and rest, or camp if he will." He believed that natural resources, like beneficial ideas, should be free as air; should belong to mankind inalienably.

For all these things, and others, Thoreau has become one of America's great. Yet among his various claims, perhaps his greatest value will remain his power to open magic casements on the verities of nature. As the lava flow of our material civilization licks up the natural beauty of earth, Thoreau's poetical, pictorial writing may become increasingly the greatest gift he bears. Each day brings its fresh discoveries, its wonder, which he delights to impart.

27. NATHANIEL HAWTHORNE

MEANWHILE, Nathaniel Hawthorne, endowed with a more earthy nature than Emerson and a more realistic mind than Thoreau, watched, not without misgivings, the divine madnesses of Concord. Toward the circle of aspiring young men at the feet of Emerson he was critical, and though he admired Thoreau's independence (together they had boated on the Concord River) he was aware in himself of no response to what he called the "wild, original strain" in this experimenter with life. In "The Celestial Railroad" he was to satirize the dreams of transcendentalism, and ·in *The Blithedale Romance* he was to delineate the follies of humanitarianism as he had witnessed them during his stay at Brook Farm. His boredom in the society of Bronson Alcott deepened in that of Margaret Fuller to active dislike. The celestial vagaries of Concord confirmed in him his own somewhat sardonic studies of a moral law which offered no millennia but only bitter proofs of its operation in the sufferings of human beings. He retreated hastily from Brook Farm; he never contributed to the *Dial*; and he remained silent in Emerson's study and at the meetings of the Saturday Club. That his writings as a whole aimed to refute or annotate the current gospels of self-reliance, the oversoul, intuition, and similar fantasies, no proof exists in his prefaces or in his fiction itself. Yet there in Concord he dwelt, a neighbor down the street, writing the romances which Emerson thought lacked "inside"; there in the midst of the transcendental storms he meditated quietly; he was silent, serene, almost quizzical. For he was, so he must have thought to himself, no prophet, no reformer, no diver into the God within him, even if he was himself in love with the invisible landscape.

Soon after Hawthorne's birth in 1804, circumstances intensified his innate Puritan characteristics: his analysis of the mind, his somber outlook on living, his tendency to withdraw from his fellows. Yet if, from the first, in the quiet household of his widowed mother at Salem, during a period of lameness which kept him out of sports, or throughout the summers in remote Raymond, Maine, he became increasingly introspective, he had few personal problems of mind or spirit. Already he was detached, and if the most characteristic paper in his juvenile magazine, the *Spectator,* concerned his own solitude, we must not conclude that melancholy had claimed him as its victim. Quite the contrary. During the four years at Bowdoin College (1821–1825) appeared that self-command which intimated that his ways of loneliness were the result of a positive choice. He had already learned to contemplate cheerfully subjects which other men as normal and healthy as he avoided. Unlike his classmate, the social, gregarious Longfellow, he was no prize winner in the curriculum; though he loved cards, wine, fishing, and shooting, his conviviality was distinctly limited, subordinate to a love of quiet. Yet these "accursed habits" of solitude, as he once called them, failed to make him unhappy. In them, as a matter of fact, lay the origins of his life of the intellect and spirit. Out of such habits, formed in the first twenty-one years of his life, were to be born Ethan Brand, Hester Prynne, Zenobia, and the other lonely children of his imagination.

This secret space in his mind, to which he ever afterward returned, and which sheltered him from the turmoil of contemporary America, had early become the center of his being. Though we cannot regard the meditative creations in his first fiction as accurate self-portraiture, it is demonstrable that he had devoted some of his early leisure to writing. He had already at Bowdoin, mentally at least, limned the college for the prose of *Fanshawe,* his first novel. There remained only one step to fix him in this course of life; and this he took on his return from Brunswick: he became a "Salemite." For, he said, "I felt it almost as a destiny to make Salem my home." The quiet streets, the lonely house, the necessity for solitude, and his innate passion for the written word, all counseled a procedure whose continuance for twelve long years has never been satisfactorily explained. Probably the reasons are not really mysterious: presumably, he had experienced no romantic disillusionment nor grief. Those eyes which Bayard Taylor said could flash fire, never viewed coldly men's lives in the busy world. Perhaps, as he wrote Longfellow later, he merely drifted into this role of recluse. Or perhaps—why not, if we think of his satisfaction in his later fame?—he meant in this Philistine America to glean the rewards of his painful solitude; namely, independence and literary success. At any rate, here he sat long in his "accustomed chamber," writing, revising, and burning the sketches and tales; perfecting his delicate craft of the symbol, of allegory, of the few themes and oft repeated character-types which were to haunt forever the minds of those who know New England.

When in 1837 he emerged from the chamber where his "fame was won," in his hand was his first published collection of prose, *Twice-Told Tales,* and primarily in his heart the image of Sophia Peabody, to whom he was married five years later, with enriching consequences to his personal life and to his writing. Neither his recognition as an author (by Poe, among others) nor his new, happy companionship in a solitude which he never really relinquished, altered his literary aims. He was, like his own Holgrave in *The House of the Seven Gables,* deepened and softened; but his broadening through associations with the workaday world as a measurer in the Boston Customhouse, as a laborer in the Brook Farm Community, and as a surveyor in the Salem Customhouse seems, in retrospect, illusory.

His daily world was real enough, of course. Few writers comprehended better the shallow objectives of the contemporary magazine; as contributor and editor, and in association with Samuel Goodrich ("the moralistic, sentimental Peter Parley"), he knew the quality of American readers. His long apprenticeship in fiction was served chiefly as a contributor of short pieces to magazines and annuals; this modified his theory of the romance and the novel and presumably influenced his techniques as a writer. By writing he earned his bread, even composing stories for boys and girls. He worked hard at Brook Farm, and in both customhouses, and he manifested a shrewd interest in local politics. Yet in spite of these concessions to everyday affairs, of an acquisitive strain in money matters and a fondness for a strong cigar or an oath, his thoughts were elsewhere. Dearer to him than these associations with the common man, in whom he was mildly interested, dearer even to him than his near-transcendentalist Sophia, who never quite entered the shadows of his darkest imaginations, dearer than all these, were his ancient vows in the lonely chamber. In 1849 he sat down and, using the craft he had learned in silence, wrote, hardly blotting a line; in four months he had finished *The Scarlet Letter.*

The mid-century mark and the two following years beheld the apogee of Hawthorne's art *(The Scarlet Letter, The House of the Seven Gables,* and *The Blithedale Romance,* as well as his best collection of tales); and the decade was rounded out by his exquisite, if rather tired, study of Puritanism in a Latin environment, *The Marble Faun* (1860). The lacuna of eight years in his formal writing we owe to a sudden dislocation in his New England life: his appointment by President Franklin Pierce to the American consulship in Liverpool, with a subsequent sojourn in Italy. Even during the English interlude Hawthorne's pen and notebooks were busy with writing fated to be posthumous: *Septimius Felton; The Dolliver Romance; The Ancestral Footstep;* and *Dr. Grimshawe's Secret.* Thus, unlike Irving, he never renounced his youthful dreams; the *English Notebooks* tell the story of his busy life but also of literary hopes deferred. Moreover, the salty vigor of this exegesis on England was an admirable substitute for a novel. As we read *The Marble Faun* and ponder over the lethargy of Hawthorne's last years, it is difficult to avoid the conclusion that in his speculations he had reached a baffling wall. Over and over in fragmentary first drafts he turned to the jejune symbols of spider and bloody footstep. Indeed, his sudden death, during a walking tour with Pierce in 1864, seemed a natural ending for a mind which could go no farther in the moral labyrinth it had entered a half-century earlier as a dreaming boy in Salem.

2

In any study of Hawthorne's art, his life story must be regarded as causative. Fixed from birth in his Puritan attitudes, he would, we may believe, have been Hawthorne had he lived for many years upon the *rive gauche* or the banks of the Mississippi. It was so in Rome; Italy failed to alter the underlying mechanisms of his Puritan mind. For he was completely integrated, until his fiftieth year, with the soil and spirit of a New England which had bred and indoctrinated his introspective forebears. He was not unlike Major William Hathorne, that "grave, bearded, sabled-cloaked and steeple-crowned progenitor,—who came so early [to America], with his Bible and his sword," or his ancestor Judge Hathorne, the persecutor of witches. Such antecedents continued to be a powerful influence in his character as a writer. We can understand New England without Hawthorne; yet Hawthorne without New England we cannot comprehend. She was literally of his blood and brain; her scenes and her people form the stuff of his romances, and his own forefathers revisit the upper shades in his pages. What he wrote of New England was not merely "local color"; rather it was the subconscious mind of the New England Hawthornes vouchsafed a voice in this unregenerate descendant of theirs.

Yes, it was the breath of his nostrils, this study of an invisible world, of whose existence he was in his way as firmly convinced as were Emerson and Thoreau. Refusing traffic with philosophic thought, both of the past and of his New England contemporaries, he clove his own path through the trackless realms of the moral life; his Puritan mind easily understood the introspective processes which made Emerson certain, Thoreau skeptical, and himself judicial concerning the meaning of life. That curiosity concerning the two fundamental relationships, of Man to God and Man to Man, which motivated the literature of New England, he shared, though his conclusions were neutral, inconclusive, even pessimistic. For he experienced with a peculiar intensity the transcendentalists' continuance of Jonathan Edwards' exploration of moral meanings. The light was the same; only the lens of Hawthorne's mind was different. Thus the spiritual questioning of his tales and novels far outweighed their ballast of New England history and background; it even subordinated his beautiful craftsmanship.

It was this memorable art of his which distinguished him from Emerson and Thoreau, an art which included his distillations of historical episodes into moods; soft color schemes of red, white, and black; rhythms of sentence and phrase which echo the harmony of his unified and reposeful life; symbols, sometimes inadequate and even absurd, but more often coefficients of the unseen moral laws which he was trying to communicate; and unforgettable case histories of men and women afflicted by guilt, or, as he called it, by "a stain upon the soul." Little of this he drew from books, apart from his beloved Bunyan, from Milton, or from Spenser, who inspired some of his allegory and even the name of one of his daughters, Una. From common incidents and from common men he wove his intricate web of the seemingly inevitable involutions of the moral pattern. Yes, except for an excusable contamination of the didactic in a few tales which he composed during his period of apprenticeship, he maintained toward all his laboratory researches into the human heart a singular detachment. His were grave and acute reflections upon the way in which the Puritan mind worked; it was, for almost the first time in American literary history, as the devoted Henry James was quick to see, the judgment of the artist upon familiar Puritan material. Thus he was akin to Poe; he anticipated James himself; and he was really the founder of the psychological novel in America.

This is a matter for mild marvel, this calm of Hawthorne amid the winds of literary doctrine. He seems to have been little affected by the conventions of the nineteenth century English novel; his indifference to the prevailing passion for the full, discursive narrative is particularly notable. In this sense, it may be argued that he never wrote what Dickens and Thackeray would have called a good story. In his beautiful letter of homage to Irving there is no trace of imitation, and his links with Charles Brockden Brown are tenuous; whatever he learned from the Gothic School he assimilated for his own precise objectives. Though different in nearly every other respect, he resembled Emerson in reading chiefly for confirmations of his own meditations: for example, his interest in the downfall of aspiring human beings through their higher natures found reassurance in Bunyan's compelling hint of the bypath to hell from the very gate of heaven. He was moved neither by the literary modes of the day nor by its criticism of his own aims. The pity recently bestowed upon him because his exposure to European culture was so belated; because, save for his sketchy intercourse with Herman Melville, fifteen years his junior, he worked alone without the give-and-take of literary peers; such pity for himself he never felt. Indeed, it may be questioned whether richer cultural influences than those of Salem and Concord would have altered either his themes or his art; these were predestinate, consecrated to his semiscientific study of the whorls of man's moral impulses.

"A most unmalleable man" he was, as he told his wife, thinking presumably of the concentration of his interests in his family, his work, and the dear lump of earth that he called New England. Yet, in a deeper sense he was, unlike Irving (or even Melville), unductile. He was a Toledo steel which bent, as in his sensibility during the writing of *The Marble Faun,* to an ancient culture, or suffered damascene ornamentation, as in his planned use of the Gothic plot in *The House of the Seven Gables*; but still steel he remained in his undeviating preoccupation with his quest for moral mysteries. This aim was the compass of his artistic life; this he followed unswervingly in his hundred-sixteen-odd tales and sketches and in his four great novels. Therefore we are not deceived by his indolence, his petulance, his intolerance of fools, or even by the deceptive softness of his prose. Our first artist in the novel had in him this vein of iron, this conscious dedication to the fulfillment of a few aesthetic-moral principles which so moved to admiration his disciple Henry James.

His is the record of a man pledged from youth to a special quest: the history, regardless of Hawthorne's provincial background, of the artistic mind. Modern scholarship has tried valiantly to right the balance, to show Hawthorne as a normal citizen of greedy, striving America. Some important readjustment of opinion has resulted: we understand better his interests in Brook Farm, the Civil War, or his own pocketbook. We certainly see him more clearly as a person, an enigmatic presence, in his dark cloak pacing the streets of Salem, but changed to robust flesh-and-blood. He was, we know, self-assured, sardonic, hardheaded. Such revaluations bring us closer to him as a man but only reaffirm the cryptic nature of his preoccupation. What was it? Sophia could not define what lay behind the veil, and his friends alluded to another Hawthorne hidden within the stalwart, outward man. He himself spoke of depths in his mind which he could neither fathom nor explain. In this transalpine region he heard the music, like Thoreau, of his own distant drummer. This intuition marked him out as a product of the New England Renaissance. In any case, no outward event in Hawthorne's biography is so important as this secret place in his mind of solitude and meditation; within this refuge, he drew the breath of life itself. When this failed him, he died.

3

The exact date of the composition of *Fanshawe* (1828), at once a culmination of Hawthorne's boyish experiments in writing and the beginning of his career as a romancer, is unknown. His later contemptuous destruction of all his amateurish work rendered this novelette—it contained only two hundred pages—a bibliographical rarity and helped to focus attention on its theme and character as a key to the origins and development of his early technique. Incidents in the awkwardly told story suggest Scott and the Gothic novel. The characters are thin and two-dimensioned, the dialogue pretentious; but a contemporary was right in declaring that in *Fanshawe* we may easily detect the weak and timid presence of all of Hawthorne's peculiar powers.

These powers were less apparent in young Hawthorne's style, which was still insecure, or in his use of plot, which was never distinguished, than in an instinctive predilection for certain basic character-types which were to reach fulfillment in a Phoebe, a Chillingworth, and a Dimmesdale. Indeed, in embryo, Phoebe, the sunny heroine of *The House of the Seven Gables,* as well as the villain of *The Scarlet Letter,* Chillingworth, and, in a lesser degree, the sullied idealist, Dimmesdale, are in this first novel. Had Ellen Langton, as has been asserted, a prototype beloved by Hawthorne in his youth, which endeared to him this type of woman, this antithesis of the sable Hester, Zenobia, and Miriam? Ellen is unmistakably the precursor of Phoebe, Priscilla, and Hilda. Another preliminary sketch is that of the "fiend-like" Butler, whose Satanism is probably derived from Hawthorne's persistent study of Milton. This crude anticipation of Roger Chillingworth confirms Hawthorne's early interest in the genus of the heartless villain, a type which he never succeeded in making altogether natural. In the end we are fascinated by the central character itself, an alloy of Byronic arrogance and Gothic gloom which Hawthorne spared his later characters. For, akin to Dimmesdale in his idealism, Fanshawe has none of the tremulous, lovable weakness of the unhappy minister:

The expression of his countenance was not a melancholy one: on the contrary, it was proud and high, perhaps triumphant.

Fanshawe is a forerunner of Hawthorne's long line of idealists (Fanshawe, Aylmer, Dimmesdale), and, though blurred by conflicting traits, the portrait reminds us of young Hawthorne himself, taking his lonely walks and imagining himself to be this solitary being, this high-minded man of thought.

Who would not desire, for an understanding of Hawthorne's art, a day-by-day record of his twelve years in the chamber while he was "the obscurest man of letters in America"? Of about sixscore pieces written during this period some were lost, some were burned, and some, he said in 1851, "might yet be rummaged out (but it would not be worth the trouble) among the dingy pages of fifteen- or twenty-year-old periodicals, or within the shabby morocco covers of faded souvenirs." All such apprentice work was unsystematic, desultory, essential to the delicate development of the artist's perceptive processes. We may deduce much from lists of the pieces in their order of publication: that about seventeen antedated the important commencement, in 1835, of the *American Notebooks*; that the rapid increase in such publications in this and the following three years (fifty-two essays, tales, and sketches) indicates a consciousness of power; that in the early years the essay seemed to be his favorite form. Yet, since the dates of composition are unknown, those stages by which Hawthorne's self-disciplines reached perfection in the few classic studies of isolation must, for the most part, remain conjectural.

4

Hawthorne's selection of nineteen pieces for the first series of *Twice-Told Tales* (1837) he based upon some fifty published contributions, and the second series (1842) upon some seventy-three; but these facts do not mean necessarily that the second volume included only later work. The third volume (*Mosses from an Old Manse,* 1846) completed, to all practical purposes, the canon of the Hawthorne short story or sketch; but five other collections, including *The Snow Image* (1852) and two posthumous volumes, were to appear before all the known fragments and bagatelles were available, and even now an occasional relic of "the accustomed chamber" is unearthed and republished.

Studying this period, we must abandon the idea of a consistent intellectual progression; we may note only over-all characteristics, and later relate these, if we can, to the more complex and sustained performances of his novels. In the sketches we detect unevenness in quality through the author's sensibility to the standards of the wretched magazines to which at first his literary fortunes were unhappily bound, and also in his early reliance upon bookish sources; and we are sometimes tempted to date the compositions according to the degree of their emancipation from these influences. Certainly after the establishment of his own unique savings bank, the first of the series of notebooks, he must have determined to lean almost wholly on those earthy observations, so characteristic of him, concerning the bizarre or the psychologically interesting:

The search [he wrote in 1844] of an investigator for the Unpardonable Sin; he at last finds it in his own heart and practice.

Here is a germ of "Ethan Brand." Indeed, in the rich soil of the notebooks may be found the seeds of many of Hawthorne's concepts concerning man in relation to man; he was no debtor to the platitudes of libraries.

The tales anticipate themes and characters in the longer narratives. If we look backward momentarily from novel to tale, the agonized, introspective Dimmesdale is in essence Parson Hooper; Chillingworth, subtly diabolized, is Rappaccini, brewer of poisons; and the perfectionist Hollingsworth carries us back to the folly of Aylmer who destroyed his wife's birthmark—and her life. Here, too, in the tales, are specimens of sins destined to reappear in the novels; in "The Gentle Boy" the Puritans cruelly persecute the Quaker child; in "Ethan Brand" the self-centered intellectual, slain in the limekiln, is found to have a marble heart; in "Roger Malvin's Burial" the youth leaves his friend to perish in the forest and is tormented by remorse. Our privilege in this early laboratory is to inspect each vial itself instead of the devil's brew in which are stirred the complicated relations of, for example, Hester, Dimmesdale, and Chillingworth.

Besides their exegetical service to the novels, the tales emphasize Hawthorne's matchless delineation of Puritanism in the seventeenth century. They constitute a minor compensation for the fact that only one of his novels deals with this epoch, with which, by reason of reading and temperament, he was so deeply familiar. "The Maypole of Merrymount," "The Gray Champion," "Howe's Masquerade," all historical pieces, give us the fruits of his profound knowledge of his ancestors' world, and intensify our regret that only *The Scarlet Letter* (though this is much) exists, among his major writings, to demonstrate his extraordinary gift for re-creating the world of the Winthrops and the Mathers. These seventeenth century tales are relatively few, but they have come to be a precious frame of reference for the great novel. Because of them we view it with more understanding, and had they never been written it assuredly would be less. Hawthorne pondered much on these Puritan precursors of his; he even wondered whimsically what they would have thought of him, their renegade romancer-descendant. Why in 1850 after the publication of *The Scarlet Letter* he wrote no more novels concerning seventeenth century Puritanism remains an enigma. The deeper Hawthorne resided in this period, and the tales concerning it are essential to our understanding of him.

Finally some of these short writings of Hawthorne's have a classic dignity —and perhaps an immortality—of their own, apart from their illumination of his craftsmanship or their record of his fealty to the seventeenth century. The number of the elect is few indeed; on the fringe of the large collection are such inanities as "Little Annie's Ramble" or such sentimentalities as "The Wedding Knell"; it is more difficult to discover divinity in Hawthorne's tales than in the early fiction of Irving or Poe. Many savor of the provinciality which seldom infects the novels. Undoubtedly the conventions of gift-book and annual shadow some of these pieces. They offer, too, very little advance in the technique of the short story; in their leisure, indefiniteness, and absence of precision they are reminiscent of Irving, whose influence over many a contemporary was no less real than it was subtly hidden. Yet for the creation in us of a single poignant mood (the quality recognized in them by Poe) they are perhaps without parallel. The utter loneliness of Parson Hooper wearing perpetually his black veil, of Young Goodman Brown who believes himself sharing the dark secrets of his friends, of Roger Malvin who deserts his comrade in the wilderness, or of Ethan Brand; the selfish perfectionism of Aylmer; the almost intolerable exposition of cruelty in "The Gentle Boy": all these moral distempers, through his special language of symbolism, Hawthorne makes us share.

In 1849 Hawthorne wrote in effortless fashion, after his long indenture to such themes and characters, *The Scarlet Letter,* his lovely novel "of human frailty and sorrow." It is too easy, from the moment that we mingle at the prison door with the women in hoods and the men in gray steeple-crowned hats until we stand beside Hester Prynne's grave, to undervalue Hawthorne's superb interfusion of fact and fancy in this tale of New England seventeenth century life: sincere in its way and aspiring, but brutish too, and often debasing, save as it could provoke the "spiritual warfare" in Hester's breast. What Hawthorne conveys of the olden time is less literal—though this element is also present, for example, in the portraits of Governor Bellingham or Mistress Hibbins—than might have been predicted from his skillful distillation of history in "The Maypole of Merrymount." Such modes of thought, our reading and the Puritan inheritance in our own minds confirm as true. There is no heavy-handed intrusion of theological doctrine or of local custom. Church, priest, sermon, court of justice, and meetinghouse are here, but all are incidental to a persuasive reality of mind. Pearl could have passed an examination in *The New England Primer* or the Westminster Catechism; but Pearl is a living child, not an animated monograph on the nature of Puritan children. All that Hawthorne had heard by word of mouth of this past, all that he had read in the Mathers or Thomas Prince, and all that he had divined through his own mind of the Puritans, make the background of *The Scarlet Letter* as accurate as a town record but also as alive as the grim beadle himself or comely Hester Prynne. Perhaps the primary virtue of *The Scarlet Letter* is stylistic: its unity and perfection of tone.

This story of Hester Prynne, this slender thread of narrative in Hawthorne's most famous novel is no great affair as to originality or complexity. When, after our introduction to her and her memories on the scaffold, she recognizes on the skirts of the crowd the then slightly deformed figure, we perceive readily that it is her wronged husband bent on his revenge. What are to be the exact terms of the punishment of Arthur Dimmesdale, Hester's lover, or what will be the ultimate fate of each of the three in the triangle (or of little Pearl), we do not know. Nor do we care particularly, so surely has Hawthorne fascinated us by his clinic, in which three superior minds exhibit the deepening stains of guilt: in one freely confessed and ennobling, in another reluctantly unconfessed and debasing, and in the third deliberately concealed and poisonously malignant, until its owner is transformed into a monster. Thus the story pauses, resumes, and pauses; it is less a narrative than a problem discussed and rediscussed by many regroupings of all the characters. One fancies a resemblance to a play by Chekhov. Even the few incidents, such as Chillingworth's harrowing interviews with Dimmesdale or the proposed flight of Hester and Arthur, are merely prolongations of Hawthorne's diagnosis of the mortal hurts of his patients. The sins of these three are assumptions merely; we are not present at their commission, but, appalled, we watch the slow, relentless fires of subsequent remorse and revenge sear them all. How strange it seems, in contrast to the luxuriance of the letter and of Hester's nature, that this writer coolly turns his back on youth and desire to show us only the complex consequences of guilt! Yet in the tales, too, the initial violations of the moral law were hypotheses.

Nevertheless, as fellow students with Hawthorne of these moral maladies we are entitled to know something of their causes. With much more amplification than in the tales he tells us all that we need to know to understand how the natural sympathy between Hester and Dimmesdale—for their temperaments are complementary—deepened into passion. On the scaffold Hester recalls her home in England, and Pearl is the ever-present reminder of her lost youth; in similar fashion Dimmesdale remembers the happy days of his scholarly renown at Oxford. We see them clearly, these lovers, and Chillingworth too, the keen-eyed seventeenth century Casaubon who married Hester to mitigate his loneliness. All such memories, so delicately conveyed, give body to the story without altering the emphasis upon the later years. We think, of course, of Shakespeare. How well we seem to know by his similar double-time schemes the early days of a Hermione or a Falstaff! This presentness of the past, suggestive of Henry James and T. S. Eliot, one of Hawthorne's oft reiterated themes and the central idea in his next novel, *The House of the Seven Gables,* prevents *The Scarlet Letter* from being a mere truncated study of the arid years of middle age. Amid the other evidences of Hawthorne's subtlety of art we should never forget this delicate balance between the present and the past.

This long foreground, woven of reminiscence and allusion, this wholeness of the story, lifting it out of the stark framework of Winthrop's Puritan colony, strengthen our conviction that we are studying no timid trio reared in a fantastic theology but rather three high-minded persons facing dilemmas as ancient and as recurrent as all common experiences. The Puritan mechanisms, such as the emblazoned **A**, are not inherent in the tragedy, but represent only an era's fashions which might have counterparts in twentieth century conventions. The sting lies not in church laws, which receive no special emphasis, but in the pangs of conscience, which have never been monopolized by any particular group, not even by the Puritans. The sin, the consequences, and the resultant quandary are of all time. The "cool familiar stare" rebuking Hester, the festering wound of Dimmesdale's hypocrisy in the pulpit, the self-torment in Chillingworth's revenge, all these human emotions transcend the seventeenth century setting in which Hawthorne has chosen to pose his questions concerning the moral law.

If the issues ring true, unconditioned by the Puritan system, they also ramify into innumerable aspects of Hawthorne's inquiry into evil and isolation. Herein lies the superiority of Hawthorne's novels to his tales. Subtle moral questions are intertwined in complex interaction. We must phrase these as questions, and, characteristically, Hawthorne obliges with no definite answers: Was Chillingworth's capitulation to a marriage for which he was unsuited a sin? If so, is not his punishment in hideous discrepancy with his small fault? Or was his anterior absorption in learning, like that of Ethan Brand, his cardinal error? Why does his plan of revenge upon Dimmesdale, upon whom his hate battens, grow into an abnormal love? How can we explain the fact that Dimmesdale's descent to folly seems to begin, in accordance with Hawthorne's favorite quotation from Bunyan, at the gate of heaven, in a spiritual attraction for Hester? Why does his cowardice in not acknowledging his fault exalt him to heights of moral counsel to his people? Why does the confession of guilt free Hester from remorse? Indeed, why does the entire experience enrich and dignify her nature? Contemplating this regenerative power of sin, which so absorbed Hawthorne in his later study of Donatello, can we wish the evil undone? One could study endlessly other chemistry in Hawthorne's experiments: the telepathy between father, child, and mother, or the mysterious violation of Dimmesdale's personality by the leech. Thinking of such crude early tales as "Egotism or the Bosom Serpent," we marvel at the foliations of Hawthorne's ideas concerning guilt as a "stain upon the soul."

In his exposition of these complicated problems Hawthorne frankly employed fiction to study psychic case histories; in him, as already hinted, was a tough, cold streak, tempting him outside the personal relationships of his characters into indefatigable analysis of these specimens of moral experience. It is true that this semiscientific study sometimes chills the characters themselves, even in the richly human *Scarlet Letter*; at times, for example, the diabolized Chillingworth seems an incarnation of the passion of revenge. Yet in other instances Hawthorne loved the people whom he had created; like the great novelist he was, he relived their experiences as persons, and he had compassion upon them. "On Hester Prynne's story," he said quietly, "I bestowed much thought." In discussing the theme which always engrossed him, the violation of one personality by another, he was as tender toward Dimmesdale under the cruelty of Chillingworth as toward Ilbrahim in "The Gentle Boy." The fact is that *The Scarlet Letter* is a nobler book than the other novels partly because we remember these four troubled characters as individuals long after we have forgotten the rise and fall of their moral temperatures.

Thus Hester Prynne has the quality of the great characters in fiction who step from the pages of a book as living, breathing human beings. She is as real as Becky Sharp or the heroines of Shakespeare's plays. Reminiscent of Beatrice in "Rappaccini's Daughter," she is also the fully formed predecessor of the dusky, strong-souled women in the other novels, Zenobia and Miriam. Tall, regal, somber-eyed, black-haired, her presence spells calm and strength, especially beside the less stable Dimmesdale, or in contrast with the thin, cold personality of the scientist Chillingworth. If in her nature there is a hint of the voluptuous, this is absorbed in the complete naturalness of her longing for the domestic life of which she has been so cruelly deprived. In her skill with the needle, in her reposeful guidance of Pearl, in her wifely (so to speak) control of the minister's hysterical emotions, in her interviews with him, with her child, or with both—interviews which seem like satires upon the fireside scenes for which Nature designed her—she is a true woman, born to comfort and command. Her tragedy is not altogether in the loss of public respect which she has learned to evaluate accurately or in that of private remorse which she has expelled in good works for others, nor even in the loss of Dimmesdale himself, but rather in the frustration, through the customs of the world, of her deep affections. Hawthorne's exposition of her spiritual development is admirable; from the timid, erring wife, shrinking before her husband, she becomes a dreamer of a new moral order, a free spirit almost disdainful of the feverish obsessions of Dimmesdale and Chillingworth.

Dimmesdale himself enjoys no such resurrection of the spirit. Yet his lineage as a character-type seems longer than Hester's: into him entered Fanshawe, Parson Hooper, and the scholar-idealists of the tales; never again was Hawthorne to paint this portrait so well. Weaker physically than Hester, he seems to demand her maternal strength. His nervous uncertainty is balanced against her repose and the intellectual assurance of the iron Chillingworth. He has the intuition, the sensitivity to moral values, which was the finest flower of the Puritan preoccupation with the invisible world; all the more terrible are the consequences of his brief concession to grosser laws. An early torment has been the corroding concealment which the stronger Hester repudiated: *vitum crescit aliterque tegendo*. The next state in this decline is his subjection to the domination of Chillingworth, until, as in the scene in the forest, he is a broken spirit, craving, unlike Hester who desires more abundant life, only release and peace. "Hush, Hester, hush, the law we broke . . ." On his breast, in effect, is the letter; gone, dead, is the dreamer of the old Oxford days; such is the penalty of guilt upon the highly wrought nature of the idealist.

Hester Prynne and Arthur Dimmesdale leave little to be desired; they are complete. The two other major characters, Roger Chillingworth and Pearl, lack finish. They suggest the benefits which Hawthorne might have received from the wise criticism of a circle of peers; there is a provincial air about them, which reminds us of the shadowy figures in the tales. The truth is that in neither of these did Hawthorne's love of the character itself transcend his interest in the abstract moral state symbolized. Chillingworth is more convincing than his prototypes, but he is still an exercise in Hawthorne's study of the process of degeneration. He is theatrical too; in him recurs Hawthorne's weakness for melodrama, which sometimes runs wild in the other novels in drowning or murder. The physical correspondence to the spiritual nature, well integrated in the studies of Hester and Dimmesdale, is in Chillingworth more rudely done, and even verges on the absurd, in the gradual growth of his hump, and the baleful red light from his eyes. Hawthorne's debts to Milton's Satan and Spenser's Archimago are apparent in this creation of an agent who must force the minister to confession. Chillingworth is a pathological study of revenge.

It is curious that Pearl too seems a product of the clinic rather than of the world of human beings in which Hester and Dimmesdale move so naturally, for she alone of the four characters is born of Hawthorne's own personal experience; Pearl is his little daughter, Una, adapted to the purposes of *The Scarlet Letter*. Her health, her elfin ways, her life and grace find parallels in the notebooks; we might expect her, for she was not the first of Hawthorne's many studies of childhood, to realize the same perfection of technique which distinguishes, for example, the portraits of the scholar-idealist. This is not so. In her beautiful union of the qualities of earth and air, in her precocious awareness of the dark currents of passion about her, she does indeed provoke reflections on the sensibilities of childhood; we think of a subtler treatment of the same theme in the story of Mamillius, in *The Winter's Tale,* who died of "thoughts high for one so tender." We are interested in the tension aroused in Pearl by the unnatural relations existing between her father and her mother, and in the strange emancipation following the latter's confession: "A spell," Hawthorne says, "was broken." Yet, as a child character, Pearl is often tedious and sometimes preposterous. Perhaps we could not give her up; her symbolic value is far from negligible; in Hawthorne's phrase she stands for "the rank luxuriance of guilty passion" and, at other times, for the youth and happiness which her mother has forever lost.

Any survey of *The Scarlet Letter* returns us ultimately to the ever-present inner compulsion in Hawthorne toward that frontier of human experience which is so close to the supernatural. In one way or another all of these unhappy persons relate their sufferings to things in heaven and earth not dreamt of in our philosophy. As the modern view has emerged of Hawthorne as realistic and even sardonic, we incline to find in his writings a half-sarcastic condescension toward man's wishful belief in a divine interference in his affairs. Certainly he seems to echo, with the implication of a negative answer, Cotton Mather's oft-repeated query: "What can I see of the glorious God in these occurrences?" From his comments upon his own tribulations, and indirectly from the novels and tales, we know that he thought living a basically grim business. It is possible that occasionally he is ironically treating as a fantastic illusion the hope that our petty fortunes elicit any attention from an indifferent, impersonal universe. There is, for instance, an air of mockery in his point of view toward Mistress Hibbins, and this skepticism he may have easily extended to the weak Dimmesdale's infantile trust in a divine guidance. Was Hawthorne at heart a realist, or even an incipient naturalist, secretly scornful of a man's attempt to ascribe his knaveries to the stars?

Though such a temper exists intermittently in his writing, it seems sense-less to believe that Hawthorne's adumbrations of the occult are merely targets which he himself set up for derision. Rather, he shared a general disillusionment of the age, and often expresses an irony which links him with the pessimism of Herman Melville and Henry Adams. His iconoclasm was profound. He reflected what his age thought of the decaying Puritanism, and his skepticism forced him back upon a kind of meliorism not unlike George Eliot's or even the ambiguous reconciliation of Melville in *Billy Budd*. Indeed, Hawthorne and Melville introduce into American literature a spirit of tragic irony. For about these mysteries Hawthorne is uncertain; he does not know, he cannot say; he repeats the eternal questions which no amount of so-called "realism" ever quite silences. He is careful not to declare his credence in divine agencies; he never, for example, is more than vaguely suggestive about the transference of Hester's badge of shame to the anguished breast of Dimmesdale. In fact, the temper of the book hints at the fatuousness of such fancies, even of the vision of the A in the heavens; as in the other novels, the fulfillment of Maule's curse in the death of Judge Pyncheon or the reincarnation of the faun in Donatello. He hints rather that these are objecti-fications or delusions held by tormented souls. So Hamlet, but no one else, sees his father in his mother's chamber. Yet Hawthorne does not deny these possibilities either. Were the portents there for Dimmesdale? Or if not there, does it matter, if to him they seemed to exist? Symbol melts into fact. Through *The Scarlet Letter* flit these phantoms, either real or the creations of the characters' dreams. Everywhere bordering on New England is another land, whose geography human beings imagine but cannot chart.

5

The Scarlet Letter was published in the spring of 1850, and in August Hawthorne moved to the "Red House" in Lenox, Massachusetts. He was now forty-six years old. Though weariness from his supreme intellectual effort and sadness from the death of his mother in the preceding year had induced a lowered tone of body and mind, he was revived by the almost immediate recognition of his novel. "Mr. Fields tells me," he set down in his notebook May 5, 1850, "that two publishers in London had advertised *The Scarlet Letter* as in press." Yet so deeply had he drawn upon his inner strength that a revulsion of feeling came over him toward the book itself.

Before him lay the most active literary period of his career, as well as his seminal friendship with Herman Melville. If we include *A Wonder Book for Girls and Boys* (1851) and his campaign biography, the *Life of Franklin Pierce* (1852), he was to publish, before his appointment in the following year to the Liverpool consulate, no fewer than five volumes. With two of these, *The House of the Seven Gables* (1851) and *The Blithedale Romance* (1852), we now leave the shadows of *The Scarlet Letter.*

"Evil will bless and ice will burn," sang the blithe Emerson. Only for the strong, Hawthorne might have replied: only for a Hester Prynne or perhaps a Holgrave. On the contrary, evil not only destroys the weak with a terrible swiftness, as in the cases of Dimmesdale and Chillingworth, but it lays its dead hand on remote generations. Maule's curse, "They shall drink blood," was uttered in the seventeenth century; the guilt of the Pyncheons—this time the hypothesis is far off—had its sequel in the nineteenth century in the marred spirits of Hepzibah and Clifford Pyncheon and in the darkened lives of Holgrave and Phoebe. *The House of the Seven Gables,* appearing only a few months after *The Scarlet Letter,* is in some ways a reaction against the sustained tragedy of the latter; and its events are spread on a vaster canvas of space and time. By comparison *The Scarlet Letter* seems but a brief episode; *The House of the Seven Gables* emphasizes the infinite reaches of retributive action from the unseen world, from the Puritan settlement to this contemporary, friendly Pyncheon garden. Hawthorne shows the ultimate wrong done the Maules (of whom the daguerreotypist Holgrave was the descendant) in the persecution of Hepzibah and Clifford by the hypocritical

Judge Pyncheon. "Shall we never," says Holgrave in a striking speech, "have done with this corpse of the past?" Hawthorne's negative is implicit; the book is a modern cancellation of the freedom of the will. In contrast to Emerson's easy "The sun shines today also," Hawthorne shows us the present as frozen, moving slowly in the inexorable glacier of past actions. In its masterly presentation of this difficult theme, this novel, despite obvious mannerisms, may well justify preference for it over *The Scarlet Letter*.

Why did Hawthorne consider this book, as he wrote to Bridge, "more characteristic of my mind, and more proper and natural for me to write"? He could hardly have referred to his plot, so obviously indebted, even in the intermezzo of Alice Pyncheon, to the Gothic romance, and so artificial in its denouement as to invite a smile at his playthings: ghostly music, manuscripts, and hidden panels. His narratives, such as the essential one in this "romance" of the Pyncheon and Maule families, are apt to be merely regroupings of characters, with solutions easily prefigured by the reader. The melodrama in Judge Pyncheon's demise is like the sensational deaths in the other novels, typical of a weaker phase of his art. What did he mean by his preference? Perhaps its quiet temper of contemplation? Perhaps the everyday events and scenes which differentiate this book from *The Scarlet Letter* and make its predominant tone as peaceful as his own tranquil days in Salem and Concord? It is a reposeful record of places and persons studied with an intimacy denied him in his imaginary companionship with Dimmesdale, Chillingworth, and Hester Prynne. Thus, in spite of ancestral curses, a theatrical villain, and a gloomy thesis concerning the past, the romance exhales a spirit of happiness as fresh as Phoebe's roses. Hawthorne's craft of the symbol now has a light, shyly humorous cast, alien from that of the macabre, crimson letter; Hepzibah's hens, the blue Davenport china, the tinkling shop bell are far from the baleful world of Chillingworth. *The House of the Seven Gables* owes little to the darkness of the Puritan past; it is "a legend prolonging itself, from an epoch now gray in the distance, down into our own broad daylight."

"The curtains are more drawn," wrote Herman Melville of *The House of the Seven Gables,* "the sun comes in more." Yet Hawthorne's recurrent themes, concerned only tangentially with the disintegration of old families and with the decay of an ineffectual New England aristocracy, suffered the usual laboratory tests through the characters. Each person in the story represents a culmination of interests explored in early writing and each is also (unlike *The Scarlet Letter*) a composite of living individuals. Here is the innocent and happy Phoebe, halfway between Ellen Langton in *Fanshawe* and Priscilla and Hilda of the later novels; Judge Pyncheon with his evident kinship to Chillingworth, Westervelt, and "the model" in *The Marble Faun*;

and, in particular, Clifford the artist, reminiscent of Peter Hovenden (in "The Artist of the Beautiful") or of Dimmesdale, without the latter's Puritan fiber. Hawthorne's investigations are, as always, double-edged; he studies not merely evil itself but its effect upon various textures of mind. The ancient wrong engraves itself in different degrees of indelibility upon different characters. "Let the black flower blossom as it may." Over the two contrasted women, the faded Hepzibah and the blooming Phoebe, the shadow of the past shifts uneasily. In poverty and loneliness the spinster is broken by the tragedy of Clifford, while Phoebe experiences a mild, nameless sadness in the aftermath of a sin in which she had no part. The range of Hawthorne's experimentation is well illustrated in this particular antithesis between the two novels: the impact of evil on Hester Prynne is direct and personal; upon Hepzibah and Phoebe it is remote, indirect, impersonal.

After the contrast of Holgrave with Judge Pyncheon—that is, of a robust goodness with a robust evil as responses to life—we are drawn irresistibly to the most memorable character in the book, Clifford Pyncheon, the hypersensitive artist, the man with his skin inside out. Disregarding the temptation to connect Clifford's suggestibility with a strain, well controlled, in Hawthorne's own nature, we observe the author's persistent interest in weak souls doomed to combat frustrations which even the strong might bear with difficulty. The nature of this unstable being is delicately suggested; he bursts into tears at the sight of a monkey, aghast at spiritual and physical ugliness. Perhaps the episode of Clifford's thirty years in prison is unfortunate; the ordeal intimates that Clifford's weakness may conceal an inner strength. He is Hawthorne's only complete neurotic; at times almost revolting, he elicits the tenderness of Hepzibah, the cruelty of Judge Pyncheon, and the wisdom of Holgrave.

Possibly the first three novels (excluding *Fanshawe*) exhibit progressively an abandonment by Hawthorne of all objectivity in the novel form. As *The House of the Seven Gables* is a step removed from the austere world of *The Scarlet Letter,* so *The Blithedale Romance* is a bolder revelation of Hawthorne's own experiences, and of his own methods as a psychological novelist. For in the pages of this tale appear, despite his denials, Hawthorne's memories of Brook Farm, and also his confessions concerning his role as a spiritual "Paul Pry":

It is not [he remarks] a healthy kind of mental occupation, to devote ourselves too exclusively to the study of individual men and women.

The personal tone of *The Blithedale Romance* is due to such autobiographical asides, to the reader's suspicion that Zenobia (and perhaps Hollingsworth and others) have actual Concord prototypes, and to Hawthorne's use, for the only time in a novel, of the first person singular. No one can positively identify Miles Coverdale as Nathaniel Hawthorne, an alienated member of the Brook Farm community. Yet his shy, thoughtful ways so closely resemble his creator's that, for good or ill, we are unable to think of Coverdale as merely the apotheosis of the observer type so dear to Hawthorne from the early sketch of "David Swan" to *The Marble Faun*. Presumably *The Blithedale Romance* is Hawthorne's most intimate study of the mind; there is something shameful, as he suggests, in knowing so well "the diseased action" of the hearts of Priscilla, Hollingsworth, and Zenobia. In fact, the tragic dialogue between the two last-named characters, like the drowning of Zenobia, comes as a shock against the quiet friendliness of the episodes at the farmhouse or at "Eliot's Pulpit."

Thus, in spite of the disarming preface, and the fact that only special traits of Margaret Fuller or of Emerson are exploited, it seems likely that Hawthorne was easing his bosom of the perilous stuff of Brook Farm. "I saw," Coverdale says of Hollingsworth, "in his shame nothing but what was odious." This portrait of a fully rounded Ethan Brand, of a humanitarian who, says Zenobia, is all "self, self, self," is not lacking in bitterness, even as the description of the Blithedale crops is not wanting in humor. The neighbors, who remarked that even the cows laughed at this spectacle, added that the Blithedale farmers

hoed up whole acres of Indian corn and other crops, and drew the earth carefully about the weeds; and that [they] raised five hundred tufts of burdock, mistaking them for cabbages; and that, by dint of unskilful planting, few of [their] seeds ever came up at all, or if they did come up, it was stern-foremost.

Certainly the book has not lessened our curiosity concerning Hawthorne's relations with the Brook Farm experiment, and his covert speculations about Emerson, Margaret Fuller, or Orestes Brownson are more exciting than his flimsy plot of mistaken identity, secret marriage, hypnotism, and suicide.

Besides studying the naïve story of *The Blithedale Romance* and its secret satire on contemporary persons and doctrines, we should look through Hawthorne's microscope at the souls of the four characters. The gold-toothed, ludicrous Westervelt is not an unworthy colleague of Hawthorne's other villains, and Coverdale is something of a prig. From his arboreal or urban perches he sees and hears more than he deserves; even if he is, as he announces in the ridiculous last line of the book, in love with Priscilla, he is, unlike Kenyon in *The Marble Faun*, a rather absurd Nosy-Parker. Yet the exposition of Hollingsworth's hardness of heart bears the imprint of Hawthorne's best work. This delineation of the reformer is too explicit, but the character is a magnificent supplement to the other investigations of those men who have surrendered themselves to an overruling purpose. Never, repeats our analyst, is the devil more ingenious than in developing egotism under the guise of philanthropy. Hollingsworth injures Priscilla, kills Zenobia, and is himself "a cold, heartless, self-beginning and self-ending piece of mechanism!" Thus we travel again the old bypath described by Bunyan; Hollingsworth's hypocrisy and selfishness began in a dream of virtue.

The Blithedale Romance depends for body and warmth upon one character. Zenobia, as imperial as her Palmyran namesake, is a freer study of the nature of women than Hawthorne elsewhere permitted himself, even in her sister-characters, Hester and Miriam of *The Marble Faun*. The three novels containing this type of Oriental, passionate woman are richer in tone, for this very reason, than *The House of the Seven Gables,* which lacks even guarded exploration of questions which could not have been absent from his singularly complete investigation of the moral impulse. The two alternating stage sets, of idyllic countryside and crowded city, are really only backgrounds for the stormy emotional experiences of this commanding character. Wearing her symbolic crimson flower, remembering some mysterious liaison with Westervelt, Zenobia is a complex of veering queenly moods, of arrogance and pity toward Priscilla, of condescension toward Coverdale, and of tempestuous love and hatred toward Hollingsworth. Zenobia is the lifeblood of the somewhat anemic *Blithedale Romance*. Into her Hawthorne poured his reflections concerning the future of woman; in her Hester's freedom of speculation becomes dynamic. Our curiosity about her kinship with Margaret Fuller is secondary to the fact that Hawthorne would create such a character. She suggests, like Miriam, his scrutiny of more violent human passions than those regarded as legitimate material for a novelist of the nineteenth century.

6

Several influences conspired to render *The Marble Faun,* Hawthorne's last work of fiction published during his lifetime, far more different from the previous novels than were these three from the preparatory sketches and tales. *The Scarlet Letter, The House of the Seven Gables, The Blithedale Romance,* all issued within a period of three years, were an inevitable culmination, in temper and technique, of this apprenticeship. Yet a space of seven or eight years, of whose nonproductivity Hawthorne is acutely conscious in his illuminating Preface, had intervened since he had meditated on Hollingsworth and Zenobia. He was older, and his age is evident not merely in the tone of *The Marble Faun,* in its note of tranquillity or resignation, but in the stiffening

of his prejudices toward the novel form. We observe, in particular, his indifference to plot in his contemptuous evasion of a solution for this story,
his disdain of adequate motivation in the obscure allusions to Miriam's past,
and his speculations concerning the twilight land of the supernatural even
to the point of ironic fantasy in the implications concerning the reincarnation of Praxiteles' faun in the modern Italian gentleman Donatello.

Secondly, the penetrating experience, not of Concord but of ancient Rome,
dyed his mind even in these later years, with tints of an older civilization.
Basic change in his outlook on life there could not be, but forum, campagna,
and Italian peasant stirred his sensibilities, creating a conflict of ideologies in
this novel absent in those rooted in the New England scene. He was now
writing, as he says in the Preface, "of a sort of fairy or poetic precinct."
Looking back toward the years in America, he set down the familiar, revealing, ironic words:

No author, without a trial, can conceive of the difficulty of writing a romance
about a country where there is no shadow, no antiquity, no mystery, no picturesque
and gloomy wrong, not anything but a commonplace prosperity, in broad and
simple daylight, as is happily the case with my dear native land.

In addition, *The Marble Faun* received the benefits of a long incubation. He
began it in Florence in 1858, but he revised the entire work on the "broad
and dreary sands of Redcar, with the gray German Ocean tumbling in upon
me, and the northern blast always howling in my ears." Thus he created
these "Italian reminiscences" out of complete maturity, out of a new life, and
out of a perspective of quiet afterthought. *The Marble Faun* was inevitably
different.

For these reasons, like a quiet river flows on the tale of Miriam, beloved
of Donatello, the child of nature and Italian antiquity; restful as a happy
dream. Sometimes, it pauses in the slack water of the guidebook descriptions
of Rome, which so endeared the book to contemporary Americans but which
bore a generation more familiar with the scenes, readers uninterested in the
forgotten travel books of a Nat Willis or a Washington Irving. In its way
The Marble Faun is identified with Rome as *The Alhambra* is with Granada.
In the catacombs, in the Forum, in the Italian plains, the book lingers, turning
to action only in the arresting episode of the Tarpeian rock when Donatello,
obeying, doglike, the bitter, unspoken wish in Miriam's eyes, hurls her
persecutor to his death.

It is disturbing to discover how the passages in Hawthorne's notebooks
on fountain, statue, and gallery, have found their way, almost unrevised, into
the novel, and how frequently the analysis of the characters is retarded by

this enchiridion of ancient Rome. Yet, in the end, we must return to his study of the moral problems of New Englanders astray amid the Latin civilization. Here are once more the old, unanswered questions: Hawthorne has changed his skies but not his riddles. Against the backdrop of the Italian campagna or the Roman carnival (instead of Boston, Salem, and West Roxbury), Kenyon, Hilda, Miriam, and Donatello experience and discuss the ruthless influences of the past, the blight of wrong upon the completely innocent, the fellowship of sinners, and the regenerative power of sin. Between the New England characters and the Roman setting exists a marked incongruity; Hawthorne's transference of his themes to Italy proclaims the persistence of his obsessions.

One unique quality of the book depends upon Hawthorne's special use of these foreign instruments to support his reasoning concerning the moral law. The splendor of the Catholic church leaves our New Englander merely curious, but in the device of the confessional he finds confirmation for his own psychological convictions; to the priest Hilda lays bare her troubled soul. In particular, since the faun belongs to the race of primitive peoples, we may study natural innocence. In Donatello's loss of the virtues of Eden by the sin of Cain, Hawthorne poses again the problem of his New England ancestors, the "Fall of Man." Not only does he study the effects of gross evil upon utter innocence, but for perhaps the only time he asks directly questions concerning the origins of evil, a kind of speculation which, for the most part, he left to his friend Herman Melville.

Whatever the causes, Hawthorne's age, his exhaustion of the normal problems in evil, or the influence of this Latin civilization, in which he must have apprehended moral depravities incommunicable to his New England readers, it is certain that in *The Marble Faun* he conveys to us by implication dark aberrations of the human spirit. Kenyon the observer, like Coverdale, may reasonably be Hawthorne himself, and Hilda is, with her exaggerated horror of "moral evil," an idealized portrait of Sophia Peabody Hawthorne. These two are as normal as Coverdale and Phoebe, whom they strongly resemble. The other three persons, however, the theatrical "model," Miriam, and Donatello, lead us into moral caverns measureless to man.

The model, least motivated of Hawthorne's motiveless villains, never, in spite of his conversations with Miriam, quite emerges from his supernatural world. Was Hawthorne thinking of the Wandering Jew? He hints that this persecutor of Miriam has a kind of immortality, that he is demonic, and that with him Miriam has been guilty of some nameless crime. Such hints and the otherwise pointless allusions to Beatrice Cenci intimate that Miriam's sin is incest, already considered obliquely by Hawthorne in one of the tales. This may account for the hopelessness of Miriam, and for the barrier between her and the reader, who never knows her with pity and understanding as he knows Hester and Zenobia. Again we reflect on the extent of Hawthorne's studies in evil, and again we speculate on possible discussions between him and Melville, in which Isabel of *Pierre* and Miriam Schaeffer, or their counterparts, may have found mention. It is unlikely that either writer refrained from frank consideration in his own mind of the depths of human iniquity.

The problem of Donatello, if more savory, is hardly less occult, except for the study of his miserable spiritual union with Miriam after the murder. As in "Young Goodman Brown," Hawthorne surveyed with puzzled excitement the wretched, almost joyous partnership of guilt. The study of Donatello's "transformation" from primitive innocence to "withering, sad, self-knowledge" is conditioned by a long preparatory definition of traits which leaves us poised in the usual uncertainty between the natural and the supernatural worlds. Did Hawthorne mean that Donatello was really a pre-Roman faun in modern dress, complete with pointed ears? The idea hardly bears phrasing; it is Hawthorne's middle world turned to fantasy, even to the whimsical. For Donatello's antics, his animallike fidelity, are not always felicitous; at best he is a heavy-footed sprite of nature. Only in his awakening experiences of sin does he take on reality, and unfortunately Hawthorne was now too explicit, explaining his parable as flatly as one of his preaching ancestors. He himself epitomized the effect on us of this beautifully written, yet unconvincing book, when he referred to it as "figures in a dream."

7

Thus Hawthorne fulfilled the impulse felt on April 22, 1858, as he stood before the faun of Praxiteles:

A story, with all sorts of fun and pathos in it, might be contrived on the idea of their [the fauns'] species having become intermingled with the human race.

To accomplish this he had laid aside a curious manuscript now known as *The Ancestral Footstep,* whose central idea was that of an American returning to the home of his English forebears. This postponement, though it yielded the rich recompense of *The Marble Faun,* was typical of the frustration of the last six years of Hawthorne's life, during which period he began without completion no fewer than four novels, until on January 1, 1864, he exclaimed bitterly:

I have fallen into a quagmire of disgust and despondency with respect to literary matters. I am tired of my own thoughts and fancies, and my own mode of expressing them.

This fatigue had a tragic outcome in his failure to finish any one of the four books; few American authors have left so incoherent a tangle of first drafts and preliminary sketches as the fragments of the posthumous novels known as *Septimius Felton* (1871), *The Dolliver Romance* (1876), and *Doctor Grimshawe's Secret* (1883). Sad indeed was this decay of the strong, sensitive mind, hopelessly retracing old paths, clumsily venturing into new ones. The artist's hand had lost its cunning.

Old dreams, old fancies! How they tormented him as he vainly sought a focus! Leaving the ancestral footstep and the tiresome old magician Grimshawe, he returned to his beloved theme of immortality. The *elixir vitae* on which Doctor Grimshawe had been working had had a long history in Hawthorne's mind, from Thoreau's legend of the deathless man and from his own story of Doctor Heidegger, until now—was this really possible?—he himself approached the fatal bounds at which a man renews his interest in the question. As one never finds in Hawthorne a personal application of his speculations on the unknown, perhaps in these years he himself was weary of life rather than eager for its continuance. It is idle, perhaps, to point out, as one example, the resemblances of the character of Septimius to other scholar-idealists, particularly to that of Fanshawe (as if the wheel had now come full circle) or, in the various fragments, of Rose Garfield to Phoebe Pyncheon, or of Sibyl Dacy to Priscilla or of Aunt Keziah to Hepzibah Pyncheon. All is repetition, uncertainty, chaos. These four novels reveal a mind whose work was done.

In the end, our study of Hawthorne leaves us with an abiding sense of the integrity of his mind and art. Few American writers have obeyed so implicitly as he the imperious, unconscious dictates of genius. In him dwelt no impatience for effect, no diversion to extraneous themes, either by emulation of other writers or by the pressures of the stormy world just outside Salem and Concord; he never strained beyond himself. From the writing of his first sketches until *The Dolliver Romance* his art, however narrow, remained supremely natural, without pretense, defying imitation. In the center of his being, deeper even than his passion for perfect expression, lay a microcosm of the New England Puritan mind; its ways of thought were integuments of himself. Indeed, he had never needed to learn how the Puritan mind worked, for to him by the time he had written *Twice-Told Tales* the revelation of its meaning was complete.

Hawthorne's quiet, independent implementing of his own beliefs concerning the objectives of the novel is remarkable if we remind ourselves of the growth and wide discussion of this form of art in the nineteenth century. Alone he achieved a pattern of high artistic excellence; alone he won the homage of Poe, Melville, and Henry James, even if, apart from his exposition of the differences between a "romance" and a novel, he bequeathed no sustained definition of his theory of fiction. At first, his idea of making it an illustration of moral concepts strongly recalls the old Puritan idea of literature as the handmaid of religion; but his freedom of speculation emancipates it from this naïve view of the art of writing which lay like a blight over such American nineteenth century poetry as that of Bryant and Longfellow. His convictions concerning these matters seem to have been unexpressed, but innate and unalterable. His imperviousness to literary fashions, to new principles, to any departure from his own instinctive way of writing is emphasized by his aloofness during his stay in England from men of letters. He had, it appears, neither desire nor need of their counsel. When we consider his long road to recognition, his loneliness in these purposes, except for the brief companionship of Herman Melville, the strength of his personality and the "unmalleable" character of his mind appear even more amazing. His was a resolute fulfillment of private artistic principles.

Yet in the America of the nineteenth century, Hawthorne's consecration to artistic purposes was not an uncommon experience. Those who live in the desert must find in their own souls secret springs. Some of our most powerful writers have been those who looked intensely within at the spiritual experiences induced by their very isolation. So Emerson himself as he walked through the snow puddles of Boston Common was "glad to the brink of fear"; and so Emily Dickinson in the brick house on the village street fell in love with Eternity—and described it, too. Possibly, then, it was Hawthorne's poverty which begot his riches. In the Puritan experience, so austere that it still moved men to fear or anger, he discovered, with his artist's eyes turned inward, the enduring fabric of art.

28. HERMAN MELVILLE

In the midsummer of 1850 Herman Melville, then thirty-one and a novelist with a considerable popular following, read, lying on the hay in his Pittsfield barn, *Mosses from an Old Manse* by his neighbor Nathaniel Hawthorne. (The two novelists were soon to meet and become friends.) As Melville read on, he was oppressed by the fact that his countrymen had not acknowledged Hawthorne's genius. Presently, in a long critical article, he tried to make American readers see that they had in their midst an inimitable man, one of "the new and far better generation of writers."

"Hawthorne and his Mosses" is a remarkably perceptive judgment of its subject, but it is more than that. In it Melville unconsciously describes his own aims as a writer. What he says of Hawthorne's work could have been said of his. "If you travel away inland into his deep and noble nature," he wrote, "you will hear the far roar of his Niagara." There is no one writing in America in whom humor and love are so developed "in that high form called genius." As the indispensable complement to these, there is in Hawthorne a "deep intellect, which drops down into the universe like a plummet." If Americans would confess the power in this man, they would "brace the whole brotherhood. For genius, all over the world, stands hand in hand, and one shock of recognition runs the whole circle round."

At the moment when Melville felt in Hawthorne the kind of genius he could admire, he was in the midst of his most ambitious work, *Moby-Dick,* a novel far greater in scope and meaning than his earlier and popular sea tales. There would be few readers who would hear in it the far roar of Melville's Niagara. For the kind of appreciative understanding which he accorded Hawthorne in 1850, Melville had to wait until the twentieth century caught up with him.

Why was it that in the years after 1852 Melville's fame was even less than that which his countrymen granted to such outragers of conventional thought as Thoreau and Whitman? Why was it so long before he joined the pantheon of American writers? His was, to begin with, a most complex nature in which divergent impulses were at war. His "ruthless democracy," as fervent as Whitman's, could make him bleed with "keenest anguish at the undraped spectacle of a valor-ruined man"; yet he was born a patrician, and all his life he loved what Thoreau despised, the company of mellow men, their champagne and cigars, their old folios and rare engravings. Even his friend Hawthorne he found lacking in the necessary "plump sphericity" of a man. "For the sake of argument," he was willing to call Emerson a fool for being so full of "transcendentalisms, myths, and oracular gibberish"; but he would rather be a fool, at that, than a wise man, and he loved all men, like Emerson, who dive. In his own plunges for truth he got into deeper and more dangerous waters than Emerson cared to dive in. As ardent a nationalist as Whitman, he shared with him, after 1865, fear for the future of American democracy.

While the other four men worked toward solutions from which they drew strength for their art, the civil war in Melville's nature grew more intense and divisive. The issues of that war came to be of greater importance to him than his art. In his quest for certainty he left the readers of *Typee* and *White-Jacket* far behind. In an age which increasingly believed in the rightness of material success and was content with the compromise of agnosticism, this spectacle of a once popular novelist who permitted his mind to "run riot amid remote analogies" was, to say the least, bewildering. Even the more troubled spirits of the day preferred the certitudes of Melville's four great contemporaries to his ceaseless search for the general equation which would solve all the relativities of his nature.

2

When the *Acushnet* put to sea from New Bedford on January 3, 1841, she had in her crew of twenty-six a new hand, twenty-two years old, who would make her voyage, transformed by his art, the most famous ever undertaken by a whaler. This was not the first time young Melville had gone to sea. In 1839 he had shipped on a merchantman bound for Liverpool. The story of that voyage he would likewise record, apparently with an equal disregard for fact, in *Redburn*. Why he was again at sea and on a whaler is no mystery. It is true that he was the son of a once prosperous New York merchant, and that his mother was a member of the distinguished Gansevoort family of Albany. Men with such a lineage did not commonly ship on whalers, for whaling was a dangerous and dirty business. But Herman Melville's father was dead, and his mother had a numerous brood to look after. The young man had his way to make in the world. He had tried and abandoned school teaching. Fortunes were sometimes made in whaling by lads who signed on at sixteen and became captains and part-owners before their beards were grown. More persuasive was the fact that Melville was tormented all his life with an "everlasting itch for things remote." A sea-captain uncle and two naval-officer cousins had told him stories of South Sea marvels, feeding his desire to "sail forbidden seas and land on barbarous coasts." Since he abominated "all honorable respectable toils, trials, and tribulations of every kind whatsoever," it bothered him not at all that he must put his hand in the tar barrel.

The *Acushnet's* voyage out was tame enough and did not at all resemble that of the *Pequod* in *Moby-Dick*. She followed the usual route of whalers bound for the Season-on-the-Line in the Pacific, touching at Santa, Peru, in June, cruising off the Galápagos Islands (of which Melville later made fictional use in "The Encantadas") in November. Captain Pease had his troubles. An unusually large number of men jumped ship before he arrived in the Sandwich Islands in June, 1843. Among the seven was Melville, who, with his friend "Toby" Greene, had dropped overboard in the romantically beautiful Anna Maria Bay on Nukuhiva, one of the Marquesas, on July 9, 1842. More than likely Melville had planned all along to look in on this South Sea paradise, well known to sailors and missionaries but still incompletely explored and described. The natives were not very friendly, and one tribe, the Taipis, were said to be practicing cannibals.

Later, in writing *Typee,* which purported to be an autobiographical record of his stay in the Marquesas, Melville mixed in plenty of fiction and a good deal of circumstantial information filched from earlier accounts of the islands; but some, at least, of the personal details are true. Toby was with him in their accidental descent into the unfriendly instead of the friendly valley. In the end Toby got away first, though Melville did not know until after his story was published whether his companion was still alive or had been killed. To make his readers believe what he tells them, Melville says he lingered against his will for more than four months. Actually he was the honored guest of the cannibals for only a few weeks, probably not more than four.

He made his escape on a decrepit but fast-sailing Sydney schooner, the *Lucy Ann,* degraded in her old age into whaling. The story of his next adventures, of a mutiny in which he was a ringleader, of beachcombing in Tahiti, that much visited but no longer sinless Pacific Eden nearly a thousand miles from the scene of *Typee,* he later set down with considerable veracity in *Omoo.* It is a skylarking book, though its high spirits were in some places achieved at the expense of several respectable persons who, after its publication, declared in print that the novelist was a libeler.

Perhaps it was homesickness, as he said, which caused Melville to leave Tahiti. We hear of him next acting as clerk and bookkeeper for a "dealer in general merchandise" in Honolulu to whom he had contracted himself for a year's service beginning July 1, 1843. A few weeks earlier the *Acushnet* had arrived in Hawaiian waters, and her captain was making affidavits about deserters. Perhaps Melville feared the arm of maritime law might snatch him back into whaling servitude. For this or some other reason he put himself under the protection of the American flag by signing on as a common seaman for the homeward voyage of the frigate *United States,* which became the *Neversink* of still another book of Pacific adventures, *White-Jacket.*

For fourteen months the *United States,* with Melville in the afterguard, cruised homeward, putting in for long periods at Callao, Peru, and Mazatlán, Mexico. The future castigator of brutalities in the American navy, as he had witnessed them on the *United States,* missed nothing of the degradation and the heroism to be seen daily around him. The man-of-war sailed into Boston Harbor on October 3, 1844, and Melville, though he had half his time yet to serve, was discharged with the rest of the crew.

The long voyage, the most momentous in literary annals, was over. Melville had seen much that other travelers had also seen and set down; but none of them—scientist, explorer, missionary, or merchant—had so clearly understood what the white man's greed and vice, and his charity, too, were doing to the primitive peoples who welcomed the pocky sailor as hospitably as the missionary's wife in her Mother Hubbard. Life on a man-of-war had helped to make him an unconditional democrat in all things. He could imagine no nobler hero than Jack Chase, captain of the maintop, to whom, in his old age, he dedicated his last work, *Billy Budd.* The impressions of these years stayed with him all his life, surviving undimmed those conveyed in later years by foreign travel and the ceaseless reading of many books.

It was inevitable, in that day when every publisher advertised a Travelers' Library in his list, that Melville should write about the wonders he had seen. He settled down to his congenial task at his mother's home across the Hudson from Albany. In 1846 *Typee, a Peep at Polynesian Life* was published by Murray in London (as *Melville's Marquesas*) and by Wiley & Putnam in New York.

Critics and readers were in the main delighted with *Typee.* Some objected to the warmth of the descriptions of Typeean women, and the franker passages on this engaging subject were removed in the new edition which was soon required. To some the story seemed too good to be true. Adventures so delightfully told and scenes so beautifully described could scarcely be trusted as the work of a deserter from the crew of a whaling ship. Actually Melville had produced a book the like of which had not been known before.

The art of *Typee,* which takes it out of the class of Stewart's *A Visit to the South Seas* (1831) to which it owes much, is evident in the first chapter. What reader can resist turning to Chapter Two after his appetite has been piqued by the anecdote about the scandalous treatment the Marquesans accorded the wife of a missionary and the account of the behavior of an Island Queen which so astounded some French sailors that they fled from the scene of so shocking an exhibition? For more than half of his story Melville keeps his readers in suspense over the fate of the two adventurers. Will they make good their escape from the whaler? Will they survive the perilous descent into the valley? Will the natives prove to be the dreaded Typees? When the adventurers find themselves among the Typees in fact, a new complex of fears arises. Will they be killed? Have they unwittingly eaten human flesh at a native feast and not the usual "puarkee" (pork)? When Toby escapes and does not return, Melville worries, needlessly, for both of them. The smoked head of a white man is whisked from his view before he can discover whether it is that of his black-haired friend.

The reader's anticipatory thrills are not always fearful. Halfway through the book Melville begins to make use of a hint he drops casually near the beginning: "I have no doubt that we were the first white men who ever penetrated thus far back into their territories." Who in 1846 could fail to read on, that he might be among the first to learn about the Marquesan marriage system (a variety of polyandry which Melville did not completely understand) and the goings-on at the Feast of the Calabashes. Melville shows in these chapters with which he fills out the middle section of his story his ability to make detail fascinating by humanizing it. It was an art he would perfect in *Moby-Dick*.

It should be noted, too, that just as Defoe makes the teller of *Robinson Crusoe* into a veritable person, so the "I" of *Typee* is not merely a reporter, but an enterprising young man, full of spirit and curiosity, and also somewhat shrewd and sly. For contrast Toby (whether Richard Tobias Greene had such a temperament or not) is represented as given to bursts of anger and moody fits. Nor are these two the only carefully drawn characters in the book. Mehevi, the chief; the aged leech; the faithful Kory-Kory; Marnoo, in masculine beauty an Apollo—all are touched into life with the finger of their creator. As for Fayaway, she was everything a romantic generation could imagine and desire a Polynesian nymph to be.

Melville's second book, *Omoo*, formed from his beachcombing adventures in Tahiti, appeared in the spring of 1847. His first publishers had turned it down, evidently fearing what the missionary world would say to Melville's attack on the Protestant stations in the South Seas. Harper, who took him on, published his next six books, and thus had the honor of putting the firm's imprint on *Moby-Dick*.

Though *Omoo* lacks the calculated element of suspense which teases along the readers of *Typee*, it is in many respects more of a novel. In place of suspense Melville uses a sequence of episodes, each one of which is naturally introduced and finished off with the self-confidence of a professional writer.

The hilarious opening chapters describing the fourth-class mutiny on the *Julia* are followed by the even more amusing pranks of the mutineers while they are confined in the open-air British jail, the Calabooza Beretanee. After their release Melville and his companion-in-idleness, the renegade Doctor Long Ghost, see the sights. This episode gives Melville his opportunity to describe "Tahiti As It Is" and to get in a word about the missionaries. His quarrel with them arose from their preposterous claims of having rescued many savage souls from the devil. He was willing to admit that they had mitigated the evils of drink, gonorrhea, and greed imported by their fellow white men, but he also knew that the missionaries had done irreparable harm in destroying the taboos which cemented the social structure of these island societies.

After the missionaries have been given their due, Melville and the Doctor move on to the island of Imeeo where for a brief time they help a Yankee and a Cockney on their potato farm. But even with three hours out each day for "nooning," work is not to be endured. They are off again on a grand tour which ends in their climactic court visit (without an invitation) to barefooted Queen Pomaree Vahinee I, who receives them surrounded by cut glass and porcelain, sabers and fowling pieces, laced hats, candelabras and decanters (all gifts from European royal cousins), and eating her fish and poi out of her native calabashes.

Beyond his new skill in developing episodes, the advance in Melville's art is evident in two qualities possessed by *Omoo*. In writing it he made almost no use of books by other travelers, depending with confidence on his own invention. He has progressed, too, in the power to characterize. In the throng of amusing characters who help to give *Omoo* its tone of irresponsible gaiety, more than twenty are sketched with a master's hand, whether Melville uses a few sentences, all he required for Old Mother Tot, or several chapters, which were needed to polish off Wilson, the blustering and high-handed deputy consul.

The third book which Melville made out of his years in the Pacific is *White-Jacket or The World in a Man-of-War*. Again as in *Typee*, Melville had novelty to offer his readers, this time in the authenticity of his picture of life at every human level on board an American warship. What he had done (in the opening chapters of *Omoo*) as the chronicler for exploited whalemen he was now doing, with much more serious intent, for the common seamen of the American navy. His faith in the innate dignity of man had been outraged by the brutal floggings and the scenes of petty tyranny he witnessed on board the *United States*. At heart a pacifist, he had been revolted by the naval laws and usages which supposedly must be enforced to make fierce fighting men out of American farm boys and mechanics. His hatred of rank could not endure without protest the parade of authority which the presence on board of a commodore required. *White-Jacket* is in places straight propaganda, and it had its small share in the reformation to which the old Navy soon had to submit in the mid-century. Melville was able to write to his friend Evert Duyckinck six months after his book appeared: "I am offering up devout jubilation for the abolition of the flogging law."

Only in a few chapters is Melville's propagandist purpose obtrusive. *White-Jacket* is the most mature book of the five which appeared before *Moby-Dick*, and ranks next to it in the completeness with which the theme is realized. It is no inconsiderable tour de force to keep the reader interested, for four hundred pages (without a plot to help), while the author explains every rite and remote compartment, every duty and activity, on a man-of-war.

Though there is no plot, there is what happens to White-Jacket, the teller of the story, whose canvas surtout makes him a marked man among his five hundred shipmates. As in *Typee,* the "I" is a person whom we like and whose fortunes we follow with sympathy. White-Jacket is "of a meditative humor," an expert lounger and time-killer, fit to be a member of the Forty-two Pounder Club to which belong the *aristoi* of the ship. He possesses an uncommon gift of satire, a gift which his creator had hitherto been able to exercise only on missionaries and pettifogging colonial officials. Subjects were rife on board the *Neversink*: the transcendental sermon of the Chaplain; the ceremonious visits of state made by the Commodore when the ship was in harbor; the rank-pulling of the five-foot midshipmen, too soon escaped from the posterior discipline of the nursery and infant school; and, most vulnerable of all, that toothless and hairless butcher of men, Surgeon-of-the-Fleet Cadwallader Cuticle, M.D.

The logbook of the *United States* has fortunately survived, so that it is possible to see what Melville transcribed from life and what he invented. Actually the last three months of the voyage home, the period which the novel covers, were so uneventful that they supplied only one important incident which he could transfer to his book. The rest is invention: Surgeon Cuticle's ghastly operation on the foretopman; the fragrant story of how eau de cologne was substituted for grog when the stores gave out; the Great Massacre of the Boards; White-Jacket-Melville's narrow escape from a flogging. The most exciting episode of all, the story of how the white jacket caused its owner to fall from the weather topgallant yardarm into the sea more than a hundred feet below, Melville coolly lifted from Nathaniel Ames' *A Mariner's Sketches,* thus causing his future biographers much pain when they discovered that he had assumed another man's death agony and passed it off as his own —or as White-Jacket's.

When Melville set to work on *Moby-Dick,* one of his main concerns was to raise the voyage of his whaler to a higher level than that of ordinary experience. His readers must find significance in a hundred routine activities. Only by investing them with universal meaning could his mighty theme be supported. In *White-Jacket,* published in the year he began writing his masterpiece, Melville experimented with this method of poetizing shipboard experience. Life on board a man-of-war had furnished him with an image of the great world. In his ship microcosm he had run the gamut of character upward from Scriggs with the picklock eye to noble Jack Chase, and of human experience from the horrors of flogging through the fleet to the pitiful moment when the "last stitch" must be sewn through his nose before a sailor may be decently buried at sea.

The world-frigate, Melville concludes, sails under sealed orders—"we ourselves the repositories of the secret packet, whose mysterious contents we long to learn." From our first embarkation its violent rolling makes every soul of us seasick, though in after life the motion becomes endurable through gradual habituation.

Oh, shipmates and world-mates, all round! we the people suffer many abuses. Our gun-deck is full of complaints. In vain from Lieutenants do we appeal to the Captain; in vain—while on board our world-frigate—to the indefinite Navy Commissioners, so far out of sight aloft. Yet the worst of our evils we blindly inflict upon ourselves; our officers can not remove them, even if they would. From the last ills no being can save another; therein each man must be his own savior. For the rest, whatever befall us, let us never train our murderous guns inboard; let us not mutiny with bloody pikes in our hands.

3

The popular success of *Typee* and *Omoo* induced Melville to make writing his profession. On this assurance that he and the reading public, in England as well as America, could get on together, he married, in the fall of 1847, Elizabeth Shaw, daughter of the Chief Justice of Massachusetts. They settled in New York where Melville was soon a member of the circle of writers whose center was Evert Duyckinck, editor, critic, and adviser to publishers. With this group, the "Knights of the Round Table," whose punch parties offered the best literary conversation in New York, the young novelist exchanged stories about South Sea wonders for talk about art, literature, philosophy, and politics. His friends and reviewers expected him to go on spinning yarns. Though *White-Jacket* (1850) had overtones which only the more sensitive of his readers could hear, Melville continued in this, his fifth book, to oblige his public with the sort of writing which it demanded of him.

The year before, in *Redburn,* Melville had gone back to his memories of his Liverpool voyage at the age of nineteen. He despised, or affected to despise, this moving tale of the sufferings of a gentleman's son who sails under a hard captain and sees for the first time the filth of a foreign seaport. Shortly after *Redburn* appeared Melville wrote to his friend Duyckinck: "[It] seems to have been favorably received. I am glad of it—for it puts money into an empty purse. But I hope I shall never write such a book again—tho' when a poor devil writes with duns all round him, and looking over the back of his chair . . . what can you expect of that poor devil?—What but a beggarly 'Redburn'!" The economics of publishing being what they were at the time, not even a writer who had lived among the cannibals, and had come home to America to tell his experiences, could support a growing family by his craft.

Yet there were signs that Melville might some day risk what security he had and strike out into a kind of writing which it was very unlikely his readers would care for. *Moby-Dick* would be in its entirety such a book, and he had premonitions of disaster while he was writing it. To Hawthorne he confided as he was slaving away on his "Whale": "What I feel most moved to write, that is banned,—it will not pay. Yet, altogether write the *other* way I cannot. So the product is a final hash, and all my books are botches." Before *Moby-Dick* he had tried to compromise—offering in part what his public wanted, in part what he wanted himself. Possibly Melville was thinking of *Mardi* (1849) as he wrote this letter to Hawthorne. His words fit it well, for it is a hash of adventure, romance, satire, and jejeune philosophizing; an annoying botch, yet to one interested in the necessary waywardness of genius, a most revealing book.

The first fifty chapters of *Mardi* reel off like those in his earlier books. This time we follow the adventures of the narrator and his companion Jarl who desert from a whaler, suffer horribly in an open boat, board and stalk a mystery-shrouded native-built ship which is later sunk in a gale. In the open boat again, they meet new adventures which are curious but not improbable. They rescue from a priest whom they kill a snow-white maiden with Golconda locks. Her story—of her more than mortal birth, of a strange captivity in the Island of Delights, of her reincarnation and deification at the temple of Apo—suggests a hand-me-down from Blake or a prose rewriting of a poem by Thomas Holley Chivers. Still, the unwary reader might suppose he was hearing a South Sea legend. He might believe, too, that the narrator was actually received as the demigod Taji at the island of Odo, even as Captain Cook was supposed by the Hawaiians to be their war god Lono. But when Taji undertakes a journey round the archipelago of Mardi in the company of a king named Media, a philosopher with the suspiciously allegorical name of Babbalanja, the historian Braid-Beard, and the poet Yoomy, at this point in the story (Chapter Sixty-six) the cat jumps out of the bag. The reader knows that Melville's little preface to *Mardi* is telling the truth: "Having published two narratives of voyages in the Pacific, which, in many quarters, were received with incredulity, the thought occurred to me of indeed writing a romance of Polynesian adventure, and publishing it as such; to see whether the fiction might not possibly be received for a verity: in some degree the reverse of my previous experience."

Into *Mardi* Melville poured the ferment of his mind in 1848. During the past seven years he had discovered the world of ideas, as he read his way through ships' libraries and the volumes in Evert Duyckinck's large collection. His new literary friendships stimulated his interest in contemporary political issues, especially the slavery impasse and the American imperialistic thrust toward Mexico and the Northwest. With the confused but insatiable curiosity of one who has had no academic training in philosophy, he delighted in juggling the technical terms of Stoicism, Idealism, Necessitarianism, Christian theology, and even Transcendentalism, though he did not heartily respect his Concord contemporaries.

Mardi is clogged with recondite allusions; with the vapid poems of Yoomy (Melville's first attempts at verse), with little essays on everything from "Time and Temples" and royal wines to the polysensuum and the physiology of genius. In spite of the intoxicated language and the amateurishness of most of the philosophical meditations, there is a new power here, and Melville is evidently exulting in the consciousness that he possesses it. The best episodes are the satirical passages about philosophers and pedants and the sequence of chapters in which Taji and his court companions explore Dominora (England) and Vivenza (the United States) and the lesser nations which made up the Mardian world in the year 1848.

Though everything which interested Melville in this American year of decision was tossed into the book, *Mardi* has a perceptible plan. The credible adventures of the first part yield to the fantastic story of Yillah. Taji's quest for her after she is stolen from him furnishes the motive for this strange voyage through the world of politics and the world of mind. The earlier satirical chapters of this section, written in a Rabelaisian vein and on traditional and universal subjects, lead to the excellently controlled satire on the superstitions, the corruptions, and the unending battle of the sects which have disgraced the Christian church for nearly two thousand years. After this long interlude Melville describes the Christian state which might be, the land of Serenia where the laws are bred, not of vengeance, but of love and Alma (Christ).

Though there was no need for him to be explicit since his chief purpose is clear enough, Melville declares in the chapter called "Sailing On" that this chartless voyage through the world of mind is as bold as that of Columbus:

That voyager steered his bark through seas, untracked before; ploughed his own path mid jeers; though with a heart that oft was heavy with the thought, that he might only be too bold, and grope where land was none.

So I. . . .

But this new world here sought, is stranger far than his, who stretched his vans from Palos. It is the world of mind; wherein the wanderer may gaze round, with more of wonder than Balboa's band roving through the golden Aztec glades.

But fiery yearnings their own phantom-future make, and deem it present. So, if after all these fearful, fainting trances, the verdict be, the golden haven was not gained; yet, on bold quest thereof, better to sink in boundless deeps, than float on vulgar shoals; and give me, ye gods, an utter wreck, if wreck I do.

What was Melville's quest? What landfall in the "world of mind" did he hope to sight? Who is Yillah, the elusive phantom whom Taji follows off the final page into an endless sea? Who is the dark and sinister Hautia who pursues the pursuer, offering him the voluptuous pleasures of this world? The symbols are vague and tritely romantic, but, in the light of the themes of *Moby-Dick* and *Pierre,* with both of which *Mardi* is affined, Melville's meaning can be discerned. He was off on his long quest for the ultimate truth. He would have an answer from the inscrutable mask of the universe. The appearance of things must be made to dissolve into the reality beyond.

When *White-Jacket* was published in London in January, 1850, Melville's fifth book was in print. He had just returned from a trip to England to which had been added a few delightful days on the Continent. Though he was abroad on business—in those days of reciprocal Anglo-American literary piracy American authors could only appeal to the generosity of their English publishers—he had filled his days and nights with pleasure: rummaging in bookstalls and, as usual, buying more than he could afford; dining with literary lions, sight-seeing, and attending the theater. London was a very different place to the now successful author of *Melville's Marquesas* from the Liverpool which had received the anonymous deck hand of nineteen. He was a full-grown literary lion himself. In his last days in England the Duke of Rutland honored him with an invitation to Belvoir. Melville reluctantly declined, so that he might return sooner to his family.

The literary society of New York had begun to disgust him. Even his faithful friends the Duyckinck brothers were deep in the business of promoting writers whom he no longer admired. In Book XVII of *Pierre* he satirizes, with some transparent allusions, this amiable society: ignorant publishers who flatter a youthful writer by bidding for the privilege of issuing his "complete works," lecture committees who beg him for an oration on any subject of his choosing (though the subject of Human Destiny is respectfully suggested), magazine editors who demand a daguerreotype to aid promotion, attar-of-roses young ladies asking for autographs.

In *Mardi* one of Babbalanja's favorite subjects for discourse is the pain of writing well. Melville makes his philosopher say that men who think deeply are giants in their genius, but dwarfs when they try to speak what they know. With his new awareness of the mysterious springs of creative power and the realization of what adventures he might experience in the world of mind, was born a contempt for the kind of fame which was already his. Of what use is fame unless it is wedded to power, money, or place? Fame is an accident, in any event, but merit is absolute. He would yet write something which would be, in its absolute excellence, beyond reach of the critics who are mules "so emasculated from vanity they cannot father a true thought."

Early in 1850 Melville embarked on a book with a mighty theme which he hoped would please himself, whether or not it pleased the critics. As if to signalize his break with the literati in New York, a few months later he moved his family to "Broadhall" near Pittsfield, Massachusetts. It was now a boarding house; but it had once belonged to a favorite uncle, and he had happy childhood memories of the region around it. Soon he found a house and farm near by which he wanted to own. For his own pleasure he added a porch to "Arrowhead" on the north where he could pace up and down and look across the meadows to the peak of the majestic mountain, Greylock, twenty miles away. When winter came he was deep in *Moby-Dick* and so full of plans for future works that he wrote in jest to Evert Duyckinck to ask if he could send him fifty fast-writing youths who could help him with his labors.

4

In the reckless mood of *Mardi,* Melville sent Ahab and his biographer Ishmael on a more fearful voyage than Taji's into the "world of mind." Readers who looked into *Moby-Dick or the Whale* on its publication in the fall of 1851, may have covered the first few chapters in all innocence, supposing they had bought just another account of a whaling voyage. Books describing the adventures of whalemen, books about the whaling industry, about leviathan himself, his anatomy and physiology, were then a staple of the book trade. But a reader could not have got through many chapters of *Moby-Dick* before suspecting that it was a very different sort of book from Frederick Bennett's *Narrative of a Whaling Voyage* (1840) or J. Ross Browne's *Etchings of a Whaling Cruise* (1846).

Moby-Dick opens properly in New Bedford, greatest of whaling ports, and the voyage of the *Pequod* begins in the most ancient home of American whalemen, Nantucket. What happens to young Ishmael while he is waiting for his ship could well have happened to any landlubber who had signed on for his first voyage—except that the details of his first hours in port are told with a livelier humor than such matter-of-fact narrators as Bennett and Browne could command. Yet there are signs even in these early chapters that the *Pequod,* that "cannibal of a craft, tricking herself forth in the chased bones of her enemies," is destined for no ordinary voyage, the end of which might be a hold crammed with casks of sperm oil transmutable into gold. Doom hangs over the ship from the start. The dark words of a prophet in faded jacket and patched trousers (his name is Elijah) beget in Ishmael all kinds of "vague wonderments and half-apprehensions." The sermon of the nautical Father Mapple, who preaches from a kind of maintop pulpit in the sailors' bethel, throws a strong beam ahead on the wayward path which, deliberately and wantonly, Captain Ahab will soon take. Like Jonah who fled from the hard command of God, obeying his own will instead, Ahab will yet know the torment which a just God visits on those who cannot say in their last breath: "O Father—chiefly known to me by Thy rod—mortal or immortal, here I die. I have striven to be Thine, more than to be this world's, or mine own. Yet this is nothing: I leave eternity to Thee; for what is man that he should live out the lifetime of his God?"

It was a bold stroke on Melville's part to draw his cast of characters from American whalemen, whose counterparts he had known on his own voyage on the *Acushnet* ten years before. His mighty theme is the equal of any attempted by Sophocles or Shakespeare, yet his cast acts it out on the oil-soaked decks of a whaler. It is his art, of course, which transforms this setting into a background worthy of the theme. But there was hidden power in the setting itself. The whaling years form one of those great episodes in our national life when thousands of Americans have been lured—by the surge of the westward migration or by the cry of "Gold in California"—to risk life and fortune on the triple hope of adventure, gold, and glory. Whaling was at its peak when Melville wrote *Moby-Dick.* The American fleet was then three times the size of the whole European fleet. We supplied the world with most of its illuminating oil, candles, and whalebone. The heroic exploits of the fishery were passing into myth, and there was at hand for Melville's use a rich literature on whaling going back even to classical times. Leviathan, most powerful and mysterious of God's creatures, had for centuries engaged the imagination of writers. All that was true and all that was myth in the lore of whalemen Melville had in his mind as he wrote in his workroom at "Arrowhead." Joined to what he had read and heard were his memories of the spirit-spout jetted into the clear moonlight, of cutting in, and of the hell-smoke of the tryworks. He would use fact, myth, and things remembered for the "honor and glory of whaling" and thus body forth the tale he had to tell of Captain Ahab, who brought destruction on his crew and on himself by pursuing private vengeance against the White Whale for the leg torn from him in their last encounter.

Such a malicious whale had in fact haunted American whalemen for years. As Mocha Dick he was described by J. W. Reynolds in the *Knickerbocker Magazine* for May, 1839. Melville himself had talked with the son of Owen Chase, whose *Narrative of the Most Extraordinary and Distressing Shipwreck of the Whaleship Essex* (1820) tells how such a ferocious whale as Moby-Dick sank the *Essex* just south of the equator in longitude 119° W. This *Narrative* may be the germ of Melville's novel. He had read it first when outward bound on the *Acushnet*.

But Ahab's White Whale is far more than a natural phenomenon to be shunned by whalers desirous of reaching home port. Ahab hates him as "the monomaniac incarnation of all those malicious agencies which some deep men feel eating in them, till they are left living on with half a heart and half a lung." He has resolved to pit himself, all mutilated, against his antagonist. In Moby-Dick he sees all evil "visibly personified and made practically assailable." He has piled on the whale's white hump all the resentment and rage felt by his race from Adam down against the divinely permitted suffering in the world.

Nor is this all. When the mild-mannered first mate, Starbuck, good Christian that he is, calls it madness, blasphemy even, to be enraged with a dumb brute, Ahab turns on him with his deeper motive. Moby-Dick may be the evil principle itself or he may be the agent of evil, but how is man to know unless he strikes through the mask of the whale's whiteness? Sometimes Ahab thinks there may be nothing beyond, but he must know for a certainty. What he chiefly hates is an inscrutable malice sinewing the White Whale's strength. Is it blasphemy to demand an answer? He would strike the sun if it insulted him: "Who's over me? Truth has no confines."

There is no one on board who can call Ahab back to sanity and divert the destruction to come, once he has nailed the gold piece to the mast and aroused the frenzy of the crew to win it by hunting down the White Whale. Ahab pauses once in his mad course to confess to Starbuck his momentary regret for the happiness with his wife and child which he wills to forgo, and to cry out at the "nameless, inscrutable, unearthly thing . . . the remorseless emperor" who commands him. But Starbuck has no power with him and, "blanched to a corpse's hue with despair," he steals from his captain's frightening presence.

Though there is no one to hold back the doom, there is one on board who apprehends its steady approach. Young Ishmael speaks for Melville. He alone survives the ship's destruction to bring back to civilization the story which he tells. It is fitting that he should be the sole survivor since he is the only man aboard who sees Ahab's monomania in its true light. At the moment when Ahab reveals his purpose to the crew, Ishmael feels himself drawn into his Captain's "quenchless feud," but as time passes he comes to realize that the mad old man's "special lunacy" has stormed his "general sanity" and "turned all its concentrated cannon upon its own mad mark." Musing on the Loom of Time one cloudy, sultry afternoon, while his cannibal companion Queequeg is weaving a mat, Ishmael decides for himself that the web of life is made up of the straight warp of necessity, the free-willed movement of the shuttle, and the play of chance which "has the last featuring blow at events." Ahab has willed his own destruction. He is not, as he believes, turned round and round in the world by the handspike of Fate.

The truth about Ahab strikes Ishmael most clearly one night when he is at the tiller while the fire and smoke from the tryworks lick the intense darkness. Stupefied by gazing too long on the face of the fire, Ishmael lets the tiller slip from his grasp. Aroused by the blow, he awakens to see that what-ever swift, rushing thing he stands on is "not so much bound to any haven ahead as rushing from all havens astern." He faces back just in time to prevent the vessel from flying up into the wind and capsizing. The meaning is clear, but Ishmael points it up for us. Ahab, from gazing too long on the artificial hell-fires of his own kindling, has permitted the "wisdom that is woe" to be inverted into the "woe that is madness." At another time, seeing Ahab burst from his cabin, driven from his intolerable dreams like a man escaping from a bed of fire, Ishmael prays to himself: "God help thee, old man, thy thoughts have created a creature in thee; and he whose intense thinking thus makes him a Prometheus; a vulture feeds upon that heart for ever; that vulture the very creature he creates."

Seen as Ishmael comprehends it, Ahab's astounding struggle to wrest from heaven the secret of human woe looks like the purest tragedy. But the tone and the intent of the book are not tragic. For one thing Melville is too much in sympathy with the Promethean mood of his villain-hero, and he sends him to his death on the third day of the chase still unreconciled to the power which suffers evil to exist. And in Ishmael himself we find mutinous thoughts which border on blasphemy and worse. In the chapter called "The Whiteness of the Whale" he meditates, close to the edge of atheism, on the "heartless voids" covered by the sinister and universal whiteness. Is there nothing but the charnel house within? Can it be that there is neither agent nor principle of good or evil behind the material, white mask? Ishmael can himself go no farther along the road to submission than to say: "For this I thank God; for all have doubts; many deny; but doubts or denials, few along with them have intuitions. Doubts of all things earthly, and intuitions of some things heavenly; this combination makes neither believer nor infidel, but makes a man who regards them both with equal eye." It is with no such faint heart that Hamlet speaks his farewell to Horatio and the world; with no such doubt does Oedipus, with blinded and bloody eyes, face his subjects and confess his unwitting crimes.

When Melville wrote in "The Whiteness of the Whale," "Though in many of its aspects this visible world seems formed in love, the invisible spheres were formed in fright," he had not said his final word about the hyperborean regions to which enthusiastic Truth will lead a mind fitted, as was his, for fearless thought. Leviathan was not the biggest fish in the sea of ideas. He had heard of krakens. He was off on his new hunt before the critics had time to express their bewilderment before *Moby-Dick*. The new novel he called *Pierre; or, the Ambiguities*—a "rural bowl of milk," as he described it, jesting grimly about the fallen innocence of his country-bred Hamlet-hero from whom the book receives its name.

The plot is as fantastic as a bare recital of it suggests. Pierre Glendinning, son of an aristocratic father now dead and a proud and adoring mother, is about to marry Lucy Tartan, a match for him in innocence and beauty. Suddenly there appears to disturb their Eden of young love the dark-haired Isabel who persuades Pierre, by hints from her mystery-veiled past, that she is the natural daughter of their father. She must be protected, and Pierre believes he must be the one to atone for the sin his father committed. To acknowledge her as his sister would undo his mother and blacken the name of his father whose memory he holds sacred. A false marriage is the only solution. This leads in the end to his mother's death and to Pierre's murdering his cousin Glen Stanly, who tries to prevent Lucy from following the hapless couple and living with them in New York. In the last act of the tragedy Lucy dies of shock and Pierre and Isabel take poison.

Melville was not writing a paper-backed thriller for "Wonder and Wen" or "The Captain Kidd Monthly," firms which sought the talents of Pierre while he was trying to live by writing a novel about Vivia who is also struggling to write a novel, the theme of which is the "pursuit of the highest health of virtue and truth." The lurid episodes of the plot and the tortured characters are intended to instruct us in what happens to a young enthusiast to Duty, who in seeking to live by heavenly absolutes discovers that he steps deeper into grief until he brings down his world around him. Like Titan, the demigod, Man is born of an incestuous union between Heaven and Earth. But the marriage was made in Heaven, and it was there that the corruption of evil first touched our nature. Innocence struggles to regain its divine birthright even by fierce escalade, but it is doomed to be thrown from the heights even as Titan was.

The theme of *Pierre* may have taken root in Melville's mind at the time he worked at *Mardi*. When the travelers arrive at the church-state of Maramma, they meet on their way to the inner shrines a youth of open, ingenuous aspect. He has refused a guide, declaring that he must seek the right way for himself. Though he may have to act counter to all monitions of wisdom, he must follow the divine instinct within. This youth who still clings to the "legend of the Peak" may well be Pierre, the Fool of Truth, of Virtue, and of Fate, in his first incarnation.

The chief of the ambiguities which the novel seeks to discuss is the sinister aspect of the visible world which breeds in the man who thinks deeply the paralyzing fear that in the Truth of Heaven the Demonic Principle has some part.

Ah, if man were wholly made in heaven, why catch we hell-glimpses? Why in the noblest marble pillar that stands beneath the all-comprising vault, ever should we descry the sinister vein?

But the word of the novel's subtitle is plural, and other ambiguities start from every chapter. Once the love idyll of Lucy and Pierre is disrupted, there is no natural love in the novel, only relations which are ambiguous indeed. Pierre and his mother are bound by a silver cord and converse with the gallantry and coquetry of old-fashioned lovers. Pierre's false marriage to Isabel soon goes beyond the brother-sister relationship which he intends it shall mask. Melville implies that it becomes incestuous, in desire if not in fact. He plays effectively, and with surprising awareness for one writing in the mid-nineteenth century, on the normal-abnormal boy friendship of Pierre and Glen which turns later to fierce jealousy over Lucy. And Lucy herself, when she succeeds in her plea to be taken as a lodger by Pierre and Isabel, transforms the strange union under the eaves in their miserable little flat into a still stranger triad.

Melville did not invent these ambiguous sexual relationships to startle such readers as may have noted them in that pre-Freudian era. They are evidently related to a theme which he states early in the book, though he does not develop it or in any other passage tie it to the theme of the ambiguous nature of ultimate reality. The passage comes just after Pierre goes to make his morning call on Lucy. It is a kind of Benedicite in praise of young love, but in its deeper meaning it declares that Love, natural love, drives the demon Principle which is the sire of Want and Woe further and further back into chaos. "All this Earth is Love's affianced; vainly the demon Principle howls to stay the banns." When Pierre deserts Lucy and love to do what he thinks is his heaven-directed duty, his chance for happiness departs. The demon Principle enters his earthly paradise.

It has often been said that an author's second novel is the turning point in his career. His first book he writes out of his experience; his second must come from his imagination. It tests whether his powers are really creative or only reportorial. In a sense *Pierre* was Melville's second novel. His earlier books, including *Moby-Dick,* came from the sea life which he had mastered as no writer who lived before him had done. Much of what had not come from his own first-hand experience, he had found in the writings of other seafarers. The books which precede *Moby-Dick* were preparatives for its greatness. But with *Pierre* he began over again. Aside from some recollections of his boyhood years among his Gansevoort relatives in Albany and his Melville relatives at Pittsfield, the novel is largely invention. He could not fall back on his endlessly delightful sea anecdotes or on his ability to interest his readers in the business of keeping a ship afloat and running before the wind.

Pierre is not a perfect book. It is not even a good one, judged by any standards. But in writing it Melville took, not altogether by accident, a road which other novelists would take thereafter. We who read *Pierre* now, with benefit of Henry James and Virginia Woolf, D. H. Lawrence, and James Joyce and the century-long tradition of symbolism, can have some idea of what his intentions were. *Pierre* is a "primitive" and will be read—by those who do not take to fiction as a substitute for life—as one of the earliest attempts to use in a prose narrative devices which before had been considered appropriate to poetry. Melville had little use for the shallow fiction of his time, novels in which "every character can, by reason of its consistency, be comprehended at a glance." Human nature, he believed, is far more complex than fiction writers then supposed it to be. Motives for action lie deep in the accidents of childhood. They cannot be directly stated and neatly reconciled but must be shadowed forth by the light projected upon them from dreams and symbols and myths.

The discordances of *Pierre,* in consequence, arise from the fact that Melville attempted to accomplish by new methods more than any novelist had previously undertaken. He was unfortunate in his choice of an incestuous relationship for the central situation of the novel, though this was probably forced on him by his allegorical theme of the incest between Heavenly Truth and the Heaven-born evil of Earth. Overt incest is too theoretical a sin to engender any terror in a modern audience. In abandoning his usual methods of narration, the autobiographical form or the device of the narrator who is close to the events yet not a whole-souled participant in them, Melville also made further difficulties for himself. Sometimes the narrator speaks as "I"; sometimes as "we." Usually the tone is that of the omniscient novelist, but occasionally a sort of chorus of pities or of ironies seems to comment on Pierre's acts or thoughts.

But these faults of method a less experienced novelist might commit or.

amend. Melville's greater failure is in his inability to bring his symbols together into a harmony of tone and to use them so that one can move through them deeper and deeper into his characters and the profundities of his theme. Some of the symbols are almost ludicrous in their effect, as is, for example, Isabel's guitar from which she plucks a dark music that is to Pierre infinitely significant but (as to the reader also) utterly unintelligible. The symbolic intention of the two portraits of Pierre's father is fully conveyed. The myth-dream of the Mount of Titans is admirable in conception, but its Enceladus theme will not quite square with the genealogy of Pierre's "heaven-aspiring but still not wholly earth-emancipated mood." Similarly the pamphlet of Plotinus Plinlimmon, which is supposed to furnish symbolic comment on Pierre's behavior, is so hedged round with satire and enigma that the critics will argue its significance perpetually.

In one magnificent section of the novel Melville uses symbolism with a power which shows us what the book might have been had he been expert enough to reach this level all the way through. Young Pierre, as a boy, had often played in the woods near a great stone, huge as a barn yet balanced so delicately on a single point of contact that it was a breathless thing to see. Pierre called it the Terror Stone. In the moment of his agony when he must decide what he is to do with Isabel, he goes to the stone, stands under it and bids it fall on him if life is a cheating dream and virtue meaningless. As his hero stands waiting for the answer which does not come, Melville transforms the Terror Stone into the Memnon Stone, built by the subjects of "that dewy, royal boy, son of Aurora, and born King of Egypt, who, with enthusiastic rashness flinging himself on another's account into a rightful quarrel . . . met his boyish and most dolorous death beneath the walls of Troy." But Pierre is not only Memnon. The symbol widens to include Hamlet and all ship-wrecked royal youths whose tragedy is that of the "flower of virtue cropped by a too rare mischance."

5

In *Moby-Dick* and *Pierre* Melville had made his bid for the kind of post-humous fame he wanted to have. Each novel fulfilled the requirements for a great and original work, as he would later define them in three chapters on the theory of the novel interjected into *The Confidence Man* (XIV, XXXIII, XLIV). He had sought to provide entertainment, but, as well, "more reality than real life itself can show." He had given his readers novelty and he had given them nature too, but "nature unfettered, exhilarated, in effect trans-formed." Pierre, as well as Ahab, was an "original character," as Melville asserted the hero of a great work of fiction should be: one who, "like a revolving Drummond light, raying away from itself all round it—everything is lit by it, everything starts to it (mark how it is with Hamlet), so that, in certain minds, there follows upon the adequate conception of such a character, an effect, in its way, akin to that which in Genesis attends upon the beginnings of things."

But there were not enough of such "minds" to praise these two novels or to buy them. *Moby-Dick* puzzled Melville's friends, though some were discerning enough to suspect that there was great power in it. Even friends and friendly critics were dismayed by the ambiguities of *Pierre*, while the simpler sort were content to be disgusted with the theme of incest. The measure of the public's desertion of Melville can be taken in the fact that his next novel, *Israel Potter*, published three years after *Pierre*, received scarcely any critical notice. Seldom has a successful author been dropped so suddenly from his pinnacle of fame.

The years between *Pierre* and Melville's removal to New York in 1863, where soon he took a job as a customs inspector, must have been the bitterest of his life. How to get enough money to support his family (which included his mother and sisters) was a constant worry. Since he was in debt to Harper's until 1864, he drew no royalties from the books which bore their imprint. The writing which he did between 1853 and 1856 could not have brought in more than $240 a year. Putnam, who issued *Israel Potter*, was forced to sell the plates in the panic of 1857. Dix & Edwards, who published *The Piazza Tales* (1856) and *The Confidence Man* (1857), went bankrupt.

Like most of his literary contemporaries, Melville tried lecturing; but his income from this source between 1857 and 1860 did not average more than $423 a year. Influential friends failed to get him a consular appointment, the quest for which took him to Washington and, incidentally, into Lincoln's presence, in March of 1861. Ill health dragged at his spirits, and there is truth in the family tradition that a breakdown soon after *Pierre* was published caused fears for his sanity. If Melville's father-in-law, Judge Shaw, had not tactfully eased matters the situation would have been desperate.

There is not very much to put into the biographical record of these years, but out of the stories and essays which he was writing one can read Melville's moods. The theme of charity recurs often enough to hint that his need of it and his resentment at having to receive it were constantly in his mind. "Maternal charity nursed you as a babe," he makes the narrator say in "The Two Temples." "Paternal charity fed you as a child; friendly charity got you your profession, . . . You, and all mortals, live but by sufferance of your charitable kind; charitable by omission, not performance."

In spite of the humiliations of these harrowing years, Melville continued to look on himself as a professional writer until 1857, the year of *The Con-*

fidence Man. He did not turn out work at the prodigious rate of the period between 1846 and 1852, when he published seven novels as well as some incidental literary criticism, but the production in five years of two novels, *The Piazza Tales* (a collection of six stories), and ten other stories and essays, is a substantial body of writing even for so fecund an author. Nor should it be forgotten that some of this writing was still of a high level. *Israel Potter,* the story of the "Revolutionary beggar" which Melville enlarged from a chapbook autobiography, is for the most part a pleasant picaresque tale, but the episode of the sea fight between the *Serapis* and the *Bonhomme Richard* is carried off with great spirit. "Benito Cereno" moves the reader step by step toward unmentionable and unimaginable horrors. It was reported to Melville that James Russell Lowell thought one of the episodes in "The Encantadas" "the finest touch of genius he had seen in prose." "Bartleby" lifts the allegorical tale above what Hawthorne could do with it to the fusion of fantasy with serious meaning which Henry James achieved in such a fable as "The Beast in the Jungle." Even *The Confidence Man,* though its narrative does not move and its tone is baffling, is redeemed by passages of sharp satire.

What one notices first in reading the work of these years is the great variety of style and theme. Possibly Melville was trying to find forms and subjects which editors would accept. "The Lightning Rod Man," for example, is close to the kind of tale with an evident but unlabored moral which made Hawthorne famous. The narrator in "The Piazza" muses learnedly and romantically on the beauties of the Berkshire countryside somewhat as the "I" of D. G. Mitchell's *Reveries of a Bachelor* (a best seller of the fifties) daydreams about his existence.

If Melville was trying to please a new public, he was also trying to release the tensions of his life in these stories. He returns again and again to themes and situations which are concerned with fears of isolation or incarceration, the dislike of taking charity, the inviolable sanctity of the human heart (his own, perhaps, in "I and My Chimney"). His narrators are men of a persistent, sometimes a perverse, integrity who hold on in spite of the contempt of the genteel world. Sometimes the teller of the tale is a moody, inquisitive fellow, withdrawn but observant, reaching out from his isolation to the poor who are, in spite of their poverty, kind, intrepid, and to a degree happy, because they have learned how to live by illusion.

As one reads these autobiographical passages one gains the impression of a man who is trying to achieve detachment and equilibrium; to be aware but not dangerously involved. The Promethean mood of *Moby-Dick* is gone, and so is the Titanism of *Pierre.* Melville seems to be struggling to stave off the disenchantment to which he finally gave way in *The Confidence Man.*

The character of Hautboy in "The Fiddler" may well be, *mutatis mutandis,* Melville as he wished to be in the year 1854. Once a famous violinist, Hautboy now "walks Broadway and no man knows him." Yet he is the most admirable of men, "honest and natural," able to hit intuitively "the exact line between enthusiasm and apathy."

It was plain that while Hautboy saw the world pretty much as it was, yet he did not theoretically espouse its bright side nor its dark side. Rejecting all solutions, he but acknowledged facts. What was sad in the world he did not superficially gainsay; what was glad in it he did not cynically slur; and all which was to him personally enjoyable, he gratefully took to his heart. It was plain, then—so it seemed at that moment, at least—that his extraordinary cheerfulness did not arise either from deficiency of feeling or thought.

From all this autobiographical writing "Bartleby" and *The Confidence Man* must be singled out for special comment, the first because it bears importantly on Melville's attitude toward his art at this time, and the second because it is the last prose work he published. After that came the long silence of thirty-four years, broken only by the four avocational volumes of verse.

Bartleby is a furtive law-scrivener, the third assistant copyist to a prosperous Master in Chancery. At first amenable enough for all his eccentric ways, Bartleby soon grows obdurate and refuses to carry out the many trivial tasks assigned to him. He will not even copy documents. He refuses, also, to be dismissed. His contrariness disrupts the whole office and at length forces his employer to change quarters in order that Bartleby and his influence may be left behind. But Bartleby stays on in his old place. Disgusted with such goings-on, the landlord has him removed to the Tombs as a vagrant. Here he dies; and all that his distressed employer can learn about him is that he had once been a subordinate clerk in the Dead Letter Office in Washington. Before a change of administration put him out, he had spent his days in opening letters full of hope "for those who died unhoping; good tidings for those who died stifled by unrelieved calamities."

From signs along the way it is clear enough what Melville means by this fable. The lawyer, we notice, declares that though he belongs to a profession proverbially energetic, he is content with his great volume of routine business; he never addresses a jury or in any way "draws down public applause." His first clerk, the overenergetic Turkey, is dangerously reckless after twelve o'clock. Yet he is invaluable to his employer in the morning, accomplishing a great deal of work in a style not easily to be matched. Nippers, the second clerk, is the victim of ambition and indigestion. Impatient of the duties of a mere copyist, he occasionally lets his imagination run wild when he should be drawing up legal documents. The Master in Chancery keeps the two clerks in his employ because "their fits relieved each other, like guards. When Nippers' was on, Turkey's was off; and vice versa. This was a good natural arrangement, under the circumstances."

"Bartleby" was the first magazine short story which Melville published. The new kind of writing he was attempting in *Harper's* and *Putnam's* resembles that of his Master in Chancery, dull business but (possibly) profitable. He is of three minds about it. Like Turkey he can keep at it until noon. Like Nippers he can be steady enough until his ambition gets the upper hand. In the character of Bartleby Melville prefigures what this new life may ultimately come to. Will its trivialities, the conventional nature of his task, impel him to follow the lonely scrivener's decision to "copy" no more? This possibility was certainly in Melville's mind in 1853. But the decision to abandon his profession, to "go to the Tombs" if that were necessary for his peace of mind, was put off until after *The Confidence Man* was published four years later.

This strange series of conversations among the passengers on a Mississippi steamboat—*The Confidence Man* cannot be called a novel—certainly does not deal with trivia, and Melville could hardly have expected it would be bought by the readers who subscribed to the family magazines in which his stories had been appearing. *The Confidence Man* begins cryptically with the emergence on deck of a deafmute who bears before him a shieldlike slate on which he has written "Charity," followed, after several erasures of the scriptural phrases belonging to the word, with his final version: "never faileth." While this is going on, the ship's barber puts up his sign—"No Trust." The ironic theme of the book has been stated, and the action, or what there is of it, begins.

A crippled Negro shuffles on, seeking alms from the crowd. Asked if there is anyone who will vouch for his poverty, he obligingly (for the reader) enumerates the eight kind "ge'mmen" who will speak a good word for him. Each is the confidence man as he will appear in one of his disguises. Every time he reenters he is a plausible fellow trying to get money or moral support out of the victims of his con game for such beneficent institutions as the Seminole Widow and Orphan Asylum or the World's Charity or the Black Rapids Coal Company. Those who are taken in are as stupid as the confidence man is vicious.

The devices of the ship-microcosm, which Melville had used in *White-Jacket* and *Moby-Dick,* and the series of episodes in each of which the confidence man makes his suave approach and fleeces his catch or is rebuffed, provide Melville with opportunity to loose his satire on missionaries, stock jobbers, universal reformers, transcendentalists, romantic nature lovers, believers in industrial progress, worshipers of the machine. He is able, through the amplitude of his structure, to work off some private grudges, as, for instance, his stab at Fanny Kemble Butler (as Goneril in the "Story of the Unfortunate Man") whose marital difficulties were the scandal of the day.

The Confidence Man is a fascinating book, in what it reveals about Melville's state of mind, for the strength of its satire, and its allusive wit. If it is a failure as a whole, it succeeds superbly in places. But one must be deeply read in Melville's earlier works to penetrate its secrets.

The clue would seem to be that Melville, having abandoned, in the course of writing *Pierre,* his confidence in the moral order of the universe, has now come to the point where he must abandon his humanist faith in the decency and dignity of man. It will be noticed that the stories written after *Pierre* deal almost exclusively with human relationships, not with metaphysical considerations. The point of *The Confidence Man* is in its title: the workers of con games make fools of those who have the wrong kind of confidence, who are, that is, made gullible through greed and softheartedness. Where can one find in the world the mutual trust and esteem, the charity, the love, which are the cement of society? In Chapter X Melville sends into the cabin "a somewhat elderly person, in the quaker dress," who distributes copies of a broadside poem "rather wordily entitled": "Ode on the Intimations of Distrust in Man, Unwillingly inferred from repeated Repulses, in Disinterested Endeavors to Procure his Confidence." If even the Quakers must give up, then it is time for all men to quit.

When Melville visited Hawthorne in England in November, 1856, after this book was completed, they talked—or Melville did—"of Providence and futurity, and of everything that lies beyond human ken." Melville informed his old friend that he had "pretty much made up his mind to be annihilated" —to become, that is, a materialist. But Hawthorne noted that he did not "seem to rest in that anticipation" and shrewdly guessed that he would not rest until he got "hold of a definite belief." Slowly and at first very tentatively, trying out the possible paths in his Civil War poems and in *Clarel* (1876), Melville worked his way to the solid ground on which he finally stood when he wrote *Billy Budd.* It was finished in April, 1891, five months before he died.

6

It is not altogether surprising that Melville should have turned, after his decision to write no more prose, to the writing of poetry. *Mardi* contains discussions of the nature of the poet's mind and art, and Yoomy is permitted to recite some of his own wobbly verses, composed in the sentimental style of the mid-century. By 1859, as Mrs. Melville notes in a letter to her mother, possibly with some dismay, "Herman has taken to writing poetry. You need not tell anyone, for you know how such things get around." When Melville left in 1860 for a voyage around the Horn with his sea-captain brother, he had a volume of verse ready for the printer. It found no publisher, though some of the verses included in it were, apparently, distributed in the privately printed volumes issued in 1888 and 1891.

The Civil War affected Melville profoundly, cured his lethargy, gave him a sense of participating in a common cause, and, above all, purged the saturnine mood of *The Confidence Man*. Like Whitman he looked on as a civilian, harrowed by the suffering and the heroism of the soldiers, brothers of a house divided. It was good for him to be lost for the time being in the joy at Northern victories and the common grief of both sides. That this was a war between Wrong and Right he did not doubt, and the steady assurance was medicine to his soul. Yet his heart went out to the misguided South, and in *Battle Pieces* (1866) he is as much the poet of the Confederate forces as of the victorious soldiers who fought for the Union. (In many of the poems the speaker is a Southerner.) But the Northern cause was indubitably the just cause. He exults as wholeheartedly as Seward or Sumner must have done in the outcome of the battle of Lookout Mountain. Many fought, he believed, in the reckless mood of Ahab.

> As men in gales shun the lee shore,
> Though there the homestead be, and call,
> And thitherward winds and waters sway—
> As such lone mariners, so fared they.

The section of *Battle Pieces* entitled "Verses Inscriptive and Memorial" tells us how constantly he brooded on the instances of individual heroism and how he desired to say in marmoreal verse the final word for those who fought with a whole heart.

However strongly Melville may have felt that in the Northern triumph there was a "type and victory of Law," he was not deluded into thinking that the Union had been saved by its success in arms. He feared the aftermath of conquest. His prose Supplement to *Battle Pieces* is a warning and a prophecy: "The years of the war tried our devotion to the Union; the time of peace may test the sincerity of our faith in democracy."

The war healed his private hurts, restoring his faith in the "Knights and Squires" of democracy whose "immaculate manliness" he had believed in while writing *Moby-Dick*. It also made him willing once more to wrestle with the metaphysical antagonists whose malign strength had finally thrown him down. The old themes appear again in *Battle Pieces,* as, for example, in the poem entitled "Commemorative of a Naval Victory":

> But seldom the laurel wreath is seen
>   Unmixed with pensive pansies dark;
> There's a light and a shadow on every man
>   Who at last attains his lifted mark—
>   Nursing through night the ethereal spark.
> Elate he never can be;
> He feels that spirits which glad had hailed his worth,
>   Sleep in oblivion.—The shark
> Glides white through the phosphorous sea.

But now there are suggestions of a way out for those who hesitate perpetually before the inextricableness of good and evil. The note of reconciliation is sounded for the first time in his writing. Nature, inexhaustible and ever renewing, heals in time some scars. What say the elms of Malvern Hill which surround the dead, grimed faces in those bloody cypress glades?

> We elms of Malvern Hill
>   Remember everything;
> But sap the twig will fill;
> Wag the world how it will,
> Leaves must be green in Spring.

Melville began to see, too, "that the 'throes of ages' may rear the 'final empire and the happier world.' " No man struggles alone. All those who have known bewilderment and despair over the nature of things are his comrades. Time, he had said in *Mardi,* is the great philanthropist. If history is fate, it may "also prove to be redemption." For Melville the road was open again. There might be refuge at its end.

In 1856–1857 Melville had made the journey to the Holy Land looked forward to by every devout or agnostic Victorian. He saw something, too, of the rest of the Near East and of Europe and England, but his record of the journey, *Journal up the Straits* (1935), proves that it was Judea which struck deep within him. His meditations on what he had seen were as decisive in his quest for certainty as the emotions aroused by the Civil War. *Clarel,* the poem which grew from them, had revolved for a long time in his mind before it was published in 1876. We know from a letter of his wife's with what anguish it was completed.

In form *Clarel* is a pilgrimage like the *Canterbury Tales.* A company of strangely assorted men journey from Jerusalem to Bethlehem, conversing as they go, their conversations provoked by their mild adventures and the odd characters, guides, monks, and other pilgrims, met along the way. The thread of narrative is attached to Clarel who, having fallen in love with Ruth, a

Jewess, leaves her for the pilgrimage when, according to Jewish custom, he is forbidden to see her for a time after her father's death. The slight story reappears at the end, with the news of Ruth's death.

Though Clarel gives his name to the poem, he is the least important character in it. As Melville's deputy he listens to the others, who are more violent in their hates or stronger in their faiths. On one side is ranged Mortmain, Swedish by birth, a disillusioned political idealist who once shared the ardor of the European revolutionaries. He has become "oblivion's volunteer" and asks only that he may die in one of the gray places of the earth. He has his wish when death comes to him in the desert. His place in the story is taken by Ungar, another of civilization's dispossessed. Blighted by the defeat of the Southern cause for which he had fought in the Civil War, he rails at the new Democracy. Having spurned the past, what can it promise for the future?

> Behold her whom the panders crown,
> Harlot on horseback, riding down
> The very Ephesians who acclaim
> This great Diana of ill fame!
> Arch-strumpet of an impious age,
> Upstart from ranker villanage,
> 'Tis well she must restriction taste,
> Nor lay the world's broad manor waste:
> Asia shall stop her at the least,
> That old inertness of the East.

Over against these lost, violent souls Melville sets the suave optimist Derwent, a Church of England clergyman. The character most fully outlined in the poem, he is as much the object of Melville's scorn as Mortmain and Ungar are of his pity. There are no issues between science and religion, Rome and modernism, paganism and Christianity which he cannot reconcile. Melville seems to dislike him most because he uses the remnants of a once strong faith to patch up his specious gospel.

Through the character of Rolfe we see most clearly the direction of Melville's own thought when he was writing Clarel. Impulsive, intellectually acute, he is the pilgrim who takes the widest view of all the questions which are debated on the journey. Though at first Clarel recoils from Rolfe's strength, he is soon drawn to him. Like his creator, Rolfe feels a deep regret that the Christian mysteries have not proved strong enough to stand in the modern world. But he knows well enough that civilization has lived through other times when faith was dim. Christ came at last to impious Rome where, to believe,

> Except for slave or artisan,
> Seemed heresy. . . .
> The inference? the lesson?—come:
> Let fools count on faith's closing knell—
> Time, God, are inexhaustible.

Amid all the conflicts of opinion which bewilder the reader of *Clarel*, Rolfe's declaration stands out clearly as Melville's own conclusion to the debate. That he sides with Rolfe is plain from the eloquent epilogue to the poem.

> Then keep thy heart, though yet but ill-resigned—
> Clarel, thy heart, the issues there but mind;
> That like the crocus budding through the snow—
> That like a swimmer rising from the deep—
> That like a burning secret which doth go
> Even from the bosom that would hoard and keep;
> Emerge thou mayst from the last whelming sea,
> And prove that death but routs life into victory.

The faith which Melville longed for while he was writing *Clarel* and finally achieved when he wrote *Billy Budd* was not the faith of his fathers. He did not receive it in a moment of conversion to any inherited system of belief. He had to construct it for himself. But it was complete and it was sufficient to satisfy him at last. That he had to make the faith by which he could live— and that he succeeded in his long effort to do so—suggests why he has been so appealing a figure to many later writers whose struggles resemble his own. War and economic chaos and the new fears aroused by atomic power have been as unsettling to men of sensibility as were the issues of Melville's day to men of his kind. Writers like Yeats and Auden, unable to rest in any traditional faith, had—even as Melville did—to construct their own. Modern man must believe or he is lost. That is the meaning of *Clarel*.

> If Luther's day expand to Darwin's year,
> Shall that exclude the hope—foreclose the fear?
>
> The running battle of the star and clod
> Shall run for ever—if there be no God.

7

At his death Melville left a mass of manuscript prose and verse sufficient to fill nearly three hundred pages in the standard edition of his works. Little of this merits attention from the literary historian. The one exception is *Billy Budd, Foretopman,* the most expertly wrought of all his stories, a tale so satisfying in the way its tragic theme is explored that it takes its place among the really great works of fiction. With good reason *Billy Budd* has been called "Melville's testament of acceptance," for much of its power comes from the fact that here at last he came to terms with the "mystery of iniquity," content to acquiesce in what he could not, as no mortal can, fully resolve.

The time is 1797; the place, the deck of a British seventy-four, H.M.S. *Indomitable.* Memories of the recent mutiny at the Nore and the hanging of the mutineers "for an admonitory spectacle to the anchored fleet" haunt officers and men alike. The Captain, the Honorable Edward Fairfax Vere, known through the Navy as "Starry Vere," is prepared to put down sternly any incipient revolt, though he is compassionate by nature. Given to dreaminess of mood, so modest in manner that if he had been on board as a civilian one might have taken him for "some highly honorable discreet envoy on his way to an important post," "Starry Vere" is nevertheless a man of positive convictions. Deeply read in history and biography, he has come to his settled views by means of those writers who, "free from cant and convention . . . honestly, and in the spirit of common sense, philosophise upon realities." Through his acts and thoughts we come upon Melville's meaning. It is young Billy Budd, innocent, fair to look upon, the victim of foulest treachery, whose death we mourn; but the tragedy falls equally upon Captain Vere who has the mind to comprehend it, as well as the heart to feel.

When the story opens, Billy Budd has just been impressed from a merchantman, the *Rights of Man.* He takes his impressment cheerfully, though he had boldly jumped up in the bow of the boat carrying him away, to salute his ship as his sorrowful shipmates look down from the taffrail: "And goodbye to you, too, old *Rights of Man."* His new mates love him for his happy-go-lucky air and his willingness to work. But he has from the start one enemy, Claggart, the Master-at-Arms. The motives which engender his dislike of Billy, Melville explains with great care, for in them lies much of the inner significance of the story.

By indirection, Claggart tries to draw Billy under the suspicion of mutiny, but the "handsome sailor" is so innocent that he does not understand the hints dropped to him. Claggart then goes to Captain Vere and accuses Billy openly. Astonished and unbelieving, Vere calls Billy to hear the accusation. This time Billy understands clearly enough. Unable to protest his innocence in words, because he is a stammerer, he speaks with his fist. The blow kills Claggart. In time of war a sailor who kills another seaman must die. Vere might take the case to the Admiral, but he chooses to accept the responsibility for a decision. A court is held, the other three officers are summoned to it, and with some reluctance, yield to Vere's decision that the law must take its course. Billy dies at dawn, crying out before the rope strangles him: "God bless Captain Vere." At the moment of his death the cloud hanging low in the east is "shot through with a soft glory as of the fleece of the Lamb of God seen in mystical vision, and simultaneously therewith, watched by the wedged mass of upturned faces, Billy ascended; and ascending, took the full rose of the dawn."

When *Moby-Dick* and *Pierre* were conceived Melville was incapable of writing tragedy, though both novels have tragic implications. It was otherwise when he came to the writing of *Billy Budd*. In the story each of the central issues of tragedy is resolved, so far as human insight will permit, and all are harmonized in Captain Vere's speech to the doubtful officers who scruple to condemn Billy. Yet it is Melville's own version of tragedy, constructed after years of painful thought, and the chief enterprise of his maturity and old age.

Claggart is the representative of evil, but this time Melville knows whence evil comes and why it is loose in the world. Men like Claggart are sick with a "depravity according to nature." They are not normal men, and in passing over to the world they inhabit one must cross "the deadly space between." Their depravity is not universal. It does not involve "total mankind." "Civilization, especially if of the austerer sort, is auspicious to it." Those who, like Claggart, are naturally depraved seem often to be subject to the law of reason. Actually they use reason to accomplish aims which "in wantonness of malignity, would seem to partake of the insane." Melville, we see, has struggled free of the fetters which once bound him to the fear that good and evil are so inextricably interlocked that men like Pierre in seeking to do good involve themselves and others in the foulest deeds.

Most men, like Billy Budd, are by nature innocent. Their sins are little sins, resembling those of sailors everywhere whose "deviations are marked by juvenility." We must not miss the significant fact that Billy is impressed from a ship named the *Rights of Man* and that he is as innocent as Adam before the fall. The ship which impresses him is named the *Indomitable* (at one time Melville thought of calling it the *Bellipotent*). Billy has left behind him the natural state of man and has entered a world at war, our world, where monomaniac depravity like Claggart's is free to roam and subvert but where, too, men like Captain Vere are sometimes in command.

Melville drops the mantle of tragedy on Billy. He gives him a tragic flaw in his symbolic inability to speak and thus throw Claggart's accusation in his teeth. Billy goes to his death manfully with a cry of blessing for Captain Vere. Melville permits him as well some recognition of the reasons for his plight, though he shuts the door upon the healing words the Captain spoke to Billy in their closeted interview.

The agony is Billy's, but only Captain Vere is capable of understanding the law which compels his suffering. To the perplexed officers of the court he expounds the law under which they live and by which they must act as its responsible agents.

Now can we adjudge to summary and shameful death a fellow-creature inno-cent before God, and whom we feel to be so?—Does that state it aright? You sign sad assent. Well, I too feel that, the full force of that. It is Nature. But do these buttons that we wear attest our allegiance is to Nature? No, to the King. Though the ocean, which is inviolate Nature primeval, though this be the element where we move and have our being as sailors, yet as the King's officers lies our duty in a sphere correspondingly natural? So little is that true, that in receiving our com-missions we in the most important regards ceased to be natural free agents. When war is declared, are we the commissioned fighters previously consulted? We fight at command. If our judgments approve the war, that is but coincidence. So in other particulars. So now, would it be so much we ourselves that would condemn as it would be martial law operating through us? For that law and the rigour of it, we are not responsible. Our vowed responsibility is in this: That however pitilessly that law may operate, we nevertheless adhere to it and administer it.

"We fight at command. If our judgments approve the war, that is but coincidence." Here Melville sets up his everlasting rest. He will not obey the first commandment. He cannot upon compulsion love the God who created the moral order in which we live. But to the rest of the decalogue he at last subscribed.

29. WALT WHITMAN

THE United States in which Emerson, Melville, and Walt Whitman spent their formative years was a group of commonwealths, loosely joined together in spite of the Constitution which was supposed to have made them one country. The federal principle had not yet been really tested, and, within Whitman's own lifetime, was temporarily to break down.

Walt Whitman was born in the intermediate land of Long Island on May 31, 1819, near the great harbor and westward-leading river of New York, with Dutch and Yankee, Quaker, and Calvinist in his ancestry. He was bred an enthusiast for the unity of his country. From his childhood in a patriotic family, he was taught to regard all men within the boundaries of the Republic as Americans like himself, differing only in their labors, fortunes, and separate personalities. In contrast to Emerson, Thoreau, and Melville, he was an American and an expansionist on a new model. Less wedded to class or region, he saw America as a whole.

There was, however, a cleavage in self-interests, in hopes for the future, or in temperament among these New World men and women more significant than the contrasts between New England and South Carolina, a cleavage which Walt too easily overlooked. In every state, and most visible of all in near-by New York, the capital of Walt's youth, an observer was sure to comment upon the difference between the settled society of Eastern merchants and landowners, and the multitude whose thoughts and energies were engaged by the great undeveloped West. Some of this multitude of the unsettled were recent immigrants on their way to new homes. Some were native Americans who, by the nature of their livelihood, or the turn of their imagination, were dominated by the idea of expansion into an unconquered continent. Many an expansionist remained where he was born, yet shared the dream of a continental, cosmopolitan state, a true New World. Such a man was Walt Whitman, and with the expansionists of geography and of politics, of body and of soul, he definitely belonged from his earliest maturity to death.

Walt Whitman was born on a farm in Long Island, a remnant of the five-hundred-acre estate of the Whitman family long settled there, near the marine village of Huntington. Just before his fifth birthday, he was taken with the family to Brooklyn, where his father, a carpenter-builder by trade, established his business. But for the next thirty years Walt was to return again and again to ramble and loaf in the fields and on the beaches of Long Island. In Brooklyn, he went to elementary school, his only formal education, and was soon apprenticed to the printing trade; there and in New York he got ink in his blood, and had opportunities to journalize on his own. From printer he grew into reporter and editor (with politics on the side), and in 1846 was given his "best sit," by which he meant situation, as editor on the *Daily Eagle,* the leading Brooklyn newspaper of his day. Here for nearly two years it was his job to round up the news of the town, of America, and of the world for local readers, and to preach to them daily on Democratic politics, morals, civic virtues, and the tendencies of the times.

He was at home in Brooklyn, a respectable member of a growing community, and placed in a typical framework of American small-town life. But the great bay of New York lay just beyond Brooklyn Ferry, crowded with shipping that swarmed with immigrants on their way to the West, especially after the opening of the Erie Canal in 1825. And New York itself was just across the ferries, already a great metropolis, cosmopolitan, turbulent, rich, incredibly growing. From Brooklyn Heights, the young Whitman could and did look at the symbol of American expansiveness, the port of New York, from which, even though art and literature still looked largely to the Old World for patterns, the trade, industry, and energetic imagination of thousands of Americans were already viewing westward expansion in terms of a continent.

The youth was a dreamer and mystic in his inner life. But as a young editor, a spokesman for the party of the plain people, he was actively concerned with the nation, and its problems which had become acute as a result of the expansions of the Mexican War, fought while he was editing the *Eagle.* As a reporter (and Whitman both in prose and in verse was always a reporter), he left daily his pleasant stall in Brooklyn to roam New York, to frequent its theaters in the years of great Shakespearean actors, and to drink in its operatic music while he watched the capture of vast audiences by the art of poetic oratory. As a Bohemian (and Whitman, who seldom lived with his family and never married, was always a Bohemian), he delighted in the crowds of Broadway, studied the "en-masse," as he called it, without prejudice, preferring workmen, farmers, the vitality of the common people, to the static and the complacent in American society. "Remember, the book [the *Leaves of Grass*] arose," he said to his friend Dr. Bucke, "out of my life in Brooklyn and New York from 1838 to 1853, absorbing a million people, for fifteen years, with an intimacy, an eagerness, an abandon, probably never equalled."

Whitman's education was partly self-education and partly vocational education, with great variety in both and few frames of reference in either. The former came by reading, the second was a by-product of his occupation as a journalist. It is difficult and unnecessary to separate the two, for while, as he grew older, he read more and more to enrich the *Leaves*—as before he had read because he was an editor and needed information—yet he read as a journalist always, finding nothing about mankind alien to his purposes and hence absorbing always the handiest books. Journalism, and especially political journalism, canalized his otherwise indiscriminate perusal of the many books that came for review into the *Eagle* editorial office, directing his attention toward all that fed his inner life, or that dealt with the rights, the opportunities, and most of all the potentialities of the common man.

We have abundant records of Whitman's reading in his many notes, not easily dated, but extending back into the formative years of the *Leaves*. As a child, he was nursed on romance, especially Scott; but when books in quantity became accessible to him and his own purposes had focused on the "long journey" of man toward personal freedom and full self-development, he foraged in history, science, general literature, and what he could take of philosophy. No year passes that some scholar does not discover a new source for the *Leaves,* in Michelet, Hegel, George Sand, Carlyle. A hundred more sources will be found, for the range, though not the depth, of the knowledge recorded in Whitman's notebooks is extraordinary.

These sources, as such, are not very important. The young man was seeking confirmation for the impulse of his inner being to become the voice of the common man who had been given at last, and on a new continent, his opportunity. Yet it is clear from the notes that, unlike the popular sentimentalists and indeed most "literary" writers of his youth, he was furnishing his imagination with facts, to be used as tools and weapons and poetic symbols. While feeding his dreams, he was collecting an intellectual arsenal for democracy, although it is probable that his first intention was to use it in editorial combats, for which, with his meager education, he had been none too well prepared.

By 1849, the Democratic Party, confused and split by the issues of slavery, no longer offered his independent mind a career in political journalism. Then he definitely turned to another objective, which was to capture not so much the opinions as the emotions and the imaginations of Americans. While still supporting himself by miscellaneous journalism, he gave his energy, his ambitions, and his deepest life to poetry. But this poetry, the *Leaves of Grass,* got much of its relevance to American life and to democracy from his reporter's training in observation and the editor's duty to be prepared for public debate on political and social issues of his day and time.

2

Although known until 1855 only as editor, or free-lance writer for the magazines, Walt Whitman had heard the call to the vocation of serious literature from his earliest youth. At first it was the wrong call, or (for him) the wrong kind of literature. Beginning at a very early age, he had endeavored to make a reputation in the conventional modes of the day—sentimental and melodramatic stories such as were being published by second-rate authors in the annuals and the magazines, orthodox poetry in the usual rhyme and meter schemes, and essays in the rhetorical-personal style then fashionable. He was successful enough to make a little place for himself in the better magazines, such as the *Democratic Review,* but, without exception, his work of this kind, including a novel on the dangers of intemperance, was commonplace, empty of real literary values, imitative, often banal, and definitely inferior to his journalism. Either the man's creative imagination had very little to say, or he could not say it. Until the late 1840's, when he was nearly thirty years old, both statements seem to have been true. Beside Emerson and Thoreau, who wrote for the same magazines, he seems shallow, facile, and ignorant. Yet in ten years Emerson was to hail him as author of *the* American poem.

The change had taken place when his inner life began to push to the surface and become articulate. We know that Whitman had been a dreamy boy, absorbed and absorptive to the point of apparent languor, so that he was often accused of laziness. Sometime in the forties, when he was most active in journalism and most prolific in attempts to be literary in the current modes, his maturing imagination began to draw upon experience lying at deeper levels. Strong influences of his childhood made it easy for him to believe in his own inspiration. The intense egoism of a young man in an expansive time encouraged him to put on the mantle of a prophet. His reading, as his notes show, supplied him with examples of the power of poetic leadership. And all this reacted upon his professional reporter's vision of the active millions of Americans around him engaged in one of humanity's great experiments. Being a writer already by profession, he began to try to make his vision articulate in poetic prose and adequate poetry, and with laborious difficulty finally succeeded.

This is not guesswork. As early as 1847, while Walt was in his "best sit," editing the Brooklyn *Daily Eagle* and lecturing the town, he began a notebook, now in the Library of Congress, which contains mingled prose and poetry, some of the poetry probably copied in from earlier records. By this time, Whitman had become completely self-expressive in good newspaper prose, and could exhort to good politics and sound morals as well as any of the journalistic tribe. Yet in this notebook is a mass of confused, apocalyptic prose writing, oracular, rhythmic, even when not written as verse, transcendental, evangelical in its earnestness. This writing, in style and subject matter, has no obvious relationship to his good if conventional editorials, or to anything known in his letters, or his personal communication with his associates. And it is definitely imperfect and experimental. The poetry in the notebook, which is written as such, is highly symbolic, rhythmic but not metrical, often unfinished, but recognizable as a first, or early, version of a part of the *Leaves of Grass*. Indeed, the dominant ideas of both the Preface and the poems of the first edition of the *Leaves* can be disentangled from the prose and verse of the first and immediately succeeding notebooks.

It is impossible to explain by any final analysis this remarkable phenomenon of the unveiling of a genius and prophet (however unformed) in the mind of a busy and successful journalist. Whitman's later friend, the Canadian alienist Dr. Richard Maurice Bucke, asserted that here was a remarkable instance of direct inspiration functioning through what he called cosmic consciousness, and many an early admirer of Whitman (and perhaps Whitman himself) was convinced by this theory of spiritual intuition. A more modest statement seems nearer the truth. There was a genius for absorption in this youth so sensitive to both his physical and his spiritual environment, and this genius became creative as soon as his rich but inchoate inner life felt the pressures of experience. His dreams became compelling and sought an expression for which his training so far was entirely inadequate. The notebooks not only record his early experiments, but show that these dreams, wherever derived and however inarticulate, had already taken form as a religion of divinity in the common man, which called for a new poet and prophet. Many of these earliest records of his inner being are meditations upon what such a poet should be like, how he should proceed, what should be the nature of his success. And it is made clear that the poet was to be himself.

Therefore, when Whitman's career as political journalist was frustrated by events, it was natural that the poet should take over the center of his life. Indeed, as one reads these notebooks, it is clearly inevitable that sooner or later this should happen. What had been a painful experiment to express the deepest in his belief and his desires, became his immediate and settled ambition. In a few years he set the motto, "Make the works," on his desk, and made ready for publication the first *Leaves of Grass,* which seems an incredible achievement for a politician and a journalist only because its long deep roots stretching back into childhood were known only to Whitman himself. This is a reasonable if not a complete explanation of one of the most surprising outbursts of genius in early middle age known in literary history.

3

But what was this *Leaves of Grass*? Whitman himself defined it many times, not always in the same terms:

An attempt . . . of a naive, masculine, affectionate, contemplative, sensual, imperious person to cast into literature not only his own grit and arrogance, but his own flesh and form, undraped, regardless of models, regardless of modesty or law; and ignorant, as at first it appears, of . . . all outside of the fiercely loved land of his birth. . . . The effects he produces in his poems are no effects of artists or the arts, but the effects of the original eye or arm, or the actual atmosphere, of tree, or bird.

I saw, from the time my enterprise and questionings positively shaped themselves (how best can I express my own distinctive era and surroundings, America, Democracy?) that the trunk and centre whence the answer was to radiate, and to which all should return from straying however far a distance, must be an identical body and soul, a personality—which personality, after many considerations and ponderings, I deliberately settled should be myself—indeed could not be any other.

Leaves of Grass . . . has mainly been . . . an attempt . . . to put *a Person,* a human being (myself, in the latter half of the Nineteenth Century, in America,) freely, fully and truly on record. I could not find any similar personal record in current literature that satisfied me.

After half a century these definitions still ring true, but they apply to the extended later editions, rather than to the original poem out of which all the *Leaves* grew, and which was crudely outlined and partly written in the 1847 notebook. This is the "Song of Myself," by no means Whitman's greatest poem, though probably his most characteristic. It is a true microcosm, and one of the most self-revealing poems in literature. He must have been working on the "Song" from the dawn of his resolve to be the poet of the New World in the "strange, unloosen'd, wondrous time" of the earlier nineteenth century—say, from about 1846 to its publication in 1855—and he heavily revised it in later editions. It is the key to an understanding of Walt Whitman.

When the "Song," the Preface, and the accompanying shorter poems were ready, Whitman became printer as well as writer. Knowing well what publishers would and would not accept, he decided to become his own publisher, fell back on his knowledge of the printing trade, laid out a book of unusual size and typography, set up some of it himself, and brought out the first edition of the *Leaves,* now a collector's item. Of this the "Song" was the outstanding feature, and was so recognized by the reviewers.

The "Song of Myself" in its final arrangement is a poem of fifty-two groups of long lines, each group a paragraph introducing a turn in the thought. Sometimes the break is abrupt, and the only reference is back to the brooding, oracular imagination of the author.

The poem begins with an assertion intended to challenge contemporary (and earlier) literature, which Whitman regarded as "class poetry" representing a world where literature had spoken for the exceptional man, not for the simple, separate person or the en-masse:

> I celebrate myself, and sing myself, . . .
> For every atom belonging to me as good belongs to you. . . .
> I loafe and invite my soul. . . .
> I harbor for good or bad, I permit to speak at every hazard,
> Nature without check, with original energy.

In an early manuscript he was more specific:

> I am your voice—it was tied in you—in me it begins to talk.
> I celebrate myself to celebrate every man and woman alive; . . .
> And I say that the soul is not greater than the body,
> And I say that the body is not greater than the soul.

This is the key passage in the poem. He proposes to be the voice of the democracy, and he intends to speak at all hazards what he finds in himself as representative of the "divine average." What does he find there?

He discovers that there is a world of sense perception in every man that is part of the eternal time stream and is far more important than what he calls the "latest dates" and the routine of daily living. Through love and its instrument, the senses, comes the knowledge that all men, with God also, are brothers. This cannot be argued, any more than the question, "What is grass?" can be answered. Yet it is certain that life and death are part of one continuous process in which every phenomenon has its importance. So leave discussion, and look at the pageant of life—wives, old maids, drivers, farmers, hunters—the Yankee clipper under her staysails, the clam digger, the trapper, the runaway slave, beautiful young men bathing and the woman who joins them in fancy, the Negro drayman with polished muscles—all these to the caresser of life are part of himself, part of a continuum both physical and spiritual. They are kin to the grass that grows wherever the land is, the common air that bathes the globe.

Therefore the self-dramatized Walt Whitman speaks for all this, sees himself in all people and all life, speaks for woman as well as man, for evil as well as good, and walking with the tender and growing night feels unspeakable passionate love for such beauty. He accepts time absolutely; in the long run, he says, it is without flaw. He accepts science which explains reality. He trusts the en-masse:

> I speak the pass-word primeval, I give the sign of democracy.
> By God! I will accept nothing which all cannot have their
>   counterpart of on the same terms.

Therefore, through him, long dumb voices of prisoners and slaves, the diseased and the despairing, the forbidden voices of sex and lust, speak at last, are clarified and transfigured. *"Walt,"* he says, *"you contain enough, why don't you let it out then?"* Which he does, first telling what he hears in the exciting world of his senses, then what he touches, both in intricate sexual imagery.

Now Whitman goes afoot with his vision. Over America, its work and festivals, he wanders, pleased with all he meets, then lifts his imagination to the past. He walks with Christ on the hills of Judaea; he is a free companion, a hero, a slave hounded by pursuers; he was at the Alamo; he fought with Paul Jones. He will save the depressed and the dying by the power of his love, outbidding those old hucksters, the heathen gods:

> I know perfectly well my own egotism,
> Know my omnivorous lines and must not write any less,
> And would fetch you whoever you are flush with myself.

Immense have been the preparations for this robust soul of his which symbolizes the soul of a new society. Nothing can stop its evolution. He will hook each man and woman around the waist and show them the endless road onward which each must travel for himself. Long enough have we dreamed contemptible dreams. As for himself, having given his message, he will depart, bequeathing himself to the dirt to grow again from the grass he loves. Somewhere, and notably in these poems, he waits for you.

This brief outline of the "Song of Myself" shows what many a reader has failed to see because of the profusion of detail and of imagery, that in spirit and exhortation, and in its long catalogues of activities, it is an expansionist poem, as expansionist as its country and its century. It is also a prophetic poem in the Old Testament sense, for Whitman is urging a vigorous country to spiritualize its energy and demanding that a society whose culture is intellectual shall find new sources of power in beautiful blood, in the ardors of sex, in a harmony, like the harmony of animals, with the physical universe. Furthermore, it is a dramatic poem. The author plays a histrionic role, like a revivalist. If he contradicts himself, he says, paraphrasing Emerson, well, then he contradicts himself. He is large, he contains multitudes. He can and does project a man of this age, great enough to feel with all, to love all, and to point them down the long brown road to full self-development. And this is the heart, though not the totality of Whitman's message. He will say it in separate poems more completely and far better, but he will never unsay any of it.

With all its extravagance, its artistic imperfections, and its incoherences (which are more apparent than real), this is an amazing poem to have come from the pen of a journalist whose literary publications hitherto had been conventional and often inferior. What was the long foreground which the wise Emerson, in his letter of greeting to the 1855 edition, intuitively felt lay behind it? What were its roots? In what spiritual and intellectual climate was it incubated? What was this "personality," this "identical body and soul," which was its dramatic center, and which Whitman deliberately settled should be himself? We can give some of the answers, without attempting to account for the essential genius which fed on the sap of environment, influence, and personal traits.

Whitman had been born in a household where radical liberalism was already familiar. His father, Walter Whitman, had been a disciple of Frances Wright, protégée of Lafayette, feminist, lecturer, and writer in behalf of labor and the common man. Walter Whitman was an intense individualist, who, though of landed stock, worked with his own hands, and liked to sleep, as he said, on floors of his own making. The family were Democrats when to be a Democrat meant specifically to vote for the rights of man and for the power of the masses against vested interests. The philosophy of this Democratic Party under Jefferson and Jackson was still revolutionary. Indeed, it was American Democrats who were to carry on a social revolution which our political Revolution had only begun. And the democracy of the Democratic Party was also a triumphant cause, never more vigorous, more hopeful, more potential than in America in the decades of the great expansion westward. A transference of the political ardor of the young political editor to the imaginative enthusiasm of a poem in which he wished to speak for the common man was natural, and carried confidence with it. Thus the background of the *Leaves* was the whole revolutionary process from eighteenth century "enlightenment" onward. For its author, the cause of the common man was a conquering religion, in which he had begun as a worker and became a priest.

It is not therefore surprising that Whitman's first characteristic poetry is not propaganda, or argument, but a chanting of victory and aspiration, in which he celebrates himself as a symbol of the "divine average." Nor that he addresses it to the "simple, separate person," the common man on common ground, who best represents a New World where oppressed human nature has already found successful release.

Yet one doubts whether the young Whitman, still so inarticulate, as his notebooks show, in the things which concern him most, would have been so confident of his inspiration or so determined to find a way to communicate it, if it had not been for his indoctrination in the mystical assurance of Quakerism. He was, of course, never a Quaker by profession; he was not made, as he said, to live within a fence. Yet he grew up in a Quaker strong-hold, his mother's family were Quakers, his father was an admirer of the great Quaker heretic, Elias Hicks, and Whitman himself was not only personally familiar with, but deeply impressed by, a religion whose only authority was the Inner Light. The essential fact is that he lived as a child and youth among men and women who took inspiration with the utmost seriousness, believing that, no matter how simple and unlearned was the voice that spoke of God, what was said was worthy of regard and should never be suppressed. He was familiar with the distinction which every Quaker made between the "I" which did the daily business of life, and the "soul" which, feeling a concern to report on the inner life of the spirit, might speak out in meeting, no matter how crudely, in the language of inspiration, a language usually rhythmic. The young Whitman had no inhibitions to overcome in writing as one inspired.

It must not, of course, be forgotten that the influence of transcendentalism, so pervasive and so powerful upon idealists, and also expansionist in its nature, was at its height in the years when the "Song of Myself" was forming in Whitman's imagination. How far this powerful transcendentalism, emanating from New England in the thirties and forties, gave form and logic and philosophy to Walt's celebration of himself, will always be in controversy. There can now be no question that Whitman absorbed from Emerson be-fore he wrote the *Leaves*. Not only is there record of essays read and lectures heard, but in the "Song of Myself," which represents the earliest stratum of his real poetry, there are echoes and paraphrases of Emerson. Whitman was definitely a fellow traveler with both the Quakers and the transcendentalists, as can be seen in the extraordinary meditations in his first notebook. Yet he was never a transcendentalist in the restricted Concord sense. Like the Quaker Hicks, he carried the ideas of man's intuitive knowledge of God and the spiritual significance of all phenomena to an ultimate conclusion, disregarding all metaphysical difficulties.

But Whitman's transcendental tendencies, though obvious, united with other tendencies much more personal to him, and emerged as a philosophy which neither Thoreau nor Emerson could accept as identical with their own, although they recognized the affiliation.

If, as Whitman learned both from the Quakers and from Emerson, a man could be God's mouthpiece, then God, so Whitman felt, must be manifest through man's body and all its impulses as well as through his soul. Soul and body were indissolubly interdependent, and blood and spirit were equally important in a true democracy. The common man, lusty, full-blooded, living, especially in America, upon hearty and varied experience, was as important as the saint, the intellectual, or the aristocrat, and in history likely to become more important. The vigorous sexual instinct which keeps the race alive was not merely a means for breeding new candidates for the Heavenly Kingdom, nor was it, as the Concordians thought, an animal remainder to be sublimated into a love transcending the flesh. No, if the soul was God, so was the body, and if democracy, and man himself, was to reach an ideal society, then the senses must have their full self-development as part of the expression of the soul. Here was an extension of transcendentalism, adapting it to the needs and the facts of an expanding democracy in a new land. When Whitman called Emerson "master," he may have meant that Emerson first gave direction and authority to his vague Quakerism. And when, later, he asserted that he was now his own master, he must have meant that he had carried his conception of God and man, body and soul, far beyond the limits of transcendental orthodoxy.

Of the personal traits which are reflected in his poems—and especially in the "Song of Myself"—one was his strong capacity for self-dramatization. Throughout life, as any careful biographer must see, he found it easy to differentiate between the "I," who was the Walt of daily relations, and the "soul," which was dramatized as Walt Whitman in the poems. The "I" was simple, natural, affectionate, often diffident and modest. The "soul," especially in his first decade of real poetry, was aggressive, brash, self-confident, violently assertive, and intensely egoistic—in addition to having many nobler qualities. Here he was representing, perhaps unconsciously, the brag and exaggeration of the frontier, the vanity of the self-taught leaders, the almost paranoiac desires of a new country aiming at greatness and clamoring for recognition. And his long and often tiresome catalogues of occupations (inventories of America, Emerson called them) are like the answers to the curious questions so frequent among immigrants and pioneers. In his vatic moods Walt clearly regarded himself as two persons, one of them under the influence of inspiration. Psychologically this, of course, was not true; but for him it had a pragmatic truth.

This accounts for the personal, prophetic element in Whitman's brand of transcendental thinking, which gave it a warmth that orthodox transcendentalism too often lacked. But the strong sensuality of the "Song of Myself" and many other poems, the deep sympathy with carnal man, indeed Whitman's whole argument for a democracy of the emotions, and particularly those emotions which are primarily sexual, unquestionably were all much influenced by his powerful body and strong but highly complicated sexual nature.

In his young manhood and early middle age, six feet in height, ruddy, not athletic, but an outdoor man, he radiated health and vigor. His best known pictures, which were taken in later years and show him "buffalo-haired" and full-bearded, a combination of Santa Claus and Father Time, give a false impression of the man in his prime. Health, vigor, lustiness are words that occur or are paraphrased throughout the *Leaves*. When most mystical, most prophetic, Walt most insists that it is his "beautiful blood" as much as his soul that is speaking. The affinities he found in his country were not among intellectuals, professional men, scholars (though these were his associates), but workmen, fishermen, farmers, pioneers, as hearty as himself, who did the work of God without analyzing. How well he knew them (and he did know them well) is not the question. It was the physical health and energy of his America in its great expansive period which stirred his imagination because he felt it in himself.

In this cult of triumphant physical vigor, Whitman was in accord with the continent-conquering energy of the mid-century, and out of accord with its most literary literature—whether the ghost-haunted narratives of Hawthorne, the polished romance of Longfellow, the febrilities of Poe, or the anemic sentimentalism of the annuals and the magazines. Most of the other writers of the age—Emerson, for example—were busy with sublimating or intellectualizing the crude energy of American physical life. Even Thoreau, who once wished to eat a woodchuck alive, was more disturbed than excited by what he regarded as the turbulent rush across the continent for land or gold. These writers were analyzing, criticizing, and portraying the first maturity of American culture. They were little concerned with the muscle, not much with the heart, except as an organ of refined or repressed passion. Though an observer and dreamer rather than forest feller and prairie breaker, Whitman had a zest for magnificent bodies, stimulated by his admiration for his own, which made him recoil from the intellectual and refined and gloat upon such manifestations as the full-bloodedness of New York—"turbulent, fleshy, sensual, eating, drinking, and breeding." He admired the immigrants bringing their muscles and little else to the new land, and was fascinated by the immense labors of pioneering, and the pageant of America at work. When, on his trip to New Orleans in 1848, he saw some of his frontiersmen along the Ohio, he was a little disillusioned by their idleness and the effects of malaria, but this did not change his dream. He believed he had more blood than his fellow writers, and better than they could feed his imagination on the strengths of the common man set loose in a free world, an aspect of America from which, he thought, literature had turned her face away, and so missed the reality of democratic advance. In an expanding democracy, the senses, he felt (and responded with his own), must take on new patterns of expression to represent the nature and needs of the "divine average," of common man on common ground of human unity.

These were some of the roots, and this was part of the foreground of this book which shocked, puzzled, amused, amazed, or profoundly impressed its few readers. But there was another source for its most challenging quality not easy to analyze. If the "Song of Myself" was symbolic of the release and expansion of democratic man, neither Whitman himself, nor some of his most characteristic poetry, was entirely representative of his fellow Americans. Physically and psychologically, Whitman was not typical of this "divine average" to which he wished to give, and did give, a voice. His love poetry was not always or often the expression of a normal sexual man. Nor was the difference merely in genius speaking, nor in a sublimation of body with spirit.

This ruddy body of Whitman's, with its electric senses, and its quick perception of passion, was not the body of an average man. Sexually, it and he (for his imagination of course was involved) belonged in the vague regions that lie in the hinterland of what a doctor or a psychiatrist would call a normal man or woman. He was physically sympathetic, mentally interpretive, for both sexes, richer perhaps than either taken alone. There is not one particle of evidence that he was actively homosexual, and when he was challenged in old age he recoiled from the idea with a horror whose sincerity is convincing. Yet from the records of his life and the testimony of the imagery of his poems, it is clear that his love went out more readily, more frequently, though not more passionately, to men than to women. With the boys he loved and cared for in the Civil War hospitals, and with young friends like the streetcar conductor, Pete Doyle, this love seems paternal. But there was often a perturbation, as he called it, a sexual arousing that does not differ from the passion between man and woman. Also, women readers of the *Leaves* have long since recognized an approach to passion that is often more feminine than masculine. Yet his love poems to women are too aglow with fervor to let one doubt that he knew also the love of women, and here in full sexual release. And to this must be added a curious worship of his own body which a psychiatrist would call autosexuality. There are patent instances in the "Song of Myself."

This sexual oversensitiveness is supernormal rather than abnormal. It made him a writer of great love poems. It made him an apostle of the love of comrades, which he believed alone could insure a durable democracy. It made it easy for him to dramatize himself as a symbol of the lusty vigor of expansionist America and of a sexuality fully developed and expressed and indispensable to the growth of a perfect society. It made it fatally easy for him to carry his sexuality beyond the bounds of reason and good taste.

Thus he became a target for the prudish; and he confused and sometimes disgusted his simpler readers, who did not like their sexual instincts discussed in terms of a religion; and he shocked beyond measure the bourgeoisie whose favorite reading was moral or sentimental novels in which sex was not so much ignored as bought off with hypocritical or lascivious hints.

4

The first *Leaves of Grass* was put on sale in Brooklyn and in New York at the shop of his friends Fowler and Wells, publishers of phrenological literature and of *Life Illustrated,* a popular magazine for which later Whitman did a series of articles. A number of copies were sent out for review and to men of influence. It was the reviews of the *Leaves,* and not the sales (which were negligible) that made American, and also English, readers aware of the appearance of a new poet, who was original if also shocking, bold if egoistic, powerful even if, in the opinion of most of the critics, powerful in wrong directions.

The first *Leaves* contained a brilliant Preface, stating a theory of poetry for democracy and for America. It contained also twelve poems, of which the first, "Song of Myself," was obviously an attempt to describe a symbolic man of the nineteenth century. This symbolic man was named in the poem, Walt Whitman, although there was no author's name on the title page of the book. Of the other poems, the most significant were (using their later titles) "I Sing the Body Electric," which was the most shocking, and "Who Learns My Lesson Complete," in which the poet steps onto the platform to explain his idea of life.

A second edition was published the next year, 1856, with new poems, some of them among Whitman's best, such as "Salut au Monde!" "Song of the Broad-Axe," "Crossing Brooklyn Ferry," "Song of the Open Road," in which his scope is notably extended. This edition failed with the buying public as completely as the first.

In 1860, Whitman issued a much more extensive volume, heavily revised, and with important additions, especially under the headings of "Chants Democratic," "Enfans d'Adam," dealing with the love of women, and "Calamus" inspired by the love of men. The outbreak of war cut short a promising sale for this edition. The Civil War, however, found its best expression in literature in *Drum-Taps,* of 1865, and the Lincoln poems, both groups included in an edition of 1867. Some of the finest of *Drum-Taps* came from Whitman's experience as a professional visitor to the sick and wounded in the hospitals in Washington where he cared for and comforted thousands of men. Though he never saw a battle, he knew soldiers intimately, and it was in the hospitals, as he said, that he first came to know from first-hand experience the virtues of the American en-masse.

In 1876, three years after his paralysis (in 1873), from which neither Whitman nor his poetic faculty ever entirely recovered, he published the sixth edition of the *Leaves,* containing the farewell poems of his creative period, "Passage to India" (separately printed earlier), "Prayer of Columbus," and "Song of the Redwood Tree," with other new poems. In 1881, the *Leaves* were given their final rearrangement in a definitive edition, and in 1892, the year of his death, got their final text in a ninth edition.

Even this briefest of bibliographical notes should make it easier to understand the unusual composition of the *Leaves of Grass.* It is not at any time, even in its ninth edition, a complete, articulated book. It is a becoming, in which the imaginative concept of the whole is to be found in the beginning, a whole which expands and gains power and control like a man's body, and which ceases, not because there is no more growth possible, but because death ends it.

Unfortunately, the courageous reader who proposes to go through the *Leaves of Grass* from cover to cover is confused not only by Whitman's occasional verbosity and frequent repetitions, but also by the aging man's rearrangements of the poems, by which a chronological order was destroyed, and poems of little vitality were inserted among the works of his great creative period. He intended to make a coordinated structure like a cathedral, but succeeded only in imitating an American World's Fair, such as the International Exposition in New York in 1853, which deeply stirred his imagination. No major author so thoroughly needs an editing as Whitman, such an editing as Arnold gave to the poetry of Wordsworth. He forbade it in his own lifetime because, with the genteel age against him, he felt that his lesson must be learned complete. There is no such necessity now for what revivalists used to call a "protracted meeting."

The first *Leaves* of 1855, which, it must be emphasized, was only the nucleus of the extensive final work, began a long battle for recognition, fought first by Whitman and then by his devoted friends. Its importance was much more generally recognized by critics in America than has been supposed, though it got plenty of blows. The selections which W. M. Rossetti made for England in 1868, from earlier editions, established Whitman's reputation there much sooner than at home. This was because the sexual poems, which had confused the prudish judgment of mid-nineteenth century America, were not included. And also, the English were naturally not offended, in fact the opposite, by what Americans regarded as a rough and raucous representation of their democracy.

The *Leaves of Grass* was one of those documents of the human spirit which appear at intervals in time, and which arouse both violent opposition and (though not always) unmeasured praise. Such documents are always the work of a pioneer, and, like the efforts of geographical pioneers, are often incomplete, defective, as full of faults as of genius. They meet with extraordinary opposition for several reasons. Even though the ideas they express may be familiar to thinkers, or drawn from the actual practice of the age, these books give these ideas their first emotional impact, take them out of philosophy or the current mores, and force them upon the imagination. It was thus with *The Prince* of Machiavelli, and the works of Rousseau. Also, it is often necessary for the writer to find, like the early Elizabethans, a new idiom in which to make his imagination articulate, and this idiom is often unfamiliar, and therefore not liked. So it was with the music of Wagner. Furthermore, if the document is literary and deals with human behavior, it is quite sure to run counter to the moral conventions, though not necessarily to the moral practices, of the locality of production. It offends because it asks for a reconsideration of what we have agreed to accept and live by. So it was with the New Testament.

All this was true of the first *Leaves of Grass,* and unfortunately the shock and clamor with which the relatively few greeted its "arrogant" verses redoubled when in the 1860 edition Whitman included his "Calamus" and his "Children of Adam," poems which, so the outraged critics thought, were only incentives to sexuality and perhaps to perversion. They neglected (with a few exceptions) new poems of moving beauty and emotional depth, such as "Crossing Brooklyn Ferry." Critics of later editions did not recognize the deepening of Whitman's religious feeling and his far saner intuitions of human nature in such superb poems of the late fifties and the sixties as "Out of the Cradle Endlessly Rocking," "When Lilacs Last in the Dooryard Bloom'd," and "Passage to India." Nor did they note, again with a few exceptions, a growth in artistry, until what had been an experiment in "Song of Myself" became in these later poems the technical excellence of a great and original creator of prosody. They let slip with faint praise (there was no general reading) the dramatic portraiture (begun in the "Song of Myself") which in *Drum-Taps* produced some of the best etched, most realistic, yet most uplifted poetry of war in English. Still confused by the outcry over Whitman's indecencies, they failed to see that democracy, which in the "Song of Myself" is only an emotional reaching toward the health and vigor of the common man, had become in "So Long!" of 1860 a religion of development, which, through the love of comrades, could make a society of realized physical and spiritual power. Nor was the profound acceptance of the will of the universe in Whitman's great poems, "Song of the Redwood Tree" and "Prayer of Columbus" (1876), adequately recognized until after his death. The critics were still discussing his sexuality, his egoism, and his exuberant optimism, while these poems, with their Hegelian antitheses of optimism, lifted faith above hope, and asserted the dream as the ultimate master of reality.

This deepening of Whitman's mind, like his growth in art, is easier to explain than the origins of his genius. His autobiographical writings, both in prose and in verse, show with painful clarity what had happened to the cheerful, confident caresser of life in the years between 1850 and 1870, so momentous to the nation. He was, it must be remembered, intensely patriotic in the most religious sense of that word. The United States, for him, was the haven of democracy, the hope of the common mass. Its unity on a continent was the great fact of the nineteenth century, and now, in the fifties, he saw his country rent apart by factions, governed by weak or corrupt politicians, hopelessly divided by the conflict over slavery, unable to meet the great emergency because of greed and selfishness in the North and arrogance in the South, and the incapacity of its leaders in both sections. When war was declared, his morale rose because the challenge to unity had been accepted, and he was soon aware of the emergence of a great man in Abraham Lincoln. But in Washington, where he arrived in 1862, he was a witness to the corruption, the self-seeking, the chaos of a government which survived only because the faults of the South, though different, were as great. Consolation was to be found only in the courage, the love, and the simple goodness of the great majority of common men as he watched over them, sick or dying, at the hospitals. In his bitter poem "Respondez" (1856–1871) he frees his heart:

Let the people sprawl with yearning, aimless hands! . . .
(Stifled, O days! O lands! in every public and private corruption!)

His later recollections, printed in Specimen Days and Collect (1882–1883), and The Wound Dresser (1898), tell of his own distresses. Only the common man and a statesman with the best virtues of the common man kept him faithful to the idealism of the earlier Leaves, but no longer egoistically confident. And to the disillusions of history must be added personal griefs and frustrations, their exact source unknown, though love and loss were evidently their source.

No one, for example, can fail to note the deepening of every noble emotion in "Out of the Cradle Endlessly Rocking" (1859). This poem, which is a reminiscence of childhood, when the "tongue's use was sleeping," is a record of loss and love far too passionate and too mature for a child's mind. The ardent sensuality of the "Song of Myself" has been sublimated in this great chant into "the unknown want, the destiny of me," and the solution is the "strong and delicious word," death, the continuum of life, the only answer to the insatiable.

Or the depth of "When Lilacs Last in the Dooryard Bloom'd" (1865), his elegy on the death of President Lincoln. This is no patriotic poem in the usual sense, nor such a triumphant celebration of the achievements of "beautiful blood" and a noble spirit in a man of the people as Whitman might well have written ten years earlier. Actually, like the far less elevated "Calamus" poems, it chants the love of comrades, which is the spiritual binding of democracy, and also the death of a "great companion," "the sweetest, wisest soul of all my days and lands." The gray-brown bird in the shadowy cedars supplies the elegiac commentary. The "powerful, western, fallen star" (Lincoln) was not extinguished with its light. The poem praises the "strong deliveress" death, and its message is always love.

Or of "Passage to India" (1871), which contains his most eloquent idealism. The theme is in the question asked by the feverish children of the modern age, "Whither, O mocking life?" The marriage of the seas in the Suez Canal, the crossing of the continent by steel, do not satisfy, they are but shadows of a greater dream. There must be passage to more than India. The soul, "that actual me," must voyage beyond its material successes in order to amplify its love, its ideals, its "purity, perfection, strength." So "sail forth—steer for the deep waters only."

Or of "Chanting the Square Deific" (1865–1866), not a great poem but an interesting commentary on Whitman's philosophy. Here is described the stern morality of a Jehovah, Christ the consolator, the Holy Spirit inspiring, and, for the fourth boundary of truth, Satan, the comrade of criminals, brother of slaves, despised, proud, equal with any, "nor time nor change shall ever change me or my words." As body and soul are aspects of the same verity, so are evil and good.

What Whitman acquired in these years when he knew, almost equally, distress and exaltation, was wisdom. Passion he had before, and more experience of varied human contacts and man's daily work than usually comes to a poet of mystic love. But his philosophy of living in the years of the first *Leaves* was what the eighteenth century would have called enthusiastic. That was its strength, the poet's exuberant faith in the onsurge of life as an end in itself and an evidence of God come from the depths of his consciousness, where it beat with his blood, and was as real as his blood. One had only to loaf and invite one's soul to know that there is not any more heaven or hell than now. It was a dangerous philosophy for a hot-blooded man who adored action as much as loafing, in a period of excited expansion like that of his youth. It was easy to oversay his philosophy, easier to shout it than to make it conform to reality, just as it was easier to describe the en-masse of America than to know the American as a fellow worker and fellow sufferer. Whitman's earlier poems have the faults of rhetorical overemphasis even though he tried so hard to make them unrhetorical. They are aggressive as a debater is aggressive who talks for points. And furthermore, as his cryptic passages too often show, he had not yet squared his own personal problems with his religion of simple and passionate love.

He needed to be broken away from his egoism by blows from without, as the enthusiast in religion needs to encounter irremediable sorrow or inexplicable sin. He needed to take into his imagination death as well as life. And being Whitman, this extension, for it was only an extension of his philosophy, had to come through no intuition of kinship with God, which was too easy for his expansive nature, but by "crises of anguish" for all who believed as he did that America was the last best hope for their fellow men. There was first the

> Year that trembled and reel'd beneath me!
> Your summer wind was warm enough, yet the air I breathed froze me,
> A thick gloom fell through the sunshine and darken'd me,
> Must I change my triumphant songs? said I to myself,
> Must I indeed learn to chant the cold dirge of the baffled?
> And sullen hymns of defeat?

And after that and equivalent experiences, a transcendence of the ego was needed, a sounder because a wiser religion, and a better understanding of "the potent, felt, interior command stronger than words," which compelled him to accept death with all it implies as passionately as life. His poetry deepened because his imagination, always sensitive to spiritual values, now reached out of his too physical world as he heard another song "covering the earth and filling the spread of the heaven."

Death began to seem as important as life, religion more important than self-expression, for only death with its extensions of spiritual continuities growing closer to the mystery of God, solved the irreconcilable contradictions of earthly life. His poetry deepened because his imagination, always aware of spiritual values, now was chastened into reaching far beyond and beneath his sensory experiences.

5

Since Walt Whitman is poet first, and an apostle of democracy and love and death only because of his poetry, the growth and maturing of his art is of the first importance in any history of the man. To understand this art it will be necessary to go back to the beginning of his career when he turned from what he called useful errands for humanity, his journalism, his surface writings, to making "the works."

Endless disputes have raged over Whitman's prosody. The truth is best ascertained by inquiring what he was trying to do, and what he actually did with the English language.

Two statements may be categorically made. What Whitman sought (and he said so more than once) was a medium in which he could express satisfactorily the expansive soul and the expansive mind and body of democratic man developing in a new continent and forming a new and different society. That a more orthodox technician could have made the conventions of rhyming or metrical verse do this, is not the question. Whitman could not, as his early verse shows. Also, his conviction that he had something new to say and describe impelled him to break away from orthodoxy in order to get an idiom which was fresh on his tongue and so could be personal and sincere. He needed to be free and lavish like his subject matter.

He did not, as he asserted, get rid of outworn poetic diction, though he refreshed it with the bold frankness and realism of his speech. He did not get much closer to the colloquial language of the people than Bryant or Longfellow. No one of his devices to achieve a unity of poetic music is original with him. Yet the result, which means the style, is unmistakable. It can be parodied and imitated, but not reproduced. It is original because it is Walt's own.

For sources, one need go no further than the flowing rhythms of the Old Testament, which, in debased form, was the emotional language of the people of Whitman's generation. And also the oratory of Shakespeare's blank verse in its more rhetorical passages, which he had heard declaimed again and again by the best actors of one of the great ages of Shakespearean presentation. Here he got his elaborate sentence structure. And, finally, the French and Italian opera, of which he was a devotee, a mixed art, both lyric and declamatory, rhythmic in both words and music. Here he found a form for many of his finest poems.

An analysis soon shows the technical contrivances of his long rolling lines, his catalogues, his exhortations, his lyrics, and his dramatic dialogues with himself. If meter and rhyme are to be discarded, some other means must be devised of securing that intense unity of impression which is an essential in poetry. Even a superficial study shows Whitman's extensive, sometimes tiresome, use of alliteration, both along the line and down the line beginnings. It shows assonance and internal rhyme, often most skillfully contrived. It shows a general trochaic and dactyllic pattern (unusual in English poetry, though not in American speech). It reveals a subtle use of the caesura, breaking the long lines into parts of differing lengths. And also a very effective play upon repetition of rhythmic patterns and of words. Rolling his lines (as we know) over and over on his tongue, until they were ready to set down, building his poems slowly with revisions that kept on until his death, he slowly perfected his use of these and other devices, the governing principle being a rhythmic pattern in his mind, which was his style.

If one reads with analytic care the extraordinarily skillful "Out of the Cradle Endlessly Rocking," it is easy to note its alliterations and its use of assonance and internal rhyme. Equally obvious, when looked for, is the structure of the whole, which is that of an opera—overture, recitative, musical meditation, and the song of the bird as lyric, until (as he says himself) "the aria sinking," the poem concludes with a finale. The verse technique of this poem or of "When Lilacs Last in the Dooryard Bloom'd" should be compared with the sprawl and pull-together of the experimental "Song of Myself," which is usually taken as the point of reference in attacks on Whitman's verse. He never wrote better than in some brief passages of the "Song," but its new prosody required the firm grip of the later poems to demonstrate its success.

The advantages of this new style (idiom, he called it) were various. Such diction responded easily to his ambitious attempt to make a voice for multitudes. It made easy rather than difficult his endeavor to put into poetry what current fashion regarded as prosaic, and what seemed, even if it was not, out of place when carried by the current forms of literary verse. It was very flexible, stretched (too readily) to any scope, and enabled him, like the makers of new literary languages, Chaucer for example, to say first and best what no one had endeavored to put into literature before, at least no one in his own land and time.

Most of all, since his personality flowed freely along these rhythms, there was an easy transference to them of the dramatized ego which he called his soul, and which was the symbol of the inner life of Walt, and also of his century and his environment as he felt them. When he "let it all out," he flowed, not into the stereotyped elocution of the orators whom he envied, but into a flexible mold already prepared.

Thus in a true sense Whitman's style may be called functional. It was admirably adapted to describe the immigrant and emigrant American on the move, the still unshaped landscape of a new continent, the energy and the romance of pioneering, the dreams of a nation sure of an illimitable future, and the revolutionary ideas of modern civilization finding their greatest release in this same America. It was also an excellent medium for his passionate nature, so often uncontrolled, and responded with a lift toward the sublime when he wrote of religion and of death.

His diction had great disadvantages also. It encouraged the occasional prose writer and the frequent preacher in the man. It tugged always at restraint, making it easy to reiterate, expand, forget the beginning in the end. In the best controlled poems, the technique became sometimes annoying because artificial. It favored ranting, encouraged padding, for anything could go in almost anywhere, and indeed Whitman frequently switched passages from one poem to another. Worst of all for him (though unavoidably) it offended good readers bred in the great tradition of poetry in English, and made his reception so difficult that in obstinate reaction he sometimes turned what was after all only a technique into an eccentricity.

Yet Whitman's poetic style must be judged by its best passages, and there it is not only as characteristic of the writer as was Shakespeare's late blank verse, but it is also a new style and often a great one.

One more commentary should be made on the growth of Whitman's art. If his own nineteenth century did not quickly rise to the flies he cast across its swirling water, one reason was that from the beginning he was often symbolic by choice and perhaps sometimes by necessity in his poetry to a degree equaled only by the much later surrealists. His endeavor was to convey the unexpressed, or the inexpressible except by indirect means, which we now recognize as a trend in modern art. One result was that his symbols were discussed in terms of their direct and prosaic (and often indecent) meanings, rather than of their indirect (Walt's favorite word) and poetical significance.

Whitman's youthful imagination was strongly absorptive, and fed upon vast, vague emotions, and upon generalized ideas about love and the varied and active reality of expanding America. He could not analyze, could not (and sometimes dared not) express himself except by finding symbols of experience which would suggest his inner meanings. There was an incapacity here which a greater artist in words, a Milton or a Tennyson, might have overcome. Yet Walt's determination to "let it all out" somehow, like his struggle to get an idiom, has given some of his best lines a symbolic force which is now recognized by world-wide quotation. In his early poetry especially, he is sometimes merely fantastic in his symbolism. Some pages could readily be added to this chapter on Whitman's lack of any true sense of humor, and his frequent absurdities in word, phrase, image and symbol—

like the "budding bibles" he hopes to find on his passage to India. Absurd, if you take him seriously, as you must, is

> By my life-lumps! becoming already a creator,
> Putting myself here and now to the ambush'd womb of the shadows.

In his early poetry he is also, and especially in sexual matters, cryptic in his symbolism beyond easy interpretation:

> Is this then a touch? quivering me to a new identity,
> Flames and ether making a rush for my veins,
> Treacherous tip of me reaching and crowding to help them,
> My flesh and blood playing out lightning to strike what is hardly different from myself,
> On all sides prurient provokers stiffening my limbs, . . .
> Deluding my confusion with the calm of the sunlight and pasture-fields,
> Immodestly sliding the fellow-senses away,
> They bribed to swap off with touch and go and graze at the edges of me.

He could also, in sexual reference, and elsewhere, be magnificent:

> Bridegroom night of love working surely and softly into the prostrate dawn,
> Undulating into the willing and yielding day,
> Lost in the cleave of the clasping and sweet-flesh'd day.

How much of his sexual imagery, which is much more abundant in his earlier than in his later poems, was a subconscious protection against the onslaughts (from which he so heavily suffered) of the prudish, or the hypocritical purity of so-called Victorianism, psychologists may decide. But it must be clear that, for him, symbolism was a native language of his poetry.

In his later poems his symbolism is no longer eccentric, and seldom erotic, and seldom confused. It should be studied in "When Lilacs Last in the Dooryard Bloom'd," which is conducted throughout by powerful and beautiful symbols, profound in their significance, so that even the imaginations of children can feel them, though they may not penetrate the meaning. The fallen western star, the perennially blooming lilacs, the thrush (it was not a thrush, but no matter) warbling death's outlet song in the pines and cedars, the pictures of active America for the walls of the burial house, the long black smoke trail of Lincoln's funeral train drifting over the daily usages of the land, "lilac and star and bird" twined with the chant—this symbolism is confident, controlled, expressive, and beautiful.

6

Walt Whitman's importance and place in American literary history can be approximately stated, although of his absolute merits it may be too soon for definitive judgment. It is clear that he was one of the significant voices of the nineteenth century, expressing in his symbolism its creative, its transitional, and its revolutionary character. Probably in poetry he will come to be regarded as its most prophetic, if not its perfect, voice. Certainly he must be named as the first powerful celebrant of the upsurge of the masses and the potentiality of the "divine average" in terms of an ideal democracy. His impulses are close to modern times—particularly in his insistence upon the vital importance of sex in human relationships, which is Freudian in its perceptions. Yet here and elsewhere his mind and style are deeply involved in the rather romantic science of his own period, and even more in that era's evangelicism and its oratory.

In trying to decide whether Walt Whitman was as prophetic as he believed and as influential as he hoped to become, it is essential to consider his prose as well as his poetry. In the poetry, a dominant theme is not so much democracy in any of its usual senses, as sex the life force which, escaping from the suppression of a false morality, revitalizes love, and makes an enduring democratic society possible, something no institutions or political or economic methods can guarantee.

In Whitman's important prose, however, the ruling theme is democracy as we all know it, and how it can get leadership and be maintained and made to grow. The powerful prose Prefaces are revealing here, especially the Preface to the first edition of the *Leaves,* afterward disintegrated and worked into the poetry of "By Blue Ontario's Shore," and now seldom reprinted and much too little read. Of the first importance also is the *Democratic Vistas* of 1871, one of the great American pamphlets, to be compared for its ideas, though unfortunately not for its style which has too much of the parentheses of conversation, with *The Federalist* papers.

In the first Preface, in singing, epigrammatic phrases, Whitman proclaims what the American poet and his poetry should be like, and his duty, which is to give voice and leadership to the dream of a fully developed man in a continent mastered for the benefit of the people as a whole. That the poet's work will be literature is only incidental. Whitman's point is, that it cannot be literature unless it makes articulate essentially American life and hopes and dreams, however conducted and wherever derived. The best American literature had too little concerned itself with the American democracy so far, and therefore is too often sterile for our own experience, and unable to speak for our New World experiment. For "America is democracy." His own hope was to become the first effective spokesman for a new race of races in a democracy, and to begin a literature for a new continent which would burst the bounds of region and class and cult. He wished to chant to the world.

Democratic Vistas was written at the end of one crisis, the Civil War, and at the beginning of another, the threatened capture of the nation by oligarchies and monopolies. In it, he carries on his theme. Democracy is not to be defined as majority rule, which may become tyrannical; it is the possibility of individual self-development, in which body, mind, and soul all proceed toward spiritual ends without loss of the material functions of living, which are as divine as the immaterial. Only a government which provides for the free functioning of every individual in every way necessary for complete being can be regarded as democratic, and such a government must rest ultimately upon the fraternity of comrades. Only such a government—and here he is more prophetic than clear—can meet and survive the difficulties of a new age in which nature has become the servant of man and can be used either to elevate or to destroy. He is realistic in describing the diseases and the collapses of our own democracy (after all, he had been a "practical" politician before he was a practicing poet). Centuries, not decades, will be required in order to mature democracy, but he has his faith.

What claim have Whitman's *Leaves of Grass,* his Prefaces, his *Democratic Vistas* to be regarded as interpreting the chief social significance of a century? The reader, too often distracted by rant and rhetoric, overwhelmed by inventories of American activities, will at first be skeptical. Yet, as gradually the lucid and powerful passages in both poetry and prose rise out of a seeming confusion, and as the self-assertive individual who calls himself Walt Whitman becomes more and more symbolic of indisputable qualities in the age of expansion, the faults begin to seem less important. Here is no typical or even representative man of the expansive age, but here, unquestionably again, is a writer of extraordinary intuition and unusual powers of expression, who could have lived in and been a product of only such a time. Whitman was quite right in saying that most of his contemporaries in authorship were running temporary errands for their fellow men, while he (so he implied) was out for immortal service. It was true that he was the bard and seer of a great idea and a great hope—even though he had some of the improvisation of the bard, and some of the extravagance in prophecy of the seer.

Was he a great poet? Many of his contemporaries, including William Dean Howells, denied that Whitman wrote poetry at all. They usually meant poetry in what they regarded as the proper form, or written upon subjects which they felt to be poetic. Even so the charge is hard to understand. His verse is sensuous and passionate and at its best simple, thus according with

Milton's famous definition. It does not fail (again at its best) when judged by the severer requirement that its form should convey its sense. True, it is difficult to find a poem in the *Leaves* which is one perfect chrysolite, yet still more difficult to deny the attributes of great poetry to "When Lilacs Last in the Dooryard Bloom'd," or "Passage to India," or many another poem or part of a poem even more characteristic of the chanter of democratic man.

The most satisfactory test of permanent value in poetry is not rhetorical, but pragmatic. If it enters into the common consciousness, exercising there the function of poetry, which is to lift the emotions by its rhythms, and to enliven the imagination by its final statements of the essence of experience, then there is not much room left for argument. This, Whitman's best lines and a few whole poems increasingly do, while the catchier meters of so many of his American contemporaries are already dropping out of memory. But even more significant is the remarkable extension of the influence of his poetry, and the welcome of that poetry itself both in its original form and in translations through so many lands and languages. This began early in his career, and has increased with each decade. He not only took his place beside revolutionary poets, his contemporaries in nineteenth century Europe, but has proved to be more expressive and more lasting.

Walt Whitman as poet and artist undoubtedly suffered from his too urgent sense of the importance of his self-appointed mission. His transcendental belief in the worth of original inspiration made him leave many a line in its first crudity, perhaps because he felt that what had come to him was inspiration, even though imperfectly caught, like radio music in a storm. His taste, too—and this was a result of self-education and a democratic disdain for refinement—was defective, as Poe's was so often in his prose. Again, in spite of powerful lines where every word was right, his feeling for words was often inferior, more often experimental, and sometimes plain bad. In this, as in his dislike of "polishing," he was a true American, with the frontiersman's disdain for too much learning or art. It was unfortunate also that Whitman's native expansiveness should have flowered in a period of literary romanticism that favored extravagance and discouraged restraint. Yet every writer should be judged by what he tries to do, provided it is worth doing. With Walt it is certain that his chants, like his favorite operas and his favorite Shakespearean plays, were never intended to be absolute art. They were written to capture his fellow men in his own time by any relevant means.

When Whitman died on March 26, 1892, his century was concluding its last quarter. The prejudices of the genteel age in America which spread burrs and prickles over his poetry were beginning to wither. A vigorous period of poetic experimentation was not far ahead, in which his rebellious rhythms were to be influential. His verse no longer offended the ear except of the most orthodox, for the industrialized world, where almost no one is illiterate, was full of new rhythms to which readers easily adjusted their senses. Shakespearean blank verse is more difficult for a schoolboy of the twentieth century than the irregular roll of Whitman's lines. After the Spanish War of 1898, national self-consciousness became the rule rather than the exception, and it was not long before Whitman, whose success (at home, if not abroad) had been a notoriety of sexual sensationalism, took his rightful place as the first poet of continental America and as the bard of democracy. The decline of religious dogmatism, so marked in this latter end of the century, also made his acceptance easier. The assumption of Godlike intentions, which had seemed blasphemous, now was seen to be only an assertion of the God in every man. Furthermore, the rising social consciousness of the early twentieth century, the acknowledgment of the rights of labor, and the emergence of the en-masse as the new factor of power in the Republic, made much of the humanitarianism and the political philosophy in the *Leaves* timely and relevant to great issues now clearly understood. Not until later, with the capture of European governments and their corruption by what Whitman had called "invaders"—those exploiters of democracy, the Mussolinis and the Hitlers—was it revealed that his fears for democracy as well as his faiths were truly prophetic.

It is still difficult to separate the gold from the mud (this is his own figure) in the heaped-up and shoveled mass of the *Leaves of Grass*. Yet the gold is easy to find, and it has become a currency which provides a common exchange of poetic ideas throughout the democratic world. We may repeat and paraphrase with confidence Emerson's remark to Moncure Conway after the publication of the now famous first edition: Americans who had been seeking abroad for some powerful expression of their phase of earth history could now come home—unto us a man had been born.

CRISIS

. . . conflict, refinement, success

30. A HOUSE DIVIDED AND REJOINED

The average citizen of the United States in 1850 held certain truths to be self-evident. Whenever he heard them uttered, from flag-draped platform or in the echoing chambers of a still-unfinished Federal Capitol, he applauded almost by reflex. He believed that God had created man with certain rights and dignities, and given him a moral law for his guidance—what Emerson in 1854 called "the constitution of the Universe." This law underlay our own Constitution, making it a document almost as sacred as the Bible, and affording us Americans the best government in the world. Mankind, in fact, was watching our experiment in democracy, to see whether it ultimately succeeded or went to smash. This government, rather than our resources of coal and iron or illimitable fields of wheat and cotton, had already made us a great people. Liberty bred self-sufficience and achievement. Liberty was greater than Equality, because it comprehended the latter—in giving every man the opportunity to rise until he became the peer of any man.

It was a fine gospel, so long as humility tempered it against smugness, and sincerity against mere lip service. If at times the behavior of average citizens— as they confronted the immigrant, for example, arriving in the Land of Promise, or the Negro long domiciled in the Land of the Free—seemed to deny some of these postulates, that contradiction merely showed that an individual, like his nation, might be a house divided. And here, as always, a split personality meant tension, frustration, unhappiness.

A conviction that their nation enjoyed a special revelation of light made some citizens look down their noses at "the old and moth-eaten systems of Europe," as young Whitman saw them from the vantage point of Brooklyn. Senator Stephen A. Douglas, pride of the Illinois Democrats, announced that, in comparison with ourselves, Europe "is a vast graveyard." In fact, the great commercial city of New York, and the new metropolis of the prairies, Chicago, from their lead in the van of materialism tended most loudly to voice this bumptiousness. But Philadelphia with its seasoned wealth, and still more Boston with its Europeanized culture, regarded such swagger with a faint distaste. Their gentry and scholars, while admitting the national genius for enterprise and invention, still granted the Old World primacy in arts and letters. James Russell Lowell, savoring a leisurely holiday in Europe in 1851–1852, reflected that our predilections were less Greek than Roman. "I cannot help believing that in some respects we represent more truly the old Roman power and sentiment than any other people," he wrote his friend John Holmes. "Our art, our literature, are, as theirs, in some sort exotics; but our genius for politics, for law, and above all, for colonization, our instinct for aggrandizement and for trade, are all Roman." Reconciled to the *fait accompli* of Manifest Destiny, the Mexican War, and California, Lowell could not help paying tribute to the expansive vigor of the great Republic, like that which had once girdled Europe, North Africa, and Asia Minor with the Pax Romana. To a few Americans, the cult of vulgar self-satisfaction was no more reprehensible than the contrary mania for cultural flunkyism. That proud Brahmin, Francis Parkman, while fretting against the commerce which in the fifties was making America powerful—grumbling that there was "no sanctuary from American enterprise"—still refused to fall a victim to the "John Bull mania, which is the prevailing disease of Boston in high places and low."

The existence of two Englands, two Europes—aristocratic and proletarian, absolutist and liberal, with very different sets of interests in the New World—became much clearer to Americans after the onset of the Civil War, with the French Emperor and the Court of Queen Victoria as frankly pro-Southern as Karl Marx, John Bright, and the mill hands of Manchester and Lyons were pro-Union. In the fifties, these demarcations had been latent but less plain. While the leisured classes of the Eastern seaboard turned more and more to the social rites of London and the elegances of Paris, in love with antiquity and the glitter of coronets, Americans in the mass were prone to sympathize with Cuba under the Spanish heel and cheered wildly for Louis Kossuth, symbol of revolt against the Hapsburgs, when as the nation's guest he visited these shores in 1851. A localized minority might share the nostalgia of Lowell's grandmother—who used to dress in black on the Fourth of July "and loudly lament our late unhappy difference with His Most Gracious Majesty" —but the majority of Americans applauded constitutional revolutions such as their ancestors had fought.

Toward economic revolution their attitude was much less friendly. Why pull down, level, destroy, when every man himself expected to be a property holder some day? Hence the arrival of Marxist socialism in the fifties, with some German immigrants, and at least one short-lived attempt to found a "Proletarierbund," roused little support. In fact, the presence of radical elements among the new immigrants, joined to prejudice against the Irish Catholics, lent fuel to the flame of nativism. From these fears and suspicions the Know-Nothing Party sprang, gathering such strength that it won the 1854 state elections in Massachusetts and nearly carried New York. For two or three years it threatened the civil liberties traditional to America. "When the Know-Nothings get control," wrote Lincoln to a friend in August, 1855, the Declaration of Independence "will read 'all men are created equal, except negroes, *and foreigners, and Catholics.*' When it comes to this I shall prefer emigrating to some country where they make no pretense of loving liberty." As he intimates, Know-Nothingism tried to link its racial prejudices with those of the slaveholding South—a move that soon cost it the roving Northern support vital to any third party's success, and so the movement collapsed.

The task of ameliorating the lot of labor, in ways less revolutionary than those of the Communist Manifesto, meanwhile engaged the attention of thoughtful Americans. Growth of the factory system in New England had shortly contrived the end of that benevolent paternalism fairly common at the dawn of Fall River industrialism—under the new hurly-burly of immigrant toilers, competitive low wages, sweatshop conditions, and quick profits. The old American fluidity of opportunity was threatened by the freezing of working classes into lasting depression. Lincoln objected to the "mud-sill" theory, that "whoever is once a hired laborer, is fatally fixed in that condition for life." In self-defense American labor began to organize, although its efforts proved feeble until man-power scarcities in the Civil War lent new leverage to its bargaining power. Up to the outbreak of war, ironically enough, the sharpest critics of the Northern sweatshop were apologists for slavery, as will be seen: writers with an ax to grind, a cause to foster, that could hardly be described as pure humanitarianism.

Other crusades and enthusiasms, platforms and shibboleths, did flourish in the North in the fifties. "Marriage reform" looking toward more liberal divorce laws and property rights, and woman suffrage as championed by Lucy Stone, Lucretia Mott, and Elizabeth Cady Stanton, enlisted minority sympathy. The opposition of the rigid minds in the male sex might be typified by Parkman the historian. Having admired the Middle Ages for their religious faith and the cult of chivalry, he caustically remarked that American vulgarity had resuscitated the one under the guise of "spirit-rapping," and the other in the form of "woman's rights, Heaven deliver us." Yet feminism found hearty endorsement from men like James Russell Lowell, husband of the poet and gentle reformer Maria White, and Henry Ward Beecher, clerical brother of Harriet Beecher Stowe. Espousing the new development of coeducation in the *Atlantic* in 1859, Thomas Wentworth Higginson, abolitionist and man of letters, argued that "woman must be a subject or an equal: there is no middle ground." Still another crusade sought to curb intemperance. Maine enacted the pioneer prohibition law in 1851; by 1855 every Northern state save New Jersey had some form of liquor control on its statute books, although aid from the courts and the machinery of enforcement often proved weak, and the experiment yielded much ground during the next decade. Wendell Phillips and Mrs. Stowe sought alike to rouse moral boycotts against wine served at public dinners. The march of the "Cold Water Army" spread propaganda through the Mississippi Valley in the fifties, invading even "the land of Dixie and whisky." By and large the South distrusted Yankee fads, rejecting them with pride and dignity, and more than a little fear of the most powerful ism of them all—abolitionism.

2

In the century's early years, the native region of Jefferson had been prone to apologize for slavery, an expedient evil that time would prune away. But from about 1830 on, following the party battles of the Jackson era, the exacerbation produced in the South by abolitionists like Wendell Phillips and William Lloyd Garrison, and the economy forged ever more tightly upon these states by King Cotton and the tribute he drew from world markets, slavery ceased to be regarded as transitional. The South's "peculiar institution" was a lasting good, vindicated by history in the glory that was Greece, and sanctioned by the wisdom of God who had created blacks to serve their white superiors. The South never tired of quoting Jefferson's praise of agrarianism, while treating with more and more neglect his devotion to natural rights, public education, and the religion of human progress. While a growing solicitude for the black man prevailed in Western Europe and the Northern states —regions where slave economy was unprofitable, as Southerners loved to point out—the spirit of Dixie moved back toward the past, taking avenues of escape into medieval chivalry, race myths, and cultural isolation. While glorifying her Anglo-Saxon stock over the mixed bloods and unassimilated immigrants of the North, and her claim of descent from Cavaliers rather than Puritans, the South increasingly regarded herself as distinctive, unique, and her way of life as the American way.

Others of course held contrary views about the essence of true Americanism, and put up strong arguments. But these rebuttals fell upon Southern ears growing more deaf through the years—as antislavery books like Hinton R. Helper's *The Impending Crisis* (1857) were suppressed south of the Mason and Dixon line, while during the fifties large numbers of Southern lads were withdrawn from Princeton, Harvard, Yale, and similar institutions, to enroll in "orthodox" colleges at home. To discussion, debate, dissent, the South began to shut its mind, fearful of apostasy among the whites, insurrection among the blacks. Its people began steadily to shift their loyalties from the nation to state and section. Under the spell of their own logic, many

Southerners in the fifties began to demand that the slave trade be reopened, and still more that slavery be spread to the Pacific. With an agrarian system and a static population (in which four million blacks had no right of franchise), Southerners saw themselves disadvantaged against a North steadily recruited by industry, immigration, and westward expansion. Short of war, only two reinforcements of their position seemed possible. The first was the safeguarding of minority rights, and the second, the establishment of slavery upon fresh soil to capture the voting strength of new states in the Union.

Thus the old wedge of the tariff yielded to the new one of slavery in threatening irreparably to split the Union along the thirty-ninth parallel and the Ohio River. And the oldest economy in the world (a staple crop agriculture on a base of slavery) found itself pitted against the newest (industrial capitalism grounded upon the wage system) within the frame of the same democratic government.

A sense of popular relief, similar to that after Munich in 1938, first greeted the Compromise of 1850 and lasted long enough to achieve the election of easy-going Democrats to the White House, Pierce in 1852 and Buchanan in 1856—the "filthy presidentiads" whose time-serving maddened the disillusioned Democrat Walt Whitman. The Kansas-Nebraska Act of 1854, referring the issue of free soil versus slavery on the Great Plains to local decision ("popular sovereignty"), looked like another victory for appeasement—although Kansas was soon won for the antislavery party by aggressive infiltration of settlers. Certainly the Dred Scott Decision of 1857, upholding property rights of slaveholders even on free soil, was a thumping Southern victory which captured that august symbol of government, the Supreme Court. In the next year, Abraham Lincoln was the Illinois Senatorial candidate of the new Republican Party—a coalition of antislavery elements, free from the old cumbering garments of Whiggism, and rejoicing in an idealistic zeal tempered by the presence of some shrewd politicians. But he was defeated by a fairly close margin, after a series of debates with his opponent, Stephen A. Douglas, through the prairie towns. Although he lost the election, these speeches helped to win Lincoln the leadership of this new party.

Despite compromise and political victories for the Southern bloc, the storm of opposition was rising steadily. In 1852 the most influential novel in all history, Mrs. Stowe's *Uncle Tom's Cabin,* was published, selling 300,000 copies in its first year. Unhappily for its cause, the South found no penman who served it with such power and persuasion as the North possessed in Mrs. Stowe, not to mention Lowell and *The Biglow Papers,* the abolition poetry of Whittier, and the fiery utterances of Emerson and Thoreau late in 1859, when John Brown stepped from the gallows into martyrdom and the battle songs of the future.

For the drift of war appeared inevitable. It was now plain that the party and leader able to unite the West with the North—as the seaboard statesmen seemed powerless to do—would win the next election and, as promised by Southern hotheads, infallibly split the Union. William H. Seward of New York, statesman of moderation, coined the phrase "the irrepressible conflict." It reverberated in the mind of the nation, along with the saying of another moderate, Abraham Lincoln, about a house divided, in his prophecy of 1858 that "this government cannot endure permanently half slave and half free." Neither then nor upon his nomination and election to the Presidency in 1860 —with hardly a single ballot from the South—did Lincoln propose to force emancipation upon the slave states. But upon two things the new President and his party were determined. There was to be no spread of slavery farther into the West, whose pioneers (in Lincoln's vivid speech) deserved "a clean bed, with no snakes in it." And the Union must be preserved. Upon this last issue the Civil War was joined—after a procession of states, led by South Carolina, seceded in the winter of 1860–1861, as the promised answer to Lincoln's election, and on April 12, a Federal expedition to relieve the garrison at Fort Sumter drew fire from the Charleston shore.

3

The leaders of North and South, most writers and thinkers, and masses of the rank and file, felt the justice of their respective causes with peculiar intensity.

The Southerner, repelling invasion from across the Potomac, fought for hearth and home, his right to freedom and self-government, and pride of race against a widely assumed threat of insurrection, rapine, and murder. Stirring songs like "Maryland, My Maryland," poems like Dr. Francis Ticknor's "Little Giffen of Tennessee" and Henry Timrod's "Ode to the Confederate Dead," exalted the spirit of self-sacrifice, often the heroism of common men. The finest poet in the South, Sidney Lanier, served through the war in uniform, was captured and imprisoned near its close. Yet under this mortal crisis, intellectual and creative life tended still more to stagnate. "Wait until you have saved your country before you make preachers and scholars," Colonel James Chesnut told some theological students seeking draft exemption. "When you have a country, there will be no lack of divines, students, scholars to adorn and purify it." Long before Appomattox, many of the best libraries had been scattered and destroyed, most colleges closed, and such vestiges of public education as the South possessed now obliterated. In the heat of war, the Southern gentry were sometimes led to exalt ideals not only of aristocracy, but autocracy as well. In a Boston speech in 1863, Oliver

Wendell Holmes seized upon a recent editorial from the Richmond *Examiner,* avowing that the embattled Confederacy had withdrawn from "the whole course of the mistaken civilization of the age. For 'Liberty, Equality, Fraternity,' we have deliberately substituted Slavery, Subordination, and Government." As the war lengthened and reversals multiplied, rifts of disillusion and disunity appeared, not only among crackers and hillbillies, but in the multitude of non-slaveholders (for, as the census of 1860 reported, out of eight million whites in the South, only four hundred thousand owned slaves). They began to say it was "a rich man's war, and a poor man's fight." The last act of the tragedy, at Appomattox, found the South bruised and bleeding, fissured geographically and spiritually, but still proud, and magnificent in her downfall.

The utterances of Lincoln, upon war aims and ideals of the Union side, made those of Jefferson Davis seem petulant and narrowly partisan. Beyond question, the man from Illinois was spokesman for the clearest thoughts and wisest judgments in the North, and became the voice of idealists throughout the world. Lesser men at first often disagreed with him; generally swung round in the end to his conclusions. The morale of the North at war is essentially the story of Lincoln's growing and deepening influence, as he thought things out for himself and expressed them, with simplicity and clarity—knowing the unimportance of malice, working all the while through the medium of democratic government, waiting for public opinion to ripen, with patience and rare skill in timing.

How literary men fell into line, and added the reinforcement of their art to his argument, may be shown by one or two instances—for, during the war, even as in its prelude, the North was richer than the South in the literature of persuasion. The pacifism with which the New England temper had opposed the Mexican War quickly yielded to the holy crusade of Sixty-one, as utterances of Thoreau, Lowell, and even Whittier the Quaker bear witness. The essayist or scholar, coaxed from his lamplit study by the controversy that heralded the war, hailed its outbreak as a great regenerative experience. A veteran like Emerson, a newcomer like Henry Adams, exulted alike in this test of strength. Typical of the New England mind in crisis was Lowell, with his second series of *Biglow Papers,* expressing in homely idiom the tenderness and pride of a nation in its costly sacrifice. Or the New England Loyal Publication Society, led by Charles Eliot Norton and other men of scholarship and letters, which undertook to mold public opinion in favor of the Union by broadsides and other propaganda angled toward small-town newspapers and border-state citizens. A kindred organization in New York, also called the Loyal Publication Society, scattered tons of pamphlets assailing both secession and pacifism. Its guiding spirit was Francis Lieber, who had left the uncongenial South in 1856 to take a professorship at Columbia University and lend his pen to glorifying the organic unity of the United States and the wisdom of her constitutional government.

Indeed the unity of this nation, and its significance in the eyes of the world, was the deepest concern of Lincoln and those who followed his leadership. It became the basic argument for the war—preservation of the Union. Lincoln had so interpreted the struggle, even before the first gun spoke. In Philadelphia's Independence Hall, en route to his inauguration in 1861, he appealed to the Declaration of Independence "which gave promise that in due time the weights should be lifted from the shoulders of all men, and that all should have an equal chance." World-wide democracy had a vital stake in the salvation of the Union. If this nation were destroyed by its domestic feuds, as Lincoln told Congress and the people time and again through the war years, the whole theory of popular self-government would be discredited forever. All nations were anxiously watching us, serfs as well as kings. The last best hope of earth here trembled in the balance.

Even after the Gettysburg dedication, some factions, of course, envisaged the war in ways less heroic than the spirit of that occasion. Certain Unionists—for example, Longfellow's great friend Charles Sumner, the eloquent senator from Massachusetts—reduced it to an invidious sectionalism, every bit as narrow as that which motivated so many Southerners. Some praised war itself as a fine, exhilarating thing. Parkman, regretting that bad nerves and eyesight kept him at home, wrote letters to the newspapers reminding Americans that "Rome grew colossal through centuries of war." Still others lost all sense of balance in sheer vindictiveness—like Parson Brownlow, the Tennessee firebrand, and Thad Stevens, the embittered Pennsylvania Congressman. But wiser, more temperate citizens in the North kept coming back to Lincoln's assertion that this was a fight not only for the Union but for world democracy, and that the only fit spirit for waging it was one of charity for all.

A second war aim, whose announcement came later, and most effectually identified the aspirations of the Union with those of world liberalism, was Emancipation. A Union reconstituted by blood and tears, in which the anachronism of slavery was still allowed to linger, was not likely to satisfy those who had sacrificed so much for victory or to enlist world sympathy. Gradual emancipation, with compensation for slave owners, which Lincoln had once favored, also became untenable in the heat and passion of war. Every passing day made compromise more improbable. "The moment came," Lincoln said, "when I felt that slavery must die that the nation might live." And so, in his cabinet meeting of July 22, 1862, he projected the Emancipation Proclamation for New Year's Day, 1863, drafting in September an announcement of the impending act. Without bating a jot of his concern over saving the Union, Lincoln saw that this new infusion of idealism would revive liberal sentiment in the North and overseas as nothing else could do. Federal acquiescence in Southern theories about the inherent superiority of whites over blacks now ended. (In the year of the Proclamation, 1863, Charles Loring Brace, pioneer New York social worker and friend of Emerson and Darwin, set forth the scientific evidence against the separate origin of races in his book *The Races of the Old World*.) Reverberations of the Proclamation were world-wide. Charles Francis Adams, American Minister to Britain, who had long breasted the current of aristocratic sympathy for the Confederacy, now felt even stronger tides flowing in favor of Lincoln and the North. His son, young Henry Adams, after attending a mammoth rally of London trade unions on March 26, 1863, organized by Karl Marx and addressed by John Bright to consolidate public opinion, wrote: "I never quite appreciated the moral influence of American democracy, nor the cause that the privileged classes in Europe have to fear us, until I saw directly how it works."

After Gettysburg and the collapse in 1863 of Lee's summer invasion of Maryland and Pennsylvania, the fall of the great Confederate river fort at Vicksburg, and in 1864 Sherman's relentless sweep through Georgia to cut the Confederacy in two, the war's outcome grew more and more apparent. Despite "Copperhead" schemes to appease the South, and counterplots by Radicals thirsting for more vindictiveness, Lincoln won overwhelming reelection in November, 1864, under the steadily growing affection of millions for Father Abraham. The assault continued, with Grant's sledge-hammer blows raining upon Lee's Army of Northern Virginia. Months before Appomattox, Union victory seemed a foregone conclusion. And, with the premature celebration so typical of American impulses, a mood of false armistice began to settle upon the North, notably in the big cities of the seaboard—with the resurgence of prosperity, extravagance, and selfishness. Moralists of press and pulpit reminded the North that her boys were still fighting and dying, but the fervent crusading spirit had already passed its peak. In the South, an almost religious exaltation—heritage of Stonewall Jackson, sustained by Lee— settled at length into grim desperation, then crumbled into the apathy of exhaustion when on April 9, 1865, Lee surrendered.

In the North, victory brought wild jubilation, and to the thoughtful, a reconsecration of patriotism. Lowell wrote to his friend Charles Eliot Norton, on April 13, that he wanted to laugh and cry at the same time, but "ended by holding my peace and feeling devoutly thankful. There is something magnificent in having a country to love. It is almost like what one feels for a woman. Not so tender, perhaps, but to the full as self-forgetful." (His feelings obviously were unlike those of the battered Johnny Reb who threw down his gun at Appomattox, and reportedly said, "Damn me if I ever love another country.") The day after Lowell wrote these words, the assassination of Lincoln transformed the jubilee of the North into a mass sorrow such as Americans had never known before. To Whitman, threnodist of the tragedy, Lincoln's death was a climax on the stage of universal time, to "close an immense act in the long drama of creative thought, and give it radiation, tableau, stranger than fiction."

4

The memory of Lincoln and the half-million war dead, North and South, lingered a little while like a benediction. Sermons, orations, poems, folklore, enshrined together in a mystic reverence the sacrifice of the nation's bitterest war and the greatest American of the century. That ardor was still strong upon Lowell when, in the summer of 1865, he was asked to write a Commemoration Ode for the war dead of Harvard College—a roll that included the poet's three favorite nephews. "So rapt with the fervor of conception as I have not been these ten years," as he confessed, Lowell read his noble poem on July 21, and before its publication in September added its most famous strophe, praising the dead leader—

New birth of our new soil, the first American.

Lowell's allusion in this Ode to "the Promised Land that flows with Freedom's honey and milk" tarnished into irony within a few years, when he wrote another poem with a bitter gibe (suppressed at the instance of friends) about "the Land of Broken Promise." For, with the backwash of postwar selfishness, the spirit already latent in the closing months of the struggle now found itself ascendant. President Andrew Johnson's attempt to carry out Lincoln's promise of charity toward the prostrate South was wrecked by the vindictive Radicals, and Johnson himself barely escaped removal from office on flimsy charges.

A stronger federal Union had been achieved, but its powers suffered abuse, as military government fastened its shackles upon all the defeated states. The carpetbagger, and his antidote the Klansman, added turmoil and violence in the later sixties. Slowly and painfully, the South began to tread the flinty road to reunion. At first, the sense of disaster seemed all-engulfing, with poverty acute among both whites and blacks, the means of production destroyed, and chaos everywhere. Speaking for the economic casualties, Sidney Lanier, the now consumptive poet who symbolized the artist's privations in those days, remarked: "With us in the South, pretty much the whole life has been merely not dying."

Emancipation was achieved, but a permanent race problem remained. Probably the most encouraging sign of the times was the zeal which the Freedmen's Bureau and Northern philanthropy brought to the education of the Negro. Within a short time, universal public education for whites as well as blacks was seen to be one of the wisest, most tangible, goals of postwar endeavor. To some observers it seemed as if that idealism which formerly had been poured into the cause of abolition now streamed into the channels of popular education, over the nation at large. A few months after Appomattox, the idol of the South, General Lee, accepted the presidency of Washington College in the foothills of Virginia, believing that education was the most important task of peace in knotting the broken threads of Southern life and enterprise. In 1867 the Massachusetts-born banker George Peabody set up an endowment of $3,500,000 to promote education in the South among all peoples.

Over the vanquished ideal of a plantation aristocracy—with its gracious manners but illiberal point of view, its appreciative but sterile humanism—arose the philosophy of success, the cult of the businessman. In the early postwar years, as the urgencies of commerce began to rebuild the first bridges of intercourse over the Mason and Dixon line, this philosophy began to infiltrate the South. But its abiding home was of course the Northeast, among the great centers of industrial capitalism. The census of 1870 revealed that the per capita wealth of the North had doubled in ten years. Some few thinkers now began to recall the wartime arguments of Lysander Spooner—Massachusetts lawyer and nonconformist—that the war had been largely a struggle for economic power, with Northern capitalism moving in to dominate the markets of the South. Ironically enough, the Fourteenth Amendment, by its "due process of law" clause, ultimately afforded more aid and comfort to the preacher of the gospel of wealth than to the poor black child—so that it seemed, by a strange jugglery of words, that Lincoln had lived and died that the giant corporation, rather than the Negro, might become a person. Though lip service to democracy survived, corporate industry—railroads, factories, oil and mining leviathans—began to arise from the demands of war and postwar technology. Organized labor, in the glut of demobilization and the short but sharp depression of 1866–1867, visibly lost ground. The immigrant, now badly needed in the expanding factories of North and West, was welcomed with open arms; the ghost of Know-Nothingism remained temporarily laid. But another concern of ante-bellum liberalism, rights for women, did not fare so well, although gains continued in higher education. Despite notable work in the war, in groups like the Sanitary Commission, women failed to win the ballot as their reward, and had to bide their time till the aftermath of the First World War.

The balance of power in America had subtly shifted. The traditional rivalry of New England with the South, in ideas and culture, as well as politics and wealth, was effectually destroyed. The defeated South was obviously in eclipse. Victorious New England had undergone changes more intangible but no less real. The Civil War had not been the pure consecrating experience that her idealists had wished for her. Its end seemed to set a term to the high noon of New England's prestige and creative power—her plain living and high thinking, her passion for reform and her literary florescence. Her culture now entered a Silver Age, when she began to produce more critics and competent editors than novelists and thinkers, more politicians than statesmen, more conservers of inherited wealth than adventurers or entrepreneurs. The new alignment—corresponding to the new flow of the nation's lifeblood of trade East and West along the rails, instead of the old North-South circulatory system along the waterways—now balanced New York against Chicago, Pennsylvania coal and iron against Minnesota wheat and Nebraska corn. The Great West had come into being. It had taken such a lion's share in raising, equipping, and feeding the vast Union armies, under pilotage of the man from Illinois, that the Middle West felt it had won the war. At any rate, its challenge in basic production, commerce, politics, and the intellectual life of the nation had now been squarely delivered.

31. THE PEOPLE'S PATRONAGE

E VEN before the onset of the Civil War, the Middle West had become a crude power, a quantitative if not a qualitative force, in the collective life of the nation—and a mission field ripe for the eager, if at times momentarily discouraged, evangels of culture from the East. Emerson at St. Louis in 1852 doubted that there was a "thinking or even reading man" among 95,000 souls; and in 1866, in an Iowa town, he perceived that, though here was "America in the making, America in the raw . . . it doesn't want much to go to lecture, and tis pity to drive it."

This impression was confirmed by some of the newspapers. Cleveland was scornful that this "perpendicular coffin" should talk to the West about the "law of success," and Detroit reported that he was palming off the "sayings of old almanacs and spelling books; . . . putting transcendentalism on stilts for the admiration of natives." Quincy, Illinois, described him as "Another Bore," and Bloomington as "Ralph Cold-Dough Simmerson." Yet, year after year, in late autumn, he set off wearily to the land of promise, pushing as far and as fast as the new railroads would take him, for like all professional lecturers he knew that he must now seek his market west of the Hudson. And year after year listeners continued to come. Perhaps they hoped that next week John Godfrey Saxe would turn up with funny verse, or Bayard Taylor with his genius for bringing Persia to Peoria, or John B. Gough to give them a near-view of a reformed drunkard. It was significant, however, that though an Iowa town might, one week, listen to Emerson on "Power" and, next week, to "Professor" Oscanyan (dressed in Turkish costume and accompanied by three females in harem pajamas) on "The Domestic Life of the Turks," it was Emerson who derived his basic income from lecturing for thirty-five years, not the "Professor." Emerson once explained, "In every one of these expanding towns is a knot of loving New Englanders who cherish the Lyceum out of love of the Charles and the Merrimac and the Connecticut rivers," but this was a limited and insular version of the truth. The fact was (and Emerson knew it) that the cultural isolationism and localism of the old Northeast was breaking down: the whole of the North, from Boston to the Mississippi, with Baltimore, Pittsburgh, and Cincinnati as a southern boundary, was becoming a cultural unit.

The key to this momentous development was the railroads which spread from the Alleghenies to the Mississippi Valley between 1850 and 1870—ten thousand new miles of them before the war. Any observant trainman (on the run from Albany to Cleveland, for example) could have seen the symbols. In the coaches were not only Emerson, but Horace Greeley, George William Curtis, and Anna Dickinson, all with lectures newly tried out in New York or in New England villages; Dion Boucicault's road company taking the successful *Colleen Bawn* from New York to the hinterland, probably unaware that in so doing they were revolutionizing the American stage; James R. Osgood, Ticknor & Fields' first traveling representative, carrying the firm's fall list to bookstores in Detroit and Cincinnati (another innovation); and subscription agents with handsome sample volumes from New York or Hartford. As they rode, many of these passengers passed the time by reading paper-covered volumes produced specifically for railroad travelers—Putnam's Semi-Monthly Issue for Travelers or Appleton's Popular Library. In the baggage car were bundles of the weekly edition of Greeley's New York *Tribune,* of Bonner's New York *Ledger,* of *Harper's Weekly* (cheaply carried in bulk under the postal regulations of 1852). In the freight train just behind were packing cases of Harriet Stowe's latest volume, a special shipment of Holmes' *Autocrat* bearing on its title page a Cincinnati book dealer's imprint along with that of the Boston publisher; and even bigger boxes of novels by Augusta Jane Evans, Miriam Harris, and Mary Jane Holmes; and certainly a consignment of *Hiawatha,* for by the middle of 1856 one-tenth of all copies printed had been bought by one Chicago jobber.

Such passengers and such freight had been moving out of the East for decades, but they had been subject to the uncertainties of river currents and floods, and to the slow plodding of horses on canal tracks and mired roads. The difference now was in quantity, speed—and direction. Northeastern migrants having moved West rather than South, Northeastern cultural goods flowed to Western bookstores, lecture halls, art galleries, and theaters. More important, perhaps, than either speed or quantity was the fact that these goods were blocked by none of the cultural embargoes and tariff walls that were appearing along the Mason and Dixon line.

What had happened to the Southern market? Up to 1840 it had been a major outlet for New York and Philadelphia book and magazine publishers, whose alliances with booksellers in large Southern cities were certain evidence of the cultural homogeneity of the Atlantic seaboard. Even in the early fifties, few Northern publishers dared to alienate Southern buyers, or failed to apply pressure to writers who were indifferent to their prejudices. In 1845, for example, a Philadelphia publisher removed Longfellow's antislavery poems from a collected edition because they would damage his Southern business. The popular "Grace Greenwood" (Sara Jane Lippincott) was warned by her Boston publisher in 1851 that the question whether her remarks on slavery would cut off the sales of her work south of the Mason and Dixon line was "one of some importance to a writer whose reputation should make her books sell extensively thro'out the country." But the lady had better business sense than her publisher. Not at all concerned about Southern opinion, she begged him to see to the distribution of her books in Western towns, where there was a constant and unsatisfied demand for them. Within a year another Boston publisher turned down *Uncle Tom's Cabin* because it would not sell in the South; when a competitor took a chance with it, the new North bought 100,000 copies in eight weeks. James T. Fields saw the point when he removed the *Southern Literary Messenger,* the most important of all Southern magazines, from his review-copy list in 1849; so did G. P. Putnam when he ignored dire threats from Southern readers of his *Monthly*: its entire sale in the South was smaller than that in Ohio alone. The fact that the enormous development of the popular lecture after 1850 took place almost exclusively in the North enforced the moral: as a literary market, the South was dispensable. As its screen against Northern thought became finer and finer, its purchasing (and therefore its cultural) power became less and less.

The Midwest not only mattered—its cultural, as well as its economic and political, influence was by the fifties beginning to be crucial. Predisposed, like the Northeast, to a threefold economy—agriculture, commerce, and manufacture—it offered no serious barriers to cultural penetration from the coast. Committed, like the Northeast, to the ideal of universal, free, and eventually compulsory education, it was destined to produce an ever larger percentage of the literate adults of the nation. Once tied by railroads to New York, Boston, and Philadelphia, the centers of cultural production and the meccas of the nation's talent, the Midwest became an integral and influential part of that powerful civilization known as "the North" which was to dominate the nation thenceforward.

The accessibility of the Western market to publishers depended as much upon urbanization as on railroads. Newspapers and magazines could reach isolated farms by mail, but the bookstore, which could flourish only in fair-sized towns, was still the publisher's chief outlet. If, now, Cincinnati, Buffalo, and Cleveland book jobbers served ever-growing clusters of towns capable of supporting bookstores, they were merely belated beneficiaries of an economic phenomenon which had been characteristic of the industrial Northeast for decades. In New England, countryfolk were flocking to Lawrence and Pawtucket, Fall River and Hartford; in New York to Albany and Troy,

Schenectady and Elmira; and in Pennsylvania to Harrisburg, Reading, and Allentown. With markets geographically so concentrated, the publishers of Boston, New York, and Philadelphia had been able to achieve a leadership in book production which they have never lost.

For the literary man, Boston had importance far out of proportion to the volume of its publishing business. New York in the fifties had 107 publishers —twice as many as either Boston or Philadelphia; but its biggest houses specialized in British and in nonliterary writings, as did its biggest magazines —*Harper's Monthly* and *Harper's Weekly*. When G. P. Putnam (the most "literary" of the New York publishers), and his *Putnam's Monthly* (the best literary magazine of its time), dropped out of the running in the middle fifties, Boston firms had few important rivals in the publishing of American belles-lettres. Admittedly, the best printing (especially of poetry) and the best proof-reading were done in Cambridge by the University Press; and the best cloth binding was done in Boston by Benjamin Bradley. Ticknor & Fields was hospitable to poets and essayists; Little, Brown & Company, to historians; James Munroe, to philosophers; John P. Jewett, to popular novelists; and Phillips, Sampson & Company, to writers in general.

Constantly improving railroad connections with the West via Albany, and the enterprise of the younger publishers (Jewett, Harriet Stowe's publisher, had a branch office in Cleveland) reduced somewhat the disadvantages of Boston's geographical position. Even so, Boston publishers could rely upon a local public long accustomed to buying and reading books, and it was a common belief among American poets that verse sold better in New England than elsewhere. Moreover, the New England public accorded to the writer a prestige which he enjoyed nowhere else in the nation; and properly introduced authors from other sections were sure of a cordial reception and good literary fellowship in dozens of homes, bookshops, and editorial offices in and near Boston. When the *Atlantic Monthly* was founded in 1857 (two months after *Putnam's Monthly* had expired), its success was assured—not only because there was enough local talent to keep its pages full (one explanation of its reputed provincialism), but because it was backed by the money and influence of publishers long accustomed to dealing with literary materials and with creative writers. Such factors as these had much to do with the renaissance of the fifties.

2

Important as were material factors in the growth of the power of the new North, education was the social foundation on which the region was building a culture radically different in quality, depth, and extent from the patrician culture which had prevailed in the old urban centers and in the South. If time devoted to formal education is an index to consumption of print, the accelerated growth of mere literacy in the North was a phenomenon of some import to the literary world. Between 1850 and 1870 the population of the country increased about 68 per cent, but attendance at public schools almost doubled—to six and one-quarter million. Educational methods, equipment, and teaching personnel may have failed to keep step with this growth, but ability to read well was an educational goal more faithfully kept in view than it is now. In spite of brave attempts in some Southern states to combat difficult conditions, the great majority of these readers were being trained in the North. Illiteracy among South Atlantic whites in 1850 was five times as great as in New England; and in the relatively new South Central states it was three times as great as in the Middle West.

A presumably more sophisticated class of readers was being produced during the period (both in the North and in the South) at an even greater rate, for enrollment in academies, liberal colleges, and other private schools more than tripled to almost a million. The academies, now for the first time enduring strong competition from public high schools, were in 1850 a far greater influence in the literary market than the colleges, which enrolled a mere 27,000. It was not only that the enrollment in academies was ten times as great, but that they were hospitable to women, as most Northern colleges were not, and to "modern" courses, of which the majority of colleges were still suspicious. Like the public high schools (during the period some sixty-five of these were established in large towns, only four of them in the South) they tended increasingly to offer a terminal education rather than a merely preparatory course. Inasmuch as the South in 1850, with a relatively small white population, had 40 per cent of the nation's private schools (Kentucky had twice as many academy students as Indiana) it is no wonder that Northern publishers resented the alienation of Southern readers.

Few colleges (total enrollment was only 56,000 on the eve of the Civil War) were doing much to improve the old classical curriculum. There was some progress in the teaching of science, modern languages, and the newer social sciences, but sectarian influence was still strong, and higher education still awaited the thorough shaking-up it was to get under new, young, German-trained presidents within a decade after the war. It was largely because the established colleges, committed to an academic program of what Veblen later called "conspicuous waste," were slow to respond to the needs of industry and agriculture, that during this period technological schools sprang up as separate entities or as independent affiliates of older institutions. Most of the twenty-two technological schools and state universities founded in the sixties got federal support through the Morrill Land Grant Act (1862), the purpose of which was "to carry the advantages of education to those engaged in manual industries." Though the South before the war had sent an even larger proportion of its white population to college than had the North, the war delayed the development of technological education in the region. At any rate, higher and "useful" education for the many, like literacy for the masses, was a typically Northern idea, one which was steadily undermining the old tradition of an exclusively classical and British culture for the few.

Paradoxically, increasing material prosperity was the major factor in the education of the most potent class of readers in the nation—women. Though few people as yet believed that women were worth educating beyond the elementary level, something had to be done with girls who did not have to become household drudges as soon as they were old enough to work. The solution was the female academy. Census figures for secondary education of the sexes before 1870 are lacking, but in that year more than half of all academy students were girls. As for women's colleges, the striking fact is that in 1870, though those in the Northeast were the best in the country, the number of girls enrolled in them was negligible; whereas the South, which had forty-two of the fifty-six women's colleges established during the period, was giving higher education to almost as many women as men. Except in normal schools, technical and professional curricula were intended for boys, with the result, momentous for the literary market, that education for the enrichment of life, as opposed to education for a job, was monopolized by girls. No one knows what percentage of the readers of poetry, fiction, and essays was female, but the signs are many that by mid-century most of the consumers of imaginative literature were women of the upper and middle classes. Whether, at this date, the younger female audience was made up of "vivid, responsive intelligences, which are none the less brilliant and admirable because they are innocent" (according to Howells), or whether it constituted an "Iron Madonna who strangles in her fond embrace the American novelist" (according to Boyesen), it was a force which affected literary history.

Of the informal varieties of education, the most characteristic of the period was the "popular lecture," which, though it grew out of the lyceum system, must not be confused with the typical lyceum lecture. By the fifties, the superior man was no longer sharing his cultural wealth, in the local lyceum, with his less fortunate townsman; he was selling it to large groups of critical strangers who demanded their money's worth. Young Men's Associations and Library Societies, which (particularly in the West) were displacing the lyceums, now paid fees of from $50 to $100 to "names" who invariably had made their reputations in activities other than lecturing, and the reappearance of these on any platform depended on their ability to talk "interestingly" on foreign travel or on social and ethical topics. This test of popularity was not necessarily corruptive. Emerson, who made only the indispensable compromises with his audience, by much effort could earn as much as $2,000 for a season. Bayard Taylor, with his popular travel lectures, often made $5,000, and magnetic personalities like Henry Ward Beecher, Anna Dickinson, and John B. Gough earned much more. Although, inevitably, such sums tempted lecturers to cheapen their wares, the public rarely tolerated charlatanism. Dr. Holland (writer of best sellers and, later, editor of *Scribner's*), who declared that "the public do not accept of those who are too openly in the market," believed that at its zenith the popular lecture was the champion of liberty and the foe of bigotry in politics and religion. From the forties until 1865 the platform was a medium for the expression of social opinion; and as such it served the great purpose of ameliorating prejudice; and, like the radio of today, it was a nationalizing force.

But the end of the war brought about a rapid if temporary degeneration of social and intellectual tone, one of the permanent effects of which was the destruction of the popular lecture. Commercial lecture bureaus, under the inspiration of publicity geniuses like James Redpath and Major J. B. Pond, quickly transformed it into "amusement business," and by 1870 the platform was reserved for exhibitions of the newly famous, "readings" by the latest or the oldest literary idol, and what Bayard Taylor called bitterly "non-intellectual diversion." In a little more than forty years a great cultural institution had outlived its usefulness. Thereafter the serious-minded turned to the Chautauqua for edification and enlightenment.

3

Journalism proved even more adaptable to social change. As business and industry destroyed the slow tempo of the old agrarian culture, American life speeded up. The great mass of literates produced by the schools sought reading matter attuned not to the ages but to the day, the week, and the month. Increasingly, writers were trained to write and readers to read, by periodicals. Not only literacy but inventions and improved news-gathering techniques enabled daily newspapers during the period to more than triple their circulation, though the war was responsible for a good part of the total of two and a half million.

Of these, much the most significant from the point of view of Northern culture was Horace Greeley's New York *Tribune,* which sold over half of its huge weekly edition outside the city, and which, according to Bayard Taylor, ranked next to the Bible in popularity in the Midwest. It is of some significance that Greeley thus sent into the hinterland the book and lecture reviews of George Ripley (who was kindly to social radicals like Emerson), the travel letters of Taylor, Curtis, and Clemens, and the more popular verse of the New York poets. But even Greeley could not counterbalance the weight of the scores of cheap weekly magazines and "Sunday newspapers" which flooded the nation in mid-century. The historian of our magazines has well said that the descending curve of illiteracy seems to have been matched by the ascending curve of popularity of the weeklies, for by 1870, 4,295 of them had a circulation of ten and one-half million—one copy for every two or three adults in the nation. Many of them, it is true, were insignificant religious and agricultural papers of small circulation, but some of those that emanated from New York were known in every downy hamlet in the land. Among those with circulations of over 100,000 were the *New York Weekly,* whose serials were the foundation of the Street & Smith dime-novel dynasty; the somewhat more respectable New York *Sunday Mercury,* which specialized in the J. H. Ingraham and "Ned Buntline" thrillers, and in the new popular humor of Ward, Billings, and Kerr; and the New York *Ledger,* which topped them all with a circulation of 400,000 in 1860. Robert Bonner, the owner of the *Ledger,* was, like Barnum, a master of the recently born art of publicity. His amusing use of gold—and brass—to lure such "names" as Henry Ward Beecher, Edward Everett, and Longfellow into the domain of "Fanny Fern" (Sara Payson Willis Parton), Mrs. E. D. E. N. Southworth, and Sylvanus Cobb, Jr., gives an intimate view of new cultural mutations.

Bonner's success was rivaled only by that of illustrated news weeklies such as *Frank Leslie's Illustrated* and *Harper's Weekly.* The latter, like the illustrated *Harper's Monthly,* were of less direct importance to American writers than weeklies of the *Ledger* type because they printed little American fiction. Nevertheless, the editorial policies of Bonner and the Harpers had considerable influence upon literature. Before the establishment of *Harper's Monthly* (1850), few American novels were serialized. By that date Cooper had serialized one of his last romances, the other major writers none. But by 1870 almost all recognized novelists were selling their work first to magazines and were making the necessary compromises in matters of chapter division, construction, arrangement of incident, style, and moral and social prejudice. In their new venture the Harpers had intended only to get ahead of their competitors by reprinting foreign novels as fast as they appeared in serial form abroad, but they soon discovered the potency of the phrase "to be continued." When other magazines like the *Ledger* (1850) and the *Atlantic* (1857) began to serialize American novels, the writer had a new and tempting source of income, for he could sell each novel twice—three times if he could get an English magazine to serialize simultaneously, four times if he could also sell to an English publisher.

Only slightly less important were other policies of the new magazines: they popularized the illustration of fiction, a development which was later to affect the work of novelists like Howells and James; they raised the rate of pay for magazine work and thus not only helped to stabilize further the literary profession but made New York the center of literary magazine production; they protected the copyright of their periodicals and thereby helped put a stop to the wholesale scissoring which in the forties had deprived Poe and Longfellow of the major rewards of their popularity; they helped break down the custom of literary anonymity, which had also militated against the author's interest; most important of all, by appealing to a national audience, they helped to destroy the narrow localism which damaged such respectable and even superior competitors as *Putnam's* and the *Atlantic Monthly*. The influence of these popular periodicals on literary production shows that, though Emerson may have been justified in his faith that "water and intelligence work down," it is just as true that popular influences work up.

4

The same forces were at work in the book world. The opening of railroad transportation in the Midwest, the campaign against illiteracy throughout the North, the habit of reading which was encouraged by lecturers, newspapers, and magazines, served to increase the sale of books on all levels. The schools contributed directly to publishers' prosperity, not only through textbooks and juveniles, which were the backbone of many a firm's list, but through district-school libraries, whose holdings increased from two and one-half to three and one-half million volumes. By mid-century these libraries had become so important in the literary market that the standard Harper contract included a clause covering school editions.

The contribution of religious education was little short of spectacular: church and school libraries in 1850 owned six hundred thousand volumes; in 1870 the number was almost ten million. The ancient alliance between the church and literary culture, inevitable in colonial and early national days when the clergy wrote much of what got into print, was perpetuated up to the Civil War by close relations between the major publishers and specific denominations—Harpers with the Methodists, Appleton with the Episcopalians, Ticknor with the Baptists, Munroe & Francis with the Unitarians. But if the churches stimulated the appetite for books they also satisfied it to some extent by doing much publishing on their own account. There were bitter complaints that such organizations as the American Sunday School Union, the Presbyterian Board, and the Methodist Book Concern, all subsidized by charity funds, were publishing and distributing general literary works of a religious cast in competition with "legitimate" houses, and that authorship suffered because copyright was paid only rarely and reluctantly.

The cycle of business expansion completed the process by which literature became an important article of commerce. The enlarged book market led printers to buy improved and expensive machinery, and publishers to compete with one another by paying higher royalties, sending agents out on the road, and advertising nationally. Increased overhead made larger sales necessary; so that publishers could no longer afford to be hospitable to the elite few who absorbed a thousand copies of a "good" book. G. W. Curtis in 1854 wrote the publishers to whom he was adviser that "nowadays a book seems hardly to be launched until it has a circulation of 5000."

For authors who were willing to consult the tastes of the five thousand the rewards were increasingly great. The almost universal royalty of 10 per cent and/or "author's risk" of the forties became, in the early fifties, 15 per cent, often 20 and sometimes 25 per cent if the writer paid for his own stereotype plates. Indeed, the years between 1850 and the panic of 1857 saw a boom of authors' profits unequaled in the whole nineteenth century, and royalty offers reached a high of 33⅓ per cent before the panic. During the sixties, they tended to slip back to a norm of 10 to 15 per cent, where they remained until the nineties. Authorship suffered during the Civil War, for new literary works were not in demand unless they had some special relation to the conflict, and the doubling of the cost of living about 1864 left many writers in bad straits. But retail book prices doubled too, and since deflation did not reduce them all the way to the old level, authors were left better off than they had been before.

Meanwhile, publishing methods had improved. By 1850 the old barter system by which bookseller-publishers exchanged their imprints for those of shops in other towns had been displaced by techniques of publishing for a national market. Booksellers were now encouraged to move their stocks through generous publishers' discounts which were adjusted to the salability of individual titles. Nation-wide newspaper and magazine advertising (Ticknor & Fields, publishers of the Brahmins, did not spurn the columns of the nationally circulated *Leslie's*), and new promotional methods undermined the vicious local review clique which had done great harm to professional authorship in Poe's day. Publishers learned how to exploit potential reader-markets more thoroughly by adjusting format and price to differing income levels. The difficulty of reaching readers in rural areas was overcome to a certain extent by the development of subscription publishing. It was chiefly biography, history, and travel that was thus issued by such firms as the American Publishing Company in Hartford and Scribner's in New York, but Harriet Stowe in 1870 daringly contemplated sending agents into the South with an illustrated edition of *Uncle Tom's Cabin*. As she wrote her publisher, "Books to do anything here in these southern states must be sold by agents. . . . Yet *there is* money on hand even down to the colored families, and an attractive book would have a history." Mrs. Stowe's experiences illustrate another comparatively new development: the growth of intimate and trusting relations between author and publisher. Many a house like Putnam, Scribner, and Ticknor & Fields now inspired such loyalty as Emerson's, who called his publisher "the guardian of us all."

Among the new duties of the friendly publisher was arranging for simultaneous publication of his titles in England. Author and publisher alike studied British copyright, so that in spite of unfavorable decisions in the House of Lords in the early fifties, shrewd writers like Mrs. Stowe made better bargains with English publishers than Irving, Cooper, Prescott, and Melville in earlier days. Setting up a few days' residence in Canada at the time a new book was published in London was one method by which American authors acquired a kind of standing in British courts, but careful preliminary arrangements with a reliable foreign house frequently sufficed to turn the trick. Publishing relations with Canada were excellent, though they were destined to degenerate in subsequent decades. A Canadian law of 1849 removed all tariffs on American books; another of 1850 permitted the importation of American reprints of British copyright works, with the provision that a 12½ per cent royalty for the benefit of the English author be collected at the border. In 1852 a correspondent reported that low-priced American books had almost destroyed the Canadian-English book trade, and that New York had displaced London as the purchasing center for the Dominion.

On the American side, reckless competition in the printing of English books had produced its own partial cure by mid-century: a system of courtesy by which a publisher who bought and announced a foreign title was let alone by other houses. Such arrangements raised the price of American editions of foreign works and gave native productions a better chance than they had had before. By 1860, at any rate, many American writers were deriving an adequate income from the home market, which had not been possible during the first half of the century even for such well established authors as Irving, Cooper, and Willis. During this period writing ceased to be a part-time avocation and became a profession capable of supporting authors in middle-class respectability.

5

The forces of education and business having combined to make the popular patronage of literature an economic fact, it was inevitable that readers and publishers should exert a shaping influence upon literary work. Bald logic would suggest that such influence must have been destructive of pure creative ideals, and that the success of T. S. Arthur, Sylvanus Cobb, Susan Warner, and Josh Billings during the period of the decline of Melville, Hawthorne, and George Henry Boker was not merely coincidental. Common sense would indicate that increased literacy might have brought the new group into being without destroying the old. Between logic and common sense lay a fact: that even the best of the older writers recognized the new reading class as a force and attempted to adjust themselves to it without compromising their integrity. Unsophisticated readers throughout the North required that writers and lecturers present themselves not on the ground of their local (if impressively urban) reputations, but on the ground that they had something interesting to say to "nonliterary," "nonintellectual," but intelligent people. The prerequisites for such an appeal were then what they must always be: simplicity, concreteness, lightness, eloquence, freshness, and a distinctive (if not distinguished) personal style. If the writer's ideals included also imagination, power, and relentless truth, so much the better: the public required only that he communicate and that he be interesting.

Emerson, who derived his living not from a little group of transcendentalists in Boston but from a public which extended from Bangor, Maine, to Davenport, Iowa, saw the validity of such standards. When Thoreau remarked in 1853 that any lecture which pleased an audience must be bad, Emerson demurred. "I am ambitious," he said, "to write something which all can read, like *Robinson Crusoe*. And when I have written a paper or a book, I see with regret that it is not solid, with a right materialistic treatment, which delights everybody." Melville recognized the requirements when he sought better terms from his publisher for *Pierre* because its "unquestionable novelty" would make it popular, it "being a regular romance, with a mysterious plot to it, and with all, representing a new and elevated aspect of American life and stirring passions at work"; and for *Redburn* because it was "a plain, straightforward, amusing narrative of personal experience . . . no metaphysics . . . nothing but cakes and ale."

It was the mark of younger and lesser writers of the period that instead of striving, like Emerson and Melville, to adapt their best gifts to the needs of their audience, they attempted a false dualism: that of subsidizing their unprofitable "art" by grinding out commercially successful work of which they were contemptuous. Bayard Taylor was humiliated that on his lecture tours women swooned, and cried, "There he is! That's *him*!" And he complained that lecturing, which built him a fifteen-thousand-dollar country house, was destroying his poetry, which he never wrote for money. Similarly, Stedman, in 1869, was conscience-stricken because he had "lately written so much poor stuff for the money's sake"; and a year later he reported that the public taste was being led astray "after burlesque, the grotesque, the transitory."

There was indeed a bigger market for "poor stuff" than ever before; but those who had genuine faith in democratic man knew that the crowd were ready for better stuff if only one would learn their idiom. Whitman and Emily Dickinson did not; Mark Twain did, and reaped his reward. Melville, who never mastered it, said bitterly in 1851: "This country . . . is governed by sturdy backwoodsmen—noble fellows enough, but not at all literary, and who care not a fig for any authors except those who write those most saleable of all books nowadays—i.e.—the newspapers and magazines." Yet he added, more hopefully: "This country is at present engaged in furnishing material for future authors; not in encouraging its living ones." But it was Emerson, as usual, who saw in true perspective the dilemma of the author in this age of Barnum, Beecher, and Bonner. When a "stout Illinoian" walked out on his lectures, he reflected that "the people are always right (in a sense), and that the man of letters is to say, These are the new conditions to which I must conform . . . he is no master who cannot vary his forms, and carry his own end triumphantly through the most difficult." The time was, indeed, a difficult one for the artist, but it was not impossible. He needed only faith and humility to see that though he himself must serve Mammon as well as God, the people served God as well as Mammon.

32. THE HISTORIANS

The effort of mid-century writers of the patrician East to meet popular taste and popular interest with important books is nowhere better illustrated than by Irving's turn, in his last years, to a many-volumed life of Washington, and in the monumental historical works of Prescott, Parkman, and Motley.

"Literary" history—when it has not meant, as it does elsewhere in this book, the history of literature—has still meant different things at different times in different countries. In the United States the adjective "literary" has generally been confined to the work of three historians, William Hickling Prescott, John Lothrop Motley, and Francis Parkman, who wrote in the middle decades of the nineteenth century. Limited in this way, the "literary" historians may be identified as men who chose themes of sweeping dimensions, collected their materials by enormous and skilled research, were concerned with a dramatic story of leaders and ideas rather than the workaday life of ordinary people, and built works of such artistic attractiveness that they have been read with pleasure by the educated public ever since. Another and more elusive quality was given to such literary history by the fact that all three of its major exponents were patricians.

2

Prescott, Motley, and Parkman began to write amid the encouragement of a boom in historical interest. By the time that the oldest of the three, Prescott, started his first book in 1829, the new nation had reached a state of self-consciousness which made its past seem exciting. Shoddy national histories and better biographies and state histories written by the previous generation were attracting an ever widening audience; a scaffolding was being built for new histories. In the early part of the century, Peter Force, a politician and printer-journalist working in Washington, was only the most important of a considerable group of documentarians who were editing and publishing materials concerning the whole period from the beginnings of colonization on the American shores to the adoption of the Constitution. They were convinced, as Force put it, that "the tendency of the present age has been justly and philosophically designated as historick," and the interest in their work—including Federal funds of more than $200,000—justified his view. The historic tendency of the age also showed itself in the critical journals. Both in its editors and in its articles, the principal critical journal, the *North American Review,* was almost as much a historical publication as a literary one from the twenties through the Civil War. In 1857 the literary historian, Prescott, helped found the *Atlantic Monthly,* and from its beginning the magazine showed a history-mindedness similar to that of the *North American Review.*

All kinds of history and biography poured from the presses, especially in Boston, the center of the new enthusiasm. There Prescott, Motley, and Parkman were joined by three quite different authors to complete the list of the period's most important historians. Of the latter group, two were literary only in the most limited sense; the other was belligerently antiliterary. The most prolific of the three, Jared Sparks, managed to produce nearly seventy historical volumes despite periods as a Unitarian minister and as president of Harvard. During Sparks' lifetime more than 600,000 Americans bought works bearing his name either as author or as editor—especially the ten-volume *Works of Benjamin Franklin; with Notes and a Life of the Author* (1836–1840), which probably contained his best writing, and *The Library of American Biography* (1834–1838), which was certainly his most skillful editorial enterprise. But Sparks' writings can claim no permanent place either as literature or as history. His research was marred by a patriotic tendency to overlook or alter facts which he considered injurious to the reputations of the great, and his writing was distinguished only by clarity.

Much more pretentiously literary was George Bancroft, whose reputation was based on a twelve-volume *History of the United States* (1834–1882). When Bancroft's first volume appeared in 1834, many a guardian of current literary taste hailed it as a classic. Edward Everett, in a review typical of many, said: "You have written a work which will last while the memory of America lasts." Almost until the time of his death in 1891, Bancroft's *History* was accepted as standard, and his prestige as a literary figure grew until Chester Arthur could say that the President of the United States is "permitted to accept the invitations of members of the Cabinet, Supreme Court judges, and—Mr. George Bancroft." A century's perspective now makes it plain that the critics and the country had been beguiled into extraordinary overpraise by Bancroft's flamboyant declamations about Liberty, Democracy, and the Nation. The best literary taste of the mid-nineteenth century was hardly represented by rhapsodies about a work from which it is quite fair to quote these sentences: "With one impulse the colonies sprang to arms. With one spirit they pledged themselves to be ready for the extreme event. With one heart the continent cried, Liberty or Death."

Bancroft's floridity produced a direct reaction in the shorter *History of the United States* (1849–1852) of Richard Hildreth, which is as matter-of-fact as a railroad schedule. Hildreth's irritation at "centennial sermons and Fourth-of-July orations" combined with an enthusiasm for English Utilitarian thought to produce history that was consciously antiliterary. Many a later historian, seeking "scientific history," hailed Hildreth as the most important American historian of the nineteenth century; his contemporaries were inclined to ignore him as a churlish fellow who reduced everything to his own dull level.

However different Hildreth, Bancroft, and Sparks were, all three were alike in having grown up outside the wealth and aloofness of patrician Boston. They lived their lives with no sense of remoteness from the hurly-burly of politics and economic change around them. Bancroft was an active Democratic politician, Hildreth an active Whig, and both operated for considerable periods at the grubbier level of politics. When they picked a theme for history they chose the history of the United States, of a United States close to them in time and in problems. They were so concerned with contemporary issues that their histories plainly voted on tariffs, central banks, land, slavery, and other public questions of their day. Even the least present-minded of the three, Jared Sparks, had served for two years as Chaplain of the House of Representatives and persistently thought of history as a kind of sermon to politicians and voters.

This sympathetic interest in their age, this sense of moving with it, Prescott and Parkman did not have; and Motley shared it only to a small degree. The background of the literary historians put them on an aloof social plateau, from which they could come down to the level of common life only by a conscious effort. All three were heirs to great wealth, and disengaged from the trading by which it had been amassed. Socially, they belonged to a circle which had hardly admitted a new name since the Revolution. Theirs was the Boston patrician routine: the gentleman's excursion at Harvard, the *Wanderjahre* in Europe, and then the return home to an exclusive social life and equally exclusive literary societies. There they discussed one another's papers over a sound supper of widgeons and teal and generous claret brought in by a ship which one of them probably owned but had never seen. None of them came to grips with contemporary economic life; the closest any of them approached to active politics was Motley's one term in the Massachusetts legislature, which revolted him, and his short periods as a diplomat, the least rough-and-tumble of government services. They varied only in the degree to which they were repelled from their age and from present-minded history by a raw industrialism and the "vulgar" politics of factory hands, small farmers, and trades-people.

Yet this Boston was too much New England, too close to its conscience-lashed past to be satisfied with fashionable dilettantism. The merely graceful life was unthinkable to the grandsons of men who had believed that idleness was sin and who had, on their own road to heaven, wrung wealth out of rocky soil and stormy oceans. The answer, the most natural answer under the circumstances, was the writing of serious books. As Prescott put it,

A person in our country who takes little interest in politicians or in making money—our staples you know—will be thrown pretty much on his own resources, and if he is not fond of books he may as well go hang himself, for as to a class of idle gentlemen, there is no such thing here.

When Prescott, Motley, and Parkman thought of writing books, a special circumstance inclined them to books of literary history. Hostile as their Boston was to raucous new America, it was alive and open to the literary interests, enthusiasms, and standards of western Europe, where the brightly colored history of dramatic men and events was the current enthusiasm. Even without the European influence, no kind of writing could have seemed more con-genial. What else was so far removed from the drab factories that were ruin-ing the charming little rivers of Massachusetts or the ragamuffin hordes that toppled over punch bowls at Andrew Jackson's inauguration? With a happy sense of escape, Prescott turned to the glamorous Spanish conquerors, Motley to the dramatic Dutch struggle for liberty, and Parkman to the technicolor story of the American forests.

3

Tall, graceful William Hickling Prescott was one of the gayest figures of young Boston, but there was never any question in his mind that he must become "habitually industrious." The loss of one eye in a Harvard frolic and the rapid inflammation of the other, which rendered him nearly blind for the rest of his life, brought no weakening of the compulsion to work. At first the industry went into sentimental short stories for his literary society "The Club"; then into carefully worked critiques of English literature for the *North American Review*. Prescott was not satisfied; none of these projects was big enough to match his conscience or his ambition. He toyed with the idea of writing a history of Italian literature, a history of Rome, and with various biographical possibilities. Meanwhile, an interest in Spain, set off by Napo-leon's raids on the Peninsula, was intensifying in Anglo-American literary circles. As Prescott entered his thirties, George Ticknor, another member of the patrician set, returned from Europe eloquent with the possibilities in Spanish subjects. Prescott listened entranced to some lectures Ticknor had prepared for a Harvard course, browsed though Ticknor's extensive Spanish library. In 1826 he made his decision. He "subscribed" to the subject of the reign of Ferdinand and Isabella.

"Subscribed" is a weak word for the dedication Prescott actually gave. To conquer the scholarly and literary problems involved and the handicap of his near-blindness, he systematically employed every kind of aid available. To overcome his love of leisure, he budgeted his life as a pauper budgets his pennies. He had his servant pull away his bedcovering at a set hour; he made bets with his secretary that he would write the allotted number of pages that day; even on his daily horseback ride he made sure that he composed history in his head. From this intense concentration came, with notable rapidity, Prescott's four major works: *A History of the Reign of Ferdinand and Isabella* (1837), *A History of the Conquest of Mexico* (1843), *A History of the Conquest of Peru* (1847), and *A History of the Reign of Philip the Second* (1855-1858)—the last incomplete at his death.

Into each of these works Prescott poured enough research to produce a hundred learned monographs. After generations of criticism, the general verdict is that his scholarly use of the sources then available leaves little to be desired. But Prescott himself would be even more pleased by the fact that after a hundred years his *Mexico* and *Peru* are still in print in several inexpensive editions, for he thought of himself primarily as a literary craftsman. As such, he carefully studied the existing models before writing a word of his first major literary history. Of course, Sir Walter Scott, whom he considered "the master of the picturesque," was given close attention. From Voltaire, Prescott took the idea of a topical rather than a chronological matrix. He found in *De l'étude de l'histoire* of Voltaire's contemporary, the Abbé de Mably, a congenial notion of the "necessity of giving an interest as well as utility to history, by letting events tend to some obvious point or moral; in short, by paying such attention to the development of events tending to this leading result, as one would in the construction of a romance or drama." Prescott also acknowledged his debt to French disciples of Scott, who heightened the readability of their histories by freely paraphrasing from colorful documents. In his general approach Prescott followed contemporary European romantic history, which sought, above all, unity of theme embellished with striking facts, a dramatic arrangement of these facts, and elaborate attention to the characterization of leading personalities. Basically, his conception of the structure of literary history was also that of Motley and Parkman.

Prescott's style at first shunned the flexibility encouraged by European romanticism and showed more of the eighteenth century English emphasis upon clarity, use of balance, antithesis and metaphor, and abstention from "low diction." When his first important work, the *Ferdinand and Isabella,* appeared, one reviewer roundly condemned him as "always on his best behavior, prim, prudish, and stiff-necked." The critic had a point. *Ferdinand and Isabella* is overfull of the balanced sentence, the studied antithesis, and the elaborate parallel; women are invariably "females," a gift is a "donative," people are married by "having nuptials solemnized," a name is an "appellation," and people are buried by being "consigned to their kindred dust." Prescott's immediate reaction was to say that the reader had to take his style for better or for worse, but he did admit that it was not as simple as it might be. As he went on writing, he simplified it a great deal and he repudiated more and more consciously the eighteenth century theory that there is only one good style. "The best rule," he came to believe, "is to dispense with all rules except grammar and to consult the natural bent of one's genius." In only one stylistic idea did he remain so rigid that he would have pleased Samuel Johnson on the Doctor's most dogmatic day; he belligerently insisted on writing English, not American. As chary of the new language as he was of the new America, he warned against "innovations, liable to spring up in a country where an active, inventive population, less concerned with books than with business, is very likely to corrupt the pure waters of 'English undefiled.'" How artificially he wrote English is suggested by the contrast between his books and his letters, which bounce along with such downright Americanisms as "whopper-jawed," and "take it easy."

Because of his tendency to use literary starch, the extraordinary effect of Prescott's writing comes largely from his successfully dramatic structure, his precision in language, and his striking ability to adapt that language to the demands of his subject matter. His military descriptions march in staccato sentences of parallel structure which are as devoid of ornament as a troop train. In a philosophical or a generalizing vein, his use of metaphor gives attractive clarity to abstruse thoughts. His paragraphs of general history vary from the lush to the spare, and are as arresting either way because the materials seem to demand just that treatment.

As literature, the *Conquest of Mexico* is undoubtedly Prescott's masterpiece. Here was a subject ideal for the medium. One man, Cortés, strides through the story in a way that would be spectacular in the coldest recital of the facts. As Prescott said:

The natural development of the story . . . is precisely what would be prescribed by the severest rules of art. The conquest of the country is the great end always in view of the reader. From the first landing of the Spaniards on the soil, their subsequent adventures, their battles and negotiations, their ruinous retreat, their rally and final siege, all tend to this grand result till the long series of events is closed by the downfall of the capital. . . . It is a magnificent epic, in which the unity of interest is complete.

As Prescott conceived the work, it presented only two serious problems of form. To describe the conquest without describing the Aztec civilization it conquered was obviously superficial; and yet such an introductory section could easily disrupt the unity of the whole work. Prescott also felt that he had to tell Cortés' life after the Conquest, and he was only too aware of the dangers of an anticlimactic effect in doing this. It was in the difficult introduction and in the difficult close that Prescott demonstrated his supreme artistry. Far from disrupting unity, his "View of the Aztec Civilization" builds into an attractive foreground a mass of facts which needed telling but would have clogged the story of the Conquest itself. Moreover, the opening, by emphasizing the barbarism of the Aztec civilization, makes its overthrow seem the more glamorous an enterprise. Far from being anticlimactic, the later life of Cortés is handled in such a way that he is made to seem fascinating even when his main work is done, and the total interest in him is thus heightened.

The earlier work of Prescott, *Ferdinand and Isabella,* offered less opportunity for dramatic unity than the *Mexico,* but Prescott did as much as could be done for literary effect by weaving the story around the theme of progress out of a "barbarous age" to a powerful and unified Spain. The work that followed the *Mexico,* his *Conquest of Peru,* presented still more tortuous literary problems. Pizarro is neither so dominant nor so attractive as Cortés. The main action, the subduing of the Incas, comes to an end long before the close of the narrative, and the rest of the story consists mainly of squabblings among the conquerors until the supremacy of the Crown is finally established. Prescott sought his unity by making the narrative a series of steps leading to the "great result" of the domination of the Spanish Crown, but, as one of his critics has remarked, this solution was more logical than convincing. The conquest of a humane people by a group that Prescott had to call the "scum of [Spanish] chivalry" could hardly be called progress toward a "great result," and the vanquished, unlike the Aztecs, were so feeble that their submission offers only sporadic drama. The story moves and shimmers, but the movement is mostly the whirl of little men and the shimmer is often the effect of artificial lighting. Prescott's last work, covering the reign of Philip II, would have taxed even his normal powers to the fullest, since its subject matter was the worst possible for a literary historian—a mass of disparate facts adding up, if they added up at all, to decay and dissolution. As it was, most of the volumes were written against the doctor's orders; and they emerge only as a collection of charming or spectacular episodes.

4

As Prescott was working on his *Philip the Second,* he received a worried communication from a young fellow Bostonian, John Lothrop Motley. Motley had started to write a history of the revolt of the Dutch against Philip II, and when he heard of the famous Prescott's project he was afraid of being completely overshadowed. In the spirit of gracious scholarship, Prescott invited Motley to a conference and encouraged him to go ahead on the basis of a division of emphasis. Prescott would use the focus of the whole reign of Philip, and Motley would concentrate on the development of the Netherlands. The field was, Prescott assured the younger man, big enough for two plows. Big enough it was, especially since there were differences between the two men's conceptions of literary history.

Not that Prescott and Motley arrived at their methods by very different routes. Motley also was born into the Boston elite; he graduated from Harvard; he went on to the inevitable travel and study abroad; and he returned to Boston contrasting the "naked and impoverished" past of the United States with Europe, "where fable and romantic legend have lent a name and a charm to every forest, mountain, rock, and river." Motley's first attempts to put this kind of charm on paper were two novels that stumbled under the burden of bad plots. Restless and in magnificent physical vigor—he was the only one of the three literary historians not to suffer serious eye trouble—Motley then tried a minor diplomatic post in St. Petersburg and one term in the Massachusetts legislature. But bleak St. Petersburg brought only homesickness and, after two years in the Massachusetts House, he recoiled from all active politics with lugubrious reflections on "rule by the dismal mob."

Meanwhile, a piece of literary criticism that he wrote for the *North American Review* led him to a more congenial field. What started as a critique of two books about Russia ended as a brilliant piece of literary history sketching the reign of Peter the Great. In a chorus Motley's friends advised him to turn to history on a large scale. The advice was sound. History did not require what Motley found it hardest to do—invent a plausible plot—and it used to the fullest his talents for picturesque language and sweeping generalization. Although he could not down the feeling that any kind of history was a job for "sappers and miners" compared to the novel-writing "lancers," Motley took the advice of his friends, and in his mid-thirties began intensive preparation for writing history. Later in life, he paused for some gentlemanly politics as United States Minister to the Austrian Empire and to England, and did considerable nonhistorical writing on the American Civil War as a struggle for a quite abstract "liberty." But the core of Motley's life was the many-volume literary history he wrote around that same thesis of liberty, worked out, by a wise choice, in terms of the history of the Dutch. Over the years, his carefully wrought volumes carried the story of the Dutch all the way from the struggle for freedom from the Spanish Empire to the struggle to reconcile freedom with nationhood. The story was told in *The Rise of the Dutch Republic* (1856), the *History of the United Netherlands, from the Death of William the Silent, to the Synod of Dort* (1860–1867), and *The Life and Death of John of Barneveld, Advocate of Holland* (1874).

Fundamentally, Motley's conception of the structure and style of literary history was the same as Prescott's. He sought above all to cut through the "confused mass of particulars" to a unity of theme, and to develop that theme by "startling and brilliant pictures." But Motley, who had spent his boyhood building miniature theaters and declaiming in and out of season, sought the dramatic so avidly that his work takes on a different tone from Prescott's. In characterizing even Cortés, Prescott preserved a certain calm and balance. Motley, imitating the "magnificent" Carlyle, made his heroes all heroic, and when he disliked a man he could write of him, "If there are vices—as possibly there are—from which he [Philip II] was exempt, it is because it is not permitted to human nature to be perfect in evil." Motley also contrasts with Prescott in belligerent didacticism. The older man was careful to insist that, while all history should flow into a unified theme, the theme should never shape the facts. Of a more simple mind and with his emotions under less restraint, Motley consciously wrote history as tract. With full-throated dogmatism, he preached the virtues of "noble," "grand" Protestant liberty as opposed to "ruthless," "decadent" Catholic absolutism.

Motley's first work, *The Rise of the Dutch Republic,* is far more sure of permanence in the national literature than anything else he wrote. Here the subject, the struggle of the Dutch for independence, lent itself to the dramatic unity of a liberty-versus-absolutism thesis; the fight of a small nation against a powerful empire made heroic language natural; and the leader of the Dutch, William of Orange, was, in fact, a character of almost Carlylean perfection. Once the Netherlands were free and William was dead, Motley himself saw literary trouble ahead. "It is difficult to scare up another William of Orange," he observed ruefully. Moreover, the action was no longer neatly confined within the Netherlands, but had to pass through most of western Europe and even push along the routes of navigators who were daring many oceans. The *History of the United Netherlands* is at best only brilliant episodes, and at worst it is grossly overwritten. In *John of Barneveld,* Motley was able to recapture dramatic unity by pitting two strong personalities against each other and by giving the outcome of their struggle tragic inevitability. His work regains some of the power of the *Dutch Republic,* though in making these men focal symbols he had to distort more than when he made William of Orange an idea incarnate.

Motley's overdramatization and didacticism, combined with research less intense than Prescott's or Parkman's, have cost his works in staying power. Scholars have largely rewritten the story of the Dutch Republic; it is the rare modern who would, for pleasure alone, read Motley from cover to cover, even his *Rise of the Dutch Republic.* But particular characterizations and episodes in his writings—notably the portraits of William of Orange and Philip II, and the descriptions of the Siege of Leyden, the abdication of Charles V, and the assassination of William—are not excelled in American literature for glint and lift and thud of language.

5

Neither Motley nor Prescott has been the subject of a full-length biography since 1905, but as late as 1942 an ambitious life of Parkman appeared, and more about him is always on the way. This interest is not surprising. Not only is Francis Parkman generally accepted as representing the literary historians at their best, the man himself is as arresting as any page he wrote.

A lanky, sensitive boy, scion of the most settled Boston, Parkman was not through Harvard when, as he says, he contracted "Injuns on the brain." Before graduating, he was off on vacation trips to the forests lying north and west of Boston. Only a few months after getting his degree, he left on horseback for a seventeen-hundred-mile trip along the Oregon Trail. In the forties, such a venture was as dangerous as crossing the Atlantic in a small boat, and Parkman reveled in the danger. Out of the trip came *The California and Oregon Trail* (1849), which, in addition to being one of the few authentic accounts of primitive Indian life at that date, is still widely read by lovers of the literature of adventure. Out of this trip also came some of the maladies that were to cut seriously into his working efficiency for the rest of his life. Medical scholars still argue exactly what was wrong with Parkman, and how much of his illness was neurotic. He certainly was afflicted for long periods with a painful arthritis, and, between near-blindness and fierce headaches, the day was rare when he could write more than a few pages.

Fighting illness, Parkman, like his admirer Theodore Roosevelt, developed an extreme hate for "weakness." To Parkman, nothing was a plainer confession of weakness than arguments for democracy, and the mores of commerce and industry were accorded equal scorn because they seemed a departure from the blunt, virile ways of an earlier world. He once called himself "a little medieval," and the description catches well his feudal disdain for the market place and the ballot box. Politically, this disdain made Parkman one of the most sweeping reactionaries in all American letters; as an author, it gave him ideological impetus to write the history of the frontier to which he was so emotionally attached. Here was a wide-open opportunity for a story of raw forces, unrestrained by strivings for democracy and, at least in Parkman's view, comparatively unaffected by the traffickings of commerce. Before he was out of his twenties, Parkman had found his way to his natural outlet—"a history of the American forest," which, more specifically, meant the struggle of France and England for the mastery of North America. Eight different works, running to a total of eleven volumes and published over the long period from 1851 to 1892, were required to complete the whole of this vast design. The series is known by the title *France and England in North America.*

Of the three literary historians, Parkman was easily the least self-conscious as a craftsman, though his preparation for his task was as conscientious as that of the others. He studied all the classics, historical and otherwise, and carefully worked out a method and style which he thought best suited to his purpose. But he had an aversion to the intricate theorizing about literary method which was characteristic of the romantics, just as he shied away from much of their ebullience. Only from occasional remarks, his prefaces, the internal evidence of his volumes, and his reviews for the *North American Review* and other journals, can the fundamentals of his conception of history be reconstructed.

Parkman believed that the facts should be collected by the most painstaking and persistent research—whenever possible, in first-hand documents and by personal visits to the scenes of the incidents. The writer was to go at his material with a determination "to imbue himself with the life and spirit of the time," to avoid moralizing and philosophizing, and, above all, to get at "the truth." The work was to be constructed on the principle of dramatic unity of theme, and both the integrity and the artistry of the book were to be safeguarded by the utmost care about proportions. The style should be "manly" and "direct," distinguished by "freedom from those prettinesses, studied turns of expression, and pretty tricks of rhetoric, which are the pride of less masculine writers."

With this conception of history, Parkman's volumes are naturally similar in many fundamentals to Prescott's and even, though in lesser degree, to Motley's. But parts of Parkman's ideal of history produced significant differences. His emphasis upon the integrity of materials ruled out Prescott's and

Motley's use of color for color's sake, particularly Prescott's tendency to prefer a chatty chronicle to a rationally determined set of facts. Parkman's aversion to philosophizing would have killed many a paragraph in Prescott and required a reconstruction of Motley's whole work. In style, his predilection for the "direct" and "manly" made him both less eighteenth century and less romantic than the other literary historians, as little disposed to balance and antithesis as to glossy adjectives and hyperthyroid verbs.

Each of Parkman's variations from the other men, perhaps intentionally, gave greater permanence to his volumes. Prescott's and Motley's conceptions of what is colorful, Motley's philosophizing, and both men's highly stylized styles have all tended to date; but the past is immortal, and Parkman's whole method may be accurately summarized as an attempt to bring back the past just as it was. To more than one critic he has recalled the remark of Michelet, that history is not narration as Thierry thought, nor analysis as Guizot thought; it is "resurrection."

Parkman's success in historical resurrection has, by general recognition, never been excelled. Time after time the reader comes close to the sense of being able actually to see and hear the incident. It is not difficult to tell from Parkman's writings that he preferred English civilization to French, the Protestant religion to the Catholic, and many features of the old regime to democracy. The discovery of additional materials has rounded out some episodes he described, such as the French explorations, and changed in important ways other incidents, like the story of Braddock's defeat. Many modern historians feel that he seriously underrated the importance of economic factors. But his research was so prodigious, his use of materials so coolly rational, and his language so objectively precise that the main body of his work has stood immune to the criticism of modern scholarship. Parkman's practice of making trips to the scenes of incidents gave his work one type of authority which no amount of modern scholarship could possibly have, for in his day many of the physical scenes were very little changed from the period of French-English rivalries. And what he learned he set down with the most timeless type of art—dramatic organization restrained by disdain for melodrama, and clarity enlivened by a sure sense of the picturesque.

The achievement of Parkman has such majesty that many a critic has overlooked the fact that his style is of uneven quality. At times the past does more than live again. It lives bombastically, as when "that savage river [the Missouri], descending from its mad career and a vast unknown of barbarism, poured its turbid floods into the bosom of its gentler sister," or when the French Revolution became "blazing hamlets, sacked cities, fields steaming with slaughter, profaned altars, and ravished maidens." This turgidity virtually disappeared as his art matured. The style which has made his writings the manual for many a wise young author is more accurately exemplified by his description of the death of Wolfe at the battle on the plains of Abraham (in *Montcalm and Wolfe*), where the drama inherent in the event reveals itself through straightforward narrative prose.

As Parkman looked back at his volumes over nearly seventy years, he was satisfied with the style he had wrought by infinite hard work. It was another literary feature of *France and England in North America,* its organization, which troubled him. According to the literary historians' ideal of structure there is a flaw, for the organization of the work is not consistent. From the dramatic point of view, the French and English conflict should revolve around the clash between dominant men and ideas. From the logical point of view, the story should move in a cause-effect series, with men and ideas subordinated to that series. Sometimes dramatic and sometimes logical, *France and England in North America* shifts perspective both within the series and within particular books of the series. Parkman, always the perfectionist, was bothered by this inconsistency, and only his death cut short a plan to revise the whole massive work.

One may wonder whether the flaw did not seem more serious to Parkman than it actually is, whether it is not more technical than real. After all, the struggle of France and England for North America was a sprawling, inchoate conflict in which the dramatic and the logical blended and clashed. Perhaps Parkman's instincts served him better than his intellect by loosening his structure in a way that approximates the wobbling of human affairs. At any rate, only a few of his most critical readers have been bothered by the organization of his work. Even Populist-minded Vernon Parrington, whose pen reached for acid as soon as it approached a Brahmin, was ready to accept *France and England in North America* as a permanently great work. The full stature of this nearly blind historian, tortured by sickness and imaginings of sickness, is suggested by the fact that no man has attempted to do again the full story of the struggle for mastery of the North American continent.

6

Well before Parkman died in 1893, the writing of history in the United States had swerved away from the Parkman concept. There were, of course, attempts to write in the tradition of literary history. John Bach McMaster, a civil engineer with the ambition to be "the American Macaulay," made the effort quite consciously in his *History of the People of the United States* (1883–1913). McMaster's bulky green volumes earned a prominent place in historiography because of their attention to the activities of ordinary people, and many a contemporary critic hailed their "vivacity"; but a ramshackle organization and an awkward style cost them any permanent place in literature. Theodore Roosevelt's *Winning of the West* (1889–1900), modeled after Parkman's work, continued the Parkman story through the Louisiana Purchase. Here again the attempt at history as literature was decidedly inferior to the earlier masters both in research, which was too often skimpy, and in style, which was frequently tumid.

More popular than the historical writings of either Roosevelt or McMaster were the eleven scattered volumes of John Fiske. Lucid and lively, his written history showed the same flair for popularization that made him one of the most successful lecturers the American platform has ever known. But even the book to which Fiske gave the most research and the most thought, his *Critical Period of American History, 1783–89* (1888), was little more than an ingenious arrangement of well established materials. Of all the historians writing toward the end of the century, the only one who produced volumes that are incontestably literature as well as important history was, appropriately enough, a latter-day Boston Brahmin, Henry Adams. His *History of the United States During the Administrations of Jefferson and Madison* (1889–1891) is a triumph of research, thought, and art.

Yet even Henry Adams did not hold the ideal of literary history. He wrote his nine volumes, as he put it, to try to fix "a necessary sequence of human movement" by the "severest process of stating, with the least possible comment, such facts as seemed sure, in such order as seemed rigorously consequent." In short, Adams, like most of his generation, wrote as a "scientific historian." The American Historical Association, organized in 1884, was dominated by a group of men who believed that history could and should be converted into a science by the most objective statement of the most critically determined facts. This "scientific history" denied to the historian the right to impose on his facts any pattern, either literary or ideological, or to add color and movement to the narrative by an imaginative handling of the materials. The American predecessor on whom "scientific history" lavished its praise was Richard Hildreth, who had shillelagh words for any historian seeking literary effects.

The lessening importance of the patrician in the historical field also undermined interest in literary history. By 1900 the overwhelming number of American historians were the sons of middle-class families who shared relatively little (when they shared it at all) the patrician type of revulsion from commercial and industrial America. Moreover, the reform enthusiasm sweeping the United States in the early twentieth century found sympathy in many professors. With this sympathy came a tendency to use the major intellectual weapon of the Reform movement, an economic interpretation of past and present affairs. Even historians unsympathetic to the reformist social program and hesitant about rigorous economic interpretations were, for the most part, in revolt against a romantic apotheosis of an undemocratic past. They too were turning to history which focused on the undramatic, workaday activities of masses of little men. The older literary history, with its emphasis upon the powerful few and the colorful incident, was ruthlessly squeezed between the "scientific" and the "social" history, both of which were combined in the typical new history.

The new history soon brought a radical change of audience. Prescott, Motley, and Parkman had been and continued to be read by the general educated public. With a few exceptions, the footnote-fettered "scientific historians" were read only by one another. Their triumph in the early decades of the twentieth century meant that the public interest in history had to be served largely by popular writers who had neither the high artistic standards of the old school nor the high scholarly standards of the new.

Obviously it was only a question of time before a still newer type of historian combined some features of both traditions. Beginning in the 1920's, the educated public was offered a rapidly increasing output of history which could challenge the work of the literary historians in readability and that of the "scientific historians" in method. Most of these books were written outside the universities; the Professor of History generally kept his eye to the microscope of monographic treatment. But, in or out of universities, these men and women wrestled, often successfully, with a problem that is fundamentally literary. It was a problem made ever more tortuous by the increasing mass of materials, the increasing demands of historical scholarship, and the increasing sophistication of historical interpretations.

This newer new history has been called a revival of literary history but it is hardly that in the sense in which the term has been used in this chapter. The newer historians of high readability chose different kinds of subject matter, treated it with a modern concern for social and economic analysis, and built their books along essentially different lines of structure and style. The literary history of Prescott, Motley, and Parkman came from a particular milieu which has never reappeared in the United States. Although many another Brahmin group has appeared, with an equal attachment to books and even an equal aversion for commercialism and "the mob," there has been only one Brahminism stirred by those cross winds of the eighteenth and nineteenth centuries which swirled through Boston at the mid-century. Men and women will always go on writing history that is also literature, but the work of Prescott, Motley, and Parkman is as unique as it is permanent.

33. THE ORATORS

ORATORY has always been a proud American tradition, a national habit. The tradition of more than three centuries links Thomas Hooker preaching in his pulpit at Hartford, Connecticut, on *The Soules Humiliation* with Franklin D. Roosevelt halting a national debacle with the sanative words of his First Inaugural: "Let me assert my firm belief that the only thing we have to fear is fear itself." We have produced oratory robustly in mass, volume, and diffuseness. In times of crisis we have also produced addresses of compelling thought and enduring beauty.

The art which the orator practices—the art of rhetoric—was defined by Aristotle as the faculty of observing (not necessarily of using) all the available means of persuasion. Our orators who have practiced this art have been men who by logical proof and emotional appeal, reinforced by all the resources of their established prestige, have persuaded large groups of their fellow citizens to adopt certain beliefs or to pursue certain policies. In America, oratory has been the great creator of loyalties. The pervading tradition of our literature, written or spoken, is a tradition of revolt, but the orator, even when leading a revolt, has always sought to arouse the indifferent or dissuade the hostile in order that he may secure the loyalty of a group. He has attempted by direct address to compel that same kind of devoted response which may come to novelists or poets only after generations of readers have read their works.

It has been said that "oratory is partly an art, partly a power of making history, and occasionally a branch of literature." Oratory concerns chiefly the public life of society, but literary critics select for survival those passages of the oration which show something of the private life that a public life preserves. To the literary critic Lincoln's Gettysburg Address is a great prose passage written by a man who brooded much in solitude, and who rose above a particular occasion to speak to the ages. But we should remember that he also seized the occasion with its powerful emotional associations to dedicate his audience to carrying on the Civil War.

We call the criticism of the work of the orators rhetorical criticism. It is not primarily concerned with permanence, nor beauty, but with effect.

Rhetorical criticism carries on near the boundary line of literature and politics. Its atmosphere is that of public life rather than the quiet of the library. It is concerned with the ideas of masses of people as influenced by their leaders rather than with the ideas of solitary thinkers or poets. It examines the wielder of public opinion as one handling a technique of power. For rhetorical criticism the personality of the orator, the history of the issues he debated, the nature of the opposition he faced, the character of the audiences he addressed are at least as important as his artistic ability to lend interest to matters whose practical importance has vanished. Necessarily, then, the critical approach of this chapter will differ somewhat from that of other chapters which are concerned with the works of thinkers or poets whose audience never crowded close around them to hear their voices.

In no period of American history was the orator so influential as during the fifty years before the Civil War. The age produced a steady stream of able speakers who by their superior eloquence attained the stature of orators and profoundly affected the direction of public affairs. Many, like Emerson and Phillips and Parker, were notable writers as well as lecturers and orators. It is appropriate, therefore, that the chapter of this history devoted to American oratory should appear at this point in the story of the development of American literature, and that it should be concerned mainly with the great figures of the golden age of American oratory. But to make the account complete, the chapter must look before and after, backward to the great Puritan preachers and forward to the day when the radio would make it possible for a national leader who was also an orator to speak directly to millions of his countrymen and move them to act.

2

The first American orators—the preachers, the colonial governors and legislators—were men well trained, as they needed to be, in the art of rhetoric which they had learned in the English universities, the Inns of Court, or the infant colleges of the New World. At Harvard in 1655 students were required to make public declamations twice each month. Lectures on rhetoric were given on Friday mornings, and all the members of the college spent the rest of the day in rhetorical exercises based on the logic of Peter Ramus and the rhetoric of Talon.

The Puritan preacher had special need of this elaborate training. The Covenant Theology which he expounded was intricate and most difficult to make plain. Too much depended on the truthfulness and clarity with which he set it forth to permit him to exceed by much the bounds of the "plain style." Curious as the sermons of Increase Mather and Urian Oakes may seem to modern readers, they were wonderfully effective instruments for explaining great mysteries to simple men.

The colonial legislatures were closed assemblies until the middle of the eighteenth century; but within the small chambers in Boston or Williamsburg the great debate between the Crown and a rebellious America had already begun. Governors sometimes spoke sharply to the people's representatives in their opening addresses, but they usually tried to argue the Crown's case well—if relations were still cordial enough to induce them to speak at all. Once the people were admitted to the galleries, the legislators learned soon enough to speak beyond the heads of the governor and their fellow representatives to the larger audience outside the walls of the statehouse.

Until the third decade of the eighteenth century most of the orators were trained in the rhetorical tradition which the Renaissance inherited from Aristotle and Quintilian and remade for its own purposes. But a new age in America in which an ever increasing audience of the plain people was eager to hear religious and political issues debated before it, now demanded a more emotional style. The preachers who induced the Great Awakening in the 1730's were bent on arousing their hearers to the dangers of their sinful state. Their instrument was enthusiasm rather than logic. When ministers of the established churches refused them their pulpits they went to the people in the open air, as George Whitefield did when Franklin heard him speak from the Courthouse steps in Philadelphia. The power of his voice on this occasion impelled Franklin's belief in the newspaper accounts of his having preached to as many as twenty-five thousand in the fields. The great orators of the Revolution likewise knew how to sway the emotions of their hearers, an art which they had learned by belaboring their opponents in law cases and by appealing to reluctant juries. Burke spoke the truth when he said in his speech On Conciliation that the American legislators were all lawyers or men endeavoring "to obtain some smattering in that science," and that their training had made them "prompt in attack, ready in defence, full of resources."

John Adams complained of the tediousness of the sessions of the Continental Congress in which "every man upon every question must show his oratory, his criticism, his political abilities"; but most of the other members agreed that he, as well as George Wythe, James Wilson, and a dozen others who spoke frequently, was good in debate and easy to listen to. Even John Witherspoon, whose voice was so low that it did not carry to the back of the room, received close attention because of the weight of his frequent speeches. Jefferson, Franklin, and Washington did not indulge in oratory but kept strictly to the issues. The great orators of the Congress, as most Americans still know, were Patrick Henry and Richard Henry Lee.

When presently the fateful issue of the Constitution was before the people, the skill of the orators who rose to defend it in the several states equaled that of the pamphleteers who also helped to secure its ratification. John Jay and Alexander Hamilton were ingenious and indefatigable in their arguments for adoption before the convention in New York State, as were C. C. Pinckney in South Carolina and Oliver Ellsworth in Connecticut. In Virginia the passionate opposition of Patrick Henry seemed at the time dangerous but was ultimately matched and defeated by the logic and lucidity of James Madison, the chief architect of the Constitution.

3

Throughout the years of the early national period there were many voices and multitudes of attentive listeners. They spoke and were heard in farm surroundings, village squares, and town halls, and only here and there in what we now call cities. For in 1830 a bare sixth of the people lived in places of over 8,000 population. It was a period, however, when men everywhere were eager to learn, eager to speak and take sides, eager to reach decisions. "The traits of intelligence, rapidity, and mildness seemed fixed in the national character as early as 1817," observes Henry Adams. And he significantly adds: "Another intellectual trait . . . was the disposition to relax severity." New horizons were ahead. The people were shifting, restless, youthfully optimistic, ambitious for better life and happier living. Literacy and learning were not widespread, but the capacity to listen to speakers and to criticize them knew no bounds.

The most important addresses of the period were made before legislative bodies, especially the United States Senate, before courts and juries, and at great patriotic ceremonies before vast audiences, like those assembled at Plymouth, 1820, Bunker Hill, 1825 and 1843, and Faneuil Hall, 1826, to hear Daniel Webster. His magnificent addresses on those occasions are without equal in the history of ceremonial oratory.

The pulpit, the lecture platform, and the election campaign likewise offered variety of subject matter ranging from instruction to entertainment. Audience taste, speech form and style, the educational equipment of the speaker combined to produce in the early years, from 1815 to as late as 1850, a characteristically ornate and diffuse kind of speaking. The same was true of the writing. By 1858, for instance, a writer in the *North American Review* took pains to explain:

It pleases our English critics to charge upon American writers in the mass— particularly upon our historians, orators, essayists, and lecturers, and the after-dinner speakers of our frequent celebrations and commemorations—what has come to be designated as "the spread-eagle style,"—a compound of exaggeration, effrontery, bombast, and extravagance, mixed metaphors, platitudes, defiant threats thrown at the world, and irreverent appeals flung at the Supreme Being. Now it is a simple slander upon us to generalize this charge, and to visit it upon American writers and speakers as such. There has been, as we all know, too much of this inflated and braggadocio utterance among us. . . . This habit of speaking, however, is now visiting the force of its own ridicule upon itself, and that will banish it sooner than will any protest of those aggrieved by it on either side of the water.

The prophecy proved correct. A youthful country may produce, it is true, a blatant and bumptious kind of oratory. But as individual speakers matured—Webster and Lincoln in particular—the powerful, simple, straightforward kind of address that befits a better educated and cultivated citizenry slowly emerged.

What kinds of subjects occupied men's minds? Wendell Phillips, the most famous of the antislavery orators, spoke during his lifetime on woman's suffrage and equal rights, temperance, capital punishment, treatment of the Indians, religious topics, education, prison reform, money and banking laws, and better wages and working conditions for labor. His consuming interest, however, was in freeing the slaves. He was typical of the age. From 1820 until Lee surrendered at Appomattox slavery was the dominating political issue. All other causes including the war with Mexico and the expansion of the West are dwarfed by the volume of speech-making produced by slavery. It carried with it, of course, discussion, debate, and dissent on the doctrines of States' Rights, Popular Sovereignty, Nullification, the Compromise of 1850, and eventually in 1860, Secession. Year by year until the Kansas-Nebraska Bill of 1854 and the Dred Scott Decision of 1857 the intensity of feeling and the convictions of evil and good mounted in the hearts and minds of men. When Lincoln and Douglas staged their joint debates in 1858 they were the final-act characters of a drama that had been playing with accelerating tempo and heightening action for fully forty years.

Throughout the process of erecting a superstructure on the foundation of the Fathers three orators were preeminent. In the beginning they were sectional figures. Daniel Webster was the North, John C. Calhoun the South, and Henry Clay the New West. But all were also nationalists, and Clay and Webster outgrew their sectionalism. Their principles came not from the inner light, nor from systematic political philosophy, but from an understanding of their constituents. Their ideas changed with changing times and interests. If they are to be criticized for having their eyes on the Presidency, they should be credited with able attempts to state ideas upon which the greatest number of conflicting interests could unite. Their power rested fundamentally upon their ability to state those ideas persuasively and impressively, and to convince their constituents that they were the ablest advocates before the bar of public opinion.

These men did not need an Emerson to remind them of "the meal in the firkin, the milk in the pan." They lived in their country homes at Marshfield, Fort Hill, and Ashland with something of the dignity of Washington at Mount Vernon or Jefferson at Monticello. They were not only attached to their lares and penates, they were practical directors of their agricultural pursuits. Their education was classical in background, and they all possessed an ardor for *respublica*. In the loyalties inspired by them the economic and political history between 1815 and 1850 may be understood, and in their devotion to country and section patriotism often rose above economics and politics.

4

Henry Clay was the first of these new leaders to talk himself into national prominence. "Harry of the West" was born in Virginia, and nurtured in Jeffersonian agrarianism. He migrated to Kentucky, absorbed the spirit of speculative expansion, entered the State Legislature, and was appointed to the United States Senate in 1806. Henry Adams notes that the twenty-nine-year-old Senator had been in the capital only two weeks when he introduced a new style into American politics by rhetorical references to the Union and the Fathers. George Washington and his contemporaries had previously been conceded greatness and had occasionally been hailed as venerable, but from now on American orators were to vie with one another in deifying them.

Clay, however, was as quick to defy Washington as to deify him. The policy of the older men had been prudence and peace, and under such a policy our army had been reduced to a small police force to guard against the Indians. Clay, as one of the sixty new youngsters sent to Congress, was determined to show what the boys could do, and he led a country without an army to attack a country whose army had been commanded by Wellington and whose navy had been trained by Nelson. "Sir," he exclaimed in the Senate two years before the War of 1812, "is the time never to arrive when we can manage our own affairs without the fear of insulting his Britannic majesty? Is the rod of British power to be forever suspended over our heads? . . . Whether we assert our rights by sea, or attempt their maintenance by land—whithersoever we turn ourselves, this phantom incessantly pursues us. Already has it too much influence in the councils of the nation."

The War Hawks, Clay included, deserved Josiah Quincy's characterization of them as "young politicians, with the pinfeathers yet unshed, and the shell still sticking upon them—perfectly unfledged." But the "Western Star," elected to the Speakership of the House immediately upon his entrance in 1811, had behind him the whole Mississippi Valley, bitter over a depression which it laid to the British Orders in Council, and the South, eager to wrest Florida and Mexico from England's ally, Spain. New England, still making profits in spite of the invasion of seamen's rights, had no desire to have its pride avenged, but its wrongs also furnished battle cries in the crusade of the West and South for war. Clay's Liberty Boys were determined to fix a national character by a second declaration of independence which should separate us from the governments of Europe. Clay had a vigorous two years of organization as well as of oratory before he could overcome the opposition of the Federalists. In his debates on the need for a navy, for a militia, for frontier mounted rangers, for equipment and supplies, he learned what a task it was to organize America's resources and create a national spirit capable of maintaining independence. The difficulties were so great that Clay and his colleagues may well be accounted foolhardy. Their policy, by all the laws of probability, should have brought defeat and ruin, but the net result, in spite of military disasters, was to establish the self-confidence of the nation, and win for it European recognition as an independent power.

Clay's expansive thinking led to large plans for the creation of a balanced economy for the United States, which he summarized as "The American System." It has been charged that it was a blind for a policy of high tariffs, but this is to fail to consider the system in its entirety. Clay's tariff was protective and it did build up manufacturing interests, which was a departure from his early Jeffersonianism. But, he argued, this would make the country self-sufficient in war, and would support a large industrial population, which in turn would provide a market for the produce of the expanding West and the plantations of the South. A substantial part of the tariff revenue was to provide funds for internal improvements in the West, thus distributing the benefits of the system to the whole nation. If the selfishness of sectional, class, and occupational interests could have been controlled, and the balance preserved, the American System might still be a tribute to Clay's powers of persuasion. But the blindness of the supporters of the National Bank, the uncompromising hostility of Jackson and the frontiersmen, and the demands of Calhoun for the South led to the Nullification Crisis of 1833. Clay saw that it was his American System against the Union, and he sacrificed what he regarded as his greatest contribution to American statecraft in order to introduce a compromise tariff.

From 1833 to 1842, during the years when Clay's powers were at their greatest, he was a leader of the opposition, and achieved little that will be remembered. His position as candidate for the Presidency in 1844, when the bitterness over the annexation of Texas compelled him to announce that he considered the preservation of the Union the paramount issue, was regarded as an unheroic straddle; his preference for the middle ground was thought to be dictated by his consuming desire for the Presidency. But when, after six years of retirement at Ashland, he was returned at the age of seventy-two to attempt again his old role of pacificator, he could remind the Senate that he was beyond ambition, could seriously deprecate the violence of party spirit, and could solemnly urge the necessity for compromise:

The final result [of Civil War] would be the extinction of this last and glorious light which is leading all mankind, who are gazing upon it, in the hope and anxious expectation that the liberty which prevails here will sooner or later be diffused throughout the whole of the civilized world.

The debate upon Clay's compromise proposals is one of the great debates in American history, or in the history of any parliamentary body. Clay, Calhoun, and Webster, all old and ill, were still the giants of the Senate, although a fiery and impetuous younger generation, including William H. Seward, Salmon P. Chase, Jefferson Davis, and Stephen A. Douglas were asserting themselves. But the older leaders symbolized their cause as no younger men could. Harry of the West was now the Great Pacificator. His sunken cheeks, pinched nose, bald head, and long fringe of gray hair falling to his shoulders, showed his age, but he profoundly moved the crowded galleries. His speeches gained in power from the fact that he was the author of the compromise proposals. He knew the extremists of both sides. He knew the temper of the nation, and no one could accuse him of ambition when he declared:

I go for honorable compromise whenever it can be made. Life itself is but a compromise between death and life, the struggle continuing throughout our whole existence, until the Great Destroyer finally triumphs. All legislation, all government, all society, is formed upon the principle of mutual concession, politeness, comity, courtesy; upon these everything is based. . . . Let him who elevates himself above humanity, above its weaknesses, its infirmities, its wants, its necessities, say, if he pleases, I never will compromise, but let no one who is not above the frailties of our common nature disdain compromises.

Clay was in his own time esteemed as the greatest orator of the day, but his speeches have had little effect as literature. His outlook on human affairs was eminently practical, and his speaking had a highly utilitarian purpose; but he understood the American mind, and he typified more than any other man of the age its strength and its shortcomings, its emotions, hopes, and ambitions.

5

Daniel Webster attained his oratorical eminence during the period 1818–1830. Elected to Congress in 1813, at the age of thirty-one, he attracted attention in his maiden speech by his historical learning and power of illustration. Chief Justice Marshall writing to a friend shortly after the speech predicted that Webster would "become one of the very first statesmen in America, and perhaps the very first." Had his career stopped short with the Second Reply to Hayne in 1830 his immense fame would have been secure. By then he was known for a score and more of speeches which made history. He had become a highly successful courtroom pleader both at the bar of the Supreme Court, as in the Dartmouth College Case (1818 *) and before criminal juries, as in the White Murder Trial (1830). But Webster's even greater reputation is based on his ceremonial speaking—the Plymouth Oration (1820), the First Bunker Hill Address (1825), the Eulogy of Adams and Jefferson (1826). These were addresses which furnished declamations for generations of American schoolboys up to the Civil War and it was that final solemn sentence of the Second Reply to Hayne, "Liberty *and* Union, now and forever, one and inseparable," that became the rallying cry of Union troops in 1861.

In appearance, in learning, in temperament and action Webster was the ideal orator. But it was his legal turn of mind, his ability to cast large ideas into musical language, and his remarkable gift of imagery that set the man apart as a speaker. Clay was the better debater and campaign orator; Calhoun was the better reasoner and political thinker. Webster was the epideictic orator par excellence. He lays down his own formula for good speaking in his Eulogy of Adams and Jefferson delivered at Faneuil Hall on August 2, 1826:

When public bodies are to be addressed on momentous occasions, when great interests are at stake, and strong passions excited, nothing is valuable in speech farther than as it is connected with high intellectual and moral endowments. Clearness, force, and earnestness are the qualities which produce conviction. True eloquence indeed, does not consist in speech. . . . It must exist in the man, in the subject, in the occasion. Affected passion, intense expression, the pomp of declamation, all may aspire to it; they cannot reach it. It comes, if it comes at all, like the outbreaking of a fountain from the earth, or the bursting forth of volcanic fires, with spontaneous, original, native force.

It was Webster's reply to Hayne in the Senate session of 1829–1830 that raised his reputation to the highest pitch. Senator Foote of Connecticut had

* Unless otherwise noted, dates of speeches in this chapter indicate the year of delivery rather than of publication.

introduced a resolution asking for an inquiry into the practical effects of limiting the sale of government land in the West. Senator Hayne of South Carolina had forcefully argued that the East had always tried to oppose the development of the West. Webster rose to defend the charge. His exordium beginning, "Mr. President, when the mariner has been tossed for many days in thick weather and on an unknown sea," is easily the most famous in American parliamentary address. The speech itself completely demolished the attacks made on Webster's character and his motives. By a strong argument the orator demonstrated his reliance upon the supremacy of the Constitution. Hayne on the other hand, Webster held, was deliberately expounding ideas which would surely lead to disunion and civil war. The final paragraph suggests in farseeing language what came to pass thirty years later:

> When my eyes shall be turned to behold, for the last time, the sun in heaven, may I not see him shining on the broken and dishonored fragments of a once glorious Union; on States dissevered, discordant, belligerent; on a land rent with civil feuds, or drenched, it may be, in fraternal blood!

The popular acclaim of the Second Reply to Hayne was extraordinary. The speech marked the zenith of the orator's career. In succeeding years Webster made many speeches, some good and a number lacking in quality. He reached a peak again, but with bitter result, in his Seventh of March speech (1850), when he deserted the abolitionist cause and in effect justified the South's stand on slavery.

The evidence now shows that the Union was in imminent danger of armed conflict in the spring of 1850. General Winfield Scott wrote General Sherman that the country was "on the eve of a terrible civil war." Similar testimony is available from such varied observers as Alexander H. Stephens, Francis Lieber, and Horace Mann. Late in February, 1850, Edward Everett wrote that "the radicals of the South have made up their minds to separate, the catastrophe seems to be inevitable."

It was with this knowledge that Webster planned the oration he called "The Constitution and the Union," but which history has named the Seventh of March speech. His opening sentence set the tone of the address: "I wish to speak today, not as a Massachusetts man, nor as a Northern man, but as an American."

The address proper required more than three hours in delivery and its published form takes up forty-one pages in the National Edition of Webster's works. In the main section the speaker calmly reviewed the grievances of the North and the South. He admitted that the North had failed to live up to its constitutional obligations to return fugitive slaves. He conceded that the abolition societies had only served to inflame feeling without effecting anything "good or valuable." He did not deny the irritating results of the resolutions to abolish slavery as drawn up by legislative bodies in the North. But the North objected to the institution of slavery which the South wished "to be cherished, preserved, and extended." And the only basis for solution, Webster argued, rested on new understandings—"a better feeling and more fraternal sentiments between the South and the North." Any attempt at "peaceable secession is an utter impossibility," he proclaimed as he turned and faced Calhoun.

With respect to an economic solution of the problem Webster announced his willingness to support a project for transporting freed slaves "to any colony or any place in the world." He also favored paying Texas a fair sum for deeding to the United States the lands adjoining New Mexico, an area always claimed by Texas as its own.

In his final appeal the orator counseled that "instead of speaking of the possibility or utility of secession" the nation should try to enjoy "the fresh air of Liberty and Union," and to preserve the Constitution and "the harmony and peace of all who are destined to live under it."

In general, it was a wise and temperate speech, not impassioned or emotional. And therein lies its strength. Webster assumed a statesmanlike position, and history has vindicated him; but his New England friends at the time, the Abolitionists in particular, never forgave him. Soon the Quaker poet, Whittier, gave to the once great Daniel the name of Ichabod and mourned for him in cutting verse as one dead:

> Let not the land once proud of him
>   Insult him now,
> Nor brand with deeper shame his dim,
>   Dishonored brow.
>
> But let its humbled sons, instead,
>   From sea to lake,
> A long lament, as for the dead,
>   In sadness make.

But the Union was preserved for another decade. If only another orator could have spoken again and preserved it, let us say, until 1870, economic forces, which we now comprehend, might have prevented the bloodshed.

6

The third of the triumvirate, John C. Calhoun, was in his prime a little later than Clay and Webster. His best speeches are in the Senate debates from 1833 to 1843 and again shortly before 1850. The most important are Against the Force Bill (1833), In Support of States' Rights (1833), Against Incendiary Publications (1836), those denouncing the Expunging Resolution and the Abolition Petitions (1837), Against the Ten Regiment Bill (1848), and his last speech, delivered just before he died, on The Slavery Question (1850).

As these titles suggest, Calhoun was generally in the opposition; as the spokesman of the South, he was against the long succession of measures designed to limit or abolish slavery. He argued in 1837 that slavery was a positive good, and he fought valiantly in the Senate to his death to maintain the balance between the slave and free states. On these issues Calhoun's excellent education at Yale, his first-class legal training under Judge Reeve at Litchfield, his lifelong reflective habits, and his analytical mind made him intellectually more than a match even for Clay and Webster.

For years Webster, the symbol of the New England manufacturing interests, and Calhoun, representing the slaveholding aristocracy of the South, were direct antagonists. (At the time of Webster's reply to Hayne, however, in 1830, Calhoun was serving as Vice President, and the Great Nullifier yielded to Hayne as the first expounder of the doctrine.) In simplest terms, Calhoun argued that a state reserved the right within its own borders to impede or to attempt to prevent the federal government from enforcing a law of the United States.

Emerson says: "There is no true eloquence unless there is a man behind the speech." Calhoun is perhaps the shining example among statesmen before the Civil War of the classical definition of the orator: the good man skilled in speaking. Even his political opponents admired his character, freely acknowledged the absence of corruption in his personal life. His voice and learning could not be bought. It is this intellectual honesty of the man that we must fix in mind to form a true estimate of Calhoun.

But I take higher ground. I hold that in the present state of civilization, where two races of different origin, and distinguished by color and other physical differences, as well as intellectual, are brought together, the relation now existing in the slaveholding states between the two is, instead of an evil, a good—a positive good. I feel myself called upon to speak freely upon the subject, when the honor and interests of those I represent are involved. I hold, then, that there never has yet existed a wealthy and civilized society in which one portion of the community did not, in point of fact, live on the labor of the other. Broad and general as is this assertion, it is fully borne out by history.

Thus spoke Calhoun before the Senate in 1837 on the question of receiving petitions in Congress for the abolition of slavery in the District of Columbia. The whole speech is typical of his style and logical structure. Unlike many speakers of his day he was not given to extensive use of emotional appeal. His use of ethical proof, the relation of the orator's character to the larger treatment of the subject, is awkward and generally not effective. But his arguments, well planned and supported, are readily followed. He is a master of cause-to-effect reasoning, and he frequently uses specific examples, analogies, and authorities to buttress the framework. The total effect is one of cold rigidity rather than of smooth persuasive appeal. Calhoun's language is not florid or effusive, as Southern oratory often is. Nor could anyone ever say of him, for example, as John Quincy Adams on a certain occasion wrote of John Randolph:

His speech, as usual, had neither beginning, middle, nor end. Egotism, Virginian aristocracy, slave-scourging, liberty, religion, literature, science, wit, fancy, generous feelings, and malignant passions constitute a chaos in his mind, from which nothing orderly can ever flow.

"The cast-iron man who looks as if he had never been born," Harriet Martineau called Calhoun. The impression explains why Calhoun never rose to the popular esteem of Clay or the brilliant eloquence of Webster. He seldom swayed votes on the issues he opposed, and his influence, not his interests, seldom went beyond sectional range. He was too severe, too humorless, too strait-laced to be a great public idol. Nevertheless his speeches deserve wider reading than they have enjoyed. They are neither dull nor ponderous, and they furnish the clue to the constitutional principles upon which the South defended slavery as an institution for the three decades before the fateful first shot at Fort Sumter.

7

In the summer of 1850 a young lawyer, Abraham Lincoln of Illinois, compiled some notes for a law lecture. What he wrote, concisely stated his character and foretold his own career:

Extemporaneous speaking should be practised and cultivated. It is the lawyer's avenue to the public. However able and faithful he may be in other respects, people are slow to bring him business if he cannot make a speech. And yet there is not a more fatal error to young lawyers than relying too much on speech-making. If anyone, upon his rare powers of speaking, shall claim an exemption from the drudgery of the law, his case is a failure in advance.

Within the next ten years Lincoln became by his own formula of diligent study and fluency in debate the people's chosen leader and the successor to the tradition of Clay, Calhoun, and Webster.

Ask any American today which of Lincoln's writings he remembers, and he will usually reply, "The Gettysburg Address and the Second Inaugural." If he happens to be a student of Speech or History he may add the Lincoln-Douglas Debates (1858), the Cooper Union Address (1860), the Farewell Address at Springfield (1861), the letter to Colonel Ellsworth's parents (1861), the letter to Mrs. Bixby (1864), and possibly others. These letters and addresses have established Lincoln as one of the masters of prose style in the English language.

Like Webster before him, Lincoln gradually came to see the strength and power of the plain style. As a young politician he was used to the ornate overspeaking of the day. But during the Zachary Taylor presidential campaign of 1848 he heard William H. Seward, later to be his Secretary of State, speak in Boston, and was impressed with his logical argument and conversational manner of delivery. We see the signs of a maturing speaker in the Peoria Speech of 1854, in the famous House Divided Against Itself Speech delivered before the Illinois Republican State Convention in 1858, and especially in the address at Cooper Union on February 27, 1860.

For this speech Henry Ward Beecher had first invited Lincoln to his Plymouth Church in Brooklyn; but the scene was later changed to accommodate the larger audience. A good share of Lincoln's argument went to answering the charges of Stephen A. Douglas that the writers of the Constitution had denied the government control over slavery in the territories. The speech did much to gain Lincoln the nomination for the Presidency. Joseph H. Choate later described its impact: "That night the great hall and the next day the whole city rang with delighted applause and congratulations, and he who had come as a stranger, departed with the laurels of a great triumph."

The Lincoln we know as President is less the orator and more the writer of masterful prose. He then habitually read his speeches from manuscript, and for this reason probably prepared and revised more carefully than ever before. The final wistfully hopeful sentences of the less often read First Inaugural Address reveal the glow of polish:

I am loath to close. We are not enemies, but friends. We must not be enemies. Though passion may have strained, it must not break our bonds of affection. The mystic cords of memory, stretching from every battlefield and patriot grave to every living heart and hearthstone all over this broad land, will yet swell the chorus of the Union when again touched, as surely they will be, by the better angels of our nature.

Edward Everett was the first to recognize the dignity of Lincoln's address at Gettysburg. He wrote to the President the next day from Washington:

I should be glad if I could flatter myself that I came as near to the central idea of the occasion in two hours as you did in two minutes.

And Lincoln courteously replied:

In our respective parts yesterday you could not have been excused to make a short address, nor I a long one. I am pleased to know that, in your judgment, the little I did say was not entirely a failure.

The general recognition of the exalted beauty of the Gettysburg Address was late in coming. So it was with the Second Inaugural Address. Yet British critics who had previously berated American literary efforts were quick to praise the poetry of the lines:

With malice toward none; with charity for all; with firmness in the right, as God gives us to see the right, let us strive on to finish the work we are in; to bind up the nation's wounds; to care for him who shall have borne the battle, and for his widow and his orphan—to do all which may achieve and cherish a just and lasting peace among ourselves, and with all nations.

Gladstone proclaimed:

I am taken captive by so striking an utterance as this. I see in it the effect of sharp trial, when rightly borne, to raise man to a higher level of thought and action. It is by cruel suffering that nations are sometimes born to a better life. So it is with individual man. Lincoln's words show that upon him anxiety and sorrow have wrought their full effect.

Here we have the judgment of an orator who has turned literary critic. His opinion is of interest because it reminds us that Lincoln is the one American orator who survives as a literary artist. His literary instinct was so true that we tend to forget his rhetorical skill. But whenever he spoke Lincoln was a persuasive man, an orator, as a study of the effect of his addresses reveals.

8

For forty-odd years before his death in 1865, Edward Everett was the great scholar-orator whose reputation was for a time on a plane with Webster's. Everett's published addresses were best sellers a century ago, and they reached a ninth edition in 1878. His famous oration on The Character of Washington was delivered nearly 150 times, and from its proceeds he donated a large sum to the Mount Vernon Ladies Association, an organization formed about 1856 to preserve Washington's estate. In all his addresses Everett exhibited the power of his classical learning both in content and in form. He was not profound, but he was never superficial. Indeed, the very weight and variety of his literary and historical illustrations add up to his greatest fault. But the audiences of his day did not object. They admired the man and devotedly gave him their attention.

Emerson complained of Everett: "He is all art, and I find in him, nowadays, maugre all his gifts and great merits, more to blame than to praise. He is not content to be Edward Everett, but would be Daniel Webster. This is his mortal distemper." Everett himself admitted in his later years the need for pruning some of his floweriness, and he added: "This operation might have been carried on still further with advantage; for I feel them [the speeches of his 1849 edition] to be still deficient in that simplicity which is their first merit."

The truth of the self-criticism is confirmed for those who have taken the trouble to read Everett's two-hour-long oration at Gettysburg. But it was far from a failure on the day of delivery. The audience received it with prolonged applause, and it is unfair to Everett's ability to inspire audiences to end a criticism of him by contrast with Lincoln. Emerson later and more wisely said of Everett that he "had a great talent for collecting facts, and for bringing those he had to bear with ingenious felicity on the topic of the moment." He was the most erudite speaker of his time, a great disseminator, before thousands of relatively unschooled Americans, of the lofty sentiments for which they hungered.

Preachers in pulpits, professional agitators, women orators, and a host of lesser persons took up the struggle against slavery. Not all of the speaking on these issues was done on the floor of Congress. A mere list of those active would include scores of names. Foremost of the preachers who were also reformers at heart were Theodore Parker, Henry Ward Beecher, and Phillips Brooks. They were all important antislavery figures, and the influence of Beecher and Brooks reached into the Reconstruction Era.

Theodore Parker espoused what came in time to be popular causes, but he helped to make them popular. He opposed the sterile rationalism of established Unitarianism; he fought the social abuses of his day; and in the fifties he spoke daringly, and acted also, against slavery. He attacked unceasingly the dominant powers in Boston: the strong remnant of Federalism, the cotton Whigs, the Democrats who accepted without a qualm the Fugitive Slave Act, the influence of Webster whom he had loved but whom he denounced the Sunday after his death in one of the strangest funeral sermons ever preached.

No living man [he said to his congregation] has done so much to debauch the conscience of the nation, to debauch the press, the pulpit, the forum, and the bar.

. . . He poisoned the moral wells of society with his lower law, and men's consciences died of the murrain of beasts, which came because they drank thereat.

From the time Parker left his church in West Roxbury to shepherd a new congregation of three thousand, in the old Music Hall in Washington Street, he was the keeper of the public conscience of Boston. He said he was the most hated man in the city, and he was often in danger of physical violence; but Emerson was near the truth when he declared him to be one of the four great men of the age.

In his theology Parker was a transcendentalist. His sermon On the Transient and Permanent in Christianity, preached in 1841, occupies a place in the history of transcendentalism comparable to that which William Ellery Channing's Baltimore Sermon of 1819 holds in the history of Unitarianism. Parker's transcendentalism was of a more logical, though much less subtle, kind than Emerson's. For this reason his presentation of the new faith reached listeners whom Emerson could not touch. He announced the "new views" with an unostentatious but careful rhetoric in which simple words and homely allusions were enriched with metaphor. In all his speaking, but in none of his causes more boldly than on the issue of slavery, he was Emerson's "Man Thinking," a great soul strong to live as well as strong to think, but one who never sacrificed "any opinion to the popular judgments and modes of action."

For tenacious persistence in conquering a hostile audience there are few better examples than Henry Ward Beecher's speech defending the North, delivered at Liverpool in 1863. The orator here adapted his arguments to his immediate hearers with amazing skill. He used luminous and convincing illustrations, historical facts and statistics, pleading all the time for fair play and the right to be heard. The speech began amidst catcalls and heckling but ended in a vote of thanks.

Beecher's Memorial Sermon on Abraham Lincoln (1865), his oration on Raising the Flag at Fort Sumter (1865), and his Yale Lectures on Preaching (1872), have survived in interest to this day. Though the gift of argumentative reasoning was not wanting in the man, his real power lay in imaginative appeal. The key to his method is made clear in his own words:

There are in any community probably six to one who will watch for the emotional and impassioned part of the sermon, saying, "That is the preaching I want; I can understand what I feel." They are fed by their hearts. They have as much right to be fed by their hearts as others have to be fed by their reason.

Among the lesser political speakers we should not neglect "Old Bullion," Thomas Hart Benton of Missouri, the defender of the rights of settlers upon the public lands and the advocate of gold and silver in preference to a paper currency; Thomas Corwin, who opposed the war with Mexico in a brilliant prophetic speech; John Quincy Adams, the ex-President, who skillfully kept alive the discussion of slavery and won permission in 1844 for antislavery petitions to be heard in the House of Representatives after a six-year period of tabling; or Stephen A. Douglas, to whom Lincoln lost a senatorship, but who established himself as "an exponent and interpreter of the essence of democracy."

The more significant individual orations dealing with the Civil War include The Crime Against Kansas (1856), by Charles Sumner; The Irrepressible Conflict (1858), by William H. Seward; On Withdrawing from the Union (1861), by Jefferson Davis; and On the Confederate Constitution (1861), by Alexander H. Stephens. Other Southern orators who gained more than sectional attention were Robert Y. Hayne of South Carolina, William L. Yancey, the "orator of secession," and Seargent S. Prentiss, a native of Maine but an adopted son of Mississippi.

Wendell Phillips, perhaps more than any other of the orators before the Civil War, typifies the mighty force of the spoken word. Neither statesman nor preacher, he was essentially a professional agitator. His famous speech on the Murder of Lovejoy (1837) was classed by George William Curtis with Patrick Henry's The Call to Arms and Lincoln's Gettysburg Address as one of the greatest American public utterances. In the fifties Phillips was preeminent among an eloquent company—Douglas and Lincoln, Seward and Sumner, Chase and Choate. His lecture, Toussaint L'Ouverture, spoken more than a thousand times during the war years 1861–1865, fascinated and enthralled even those bitter with race prejudice. Designed to show the potentialities of the colored man, it served to improve understanding of the Negro and to instill a sympathy for him as a freeman.

Nor can the effect of the women agitators during the forties and fifties be underrated. Many of their best speeches have not been preserved, and until recent years their contribution has escaped the historians. But Frances Wright, the Scotchwoman lecturing on free inquiry, Angelina Grimké, the refined South Carolinian speaking out against slavery, and Abby Kelley, the New England schoolteacher turned Abolitionist, were persuasive personalities a century ago. Even more influential in a slightly later period were those earnest and skillful platform speakers, all trained at Oberlin College, Lucy Stone, the advocate of women's rights, Antoinette Brown and Sallie Holley, crusaders in the antislavery cause.

The law, too, contributed distinguished speakers during these years. Rufus Choate was a foremost jury orator; Jeremiah H. Black was a defender of civil rights before the Supreme Court; and William M. Evarts was government counsel in privateering cases and other litigation following the Civil War.

Choate is known also for his Eulogy of Webster at Dartmouth College (1853). The speeches of Black and Evarts are not literary masterpieces, but as speakers both men were effective legal thinkers dealing with complex issues and adapting them by artful use of invention in the best Aristotelian tradition to the audience at hand, whether it was composed of trained jurists or common-sense citizens.

Viewed in the mosaic of history, political and literary, American oratory of the period 1815–1865 deeply influenced our national destiny. We now know that many of the mighty movements that have affected the common man began in obscure places. Likewise many of the speakers in this distinctly oratorical age began as obscure persons. They became known and gained leadership by the greatness and intensity of the issues they discussed and by their mastery of the rhetorical art. But behind those we have briefly considered were thousands, now forgotten, who within their own small spheres commanded respect, created loyalties, and moved men to action.

Oratory was a political instrument. In fact, the national consciousness was created and established, policies for the development of the West were formulated, the rise of the common man was effected, the slave power was consolidated and then broken, all through the democratic processes of public address—ceremonial, controversial, deliberative. As we glance back we realize that the effect of even inspired speaking is often transient. The speech is heard and forgotten. But Americans of the years before the Civil War heard, mulled over, read aloud, and committed to memory their favorite orators. "It was the noble passages from Webster learned in school by Northern boys that prepared them to respond, with arms in their hands, when Lincoln called them to support the National Government and to save the Union."

9

The Radical leaders in the Republican Party were the victors in the Civil War. For twenty years after 1865 the Republicans controlled the life of the nation so absolutely that they had little need of orators to defend their rule. All that was required of a political speaker was ability to wave the Bloody Shirt at the climactic moment. For political rallies and anniversary dinners the speakers most sought after were Civil War generals, whose mere presence was sufficient to revive memories of Gettysburg and Atlanta and bring audiences to their feet singing "Marching Through Georgia." In consequence, the tradition of political oratory declined during these years to its lowest point. James G. Blaine is the only political leader whose ability as a speaker is remembered. A master in debate rather than an orator, his strategy of attack, surprise, and sarcasm often overreached itself.

As the Democrats slowly regained power, new issues, such as populism, free silver, imperialism, and the power of the trusts, replaced the problem of reconstruction, and a new generation of orators came forward to debate them. For thirty-seven years William Jennings Bryan carried the arguments of the Democrats to the American people with his rich and tireless voice. As one historian has noted, probably Samuel Adams alone excelled him in the power of manipulating the masses; and Adams never spoke as Bryan did to audiences of fifteen thousand, making sometimes as many as thirty appearances in one day. Bryan's effectiveness as a speaker came from the biblical simplicity of his language and from his appeal to the emotions of his listeners, who saw in him a great champion of the West and the South against the money power of the East. He said little that was new and he did not deign to argue. He simply assumed the wisdom of the cause he was advocating and used all his oratorical powers to enlist the faith of his hearers.

Matched against Bryan for ten years after 1896 were two Republicans who became the leaders of the Progressive movement, Theodore Roosevelt and Albert J. Beveridge. Both were great "spellbinders," but as they matured in public address they adopted a more blunt and conversational style without losing any of the vigor for which they were noted. The listener's initial astonishment at T. R.'s squeaky voice, which often broke in moments of great excitement, was soon forgotten in admiration of his sharp, driving style and the energy with which he attacked the "interests" and defended his ideal of a militant imperialistic America.

If, with few exceptions, great political orators were lacking between Lincoln and Wilson, there were many able men who spoke eloquently for particular causes, and certain of their speeches created historical moments in the life of the nation. The Atlanta Exposition Speech (1895) of Booker T. Washington won him wide support among whites, North and South, who approved his proposal that the Negro should "put brains and skill into the common occupations of life." This policy, ably set forth in the Atlanta speech, aroused at the same time the opposition of the militant Negroes and defined an issue which still divides the race. The Atlanta editor Henry W. Grady achieved a national reputation with his adroit speech on The New South delivered before the New England Society of New York in December, 1886. There are few occasions in the history of American oratory to match this one when a suspicious audience, made up of men who wielded great financial and political power, was won over completely to the speaker's side. Grady proved not only that the loyalty of the New South to the Union could be trusted but—what may have been more important to J. P. Morgan, Russell Sage, and other capitalists at the table—that its business capacity warranted the investment of Northern capital in the reconstructed South.

During these years Samuel Gompers, organizer of the American Federation of Labor, ruled and advanced the power of the organization in large part by speeches which played upon the discontent and frustration of labor. Revolt within the Federation he controlled by blunt speaking and invective. Workingmen still hear of his momentous speech at the Convention of 1903 when he headed off a strong Socialist offensive organized to seize control of the American Federation of Labor.

Of all the pleaders for special causes in this era, none had so large a popular following as Robert G. Ingersoll—to millions of the pious a notorious infidel, to other millions the preacher of a new gospel which had released them from superstition and bigotry. Ingersoll was an effective trial lawyer, and as a political orator he helped to elect three Republican Presidents; but he will be remembered as the great agnostic, impressing his vast audiences as terribly in earnest, a humane, big-hearted man who sought to rescue the reputation of the Deity from "the aspersions of the pulpit." Redpath, the lecture-manager, declared that he was the "best card" in America, and that his last house in San Francisco had "more money in it than any lecture ever yielded since lecturing began."

Though there were some giants in the years between 1865 and 1912 to carry on the oratorical tradition of Clay, Calhoun, Webster, and Lincoln, admiration for the art of oratory declined year by year. Professors of Rhetoric and Oratory in the colleges were looked upon as little better than teachers of elocution, which, indeed, most of them were. Their once proud profession was despised by their academic colleagues. The college debating societies, which had trained many of the great orators, and in whose activities students had found more intellectual stimulus than in their regular classes, fell to low esteem among extracurricular campus organizations. Yet it was a new national leader, nurtured in this matrix of the American orator who restored confidence in the art. From his boyhood Woodrow Wilson aspired to lead men by his eloquence. His father, who read the orators with him, trained him in precise speaking. At Princeton, Johns Hopkins, and Wesleyan he led in organizing student debating and speaking. As a professor at Princeton he was voted the most popular lecturer, year after year; and he believed that no teacher, no matter how learned, can stimulate young men unless he is an orator. At the time Wilson became President he was already nationally known as a speaker. When the country faced the crisis of war, he was able to lift the nation to the level of his ideals, even as his masters, Burke, Bright, and Gladstone, had done in critical moments of British history. It is a fact to be remembered that if Wilson's eloquence had not so thoroughly convinced his countrymen that they were engaged in a great crusade to make the world safe for democracy, the disillusionment which followed the shattering of his ideal of a world government would not have been so profound and pervasive.

The invention of the radio brought to the orator a great access of power. It also tested his resources severely. Voices effective before ordinary audiences sometimes came over the air ruinously distorted. Gestures and facial expression did not come over at all. Some political speakers, like Governor Alfred Smith, acquired additional force when faced by the microphone. Few who heard him, in the 1928 campaign, attack the Republican misdeeds with his nightly "Let's look at the record" will forget how even his East Side New York accent helped him as a radio orator. The radio also created a new profession for the public speaker, that of news commentator. Each listener had his favorite, but the one most admired was Raymond Swing, who, night after night during the Second World War, brought comfort to millions here and in England. His grave and measured words were adequate to the issues and events which he analyzed for his anxious listeners.

But the master of all the radio orators was President Franklin D. Roosevelt. The radio technicians who set up the equipment for his speeches and fireside chats marveled at his imperturbability under all sorts of difficult conditions of delivery. To the millions who listened to him his humanity came through as well as his power. No nuance of humor or sarcasm or emotion was lost. When speaking from fireside to fireside he seemed to be near by, beside the listener. This sense of his having been, time and again, in one's home accounts in large measure for the personal loss which his fellow Americans felt when he died. It was well known that he had expert assistance in the preparation of his speeches, as do most men in public life; but the tone and the watchwords were always his. Quite as much as Wilson, he contributed memorable phrases to American life. The barbs of irony stayed in the hides of his opponents, as he intended they should, but he could also lift the nation with his eloquence. Most telling of all was the sense he conveyed that he was speaking to and for the whole nation, seeking to unite and fortify its strengths. In this respect he belongs with the orators of the golden age, with Clay and Webster and Lincoln who would recognize their hope for a united America in words which Roosevelt spoke during the presidential campaign of 1940:

We are a nation of many nationalities, many races, many religions—bound together by a single unity, the unity of freedom and equality. Whoever seeks to set one nationality against another, seeks to degrade all nationalities. Whoever seeks to set one race against another seeks to enslave all races. Whoever seeks to set one religion against another seeks to destroy all religion. I am fighting for a free America—for a country in which *all* men and women have equal rights to liberty and justice. I am fighting, as I always have fought, for the rights of the little man as well as the big man—for the weak as well as the strong, for those who are helpless as well as for those who can help themselves.

34. LITERATURE AND CONFLICT

Thus historical writing and oratory rose
to perhaps their greatest literary heights in those troublous mid-century years
when national feeling was both intensified and strained by civil war. But on
literature less immediately connected with domestic issues, the effect was not
so clear-cut. Many writers like Emerson and Hawthorne lost power or died;
others like Lowell and Whittier turned their energies and their arts at least
temporarily to the service of the cause of the day.

When President Lincoln greeted Harriet Beecher Stowe with the words,
"So you're the little woman who made the book that made this great war," he
was speaking as a political realist who had learned by experience to respect
the power of the pen. It was not for him to refer slightingly to "mere literature." Without *Uncle Tom's Cabin,* in the opinion of Sumner, there would
have been no Lincoln in the White House.

But the historian must avoid hyperbole. In spite of the enormous vogue
of Mrs. Stowe's novel, it is doubtful if a book had much power to change
the course of events. More persuasive than her tender pleadings was the harsh
propaganda carried on by Abolitionists for over thirty years. And mightiest
of all was the trend of liberal opinion through the nineteenth century, which
was bound to sweep out of existence even the most beneficent and patriarchal
of feudal survivals. In the last analysis slavery was abolished because men
could no longer endure the thought of it. Shrewd common people were the
first to sense how the tide was running.

2

"A small, shallow, and enthusiastic party preaching the abolition of slavery
upon the principles of extreme democracy"—so John Quincy Adams in 1835
appraised the Abolitionists. He was not one of them. At that date few people
of social standing were numbered in their ranks. The protest against the
wrong of slavery was not initiated by men of wealth, or politicians, or the
clergy, who were the customary molders of opinion. It was begun by humble
men who, though living by the work of their hands, did not let their minds

lie fallow. A journeyman printer and newspaper editor, a shoemaker poet, and a Yankee peddler were promoters or convinced adherents of the first anti-slavery societies. Their names were William Lloyd Garrison, John Greenleaf Whittier, and Bronson Alcott. Intellectual aristocrats came later.

The early Abolitionists were plain people who took their Christian and democratic convictions seriously. They believed in the power of moral suasion, and hoped to sway the policy of the nation by appeals to reason and right principles. The small cost of establishing a four-page weekly newspaper made it easy for them to place their ideas before the public. As early as 1821 an Abolitionist journal, the *Genius of Universal Emancipation,* was started by the Quaker reformer Benjamin Lundy, and thereafter was issued at irregular intervals whenever the peripatetic editor could avail himself of a printing press. Ten years later Garrison, who had been jailed in Baltimore while working as Lundy's partner, founded in Boston the most intransigent of antislavery organs, the *Liberator,* which sounded an uncompromising demand for the immediate freeing of the oppressed. After the formation of the American Anti-Slavery Society in 1833 at least a score of journals of opinion dedicated to the cause of emancipation sprang up throughout the Northern states.

The proslavery element, which insisted on a strict construction of the Constitution where its own interests were concerned, had no scruples about denying to its opponents the constitutional guarantees of free speech and a free press, the right of assembly and the right of petition. Abolitionist agents and speakers were mobbed on numerous occasions, and meetings broken up by violence. But the attempt to muzzle opinion brought important recruits to the antislavery cause. John Quincy Adams waged a bitter struggle in the House of Representatives to prevent the petitions of his constituents from being laid on the table without a hearing. When Elijah P. Lovejoy, the editor of the Abolitionist *Observer* of Alton, Illinois, was killed while defending his printing plant, it became dramatically evident that slavery and the free discussion of slavery could not exist side by side. The indignation meeting in Boston inspired by Lovejoy's death brought out the most effective of antislavery orators in the person of Wendell Phillips. Prominent clergymen, scholars, men of letters, lawyers, and statesmen were gradually drawn into the movement.

Only when such recruits as Theodore Parker and William Ellery Channing, Edmund Quincy, Lowell, Emerson, Longfellow, and Charles Sumner were secured from the educated classes did the Abolitionist propaganda overflow to any considerable extent into literature. Even then its staple remained direct and practical, taking the form of manifestoes, resolutions, petitions to legislative bodies, newspaper paragraphs, circular letters, tracts, lectures,

speeches, sermons, and political songs. Its tone may be represented by some
lines written by Garrison to be sung to the tune of "Auld Lang Syne":

> I am an Abolitionist!
>   The tyrant's hate and dread—
> The friend of all who are oppressed—
>   A price is on my head!
> My country is the wide, wide world—
>   My countrymen mankind:
> Down to the dust be Slavery hurled:
>   All servile chains unbind!

The first men and women of letters who became interested in the cause of the
slave were at once deflected from their literary careers. The hope of reforming
the world, leading to emotional identification with the downtrodden, proved
to be then what Robert Frost has since called it, "poetry's great anti-lure."

Mrs. Lydia Maria Child may be cited as a typical example of what was
happening to many minor writers. Born in 1802 into a family of Boston intellectuals, a sister of the transcendental Convers Francis, this lady when hardly
out of her teens was producing successful historical fiction by the simple device
of confronting herself with a quire of blank paper. She also made a promising
start with a magazine for children. But marriage to the Reverend David Lee
Child, a serious thinker, turned her mind to social problems. In 1833 she shattered convention by issuing a forthright *Appeal in Favor of That Class of
Americans Called Africans,* in which emotional fervor and common sense,
sound economics and fanciful anthropology, were equally harnessed to the
cause of emancipation. Thereafter Mrs. Child was marked as a dangerous
woman. As Thomas Wentworth Higginson recalled, "She seemed to be
always talking radicalism in a greenhouse." Though she was fertile in devis-
ing all sorts of antislavery propaganda, she lent herself freely to other causes,
such as the movement to abolish capital punishment, in her popular *Letters
from New York* (1843, 1845). Only toward the close of her career did she succeed in fusing philanthropy and literature in the belated Abolition novel
entitled *A Romance of the Republic,* which did not get into print until 1867.

But poets and novelists were, on the whole, slow to turn their attention to
slavery. In the North it was long considered bad form, and also unprofitable,
to expose the skeleton in Freedom's closet. The Negro might be sketched as
a comic figure, as by Fenimore Cooper in *The Spy,* or a certain romantic
pathos might be extracted from the picture of the untamed savage doomed to
a bondage which he is too noble to endure, as in Bryant's early poem, "The
African Chief." But even stanch opponents of the extension of slavery like
Bryant kept their controversial sentiments out of their poetry. Edmund

Quincy, an editor of the *Liberator,* though he composed a small group of polished tales dealing with servile insurrections and the devotion of slaves to their masters, yet preferred to amuse his fancy with the elegances of bygone days in his chief novel *Wensley,* which preserves as if under glass a picture of colonial society.

Soon after 1840 several prominent New England poets followed Whittier's lead in the production of antislavery poems. Longfellow on a stormy return voyage from Europe conjured up seven of the eight lyrics contained in his tiny paper-covered pamphlet, *Poems on Slavery* (1842). Eight years later his fears for the safety of the Union inspired his much quoted apostrophe, "Thou, too, sail on, O Ship of State." His relation to the abolition movement was never more than that of a sympathetic bystander. Emerson likewise remained somewhat apart, saving his strength for the freeing of souls from a more universal bondage than that suffered by the Negro.

Lowell, though serious workers for the cause considered his tone regrettably playful, took a more than passing interest in the subject of slavery. Over fifty editorials from his pen appeared in Abolition journals at the time when the annexation of Texas was being debated, and in the first series of *The Biglow Papers,* begun in the Boston *Courier,* June 17, 1846, he voiced with homely effectiveness the protest of New England idealists against a war in the interest of the slaveholder. The resolute expression of Lowell's democratic and pacifistic principles in the mouth of the rustic Hosea Biglow was partly obscured by the swathings of prose commentary written in the character of Parson Wilbur. But enough wit penetrated the prolixity to make the satire count. Nothing that Lowell wrote with more serious intent on questions of the day, and nothing in the revived *Biglow Papers* which dealt with the Civil War, equaled the first impromptu outbursts of his indignation.

Hosea Biglows in the flesh were not wanting. In vigorous protest against the government's official policy of appeasing the South by permitting the expansion of slavery into the lands newly wrested from Mexico, Bronson Alcott declined to pay his taxes and was briefly lodged in Concord jail. A little later Henry Thoreau followed his example. The latter's "Civil Disobedience," written as a result of this experience and delivered as a lecture in 1847, has become the classic defense of the individual's integrity against the moral degradation of the state. The hard intellectual intransigence of Thoreau in this essay and in his "Plea for Captain John Brown" is in sharp contrast to the sentimental humanitarianism of much Abolitionist literature.

Until after the spectacular success of *Uncle Tom's Cabin,* antislavery novels hardly existed. The only one of possibly half a dozen examples that calls for mention is *The Slave: or Memoirs of Archy Moore* (1836) by the Federalist historian Richard Hildreth, which recounts representative vicissitudes in the life of a light mulatto, at once son and slave of an aristocratic Virginia colonel. All the stock cruelties are visited on Archy, and in particular the sexual abuses incident to slavery are handled with considerable freedom. But the first-person narrator of the story is all too clearly a New England intellectual.

A flood of fiction attacking or defending slavery was released by Mrs. Stowe. Most of the Abolition novels made the mistake of selecting an exceptional situation, as of a white child kidnaped into slavery, or of presenting an impossibly idealized hero or heroine. The "anti-Tom" novels, which originated less often in the South than in Philadelphia, were hardly more impressive. The blandest of the many counterblasts was Mrs. Mary H. Eastman's *Aunt Phillis's Cabin* (1852), a book rightly described as insipid.

In the South slavery remained a debatable issue until about 1830 at the latest. Opinion then crystallized, and the allegiance of the region to its "peculiar institution" remained unshaken. The social philosophy of the plantation owners, first formulated by such men as Thomas R. Dew and William Harper, was given persuasive political application by John C. Calhoun and glorified with golden oratory by William L. Yancey. By 1854 George Fitzhugh, the author of *Sociology for the South,* could confidently predict, "Slavery will everywhere be abolished or everywhere be reinstated"—and the first of these alternatives was evidently unthinkable. Firmly assured that their social system would be envied and imitated the world over, Southern leaders paid no heed to protests in the name of the poorer farmers and landless whites such as Hinton R. Helper's *The Impending Crisis of the South* (1857). The wide circulation given this work by Northern reformers only added to the fury directed against the Abolitionists.

But it is important to note that the antislavery crusade was almost as much resented in the North as in the South. Many Northern leaders were perfectly content with the compromise embodied in the Constitution. Slavery was not more ardently defended by the Charleston intellectuals Hugh Swinton Legaré and William Gilmore Simms than it was by Washington Irving's friend, James K. Paulding of New York. Even in Boston the circle of George Ticknor viewed with extreme disfavor the promoters of social agitation on this subject. Francis Parkman could write in 1850:

For my part, I would see every slave knocked on the head before I would see the Union go to pieces, and would include in the sacrifice as many abolitionists as could be conveniently brought together.

This latter sentiment was cordially endorsed by William J. Grayson of South Carolina in his sizzling verse-satire *The Hireling and the Slave* (1854) and by John Beauchamp Jones, a Southern journalist, in *Wild Southern Scenes*

(1859), a fantastic picture of an imagined civil war fought over the issue of slavery. Even after the outbreak of hostilities a Boston antiquary and temperance reformer, Lucius M. Sargent, a "late George Apley" of his day, could write in *The Ballad of the Abolition Blunder-buss* (1861) a scathing Hudibrastic satire in the best doughface tradition. It was not the comfortable classes, North or South, who took pity on the slave.

3

"An afflatus of war was breathed upon us," wrote the young Confederate private Sidney Lanier in *Tiger-Lilies* (1867), a first novel largely composed while the writer was in camp:

> To obscurity it held out eminence; to poverty, wealth; to greed, a gorged maw; to speculation, legalized gambling; to patriotism, a country; to statesmanship, a government; to virtue, purity; and to love, what all love most desires—a field wherein to assert itself by action.

In the North, Robert Gould Shaw's sister, at seventeen, felt the same ebullience, even after the Union forces had recoiled from Bull Run:

> These are extraordinary times and splendid to live in. . . . This war will purify the country of some of its extravagance and selfishness, even if we are stopped midway. . . . We, as a Nation, are learning splendid lessons of heroism and fortitude through it that nothing else could teach.

At the outbreak of hostilities the emotional pressure on both sides demanded instant outlets. Pure chance rather than intrinsic merit settled upon the music-hall song of "Dixie" and the camp-meeting chorus of "John Brown's Body" as the vehicles of opposing sentiment. Hardly less fortuitous was the later choice of Julia Ward Howe's "Battle-Hymn of the Republic" and James Ryder Randall's "Maryland, My Maryland" as the supreme expressions of the North's crusading zeal and the South's defiance. Each of these poems was destined to become the one piece by its author that posterity has cared to recall. Entirely forgotten are such fervently patriotic songs as William Ross Wallace's "The Sword of Bunker Hill" and "Keep Step with the Music of the Union," which as marching songs attained a wide popularity in 1861. These and many other ephemeral outpourings hurling heated epithets filled the pages of the early anthologies of war poems, Union and Confederate alike. Not until the publication of Francis F. Browne's *Bugle-Echoes* (1882), the prototype of later collections of Civil War poetry, were the memorable occasional poems of the war separated from the chaff and arranged in relation to the episodes that inspired them.

The established poets of the North responded variously to the emotional impact of the war. Bryant was startled out of his calm to write two stirring lyrics in "Not Yet" and "Our Country's Call." Thereafter he contented himself with a single poem on "The Death of Slavery." Emerson likewise celebrated the emancipation of the slaves in his "Boston Hymn." Longfellow's single utterance, on the loss of the sloop-of-war *Cumberland,* ranks with the finest of patriotic elegies. Holmes, who had previously written little on public questions, scattered his fire, and neither his marching songs for Armageddon nor his furious invectives against traitors and stay-at-home rangers attained distinction. Lowell, besides his rather labored revival of *The Biglow Papers,* expressed the dark forebodings of the early war days in "The Washers of the Shroud."

On the Confederate side the coming of war and the invasion of the Southern states by Federal troops had a profound effect on Henry Timrod, the leading poet among the younger writers of Charleston. At its best his early verse was scholarly and overdelicate, at its worst derivative and formal. But the war made him the spokesman of a nation struggling to be born. Though he opposed secession, Timrod was fervidly loyal to South Carolina. His "A Cry to Arms" paralleled Bryant's "Our Country's Call" as a tocsin of patriotic feeling. His "Ode" sung at Magnolia Cemetery holds the same relation to the Confederate dead as Lowell's "Commemoration Ode" to the fallen soldiers of the North. The contrast between its twenty chiseled lines and the orotund amplitude of Lowell is impressive.

> In seeds of laurel in the earth
> The blossom of your fame is blown,
> And somewhere, waiting for its birth,
> The shaft is in the stone!

Fewer than a dozen poems contain Timrod's poetic response to the war, but they remain a monument to the Southern ideal of classic grace united with deep emotional fervor.

Paul Hamilton Hayne of Charleston, whose memory is kept fragrant by his chivalrous devotion to his section, was a poet of lesser stature and was seldom at his best when writing of the war. Though he duly celebrated the sacrificial zeal of the Southern arms, his gentle nature inclined him to pursue a beauty detached from the hard realities which he uncomplainingly endured. After the war he was able to prepare the way for the reconciliation of the North and the South through his cordial relations with Whittier, Taylor, and other literary men. More notable than any collection of his own verse was his edition of the poems of Timrod.

As the war dragged to its close the sufferings of Southern womanhood were epitomized in *Beechenbrook* (1865), a popular narrative poem richly freighted with sentiment by Margaret Junkin Preston, the Pennsylvania-born sister-in-law of "Stonewall" Jackson. A proud allegiance to the lost cause throbbed in "The Conquered Banner" by Father Abram Joseph Ryan and "The Land Where We Were Dreaming" by Daniel Bedinger Lucas, to mention only two of the many dirges for the Confederacy. Long before the end the soldier songs lost all traces of vivacity. The plaintive melody of "Tenting on the Old Camp Ground" expressed the most pervasive emotion of both camps, weariness of the protracted struggle and an overmastering desire to go home.

The factual record of the Civil War in diaries and narratives of personal experience was extremely voluminous, but seldom reached a literary level or even the level of expert reporting to which the two world wars of the twentieth century have accustomed us. The Confederacy produced a minor Pepys in John Beauchamp Jones, who deliberately prepared for posterity the account of life in Richmond, published as *A Rebel War Clerk's Diary* (1866). Gamaliel Bradford has not unaptly likened the commonplace and average temper of the war clerk's mind to the conventional choral figure of Greek tragedy. Money troubles and an increasing dissatisfaction with political leaders form the burden of his testy plaint: "Never before did such little men rule such a great people."

Theodore Winthrop, the writer of several novels, should have pictured the war from the Union ranks, but his brilliant sketches were soon terminated by his untimely death in battle. Walt Whitman's graphic but inconsecutive impressions convey the feeling of war-torn Washington. Perhaps the palm for literary reporting should go to Thomas Wentworth Higginson for his *Army Life in a Black Regiment* (1870), though almost as readable is the realistic *Camps and Prisons* (1865) by Augustine J. H. Duganne, a writing colonel who elsewhere undertook to memorialize each important clash of the armed forces in indifferent rime. Henry Howard Brownell gained eminence as a "Battle-Laureate" for his accounts of the naval actions at New Orleans and at Mobile Bay written under the immediate impulse of the occasion in facile but stirring verse. Of some thirty poems dealing with the war his best are "Bury Them," a tribute to Robert Gould Shaw, and "Abraham Lincoln," which pictures the long file of the nation's dead passing in review before the martyred President while the review of the Grand Army sweeps through the capital. Brownell owes his place in American literature entirely to his poems inspired by the struggle.

Previous to the war the prevailing tone of polite fiction had been tearful and sentimental, while a vigorous school of backwoods humorists created realistic sketches of illiterate rascals of the Simon Suggs and Sut Lovingood type. The humorists of the war years, however, specialized less in character than in opinion. Like Lowell in *The Biglow Papers* they wrote what were in effect editorials from behind the mask of a comic personality. David Ross Locke ("Petroleum V. Nasby"), Robert H. Newell ("Orpheus C. Kerr"), and Charles G. Halpine ("Miles O'Reilly") for the North, and on the other side Charles H. Smith ("Bill Arp") did much by their witty comment on current happenings to sustain the morale of men whose nerves were worn ragged by the stresses of the hour.

Meanwhile fiction discarded the trappings of sentiment and tended to become more realistic. Though the war novels of John Esten Cooke were still of the romantic cloak-and-sword type, he made an effort to introduce actual characters and incidents and to report verbatim the words spoken by Jackson, Jeb Stuart, Ashby, and other Southern immortals. Still more authentic was the picture of the sufferings of Union sympathizers under the Confederate regime as presented by William Mumford Baker, the manuscript of whose *Inside: A Chronicle of Secession* (1866) had several times to be buried to keep it from falling into the wrong hands. A much more powerful treatment of the Southern Unionist was written by the Alabama politician Jeremiah Clemens in *Tobias Wilson* (1865), a novel which deserves to be rescued from the oblivion that has befallen it.

But the best of the Civil War novels and one of the most notable achievements in American fiction is John William De Forest's *Miss Ravenel's Conversion from Secession to Loyalty* (1867), a book that for lifelike portrayal of scenes of action, firm grasp of character values, and penetrating interpretation of the issues of the time can hardly be too highly praised. Considering the fact that the novelist was a Union officer, he maintained a remarkable objectivity in his picture of high purposes mingled with inefficiency and corruption at the North and of chivalry badly flawed by moral laxity at the South. De Forest was a pioneer realist too honest for his own good in an age that expected conventional falsifications in works of imagination. In particular his habit of treating his women characters as responsible human beings who must make their own decisions and abide by the consequences was not popular. In *Kate Beaumont* (1872) and *The Bloody Chasm* (1881) he again drew unsparing pictures of Southern scenes and characters, while in *Honest John Vane* (1875) and *Playing the Mischief* (1875) he exposed the vicious deterioration of political life in Washington.

Reflective interpretation of the meaning of the war was carried to an ultimate contemporary extent in Walt Whitman's *Drum-Taps* (1865) and Herman Melville's *Battle Pieces* (1866). The brief prose supplement appended to the last-named has been likened to Lincoln's "Second Inaugural" because of its noble perception that "the glory of the war falls short of its pathos—a pathos which now at last ought to disarm all animosity." Melville states that his poems "originated in an impulse imparted by the fall of Richmond," and that they record the variable moods induced by memories of the conflict much as a harp placed in a window might respond to wayward airs. But beneath the temporary heightening of emotion and the sense of dedication to a great cause which *Battle Pieces* shares with much other war poetry there may be detected an undernote of apprehension, even in the moment of victory. Musing on his country's ills, "On the world's fairest hope linked with man's foulest crime," Melville cannot convince himself that a spiritual regeneration will necessarily follow the resort to the sword. It may be that the war will bring only a release of "power unanointed," a triumph of sheer Mammonism before which "the Founders' dream shall flee" and "the Dark Ages of Democracy" be ushered in. Oppressed by thoughts like these, Melville like another Prospero cannot still his beating mind.

No such prescient fears afflicted Whitman. Though he knew more immediately than many of his contemporaries the terrible cost of the war in human suffering, he was possessed by visions of apocalyptic grandeur, seeing

How DEMOCRACY with desperate vengeful port strides on, shown through the
    dark by those flashes of lightning!

"I have lived to behold man burst forth, and warlike America rise," he jubilates. "Never was average man, his soul, more energetic, more like a God." For America, the mistress, he was ready to chant a greater supremacy, confident that "affection shall solve the problems of Freedom yet." Even while exulting in these affirmations of upsurging power, Whitman could still pause to caress the grief of stricken families in "Come up from the fields, father," and to write for the dead Lincoln the tenderest tribute that any statesman has ever inspired.

Melville's brooding concern and Whitman's passionate love of country were fused, though somewhat diluted, in the exalted sentiment of Lowell's "Commemoration Ode," admittedly the finest example of official poetry in the literature of the United States and the inevitable epilogue for a discussion of the writing inspired by the great conflict:

O Beautiful! my Country! ours once more!
            .   .   .   .
        What were our lives without thee?
        What all our lives to save thee?
        We reck not what we gave thee;
        We will not dare to doubt thee,
        But ask whatever else, and we will dare!

4

After Appomattox the development of realistic fiction was carried on chiefly by writers associated with the North and West, like William Dean Howells, and by the few Southerners who along with George W. Cable found a congenial refuge in the North. The prevailing mood of Southern fiction for a full generation was nostalgic and sentimental, a turning back to what had been. The vogue of local color and dialect stories only slightly modified, as in Joel Chandler Harris' Uncle Remus tales, the fond recollections of ante-bellum days on the old plantation.

Fiction dealing with the problems of Reconstruction was written chiefly by De Forest and by Albion W. Tourgée, both Northerners with first-hand experience of life in the South. Women realists such as Rose Terry Cooke and Rebecca Harding Davis also drew upon the war and its aftermath for subjects. The latter, though straining too hard to impress her message, barely missed creating a great novel in *Waiting for the Verdict* (1868), which pictures the helpless predicament of the Negro when the North, after emancipating the slaves, turned its back on the social problem it had brought into being. A bitter arraignment of the collapse of Southern integrity under the shock of defeat and poverty was composed by John S. Wise, the son of a former governor of Virginia, in *The Lion's Skin,* but this book was not published until 1905.

The most persistent efforts to embody in fictional form a review of the breakdown of the slaveholders' empire and the chaos that followed were made by Tourgée, a Union officer born in Ohio who returned to the South after the war. As a political judge in North Carolina he soon earned the hostility of his fellow citizens, a sentiment which he cordially reciprocated. His novels, consequently, are colored by violent partisanship, especially in their opposition to Ku Klux activities in the reconstructed states. At no time did Tourgée reveal any comprehension of the complex psychological strains that Southerners were forced to undergo.

In the order of the events they dramatize, Tourgée's polemical novels begin with *Hot Ploughshares* (1883), which deals largely with the efforts of a conscientious slave owner to emancipate his Negroes in defiance of sectional prejudice. *Figs and Thistles* (1879), a fictional treatment of the career of James A. Garfield, is set in Ohio during and after the war and pictures the relations of a rising politician to the manipulators of finance and industry who are his backers. *'Toinette* (1874), rechristened *A Royal Gentleman* (1881), is a sentimental exploitation of the dilemma of a nearly white Negro woman who cannot marry her lover, a patrician Southron, because of his ingrained horror at any pretense of equality between the races. *A Fool's Errand* (1879) and

Bricks Without Straw (1880) analyze the political and social problems of Reconstruction, particularly the plight of the Negro who has been left without adequate provision for his free development. The novelette *John Eax* (1882) develops a story of Southern family pride in conflict with the hero's vigorous individualism. Tourgée's plots have elements of the sensational, and his books are overweighted with didactic passages, but the backgrounds are drawn with an instinctive faithfulness to actuality that gives these novels some importance as social documents.

Tourgée was by no means unique in desiring to impress a partial interpretation on the events of history. Ex-Confederates felt an even stronger compulsion to make palatable by dialectic the bitter blow to its pride that the South had experienced. The long process of glorifying the lost cause and explaining away its defeat, a process which still continues, was begun by the brilliant Alexander H. Stephens, the former Vice President of the Confederacy, in his *Constitutional View of the Late War Between the States* (1868–1870).

The Southern man of letters who most gallantly faced the facts of Reconstruction and tried to find a remedy for the economic ruin of the South was Sidney Lanier. This young poet, who had proclaimed himself "a full-blooded secessionist" at the beginning of hostilities, recorded in half a dozen poems written in 1867–1868 his agonized awareness of the complete prostration of his section: "We lie in chains, too weak to be afraid." In urging a greater diversification of crops in "Corn" and other poems Lanier may seem to have adopted a grotesque expedient; but when men harnessed themselves to the plow for want of draft animals it was not altogether inappropriate that the muse should be similarly employed.

What has often been called an American renaissance took place at the time when the Abolition movement was gathering strength; but it is doubtful if the increased tensions due to public agitation had any demonstrable effect on the concurrent production of literature. In general, national convulsions are not favorable to the arts. The strong emotions they arouse are exhausting rather than stimulating. So much fuel is used up for heat that little remains for light. The antislavery crusade may be held directly responsible for *Uncle Tom's Cabin,* which in its stage version has become a part of America's folklore. Out of the Civil War came some stirring lyrics, two or three fine volumes of poetry, and one first-rate piece of fiction. When one considers the sacrifice of blood and treasure, the surges of passion, the heroism, and the broken lives, the disproportion between the great conflict and its immediate results in literature seems to indicate that the war tended to stifle the creative expression, at least of relatively minor writers.

How participation in controversy may channel a vigorous writer's energy in a single direction, and so limit the full rounding of his nature, may be shown by an examination of the careers of Whittier and Mrs. Stowe. The Civil War and the agitation that preceded it have often been pictured as a conflict between Union and Secession, between North and South, between slave and free. The literature of the struggle, however, reveals most emphatically an ideological difference between plain and privileged people. The Abolitionists in all sections of the country were revolting against aristocratic and conservative leadership. It was not inappropriate that the movement should find its major literary spokesmen in a homespun poet and a daughter of Puritan levelers, both of them gifted with uncommon powers of expression.

5

In the course of his eighty-five years John Greenleaf Whittier, though deprived of most advantages that foster a writer's labors, managed to produce well over forty books of prose and verse, in addition to a large quantity of journalistic writing which remains uncollected. He came of New England farmer stock, was largely self-educated, and after his early thirties could seldom count on two successive weeks of good health. Yet within a long lifetime he ran through several literary careers, turned out an amount of work that would have done credit to a robust man, and maintained a level of good craftsmanship that commanded the respect of his peers.

Between 1826 and 1832 Whittier was primarily an editor of country newspapers and a writer of newspaper verse. Except for three early books, which he would have gladly disowned in later years, little of the product of this period has been preserved. From 1833 to 1860 he was engaged in the antislavery campaign as an active agent, an editor of reform journals, and a writer of polemics in prose and verse. His antislavery poems and his political prose constitute an important section of his collected works. Finally from about 1850 until his death in 1892 Whittier's chief interest was again centered in poetry. During this period he wrote the majority of the pieces for which he is best known.

Whittier's prose is subsidiary to his verse. His Abolitionist pamphlet *Justice and Expediency* (1833) is of biographical importance as announcing his decision to throw in his lot with the unpopular friends of the slave, but it does not stand out above the level of antislavery tracts as his polemical poems rise superior to most productions of the sort. *Margaret Smith's Journal* (1849) is a charming sketch of life in colonial New England as seen through the eyes of a descendant of Quakers. The remaining biographical, historical, and miscellaneous papers included in his works are of slight importance. His letters, which remain largely in manuscript, show that he possessed a gift of personal humor which rarely appeared in his public writing. But as an American poet Whittier is remembered for three kinds of poetry: his antislavery poems, his New England ballads and idyls, and his personal and religious lyrics.

The most vigorous and formative years of Whittier's life were so bound up with his activities as an antislavery agitator that the poet himself was inclined to rate his part in the great humanitarian crusade as his chief claim to distinction. He was prouder to have signed the Declaration of Sentiments adopted at the first convention of the American Anti-Slavery Society than to see his name on the title page of any book. In the modest "Proem," written in 1847 for a forthcoming collection of his poems and retained in all subsequent editions, he denied that his verse possessed any "rounded art" or "seer-like power," but emphasized his unqualified devotion to freedom and human brotherhood. "I am a *man*," he wrote to his first biographer in 1883, "and not a mere verse-maker."

But one may protest too much. Poets are not normally reluctant to accept whatever share of glory may fall to their lot. Whittier's repeated disclaimers of "a selfish pursuit of literary reputation" rouse the suspicion that he was constrained to seek compensation in the cause of Abolition for some secret disappointment.

It is remarkable that about one-third of Whittier's total poetic output, measured in terms of number of poems, was written before he was twenty-five and was published in newspapers. Some of these pieces were jocular or trivial, but most of them were serious exercises in exalted rhetoric, the work of a young man who considered literature as a realm of ideal values apart from and superior to the commonplace of daily existence. At this time Whittier was apparently dreaming that in some vague way he might attain through poetry the kind of sudden fame that had come to Burns and Byron. But verses in the poet's corner brought him neither renown nor a livelihood. There was clearly no future for him as a man of letters. Under the sting of this disappointment he renounced literature, writing with just a shade of bravado to his friend Jonathan Law: "I have knocked my Pegasus on the head, as a tanner does his bark-mill donkey, when he is past service, and the crows—alias, critics—may have the picking of his bones."

But if poetry was closed to Whittier there remained the vocation of newspaper editing, for which he had shown a considerable aptitude. He entered journalism as an awkward and ill educated youth from the country, but he had tact and modesty and the ability to learn quickly by experience. He proved to be a vigorous and able editor, and no doubt would have remained an editor had his health permitted. He was also a natural politician whose astuteness made him a useful though prickly ally of Caleb Cushing, the Whig, and Robert Rantoul, the Democrat, and later a discerning friend of Charles

Sumner. As an ardent supporter of Henry Clay and the American System he had learned how to gauge public feeling and how to make effective use of key phrases and striking incidents to enlist the popular imagination. This ability acquired in the tough school of Essex County politics Whittier brought to his work as a writer of rhymed propaganda for the Abolition cause.

His antislavery poems are not literary in the bookish sense, though they contain biblical echoes. They are packed full of explosive slogans: "Our fellow-countrymen in chains!" "No fetters in the Bay State!" The several poems are skillfully adapted to a variety of readers. "The Yankee Girl," for example, is purely the equivalent of a campaign poster, using the gaudiest colors and appealing to vulgar sentiment. On a higher level "Clerical Oppressors," written to castigate the clergy of Charleston, and "The Pastoral Letter," reproaching the Congregational ministers of Massachusetts for failing to bear witness to the evils of slavery, sound a note of Hebraic indignation. "A Sabbath Scene" makes a vigorously effective contrast between the Christian doctrine of brotherhood and the hunting down of fugitive slaves. The seizure of an alleged runaway in Boston was the occasion for an outburst of genuine local pride in the powerful "Massachusetts to Virginia." And when Webster betrayed the hopes of Northern idealists in his notorious "compromise" speech, Whittier's withering scorn in the incisive lines of "Ichabod" brought invective to the level of high art. Few of the antislavery poems are more than earnest propaganda, but in writing them Whittier learned to crystallize his meaning in clear and sharp-edged phrases. As an Abolitionist agitator he attained a power of expression that he could never have reached as an imitator of Mrs. Hemans and Mrs. Sigourney.

But his advance in power was not achieved without cost to his development in other directions. Thirty years of intense absorption in humanitarian reform left their mark on Whittier. He had little time for general reflection and his principles, once adopted, remained fixed. Beneath his temperamental tolerance and sympathy one can sense a trace of the stiffness that showed itself most baldly when he decided not to marry a Quaker woman whom he had been fond of for many years because of divergences in their religious views. His *Songs of Labor* are innocent of any such comprehension of the problems of the American workman as Orestes A. Brownson, for example, possessed. He had no such suspicion of material progress and invention as Thoreau. To the end he apparently remained unaware that the Industrial Revolution created situations which could not be solved in terms of a simple personal morality. It was in part an evidence of limitation that Whittier turned to the New England past and to religion as the favorite subjects of his late maturity.

More than most poets Whittier was identified with the region that produced him. When he was born in 1807, the second child and eldest son of a farmer in the township of Haverhill, Massachusetts, he had behind him four generations of Whittiers who had occupied the same spot. The family home-stead, later pictured in *Snow-Bound,* had been built in 1688 by the Thomas Whittier who, some fifty years earlier, had left his native Wiltshire and had prospered and begotten ten children in the new land. The house had been passed down, in defiance of primogeniture, from youngest son to youngest son until it came to John Whittier, the poet's father, who worked the farm jointly with a bachelor brother. In his boyhood Greenleaf heard, from the elders of the household and from rare visitors, tales of adventure and hardship, of witchcraft and persecution, that made up the lore of the countryside. There was no trace of either clerical or mercantile leanings among Whittier's fore-bears. They were plain Yankee farmers rooted in the soil of Essex County.

In only one respect was the family not typical of New England yeomanry. For three generations the Whittiers had professed a sturdy adherence to Quaker principles. The fact that they belonged to a minor and once persecuted sect encouraged a certain critical detachment in the poet when he contem-plated the New England past, and at the same time it encouraged a habit of "inwardness" which deepened his inherent tendency to mysticism.

Both incidents in Quaker history and traditions of colonial days in general furnished Whittier with material for local ballads and narrative poems. He did not attempt, as Hawthorne did, to inject symbolic meanings into historic episodes, but contented himself with reviving the atmosphere of a bygone time and portraying scenes and characters as vividly as possible. He seldom made alterations in the stories as he found them. His revisions were generally amplifications. He was no antiquarian and seldom took pains to verify his information. Consequently a highly successful piece of poetic craftsmanship like "Skipper Ireson's Ride" wrings from the professional historian the acid comment: "In 1808 occurred the regrettable incident of Skipper Benjamin (not Floyd) Ireson, for his crew's cowardice and lying (not for his hard heart), tarred and feathered and carried in a dory (not cart) by the fishermen (not the women) of Marblehead." But Whittier chose to tell the tale as he heard it from the lips of a schoolmate from Marblehead, partly because in its oral form it was already on the way to acquiring the quality of folklore.

Along with his historical and legendary narratives Whittier produced a number of country idyls, of which "The Barefoot Boy," "Maud Muller," and "Telling the Bees" are familiar examples. As early as 1847, in reviewing the poems of his Abolitionist friend William Henry Burleigh, he had deplored the lack of "Yankee pastorals" and had called attention to "the poetry of human life and simple nature, of the hearth and the farm field" as a type of writing that might well be attempted, not by the "amateur ruralist," but by one who was himself part and parcel of the country life of New England. He thus became a pioneer in exploring the ground which in our own time has been more expertly cultivated by Robert Frost.

He also celebrated in verse the sea beaches at the mouth of the Merrimack, the landscape of ridges and pleasant valleys around Haverhill, and the loftier mountains of the interior. But he was not well equipped to be a nature poet. Too color-blind to distinguish red from green, he was not by temperament a man who lived a full life of the senses; nor did he possess the Wordsworthian faculty of finding thoughts too deep for tears in a wayside flower. His impulse was to value external nature purely in terms of its human associations; as in "Monadnock from Wachuset,"

> We felt that man was more than his abode,—
> The inward life than Nature's raiment more.

Only rarely, as in the later poem "Sunset on the Bearcamp," did he even approximate a feeling of identity between the light of setting suns and the mind of man.

His interest in public affairs made it inevitable that he should comment in verse on various aspects of the Civil War. At its outbreak he regarded the resort to arms as a spiritual disaster. "The sad war drags along," he wrote in a letter of November, 1861. "I long to see some compensation for its horrors, in the deliverance of the Slaves. Without this, it is the wickedest war of the nineteenth century." Yet he was patriotically stirred by the legendary heroism of Barbara Frietchie, which he recounted in a highly successful ballad. The most heartfelt of his war poems, however, was the fervent "Laus Deo," which sang itself as he heard the bells ringing to celebrate the passage of the constitutional amendment abolishing slavery. His long campaign was finished, though not by the means he would have chosen.

The death in 1864 of his sister and companion Elizabeth, who in some measure shared his poetic gift, left Whittier solitary and by the same token turned his thoughts back to the close-knit family life of his boyhood. Out of his loyalty, not alone to vanished faces, but to the fulfillment of personal relationships which his boyhood home symbolized, he wrote *Snow-Bound* (1866), the finest of his Yankee idyls, a faultless integration of precisely remembered detail and tender devotion. In a general way this poem is the New England analogue of Burns' *The Cotter's Saturday Night*, with which it compares favorably both for its wealth of homely description and for its genuineness of sentiment. But against the background of a nation fast adapting itself to urban ways the poem appears something more than a cold pastoral. It is a quiet tribute to a form of civilized living that was passing. Here embodied in glowing terms was the Jeffersonian dream of the virtuous small landholder and his household, beholden to no one and winning an honest, laborious livelihood from the soil. Long before the Presidency of Grant this ideal pattern of a good life that might have been realized on an unpre-empted continent had been shattered; but it still continued to haunt the minds of country-born dwellers in the expanding cities whose simple upbringing had not prepared them for the complex problems of an industrial era. In Whittier's idyllic picture of an existence totally untroubled by the fevers of getting and spending, many Americans recognized with wistful regret an Eden from which they were forever debarred.

Significant also of a quality of mind that was rapidly becoming old-fash-ioned was the naïve directness of Whittier's poetic technique. With no obeisance to the method of suggestiveness illustrated by Whitman in "Out of the Cradle Endlessly Rocking," where a reminiscence of childhood is analyzed into its component sensuous images and then freely recomposed into a globed and harmonious work of art, Whittier developed Snow-Bound by a linear or melodic progression of one image after another. Very little is conveyed by hints or implications, but each mood and moment is defined with stark integrity. Behind this way of writing may be felt, not merely personal inno-cence, but a deep-seated racial conviction of the virtue of plain speaking, a conviction that for Whittier was reinforced by his Quaker breeding. As a man of undefeated spirit, he was not concerned to explore the devious hinter-land of consciousness that could only be expressed by innuendo, suggestion, or symbol. What he felt he could say.

Not all of Whittier's poems are limited to a New England setting. He took an interest in the struggle for freedom all over the world, in Italy, in Brazil. He found many subjects for ballads in Scandinavian or Oriental stories drawn from his wide reading. Hardly less intrinsic than Snow-Bound in its simplicity and genuineness is his account in The Pennsylvania Pilgrim (1872) of the pious German community established by Pastorius near William Penn's newly settled Quaker colony, with which it soon merged in religious affiliation. From this group of perfectionists came the first protest against slavery made by any religious body. Whittier himself considered The Pennsylvania Pilgrim "as good as (if not better than) any long poem" he had written, and surely no poem in the language has succeeded better in evoking a sense of the charm and sweetness of social intercourse that becomes possible when for a brief moment men have managed to reconstitute some semblance of a Golden Age.

The virtue of Whittier's poetry at its best lies in its firm texture of sincerity. He wrote about things that he knew intimately. His feelings were based on sentiments tested by the strains of life and driven down until they rested on bedrock conviction. His religious perceptions especially rested on a very real sense of divine immanence.

For these soundings, these often meditated inward truths, Whittier could find compact, simple, moving, and very nearly ultimate phrases. Much as he concerned himself with the outer world of politics and men's daily occupations, his deepest resources were of the spirit; in the poems which he called "subjective and reminiscent" and in his religious lyrics is his most distinguished writing. The autobiographical stanzas from "My Namesake" might be cited as a high point; but more fervent and more touching are the lines from "My Triumph," in which the poet foresees his own fulfillment in the eventual perfection of human society.

> The airs of heaven blow o'er me;
> A glory shines before me
> Of what mankind shall be,—
> Pure, generous, brave, and free.
>
> . . . .
>
> I feel the earth move sunward,
> I join the great march onward,
> And take, by faith, while living,
> My freehold of thanksgiving.

With equal honesty Whittier recorded his occasional religious doubts and his more characteristic seasons of transcendent confidence. His vital experience of God's nearness inspired such devotional lyrics as "The Eternal Goodness," "Trinitas," "Our Master," "Questions of Life," "The Over-Heart," "The Meeting," and "My Psalm," to mention only some of the best loved. Though Whittier was specifically a Quaker and a Christian, his faith was as free as any man's can be from the trammels of formalism. He turned to God with a childlike passion of trustfulness that needed no support or creed. Among the finest hymns of the nineteenth century is that beginning "Dear Lord and Father of mankind," a selection of stanzas from "The Brewing of Soma." Stronger than the local attachments that led Whittier to join with Hawthorne and Longfellow in awakening a romantic interest in the New England past, and deeper than his humanitarian dedication to the relief of the oppressed among men, was his sense of "the silence of eternity interpreted by love" and the beauty of God's peace.

6

Unlike the homespun Whittier, Harriet Beecher Stowe was a product of the intellectual aristocracy of New England. Her father, the Reverend Lyman Beecher, a militant evangelist in the pulpit and a diligent promoter of multifarious good causes in his spare time, followed Jonathan Edwards as a stalwart upholder of Puritan orthodoxy. Six of his sons became clergymen, four of them nationally known. His eldest daughter, Catharine, after the untimely death of the professor of mathematics she should have married, devoted her life to the higher education of women. A younger daughter was an early advocate of women's rights. Any of the Beechers, if cast away on a cannibal island, would have been capable of organizing a church, a school, a temperance movement, and a ladies' aid society before help could arrive. They were all public characters.

Harriet, the second daughter of the family, was born while her father was pastor of the important church at Litchfield, Connecticut. She never outgrew the effects of her upbringing under the rigid restraints of Puritan discipline, which turned her nature inward upon itself and left her acutely imaginative and morbidly introspective. To such a nature the experience of religious conversion occurred with hardly a perceptible shock. She had absorbed Calvinistic doctrines from her earliest years, and all her days were full of upward strivings and self-abnegations. This program of austere improvement was only slightly mitigated by country outings, by some acquaintance with the novels of Scott, and by the liberal teachings of an uncle, Samuel Foote.

At sixteen Harriet went to Hartford to become a pupil and shortly a teacher in her sister Catharine's school for young ladies, while her father, translated to Boston, stirred the dry bones of Unitarianism by his rattling revival sermons at the Hanover Street Church. In 1832 he accepted a call to Cincinnati, Ohio, to establish Lane Seminary in order that ministers and home missionaries might be trained to cope with the alarming heathenism of the American frontier. With him went the whole "Beecher caravan," and once in possession of the ground they proceeded to act very much as though Cincinnati were the hypothetical cannibal isle. Catharine and Harriet attended to the school part. It was while she was living in virtual exile from her girlhood home that Harriet began writing for the religious press little tales of the New England life that she passionately loved and of the village people whom she had known. A collection of these stories, which were about equally compounded of conventional piety and sharp factual observation, was issued as *The Mayflower; or, Sketches of Scenes and Characters Among the Descendants of the Pilgrims* (1843).

Meanwhile Harriet had found a husband in the Reverend Calvin E. Stowe, her father's colleague at the seminary, a widower at once childlike and incredibly learned, a kind of theological cherub in a frock coat. The Stowes had six children. Mrs. Stowe as a busy mother and frontier housekeeper had little time for writing, but under the most adverse circumstances she was always able to produce a thin trickle of copy for the sake of adding a few dollars to the family income. She made a brief visit to Kentucky, in the course of which she saw something of slavery in its gentlest form. In Cincinnati she had become aware of the help afforded to runaway slaves by the "underground railroad," and without committing themselves to an unpopular position in public she and her husband had both become sympathetic to the antislavery agitation. Her brother Edward Beecher was an out-and-out Abolitionist, a friend and associate of the martyred Lovejoy.

In 1850 the Stowes' long exile ended when Professor Stowe was appointed to the faculty of Bowdoin College in Brunswick, Maine. Surrounded again by the decencies of New England village life, Harriet brooded in her apocalyptic way over the tales of violence and oppression that she had read in antislavery tracts and had in small part heard confirmed from the lips of fugitive Negroes. A letter from Mrs. Edward Beecher besought her to dedicate her fluent pen to the deliverance of the dusky Israelites. Filled with deep and vague emotions while attending a communion service, Mrs. Stowe unexpectedly saw unrolled before her as in a vision the scene of Uncle Tom's pathetic death and Christlike forgiveness of his persecutors. In that exalted moment the greatest of American propaganda novels was conceived.

Uncle Tom's Cabin (1852) was great in its social effects rather than in its artistic qualities. Its author's resources as a purveyor of Sunday-school fiction were not remarkable. She had at most a ready command of broadly conceived melodrama, humor, and pathos, and of these popular elements she compounded her book. In spite of the intensity of her feelings while writing, Mrs. Stowe showed admirable tact in refraining from attacks on the people of the South. All the villains of her story are Northern renegades. Her emphasis was clearly placed on the unavoidable evils of slavery, the separation of Negro families by sale and the brutality inseparable from the pursuit and recapture of fugitive blacks. Abolitionists at first considered her book too gentle, and Southerners saw no reason to resent it—until the extent of its effect on the public became evident. Nothing attributable to Mrs. Stowe or her handiwork can account for the novel's enormous vogue in the Northern states, in England, and throughout the world. When she went abroad, the reception accorded her was little short of hysterical. She had become a symbol.

In her second antislavery novel, *Dred: A Tale of the Great Dismal Swamp* (1856), she conscientiously attempted to construct a story complementary to her first, in that she now focused attention on the effects of slavery on the slaveholders. But she was betrayed by weaknesses which had somehow been overcome by the sheer fervor of her vision when she wrote *Uncle Tom's Cabin,* a fervor that could not be indefinitely sustained. Her plot is a tissue of unlikelihood. She was unable to fuse into any sort of unity the double story of the sensitive Nina Gordon and her lover in their efforts to prepare the way for eventual emancipation and of the defiant Negro insurrectionist Dred, who lurks in the swamps to provide a refuge for runaways. The novel alternates between scenes of fantastic melodrama and stretches of too-conscious homily.

Mrs. Stowe had now said all she had to say on the subject of slavery. Even before the outbreak of the war, which in Lincoln's eyes she had done much to provoke, she turned to other themes. After a second trip abroad marked by scarcely less acclaim than the first, she settled down in Andover, Massachusetts, and later in Hartford, to continue her career as a popular author. She did an immense amount of journalistic and pietistic hack writing, some of which found its way into published books. From the mass of indifferent and hasty scribbling her New England novels stand out.

In *The Minister's Wooing* (1859) she returned to the subject most suited to her capacities, the delineation of the mind and manners of New England village folk during the period when its clergymen, like Jonathan Edwards when he left his Northampton pulpit, were led to follow theological counsels of perfection without regard to the temper of the time or the vital needs of their people. The ensuing collapse of Calvinistic dogma may have inspired Holmes to write his mischievous parable of "The Deacon's Masterpiece, or the Wonderful One-Hoss Shay." But Mrs. Stowe knew better than anyone else how much earnest striving and high-minded self-discipline had been consecrated by descendants of the Puritans to the cause of spiritual perfection —and what the effort had cost in human terms. Particularly she understood what repressions women had undergone in the vise of uncompromising convictions, and what psychological adjustments they had been obliged to make in the struggle to survive and keep their sanity. *The Minister's Wooing* with its plot based on a succession of fine-spun renunciations is not a great novel, but it is a masterly revelation of the springs of Puritan character. The light it throws on the inner life of an intensely native New England poet like Emily Dickinson can never be too insistently brought to the attention of readers who have not cultivated a historical imagination.

A plot that suffers from idealistic manipulation is combined in *The Pearl of Orrs' Island* (1862) with Dickenslike portraits of well weathered characters on the Maine coast. Mrs. Stowe knew human nature instinctively and thoroughly, but she was constantly hampered in her presentation of the figures that she could create at will by her desire to make them illustrate the moral prepossessions that she had been brought up to regard as sacred.

This handicap was less in evidence when she undertook to embody in fiction her husband's recollections of his boyhood in the little Massachusetts town of Natick. The resultant leisurely exposition of New England ways in *Oldtown Folks* (1869) crowned her work as the interpreter of a peculiar people whose institutions and habits of thought had for nearly two centuries suffered little by abrasion from the rest of the world. The descriptive chapters in this novel and its varied gallery of village characters place Mrs. Stowe at the head of the school of New England realists. Her later transcriptions of local material in *Sam Lawson's Oldtown Fireside Stories* (1872) and *Poganuc People* (1878), the latter a re-creation of the Litchfield of her childhood, confirmed her control of background and character without in any way improving on the penetrating insights that she had already recorded.

In a certain sense Mrs. Stowe has been a victim of her own enormous success, since the world-wide celebrity of *Uncle Tom's Cabin* has tended to distract attention from the field where she was most at home. The merits of her New England novels should be rediscovered. It is doubtful, however, if Mrs. Stowe was capable of realizing the limitations of her talent. Her Italian novel, *Agnes of Sorrento* (1862), was simply an unqualified mistake. Her embroilment in a minor but acrimonious controversy over Lord Byron's marital troubles led to the ill considered publication of *Lady Byron Vindicated* (1870), a book which demonstrates both the author's conscientious officiousness and her indifference to worldly prudence. Though her society novels published in the seventies achieved a contemporary success, they are ephemeral in quality. A Freudian analysis of them, however, might cast a startling light on long repressed urges in Harriet Beecher Stowe.

Conflicts between the rigid standard of conduct in which the Beechers had been reared and the desires natural to opulent and creative personalities were not infrequent and sometimes led to amusing evasions of the code. Mrs. Stowe, for example, concurred in her father's view that the theater was the devil's instrument; but when a dramatic version of her own *Uncle Tom's Cabin* visited Boston in the winter of 1852 or 1853, she could not repress a wish to see it. Francis H. Underwood escorted her to the manager's box—"and we entered privately, she being well muffled." Mrs. Stowe was entranced. "I never saw such delight upon a human face as she displayed," said Underwood; but the New England conscience must have received a mortal wound. Less clandestine but equally funny was the *Atlantic* dinner when women contributors were for the first time invited. Mrs. Stowe agreed to attend with the ironclad stipulation that no wine should be served, and then, according to the report of one of the thirsting guests, made her appearance wearing "vine-leaves" in her hair. Mrs. Thomas Bailey Aldrich, finally, records a delicious anecdote of Mrs. Stowe's early arrival at an afternoon party on a sweltering day, of her innocent partaking of a refreshing punch and feeling a subsequent drowsiness, and of the hostess' horror when she had to receive her guests in the small drawing room close to the alcove where on a sofa, in hoop skirt and lace mitts, the author of *Uncle Tom's Cabin* lay sleeping off her potations.

Obviously Harriet Beecher Stowe was neither a great personality nor a great artist; yet the words set down by her hand appeared to convulse a mighty nation. She herself solved the paradox with charming simplicity by saying of her world-famous book, "God wrote it!" She was only the amanuensis of the Eternal. To a mind grounded in Hebrew Scripture, there was nothing impossible in the thought that God should choose the foolish things of the world to confound the wise, and the weak things of the world to confound the things that are mighty.

35. THE NEW ENGLAND TRIUMVIRATE: LONGFELLOW, HOLMES, LOWELL

NEITHER the issue of slavery nor the fact of civil war could stir very deeply the peace which pervaded the country town of Cambridge, near Boston, in the middle years of the century. Around the disorderly College Yard and its seven red-brick "Muses' factories" sprawled the "Village," which Lowell was to describe in one of his sprightliest essays, "Cambridge Thirty Years Ago." It was in fact a country town, quite separate from Boston, and though perhaps not beautiful, certainly not ugly. To the casual visitor it would have seemed to differ from other New England towns mainly in its vivid recollections of the Revolutionary War and in the pride it took in the college. On closer acquaintance one would have found it a place in which scholarly attainments outshone every sort of worldly success. Democratic enough for the president of the college to serve happily as major in the company of militia of which his own manservant was the colonel, it possessed and highly respected its own intellectual aristocracy.

Cambridge was also a friendly place, a true society, in which the loneliness endured by most American thinkers and creative workers could have little excuse. The intensity of the Puritan past, now sluiced into other channels, was still evident there. Somewhat provincial the place may have been, and a little out of the main American current; yet one would be at a loss to say where or when America has provided a pleasanter residence for a scholar, a thinker, or a man of letters. Even a young poet, if by chance he should turn up there, would not be laughed or frozen into silence.

Three young poets—Henry Wadsworth Longfellow, Oliver Wendell Holmes, and James Russell Lowell—lived there and in Boston in the thirties. The good fortune that was to persist throughout their long lives began with the time and place of their birth. The New England of their early years was a rural and agricultural region, yet strongly sea-minded. It was remarkably homogeneous in population and had a history and tradition of its own. In two centuries of toil this region had accumulated a moderate, well distributed wealth. Nowhere in the world had the elements of education been made more accessible. At no time since the great age of Athens had any community worked out a better balance of individual liberty with the sense of social and political obligation. This New England was composed not so much of states and cities as of towns, and of towns so nearly independent, so stoutly supported within by citizens fully aware of their rights and duties, that a clear-eyed foreign observer, Alexis de Tocqueville, could regard them in 1835 as almost perfect examples of democracy. Such a New England town was Cambridge—with the difference that it had an ancient college.

In such surroundings, a poet could be in harmony with the present and at the same time devote his energies to the exploration of the past. Cooper and other early American writers had complained that the young nation could not produce a really great literature until it had a cultural tradition of its own, rooted deeply in the past. Only then would there be a society of readers who had assured and common thoughts, and emotions with which to respond. In Longfellow, Holmes, and Lowell such "great writers" seemed to be in the making.

With equal success these three poets managed to reconcile the conflicting demands laid upon the scholar, the creative writer, and the gentleman. One and all, they were sound literary craftsmen, industrious and fluent and prolific in prose and verse. They were good men in nearly every sense that the word "good" can bear. Each of them descended from dignified and long-established New England stock, they were highly respected in their day and so could do much to make literature "respectable" in a country preoccupied with quite other things. Their inheritance of New England's version of the eighteenth century, during which the more acrid juices of Puritanism had considerably mellowed, made them optimistic, serene, and sweet-tempered, so that the widespread admiration they won in their time was always warmed by affection. Although their unquestionable patriotism was deeply rooted in their native region, each of them in his way was a transplanter of Old World culture. Moreover, they moved in the same circles, heard the same talk, and read the same books for half a century. They even read and liked and praised one another's books, and often met as members of the Saturday Club of Boston, which came to be called a "mutual admiration society."

In writing deliberately for an audience which they knew and which they wished to address in terms that would be widely understood, Longfellow and Holmes and Lowell had good and numerous company. To oversimplify an intricate matter, many poets of the years after the First World War talked to themselves not so much because they despised a larger audience as because they despaired of one. But the Cambridge and Boston triumvirate had no reason for any such despair. Their natural and easily defensible wish to be understood, to be liked, to be even influential, was fully gratified. They were as sure of their audience as a minister composing his Sunday sermon, and out of this assurance came the tone of public address that we hear in much of their verse. Thence too, no doubt, came the platitudes and sentimentalities, the threshing of thrice-tossed straw, the smooth slipping along old greased grooves, that have lowered the repute of their verse with a later generation; but in counting the cost we should not forget that much was gained when these men showed that poetry of a sort could be written in America and made intelligible, even enjoyable, to common and workaday understandings.

2

Longfellow was twenty-nine years old when, in 1836, he took up his duties at Harvard College as Smith Professor of Modern Languages. His preparation for those duties had not been of the sort that provides severe mental discipline or produces what would later be called accurate scholarship. Born in 1807 at Portland in the District of Maine, the son of a successful lawyer and grandson of a patriarchal hero of the Revolution, he had graduated at Bowdoin College in the same year as Nathaniel Hawthorne and then had spent three years of random travel and study in Europe. There had followed five years of teaching at Bowdoin, his marriage to a Portland girl, a second stay in Europe, and the death of his young wife. By the time he arrived in Cambridge he had written and published a number of conventional poems, several magazine articles, certain textbooks for the use of his college classes, and a slight volume of travel essays in Irving's manner entitled *Outre-Mer*. It was clear that he was quite determined to succeed in some as yet unspecified way, but nothing he had yet done showed remarkable originality or creative power.

Short in stature but good-looking and graceful, quiet and modest in manner but not unduly reticent, very careful in matters of dress, laughter-loving and with plenty of humor though not much wit, highly appreciative of creature comforts, always sociably inclined, the young professor made friends easily and held them long. He had enough personal dignity to command respect but not so much as to prevent affection. His colleagues and students liked him from the start, even though there might be something slightly exotic about his florid waistcoats and flowing hair. His unconcern with the contemporary American scene could easily be explained to his credit as the result of his two long sojourns abroad. Though so young and gay and accessible, he brought with him into the provincial college town a hint of romantic distances. He had walked the Rialto and the streets of old Madrid. He had lingered long among the "last enchantments of the Middle Age" as they were to be found— or so young America was beginning to surmise—at Göttingen and Heidelberg and along the castled Rhine. "The Old World," as he had written years before in his neatly kept private journal, was to him "a kind of Holy Land"—a feeling which would by no means impede his success in a Cambridge and a New England in which the old Hebraic sanctities were slowly giving way before a Europeanized culture. And indeed it was impossible to regard him as an outsider. His father and his grandfather had been Harvard men, and four of his maternal ancestors, including John Alden, had "come·over in the *Mayflower*."

Professor Longfellow performed his college duties faithfully but without enthusiasm. He was neither a brilliant teacher nor a dull one. His lectures on the literatures of modern Europe, quiet in tone yet warmly appreciative, contributed less to the scholarship of his auditors than to their "general culture." There was a suggestion in them that a gentleman would no more flaunt his scholarship than he would his bank account, and for criticism Longfellow had little taste or ability. "Doubtless criticism," he was later to remark in his *Table Talk,* "was originally benignant, pointing out the beauties of a work, rather than its defects. The passions of men have made it malignant, as the bad heart of Procrustes turned the bed, the symbol of repose, into an instrument of torture."

Several passages in his early letters show that Longfellow had acquired, probably in Europe, a theory of higher education in advance of anything to be found in practice at Bowdoin or Harvard, but this did not make the routine of classroom teaching any the less irksome to him. Before he had been two years at Harvard he confided to his Journal: "Perhaps the worst thing in a College Life is this having your mind constantly a play-mate for boys . . . instead of stretching out and grappling with men's minds." These words have an odd sound as coming from a man who seldom grappled with anything and was never remarkable for "stretching out." They are as surprising as the line "Let us, then, be up and doing" in "A Psalm of Life," his most famous but perhaps least characteristic poem. For Longfellow was in no sense a man of action. His life and work seem to have been actuated by two diverse desires. On the one hand he emphatically wanted to make and to leave his mark, to succeed in the world's opinion; but on the other he wanted, perhaps less consciously, to spend his life in the leisurely reading of old books and in the kind of rumination and reminiscence that went to the making of his poem "My Lost Youth." His problem was, how to satisfy both of these apparently contradictory wishes, and rather early in life he found the answer: by success as a poet. His work at Harvard could not satisfy either one of them. In 1854 he resigned his professorship.

To meet the objection that this view of Longfellow's career suggests a cool calculation, not to say an opportunism, seldom found in poetic minds, one might easily cite a number of instances in which he showed himself an astute manager of his worldly affairs while at the same time closely guarding the treasure of his dreams. His choice and rejection of poetic themes, the timing of his publications, his dealings with publishers, and most of all his accurate knowledge of the public taste, show that the tendency to what he called "daydreaming" which he seems to have inherited from his mother was well balanced by the practical gifts that had made his father a successful lawyer and politician.

Longfellow, moreover, was not a poet by compulsion of inward and innate necessity. Year after year in his early manhood he wrote verse hardly at all, and his first collection of poems was not published until he was thirty-two. There is of course no doubt that he loved poetry and delighted to write it; but he had to be assured that the writing of it would amount to something more than mere "daydreaming." When at last that assurance came, when he saw that poetry would provide a dignified and leisurely way of making his mark without the necessity to be "up and doing" or to "be a hero in the strife," he settled down to become America's first professional poet—a phrase which involves a contradiction in terms.

An interesting example of Longfellow's ability to advance his worldly fortunes while serving the needs of the heart is seen in his long courtship of Frances Appleton. One would not suggest that his love for this charming woman was alloyed by any materialistic consideration, and yet it is at least worthy of record that she was a daughter of one of the wealthiest merchants in Boston and that when, in 1843, she finally became his wife, she brought him as a wedding gift the handsome Craigie House and grounds in Cambridge, once the headquarters of General Washington.

In asking himself whether he ought to allow his daughter to marry a man who, besides being a college professor, was known to have written verses, Nathan Appleton, the prosperous merchant of Beacon Hill, had to consider that by 1843 Professor Longfellow was rapidly becoming a famous man. His first volume of poems, *Voices of the Night,* published in 1839, had sold 43,000 copies, and several poems in it, such as "A Psalm of Life" and "The Reaper and the Flowers," were already widely popular. Such success would assuage the wound caused by Longfellow's prose romance *Hyperion,* also of 1839, in which the professor had shown definitely bad taste by narrating, under a thin disguise, the early stages of his affection for Nathan Appleton's daughter. In 1841 there had appeared *Ballads and Other Poems,* considerably more vigorous than the first book and including two well told tales of the sea, "The Wreck of the Hesperus" and "The Skeleton in Armor," which any businessman could understand. Here, too, was the sweetly sentimental "Maidenhood," the platitudinous "Rainy Day," and "The Village Blacksmith" with precisely the right tone of gentlemanly condescension toward the laboring classes. These lines were fitted out at the end with a moralistic tag which, though its relation to the main substance of the poem was slight, would mitigate the curse of poetry for those who preferred sermons. In short, there seemed to be something in the little book for almost every taste, and the poem called "Excelsior" was really a masterpiece in the profitable art of pleasing everybody at once. For the youth who bore "the strange device" in that poem might, if one pleased, be thought of as climbing toward heaven, toward the summit of Parnassus, toward the full development of his own powers, or, equally well, toward the presidency of a bank, a railroad, even a college. At any rate he was climbing, hoping, aspiring, and so could be taken as the perfect symbol of a young ambitious country that hardly knew as yet where it was going but felt sure that it was on the way.

The poems in these first two books of verse sank so deep into the national memory, soon attaining there almost the currency of proverbs, that we usually think of them even today when we remember Longfellow at all—and then perhaps decide that he is not worth remembering. The deeper reasons for their popularity, though not recondite, may be left to the historians of American culture. Perhaps the most charitable thing that the literary critic can say about them is that they were, in the language of seventeenth century musicians, hardly more than toccata pieces written to try out the range and sonority of the instrument. In other words, a mind in which there was little of its own that was really burning for utterance was here trying to find out, by trial and error, what themes, what moods, what literary effects, would be acceptable to a reading public with which no one as yet was familiar. It was engaged in the task of discovering about America certain basic things which America herself did not know. Little wonder that for a while it fumbled and groped almost blindly here and there, trying all things but determined to hold fast what it found good.

Longfellow's love for Frances Appleton brought him an experience of passion, and also, for a time, of pain and apparent failure, which deepened and strengthened his whole nature. Its successful outcome brought him inward peace and released him from the need, real or imagined, to strive for the approval of everyone. During the long and mainly serene remainder of his life, his writing in verse gradually developed admirable qualities of which the early poems had not given clear promise. Completely happy at home, surrounded by friends such as Lowell, Sumner, Norton, and Agassiz, with his fame steadily spreading through the two Americas and England and Europe, he poured forth his poems with an almost effortless ease. *The Belfry of Bruges and Other Poems* (1845) contained, besides such popular things as "The Bridge" and "The Old Clock on the Stairs," a really fine sonnet called "Mezzo Cammin" in which he surveyed his past accomplishment with characteristic modesty and manly candor. Two years later his *Evangeline,* a long and rambling narrative in loose hexameters, gave notice that here was an American poet, at last, who regarded the making of poetry as his life's work. The luster of its success was undimmed by the appearance of *Kavanagh* (1849), an unfortunate excursion into prose fiction which showed how inadequate the poet's thought appeared when the cunningly woven veil of his verse was drawn aside. Longfellow reached the height of his powers in extended versified narrative in *The Song of Hiawatha* (1855) and *The Courtship of Miles Standish* (1858), both of which, like *Evangeline,* did something to stay if not to satisfy America's hunger for a past, a legendry, a body of myth, of her own. So, in part, did the *Tales of a Wayside Inn* (1863), bringing together stories from many lands, including New England, in a "framework" suggested by Chaucer and Boccaccio, and relating them as though through the mouths of New England speakers round the fireside of a Massachusetts tavern.

Not only the narrative methods but also the themes of these *Tales* illustrate what one may call the antiquarian habit of Longfellow's mind. A few of the stories, like the inaccurate but highly effective "Paul Revere's Ride," are American and almost "local," though everything possible is done to make them look old. All the rest deal with the far away and the long ago, and the "Saga of King Olaf," the best item in the series, has an air of all but mythological antiquity.

One need not urge the absurdity of the supposition that a group of nineteenth century Americans would tell such tales to one another while sitting at ease round a New England fireside, for it is obvious that Longfellow was little concerned with verisimilitude either here or elsewhere. He had almost none of the respect for concrete fact that gives body and verve to the work of Chaucer, his chief model in the composition of the *Tales,* and apparently it never occurred to him that the poetic imagination might and should be used not for escape from the facts of life, as he used it, but for penetration and inward illumination of them. At any rate, nothing seemed poetical to him until all taint of modernity had been cleansed or hidden away. When he did occasionally single out a recent event for imaginative treatment his first and instinctive act was, so to speak, to dip it in "time's ever-rolling stream." Thus in writing "The Wreck of the Hesperus," less than two weeks after the incident it describes and within fifty miles of its scene, he made it sound as much as possible like a medieval popular ballad. The scenes of his three long narrative poems with an ostensible American setting might almost as well have been laid in ancient Arcadia, so devoid they are of sharp factual detail and contemporary reference. Only once, and then reluctantly, at the request of his friend Charles Sumner, did he make an approach to a living national issue. The unsatisfactory result was his *Poems on Slavery* (1842).

This antiquarian habit was of course by no means peculiar to Longfellow.

We see it clearly in Irving and Hawthorne, and it is a familiar characteristic of the Romantic Movement throughout its long course. Yet, in American literature at any rate, Longfellow is an extreme example of this "devotion to something afar from the sphere of our sorrow." His homesickness for the glamorous twilights of the past is often attributed to the influence of his early wanderings and random readings in Europe, especially in Germany where the Romantic Movement began and lingered longest. But this is to confuse cause and effect. Longfellow's romantic tendencies were already well developed when he first went to Europe, and if they had any literary source it was probably Irving's *Sketch Book*—a work he read with delight in his boyhood, began at once to imitate, and never outgrew. More probably, however, his romanticism was fastened upon him by the choice he made between his mother's "daydreaming" and his father's clear-eyed worldliness. For the latter he never lost respect; but he saw that it involved a vigor and persistence in action "still achieving, still pursuing," which was not congenial to his nature. Poetry or daydreaming, on the other hand, required no coarsening contacts with the world's work. In the words of Ossian, one of the favorite poets of his boyhood, it was to him "a tale of the times of old, the deeds of the days of other years."

The source of Longfellow's antiquarianism, however, is not nearly so important as the fact that the true habitat of his thoughts was neither America nor Europe but the past, and not the past as reconstructed by historical scholarship or as revived by an alert historical imagination but an unchanging and timeless and quite unbelievable epoch of his own creation. This has meant that Longfellow's writing, for all its great vogue, has done nothing to correct but rather much to confirm a notion to which America has long been prone—the notion that poetry and the other arts have no bearing upon actual life and that, like "religion," they may be consigned to rainy Sundays and to otherwise unoccupied females.

After the dreadful death of his wife, by fire, in 1861, Longfellow "took refuge," as he wrote to a German friend, in the work of translating Dante's *Divina Commedia*. The result, published in three volumes from 1867 to 1870, was an adequate rendering of the Florentine's words but not of his cramped and fiery force. Longfellow was not using his developed powers and what should have been the most fruitful years of his life to advantage, either in this quite uncreative task or in his several attempts at poetic drama. His *Christus: A Mystery* (published as a whole in 1872) is a loosely connected trilogy of "closet dramas" in verse which, we are told, he regarded as his most important work. Only the second part, entitled "The Golden Legend," is today easily readable, and it reads like an extremely mild dilution of Goethe's *Faust*. Longfellow was working closer to his true vein in the simple and dignified "Morituri Salutamus," which he wrote for the fiftieth anniversary of his class at Bowdoin College.

Old age brought Longfellow a quiet culmination. His last two collections of verse, *Ultima Thule* and *In the Harbor* (1880 and 1882), had in them a number of poems far better than anything in his first one. He was, and modestly knew himself to be, the most popular poet in America or in the world. He was as widely beloved as he was famous, and must have been aware that he had done much good for multitudes of people. Letters of praise and gratitude, always courteously answered, poured in upon him from many lands, in many languages. His seventy-fifth birthday was celebrated in every school-house in the United States. Two weeks later he wrote his last poem, "The Bells of San Blas." Ten days later still, on March 24, 1882, he died.

The perennial question with regard to Longfellow's "Americanism" is not so difficult as it has been made to seem. Surely the best proof that a man belongs to his people is given when they accept him as their representative and beloved voice. By this test Longfellow is the most American poet that America has ever had. He is so much of our kind that a close reading of him helps our understanding of ourselves, not always in a flattering way. The sentimentalities, the platitudes, and the lugged-in moralisms that mar his earlier writing are faults that he came by, as we say, "honestly." He reminds us of deep-drawn traits in the American character by his antiquarian delight in the shadowy past, by the superficial melancholy that never really darkens his essential optimism, and perhaps most of all by his occasional awaking from daydreams with the injunction that one must "act,—act in the living Present." One would say, therefore, that not to know Longfellow, or to be contemptuous of him, is to lose some part of one's national heritage.

Yet after all it is not a poet's main business to represent his time and his country, to have witty or profound ideas, or even to hold sound opinions. The elementary but oft neglected fact that a poet must make poems was fully understood by Longfellow, and in his best work he showed himself a conscientious and deliberate artist. He was a master of the orthodox technique of versification, ranging easily and with a skill that concealed itself through a wide variety of meters and stanzaic structures. He could versify a long story like *Evangeline* with many a subtle modulation in the verbal music and the mood. He could narrate a short story like "Paul Revere's Ride" in a verse that races and rings. In later life he made a dozen or more sonnets, notably the one entitled "Nature" and the six composed to accompany his translation of Dante, that give the effect of massive and grandly modeled bronze. His expression, moreover, was always as clear as he or anyone could make it, and whatever he wrote, well or ill, he always seemed to write easily, without the least strain or strut. To borrow a metaphor from Thoreau, he struck not with the end but with the middle of his stick. Thus he sometimes achieved, especially in old age, a grand simplicity of style which seems the perfectly natural expression of his own essential goodness, his serenity, and his peace of heart.

3

Longfellow took twenty-nine years in reaching Cambridge, but Oliver Wendell Holmes saved time, as he himself might have said, by being born there, in an old gambrel-roofed house between the common and the college. He remained a Cambridge boy to the last of his many years, notwithstanding the fact that he was also emphatically a Boston man. In 1829 he graduated from Harvard College at the age of nineteen, and in the following year, while "yawning over law books," wrote the vigorous poem "Old Ironsides" which carried his name for a time far beyond the confines of New England and saved the old battleship *Constitution* from threatened destruction. Soon abandoning the law, he took up the study of medicine, at first in Boston, and in 1833 he went to Paris for two and a half years of close application to anatomy, surgery, and medicine under the foremost teachers that the world at the time afforded. These were the years, as his letters show, in which Holmes grew up. With a purpose far more precise than that with which Longfellow had gone to Europe some years before, he got more definite results. Besides a solid grounding in his chosen profession, he gained enough knowledge of Parisian life, and saw enough in brief glimpses of England, Scotland, and Italy, to prevent him from ever becoming in fact the provincial Bostonian that he sometimes humorously pretended to be.

During the first year, 1836, after his return from Europe, Holmes took the degree of M.D. at the Harvard Medical School, began his medical practice, published his first volume of poems, became a member of the Massachusetts Medical Society, published a dissertation on Intermittent Fever in New England, won a Boylston Prize at Harvard, and wrote for the Harvard Commencement a Phi Beta Kappa Poem that filled—allowing for the applause—an hour and ten minutes in the recitation. This year, except that it represented only a few of his later acquirements and activities, was a swiftly drawn sketch of the always eager, gay, and multilateral life that Dr. Holmes was to lead in Cambridge and Boston for more than half a century.

And yet neither in youth nor in age were his interests merely miscellaneous. They had a center, a burning focus indeed, from which not even the later fame of his prose and verse could deflect him. First of all he was, and he remained, a doctor, although he interpreted that title in a sense more inclusive than the one it usually bears. His medical practice, never extensive, was abandoned before he reached middle age, and he was never eminent in original medical research; but as a teacher he did his most completely devoted, enthusiastic, and influential work. It was said of Lowell that he sometimes yawned when entering the classroom, and one fears that Longfellow's students occasionally did the same in the midst of a lecture; but the wit, the Yankee common sense, and the completely humanized erudition of Professor Holmes were a prophylaxis against the germs of boredom. First at Dartmouth from 1838 to 1840 and then at the Harvard Medical School from 1847 to 1882 he taught anatomy and physiology with a deep, abiding sense of the teacher's privilege and obligation. One judges from the testimony of his pupils that his teaching was actuated by an unmistakable intellectual passion for what he proudly called "Science," and also by a keen aesthetic delight in the intricate order and symmetry of Nature, especially of the human body, which science was in his time slowly revealing.

If therefore we find that Holmes' prose and verse lack intensity, we do well to infer not that the Doctor himself was quite without that quality but that it had been directed elsewhere. Diminutive in stature, chronically adolescent in appearance, charmingly egotistical and avid of praise as a school-boy, bestrewing his long path through life with puns and quips and bons mots, always cheerfully convinced that the main thing about a cloud is its silver lining, the doctor and professor and poet and prose-master called Holmes was a little hard for people who saw only the surface of him to take seriously; but to those who knew him well it was observable that when he sallied forth to assail bigotry in any of its forms—it might be the bigotry of medical doctors of the old school against which in 1843 he launched his fierce and brilliant essay on "The Contagiousness of Puerperal Fever," or that of Calvinistic theologians whom he attacked again and again, as in his essay on Jonathan Edwards and his poem "Wind-Clouds and Star-Drifts"—his works carried the concentrated force of a hornet. His hatred of disorder and confusion and darkness and cruelty was the inevitable antithesis of his strong love of order and clearness, that intellectual light and beneficence which he believed modern science was offering to mankind. We are right, no doubt, in calling him a conservative, and he called himself that; but at the core of his caution and temperamental dislike of change there was an ardency, an audacity of the kind by which revolutions are made. One of the public testimonials of which he may well have been proudest was a vote taken by the members of the Massachusetts Medical Society after he had read his paper on "Currents and Counter-Currents in Medical Science." In that vote it was "resolved that the Society disclaim all responsibility for the sentiments contained in this Annual Address."

What Holmes chiefly brought back from Europe and strove to transplant in the soil of American culture was a resolute and unqualified faith in Science.

The word "faith" is here exact, for he felt and thought and wrote about Science—a word he habitually capitalized—as New England ministers of the past had done about religion. He held it to be nothing less than a new revelation of the divine mind, in terms of which all real or alleged foregoing revelations would have to be reconsidered. "The attitude of modern Science," said he, "is erect, her aspect serene, her determination inexorable, her onward movement unflinching; because she believes herself, in the order of Providence, the true successor of the men of old who brought down the light of heaven to men."

Holmes' faith in Science led him more than once out of his natural conservatism and into the ranks of the reformers. It was partly with scientific weapons that he fought his long battle with the lingering representatives of Calvinistic theology, although he did not neglect to put on also the whole armor of his learning, reason, common sense, and wit. He used scientific methods and data to show that criminals, vicious persons, and "sinners" in general, because they were not wholly responsible for their evil doing, ought rather to be educated than punished. His three novels, *Elsie Venner* (1860-1861), *The Guardian Angel* (1867), and *A Mortal Antipathy* (1885), were written with this primary intent. In fact he laid so strong an emphasis upon heredity and environment that he often seemed to be teaching a materialistic determinism no less binding than the Calvinistic predestination which he ridiculed.

But Holmes was never completely a materialist. He left some room for the freedom of the will and never lost his belief in a beneficent Deity. According to his chief biographer, John T. Morse, Jr., who knew him intimately, he was always more attracted by theology than even by literature and medicine. To those who regard him as merely an amiable jester, his theological lore is likely to be the most surprising item in his accurate and various learning. His own religious beliefs, to be sure, were neither precise nor numerous, and he once said that he could sum them all up in the first two words of the Lord's Prayer, yet he apparently found them sufficient. For all the little man's bustle and bristle, it was clear that he had in his heart the peace of God which passed even his understanding. In this regard he reminds one of certain minor poets of England's eighteenth century—men like Parnell and Gray, the Warton brothers, and William Shenstone, who were so careful to avoid all outward show of "enthusiasm" that their real religious faith seldom came to the surface.

Holmes recalls England's neo-classical period in several ways. Like Addison and Steele, he based his admirable prose style upon the best of the talk —and that would be largely his own—that he could hear in his time. In verse his favorite form was the heroic couplet. Like Pope, although not to the same extent, he depended for his effects chiefly upon wit—a term within which he would have included both reason and good sense. His feeling for Boston, where a faint aroma of the eighteenth century still lingered when he was young, was like that of Dr. Johnson for London. Moderation, urbanity, and serene self-control meant as much to him as to Lord Chesterfield. He might have excelled in the writing of satire like that of Swift if his convictions had been more fervid and his heart less warm. Even his devotion to science makes one think of the eighteenth century Deists who saw in the laws of nature a second revelation of the Creator's mind and purpose. His prevailing optimism, based upon an assurance that the human mind can comprehend and in some degree control the physical world in which it finds itself, closely resembled that to be seen in the immediate followers of Sir Isaac Newton.

One of the few outstanding events in Holmes' life was the request that came to him when he was nearing fifty that he contribute to the newly founded *Atlantic Monthly,* edited by his friend James Russell Lowell. At that time, in 1857, Holmes was little known outside the Boston region, and even there his reputation was that of an able physician and teacher who, as an amateur of letters, could be counted upon to turn out at short notice a string of amusing verses for the annual meeting of his Harvard class or almost any other such festive occasion. In *The Autocrat of the Breakfast Table* (1857–1858), however, he established his own fame and that of Lowell's new magazine at one stroke.

American literature had never before been suddenly enriched by an extended piece of writing at once so wise and gay, so felicitous in swift mingling of fact and fancy, so crackling with wit while remaining so warm, so kind. For this work and its two successors, *The Professor at the Breakfast-Table* (1860) and *The Poet at the Breakfast-Table* (1872), Holmes developed a literary form admirably calculated for the exhibition of his own powers. By combining the techniques of prose fiction, drama, and the essay, he made for himself a literary method by means of which he could sketch character, tell stories, present his favorite ideas and prejudices, parade his erudition, praise Boston, smite stupidities, and indulge in an endless monologue without fear of interruption. It was a method that made miscellaneousness a virtue and changed what might have looked like ostentatious egotism—for in fact it was something rather like that—into pure charm. And yet in admiring the method or form of the Breakfast Table series one must not ignore the contribution of Holmes' prose style, elastic and delicate and strong as a strand of spider's web. There is little to subtract from the statement made long ago in the Boston *Advertiser* that it has "the spring of the hickory, the smack of the cider, the tonic of the climate, and the vigor of the type of men hardened by the struggle that has formed our national character."

The Autocrat of the Breakfast-Table is one of the most highly civilized books ever written in America. It is a book in which the seeds of factual knowledge spring up into thought, and thought bears the fruit of wisdom. It is the product of an epoch and a place. It is a masterpiece, a triumph, of wit. One sees this mainly in the blaze of the metaphors with which it is, so to speak, encrusted. Yet they are never used for mere display. One laughs at them, if at all, in pure admiration, sharing Holmes' own manifest delight and surprise at their aptness. For he himself was amazed at his own discoveries of this kind. "What happens," he asks in *Mechanism in Thought and Morals,* "when one idea brings up another? . . . What is this action which . . . in men of wit and fancy connects remote ideas by partial resemblances? . . . There is a Delphi and a Pythoness in every human breast."

Holmes contained in himself the man of wit, the man of imagination, and the man of science, and all three of them were continually diving into what he calls "the infinite ocean of similitudes and analogies that rolls through the universe." No doubt it was this triple equipment that enabled him to make his unerring gannetlike plunges out of the skies of abstract thought upon the one minute and distant object that could best illustrate and drive home his meaning. For he was quite wrong, of course, in implying that everyone can do this sort of thing. He came near the truth when he said, "Just according to the intensity and extension of our mental being we shall see the many in the one and the one in the many."

Whatever may be thought of Holmes' intensity, he had a remarkable mental extension. He was erudite not only in medicine and anatomy, in theology, and in the English literature of the eighteenth century, but in the dialect of New England, the records of trotting horses, pugilism and photography and rowing, rattlesnakes, elm trees, prenatal influences, heredity, the Harvard Class of 1829, and microscopes. Nothing Bostonian was alien to him. He was at the same time bookish and social, a hard worker and a man of endless leisure who loved to have his talk out. He could talk with any man on any man's own topic while holding back large reservoirs of professional knowledge to which few others could pretend.

One may suspect that Holmes was kept from being in the full sense a poet by what the French would call a "defect of his qualities." He tried to be one, but laughter was always breaking in. He reaches full-throated song perhaps only in "The Chambered Nautilus." He wrote a large number of "occasional poems," all highly successful, no doubt, when first read by him in public but now for the most part lifeless. He really excelled in a dozen or fifteen tiny masterpieces—"The Last Leaf," "Dorothy Q," "Contentment," "Aunt Tabitha," and "The Organ-Blower" among them—as ingeniously wrought as a Chinese ivory carving.

Dr. Holmes knew his limitations. He accepted, he obeyed, and he even enjoyed them, often making them look like positive advantages. Thus, realizing that his profession and the asthma with which he suffered all his life would confine him to the region of Boston, he assured himself and the world that "identification with a locality is a surer passport to immortality than cosmopolitanism is," and also that the "Boston State-House is the hub of the solar system." In the same way he made his peace with the boundaries that nature had set for his intellectual and artistic aspirations.

4

The symmetry of Holmes' career is even more apparent when one compares it with that of James Russell Lowell. More versatile than Holmes by far, more deeply and highly gifted, Lowell did not willingly accept any limitations, any discipline or routine whatever. Although he gained a remarkable erudition from a lifetime of reading in half a dozen languages, he never was subjected, by himself or by others, to an arduous training. This may be one reason for the fact that he makes a blurred impression, and that one rises from a study of his manifold life, his brilliant essays, his verse of many kinds, and his wholly delightful letters, with the feeling that he was, in both the good and the bad sense, "a man of parts."

Like Holmes, Lowell was a native of Cambridge and the son of a Congregational clergyman. He was born on February 22, 1819, in a substantial pre-Revolutionary house called "Elmwood," standing in ample grounds about a mile west of Harvard College. On the paternal side he came of New England stock already distinguished and destined to be more so. His father was a man whose political and social opinions made it appropriate that he should live in a part of the town known as "Tory Row." His mother, from whom he derived his poetical talent, was descended from families that had lived for several generations in the Orkney Islands.

After a happy childhood in which he unconsciously gathered from the natural beauty about him many of the poetic images that were to enrich his later writing, Lowell entered Harvard at the age of fifteen. The letters of his college days show him as a scatterbrain, eagerly enthusiastic, devoted to his friends, gay, and averse to hard work. Toward the end of his senior year he was rusticated for a breach of college discipline and was required to spend the following six weeks at Concord. There he met Emerson, of whom he reported to a college friend: "He is a good-natured man in spite of his doctrines."

In 1840, having graduated at Harvard College and also at the Harvard Law School, Lowell became engaged to Maria White, a highly intelligent young woman of poetic talent who seems to have increased his already nascent interest in the current liberal and humanitarian movements, including Abolition. His first book of verse, *A Year's Life and Other Poems,* appeared in 1841; and when it was followed by *Poems,* three years later, his reputation was such that N. P. Willis could speak of him as "the best-launched poet in America." Meanwhile he had begun his varied editorial career with a short-lived journal called *The Pioneer,* published in Boston. After his marriage he lived for a time in Philadelphia, contributing to various liberal journals. In 1848 he put forth a two-volume edition of his poems, *A Fable for Critics,* the first series of his *Biglow Papers,* and *The Vision of Sir Launfal,* thus establishing his fame before he reached the age of thirty. There followed a long period of travel in Europe, shortly after which his wife died. This event, as he said in his old age, broke his life in two. It deprived him of the only companion and guide who was ever able to give direction to his random energies and miscellaneous interests.

Lowell fell back, as Longfellow had done under similar circumstances, upon the literary past. Since boyhood he had been a bold adventurer in the wilderness of books, but now he became, as he said, "one of the last great readers." In 1855 he accepted the professorship at Harvard recently vacated by Longfellow, thus turning his addiction to old books into a duty. He taught his classes faithfully though not with all his strength, and in 1857 became the first editor of the *Atlantic Monthly.*

Far more public-minded than Holmes or Longfellow, Lowell was profoundly stirred by the tragedy of the Civil War, in which he lost three beloved nephews. It roused him to write a second series, more mature than the first, of *Biglow Papers* (1866), and to contribute a number of deeply thoughtful articles on the topics of the times to the *Atlantic* and the *North American Review.* Thus he returned to the concern with social and political questions which he had shown in his younger manhood, gradually acquiring reputation as a public figure. He was one of the first American men of letters to recognize and proclaim the greatness of Abraham Lincoln. The noble sixth section of his *Ode Recited at the Harvard Commemoration* (1865), devoted to Lincoln entirely, may well outlast all his other writing.

Lowell's central thought with regard to democracy was that it can be saved from its tendency to "level downward" only by the constant presence and pressure within it of an aristocratic leaven. This was approximately Thomas Jefferson's position, but Lowell probably reached it through acquaintance with the New England scene. In his address on the two hundred and fiftieth anniversary of the founding of Harvard he spoke a vivid paragraph or two in praise of the early ministers of New England, asserting that they composed "a recognized aristocracy," and that "never was there an aristocracy so simple, so harmless, so exemplary, and so fit to rule." If this is a conservative opinion, then Lowell was conservative all his life, and the attempts sometimes made to divide his political and social thinking into several "periods" do not reach to the ingrained and possibly innate habit of his mind.

In spite of the disgust he felt at the political corruption of the North in the postwar years, Lowell continued to write extensively. A long poem called *The Cathedral,* one of his most ambitious, appeared in 1870. In the next year he published *My Study Windows,* a delightful collection of familiar essays. The two series of essays entitled *Among My Books* (1870 and 1876), with their extended studies of Dryden, Milton, Wordsworth, Dante, Spenser, and Keats, established his reputation as a literary critic and as one of America's foremost men of letters.

But literary fame could not satisfy this mind that never found its own center. In 1877 Lowell gladly accepted from President Hayes an appointment as Minister to the Court of Spain, and from 1880 to 1885 he served as American Minister in England. He was highly successful in both countries as a diplomat and as a spokesman for America, keenly enjoying his work, making many friends, and gradually abandoning the tendency to heckle John Bull so evident in the second set of *Biglow Papers* and in the political essays he had written before and during the Civil War. England, indeed, became to him almost a second home, and he returned to that country four times in the last five years of his life. The loss of his second wife in 1885 left him a lonely and heartbroken man. His health, which had always been remarkably robust, was destroyed by successive attacks of gout. On August 12, 1891, he died at "Elmwood," in the house of his birth.

The more one knows about this brilliant career, in so many ways so decidedly successful, the more one is inclined to call it a failure. What Lowell most deplorably lacks is coherence—and this not merely in the style of his prose and verse, but in his life, his thought, his beliefs, even his character. Lowell's mind was certainly one of the most brilliant that America has produced; but it was brilliant in the way of a shattered mirror, or, let us say, in that of the vividly colored bits of glass in a kaleidoscope that give the effect of a new geometrical pattern at every slight turn of the tube. "He did not, indeed, make one impression upon me," said William Dean Howells, "but a thousand impressions, which I should seek in vain to embody in a single presentment." Continually while reading Lowell, and even when most delighted by the incessant glitter and glint of his style, one is perplexed and vexed that a man with such powers could not draw them together and so make more of them.

Lowell was himself aware of his failure, and wrote in his old age: "I feel that my life has been mainly wasted—that I have thrown away more than most men ever had." For this failure he gave, early and late, a number of reasons. Thus, he felt that his teaching at Harvard, his work as a literary editor and critic, perhaps even his erudition, tended to inhibit his creative faculties. "I know so well how certain things are done," he told a friend, "that I can't do them." Now and then he complained that the necessity of making his livelihood with his pen had left him little continuous leisure for doing his best work. He knew also that his remarkable fluency in composition, or what he called his tendency to "improvise," was hostile to real excellence. More than once he inveighed against his penchant for "preaching." But he comes closer to the truth when he confesses the natural "indolence" which underlay his random bursts of last-minute energizing. The number, bulk, and variety of his "Works" do not conceal the fact that we seldom find him really working. He postpones the labor of the mind with such experienced grace, he veers away from it with such a veteran skill, as almost to persuade us that labor has been done; but one need only watch him closely for a typical page or two in order to see how prone he is merely to quote and paraphrase and remember when he ought to be thinking.

Another source of Lowell's failure may have been that incorrigible youthfulness which he, like many of his countrymen, seems to have mistaken for a virtue. "I continue as juvenile as ever," he wrote to his daughter at the age of sixty-nine. "I was passing a Home for Incurable Children the other day, and said to my companion, 'I shall go there one of these days.'" "Happy the young poet who has the saving fault of exuberance," said Lowell, "if he have also the shaping faculty that will sooner or later amend it." But Lowell himself never acquired that faculty. His intellectual life was not a development but a long vagrancy. His poetry shows nothing like the growth to be seen, for example, in that of Longfellow.

At the end of his life Lowell did not overestimate the value of his own verse, but he often saw and said, quite truly, that it contained "good bits," or "a good strain here and there." These were usually connected in some way with the vivid sensuous images he had gathered in childhood, before he had loaded his mind with other men's words or thought it necessary to be witty or wise or persuasive. Occasionally he has the courage to let these "invitiate firstlings" stand alone, as in "The First Snow-Fall," "To the Dandelion," "The Courtin'," and "Sunthin' in the Pastoral Line," and at such times he is likely to make a good poem. For the most part, however, he embeds them in oddly incongruous contexts. In "The Vision of Sir Launfal," surely one of the worst constructed poems in English, he foists upon a story about a medieval knight a lavish description of June in Massachusetts; and he begins his poem about the Cathedral of Chartres still more "doubtfully and far away" with a hundred admirable lines about his childhood in Cambridge.

The *Biglow Papers,* written from the Yankee point of view and partly in a carefully studied Yankee dialect, owe their unmistakable vitality and tang to Lowell's deep love of home. The poems of the two series are uneven in quality, and some of them, now that the once-burning issues they discuss are nearly forgotten, are positively dull. There is little poetry in them. Their rattling verse, though often clever, is in no way distinguished. The rustic dialect often seems to be overlaid, as a veneer, upon habits of thought and feeling that are by no means rustic. Yet the *Biglow Papers* have more life in them than most of Lowell's work in verse because they give free play to his learning, his humor, and that inveterate provincialism which he had in common with Holmes.

Most of Lowell's more ambitious poems are products of a nimble, well stored, but undisciplined mind in quest of a topic and a poetic emotion. His "Rhoecus" and "Columbus" and "Endymion" leave no definite impression. The "Agassiz," though warmer, is also more garrulous. "The Present Crisis," once widely popular and often quoted in American pulpits, is a noisy and platitudinous declamation which owes as much to Emerson's thought as it does in versification to Tennyson's "Locksley Hall." The famous "Commemoration Ode" is superb versified oratory designed for a solemn public occasion.

Lowell's prose at its best, as in his always admirable letters, has a sparkle and effervescence. Like the prose of Holmes, it has the virtues of excellent talk. Yet it lacks continuity, and the effect of steady purposeful march. Of his criticism there have been conflicting opinions. J. J. Reilly concludes a book on the subject with the statement that Lowell is not a critic at all. Norman Foerster asserts that he had "the sanest and most comprehensive conception of literature formed in America prior to the twentieth century." These two opinions do not necessarily contradict each other, for it takes more than a sane and comprehensive conception of literature to make a critic. Lowell's theory of literature was undoubtedly sound, but his practice of it in his own writing and in his estimates of other writers was spasmodic, impressionistic, and inconsistent.

Lowell's influence upon literary scholarship and criticism in America has been deep and pervasive, but it has not been the influence of a mind that reaches firm conclusions and renders consistent judgments in accord with them. It has been the influence of a sensitive and volatile temperament indulging itself in a lifelong intellectual vagabondage. In the sheer enjoyment of literature—hearty, robust, and, at any rate with regard to writers of the past, open-minded—Lowell has only such men as Lamb and Hazlitt for equals, and he has no superiors. His love of books was his nearest approach to a passion, and his devotion to them came nearer than any other of his enthusiasms to giving his life a shape and a focus. Moreover he did a great deal, by precept and example and by the contagion of his own delight, to spread the love of books in America. This was his main contribution to the task of "transplanting European culture." Thus, like Longfellow and Holmes, he did in his own way the indispensable work of all sound conservatism—conservation.

36. MINORITY REPORT: THE TRADITION OF THE OLD SOUTH

Ɪꜰ the New England poets seemed to be engaged in a literary exercise when they borrowed an Old World glamour to cast over the American myth they were attempting to create, Southern writers seized upon the romance of feudalism with desperate seriousness in constructing their counter myth. As an earlier chapter has noted, the literature of the plantation South began in the 1830's as the expression of far-reaching changes in the Southern economy. The Industrial Revolution, creating an apparently limitless market for cotton in England and New England, had revived the declining institution of slavery, given fresh momentum to the expansion of the plantation system into the Southwestern interior, and transformed the South into one of the largest colonial areas yet seen in the world. The dominant note of these processes was rapidity of change. The whole history of that Old South which has survived in popular memory lasted only about thirty years before it was cut off by the outbreak of the war in 1861.

The literature of this society was evidently not allowed to reach fruition. Many of its impulses failed to develop beyond the stage of manifestoes and critical discussions. Furthermore, Southern writers were forced to struggle against a number of hampering influences, all of them noted by contemporary Southern critics. The most serious was the absence of cities that might have functioned as literary centers. If it is not quite true that the arts are a product of overcrowding, at least literature depends in modern times upon certain urban institutions—magazines, libraries, publishing houses. But the plantation economy of the South did not produce cities. This was a consequence of the colonial nature of that economy, which in another direction imposed upon the Southern writer a severe psychological handicap. No section of the United States had been able to develop enough self-confidence before 1820 to emerge from intellectual and literary dependence on Britain. In the South this state of affairs was indefinitely prolonged. Regardless of political forms, the region was a colony of Britain and of New England down to the Civil War. Jefferson Davis, in his First Inaugural, drew an explicit parallel between the position of the seceding Confederate States and that of the British colonies of 1776. One does not have to be a very energetic believer in economic causation to perceive the relationship between the South's economic position and its dependence on British and Northern literature.

Another consequence of the structure of Southern society was the exclusion of a majority of its peoples from the ranks of potential readers of books and magazines. The slaves were excluded as a matter of course. In addition, the meagerness of popular education in the South kept a large fraction of the white population illiterate. And the remaining potential audience, an often highly cultivated, aristocratic minority, had archaic tastes and was inclined to give the English classics preference over fumbling and uncertain writers like William Gilmore Simms who were trying to develop an American or a Southern literature. A writer in Hugh S. Legaré's *Southern Review* in 1831 deplored the growing evidence of a spirit of American literary nationalism, declaring, "We have no need of a separate literature." As for Southern writers, the critic was devastating:

The general feeling of aversion to authorship in the South, may be said to prevail, for the greater part, precisely in proportion to good education and cultivated taste.

To mention only one other difficulty in the path of the man of letters in the Old South, when he was given any encouragement at all he was usually exhorted to write according to a stated program. The critics who came to support the idea of a Southern literature made every effort to enlist the literary imagination in the service of a rigidly prescribed social goal—the defense of slavery, or at any rate of Southern society, against outside attack. While no important Southern writer rebelled against this imposed discipline —all of them, from Poe to Simms and John Esten Cooke, were defenders of slavery—one can at least guess that the steadily increasing sense of crisis and urgency, of the need to mobilize all forces to repel attack, interfered to some extent with free play of the imagination.

2

During the period 1830–1860, what were Southern writers able to achieve within these limitations? It can be said at once that the often demanded literary defense of the slave society was never adequately provided. When *Uncle Tom's Cabin* appeared in 1852, Southern critics winced. Here was no assault that could be met by analytical power or oratorical skill in the halls of Congress. The only defense, they realized, would be a comparable achievement on the plane of the imagination. But there was no Southern writer or school of writers capable of making this defense. The South lost the literary battle before actual hostilities began.

On the other hand, if the demand for a literary defense of slavery was not satisfied, Southern society between 1830 and 1860 did produce a far from negligible literature. Even more important was the fact that it set in motion certain trends which were pregnant with consequences for American literature and thought in later periods.

The most important literary achievement of the Old South was of course the work of Poe. The nightmare quality of Poe's recurrent symbols can be read—if one is so disposed—as testimony from the unconscious of a poet to the Southern sense of despair, of a lost battle and an imminent doom. Much of this quality proved capable of being transmitted to Europe, so that some imaginative energy originating in the experience of the Old South outlived the destruction of the slavery system as an element in French symbolism and its English and American consequences. Yet the work of Poe is not a finished achievement. In addition to its archaic strain of Gothicism and its cult of a rationalism derived from the Enlightenment but stripped of social implication, Poe's work shows a straining after effect, an ostentation of learning, in a word the touch of "vulgarity" noted by Aldous Huxley, that mark it as provincial.

The other permanently valuable literary achievement of the Old South makes a virtue of provincialism and vulgarity by pursuing them to their ultimate consequences in an intense localism of language, characters, and setting. The humor of the Old Southwest, product of the turbulent frontier of the cotton economy as it moved out into the Gulf plains of western Georgia and Alabama and Mississippi, overshadows the contemporary development of "Down East" humor both in imaginative power and in influence upon the future course of American literature. This frontier humor contained the germ of an American literary prose based upon the vernacular instead of upon a literary tradition. It likewise adumbrated the invention of local color literature after the Civil War. Most important of all, because embracing these impulses and going beyond them, was the contribution of Southwestern humor to a folk tradition destined to flower in Mark Twain. In assessing the potentialities latent in the Old South one must remember that Mark Twain grew up in a slaveholding community, that he served for a brief period in the Confederate Army, and that his greatest book, *Huckleberry Finn,* derives its central theme from slavery and is laid in slave territory. If Mark Twain meant to denounce the South, as at least on certain levels of his mind he did, his would not be the first instance of an artist formed by his gesture of protest against the society which produced him. It would probably be more discerning to see in him an ambivalence of attitude, a ferocious but artistically fruitful interplay of attraction and repulsion not unlike William Faulkner's attitude toward the South.

Except in a dozen poems of Poe, the vein of lyricism that runs through

Southern literature of this period is not often interesting. It produced a few poems that leave an odd impression of being happy incidents, yet the imposing presence of the sentimental Mrs. Hemans hovers everywhere over the scene. But in historical fiction the Southern achievement was more notable. The Southern disciples of Cooper include his principal American follower, William Gilmore Simms, and such epigoni as William Caruthers, John P. Kennedy, Philip Pendleton Cooke, and his better known brother John Esten Cooke. Indeed, the line of filiation that connects Cooper with the rebirth of historical romance near the end of the century in Maurice Thompson, Mary Johnston, and Winston Churchill is precisely this Southern succession. Cooper's adaptation of the Scott formula to American materials evidently had a special meaning for the South. For other regions Cooper was important because he discovered landscape and adventure in the American forest; for the South he was important because he discovered the past.

3

The best known early Southern novels in the Cooper tradition, such as Simms' and Kennedy's tales of the Revolution, were not markedly sectional in tone. Like the frontier, the Revolution was usually a national theme. The historical romance could not be made into an expression of sectional feeling unless some peculiarly Southern symbol could be discovered in the past. Such a symbol was the Virginia Cavalier. The development of the cult of the Cavalier on the plane of polemic discussion can be illustrated in the writings of Nathaniel Beverley Tucker, Professor of Law at William and Mary College, and one of the first generation of fire-eaters. When George Bancroft of Massachusetts began publishing his *History of the United States* in 1834, Tucker conceived the notion (a mistaken one, as it happened) that the historian had represented the seventeenth century Virginians as going over to the side of Parliament after the execution of Charles I. This seemed an intolerable insult, for Tucker took great pride in his ancestors' unswerving loyalty to the Stuarts.

There are those [he wrote] who will say that there is great arrogance in thus claiming for them a place among the generous and brave and faithful. Others will call it folly to insist, *at this day,* on their fidelity to a *king,* and especially to one who had lost all means of rewarding, or even of using their zeal.

But he demanded to be "allowed to speak of our fathers as they were." And the account of what they were is taut with meaning:

If we know anything (and we think we do) of the character of the early settlers of Virginia, they were a chivalrous and generous race, ever ready to resist the strong, to help the weak, to comfort the afflicted, and to lift up the fallen. In this spirit they had withstood the usurpation of Cromwell while resistance was practicable, and, when driven from their native country, they had bent their steps toward Virginia, as that part of the foreign dominions of England, where the spirit of loyalty was strongest. We learn from Holmes . . . that the population of Virginia increased about fifty per cent. during the troubles. The newcomers were loyalists, who were added to a population already loyal. Could *they*, without dishonor, have been hearty in favor of the new order of things? *They* whose principles had driven them into exile? *They* who, had they remained, would have fought and fallen with Montrose?

The bare facts were commonplace; Abiel Holmes of Cambridge, father of Oliver Wendell Holmes and author of *The Annals of America* to which Tucker refers, states that the increase in the population of Virginia from twenty to thirty thousand during the Civil War in England was due to the emigration of "cavaliers." But in Tucker's mind the fact has acquired portentous overtones. His Cavaliers are not merely chivalrous and generous; they are loyal with the crazy but pure loyalty of men devoted to a lost cause— perhaps for the precise reason that it is lost.

The character of the seventeenth century Cavalier is a crucial matter because it accounts for "those peculiarities which, at this moment, form the distinctive features of the Virginian character." The Virginian character is unique, and it is doomed:

How long it shall be before the *"march of mind,"* as it is called, in its Juggernaut car, shall pass over us, and crush and obliterate every trace of what our ancestors were, and what we ourselves have been, is hard to say. It may postpone that evil day, to resist any attempt to impress us with false notions of our early history, and the character of our ancestors.

It is important to keep in mind, finally, that the object of the Virginia Cavaliers' devotion was not intrinsically good:

None can feel more deeply than we do, how utterly unworthy of this steady and passionate loyalty, was the wretch who was its object. But they knew not his faults. They only knew him in his lineage and his misfortunes. . . . We are more proud to be descended from the men who stood forward in the business of that day, than we should be to trace ourselves to Adam, through all the most politic and prudent self-seekers that the world has ever seen.

The politic and prudent self-seekers are the New England descendants of the Cavaliers' Roundhead enemies, penny-pinching children of this world who will always triumph in their generation over the children of light. The Virginian's loyalty to the past, even though the past may be embodied in an indefensible institution like absolute monarchy (or slavery), isolates him in a modern world moving in a wrong course: the march of mind leaves him to one side and makes of him a more and more helpless minority. The Virginian's honor, in fact, reaches its full development and becomes entirely pure only as it binds him to a lost cause and a drooping banner. From this point of view, the economic prosperity of the North was simply a tradesmen's vulgarity.

Although Tucker's thought was centered in Virginia, the symbol of the Cavalier could easily be expanded to shed its glory on all the South. In 1843 an anonymous writer in the *Southern Literary Messenger* announced:

A chivalrous daring—a spirit that may break but never bend—an estimate placed upon individual honor which counts all else as dust in the balance—virtues, such as these, are the peculiar birthright of the Southern people. They hold them as a direct inheritance from that bold race of cavaliers who emigrated from all parts of Europe and settled in the Southern colonies. Nor have they been impaired in the transmission.

The myth of the Cavalier lent itself admirably to literary use through the historical romance; indeed, the suggestion has often been made that it was an outgrowth of historical fiction in the first place, especially the novels of Scott and Bulwer-Lytton, so that the adaptability of the symbol to literary use is hardly surprising. At any rate, the Virginia Cavalier makes his entrance into fiction in the 1830's, concurrently with the general antidemocratic revolution in Southern thought. The first historical romance exploring the theory of Cavalier origins was William Caruthers' *The Cavaliers of Virginia* (1834–1835), dealing with the period of Bacon's Rebellion, a determined but wooden effort to say through the mechanism of plot and characters what Tucker was saying through his expository treatment of seventeenth century history. Yet if the historical novel in the Cooper tradition gave ample scope for swashbuckling adventure in the remote past, it was not an ideal form for celebrating the virtues of a contemporary society based on slavery. The value to be defended was not physical courage or aristocratic swagger, but a system of social relationships—the pastoral bliss of an orderly feudal regime. To this end the sentimental tradition was much more efficacious. The mood of Irving had somehow to be incorporated into the narrative framework of Cooper.

The sentimental treatment of the Southern plantation, without the narrative framework of the historical romance, made its first significant appearance in Kennedy's loosely constructed, Irvingesque sketches grouped under the title

Swallow Barn (1832). Given some development by Tucker in his *George Balcombe* and *The Partisan Leader,* both published in 1836, and by Philip Pendleton Cooke, as in his novelette "The Two Country Houses" (1848), the theme of the social unit of the plantation comprising devoted slaves, gallant masters, and spirited heroines was ready for merging with the historical romance of adventure in John Esten Cooke's novels. In a single year, 1854, Cooke brought out three novels—*Leather Stocking and Silk* (with a "stalwart mountaineer," John Myers, "the living type of the old border past," as an explicit reference to Cooper), *The Virginia Comedians,* and *The Youth of Jefferson.* Stilted as these romances seem to a modern reader, they carried great conviction to an age accustomed to a constant seasoning of sentimentalism in its fiction, and above all they had a pointed relevance to the sectional tensions that dominated the public mind in the year of the Kansas and Nebraska Act. Cooke merely glances at the institution of slavery, but it is everywhere presupposed, whether the setting be eighteenth century Williamsburg or the Virginia back country a hundred years later; and the glimpses of it that we get always reveal happy, indolent slaves bound to their masters by the strongest ties of affection.

Cooke's career, bisected by the Civil War, carried the plantation formula on down into a period of intensified nostalgia when a new generation of Southern writers captained by Thomas Nelson Page found a national audience for fiction dreamily recounting the virtues of the institution of slavery which the nation had just spent four years of agony to destroy. A close examination of this paradoxical phenomenon will suggest the final contribution of the prewar Southern tradition to American literary and intellectual history. For the pleasure which readers in all sections during the seventies and eighties took in stories about a vanished Golden Age in the South seems almost certainly a reaction against the ugly adolescence of Big Business. The theme of the plantation embodied graces and social harmonies to which an urban industrial society could not aspire. Although the point was obscured in the sentimental haze of plantation fiction, the feudal and now defunct Old South had embodied the only serious challenge to the triumph of finance and industry in American society.

4

It was true, as antislavery propagandists declared, that slavery was an unendurable anachronism in the modern world, a wickedness outmoded for more than a thousand years. The affirmations of Southern social theory were of little consequence because they were exercises in rationalizing an indefensible institution. But the negations implicit in the Southern tradition were much more valid. The apologists for slavery called attention to weaknesses in the Northern position that were likely to go unnoticed precisely because they were a part of the dominant "march of mind." For Northern thinkers as well as Southern were victims of the sectional rivalry. Few of them could resist reading in the depravity of the South a contrasting virtue in their own section. If the issue was between slavery and free labor, and if slavery was wrong, then free labor was right. And free labor implied the entire system of industrial capitalism.

But was the Industrial Revolution indeed an unqualified blessing, the glittering goal of the march of mankind up from the jungle? The Southerners were prepared to say no. Reports of Parliamentary hearings on the appalling misery of British industrial workers during the thirties—which were to provide so much of the documentation for the denunciatory passages of Karl Marx's *Capital*—and the scattering accounts of comparable conditions in American cities published by pioneer philanthropists in the same decade threw a somber light on the outcome of industrialization. It was not yet time for an American to declare that progress brings poverty, but the most astute apologists for slavery were beginning as early as the forties to proclaim "the failure of free society."

On the other hand, they were far from being in agreement with the Northern reformers who were likewise pointing to the evil consequences of industrialism. Southern thinkers considered all Utopian schemes for social reform futile and dangerous. Horrible as the ills of free society might be, they could not be alleviated by the remedies proposed in philanthropic programs. George Fitzhugh, the Virginia lawyer who proved to be the most fertile Southern polemicist, perceived that when the reformers denounced industrial society in the name of the "sovereignty of the individual," they were but carrying to an extreme the ideas which the school of Adam Smith had taken over from John Locke. Their programs, however various, could be enacted only after they had "dissolved and disintegrated society, and reduced mankind to separate, independent, but conflicting monads, or human atoms." An argument similar to that of Fitzhugh's *Cannibals All! or, Slaves Without Masters* (1857) was directed especially against Herbert Spencer's *Social Statics*, by George Frederick Holmes in *DeBow's Review* of the same year. The Southern case against industrial capitalism rested on exactly opposite premises. In its most telling form it proclaimed an alternative to the anarchy of individualistic competition in an organic theory of society. This Aristotelian insight lay at the base of what was permanently interesting in Calhoun's political theory, as distinguished from his fantastic checks and balances. Fitzhugh, with the not always happy aid of Carlyle, fumbled toward it once or twice.

Man, and all other social and gregarious animals [he wrote], have a community of thought, of motions [*sc.* emotions?], instincts and intuitions. The social body is of itself a thinking, acting, sentient being. . . . The great error of modern philosophy is the ignorance or forgetfulness of this fact.

But the thinkers of the Old South did not carry through their repudiation of liberalism, perhaps because it constantly led them against their will toward the general position of the Utopians. After the Civil War, the leaders of Southern thought were even less inclined to challenge the business economy. In return for the tacit but important Northern surrender of the problem of the Negro to Southern handling, the New South group led by Henry W. Grady took over the doctrines of Northern capitalism and energetically set about industrializing the South. The ideas of most articulate Southerners became indistinguishable from those of official Republican spokesmen except for an occasional polite difference of opinion about the tariff.

The logic of Southern dissidence was nevertheless still there, and after the War it was acknowledged by some of the most perceptive minds that appeared in this country during the nineteenth century. In order to throw into relief the corrupt political practices of Senator Silas P. Ratcliffe of Illinois, "The Prairie Giant of Peonia," Henry Adams chooses as the hero of his novel *Democracy* (1880) John Carrington, a Virginian "of the old Washington school" and a veteran of the Confederate Army. Carrington exposes Ratcliffe to Mrs. Lightfoot Lee, the heroine, and at the end of the novel receives the author's stamp of approval by being designated as a probably successful suitor for Mrs. Lee's hand. It is clear that Adams found in the Southern tradition some support for his repudiation of the politics of postwar America. Henry James' *The Bostonians* (1886) also has a Southerner for a hero. Basil Ransom of Mississippi succeeds in rescuing the heroine Verena Tarrant from the "mediums, and spirit-rappers, and roaring radicals" who are the heirs of the New England tradition of social reform. The conservative Southerner's freedom from shallow fads masquerading as philanthropy is held up as a saving principle of health. The reformers of the second generation are, by implication, either frauds or neurotics.

Most interesting of all is Melville's use of the Southern point of view in his long narrative poem *Clarel* (1876). Through the lips of Ungar, "the clouded man," an expatriate and unreconstructed Southern soldier of fortune, the author utters the bitterest of his diatribes against American society in a period of "sordid mercenary sin." In turn Ungar denounces mill owners who destroy children for the sake of profits, social reform, the idea of democracy ("Arch strumpet of an impious age"), and universal suffrage. When another character urges technological advance as evidence of Progress, Ungar exclaims,

> Your arts advance in faith's decay:
> You are but drilling the new Hun.

In the future Ungar sees "a civic barbarism," with

> Man disennobled—brutalized
> By popular science—atheized
> Into a smatterer—

a "dead level of rank commonplace," "an Anglo-Saxon China" which

> May on your vast plains shame the race
> In the Dark Ages of Democracy.

Without raising the question whether a society based on Negro slavery would be preferable, one can readily acknowledge that Melville's Ungar is the intellectual heir of the Tuckers and Holmeses and Fitzhughs of the Old South.

5

The implications of the Southern tradition which Adams, James, and Melville perceived were phases of a minority protest—a suspicion of humanitarian enthusiasms, a revulsion from the practical politics of democracy, a skepticism concerning the outcome of scientific and technological "progress." Its affirmations—its concern for intellectual distinction and for a religious view of man—were not so fully worked out.

One of the first evidences that the tradition of the Old South was thus moving in postwar Southern writers themselves from a nostalgia for a lost era to a protest against an industrial economy appeared in the poems of Sidney Lanier, "Trade" and "The Symphony." Lanier reflected both aspects of the tradition, as well as the concern for technique that seems, in some unexplained way, to have been its constant by-product from Poe to the present. There were, however, too many romantic elements in Lanier's agrarianism to make it more than a portent.

The tradition as a mature cultural phenomenon came to the surface in the twentieth century in the Nashville Agrarians. The Agrarian movement had its inception soon after the First World War in a group of teachers and students associated with John Crowe Ransom at Vanderbilt University who called themselves "Fugitives" and devoted themselves to writing and discussing poetry. The Fugitives were not consciously sectional in their program, but several of them later became leaders in an effort to restore an economy of subsistence agriculture in the South as a means of escape from the ills of industrialism. Besides a manifesto published in 1930 under the title *I'll Take My Stand,* the Agrarians have written such books as Ransom's *God Without Thunder* (a critique of "liberal" Christianity), Allen Tate's *Reactionary Essays on Poetry and Ideas,* and Donald Davidson's *The Attack on Leviathan.* Although it is difficult to conceive of a Southern movement of any kind that is not in some way political, the Agrarians have found a much wider audience for their theories of literary criticism than for their political ideas. In the *Southern Review,* edited at Louisiana State University by Cleanth Brooks and Robert Penn Warren during the later 1930's, the Agrarian program for the South was overshadowed by a nonsectional concern with aesthetics, especially with the interpretation of "difficult" contemporary poetry. The *Southern Review's* successor, the *Kenyon Review,* edited by Ransom since 1939 at Kenyon College in Ohio, could not be called Southern in tone.

Although by the middle forties many of the Agrarians had left the South and were dispersed as teachers in colleges in the North, they and their allies had by that time published a body of writing which for its consistency of tone and intention is unique in American literature. In the novels of Robert Penn Warren and Caroline Gordon and in the poems of Tate, Warren, and Ransom, voices from the Old South are heard again eighty years after the surrender at Appomattox. If to the work of these writers is added the fiction of William Faulkner and Katherine Anne Porter and of a host of lesser figures, it becomes evident that the South too has had its literary renaissance, though it was long delayed.

37. HEARD FROM THE NEW WORLD

By the end of the Civil War most literate Americans were beginning to be aware of the fact that there was already in existence an American literature. There was no longer need for protestations of cultural independence or demand for the appearance of native authors. A cycle of literary growth, coincident with the rise of a Romantic Movement and deriving its chief inspiration from the matured civilization of the Atlantic seaboard, had reached the stage in which its authors were recognized for their intrinsic worth rather than merely as spokesmen for an experiment in political theory. The reputations of Irving and Cooper were secure. Hawthorne, who had died just before the war ended, had his first measure of fame. Emerson's followers were often idolaters. Even Poe, dead at forty in 1849, had ceased to be notorious and was beginning to look like a classic. It was evident, too, that the younger men—Longfellow, Holmes, and Lowell—were carrying on what had by now become a tradition. The niches in the pantheon of American authors were filling rapidly.

Certainly this sense of achievement and fulfillment was strengthened by the change of attitude toward American writing on the part of European critics, creative writers, and even the mass of readers. In the early part of the century European liberals who wished America well could only hope that some day the magnificence of our experience would find its poets and novelists. By the time of the Civil War their hope had been justified.

A library not yet written would be needed to contain the history of the reception and influence in Europe of the classics of nineteenth century American literature. Thus far European scholars have had more will and energy for the task than have English or American scholars. It is a story that involves both the excitement and the apprehension of Europe and England over our democratic experiment, and it goes beyond the world of letters into every world of the mind. Of the digesting of reviews and articles, of bibliographical inventory, of the influence of one author on another, we have much; but we must have more before coherent literary history can be written. Here an outline alone can be laid down, from the evidence thus far collected.

At the beginning of the century the European, however he might be

618

engaged by the spectacle of the political experiment across the Atlantic, could feel little obligation to deal with American literature, for he found none— practically none—to deal with. The British critics were not alone in their denial of our possession of a literature. In Tocqueville, Chasles, and lesser commentators there persisted a graver speculation: perhaps a democracy, by definition, cannot produce a literature. Not, at any rate, until it achieves a society. America had thoughts for poetry, yes, but the poetry that America wrote was European.

Carlyle wrote to Emerson of the lean tough Yankee settlers steering over the Western mountains with unsubduable fire in their bellies, and every eager European critic felt the splendor of the American myth. If he were English, he was inclined to discount its possibilities for literature; if he were continental, he would deplore our Anglophile timidity, and remind us that until we should throw off our mother ties, we could have no hope for a literature of our own.

As has been said in an earlier chapter in this work, the great fact to the European was not what America wrote, but what America was. It was fixed in the general imagination as the land of great forests and mighty rivers where the Red Man still contended with the pioneer. It was also fixed, in Goethe's words, as "the Eldorado of all who found themselves restricted in their present circumstances." Brighter than the promise of romantic scenery was the promise of a decent life, lived in innocence and freedom. Was America's democracy workable? Could the dignity and worth of the common man find there its true chance for fruition, unblighted alike by political tyranny and the sharper tyranny of caste? This was the great question. It was not for beautiful letters that Europe looked to America; it was for a better life.

For this reason the books and pamphlets of the new country, the countless travelers' reports (more than three hundred from England alone up to 1860), the flooding stream of letters from emigrants, were scrutinized not as literature but as documentation. If Europe was done with, as Jefferson had thought, and America was indeed the symbol of freedom, then our derivative literature need not matter. This was a shortsighted view, and Emerson was not the first to see that the whole inner strength of a people is revealed in its imaginative genius; but in the beginning criticism was bound to turn to our political and social expression. Even Cooper declared that the only peculiarity of American literature was its distinctive political opinion, and that in taste and form English and American literature must be fashioned after the same models.

As political expression American literature received high praise from the time that Lord Chatham admired the papers of the American Congress of

October, 1774. Before the War of 1812, American histories, state papers, and congressional reports had good sales in England, and biographical studies of the founding fathers were eagerly sought. Washington and Franklin were Europe's heroes—the choice of Goethe, her greatest poet, and Sainte-Beuve, her most influential critic. Political judgment of course controlled the British magazines. The *Edinburgh Review,* brilliant and caustic, was actually less harsh toward American literature than toward more immediate targets at home. Its Tory rival, the *Quarterly Review,* like the *Anti-Jacobin* review and the *Literary Gazette,* deliberately baited all things democratic. *Blackwood's* and the *Athenaeum* were tolerant but patronizing, and the *Westminster Review* could be even extravagant in praise. Organs of the Established Church were stand-offish, and the dissenting journals were inclined to be friendly. Literary opinion was party opinion.

This is not to say that Europe and the mother country were wholly oblivious of a native literature. On the contrary. The Connecticut Wits who had set out to furnish it were rated in England beyond their strict desert. Joel Barlow's inflated *Columbiad* received respectful British reviews, and so did Timothy Dwight's *Conquest of Canaan,* although the English knew it to be feeble stuff. John Trumbull's *M'Fingal* had the best hand of all, as it deserved. Charles Brockden Brown won European praise early, the London edition of his works calling forth a good deal of talk about neglected American genius. Brown was an author's author. Percy and Mary Shelley fed on his romances, Keats praised him, Scott admitted his "wonderful powers," Hazlitt thought him a real genius. John Neal, American journalist extraordinary, creating his own "American literature" in his *Blackwood's* articles of 1824 and 1825, was proud to say that only Brown, Paulding, and himself were the genuine American article. A true forerunner of Hawthorne, Brown was read widely in Germany and France where his best work was recognized as "a conscientious study of the heart of man, of its mysterious raging, its resistless flights."

2

By the end of the War of 1812 American literature was already enough of an entity to pose the great question of its real existence, a question over which was to rage an unholy war whose fires were dampened but not extinguished in the burgeoning years from 1820 onward. It was largely England's war, not Europe's, for only a parent could take the issue so to heart. The English, alarmed alike by our competitive power and their own loss from emigration, were quick to impugn our nationalism, quick to see our almost morbid desire to have it confirmed. On our side the issue of a native literature at once became confused with the issue of patriotism. The quarrelsome aspects of the problem, with its jaded and tedious history of English abuse and American deference, need not detain us here. Across the Atlantic too much talk came from bookmen who had little information about America, and wanted none. In this country too much came from aroused patriots. Therefore most of it had nothing to do with genuine critical insight, which would have been concerned with the effect of the American experience upon imaginative expression.

The major documents in the case—Irving's "English Writers on America (1820), Bryant's "Lectures on Poetry" (1826), Channing's "On National Literature" (1830), Longfellow's "The Defence of Poetry" (1832), Emerson's *American Scholar* (1837), Melville's "Hawthorne and His Mosses" (1850), Thoreau's essays, Whitman's *Democratic Vistas* (1871), and the whole import of their other writings—are evidence that these men understood how vital it was to evaluate American literature in terms of the forces which shaped it at home. The writers of magnitude were nourished more by their differences from anything in Europe than by their similarities; and foreign influence upon them was powerful only as it accorded with native purpose. They could not but question what the European took as a matter of course, and instead of showing that American literature is only English literature written in America, their work shows that all influences which make the total experience of a nation must shape its expression.

They were in the current of the future, but against them were opposed powerful countercurrents. One was the persistent American nostalgia for the old European culture, for the institutions and forms of a traditional society with its high civilization and picturesque accompaniments. This adoration of the old was so plain in the pages of Irving and Willis that Englishmen were amused by the American worship of ways which they were passing by. In later years Howells spoke contemptuously of those American romancers who tried to be little Londoners. The little Londoners were rife in American cultural centers, especially in the colleges where American literature was largely ignored until the end of the century.

The copyright problem, of course, accentuated our dependence on the foreign market. One of Emerson's English friends remarked, "As long as you do not grant us copyright, we shall have the teaching of you"; and he was right, for the lack of an effective international agreement meant that not only the English rights of American authors were ignored, but the American market was flooded with pirated English books, many of them reprinted in cheap "mammoth" newspapers. In vain did both American and English authors protest. Under piracy the printers made money, and from them came the specious cry of free books for free men and the foolish charge that international copyright would turn the native business to foreign control. Not until 1891 was a comparatively decent copyright act written into American law.

Despite the injustice there were gains. American authors, injured in the book market by pirated English competition, turned to the American magazines, which not only developed the short story to a superb technique but became so stimulating that they were frankly imitated in England. Unquestionably, the international reputation of authors like Poe, Willis, and Longfellow was immeasurably increased by piracy, which also made possible the enormous traffic in English reprints of "cheap book" series of American authors by British publishers. The same story held true on a lesser scale in France, and in Germany where the Tauchnitz series swelled the account.

Irving was the first American author to interest all Europe. We are inclined to forget how powerfully he influenced his time, how he set in motion a whole school of imitators—Willis, Paulding, Longfellow, Kennedy, Cooke— but his contemporaries knew it, even those who, like Emerson and Poe, felt his limitations.

Salmagundi and *A History of New York* had delighted Coleridge, Byron, and Scott; but neither they nor Irving's other English readers were prepared for the spectacular success of *The Sketch Book*, which in 1820 precipitated the mood of an age. Samuel Rogers could cry, "Addison and water!" as Melville was later to cry, "An appendix to Goldsmith!" but Irving had really found a manner that was never to lose its adjustment to the popular response. The British were surprised that he could write so pure an English, and the Americans were proud that he did. *The Sketch Book* was the beginning of Irving's international reputation. John Murray, who had refused it, offered 1,200 guineas for its successor *Bracebridge Hall* (1822), and both books were quickly translated into French and German. Presently Irving found himself admired as a great man of letters in London, Dresden, and Paris.

Goethe read him although he preferred Cooper; Heine praised him, the Queen of Saxony hoped he would do a "Bracebridge Hall" for her own country. Irving hoped so, too, and tirelessly collected the legends which were to go into the *Tales of a Traveller* (1824). The Germans, who had regarded him as an English purveyor of English legends, were pleased that the *Tales* was allegedly indebted to Teutonic sources, but the English critics damned it so heartily for the same reason that Irving found little comfort in Murray's 1,500 guineas. The *Tales* was indeed a flawed performance, but now no single failure could halt the momentum of Irving's reputation. The *Collected Works* began to be edited in Frankfort by 1826, and in France the translations mounted steadily, thirty-eight separate editions being published by

1842. There were dissenting voices, of course—critics who thought he made the most of "a small talent and a small spirit." Nevertheless Irving was a standard author, and on European terms. This was his chief glory to many Americans, though not to Cooper, who thought him a sycophant.

In Spain, from whose history five of his books were to come, and where his skill as a diplomat was greatly respected, he had a surprisingly slight audience. *The Alhambra* (1832) did not appear in a complete Spanish version until 1888 although some of its tales, as well as adaptations from *The Sketch Book,* appeared in separate translations. Both *A History of the Life and Voyages of Columbus* (1828) and *The Conquest of Granada* (1829) were agreeably received, but the fact is that Irving's Spanish editions make a small showing, and Spanish knowledge of him came largely from French translations. The Spanish admired Irving, but they do not appear to have read him. Nevertheless, Irving has continued to live in all the European countries, even in Russia where his books have been popular since the Revolution.

Irving's European reputation began under English auspices and thrived on English prestige, but Cooper's began with the rejection of English imitation and disdain of foreign opinion. He resented the charge that his success at home was owed to his success abroad, and he resented even more the label of "The American Scott," which became a stereotype not only of English but of French, German, Spanish, and Italian critics as well. For six years he carried a chip on his shoulder through Europe, and when he returned it was still there. He was a social critic, who wanted Europe to know the characteristics of the American man, and America to know those of the gentleman. It was ironical, then, that his prodigious renown rested only upon the spell of his forests and prairies, his Indians and pioneers, but it was a powerful enchantment. From the first he appealed to the European as a great teller of tales, whose stylistic blemishes were lost in translation, and whose readers cared nothing for the opinions of critics.

When Cooper went to Europe in 1826 to get foreign rights for his books he was just in time. By 1829 all his first six novels had been published in England and translated into French and German as well as Italian, Danish, and Swedish. Four years later he was being marketed in thirty-four European cities. He was mighty on the Continent, but in England he ran into stormy weather. His honest *Notions of the Americans* (1828) pleased neither the English nor the Americans. Where Irving had been suave he was militant. He exulted that the American people cared no more for a lord than a woodchuck, and in his *Gleanings in Europe* (1837) he continued to offend. Despite the critics' war, Cooper never lost the regard of England's authors who, from Scott to Conrad, have praised his creative power. At least fifty editions of his work appeared in England in the last twenty years of the nineteenth century, and generations of English schoolboys have played Indian because they read Cooper.

In Germany his novels confirmed in young minds the romantic America of Chateaubriand. After *The Spy* and *The Pioneers* appeared in 1824, the translations multiplied until by 1850 there were more than a hundred, and a whole school of German novelists were influenced by him. In France there was the same ardent appreciation, especially from Balzac, and the mystery of Cooper's forests, the outlawry of his savages has been felt in the pages of Hugo, Dumas père, and many other French romancers. Although *The Bravo* (1831) was bitterly attacked in Italy as misrepresenting the tyranny of Venice, both this novel and others were read by Italians who took their knowledge of America from Cooper's stories. In Spain, where his novels were taken from French versions, he received little serious criticism, but he was read more widely than Poe. His full fame, arriving with the Madrid publication of *The Red Rover* in 1839, lasted for two decades. In Russia, where he was hailed by the powerful critic Belinsky in 1839, he has long been standard, thirty-two Russian editions appearing by 1927. To Russia, as to all Europe, Cooper's fame rests on his entrancing portrayal of a primeval America.

3

In mid-century, 1852, the fabulous reception of *Uncle Tom's Cabin* began in piracy and exploded into unequaled drama. Mrs. Stowe had herself prepared it by sending copies to England's great—Prince Albert, Dickens, Macaulay, Kingsley, and others—and kept it at top pitch by her triumphal tours abroad. One publisher among the forty who issued it in England estimated the aggregate English sales at a million and a half copies, most of them unauthorized. In fact, the book's phenomenal success inaugurated the best-seller era in England. British song writers flooded the market with tearful lyrics about slavery, and queues lined up at London theaters to see *Uncle Tom* dramatized—"Tom-mania," pronounced the *Spectator*. In England both *Uncle Tom* and *Dred* (1856), which sold 100,000 copies in four weeks, became arguments in the campaign for the emancipation of English labor that ended in the Reform Act of 1867. Even Mrs. Stowe's notorious attack on Lord Byron, the most widely discussed article in nineteenth century England, could not halt her march. She herself thought the French had a finer appreciation of her "subtle shades of meaning" than the English. And no wonder. George Sand dismissed the question of talent to call her a genius. Alfred de Musset cried, "This leaves us all behind—all, all, leagues behind!" Turgenev was charmed to meet her in Paris where *Uncle Tom* was serialized daily. At the same time a dozen other European countries were taking it up, and the exiled Heine avowed that he knelt with his black brother in prayer. From Sweden Fredrika Bremer wrote to Mrs. Stowe of its serialization in the Stockholm press. The authorized biography of Mrs. Stowe lists translations of *Uncle Tom* in twenty languages from Armenian to Welsh, omitting Hindu and Javanese which also exist. In Russia no other foreign book has enjoyed such a sympathetic audience as *Uncle Tom,* which first appeared in 1857, and has had many stage versions, including Communistic adaptations.

Mrs. Stowe moved the heart of Europe, but Emerson moved its mind. He knew that "the soul makes its own world," and his profound individualism absorbed whatever in European thinking confirmed his own faith. He had responded to the muscularity of seventeenth century English literature, and to Coleridge and Carlyle. He read Kant as early as 1820, Goethe in 1834, Böhme and Swedenborg by 1835, Jacobi, Schleiermacher, Schelling, Hegel, and Michelet in the thirties and forties. All these were voices to be listened to, but to be obeyed only at the soul's prompting. His own voice was demanding its listeners.

In England the listeners were at first the ardent younger men who had set forth or were about to set forth upon their own crusades: Carlyle, who through the long years could never forget the "clear high melody" of the American voice; Matthew Arnold, who heard the voice at Oxford, and who was to call the *Essays* the most important work done in prose during the century; Clough, who thought Emerson to be the only profound man in America; Froude, who credited Emerson with breaking from him the fetters of the church; John Sterling, to whom he was "the teacher of starry wisdom"; Spencer, who wanted Emerson's judgment on his philosophy; Tyndall, who avowed, "Whatever I have done the world owes to him." And there were others equal to the giants in their discipleship, such as George Searle Phillips, whose 1855 study of Emerson—*Emerson, his Life and Writings*—was the earliest in print, and Alexander Ireland of Edinburgh whose insistence brought on the famous tours of 1847 and 1848 that introduced Emerson to the English. In twenty-five towns Emerson lectured sixty-four times to audiences largely composed of the members of the Mechanics' Institutes. Along with the wealthier sponsors were the rank and file, the unprofessional people whose support was more significant than the fashionable following in London. In the long run Emerson's English reputation was solidly grounded among the dissenters—the Unitarians and the Reformists, who read him as sacred literature.

On the Continent Emerson's influence was felt from the time the Polish revolutionary poet Mickiewicz lent *Nature* in 1838 to the brilliant French historian Edgar Quinet; and when these two men, together with Michelet, began attacking Jesuitism at the Collège de France a few years later, they found in Emerson's principles a powerful ally. Mickiewicz also inspired the Countess d'Agoult, who published in July, 1846, the first French estimate entirely devoted to Emerson, although Chasles and Montégut were already discussing him in their reviews. A generation later another woman disciple, Marie Mali, who belonged to an advanced coterie in Brussels including Maeterlinck, Verhaeren, Verlaine, and Vielé-Griffin, initiated a Belgian vogue for Emerson. Her *Sept Essais d'Emerson* (1894), introduced by Maeterlinck, was a weapon against European pessimism. Emerson's power over French thought is widely dispersed—in the meditations of Amiel, in the creative philosophy of Bergson, in French liberal Protestantism, even in the desperate attempts of Baudelaire to find a guiding principle. Some of this influence carried over to Spain, where no editions of his work were published before 1900, but where he was read in French translation. The best Spanish criticism of Emerson belongs to the twentieth century, particularly Cebriá-Montoliu's introduction (1910) to the Catalan version of *Self-Reliance* and *Friendship*.

In Germany where Emerson was studied by many scholars his most loyal disciple was Hermann Grimm, his most influential was Friedrich Nietzsche. Grimm published an essay on Emerson six years after he first came upon the writings where he found his "own secret thoughts." There followed a warm correspondence between the two men, culminating in a meeting at Florence in 1873. Nietzsche, exiled at Pforta, came upon Emerson's essays in 1874, and, like Grimm, found thoughts he could not distinguish from his own— the gay wisdom of his own Zarathustra. Tolstoi felt Emerson's force in Russia, and from Indian leaders came testimony of the closeness of his thought to Hindu philosophy. The light from Concord had gone round the world.

Emerson traveled and lectured abroad; Thoreau, who traveled much in Concord, stayed at home. Nevertheless the light of his *Dial* essays and the later lectures was visible across the Atlantic, and *Walden* was to be often reprinted in England and translated abroad. Hawthorne rejoiced that it was one of the few works he could recommend to the English as having original American characteristics. The book became a bible of the English labor movement, deeply influencing Blatchford's *Merrie England* (1895), which sold two million copies; and Gandhi, a half-century after Thoreau's death, found his "Civil Disobedience" to be a weapon in his hand.

Foreign criticism rarely made Lowell's mistake of regarding Thoreau as a lesser Emerson. Tolstoi marked nearly every page of *Walden*; George Eliot found plenty of sturdy sense in his unworldliness; Stevenson, trying to reduce him to one word—"skulker"—confessed that he could scarcely write a sentence which would not show the influence of Thoreau; Froude saw in his pages hope for the coming world; and Thoreau's English biographer A. H. Japp could not but regard him as a sort of nineteenth century St. Francis. Yeats tells how his father's reading from *Walden* induced the boyhood dream of Innisfree, and in France Proust wrote of his admirable pages. It was an Englishman, Thoreau's friend Thomas Cholmondeley, who gave him his most valued gift from abroad, a library of Hindu classics, and another Englishman, H. S. Salt, who in 1890 published the first sound biography of Thoreau.

There were hostile gestures too. Thoreau was a strange bird to others besides Stevenson who, like Watts-Dunton, thought him as bizarre as Hawthorne's Donatello. Yet his strangeness and his strength alike have cut across boundaries in a way that his own time, not fully aware of his edge, could hardly predict; and it is not surprising to learn that, of all writers in English, Thoreau translates with least loss of value into Chinese.

No European critic of Hawthorne had the fiery penetration into his work of his own countryman, Melville, but both of them found perceptive readers abroad. To Europe Hawthorne has been from the beginning a man of high artistry whose prose has been analyzed with delight by minds as diverse as Arnold, Trollope, and George Moore. In the fifties he sold rather better in England than at home, his novels creating the high excitement there that the Brontës had aroused but a few years before. By 1851 five English editions of *Twice-Told Tales,* three of *The Scarlet Letter,* and two of *The House of the Seven Gables* had appeared. Only *Our Old Home* (1863) was to displease the English, a reaction surprising to Hawthorne, who thought his occasional sardonic reflections had not concealed an underlying affection. But abroad he was, like Cooper, a sensitive provincial who half resented the undeniable attraction of Europe. He was really never happy abroad, he especially distrusted the Italian scene, and his one novel about Europe, *The Marble Faun* (1860), while it sold better in England than in America, was felt to be a disappointment, though an admirable guide to Italy.

The French were also reading his stories in the fifties, one of them being plagiarized by the elder Dumas. Among early critics the most acute were Montégut, who felt Hawthorne's melancholy, and E. D. Forgues, who especially admired *The Scarlet Letter.* In him as in Poe the symbolists were later to find provocations to fantasy. The Spanish translated him early and enthusiastically, relying for once not on French hack work, but deriving their versions from Germany where *The Scarlet Letter* and *The House of the Seven Gables* appeared in 1851. For many years *The Wonder Book* has been read in the primary schools of Argentina and Chile; and it is also popular in Russia. Almost all of Hawthorne appeared in Russia in the ten years following 1852, and the evidence is clear that Dostoevski felt his influence as a great explorer of the conscience.

About Melville has grown the erroneous legend of a hostile reception both here and abroad. Actually *Typee* (1846) and *Omoo* (1847) were acclaimed in England as lively travel fiction; and when Melville went there in 1849, having published *Mardi* and *Redburn* and about to publish *White-Jacket,* he was entertained by the celebrities of the literary world. Only the sectarian journals had not liked *Typee* and *Omoo* because these tales had satirized the South Sea missionaries. *Mardi* troubled some of the critics with its allegorical thrusts at English imperialism, *White-Jacket* pleased nearly everybody, and so did *Redburn*. Across the channel Chasles and Forgues wrote of him in the *Revue des Deux Mondes*. Melville was being "typed" as a writer of adventure stories, and nobody was prepared for the monstrous apparition of *Moby-Dick*. In England it was called *The Whale,* and although the book was bowdlerized it was still monstrous. The critics on both sides of the Atlantic were dismayed, but of three friendly reviews one was English —the *London Leader* asking, "Who knows the terrors of the seas like Herman Melville?" But as Melville reached the height of his powers, the critics fell away. With the affronting *Pierre* (1852) his following disappeared, and he was never to know its inevitable return, although he continued to have a subterranean reputation among discriminating readers.

On the Continent Melville had been neglected, the first full study of him in a foreign language—K. H. Sundermann's *Herman Melvilles Gedankengut* —not appearing until 1937. But in England, as more belatedly in this country, his genius has demanded its followers, who have passed their discovery on to others. In this way, he has been sought and praised by a company of English admirers whose words are worth seeking out: Thomson, Morris, Salt, Dobell, Birrell, Lucas, Forster, Tomlinson, Meynell, Woolf—others. Melville's Pierre had learned that mediocrity and commonplace "hath its fire and sword for all contemporary Grandeur." Melville was in this respect Pierre, but time has revenged him.

4

Melville was a candidate for the future. Not so Longfellow, who was the poet—in Whitman's words—of the mellow twilight of the past in Italy, Germany, Spain, and northern Europe. New England's other bards—Lowell, with his immense prestige in the fashionable world; Holmes, who shared with Lowell first honors as a transatlantic wit; Whittier, who followed next in English popularity; and Bryant, whom Irving introduced to Englishmen as belonging to the best school of English poetry—had their strong roots in English affection, but Longfellow's following was incomparable.

The statistics are staggering: more than seventy British publishers, largely piratical, nearly three hundred editions in England alone in the second half of the century, at least a hundred separate book translations into eighteen different languages by 1900, and in Latin America at least eighty-seven of his poems in one hundred seventy-four separate versions by fifty-three translators. He surpassed Tennyson as the household laureate; and *Evangeline* (1847), *The Golden Legend* (1851), *Hiawatha* (1855), and *Miles Standish* (1858) became the common property of Englishmen everywhere, from the British Isles to the Antipodes. English criticism was polite before this phenomenon—more polite than Poe and Margaret Fuller in America. But his faults did not go unnoticed. Lockhart, the Rossettis, the Earl of Lytton, Harrison, and Swinburne, among others, complained of his didacticism, his sentimentality, his lack of original force. Trollope admitted that of the poets of the day he was "the last that I should have guessed to be an American." None of them denied his skill. The last word was with the general reader who, after all, was responsible for the Oxford and Cambridge degrees and the bust in Poets' Corner.

On the Continent his popularity was unmatched—even by Poe. In France his poems, especially *Evangeline,* were widely dispersed. In the northern countries he was a favorite—"Tell him," the word came, "that Iceland knows him by heart." In Spain where his books came untouched by French influence, both from Spanish America and directly from the United States, he was more influential than Poe, who was regarded mainly as a story-teller. In Italy his foreign editions outnumbered those of France. But Germany took him over as a German poet. There his works went into more editions than anywhere else in Europe, except England. The poet Freiligrath, with whom Longfellow corresponded affectionately after their first meeting in 1842, assured him that his German popularity increased daily. "There is no anthology in which you are not plundered to an excess." Freiligrath translated *Hiawatha* in 1858, a year after Elise von Hohenhausen had translated *The Golden Legend*; and many other translators followed suit. In Russia, where with Mark Twain and Cooper, Longfellow has long been standard, Ivan Bunin has transposed his *Hiawatha* with great distinction. In Latin America Longfellow, at the height of his vogue between 1870 and 1900, is now slowly losing ground to Poe and Whitman. He remains the poet of the common reader, for whom he made a legendary past.

Longfellow's gift is an inheritance, but Poe and Whitman provided a working capital of such potential that the history of their influence is still largely unwritten. Only the barest outlines can be indicated here. Of our poets they are the most seminal because both had innovating genius, and both thought through and announced the principles from which grew their practice.

Much European criticism of Poe is affected by half-truths—that his genius was independent of his environment, and that he died unappreciated. Actually, he was a skilled professional in the current of his time, alive to events, and drawing on the Gothic fashion to not inconsiderable applause. Griswold's slander confirmed error, and "genius allied to vice" was a common British formula for Poe before John Ingram rehabilitated him with his admirable biography of 1880, preceded by the faithful editing of his works.

Nevertheless the praise of English writers was early and unstinted. Swinburne delighted in his "short, exquisite music"; Lang pronounced him America's greatest literary genius; Tennyson thought him to be our most original writer; the Rossettis recited him; Stevenson, Conan Doyle, and others reflected him in their fiction; George Bernard Shaw, characteristically, expressed amazement that America could produce him; and with the Poe Centennial of 1909 the British voice was heard in full chorus, "We offer tribute to one of the great artists of the English language."

But France has taken Poe for one of her own ever since Baudelaire found in him the enchanted mirror of his own daemon. In a remarkable essay published in 1852 and revised to preface his translations *Histoires extraordinaires* (1856) and *Nouvelles Histoires* (1857), Baudelaire, excoriating the gas-lighted barbarity of America, saluted the neglected genius who "writes for our nerves." Thus he set a pattern—genius amid neglect—which, while it did not affect the judgment of Taine or Sainte-Beuve, was taken over by many critics, including d'Aurevilly and Villiers de L'Isle-Adam. Baudelaire's sensual genius was not, after all, Poe's, and it is often forgotten that before his powerful identification, E. D. Forgues had already (1846) subjected Poe's work to penetrating analysis. Poe's logic attracted Forgues, and it is the logic of Poe, more than any other quality, which accounts for his French prestige. The Parnassians adopted his brilliant theorizing in aesthetics; the decadents and the surrealists found in Poe what they were looking for—the night side of the mind; and the symbolists studied his power of rhythmic suggestion. Mallarmé's adaptations of Poe's "Raven" and other poems have greatly stimulated French experimentation in free verse. The French have never regarded Poe as a jingle man.

It is impossible here even to indicate the scores of French writers who have been drawn to Poe, or to trace the influence evident in Baudelaire, Verlaine, Rimbaud, Villiers de L'Isle-Adam, Huysmans, Schwob, Maeterlinck, Valéry, and others. The problem is under constant review, and Poe has commanded brilliant criticism in recent years from men like Lauvrière, Lemonnier, and Mauclair. Even before the end of the century nearly fifty critical studies of Poe came from France.

Baudelaire's translations were the chief means of introducing him to Spain, where in 1858 they excited the novelist Alarcón, who wrote an essay full of enthusiasm and misinformation. Spanish interest in Poe, mounting with the modernist movement, has not abated, but in Spanish America, where the lyrics are preferred to the tales, Poe's influence has been more profound than in the mother country. The Spanish-American poets—among them Bonalde, Díaz, Darío, Silva, and Nervo—have devotedly translated him. Still awaiting full study is his influence upon such important Spanish writers as Villaespesa, Carrere, and Baroja.

In Germany Baudelaire also served as Poe's intermediary for readers who found in him the macabre vein they loved in Hoffmann. The novelist Spielhagen pondered his structural principles, Elise von Hohenhausen, Strodtmann, and others translated him, and "The Raven" was almost as popular in Germany as in France. The Russians read Poe by the late 1830's, long before he was taken up in France. Dostoevski called attention to the psychological penetration of his tales in his magazine *Wremia* (1861), and the Poe influence is manifest in *Crime and Punishment,* as it is also in the work of Chekhov and Andreev, who knew Poe and studied his technique. But Poe's foremost spokesman in Russia has been the poet Balmont, who began translating the complete works in 1906, and whose ardent but uncritical praise has played in Russia the Baudelairean role.

5

In foreign regard the name of Poe has meant craftsmanship, the name of Whitman has meant a message. To Europe Whitman is a symbol, even a myth, and the myth consists both in the projection of himself, the lover and encourager, and in the dream of man's brotherhood. In avowing him to be the prophet of man's aspiration toward a better society, the testimony of foreign criticism is overwhelming. His "literary" performance has abundant recognition, its skill and power affirmed by the poets from Swinburne to Hopkins and Lawrence and his prosody elaborately analyzed by scholars like Jannaccone in Italy and Bazalgette and Catel in France, but it is his redeeming force, a religious more than an aesthetic ascendancy, that is insistent in Whitman criticism.

Not even the outlines of his story abroad can find room here; but when it is written it must embrace the whole theme of the interaction of European and American thought, for Whitman's origins are in Europe as well as in America, and Europe's hopes are found in him. It is not yet a story of the great audience Whitman had adumbrated, but of scholars, intellectuals, and poets drawn by a genius too baffling for the common reader. In Europe Whitman became a classic, not a best seller. Yet this truth needs qualification, for his following was unconventional and dispersed.

His English reception, often cited to American disadvantage, glittered with the names of Dowden, Rossetti, Symonds, Buchanan, Rhys, Saintsbury, Ellis, Carpenter, but he was also a "penny poet" in England, available in cheap reprint and influential among Blatchford's labor disciples and the fellowship groups of industrial centers. In Germany, where Freiligrath discovered Whitman in 1868, translating rather ineptly from the Rossetti edition, many scholars and poets spread his word, most notably Johannes Schlaf (1907, 1919), who became the center of a Whitman cult, and Hans Reisiger (1922), for whose admirable translation Thomas Mann expressed his gratitude. But here too, as in England, Whitman has been the inspirer of the dispossessed and the ardent young—such worker-poets as Engelke, who fell in the First World War, Bröger, Grisar, and Lersch.

In France early criticism of Whitman was mistrustful until the symbolists—La Forgue, Vielé-Griffin, Mallarmé, and others—began to translate and make available the accurate text of *Leaves of Grass* as an innovating experiment in form. Closer to Whitman's own emphasis was Bazalgette's influential biography of 1908, followed in 1909 by his translation (of which Gide was critical), and in 1921 by his analytic study. To Bazalgette Whitman was an evangelist, and his discipleship affected the earnest group known as the Abbaye—Romains, Vildrac, Duhamel, and others for whom Whitman became the poet of the new age. French soldiers took *Leaves of Grass* into the trenches; in 1926 a "Comité Walt Whitman" was founded; and such later interpretation as Catel's psychoanalytic study of Whitman's personality and his "vocal style" has strengthened a recognition which finally eclipsed that of Poe.

In Russia Whitman was frankly turned to Soviet doctrine, the Moscow poet Chukovsky's translation of *Leaves of Grass* reaching a sixth edition by 1923. After the Revolution his poems honoring "humanity" and the "machine" were declaimed all over the country, and such class-conscious poets as Mayakovsky, Meyerhof, and Gastev own his kinship. In earlier days Turgenev had thought of translating him, Tolstoy deemed it necessary to criticize his lack of clarity, the poet Balmont translated him in a mood of mystic ecstasy, misinformed biographical sketches appeared in the press, and Chukovsky's own first translations were censored by the police. His influence spread irresistibly, and carried over to Hungary where Pasztor, Gaspar, and others translated him, and such poets as Kosztolányi, Babits, and Margit Kaffka were affected by him.

The mounting list of Whitman's partisans may not even be sketched here —merely instanced: Jensen and Schyberg in Denmark; Gamberale, Jannaconne, Praz, and Nencioni in Italy; Mann and Werfel in Germany; Verhaeren in Belgium; Brossa, Guerra, and Cebriá-Montoliu in Spain; Darío in Spanish America. Like Thoreau's *Walden* and Emerson's *Essays,* Whitman's word has been procreant in the Orient—in India, China, and especially Japan, where *Leaves of Grass* has been regarded as a text of Western democracy. It may be, as Whitman hoped, that he will reach, more than any other American poet, to "the bulk-people of all lands."

6

At Whitman's own urgency Europeans had made a mythic figure of him— a bearded divinity, compelling and resolute, who, if not representatively American, was what America ought to produce. Something of the same expectancy was operative in the foreign reputation of the Western writers who emerged after the Civil War: Artemus Ward, Miller, Harte, Bierce, and —above all—Mark Twain. Their "aura" was theatrical and flamboyant, as befitted travelers from a region of fantasy; and they were all indiscriminately assigned to the tradition of humorous exaggeration which went back to the early coon songs and yokel buffoonery of the comedian Charles Mathews, to Haliburton's Sam Slick, to Davy Crockett's exploits, to countless pirated collections of Yankee drolleries, and on to the *Biglow Papers* of Lowell, the wit of Holmes, and Leland's Hans Breitmann.

The list is partial: the point is that when Artemus Ward faced his first London audience on the night of November 13, 1866, it expected the kind of performance it got. All England was being flooded with Western humor by enterprising publishers, chief of whom was the pirate Hotten who issued all of Ward he could steal, one compilation selling 250,000 copies. The English loved Ward's gentle absurdity, the highly personal art that shone from his letters to *Punch,* and the wonderful lectures that wore out his brief life. They were also taken, the fashionable world in particular, with the red shirt and gusty verse of Joaquin Miller (*Pacific Poems,* 1871, *Songs of the Sierras,* 1871, *Songs of the Sun-Lands,* 1873), whose appeal was elemental—and brief. Upon his final visit in 1878, England, whom Miller had publicly thanked for her noble treatment, turned a cold shoulder. Ambrose Bierce, who hated humor, enjoyed repute as a wit and raconteur during five London years (1872-1877) as a journalist and staff writer for Hood's *Fun.* His first three books, all published in England, won praise, even from so important a man as Gladstone, but Bierce needed better criticism than his Fleet Street confreres could give him. His Western air suffered a sea change in London, acquiring a Tory cast.

Bret Harte's triumphal progress eastward upon the phenomenal success of "The Luck of Roaring Camp," "The Outcasts of Poker Flat," "The Heathen Chinee" was marked in England as the emergence of a new trans- atlantic genius. Hotten's pirated edition of his works sold heavily, and when Harte later turned up in England (1879), his American prospects fallen away, he found a ready audience whose interest in his performance lasted until death ended his exile in 1902. "England never got tired of that lariat," said Aldrich. Harte thought he could say some new things of England, but he never did. He remained to the English a mercurial and puzzling fellow who could combine sentiment and humor in the right proportion. In Germany, where Harte had been consul at Crefeld in 1878, his vogue was extraordinary; and it was the conspicuous success of the German edition of *Tales of the Argonauts* (1873) that persuaded Harte's Leipzig publisher to chance the first publication of Mark Twain. Up to the end of the century Harte's German editions actually outnumbered those of his great compatriot.

Mark Twain went to England in the summer of 1872 with two purposes: to protect his copyright, and to deal as freely with English manners and customs as the "Innocent" had dealt with Europe. He assailed Hotten satisfyingly enough, but his second purpose, which had been common talk among the English themselves, was never achieved. Why? His own answer was that he could not write critically of people whose hospitality he had accepted, an excuse that had deterred neither Emerson nor Hawthorne. The real answer seems to be that his immense success in England—the endless sales of his books, the crowded lectures, the innumerable occasions when his wit played across the festal board, the friendships with England's great, the impressive honors culminating in the Oxford degree—forced him inevitably into the role of international jester. More than this, he fitted with consummate grace into the role of unofficial ambassador to England from America.

It was a great service he performed because he had the gift of remaining himself, of actually being what he seemed to be. His experience abroad simply confirmed and accentuated his national characteristics because he carried with him, as one critic said, the same habits of life that sufficed him in Connecticut. Yet the discerning were uneasy that he should play the amiable part merely. Men like Bernard Shaw and Thomas Hardy saw in him more than the entertainer; they saw his kinship with Cervantes and Swift. Had they seen his notebooks they would have been reassured, for here his private rages, his resentment against the hypocrisies of hereditary privilege, boiled over. But publicly Mark Twain tilted only against England's medieval institutions— as in *A Connecticut Yankee in King Arthur's Court* (1889), which was criticism in motley. The English public did not like the *Yankee,* but it liked nearly everything else of Mark Twain's, tending, like the American public, to praise most what most complied with conventional taste.

All over the world Mark Twain's "place" was that of public entertainer. He had always hunted, he told Lang, for bigger game, for the masses; and to the masses everywhere he became a legend. In Germany, where his popularity, associated with Harte's, was cultivated by the publishers' campaigns of